# AMERICAN HISTORY

Patrick Carter, Fiorella Finelli, Derek Grant, David Nagy

2008
Emond Montgomery Publications Limited
Toronto, Canada

Emond Montgomery Publications Limited
60 Shaftesbury Avenue
Toronto ON M4T 1A3
http://www.emp.ca

Printed in Canada.

We acknowledge the financial support of the Government of Canada through the Book Publishing Industry Development Program (BPIDP) for our publishing activities.

ISBN 978-1-55239-218-8

**Publisher**
Anthony Rezek

**National sales & marketing manager**
Lindsay Mascherin

**Developmental editors**
Ed O'Connor
Kate Hawkins
Tanjah Karvonen
Shirley Tessier

**Consulting editor**
Ian Hundey

**Contributing writers**
Ian Hundey
Damon Monteleone
John Myers
Laurence M. Olivo

**Managing editor**
Jim Lyons, WordsWorth Communications

**Production & copy editors**
Sarah Gleadow
Francine Geraci

**Image researcher & permissions editor**
Lisa Brant
Christina Beamish

**Maps**
Visu*Tron*X

**Cover designer, interior designer, & compositor**
Tara Wells, WordsWorth Communications

**Proofreader & indexer**
Paula Pike, WordsWorth Communications

# Reviewers

**Dave Alexander**
Owen Sound Collegiate and Vocational Institute (Bluewater DSB)

**Dimitry Anastakis**
Trent University

**Brent Austin**
Mississauga Secondary School (Peel DSB)

**Lee Ann Benson**
Dryden High School (Keewatin Patricia DSB)

**Vince Dannetta**
University of Toronto

**Trevor Elmslie**
Preston High School (Waterloo Region DSB)

**Erin Fenlong**
Smiths Falls District Collegiate Institute (Upper Canada DSB)

**Allan Hux**
District-wide Coordinator, Toronto District School Board

**Anyta Kyriakou**
Mary Ward Catholic Secondary School (Toronto Catholic DSB)

**Maureen Matchett**
F.E. Madill Secondary School (Avon Maitland DSB)

**Taresa Matchett**
Collingwood Collegiate (Simcoe County DSB)

**Mary Maurice**
White Pines CVS (Algoma DSB)

**Jory Vernon**
Community Hebrew Academy of Toronto (Private School)

**Peter Voight**
George S. Henry Academy (Toronto DSB)

**Tim Waterhouse**
Arnprior District High School (Renfrew County DSB)

**Scott Wear**
Sandwich Secondary School (Greater Essex County DSB)

**Tim Zander**
Perth & District Collegiate Institute (Upper Canada DSB)

# Contents

## Chapter 4 Birth of the Republic (1789–1828)



# Unit III Nationalism and Sectionalism

## Chapter 5 Manifest Destiny (1828–1850)



## Chapter 6 The Crisis of the Union (1850–1865)

## Chapter 9 The Progressive Era and World War I (1900–1920)



## Chapter 10 Between the Wars (1920–1940)



# Unit V World Power

## Chapter 11 World War II and the Cold War (1941–1960)

## Chapter 14 Into a New Century (1989–Present)



## Appendix

# Features of This Text

The history of America is a story of dynamic change, of a nation and its people moulded by different economic, social, political, and philosophical forces. In this book you will examine American history through the lens of one guiding concept: *The United States is a nation shaped by ideas.* America has always been a country defined not just by its borders or the background of its people, but by powerful ideas. Among the ideas that have guided America's development are *liberty*, *democracy*, *equality*, and *opportunity*. You will find this guiding concept in all aspects of American history and identity—in technology and the arts; in the stories of immigrants and the treatment of different racial, social, and religious groups; in the push toward the frontier, wherever it may be found; and in America's interactions with Canada and the wider world. Above all, the United States is a modern state that has been profoundly shaped by its past. To fully comprehend the nation and its people, you must begin by examining its history. The features of *American History* open windows onto significant events, movements, people, and texts, define the dimensions of historical inquiry, and allow you to assess your understanding of the material.

**AMERICAN ARCHIVE**

**American Archive** explores significant official documents, many of which resulted from the collaborative efforts of a group of people. In each case, actual excerpts from the documents are reproduced and analyzed.

**Culture Notes**

**Culture Notes** provides a description and analysis of landmark works in the visual arts, literature, music, and architecture, and explores the significance of these works in terms of their connection to key ideas, events, or struggles of the time.

**49th Parallel** illustrates the close connection between the histories of Canada and the United States, the interdependence of their economies, and Canada's long struggle to remain culturally independent of her more populous and powerful neighbour.

PAST VOICES

**Past Voices** presents an individual point of view—through excerpts from speeches, letters, diaries, newspaper editorials, and works of fiction and non-fiction—to articulate the thoughts and views of Americans at a particular time.

WE THE PEOPLE

**We the People** profiles a diverse selection of American leaders in areas such as politics, the economy, philosophy, technology, social reform, and the arts to provide you with an overview of their achievements as well as a sense of who they were, the challenges they faced, and the historical significance of their accomplishments.

CHECK YOUR UNDERSTANDING

**Check Your Understanding** allows you to assess your progress at the end of each major section in a chapter.

SOUND BITE

**Sound Bite** offers brief, high-interest quotations related to the main text on the page.

WEB LINKS

**Web Links** points you to useful websites that allow you to further explore a particular topic.

THE HISTORIAN'S CRAFT

**The Historian's Craft**, a full-page feature near the end of each chapter, guides you through the theory and practice of historical inquiry, research techniques, methods for detecting bias, academic documentation, ways of generating a thesis, using primary and secondary sources, and conducting research on the Internet. (See the Introduction to this feature on page xii.)

STUDY HALL

**Study Hall** provides an extensive set of end-of-chapter activities covering Thinking, Communication, and Application skills.

# Introduction to The Historian's Craft

The Historian's Craft features focus on the nature of historical thinking and the work of the historian. Their premise is that the most valuable studies are those that are authentic—that require you to work in the same way as practitioners of a craft. In these features you will read how historians approach their work, undertake research, interpret evidence, use historical imagination, refine their thinking, and present their conclusions. You will also consider how historians help us understand today's world and speculate about the future. Each feature includes questions that relate The Historian's Craft to the chapter content and that require you to think and act as a historian.

A common theme running through all of these features is the recognition that historians act out of intellectual curiosity. Even when they are expert in a topic, they are predisposed to look more deeply into matters. This questioning mind is the backdrop for formal inquiry. From your previous studies in history you know that inquiry involves researching historical sources. You also know that these sources fall into two categories. Primary sources are those that were produced at the time of historical events. Secondary sources are those works that are produced after the events and are based on primary sources and earlier secondary sources. In writing this book the authors have used both kinds of sources, but have taken care to include a wide range of primary sources.

A history textbook from a hundred years ago would not be as rich in primary sources as this text. If such texts included primary sources at all, they were limited to legislation, proclamations, and other official documents. In this book, however, you will find not only official documents but other kinds of written evidence as well, such as song lyrics, diary entries, and newspaper articles. You will also find primary evidence beyond written sources—for example, video clips (via Internet links), paintings, cartoons, contemporary maps, and photographs. It is important to include such a range of primary evidence for two reasons. First, the past voices of those both verbally and visually literate are allowed to speak. Second, such a wide range of evidence helps you and your classmates—with your varied learning preferences and multiple intelligences—engage with American history in more meaningful ways.

The Historian's Craft features reinforce the importance of primary sources and focus on key examples throughout the chapters. In doing so they allow you to deepen your appreciation of the historian's craft.

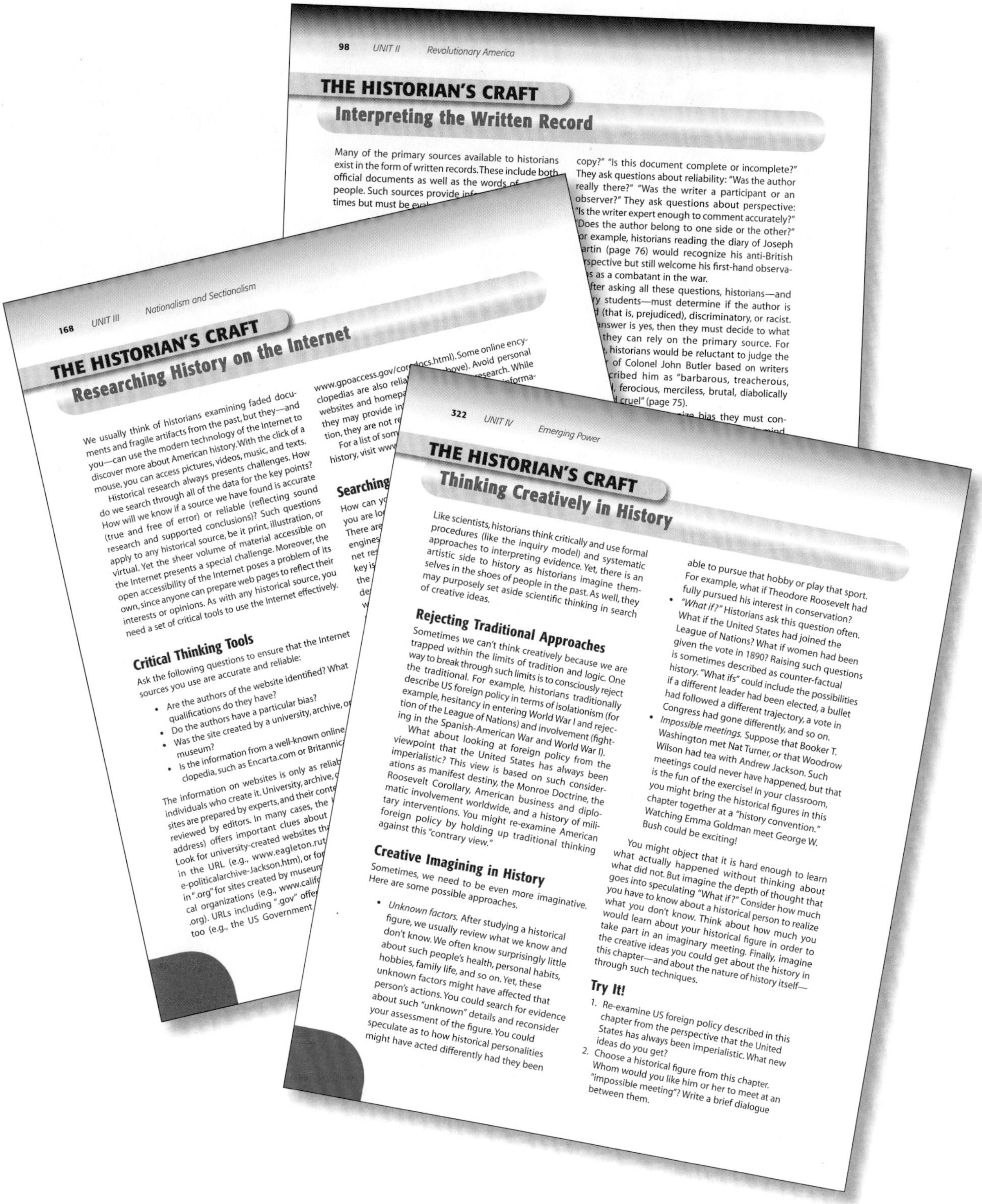

98 UNIT II Revolutionary America

## THE HISTORIAN'S CRAFT
### Interpreting the Written Record

Many of the primary sources available to historians exist in the form of written records. These include both official documents as well as the words of ... people. Such sources provide inf... times but must be eval...

copy?" "Is this document complete or incomplete?" They ask questions about reliability: "Was the author really there?" "Was the writer a participant or an observer?" They ask questions about perspective: "Is the writer expert enough to comment accurately?" "Does the author belong to one side or the other?" ...or example, historians reading the diary of Joseph ...artin (page 76) would recognize his anti-British ...rspective but still welcome his first-hand observa...s as a combatant in the war.

...fter asking all these questions, historians—and ...y students—must determine if the author is ...d (that is, prejudiced), discriminatory, or racist. ...answer is yes, then they must decide to what ... they can rely on the primary source. For ..., historians would be reluctant to judge the ...r of Colonel John Butler based on writers ...cribed him as "barbarous, treacherous, ..., ferocious, merciless, brutal, diabolically ...d cruel" (page 75).

...ize bias they must con-...

168 UNIT III Nationalism and Sectionalism

## THE HISTORIAN'S CRAFT
### Researching History on the Internet

We usually think of historians examining faded documents and fragile artifacts from the past, but they—and you—can use the modern technology of the Internet to discover more about American history. With the click of a mouse, you can access pictures, videos, music, and texts.

Historical research always presents challenges. How do we search through all of the data for the key points? How will we know if a source we have found is accurate (true and free of error) or reliable (reflecting sound research and supported conclusions)? Such questions apply to any historical source, be it print, illustration, or virtual. Yet the sheer volume of material accessible on the Internet presents a special challenge. Moreover, the open accessibility of the Internet poses a problem of its own, since anyone can prepare web pages to reflect their interests or opinions. As with any historical source, you need a set of critical tools to use the Internet effectively.

#### Critical Thinking Tools

Ask the following questions to ensure that the Internet sources you use are accurate and reliable:

- Are the authors of the website identified? What qualifications do they have?
- Do the authors have a particular bias?
- Was the site created by a university, archive, or museum?
- Is the information from a well-known online ... clopedia, such as Encarta.com or Britannic...

The information on websites is only as reliab... individuals who create it. University, archive, ... sites are prepared by experts, and their conte... reviewed by editors. In many cases, the ... address) offers important clues about ... Look for university-created websites th... in the URL (e.g., www.eagleton.rut... e-politicalarchive-Jackson.htm), or fo... in ".org" for sites created by museum... cal organizations (e.g., www.calif... .org). URLs including ".gov" offer... too (e.g., the US Government...

www.gpoaccess.gov/cor...docs.html). Some online encyclopedias are also relia... ...bove). Avoid personal websites and homepa... ...esearch. While they may provide in... ...informa-tion, they are not re...

For a list of som... history, visit www...

#### Searching...

How can yo... you are loo... There are... engines... net re... key is... the... de... w...

322 UNIT IV Emerging Power

## THE HISTORIAN'S CRAFT
### Thinking Creatively in History

Like scientists, historians think critically and use formal procedures (like the inquiry model) and systematic approaches to interpreting evidence. Yet, there is an artistic side to history as historians imagine themselves in the shoes of people in the past. As well, they may purposely set aside scientific thinking in search of creative ideas.

#### Rejecting Traditional Approaches

Sometimes we can't think creatively because we are trapped within the limits of tradition and logic. One way to break through such limits is to consciously reject the traditional. For example, historians traditionally describe US foreign policy in terms of isolationism (for example, hesitancy in entering World War I and rejection of the League of Nations) and involvement (fighting in the Spanish-American War and World War I).

What about looking at foreign policy from the viewpoint that the United States has always been imperialistic? This view is based on such considerations as manifest destiny, the Monroe Doctrine, the Roosevelt Corollary, American business and diplomatic involvement worldwide, and a history of military interventions. You might re-examine American foreign policy by holding up traditional thinking against this "contrary view."

#### Creative Imagining in History

Sometimes, we need to be even more imaginative. Here are some possible approaches.

- *Unknown factors.* After studying a historical figure, we usually review what we know and don't know. We often know surprisingly little about such people's health, personal habits, hobbies, family life, and so on. Yet, these unknown factors might have affected that person's actions. You could search for evidence about such "unknown" details and reconsider your assessment of the figure. You could speculate as to how historical personalities might have acted differently had they been able to pursue that hobby or play that sport. For example, what if Theodore Roosevelt had fully pursued his interest in conservation?
- *"What if?"* Historians ask this question often. What if the United States had joined the League of Nations? What if women had been given the vote in 1890? Raising such questions is sometimes described as counter-factual history. "What ifs" could include the possibilities if a different leader had been elected, a bullet had followed a different trajectory, a vote in Congress had gone differently, and so on.
- *Impossible meetings.* Suppose that Booker T. Washington met Nat Turner, or that Woodrow Wilson had tea with Andrew Jackson. Such meetings could never have happened, but that is the fun of the exercise! In your classroom, you might bring the historical figures in this chapter together at a "history convention." Watching Emma Goldman meet George W. Bush could be exciting!

You might object that it is hard enough to learn what actually happened without thinking about what did not. But imagine the depth of thought that goes into speculating "What if?" Consider how much you have to know about a historical person to realize what you don't know. Think about how much you would learn about your historical figure in order to take part in an imaginary meeting. Finally, imagine the creative ideas you could get about the history in this chapter—and about the nature of history itself—through such techniques.

#### Try It!

1. Re-examine US foreign policy described in this chapter from the perspective that the United States has always been imperialistic. What new ideas do you get?
2. Choose a historical figure from this chapter. Whom would you like him or her to meet at an "impossible meeting"? Write a brief dialogue between them.

# UNIT I EARLY AMERICA

# 1 Aboriginals and Europeans (1000–1700)

## KEY CONCEPTS

In this chapter you will consider:

- The nature of Native American societies before the arrival of Europeans
- The role of political, social, and economic developments in Europe in encouraging exploration of North America
- The contrasting early experiences of Spain, France, and England in the Americas
- The formation of the first English colonies in Virginia and Massachusetts
- The variety of English colonies established in North America
- The impact of European settlement on Aboriginal peoples

## The American Story

The early history of European settlement in North America is a story of contact between two established societies: Aboriginal and European. European colonization transformed both groups. Aboriginal societies were devastated by disease and drawn into struggles between European powers for control of North America and its wealth. Europeans faced the hardships of surviving and thriving in a new environment. Yet by the end of the 17th century the English in particular had established a number of colonies along the Atlantic coast. Their diverse characters would help chart the future course of American society and politics.

## TIMELINE

| 1451 | 1516 | 1607 | 1608 | 1609 |
|---|---|---|---|---|
| ▸ Iroquois Confederacy established | ▸ Smallpox arrives in the Americas | ▸ Jamestown founded (English) | ▸ Quebec founded (French) | ▸ Santa Fe founded (Spanish) |

## IMAGE ANALYSIS

**Figure 1.1** This is a drawing of the Aboriginal village of Secoton in 1585 by an Englishman named John White. Later in this chapter you will read more about White and the colony he founded near present-day Roanoke, Virginia. As the leader of the first English colony in North America, White kept careful records, both written and visual.

As you examine this visual record, put yourself in the place of a historian and let your curiosity go to work. What questions do you have about the Aboriginal peoples who lived here? Notice the three cornfields on the right side of the drawing. The one at the top is for ripe corn; the one in the middle is for green or unripened corn; and the one on the bottom is for corn that has just started to sprout. What does this tell you about the abilities of these people as farmers? What other evidence in the drawing shows that Native Americans had sophisticated and well-organized societies at the time of their first contact with Europeans?

- ▸ Pilgrims arrive — **1620**
- ▸ English capture New Amsterdam — **1664**
- ▸ King Philip's War — **1675**
- ▸ Bacon's Rebellion — **1676**
- ▸ Salem witch trials — **1692**

# INTRODUCTION

This book invites you to take an active role in studying American history—not just reading the words on the page, but thinking, questioning, interpreting, and theorizing about the people and events of this large and fascinating country just to the south of Canada.

Think about this for a minute: There were several people your own age in the group of English settlers that John White led to Virginia in 1585. How do you imagine they felt about going to live in a place that was completely unknown to them, among a people with different customs, beliefs, and language—a whole different worldview—from their own?

Now consider this: At one point White had to return to England, leaving about a hundred colonists behind in a tiny village on the edge of a vast continent. When he returned several years later, he found the colony abandoned and no trace of the settlers. Their disappearance has become one of the great mysteries of American history.

Such mysteries, while fascinating in their own right, often lead to larger questions. Why, you might wonder, were relations between European settlers and Aboriginal peoples so often marked by hostility and violence? Was war inevitable, or could the Europeans and Native Americans have coexisted peacefully and for their mutual benefit? These are the kinds of questions you will be invited to consider, and offer your own ideas on, in this chapter and throughout the rest of the book.

# AMERICA BEFORE EUROPEAN IMMIGRATION

Before Europeans arrived in North America, the population of the continent was made up of a range of Native American societies. Despite significant cultural differences, these societies had much in common with early modern societies in Europe and Asia.

## Aboriginal Societies and Cultures

In order to fully appreciate the impact of the arrival of Europeans, one key fact must be remembered: during the centuries preceding their arrival, North America was home to several significant Native American societies. While archaeologists dispute the precise dates of these societies, their research and excavations reveal that a range of impressive societies flourished across North America in the centuries before Europeans arrived. From the Anasazi to the Mississippians, these Native American groups possessed distinctive cultures that shared many of the characteristics of contemporary European civilization, including major urban centres, sophisticated agricultural and trade economies, and advanced political organization.

## Southwest Society

Between 1000 and 1300 CE a group called the Anasazi lived in what became the southwestern United States, in the area where the modern boundaries of Arizona, New Mexico, Colorado, and Utah meet. The Anasazi established hundreds of settlements connected by a network of roads, and developed sophisticated irrigation systems to grow crops such as maize in the semi-desert areas. They were known above all for their multi-storey cliff dwellings, which the Spaniards called *pueblos.* A number of these settlements, some from as early as the 12th century, still survive.

In the two centuries after 1300 CE the Anasazi culture was threatened by drought, and by invasion by the warlike Athabascans. The Athabascans had moved steadily southward during the previous century from their origins in the subarctic (present-day Alaska and northern Canada). Armed with superior technology such as bows and arrows, the Athabascans repeatedly raided Anasazi settlements until, by 1500, they had forced the Anasazi from their lands. The descendants of the Athabascans, the Navajos and Apaches, continue to occupy these lands today.

## Mississippian Society

While the Anasazi were establishing *pueblo* settlements in the deserts of the Southwest, another society was emerging in the Mississippi River Valley. Like the Anasazi, the Mississippians had an agricultural society based on the cultivation of maize. The Mississippians created large settlements along the rivers, exercised power over the surrounding countryside, and traded with neighbouring communities and those further afield. They also appear to have fought with their neighbours for control over trade.

The largest Mississippian settlement was Cahokia, situated opposite modern-day St. Louis. With an estimated population of 20,000 at its peak around 1200 CE,

**Figure 1.2** An artist's impression of the Mississippian settlement of Cahokia, ca. 1200 CE. Note the wide Mississippi River in the upper left corner. What evidence of the level of Mississippian civilization do you see in this image?

Cahokia was almost certainly the largest urban centre in North America before the arrival of the Europeans, and would have rivalled many contemporary medieval European cities in size. To control their trade networks, Mississippian communities appear to have developed sophisticated political structures ruled by powerful chiefs, who built residences on flat-topped mounds in the centres of their towns. These city-states had hierarchical societies, with rulers, priests, and **artisans**. But by the 15th century Cahokia had vanished and the Mississippian culture had almost entirely disappeared. Europeans introduced diseases that wiped out the last remnants of the Mississippian peoples, leaving only earthen mounds and archaeological evidence of this society.

### The South

In the Southeast of North America, between the Mississippi delta and the Atlantic coast, a number of significant Native American nations flourished in the centuries before the arrival of Europeans. Throughout the South, the mild climate and rich soils made extensive farming possible and encouraged substantial settlements, which were often home to hundreds of residents. These nations included the Creeks, who lived in present-day Georgia, and the Cherokee, who hunted in the hills of Tennessee. Both these societies would be profoundly affected by the arrival of European settlers. The surviving members of the Mississippian culture, the Natchez, lived in the lower Mississippi Valley. With their clear class distinctions and advanced political structures (which included a ruler known as the "Great Sun"), the Natchez survived until the 18th century, when they were destroyed in a war against the French.

## Eastern Woodlands

Although the Anasazi and Mississippian cultures had largely vanished before Europeans arrived in North America, the first Europeans did encounter the Aboriginal peoples of the eastern woodlands, a region stretching from the Atlantic coast to the Great Lakes and from the Gulf of St. Lawrence to the Carolinas. Two main Aboriginal groups coexisted in this area: the Algonquin and the Iroquois. The interaction between Europeans and the Native Americans of the eastern woodlands had a profound impact on both groups and helped shape the early history of European settlement in North America.

### The Algonquin

The Algonquin were a group that included the Mi'kmaq, Cree, and Montagnais. They engaged in only limited farming, relying more on hunting and foraging in the forests of eastern North America. With a semi-nomadic lifestyle, they lived in small bands usually numbering no more than several hundred members, and most of their settlements were modest and temporary. Some of the Algonquin groups became ready partners in the fur trade with the Europeans, as they were already accustomed to hunting and travelling through the interior of the continent. In New England, Algonquin groups included the Narragansetts and Pequots, while further south along the Atlantic coast was the Powhatan Confederacy. These were among the first Native Americans to encounter the English and French during the 16th and early 17th centuries.

## The Iroquois

The Algonquin were the first to make contact with the new European arrivals, but the Iroquois had a greater and more lasting impact on the early history of European settlement in North America. Unlike the Algonquin, the Iroquois had developed an agricultural economy, cultivating maize and other crops. This intensive farming led to the growth of large villages, which were often composed of several hundred families. Women dominated the farming economy and exercised considerable leadership within the family and village. At the same time a warrior culture developed, and neighbouring villages were raided regularly.

By the 15th century this warfare had reached a dangerous level. As a result, around 1451 the five main Iroquois nations (Mohawk, Oneida, Onondaga, Cayuga, and Seneca) agreed to form an alliance—the Iroquois League. According to oral traditions, the eloquent Mohawk chief Hiawatha deserves most of the credit for negotiating the agreement. Members of the League agreed to resolve their disputes peaceably and take some decisions collectively, while each of the nations retained its independence. Each nation was represented in the League's council by its chief and by specially selected men known as **sachems** (SAY-chums).

Some have argued that the League, which combined a central authority with local autonomy, served as an early model for the federal structure of government later adopted in the United States. Whatever the case, the Iroquois' advanced political and military organization enabled them to respond more effectively to the challenges posed by the arrival of the Europeans on the shores of North America.

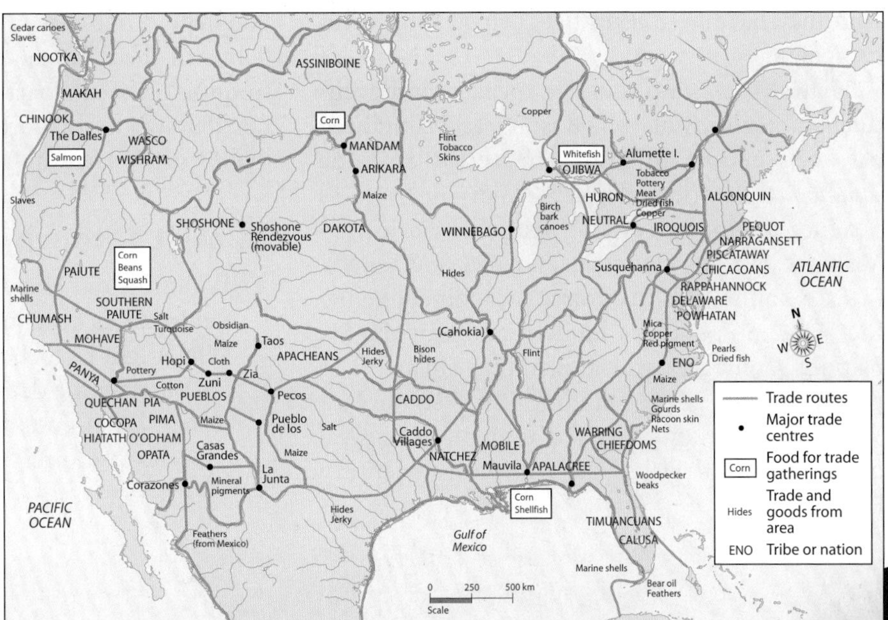


**Figure 1.3** This map shows the Native American territories and trade routes in North America at the time of the arrival of Europeans. Who would be the first to make contact with Europeans?

# WE THE PEOPLE

## Hiawatha, Iroquois Leader

**Figure 1.4** An artist's impression of Hiawatha.

Among the earliest Native Americans known to historians is Hiawatha, an Iroquois orator and political leader who lived in North America more than a century before the arrival of Europeans.

Much of Hiawatha's life is shrouded in legend, but it is clear that he was a historical figure. Iroquois oral traditions identify him as a member of the Onondaga nation living near Lake Ontario during the mid-15th century. His name means "he who seeks the wampum belt"—that is, someone who seeks wisdom. During a time of considerable conflict between various Iroquois nations, the middle-aged Hiawatha worked to promote peace. His early efforts to win the support of his own nation, however, were thwarted by the suspicion of the Onondaga chiefs and their powerful leader, Atotarho. Undeterred, Hiawatha turned to other Iroquois nations, travelling from one council to another urging the formation of a permanent **confederacy**. Another Iroquois leader, Dekanawidah, who may have been a relative, helped him in his campaign.

Hiawatha was a persuasive speaker, and eventually overcame Atotarho's hostility and convinced his own people to join. The result was the *Haudenosaunee* (haw-da-na-SAW-ni), or Iroquois League, composed of five Iroquois nations—Mohawk, Oneida, Onondaga, Cayuga, and Seneca. A sixth nation, the Tuscarora, later joined, giving the Haudenosaunee its modern name of the Six Nations Confederacy. The resulting alliance was governed by the Great Binding Law (see the Past Voices feature) and survived even the upheaval caused by the arrival of the Europeans a century later.

Hiawatha was soon adopted by the Mohawk nation as a chief in recognition of his efforts. Iroquois oral traditions emphasize his wise leadership within the confederacy, but little is known of his later life. Hiawatha's accomplishments included arranging the clearing of streams and waterways to ensure that these vital travel and communication routes remained passable.

In 1855 the American poet Henry Wadsworth Longfellow published "Hiawatha," an epic poem telling of the fictional exploits of an Ojibwa (not Iroquois) leader. Apart from the name, however, Longfellow's work bore no direct connection to the historical Hiawatha.

### Think It Through

1. What role did Hiawatha play in establishing the Iroquois League?
2. Why might historians have difficulty establishing the details of Hiawatha's life and career? What does this tell us about Native American culture?

## PAST VOICES

# The Great Binding Law of the Iroquois

After Hiawatha had succeeded in creating the Iroquois League around 1451, representatives of the five nations met for the first time under The Great Tree of Peace and formed the Council of Fifty. This assembly was led by chiefs from each nation, and would rule according to the Great Binding Law for centuries.

Adhering to the Great Binding Law, or *Gayanashogawa*, the Iroquois League practised a form of government that celebrated **democracy**—a decentralized government with checks and balances, and leadership based on merit rather than heredity. The Law reveals much about Iroquoian society and government before the arrival of the Europeans. For example, women were highly respected in Iroquois culture and played a vital role in selecting the tribe's Council Chiefs:

> The right of bestowing the title shall be hereditary in the family of the females legally possessing the bunch of shell strings and the strings shall be the token that the females of the family have the proprietary right to the Lordship title for all time to come.

The Law established a highly organized system, with checks and balances, for bringing up issues and for debate. While discussion in matters of common concern such as war, peace, and treaties was open to all, the Council could not interfere with the internal affairs of each tribe. At the same time the leaders of the League were to rule in the best interests of the Five Nations, for:

> The Lords of the Confederacy of the Five Nations shall be mentors of the people for all time. Their hearts shall be full of peace and good will and their minds filled with a yearning for the welfare of the people of the Confederacy.

**Figure 1.5** This illustration, published in 1796 by writer and artist Jacques Grasset de Saint-Saveur, attempts to show an Iroquois man before European contact.

Most significantly, the people of the Five Nations retained ultimate sovereignty over Council decisions:

> Whenever a specially important matter or a great emergency is presented before the Confederate Council ... the Confederacy must submit the matter to the decision of their people and the decision of the people shall affect the decision of the Confederate Council.

Some scholars believe that the Great Binding Law was the single most important model for later constitutional documents, including the US Constitution. While some similarities do exist between the Iroquois League and later American political institutions, it remains unclear how much influence the Great Binding Law had on the development of the American form of government. The colonists had extensive treaty and trade interactions with the Iroquois and were familiar with their form of government. The Iroquois leader Canassatego had advised the colonists during treaty negotiations in 1744:

> Our wise fathers established a union and amity between the Five Nations that has made us formidable. We are a powerful confederacy and by your observing the same methods ... you will acquire much strength and power.

### Think It Through

1. Describe some of the important characteristics of the Great Binding Law of the Iroquois.
2. What evidence is there to suggest that the Iroquois League had an influence on early American unity and politics?

### CHECK YOUR UNDERSTANDING

1. Why did the Anasazi disappear?
2. What were the key elements of Mississippian culture?
3. What features of Native American culture demonstrated their possession of the land?
4. What was the Iroquois League and why is it considered significant?

# AGE OF EMPIRES

In the 15th century European nations began to explore beyond the limits of Europe and the Mediterranean world. This push to expand the boundaries of the world known to Europeans led to an age of discovery and empire. The arrival of Europeans in the Americas would transform continents on both sides of the Atlantic.

## European Expansion

During the later **Middle Ages** Europe had experienced a period of economic and cultural expansion and development. Merchants from Italy gained control over the valuable trade in spices from Asia (such as nutmeg and pepper) that travelled overland through the Middle East to the Mediterranean. The resulting wealth stimulated the development of banking systems and the growth of commercial and political power.

Three crucial inventions accompanied the spices and other luxury goods: gunpowder, the compass, and the technique of printing with movable type. Gunpowder revolutionized warfare and gave European nations a powerful military advantage over their opponents. The compass, combined with advances in ship design, enabled voyages of exploration and encouraged eventual European dominance over a large portion of the globe. Printing with movable type allowed scientific and other knowledge to spread faster than before, further promoting the intellectual flowering of the **Renaissance**.

Christian Europe's control of the Middle East following the **Crusades** was crucial to the smooth functioning of the spice trade and to the profits and benefits it provided. In 1453 Europe was shaken by the news that the Ottoman Turks had captured the city of Constantinople (present-day Istanbul). Constantinople lay at the frontier between Europe and Asia, and was a crucial link in the overland trade route to Asia. When the new Islamic rulers of Constantinople prohibited Christian European traders from using their traditional routes, European merchants and princes began to look for new ways to reach the spices and riches of Asia.

**Figure 1.6** On May 29, 1453 the Ottoman Turks captured Constantinople, the capital of the Byzantine empire. The event sent shockwaves through Europe and encouraged European merchants and rulers to seek alternate trade routes to Asia.

## A New World

During the late 15th century improvements in shipbuilding and navigation allowed European mariners to explore the west coast of Africa and eventually sail around the continent to reach the Indian Ocean. Portugal was the first kingdom to dominate this Atlantic trade, bringing slaves from West Africa to work in sugar plantations in Madeira and the Azores. One of the adventurers involved in this trade was the Italian mariner Christopher Columbus, who approached various European rulers with a proposal to avoid the dangerous African route by sailing westward to reach India. Initially he found little support for his proposal. Most geographers scoffed at Columbus's plan, arguing that he had greatly underestimated the distance to Asia sailing westward. (Contrary to popular myth, Columbus did not prove the earth was round—this fact was already well known by geographers.) Columbus eventually convinced the Spanish monarchs Ferdinand and Isabella to finance his voyage, and set out with a fleet of three ships in August 1492.

**SOUND BITE**

"Columbus did not discover a new world. He established contact between two worlds, both already old."

—Historian J.H. Perry

**Figure 1.7** This Spanish map shows the Atlantic world in the mid-16th century. Which parts of the Americas were most familiar to Europeans at the time? Why?

**Figure 1.8** Christopher Columbus landing in the "New World." In what ways might the scenes in this engraving foreshadow future relations between Europeans and Native Americans?

In October of that year Columbus reached the Bahamas. Believing he had landed in China, he explored the coasts of the islands of Cuba and Hispaniola and returned home. While it was clear that Columbus had failed to reach the Indies and its spices, he nevertheless argued that the Native Americans he had encountered could provide a valuable source of slaves. Initial hopes of gold and other riches were never realized, and most of the enslaved Native Americans soon became ill and died. Spain eventually withdrew its support of Columbus but he continued his search for a new route to the Indies, making several subsequent voyages. One of the first Europeans to realize that this was a "New World" was the Italian explorer Amerigo Vespucci. Geographers in the 16th century would name the new continent America in his honour.

## New Spain

Columbus's explorations on behalf of Spain soon led to conflict with Portugal, the principal nation involved in overseas exploration and trade at the time. In 1494 Pope Alexander VI issued a decree to limit competition between

Portugal and Spain for imperial supremacy. The Treaty of Tordesillas drew a line from pole to pole dividing the world between the two powers. Spain received most of the Americas, while Portugal received Brazil, Africa, and the East. The Spanish soon took advantage of the terms of the treaty to establish a permanent presence in the Americas.

## Conquistadors

During the early 16th century a succession of private Spanish adventurers and soldiers known as **conquistadors**, or conquerors, occupied the islands of the Caribbean seeking gold and other riches. The Aboriginal peoples of the islands were massacred, enslaved, or died of disease. Many Spaniards disapproved of this murderous treatment. A few, including the Spanish priest Bartolomé de las Casas, argued that the primary objective of the Spanish empire should be to convert the Native populations to Christianity. They lobbied for more humane treatment of the Aboriginal inhabitants, but with limited success. Indeed, Spanish actions in the Caribbean were only a prelude to the principal Spanish conquests on the mainland.

In 1519 the conquistador Hernan Cortes led a band of 500 soldiers into Mexico, which was ruled by the fierce and warlike Aztecs. Cortes entered Tenochtitlan (te-NOTCH-tee-TLAN), the Aztec capital, and seized the Aztec ruler Montezuma. The Aztecs resisted, but two factors helped the Spanish win. First, they successfully allied themselves with the Aztecs' enemies. Second, they brought with them **smallpox**, an acute contagious viral disease, which decimated the Aztec population in 1520. It was estimated that half of the Native Americans infected with smallpox died as a result. Within two years of Cortes's arrival, the Aztec empire collapsed and the Spanish established the capital of their empire, Mexico City, on the ruins of Tenochtitlan. Following a familiar pattern, one powerful empire replaced another. The Spanish soon established extensive silver mines in Mexico and Peru. In the following century these would become the main source of income for the Spanish government.

## New Mexico

While Mexico and Peru remained the focus of the Spanish imperial effort, other Spanish conquistadors explored the coast of North America. In 1513 Ponce de Leon claimed the most southerly part of the Atlantic coast for Spain, calling the land Florida. The Aboriginal peoples in the area proved more than a match for Ponce de Leon, however, and he was killed in 1521. Other conquistadors explored the lower Mississippi Valley and encountered similar fierce resistance from the Native populations. Still other conquistadors moved north from Mexico seeking the riches of another empire like that of the Aztecs. Instead they found only deserts and small communities of Native Americans along the Rio Grande River.

The Spanish took steps to defend their American empire from any threats. A group of French Protestants had established a base on the coast of Florida from which they attacked and seized Spanish treasure ships transporting silver to Europe. In 1565 a Spanish expedition was sent to destroy the French settlement. The Spanish executed the French inhabitants and founded a fort at St. Augustine to prevent future settlements. St. Augustine remains the oldest continuously occupied European town in North America.

In 1598 an expedition was sent north from Mexico, seeking gold and silver and intending to spread Christianity to the local native Pueblo population. When the Spaniards met with resistance, they captured several towns, massacring most of the inhabitants and enslaving the remainder. The search for precious metals was in vain, but the Franciscan priests who accompanied the expedition convinced the Spanish authorities to support their **missionary** work in this territory of New Mexico. Santa Fe became the capital of the Spanish colony of New Mexico in 1609. New Mexico attracted few new settlers, as it possessed little economic significance. The Spanish population remained small, farming, raising livestock, and working as missionaries in the surrounding Pueblo villages. New Mexico remained an isolated outpost of the mighty Spanish empire.

## Fish and Furs

While Spaniards were mining silver and striving to convert Native Americans to Christianity, other nations began to threaten Spanish dominance of the Americas. Both France and England were seeking a foothold on the continent to the north of the Spanish colonies. Pursuing gold and silver, the English and French instead found other riches: fish and furs. In time these commodities would form the foundation of two European empires in North America.

### New France

France, which had not signed the Treaty of Tordesillas, began exploring the Atlantic coast of America during the 1520s. In 1534 and 1535 Jacques Cartier explored the St. Lawrence and claimed the northern portion of the continent on behalf of the king of France. Initial attempts to plant a permanent colony failed, and for the next half-century the French limited their efforts to sending fleets to fish in the Gulf of St. Lawrence and the North Atlantic. In 1603 a settlement was established at Port Royal on the Bay of Fundy. Five years later a French expedition led by Samuel de Champlain sailed up the St. Lawrence to establish a fort at Quebec with the aim of controlling the fur trade more effectively. Even as small numbers of settlers arrived to farm along the St. Lawrence, the French concentrated on the fur trade throughout the 17th century, sending repeated expeditions along the Great Lakes and as far as the Mississippi Valley. The French would eventually create an empire that dominated the interior of North America and presented a significant obstacle to the future expansion of English colonies along the Atlantic coast.

## 49th PARALLEL

# La Salle and the Mississippi

**Figure 1.10** René-Robert Cavelier, sieur de La Salle.

While English settlement in North America was largely confined to coastal areas, France dominated the interior of the continent. The Mississippi and Ohio rivers formed part of a trade network centred on the Great Lakes and the St. Lawrence, with its headquarters at Montreal. Few contributed more to the creation of the French empire in North America than René-Robert Cavelier, sieur de La Salle.

La Salle was obsessed with finding an overland route to China. He even named his lands on the island of Montreal "Lachine," or China. He was determined to follow the paths of earlier French traders and missionaries who had explored the Great Lakes and had seen a great river, the Mississippi. Hoping that this would lead to Asia, in 1679 La Salle and his men constructed the first sailing vessel on the Great Lakes, near present-day Buffalo, and sailed aboard the *Griffon* as far as Lake Michigan.

In 1681 La Salle set out again in search of the mouth of the Mississippi. The expedition crossed the upper Great Lakes, through Illinois, and then down the Mississippi. La Salle's determination paid off. On April 7, 1682 he reached the river's mouth and claimed the entire Mississippi Valley for France, calling it Louisiana in honour of the French king. Despite this sweeping claim to Louisiana's many "nations, peoples, provinces, cities, towns, villages, mines, fisheries, and rivers," Louis XIV dismissed La Salle's territory as "quite useless." La Salle deliberately falsified his report, suggesting that the mouth of the Mississippi was far west of its true location and therefore closer to Asia. He hinted that it could provide a base from which to continue the search for China while raiding Spanish territories and their gold mines further south. Despite the doubts of the king and his ministers, La Salle was appointed commander of the territory and given men and a ship to continue the search.

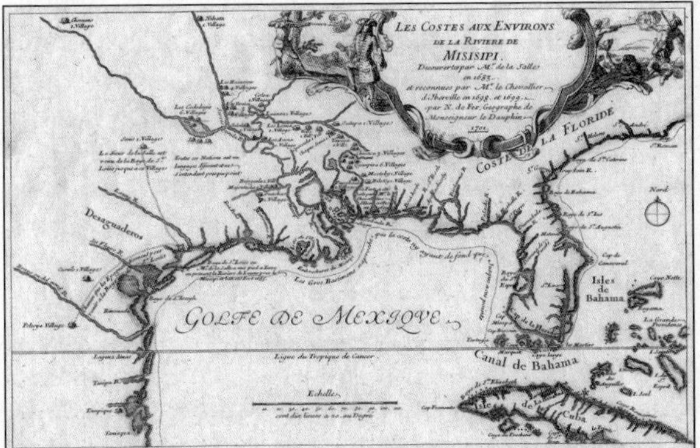


**Figure 1.9** This map shows the Mississippi Valley explored by La Salle during the 1680s, with details of the Native American settlements he encountered.

La Salle's return proved ill fated. For almost two years he wandered through present-day Louisiana and eastern Texas, pressing his men forward in a fruitless search for riches. Some men died of disease in the swamps of the Mississippi delta, while others revolted against La Salle's autocratic leadership. Eventually, having endured enough, they murdered La Salle on March 19, 1687.

While La Salle failed to find an overland route to China, he did succeed in establishing a French presence in the interior of North America from the Great Lakes to the Gulf of Mexico. The lands he claimed for France would, for the most part, remain under French control until the Louisiana Purchase in 1803 (see Chapter 4) and profoundly affect the development of the American nation.

## Think It Through

1. How did the search for a shorter route to China influence La Salle's career?
2. Why might Louis XIV have described La Salle's discoveries as "quite useless"?

## CHECK YOUR UNDERSTANDING

1. How did trade with Asia transform Europe during the later Middle Ages?
2. What was the impact of the capture of Constantinople by the Turks?
3. What was the purpose of the Treaty of Tordesillas?
4. What factors contributed to the rapid success of the Spanish in creating an empire in the Americas? Why did the Spanish establish the province of New Mexico? Why did it enjoy only limited success?
5. What was the basis of economic development in the French and English colonies?

# THE ENGLISH EMPIRE

By the mid-16th century Spain had established a significant empire in the Americas and France was beginning to dominate the trade in furs. England, however, appeared to have few realistic imperial ambitions in the Americas. In 1497 the Italian mariner Giovanni Caboto, or John Cabot, had sailed for England as far as Labrador. He discovered a rich fishery in the waters around Newfoundland, but the English Crown made little attempt to establish a permanent presence in North America. By the 1560s English sailors were participating in the slave trade to the Caribbean and raiding Spanish treasure ships en route to Europe.

During the reign of Elizabeth I in the late 16th century commentators such as Richard Hakluyt (HAK-loot) advocated the establishment of English colonies on the Atlantic coast of America. Hakluyt argued that colonies would provide bases to attack Spanish fleets, offer new markets for English goods, and provide a destination for "loiterers and idle vagabonds" who would otherwise live in poverty in England. Finally, establishing colonies in America would show the world that the England of Elizabeth I and her successors was a true maritime power. During the 1570s and 1580s a succession of voyages of exploration were sent to discover the best prospects for an English empire in North America.

## Early English Colonies

Two models shaped early English settlement of North America. The colony of Virginia was a commercial venture intended to make a profit for English investors. The colony of Massachusetts was created as a refuge for religious dissenters who wished to escape the control of the English church. These two types of colonies laid the foundation for the American colonial experience.

## Roanoke: The Lost Colony

Although English explorers and adventurers had sailed to the New World several times during the 16th century, England did not attempt to establish permanent settlements until the 1580s. An expedition to Newfoundland failed when the ship was lost on the return voyage to England, but a subsequent expedition to the coast of North Carolina reported a promising location for a colony. The English courtier Walter Raleigh dreamed of creating an English empire on Roanoke Island to rival that of Spain. In 1585 a group of settlers travelled to Roanoke with plans to trade for furs, establish farms, or perhaps mine for gold and silver using Native American labour as the Spanish had done. As would happen again in later years, early cooperation with Native Americans, who at first shared precious food and supplies with the English settlers, soon turned to mistrust and then to violence. Armed colonists eventually captured and killed the local Native American leader Wingina.

In 1587 a new group of colonists, led by the explorer John White, settled in Roanoke. This time the colonists found their Native American neighbours far less eager to assist. Spurred on by the fearful colonists, White sailed back to England but found little help for the colony. England's struggle against Spain was growing more pressing (in 1588 the Spanish king launched a massive invasion fleet against England—the Spanish Armada). When White returned to Roanoke in 1590 he found the colony deserted and no trace of the more than 100 colonists he had left three years earlier. To this day, their fate remains a mystery. Some have argued that Native Americans killed them in an attack. Oral traditions also persisted that the surviving colonists, believing themselves abandoned by White and the English Crown, left the colony and were adopted into the local Aboriginal communities. Regardless of the true story, the disastrous Roanoke experience did little to encourage settlement. England would not attempt to establish another colony on the Atlantic coast of North America for almost two decades.

## Virginia

In 1607 a group of London merchants known as the Virginia Company sent an expedition to found a colony on the coast of Virginia. These investors hoped to profit from the gold and silver the colonists would discover and mine. On the shore of Chesapeake Bay the group of colonists, led by John Smith, established Jamestown, named in honour of King James I of England. The hundred male colonists, however, chose a poor site. Jamestown was situated in a swampy area infested with disease-bearing mosquitoes.

At first the Algonquin peoples living in the area, who formed a confederacy led by Powhatan (pow-a-TAN), welcomed the arrival of the English. Powhatan hoped that by providing the English with food and supplies he would profit through trade. He also hoped to gain English support for his own wars against competing Algonquin groups. Relations between the colonists and their Algonquin neighbours, however, deteriorated rapidly with the departure of Smith, who had cultivated a friendship with Powhatan. The English settlers, who lacked sufficient supplies to survive the harsh winters, soon began to steal food. Powhatan cut off further assistance and the colonists starved, with fewer than 60 of the 500 surviving the bitter winter of 1609–10.

**SOUND BITE**

"Why should you take by force that which you can have from us by love? Why should you destroy us who have provided you with food? What can you get by war? We can hide our provisions and fly into the woods. And then you must consequently famish by wrongdoing your friends."

—Chief Powhatan, addressing John Smith in 1609

The Virginia Company sent more men and weapons to the colony and began a war against Powhatan. Peace was restored temporarily in 1614 with the marriage of Powhatan's 19-year-old daughter Pocahontas to John Rolfe, a leading colonist. Within a few years, however, both Pocahontas and Powhatan were dead, and as more settlers arrived the English demands for land caused frequent clashes between the English and Algonquins. Algonquin attacks in 1622 and 1644 killed hundreds of colonists. At the same time the combination of warfare and diseases introduced by the English devastated the Algonquin peoples, who were almost entirely wiped out. In 1607 the Chesapeake Bay area had been home to more than 20,000 Algonquins and fewer than 100 English colonists. By 1670 the proportions had dramatically reversed, with more than 40,000 colonists and barely 2,000 Algonquins.

The Virginia colony was established for profit. While hopes of gold and silver were never realized, Virginia proved to be ideal for growing tobacco. Smoking tobacco had recently become wildly popular in England, although a few individuals, including King James I, denounced its negative effects on health. Before long the Virginia colony was fixated on tobacco farming. Members of the Virginia Company began to profit from their investment, but tobacco had a profound and largely damaging impact on the colony's early development.

The sizable profits available from tobacco discouraged colonists from other farming. Rather than growing necessary food, every available plot was devoted to this cash crop and winters brought food shortages and widespread starvation. Tobacco farming also rapidly depleted the soil, leading to a constant demand for fresh lands and increasing tensions with the colony's Algonquin neighbours. Finally, tobacco cultivation was very labour-intensive. In order to succeed the colonists had to import workers.

Ætatis suæ 21. Aº. 1616.

Matoaks als Rebecka daughter to the mighty Prince Powhatan Emperour of Attanoughkomouck als Virginia converted and baptized in the Christian faith, and Wife to the wor.ll Mr Tho: Rolff.

**Figure 1.11** Pocahontas, daughter of the Algonquin chief Powhatan, portrayed as an English gentlewoman. Her marriage to an English colonist at the age of 19 was meant to symbolize harmony between two peoples. She eventually travelled to England, where she fell ill and died at the age of 22. What messages about Native American culture might this portrait have intended to convey?

**Figure 1.12** This contemporary illustration depicts the arrival of Englishmen at Jamestown in 1607. What dangers, real and imaginary, did 17th-century seafarers face?

**Figure 1.13** An image of a Native American warrior from Virginia at the time of the Roanoke colony.

In the early years wealthy colonists brought **indentured servants** (men and some women) to Virginia to provide a source of labour. The colonists paid for the costs of the servants' voyages and provided them with food and shelter in exchange for their labour for a period of time, usually from 7 to 14 years. Life for indentured servants was very hard. Many died in Virginia, and most of those who survived returned to England as soon as they were free to do so and could afford the voyage home. The obvious drawbacks of indentured service in Virginia eventually made recruiting sufficient white indentured servants difficult and encouraged tobacco farmers to import African slaves to meet the demand for labour. This profoundly affected American history in the succeeding centuries.

Explore the world of the early Jamestown colony and its Aboriginal neighbours by visiting www.emp.ca/ah.

## Massachusetts

During the mid-16th century England underwent a Protestant reformation. Following this, many people believed that the Anglican Church, the established state church in England, still retained too many vestiges of Catholicism, including bishops and some religious ceremonies. So-called **Puritans** wished to further purify the English church. In the early 17th century some more radical Puritans began to leave England for Europe, seeking freedom from the Anglican Church and its laws. Others began to explore the possibility of America as a refuge where they could create ideal religious communities.

In September 1620 the first group of Puritan colonists, known as **Pilgrims**, sailed for America from Plymouth, England aboard the *Mayflower*. The voyage was led by William Bradford and sponsored by the Virginia Company, which had also founded the colony at Jamestown. In December 1620 the Pilgrims reached Massachusetts Bay and established a settlement they named Plymouth. The combination of disease, malnutrition, and the harsh winter killed almost half of the settlers within a few months. As at Jamestown, the colony survived only with the aid of the local Algonquin peoples, the Wampanoags, who hoped to ally themselves with the English against their neighbours.

The key figure in forging the alliance was Squanto, an Algonquin who had been kidnapped by an earlier English expedition and had spent time in Europe. He exploited his understanding of the Algonquins and the English in an attempt to increase his own influence and power before, like thousands of others, he succumbed to an epidemic. The Plymouth colony did not make a profit for the Virginia Company, but it slowly grew and eventually became economically self-sufficient due in large part to Bradford's leadership. It remained a small but independent colony until it was united with the larger Massachusetts Bay colony in 1691.

As political conditions in England deteriorated during the 1620s, wealthy Puritans planned to found another colony or refuge in America. In 1629 they established the Massachusetts Bay Company and began to organize a large-scale emigration from England. Over the following 15 years about 20,000 Puritan colonists crossed to Massachusetts in what became known as the Great Migration. Led by the lawyer John Winthrop, they founded the town of Boston in 1630 and within ten years had extended their settlements almost 100 kilometres inland. By exploiting a legal loophole in their **charter** and moving the Company's headquarters to America, the Puritans in Massachusetts were able to establish their own government, largely free of any interference from England. As governor, Winthrop declared that all male heads of households (freemen) who were church members could vote to select delegates to the General Court, which drew up laws for the colony. This early form of democracy served as a model for future political developments in the colonies and helped make Massachusetts a centre of resistance to British imperial control during the American Revolution.

While sailing from England in 1630 Winthrop had preached a sermon in which he stated his vision for the new Puritan colony as a model of a religious community. He reminded his companions: "we shall be as a city upon a hill, the eyes of all people ... upon us." This vision of a "city upon a hill" would resonate throughout the following centuries, both as a powerful expression of American **exceptionalism**—the idea that the creation of America was a unique historical experiment and that America holds a special position in the world—and as a metaphor for the nation's role as a model for other peoples and nations.

AMERICAN ARCHIVE

## The Mayflower Compact

In September 1620 a small band of religious dissenters sailed from Plymouth, England on board the *Mayflower*. They were going to establish an English colony in America. While on board the ship, the male members of the expedition composed the **Mayflower Compact**, a document they hoped would preserve their freedom in the new colony. When the ship veered off course from the original destination in Virginia, the legal patent granted to the colonists was no longer considered binding in Plymouth. The Pilgrims, who understood the challenges of carving a community out of the New England wilderness, were determined to establish a legitimate form of government.

Although the authority of the government came from God and the Pilgrims' loyalty to the king remained, the legitimacy of the governing compact came from those who signed it: "We whose names are underwritten, the loyal subjects of our dread sovereign Lord, King James ... do by these presents solemnly and mutually in the presence of God, and one of another, covenant and combine ourselves together into a civil body politic." The Pilgrims acknowledged that a government should be created by and for the citizens for whom it governed. Thomas Jefferson would champion this underlying principle in the next century.

The compact emphasized both preserving order in an untamed, faraway colony and the philosophy of justice and equality in law: "for our better ordering and preservation and furtherance of the ends aforesaid; and by virtue hereof to enact, constitute, and frame such just and equal laws, ordinances, acts, constitutions, and offices ..." Governments continue to have the dual responsibility of protecting and providing for the governed while maintaining their civil rights and liberties. The Pilgrims also understood that in order to preserve the common good of the community, they had to create a compact where citizens would submit themselves to a government: "from time to time, as shall be thought most meet and convenient for the general good of the colony, unto which we promise all due submission and obedience ..."

Although the Mayflower Compact is often referred to as the first constitution in American history, it established no rules of government. Instead, its significance is the idea that government is a contract between those who govern and the governed, and that the legitimacy of a government must be based on the consent of the citizens. During the Revolutionary War the Mayflower Compact served as vital political propaganda, since it was an early example of direct democracy. John Quincy Adams, a descendant of the Pilgrims, later described the compact as "the only instance in human history of that positive, original social contract." Consequently, some historians view the Mayflower Compact as the first step on the road to the Declaration of Independence and the creation of the United States.

### Think It Through

1. Why did the Pilgrims feel it was necessary to create a written governing contract prior to landing in Plymouth?
2. What fundamental principles of government did the Mayflower Compact establish?

**Figure 1.14** This 1939 painting by N.C. Wyeth of the signing of the Mayflower Compact commemorates a key moment in the idea of American government.

The economic success of the Massachusetts Bay colony and the constant arrival of new colonists led to a growing demand for fresh lands, creating friction with the Algonquin peoples who lived in the area. The Native Americans did not always understand the documents they were pressured to sign surrendering lands to the colonists, and the colonists often used dishonest means to gain land. Native Americans held that land was communal property, and therefore believed that they were simply agreeing to share access to and usage of the land with the settlers. These different concepts of land ownership would lead to recurring problems between Native Americans and Europeans. The colonists' efforts to displace their Native American neighbours were aided by epidemics of smallpox (as in 1633–34) and other diseases, as well as wars between rival Algonquin peoples.

Following the English Civil War the Puritans seized power in England. Their supporters no longer had any reason to flee to America, and in the mid-17th century immigration declined. Initially this created problems for the colony, which had come to rely on the steady stream of settlers. However, as the economy diversified into shipbuilding, fishing and overseas trade, and agriculture, Massachusetts prospered again and established itself as one of the wealthiest English colonies in America.

**Figure 1.15** This 19th-century engraving shows the landing of the Pilgrims at Plymouth in December 1620. What challenges did the Pilgrims face? Does this illustration tell you anything about the character of the Pilgrims, and the reasons for their eventual success?

# Culture Notes

## Limners and Early Colonial Portraits

Throughout the nation's history, the arts—including painting, architecture, and music—have played a significant role in illuminating the changing character of American society. They illustrate both the influences of established European society and culture, and the emergence of a unique American identity. Artistic developments highlight significant trends in American history and help us understand the evolution of American culture.

Art in 17th-century Puritan New England was strongly influenced by the contemporary portrait painting of England known as "limning." In early colonies such as Massachusetts, most of the limners, as these portrait painters were known, were untrained. They travelled from community to community offering their services. Most limners were anonymous and are identified now by the subject of their works, like the painter of the Freake family who worked in Boston in the early 1670s. The success of limners reflects the emergence of a prosperous merchant class in New England colonies able to afford portraits. It also illustrates the success of the New England trading economy by the late 17th century, with the growth of towns such as Boston and Salem.

The limners' work is evidence of the devotion of New England society to traditional social and religious values. In their theology the Puritans of New England emphasized material prosperity as proof of divine favour and the product of personal piety. Rather than a statement of social and economic success, a family portrait illustrating the wealth and possessions of the sitters served as a declaration of personal religious conviction.

By 1700 the work of the limners was regarded as old-fashioned, even in New England. New styles of portraiture were adopted that reflected changes in artistic taste in Europe. The limners and their art began to disappear, leaving later generations a glimpse of domestic life for the colonial elite in the late 17th century.

### Think It Through

1. How did the work of limners reflect the colonial society in which these artists worked?
2. Examine the painting of the Freake family. What impression is given of Mrs. Freake and her daughter by their dress? Would it be easy to identify them as Puritans? Why or why not?

**Figure 1.16** This portrait of the young wife and daughter of the Boston merchant John Freake was completed in the early 1670s. It appears that the baby, Mary, was added to the painting later.

## CHECK YOUR UNDERSTANDING

1. Why did England decide to join other nations in establishing colonies in the Americas?
2. Why did Powhatan cooperate with the first English settlers?
3. What factors hurt the early development of the Virginia colony?
4. Why did the Puritans move to Massachusetts?
5. How did different views of land ownership lead to conflict between the Algonquin peoples and the Massachusetts colony?
6. Given the purposes of Virginia and Massachusetts, what two values were established in the colonies from the beginning?

## New Colonies

While profit and piety were the two primary motives of early English settlement in North America (in Virginia and Massachusetts), the most striking characteristic of the American colonies as a whole was their diversity. Some were established by the Crown, while others were "proprietary," or controlled by a single individual or small group. Some were established by men and women seeking greater political or religious freedom, while others were an attempt to recreate the societies that the settlers had previously known in Europe or the Caribbean. These differing colonial histories mattered, for they prevented the growth of a common American identity during the 16th and early 17th centuries and generated **sectional** differences that would endure far longer.

### Puritan Refugees: Connecticut and Rhode Island

The Puritans crossed the Atlantic as refugees fleeing religious persecution in England, hoping to found a "godly commonwealth" in North America. Once they had established political control, the Puritan authorities proved hostile to any who challenged their control or refused to conform to their theological vision. The most outspoken dissenters were banished from the colony. A few set up colonies themselves where they could follow their beliefs freely.

Thomas Hooker, a Puritan minister who objected to the policy of limiting political power to church members, was one of the earliest refugees. In 1636 he led a group west to the Connecticut River where they founded a new colony. That same year another Puritan minister, Roger Williams, was banished for criticizing the authorities. Williams believed in religious toleration and in the separation of church and state, or the idea that religious and civil authorities should be distinct. He also protested the colonists' poor treatment of Native Americans, arguing that the latter should be fairly compensated for their lands. Williams and his followers left and established the settlement of Providence. Williams was soon joined by Anne Hutchinson, a Boston merchant's

**Figure 1.17** A 19th-century wood engraving depicting Thomas Hooker and his followers reaching their new settlement, which would become the colony of Connecticut.

wife who had publicly rebuked the religious leaders of the Massachusetts colony for their behaviour. Angered by the criticism, the authorities **excommunicated** and banished Hutchinson and her supporters. In 1644 Williams was granted a royal charter for the new colony of Rhode Island. Subsequent charters guaranteed complete religious freedom in the colony.

"God requireth not a uniformity of religion."

—Roger Williams, founder of Rhode Island

## Proprietary Colonies: Maryland and Pennsylvania

Several English colonies were created by royal grants of lands to powerful individuals or groups. These proprietary colonies became the personal property of the recipients, who controlled settlement and directed the colonies' early development. Two of the proprietary colonies, Maryland and Pennsylvania, had distinctive religious characters that reflected the beliefs of their founders.

In 1632 King Charles I granted four million hectares of land on Chesapeake Bay to William Calvert, Lord Baltimore. Calvert, a prominent Catholic nobleman and supporter of the king, in turn made large grants to a group of Catholic noblemen. These noblemen dominated the colony's government. Calvert encouraged Catholics—who were facing discrimination in England—to settle in the colony, which was named Maryland in honour of the king's wife, Henrietta Maria, who was also a Catholic. Maryland's substantial Catholic minority made it unique among English colonies. Its economy was based on tobacco cultivation, mirroring that of neighbouring Virginia.

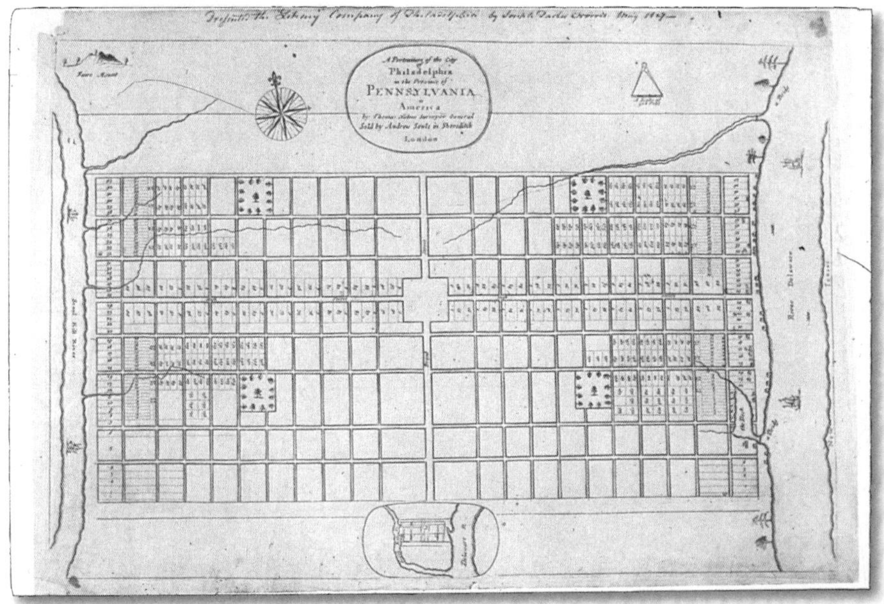


**Figure 1.18** The plan prepared by William Penn in 1683 for his new city of Philadelphia. Notice how ordered it is, with straight streets and a central square, compared with the wilderness of North America.

Like his father, King Charles II used land in America to reward his friends and supporters. Owing a large personal debt to one of his friends, in 1681 the king granted a huge tract of land west of the Delaware River to his friend's son, William Penn. Penn and his family belonged to the Quaker sect, a religious group that favoured religious toleration and pacifism. Quakers were persecuted in England for their unwillingness to pay taxes to support the English military or the established Church, so Penn opened his colony, called Pennsylvania, to anyone seeking refuge from persecution, including Quakers.

Penn took a strong personal interest in the early development of his colony. He drafted a constitution that protected religious freedom and guaranteed popular democracy. He also prohibited further settlement in the colony until the Native inhabitants had received fair compensation for their lands, in an effort to ensure that the Native Americans were treated fairly. Reflecting the spirit of the new colony, Penn drew up plans for Philadelphia, whose Greek name means "city of brotherly love." Pennsylvania attracted many farmers from England and Germany and its agriculture flourished. In 1704 Penn approved the establishment of a second colony, Delaware, along the Delaware River, partitioned from Pennsylvania.

## The Carolinas

In 1663 King Charles II chartered a new colony between the southern limits of Virginia and the Spanish colony of Florida. The colony was named Carolina from the Latin for Charles, Carolus. Virginians settled in the northern part of the colony, establishing small farms and larger tobacco plantations on the fresh lands. By 1675 North Carolina had a population of over 5,000. Further south, English settlers from the overpopulated Caribbean island of Barbados founded another colony. The settlers brought many slaves who made up almost half of the colony's population by the end of the 17th century. With its larger plantations and slave economy, South Carolina more closely resembled English colonies in the West Indies than the more northern American colonies, underscoring the economic and social differences between the English colonies.

### New York

During the early 17th century the newly independent Netherlands established a fur-trading colony along the Hudson River with a settlement at the mouth of the river—at the tip of Manhattan Island—called New Amsterdam. While some Dutch aristocrats dreamed of establishing a feudal society along the Hudson River similar to the seigneurial system in New France, the Dutch West India Company's commercial alliance with the Iroquois soon enabled it to dominate the fur trade throughout the Great Lakes.

In the mid-17th century England and the Netherlands struggled to dominate international trade. Competition with England for control of trade along the Atlantic coast soon led to war, and in 1664 a small English fleet captured New Amsterdam (without firing a shot). King Charles II granted the colony to his brother James, Duke of York, and it was renamed New York in his honour. The following year the portion of the colony along the Delaware River was separated to form the colony of New Jersey. Under English rule, New York continued to prosper as a port, particularly through the export of grain and flour from the farms of the Hudson Valley.

## Societies in Conflict

In the early years relations between Native Americans and Europeans were relatively good, and many of the early colonies could not have survived without assistance from Native Americans. This initial harmony, however, did not last. European diseases devastated Aboriginal populations, and it was not long

**Figure 1.19** The settlement of New Amsterdam, at the tip of the island of Manhattan (1664).

before disputes over land erupted into violence. Shortly after contact, European and Native American societies were in conflict.

### King Philip's War

Relations between colonists and Native Americans steadily deteriorated through the mid-17th century. As the growing numbers of settlers demanded more and more land, pressures on the Algonquin to end their earlier accommodations with the colonists increased. In the early 1670s the Pokanoket leader Metacomet, whom the English called "King Philip," persuaded several Algonquin groups to confront the colonists. In response, in 1675 an alliance of New England colonies and New York launched an attack on Metacomet and his supporters. The resulting conflict, King Philip's War, was marked by fierce fighting and substantial destruction on both sides.

**Figure 1.20**
Metacomet, known to the English as "King Philip," responded to pressure on the Pokanokets by organizing and leading armed resistance to the English settlers of the Plymouth colony.

Initially the colonists suffered significant losses as Metacomet's warriors attacked and burned settlements across New England. Soon, however, the colonists organized a military response and gained the upper hand. The Iroquois ignored Metacomet's appeal for help and instead joined forces with the colonists in a calculated effort to unseat the Algonquin nations and dominate the fur trade. Metacomet's army was destroyed in the summer of 1676, ending the Native American challenge to expanded European settlement. The struggle had cost more than 6,000 lives, including the lives of 4,000 Algonquins, and destroyed dozens of settlements. It also helped the Iroquois establish control over the interior and the lucrative fur trade, and demonstrated their ability to use their alliance with the English colonists to solidify their own dominance. Finally, the struggle demonstrated the success of colonial leaders in setting Native American groups against each other.

During the 17th century the government and merchant leaders in London wanted to incorporate the Aboriginal peoples as partners—albeit subordinate ones—in the colonial enterprise. Their goal was to spread European "civilization" to the New World, an objective founded on the belief that Native American societies were "uncivilized." Many in England envisioned an American empire where all residents, European and Native American alike, embraced English law, customs, and religion, and the economy was organized to profit the mother country. Population pressures and the resulting demand for land combined with a widening cultural divide to frustrate these plans. Instead, despite an early harmony, relations between Europeans and Aboriginal peoples in North America rapidly deteriorated. A pattern of frontier conflict began that would continue for centuries.

## Colonial Tension

Social and political tensions grew as new settlers arrived and the colonies expanded. The issues were different in each society, reflecting the variety of colonial experiences. In Virginia, for example, conflict arose between the prosperous established **planters** along the Atlantic coast and the poorer colonists in the interior along the **frontier**. In Massachusetts the crisis focused on the changing religious character of the colony and the resulting political turmoil.

## Bacon's Rebellion

During the 1670s in Virginia, backcountry colonists, led by wealthy farmer Nathaniel Bacon and seeking fresh lands, began a frontier war against the Susquehannock people. As in New England during King Philip's War, both sides carried out violent raids. The governor of Virginia, Sir William Berkeley, saw the colonists' raids as provocative and as a threat to the peace he wished to preserve with neighbouring Native groups, and ordered an end to the raids. The conflict revealed a split within Virginia's population. Many wealthy planters living in coastal areas, who no longer lived with the threat of raids, also opposed the frontier war. The backcountry farmers, led by Bacon, protested the governor's lack of support for their quest for fresh lands and protection from Native raids.

In the spring of 1676 Bacon led several hundred colonists in a revolt against Berkeley and the planter elite, calling for the removal of all Native Americans from the colony. Bacon also demanded an end to control over the colony by the wealthy coastal planters, whom he denounced as "parasites." The rebels attacked and burned Jamestown, forcing Berkeley to flee. The rebellion fizzled out, however, when Bacon fell ill and died. The other leaders of the rebellion were rounded up and executed. Although Bacon's Rebellion failed, it revealed the social tensions that existed in colonies such as Virginia between wealthy established colonists and poorer farmers living on the frontier. It also encouraged colonial authorities to be more active in helping colonists eliminate Native Americans from their territory in order to avoid future troubles. The different interests and attitudes of the frontier and the established centres would remain an important theme in the following centuries as America continued to expand westward.

## Salem Witch Scare

While Virginia was divided over policy toward Native Americans and political differences between established coastal plantation owners and frontier farmers, the Massachusetts colony was experiencing its own social and economic tensions. In 1685 the English government of the Catholic King James II revoked the Massachusetts charter. A new royal governor was sent with a plan to unite many of the colonies into a Dominion of New England. Governor Edmund Andros took steps both to reduce the powers of the local government in Massachusetts and to end Puritan dominance within the colony, even sanctioning the first public Christmas celebrations in the colony (long prohibited by the Puritan authorities). In the Revolution of 1688 the Protestant King William III replaced King James II as king of England and Andros was removed. The new English government, however, still required the colony to extend religious toleration and allow non-church members to vote in elections. While most new immigrants to Massachusetts welcomed these changes, many Puritans feared that the colony's unique character as a Puritan "city upon a hill" was threatened.

**Figure 1.21** This 19th-century painting shows an accused witch being questioned. Why might accusations of witchcraft have attracted such widespread interest in colonial communities?

Fear of the end of the Puritans' "godly commonwealth" was expressed in one of the most bizarre incidents in colonial history: the Salem witch scare. In late 1691 several young women in the Massachusetts port of Salem were accused of witchcraft. Throughout 1692 the community was in turmoil, with over 100 women and a few men accused of involvement in witchcraft. Twenty individuals were convicted and executed for witchcraft before the new governor ordered a halt to the trials.

While accusations of witchcraft were not uncommon in New England (there were more than 300 prosecutions during the 17th century), the events in Salem were without parallel in their scope. Most commonly those accused of witchcraft were old women, unmarried or widowed, who were denounced by their neighbours out of fear or jealousy. The Salem accusations, however, involved both old and young women and men, and likely reflected deeper social and economic divisions within the community. The accused were generally from the more prosperous commercial parts of the town and were members of religious minorities, such as Anglicans or Quakers. Their accusers were largely from areas of the town that were suffering economically, and were mostly Puritans. Moreover, one of the first young women accused was an African-American slave who had recently arrived in Salem, reflecting further fears about race within the community and perhaps the threat to local employment posed by the spread of slavery. Like Bacon's Rebellion, the Salem witch scare revealed the social and economic stresses that afflicted established colonial societies.

**WEB LINKS**

To discover more about the shocking events in Salem in 1692 and read eyewitness accounts of the trials, visit www.emp.ca/ah.

## King William's War

Wider imperial conflict soon matched the social and political tensions within the colonies. In the final decade of the 17th century a lengthy struggle began between France and England for control of North America. This was part of a wider competition between the two powers for imperial dominance around the world. The first part of the conflict, known in North America as King William's War, began in 1689 when a combined force of English and Iroquois attacked Montreal. The following year the French and their Algonquin allies responded with raids on frontier settlements and Iroquois communities in New York and New England. Further English attacks followed, including the brief capture of Port Royal in Acadia. Peace came in 1697 with the Treaty of Ryswick, but after only five years war erupted again.

King William's War both foreshadowed the imperial struggle of the 18th century and led governments to increase their control over the American colonies in order to ensure a more coordinated defence. In 1701 the English Crown took direct control of all remaining proprietary colonies (although William Penn did successfully petition to regain control of Pennsylvania), ensuring that each colony had a royal governor. The combination of growing imperial conflict and England's increasing control over its colonies would become the predominant theme in the history of the American colonies during the 18th century.

## Emerging Patterns

By the end of the 17th century many of the fundamental themes of the American story were becoming clear. The first was the impact of continuous contact between existing societies and new arrivals. Native Americans struggled to adjust to increasing European settlement, while European attitudes toward Aboriginal peoples changed from a wish for partnership to a desire to dominate. Relations between the two peoples began as alliances of equal nations but by 1700 this equality was already disappearing. A second crucial pattern emerged from the importance of dissent. Many of the early European arrivals came to North America seeking economic and religious freedom, and that desire for freedom (or liberty) would become a key characteristic of American society. Finally, the diversity of American society was already evident as each colony acquired its own unique character. Significant differences were also emerging between urban and frontier society, a tension that would shape America in the decades and centuries to come.

### CHECK YOUR UNDERSTANDING

1. What reasons did Roger Williams and Anne Hutchinson have for leaving Massachusetts and establishing a colony in Rhode Island?
2. Why were the colonies of Maryland and Pennsylvania founded?
3. What were common factors in King Philip's War, Bacon's Rebellion, and other conflicts with Native Americans?
4. How did the Iroquois make use of their relations with the English?
5. How did the appointment of Governor Andros by King James II challenge the Puritans?
6. What relationships are shown between the Native Americans and the English and French in King William's War?

# THE HISTORIAN'S CRAFT

## Inquiring and Imagining

### Curiosity and Inquiry

If historians typically exercise intellectual curiosity (see Introduction to The Historian's Craft, page vi), what makes them ask new questions or start a new line of research? They may pursue new ideas after reflecting on their own work or be inspired by others' discoveries. For example, a historian who studies Aboriginal settlements in the southwest United States might read about a new archeological discovery in a professional journal or see a TV news report about recently discovered artifacts. This new information raises questions in the historian's mind about how these discoveries fit into existing knowledge about early Native American life.

When you study history you need to approach it as a historian. First, you must become knowledgeable enough about a topic to arouse your intellectual curiosity. You need to know enough about the Salem witch scare (pages 29–30) to ask questions such as "what happened next?" or "why did that happen?" or "what was the result?" Some of these questions lead to immediate answers, while others prompt you to make inferences (tentative conclusions) or reasoned deductions. For more definite answers to these latter questions, historians research to find relevant historical evidence.

Historians prepare for research by moulding their inferences into a hypothesis (e.g., "Economic and social tensions explain the Salem witch scare") or into an inquiry question (e.g., "What best explains why the Salem witch scare happened?"). An inquiry question is one worth researching and that suggests a number of feasible alternative answers. Historians then gather evidence for each alternative.

### Scientific Method and Historical Imagination

As historians research they are rigorous, looking for evidence that not only supports their hypothesis but that may weaken or disprove it. This process may lead to a revised hypothesis. When pursuing an inquiry question historians gather evidence for all alternatives, sometimes developing new alternatives or an entirely new question if the evidence warrants. Once they have gathered their evidence, historians ask critical questions about its reliability (see The Historian's Craft features in Chapters 2, 3, and 4). Then they consider whether they have left out other possibilities, or interpreted the evidence carefully enough. So, historians critically interrogate their starting points, their evidence, and their research methods. Only then do they make conclusions and communicate their findings.

All of this sounds very scientific, but historians use historical imagination, too. They imagine what life was like at the time and feel empathy for the people in history. For example, they put themselves in the shoes of the residents of Salem to understand the atmosphere in which the witch trials were conducted. As they read the evidence they imagine how people felt limited by social and religious constraints that are unknown in today's society.

As you work through this text, "doing" history, you too will exercise both the scientific and the imaginative aspects of the historian's craft.

### Try It!

1. Review the characteristics of an inquiry question. Develop an inquiry question for the topic: the decline of the Mississippian culture.
2. Inquiry question: *What best explains the success of the Massachusetts colony?* Alternative explanations: the strong sense of community among the Puritans; help from Native Americans; the development of self-government; diversification in the economy. Research these alternatives and write a statement to answer the inquiry question.
3. Exercise your historical imagination: (a) review your knowledge of conditions in the Massachusetts colony (b) put yourself in the shoes of a Puritan in England. Would you have emigrated to America? Explain and justify your answer.

# STUDY HALL

## Thinking

1. In a graphic organizer compare the Native American societies of the Southwest, Algonquin, and Iroquois under the headings: Location, Economy, Organization/Government.
2. How important were economic concerns in the development of the Spanish and French colonies? Were they as important as religious concerns? Why?
3. "The process of exploration and colonization profoundly transformed both European and Native American societies." Do you agree or disagree with this statement? Why?
4. Make a graphic organizer to compare the Virginia and Massachusetts colonies with headings such as Location, Date of Foundation, Purpose, Economy. What other headings can you add?
5. European and colonial politics and policies had an enormous impact on Native American peoples. What influence did Native American peoples have on the growth and development of the colonies?
6. Is it correct to say that the Puritans were champions of religious toleration and freedom? Why?
7. Can contact between Native Americans and Europeans be described as a disaster? Explain.
8. Were indentured servants and slaves the same? Discuss the similarities and differences.

## Communication

9. What would be the Native American point of view of the arrival of the Spanish and their conquest of the Aztec empire? Create a skit that shows what a Native American television news show might have been like in covering this story.
10. Imagine that you are a Native American living near the Atlantic coast in 1700. Briefly recount and evaluate the impact of English colonization on your society and culture during the preceding century.
11. Is it possible today to compensate Native Americans for the losses they faced when Europeans arrived? Conduct a debate.

## Application

12. Which word better describes the principal motivation for European colonization in the Americas, "profit" or "piety"? Explain your choice.
13. First contact between cultures has always been a great challenge. How would you have managed the contact? Write a set of guidelines for people who are meeting another culture for the first time. How would your guidelines have changed first contacts as described in this chapter?
14. In what ways does the United States today represent a "city upon a hill" to the rest of the world? Consider its culture, economy, government, and institutions.

# 2 Colonial America (1700–1775)

## KEY CONCEPTS

In this chapter you will consider:

- The impact of the struggle between France and Britain for control of North America
- The changing economic and political role of the American colonies within the British empire
- The significance of slavery for the colonial society and economy
- The evolving relations between Europeans and Native Americans along the colonial frontier
- The influence of the Great Awakening on American religious and social life
- The development of British policy toward the colonies and its results

## The American Story

The 18th century was a time of social change and political upheaval in the American colonies. The costly struggle between Britain and France for dominance in North America ended in victory for Britain, but rather than a new era of peace the result was further turmoil. New political and religious ideas swept through colonies already transformed by growing populations and economies. The result was a widening gap between the interests and outlooks of the colonists and those of the British government, which would ultimately lead to revolution and independence.

## TIMELINE

|  |  |
|---|---|
| 1704 | Deerfield Raid |
| 1738 | George Whitefield begins preaching tours |
| 1754 | French and Indian War begins |
| 1759 | Capture of Quebec |
| 1763 | Proclamation of 1763 and Pontiac's Revolt |

## IMAGE ANALYSIS

**Figure 2.1** This painting depicts the death of General James Wolfe at the Battle of Quebec on September 13, 1759. The British capture of Quebec may have been the most important battle in Canadian history but it was a pivotal moment in American history, too. After five years of war between England and France, the American colonies were finally free of raids by French armies and their Aboriginal allies.

The American artist Benjamin West painted this picture to portray the British General Wolfe as a great American hero. How has West used light and darkness, and the other figures in the painting, to focus attention on the dying Wolfe and make his death seem tragic? The American colonists would not forget Wolfe's sacrifice—they immortalized the young commander in ballads, and named taverns and streets in his honour. Yet within six years of Wolfe's death the passage of the Stamp Act would turn many colonists against Britain, sparking a movement that would end in open rebellion.

| ▸ Stamp Act | ▸ Townshend Duties | ▸ Boston Massacre | ▸ Boston Tea Party | ▸ Coercive Acts and Quebec Act |
|---|---|---|---|---|
| 1765 | 1767 | 1770 | 1773 | 1774 |

# INTRODUCTION

In this chapter you will read about several incidents that marked a deteriorating relationship between Britain and its American colonies. One of these has gone down in history as the Boston Tea Party. On this occasion a band of **Patriots** disguised as Mohawks boarded three ships in Boston harbour and dumped their valuable cargos of tea into the water. The Patriots did this because they objected to the monopoly on tea imports the British Crown had given to the British East India Company, denying American merchants any share in the profitable trade.

Notice the use of the word "Patriots." This is what American colonists who favoured radical action against the British authorities called themselves. In Britain, however, the same people were called "rebels." Have you ever been in a situation where what you did seemed right to you but was criticized by others?

As you read through this chapter, try to decide where your sympathies would have been at the time. Would you have identified with the Americans who participated in the Boston Tea Party and other acts of protest as Patriots fighting for their rights and freedoms? Or would you have viewed them as rebels who were defying the British Crown and threatening the economic well-being of the empire?

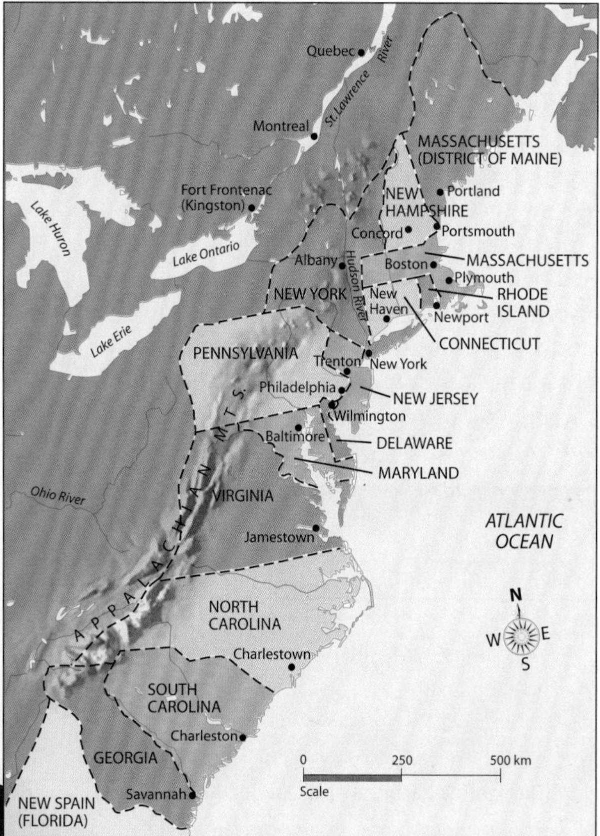


# COLONIAL LIFE

By 1700 a variety of British colonies flourished along the Atlantic coast of America, from Massachusetts in the north to Georgia in the south. While most communities relied on agriculture, a number of significant towns had appeared, including Boston, New York, Philadelphia, and Charleston. The colonies contributed substantially to the wealth and prosperity of the British empire and were an integral part of the Atlantic economy. Steady immigration was altering the population profile of many colonies, creating a society more diverse than Britain.

**Figure 2.2** A map of the American colonies before the Treaty of Paris, signed in 1763. What physical and political barriers do you notice to the expansion of the colonies?

# Trade and Economy

During the first half of the 18th century the economy of the American colonies expanded dramatically. The colonies clearly profited from their relationship with the British empire, while Britain's prosperity depended on the colonies. Under the theory of **mercantilism** the wealth of a nation was based on the value of the gold and silver it earned from exports. Colonies provided ready markets for exports of manufactured goods and in turn served as a source of raw materials for the mother country. The success of the mercantilist system depended on heavy government regulation of economic activity in the colonies. This regulation allowed the American economy to grow but also became a source of tension and conflict.

## Colonial Trade and Mercantilism

By the mid-1700s the American colonies had developed a diversified export economy, supplying a range of agricultural and other products to Britain and other parts of the empire. New England provided fish and meat; the middle colonies of Pennsylvania and New York exported grain, meat, and dairy products; and the Chesapeake region (chiefly Virginia) produced tobacco and grain. Plantations in southern colonies supplied rice and indigo, a plant used to make blue dye. Increasingly this trade used American-made ships, and by the middle of the century a third of all vessels involved in the British Atlantic and coastal trade had been built in the American colonies.

The mercantilist system was enforced by the Navigation Acts, a series of British laws that set out rules for trade during the later 17th century. The Acts prohibited foreign vessels from carrying goods between Britain and its American colonies. Many goods could only be exported to or imported directly from Britain, limiting inter-colonial trade. In practice, however, these restrictions were usually ignored in the interest of economic development. Colonial merchants grew accustomed to substantial profits and few restrictions on trade. Merchants in Philadelphia, New York, and Boston increasingly supplied farmers and plantation owners in Virginia or the Carolinas directly. New England distilleries, supplied with sugar directly from the Caribbean contrary to the Navigation Acts, were exporting rum throughout the British empire. Britain's lax enforcement of trade laws, a policy known as **salutary neglect**, encouraged rapid economic growth. Between 1700 and 1760 exports from the colonies increased more than 150 percent and imports from Britain by more than 400 percent.

## Slavery in Colonial America

Arguably the greatest contributor to the prosperity of the Atlantic economy during the 18th century was slavery. Slave labour was essential to the cultivation of tobacco, rice, indigo, and sugar in the British West Indies and the southern and Chesapeake colonies. Together these colonies contributed almost 95 percent of the total value of exports from America and the West

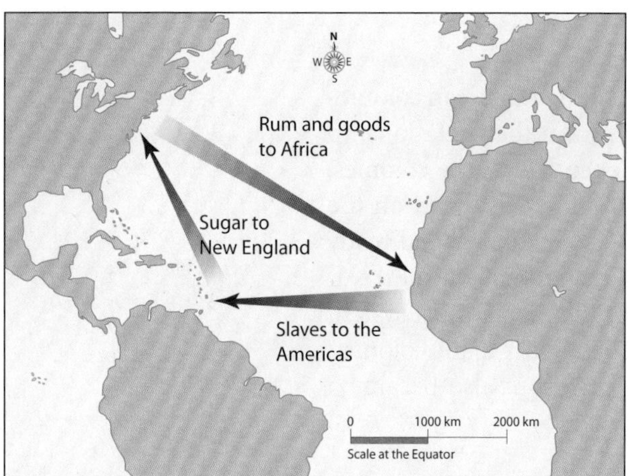


**Figure 2.3** The so-called Triangle Trade of slaves, sugar, and rum linked merchants in colonial New England with the Caribbean economy and the slave trade from Africa, as part of the wider British empire system.

Indies to Britain. The middle colonies and New England were involved in this trade as well. Merchants provided necessary financing, and ports such as Boston and New York were important distribution points.

During the 18th century tens of thousands of men and women were shipped from Africa as slaves each year. In all, almost 600,000 Africans were brought to the American colonies before the slave trade was finally abolished in the early 19th century. Yet this enormous number represents barely 5 percent of the total number of Africans who crossed the Atlantic as slaves. Most were sent to plantations in the West Indies or Brazil.

Slaves were brought from the coast of West Africa across the Atlantic to the Caribbean and America. They were crammed aboard slave ships built for 400 or 500 people but usually carrying many more. The horrors of the Middle Passage, as the slave voyage to America became known, were almost unbearable. Sanitation was virtually non-existent, and the stench of disease and death was inescapable—it was said that a slave ship could be smelled five miles away. Perhaps one African in six did not survive the journey in such appalling conditions. Some threw themselves into the sea in despair rather than face the voyage and the hardships that awaited them.

**WEB LINKS**

To learn more about the transatlantic slave trade and its impact on colonial America, visit www.emp.ca/ah.

Slavery was a key factor in shaping colonial American society during the 18th century. In the first decade of the 1700s more slaves were imported than during the entire previous century, and by 1770 slaves accounted for one-fifth of the colonial population. A healthier climate and better care for slaves in the American colonies helped ensure a growing native slave population by the mid-1700s. By then almost 80 percent of slaves in Virginia had been born in America.

Because slave labour was essential to the cultivation of tobacco, rice, and other cash crops throughout the Chesapeake and southern colonies, slaves were a crucial investment for plantation owners. To protect slaves—as one would protect any other valuable property—politicians ensured that laws governing the ownership and treatment of slaves were **codified**. The high cost of slave ownership created growing divisions within colonial society between an elite group of plantation owners, who often owned hundreds of slaves, and poorer farmers who could not afford the investment. The southern colonies' reliance on slavery as the foundation of their economies set them apart from those in the North. This difference would grow more pronounced in the years to come.

Slavery was also common in New England and the middle colonies, though most owners there possessed only a small number of slaves. Slaves worked as personal servants, and as labourers in towns and ports such as

Boston and Philadelphia. The first major slave revolt in the American colonies occurred not on a southern plantation, but in New York City in 1712. Slavery was widely accepted throughout the colonies as a natural part of American colonial society and its economy, and few Europeans openly questioned the institution.

**SOUND BITE**

"We were all put under the deck … The closeness of the place, and the heat of the climate, added to the number in the ship, which was so crowded that each had scarcely room to turn himself, almost suffocated us … This wretched situation was again aggravated by the galling of the chains now become insupportable; and the filth of the necessary tubs [toilets], into which the children often fell, and were almost suffocated."

—*Memoirs* of Olaudah Equiano, an Ibo from West Africa who was taken on an English slave ship to Barbados

## Society

As with trade and commerce, the 18th century was a time of dramatic change in colonial society. Population growth and steady immigration changed the character of American society, creating new economic conditions and promoting urban growth and settlement expansion along the frontier. Immigration and the frontier would become significant factors in shaping the future of American society.

### Population Growth

During the 18th century the population of colonial America grew at an impressive rate, more than three times as quickly as that of Europe. In 1751 Benjamin Franklin accurately calculated that "our people must at least be doubled every twenty years." Indeed, in 1700 the population of the American colonies was less than 300,000 but by 1750 it had reached almost 1.3 million. Why?

The population increase was partly due to the fact that living conditions in America were better than those in Europe. Less overcrowding and greater food supplies reduced deaths from disease and malnutrition and encouraged larger families. More significantly, the British actively encouraged immigration to their colonies by British residents as well as foreigners. This policy differed from the colonial policies of the French and Spanish, who regularly restricted immigration. Many British merchants actively encouraged foreigners to come to America, as a way of filling their empty vessels en route to America with paying passengers.

In addition to Englishmen and the hundreds of thousands of Africans brought as slaves, two other groups stood out: Scots-Irish and Germans. The Scots-Irish had left Scotland to settle in Ulster (Northern Ireland) during the 17th century. Facing religious persecution and economic hardship in Ireland, however, many eventually emigrated to America. In the 1680s William Penn had begun encouraging immigration by German Protestant refugees and this continued throughout the 18th century. Most German immigrants settled in Pennsylvania, where they were known as Dutch (a corruption of "Deutsch," meaning German). This immigration resulted in remarkable ethnic diversity in colonial America. In 1700, 80 percent of the population was English and Welsh, but by the end of the century these groups accounted for only 49 percent. Africans—almost all slaves—made up 19 percent, Germans 7 percent, and Scots-Irish a further 5 percent.

Immigration accentuated the differences between the colonies. While New England's population remained predominantly English, Pennsylvania was nearly 40 percent German and African slaves made up the majority of the population in many areas of the South. The colony of New Jersey, for example, was home to a diverse population that included communities of English Quakers (and their slaves), Swedes, Germans, Jews, and other groups.

## Settlement

The most obvious difference between colonial and European society was the abundance of cheap land in America. Ready labour was needed in the countryside and in towns to exploit this opportunity, and as you have already seen some relied on slaves. Immigration by indentured servants was equally important during the 18th century. Most were unmarried skilled tradesmen who agreed to work for a master for four or five years in exchange for free passage to the colonies and, often, a grant of land at the end of their service.

During the 17th century most indentured servants returned to Europe at the end of their service. In the 18th century the expanding colonial economy and opportunities for acquiring farmland persuaded more than half of indentured servants to settle in America following their service rather than return home. Many enjoyed greater economic prosperity than they would have in Europe.

While some farms in the South and even in middle colonies such as Maryland and Pennsylvania produced crops (rice, tobacco, wheat, and rye) for export to other colonies or overseas, most colonial farmers grew crops for themselves or to barter for items at local markets. Farmers aimed to be as self-sufficient as possible and some worked as blacksmiths or practised another craft to supplement their incomes.

Colonial craftsmen—from shoemakers and shipwrights to printers and glaziers (window glazers)—practised their trades in the growing number of towns. Most began as apprentices who learned their trade from a master craftsman over a period of years before being free to seek employment in a

**Figure 2.4** Farming was the foundation of the colonial economy. Colonial farmers produced food for the growing American population and to export to Britain and the Caribbean.

shop. Such journeymen spent years saving their wages in the hope of accumulating sufficient **capital** to open their own shops as masters and perhaps take on apprentices of their own. This system mirrored the practice in Europe, but craftsmen in colonial America often had greater opportunities to establish independent workshops than in Britain, where entry into trades was more tightly controlled.

**Figure 2.5** Most colonial craftsmen, like this shoemaker, worked in small shops aided by one or more apprentices. Apprenticeship was the primary means of learning a trade in America during the 18th century.

### Colonial Women

While most women in colonial America possessed few legal rights, many fulfilled important economic roles and exercised considerable influence. Farmwomen traded produce and managed households. In addition to raising children, some women worked as midwives, caring for women in childbirth. Work on most farms was divided equally. Out of necessity, women helped with even the most difficult tasks. Two common terms for wives in 18th century New England were "deputy husbands" and "yoke mates," suggesting a high degree of partnership.

Widows enjoyed considerable freedom and even greater rights than married women. They received a third of their late husbands' estates and many operated farms or businesses on their own, sometimes employing apprentices and journeymen. Few expressed their independence better than a group of New York City widows in 1733. The widows protested their exclusion from political affairs, declaring: "We are housekeepers, pay our taxes, carry on trade and most of us are she Merchants." Such fierce determination would ensure women a prominent role in organizing and encouraging colonial American resistance to British policies in the decades to come.

## Religion

Although many colonies (from Massachusetts to Maryland) had been established by colonists seeking religious freedom, the importance of religion in everyday life had decreased considerably by the early 18th century. Weekly attendance at services was declining and many clergy began to emphasize the importance of good works rather than strong personal belief. A shortage of clergy to minister to growing populations compounded the crisis.

Wealth and social status—not religious fervour—were the new chief requirements of membership in many congregations. Religion had become an intellectual affair, devoid of passion. With churches dominated by scholars and the wealthy elites, young people and the poor felt excluded from religious life. Even in traditionally Puritan New England it was estimated that only 20 percent of colonists were members of established congregations.

## The Great Awakening

In the 1730s a religious revival that became known as the Great Awakening swept through the colonies, shaking the colonial religious establishment. One of the men who helped initiate the movement was Jonathan Edwards, the minister of Northampton, Massachusetts, who began preaching emotional sermons to the youth and poor of his district determined to "have their hearts touched." Edwards enjoyed dramatic success with his message of personal faith and "enthusiasm." Attendance at his meetings swelled, and other preachers were soon conducting similar meetings throughout New England.

The arrival of the English minister George Whitefield in 1738 led to an expansion of this religious revival throughout the colonies. Whitefield toured the colonies, preaching to enormous crowds; one outdoor meeting in Philadelphia drew an audience of 30,000. Many of Whitefield's listeners responded dramatically: "Some of the people were as pale as death; others were wringing their hands; others lying on the ground; others sinking into the arms of their friends." While some in the religious and social establishment ridiculed such displays of religious zeal or regarded them suspiciously—as "common disturbers of the peace"—many ordinary colonists responded to the personal and emotional message with great enthusiasm. The Great Awakening transformed colonial society, leading to a dramatic increase in church membership, particularly among the young.

The Great Awakening had a deeper impact on the development of colonial society beyond reinvigorating religious life in America. As a mass movement, the revivals represented one of the colonies' first widely shared experiences, helping to forge greater solidarity between their societies. The Great Awakening also represented a considerable challenge to the control of religious life by the colonial elites, both clerical and lay. Groups normally excluded from social influence, such as women and slaves, shared in the revival. At the same time, the emphasis on personal faith rather than institutional religion represented a potential challenge to all authority. Finally, the Great Awakening demonstrated the potential of passionate oratory to stir the common people—a lesson that political **radicals** would remember in the decades ahead.

**Figure 2.6** Outdoor preaching was common during the Great Awakening. Note the differences in dress among the preacher's audience. What might this tell us about the appeal of the Great Awakening?

## CHECK YOUR UNDERSTANDING

1. How did the economy of the colonies benefit from mercantilism?
2. How did slavery degrade human beings? Make a list of examples.
3. What factors helped the colonial population and economy grow?
4. What was the Great Awakening and how did it shape the colonies?
5. How did colonial women forge an important role for themselves in everyday colonial life?

# THE STRUGGLE FOR EMPIRE

The early years of settlement in North America had been shaped by the encounters of Europeans with the wilderness and with existing Native American societies. The history of 18th-century America would be shaped above all by the conflict between Britain and France for control of North America, and by the consequences of victory for British policy.

## Frontier Conflict

Throughout the first half of the 18th century Britain and France fought a series of wars along the frontier between their colonies in North America. These wars were partly associated with simultaneous wars in Europe, but in North America their causes were generally local. The conflict focused on control over the lucrative fur trade and French efforts to thwart British and American expansion into the interior of North America. Each side relied on its Native American allies to conduct much of the fighting. Native Americans in turn attempted to protect their own territorial interests by playing the European powers off against each other, with varying degrees of success.

### From Deerfield to Louisbourg

In 1702 an uneasy truce along the frontier ended with the outbreak of Queen Anne's War, known in Europe as the War of the Spanish Succession. The most notorious incident in the war, the Deerfield Raid, occurred on February 29, 1704 when an alliance of Abenakis and French attacked the settlement of Deerfield, in Massachusetts. Fifty settlers were killed and more than 100 were taken captive, including the town clerk Thomas French and his family. The settlers were forced to march as captives through the snowy forests to Montreal. Some—including French's wife, Mary—were murdered en route. Of those who survived the winter trek, Thomas and many hostages were later ransomed and returned to Massachusetts. Others, like Thomas's eight-year-old

**Figure 2.7** The French and Abenakis raiders attacked Deerfield in the early morning hours of February 29, 1704. Why would it have been difficult for the British to defend farms such as this on the frontier?

**WEB LINKS** 

Discover more about the Deerfield Raid and the experiences of the English, French, and Native American participants by visiting www.emp.ca/ah.

daughter Martha (renamed Marguerite), remained permanently in New France, while still others, like Thomas's six-year-old daughter Abigail, were adopted into Aboriginal communities.

The French retained control of Île Royale, now Cape Breton Island, and constructed a large fortress called Louisbourg. From this base they protected the entrance to the St. Lawrence and harassed shipping between the American colonies and Britain. In 1740 King George's War, known in Europe as the War of the Austrian Succession, broke out. Britain organized an expedition to attack Louisbourg and end the threat it posed. In 1745 the objective was achieved when colonial troops from Massachusetts, assisted by the British navy, captured Louisbourg. Colonial rejoicing proved short-lived, however, for in 1748 Louisbourg was returned to France under the Treaty of Aix-la-Chappelle. New England merchants who had paid for the expedition and who welcomed the removal of the French threat were incensed. The British government appeared to have taken their efforts for granted and overlooked their interests. It would not be the last time the American colonists would feel marginalized.

## French and Indian War

For decades France and Britain engaged in a battle for supremacy in North America with a series of wars punctuated by periodic truces. These wars were part of a wider quest for global dominance. In 1754 a struggle began between American colonists and the French and their Native American allies for control of the Ohio Valley. The dispute would ignite a final clash of empires, a world war that would lead to British victory and the end of French control in North America and elsewhere. As the British statesman Horace Walpole later commented: "The volley fired by a young Virginian in the backwoods of America set the world on fire." The French and Indian War would become

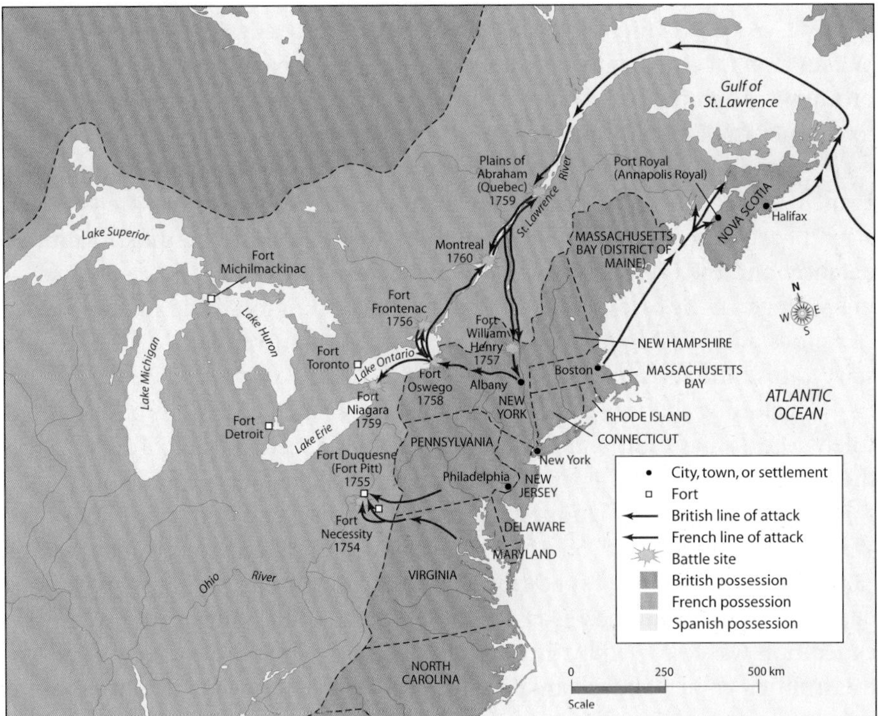


**Figure 2.8** As this map shows, most of the fighting in the French and Indian War took place along the frontiers of western New York and Pennsylvania. This was an area where English settlers, French traders, and various Native American groups collided.

part of a wider conflict known as the Seven Years War (1756–1763). In addition to in Europe and North America, British and French forces fought on the Indian subcontinent, in West Africa, and in the Caribbean.

While Britain sought global primacy and an end to French military and commercial challenges to its interests, the American colonists' objective was more local. During the French and Indian War their main goal was to end Native raids on their colonies and open the Ohio River Valley to settlement. In order to accomplish this, French support had to be eliminated.

In June 1754 representatives of the northern colonies met at Albany, New York to discuss the threat posed by the French, who "have advanced further towards making themselves masters of this continent within the past five or six years." A few delegates, including Benjamin Franklin, argued that the colonies should unite to face the French threat (see the cartoon on page 91). This initial attempt to develop a common colonial system, however, did not succeed. Instead, individual colonies asserted separate claims on the lands of the Ohio River Valley and organized their own military expeditions and settlements.

## Washington and Braddock

In the mid-1700s the French, concerned that English traders and colonists might encroach on the interior (the Ohio Valley), began to build a series of forts and reinforce their garrisons. These included Fort Duquesne on the Monongahela River, at the site of present-day Pittsburgh. Colonial authorities in Virginia saw the heightened French military presence as a threat, and in October 1753 Governor Robert Dinwiddie sent a young Virginia **militia** officer named George Washington to spy on the French and deliver a warning to them. Washington returned with alarming news of French expansion, and Dinwiddie promptly promoted him and sent him back in command of a militia regiment to counter the French threat.

Washington's expedition was a failure. After ambushing a small party of French soldiers and murdering their commander, Washington's men erected a fort: Fort Necessity. The poorly situated fort had only the most primitive defences and the French soon arrived with their Native American allies seeking revenge. In the brief battle that followed, Washington's side suffered many casualties and Washington himself was forced to surrender—a humiliating start to his military career.

Concluding that the campaign against the French could not be entrusted solely to colonial militiamen and their inexperienced officers, in early 1755 the British dispatched General Edward Braddock and a large force of trained soldiers to capture Fort Duquesne. Braddock, however, fared little better than Washington. On July 9, 1755 a force of French soldiers and their Native American allies ambushed the expedition. In the ensuing battle the British force was decimated and Braddock was fatally wounded. The failure of Braddock's expedition was followed by increased attacks on American settlements along the frontier from Pennsylvania to the Carolinas. Hundreds of settlers were killed or captured in raids conducted by the French and their Native American allies, and many more fled eastward as refugees.

Although the British colonial authorities tried to protect the frontier by building a string of forts along the Allegheny Mountains, the continued French presence remained a major threat. In 1758 another major British expedition was sent against Fort Duquesne and this time the British took no chances. First, they persuaded the local Native American groups to abandon the French in exchange for British protection. By the time the British reached Fort Duquesne it had been abandoned. The British erected Fort Pitt (Pittsburgh) in honour of the British prime minister, William Pitt, in its place to secure their control of the Ohio Valley.

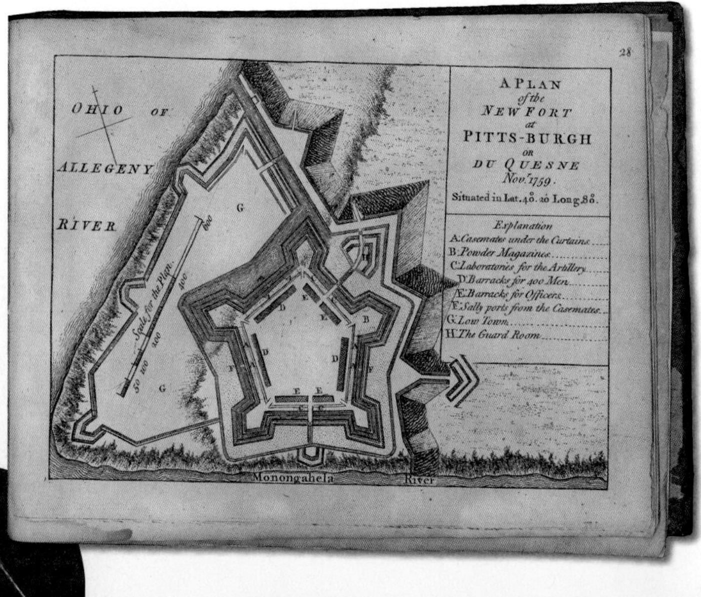


**Figure 2.9** This British fort at Pittsburgh replaced the French Fort Duquesne. Note the extensive walls and fortifications, reflecting the site's strategic significance to the British.

## British Victory

Although the guerrilla war waged by colonial militias and British soldiers in the Ohio River Valley was costly, elsewhere the British enjoyed greater success. The destruction of Fort Duquesne in 1758 coincided with the capture of several other French forts, including Fort Frontenac near present-day Kingston, Ontario. That same year, the British also captured the massive French fortress of Louisbourg. The long threat to American shipping was finally ended and the St. Lawrence Valley lay open to British attack. The next year, General James Wolfe led a British siege on Quebec and the city was captured following the Battle of Quebec on September 13, 1759. The losses of Louisbourg and Quebec sealed the fate of the French empire in North America. The French threat was finally eliminated with the fall of Montreal to a British force in 1760.

**Figure 2.10** This sign hung outside one of many taverns named in honour of General Wolfe during the 1760s. Why would Wolfe have been regarded as a hero in the American colonies?

## Pontiac's Revolt

As in the Fort Duquesne campaign, British victory over the French in the Seven Years War in North America owed much to their success in persuading the traditional allies of the French to remain neutral or switch sides. In return for their support, Native American leaders were promised that the British would respect these agreements and protect their traditional territories from further settlement.

The creation of new British forts and apparent British reluctance to discourage colonial expansion, however, soon caused Native American leaders to question British and American intentions. Many also protested the 1763 French surrender of the Ohio territory—land the Native Americans regarded as theirs—declaring indignantly: "the French had no right to give away [our] country." The British authorities made the situation worse by ending the practice of regular gift-giving that had helped build positive relations between European and Native American communities. Until 1763 Europeans had generally regarded Native Americans as allies, almost as equals. Increasingly this was no longer the case, and Native Americans found themselves treated as subjects whose interests and rights were regularly ignored.

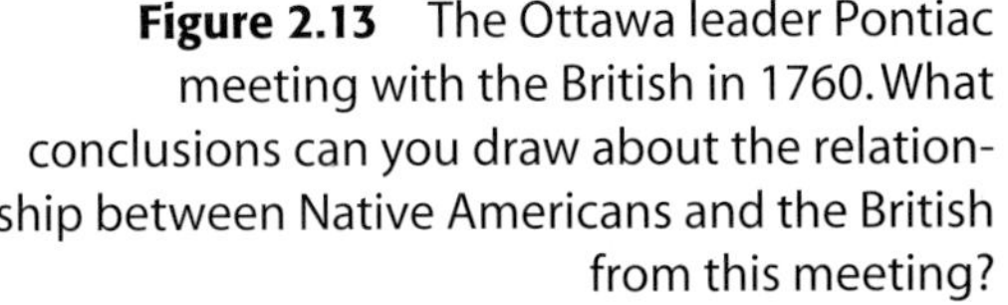

**Figure 2.13** The Ottawa leader Pontiac meeting with the British in 1760. What conclusions can you draw about the relationship between Native Americans and the British from this meeting?

The Native spiritual leader Neolin, whom the English named the "Delaware Prophet," emerged from this climate of distrust and discontent. His calls for an end to European influence over Native American society and the expulsion of settlers attracted great interest. Allied with Neolin was the Ottawa chief Pontiac, who used his political skills and oratory to organize a confederacy to attack British forts. In May 1763 the confederacy captured Fort Michilimackinac, south of present-day Sault Ste. Marie, and within weeks a number of other forts were attacked, including Niagara and Detroit. Settlements were burned and at least 2,000 settlers died. The British responded with attacks on Native communities that included the distribution of blankets infected with smallpox, an early example of biological warfare. The resulting epidemic caused hundreds of deaths among the Delaware and Shawnee nations. Eventually each side realized it could not entirely defeat the other and an uneasy peace was restored on the frontier.

Although the Native Americans failed to remove the British from the Ohio territory in Pontiac's Revolt, as the events of 1763 became known, they did secure a significant concession. In an effort to reduce tensions on the frontier, the British government issued the Royal Proclamation of 1763, which prohibited European settlement west of the crest of the Appalachian Mountains. The Proclamation was designed to prevent another revolt by protecting Native American lands from encroaching settlers, to ensure that "the several nations or tribes of Indians, with whom we [the British Crown] are connected, and who live under our protection, should not be molested or disturbed." The British government also hoped that this policy would preserve the lucrative fur trade and renew previous alliances.

Unfortunately, the colonial farmers' demand for land to replace "our old land which we have worn out" (through excessive cultivation) and to satisfy the needs of a growing population made the pressure to expand unstoppable. Moreover, the British proved unwilling to pay for sufficient soldiers along the frontier to control settlement. Despite British intentions, the Proclamation of 1763 was a failure. It created deep resentment on the part of colonists who were hungry for fresh farmland and angry that the end of French control in North America did not open these territories to settlement. Nor were the Native Americans happy, since British guarantees to protect their lands proved worthless.

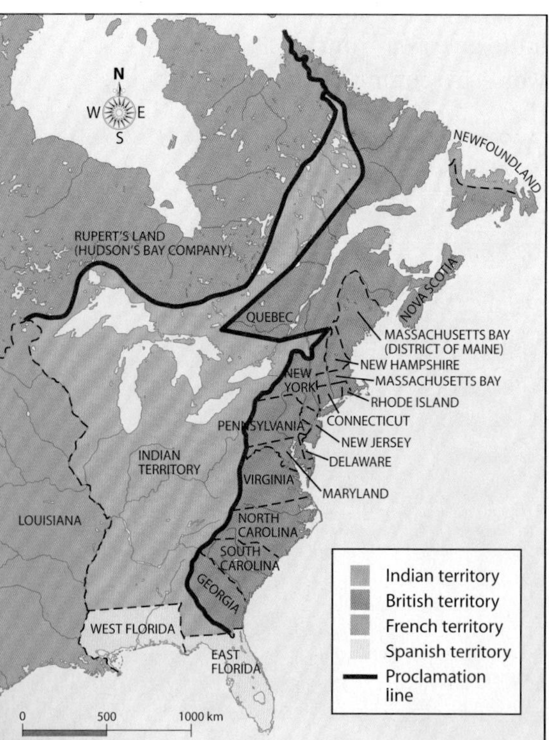


**Figure 2.14** The Proclamation of 1763 was intended to reserve the interior of North America for Native Americans following Pontiac's Revolt.

## 49th PARALLEL

# The Expulsion of the Acadians

**Figure 2.12** The statue of Evangeline at Grand Pré, Nova Scotia commemorates the expulsion of the Acadians.

During the 17th and early 18th centuries as wars between Britain and France led to mounting tension, the prosperous French farmers of Acadia (along the Bay of Fundy) enjoyed close trading relations with the New England colonies. Reflecting their ambivalent relationship, the Acadians referred to their New England neighbours as *nos amis l'ennemi*, or "our friends the enemy." In 1713 France ceded Acadia to Britain under the Treaty of Utrecht. The Acadians, who saw themselves as Catholic subjects of the king of France, refused to swear an oath of allegiance to the Protestant British Crown. They were allowed to remain on their farms despite this, but the British authorities viewed them with suspicion. In 1730 the Acadians swore allegiance to Britain on condition that they would not be required to take up arms against France. As the struggle for control of North America intensified, however, this neutrality would prove unsustainable.

The British authorities were fearful that the Acadians might support a French invasion of the colony. They also faced pressure from New England colonists anxious to occupy the rich farmland along the Bay of Fundy. In July 1755 Governor Lawrence of Nova Scotia demanded that the Acadians swear a new oath without any conditions. When they refused, Lawrence ordered the Acadians deported. Colonial troops from Massachusetts oversaw the removal of the Acadians from the colony. They were placed on ships, while their farms and villages were burned. In many cases, families were split up. One officer described the scene: "We have started moving the inhabitants out. The women were very distressed, carrying their newborns in their arms; others brought along in carts their infirm parents and their personal effects. In short, it was a scene in which confusion was mixed with despair and desolation."

**Figure 2.11** The Expulsion of the Acadians in 1755. What sufferings does the artist depict?

During 1755 almost 7,000 Acadians were deported. Further deportations occurred in the following years, known as *le grand dérangement*. Several thousand Acadians were sent to France and Quebec while others were dispersed throughout the American colonies, including 1,000 to Massachusetts and a similar number to South Carolina. Arriving in the English colonies in the midst of the French and Indian War, as French Catholics the Acadians were unwelcome. Their new neighbours regarded them as enemies who were "murdering and scalping our frontier settlers." In fact, most of the Acadians deported to Virginia were later sent to England as a result of opposition from the colony. Some eventually returned to Nova Scotia; others settled in Louisiana, where their descendants became known as Cajuns.

In 1847 the American poet Henry Wadsworth Longfellow (1807–1882) published his epic poem "Evangeline." The poem relates the fictional tale of a young Acadian woman whose idyllic life with her fiancé in Acadia comes to an end when they are separated in the Expulsion of 1755. Evangeline searches for her lover throughout the American colonies. She finally finds him in Philadelphia, where he lies dying of an epidemic; Evangeline herself dies soon after from grief. "Evangeline" became a classic of 19th-century American literature, helping establish Longfellow as a great American writer and immortalizing the story of *le grand dérangement* in history.

### Think It Through

1. What was the significance of the Acadians referring to the New England colonies as *nos amis l'ennemi*?
2. Consider the British perspective. How would the British authorities have justified their expulsion of the Acadians?
3. What impact did the Acadians' arrival have on the American colonies? Why?

### CHECK YOUR UNDERSTANDING

1. Explain the North American causes of conflict between the British and the French.
2. How did the American colonists benefit from British victory in the Seven Years War?
3. What role did Native Americans play in the wars between the British and the French?
4. What role did the American colonists play in defeating France?
5. Why was General Wolfe's victory at Quebec important for the American colonists?
6. What was the purpose of the Proclamation of 1763?

## GROWING DISCONTENT

In October 1760 American colonists celebrated the crowning of a new monarch, George III. The new king was young and vigorous—a perfect symbol for an empire that now controlled all of eastern North America since the capture of the final French stronghold at Montreal a few months earlier. Yet the euphoric reaction to the news on both sides of the Atlantic masked growing differences in outlook and interests between Britain and its American colonies. Britain was determined to exert greater control over the colonies in order to solidify the gains of the Seven Years War. Such policies, however, threatened the relative autonomy the colonies had enjoyed for decades.

### A Crisis of Empire

As a result of the Seven Years War, Britain's national debt had increased to a staggering £145 million (about $39 billion in current dollars). This, coupled with the costs of stationing 10,000 troops in the colonies to guard against threats from Native Americans after Pontiac's Revolt and potential unrest in the newly conquered Quebec, prompted the British government to look to the American colonies for tax revenue. While the British considered it fair that the colonies should help pay for a war whose outcome—the defeat of France—directly benefited them, the American colonists disagreed. The issue of taxation would quickly undermine the harmony of the British empire.

**Figure 2.15** A portrait of the new British king, George III, by Allan Ramsay in 1760. What political message(s) might the artist be attempting to convey in this painting? Why is it effective?

## Sugar and Stamps

The British Chancellor of the Exchequer (finance minister), George Grenville, began cautiously. Noting that the costs of collecting customs duties greatly exceeded the revenue collected, in 1764 Grenville determined to *reduce* the duty in the colonies on molasses, the key ingredient for rum. At the same time, more powerful courts and stricter documentation would allow for tighter enforcement and collection of the new lower duty and the colonies would begin to generate needed revenue for the British Crown. The Revenue Act of 1764, known as the Sugar Act, was opposed by merchants who had grown accustomed to the previous lax administration. Under such administration, most had been able to avoid the older higher duty. Some towns began **boycotts** of British goods to protest the new tax regime. Petitions were dispatched claiming that the new impositions threatened colonists' rights.

Undeterred by colonial opposition, Grenville introduced a further tax in the colonies the following year. The Stamp Act required all legal documents, pamphlets, playing cards, newspapers, and other printed materials to be produced on paper bearing a stamp indicating that a tax had been paid. Specially appointed officials in the colonies would be responsible for distributing the paper. While a similar tax already existed in Britain, its extension to America was new. The American colonies' response was swift and clear. During the six months between the passage of the Stamp Act and the imposition of the tax in November 1765, boycotts of British imports began. Local distributors of

**Figure 2.16** Opponents of the Stamp Act did everything possible to voice their unhappiness and encourage resistance, including producing teapots with clear political messages. Why might a teapot be a particularly powerful symbol? Can you think of modern examples of popular everyday items with political slogans?

The TIMES are Dreadful Doleful Dismal Dolorous, and DOLLAR-LESS.

Thursday, October 31. 1765 — THE — NUMB 1195

# PENNSYLVANIA JOURNAL; AND WEEKLY ADVERTISER.

EXPIRING: In Hopes of a Resurrection to LIFE again.

I am sorry to be obliged to acquaint my readers that as the Stamp Act is feared to be obligatory upon us after the *first of November* ensuing (The Fatal To-morrow), The publisher of this paper, unable to bear the Burthen, has thought it expedient to stop awhile, in order to deliberate, whether any methods can be found to elude the chains forged for us, and escape the insupportable slavery, which it is hoped, from the last representation now made against that act, may be effected. Mean while I must earnestly Request every individual of my Subscribers, many of whom have been long behind Hand, that they would immediately discharge their respective Arrears, that I may be able, not only to support myself during the Interval, but be better prepared to proceed again with this Paper whenever an opening for that purpose appears, which I hope will be soon.

WILLIAM BRADFORD.

Adieu Adieu to the LIBERTY of the *PRESS*.



**Figure 2.17** The publisher of this Pennsylvania newspaper chose to close his newspaper rather than submit to paying the stamp tax. How has he made his opposition clear?

stamped paper were intimidated into not collecting the tax. Colonial lawyers and merchants opposed to the Stamp Act united as the "Sons of Liberty" to organize campaigns against the new taxes.

At the same time as the merchant and political elites in Boston, New York, and other towns were coordinating their opposition, crowds in those same communities were taking matters into their own hands. Throughout the summer of 1765 the homes of royal officials and stamp distributors, such as the hated Andrew Oliver in Boston, were ransacked and torched by crowds of labourers. Oliver himself was burned in **effigy** and then publicly humiliated, being forced to resign his commission. In Annapolis, Maryland mobs destroyed the warehouses of the stamp distributor Zachariah Hood and forced him to flee the colony. Similar protests occurred from Newport, Rhode Island to Charleston, South Carolina.

More ominously, the demonstrations blended opposition to British policies with attacks on colonial elites. The merchants and lawyers who formed the Sons of Liberty struggled on occasion to contain the fury of "mobs" whose humbler members took advantage of the protests to settle scores with members of the elite whose wealth and privileges they resented, such as Oliver and Hood. Such intimidation prompted most stamp distributors to abandon their work, frustrating British efforts to collect the tax.

## No Taxation without Representation

British efforts to extract taxes from the colonies raised fundamental issues that were hotly debated on both sides of the Atlantic. Most colonists rejected Parliament's right to impose taxes *within* the colonies. In part this was because taxation had long been the sole responsibility of colonial assemblies—a power they jealously guarded. At the same time there could be "no taxation without representation," and the colonists did not elect members to the British Parliament. The British government responded by arguing that members of the British Parliament represented the entire empire through "virtual representation," and could therefore impose taxes throughout the empire without requiring colonial consent. Britain's arguments were swiftly rejected by many, and by late 1765 the assemblies in nine colonies had passed resolutions denouncing the Stamp Act and affirming the principle of "no taxation without representation." When delegates from the American colonies met in New

York in October 1765 in the so-called Stamp Act Congress, they reiterated their opposition to such taxation, although they did grudgingly acknowledge Parliament's right to regulate trade.

## Townshend Duties

Effective **lobbying** by colonial leaders combined with the crippling impact of boycotts of British goods soon produced the desired effect. In March 1766 Parliament revoked the Stamp Act, prompting public celebrations throughout the colonies. Political disputes in Britain, which had undermined Grenville's government and his policies, had contributed to the decision. As well, Benjamin Franklin had successfully urged Parliament to reconsider the tax, arguing that the colonists opposed internal taxes but did not challenge the British government's right to tax trade. The British Parliament passed the Declaratory Act in response to the crisis, affirming Parliament's right to make laws concerning the colonies.

Still desperate for revenue, following Franklin's suggestion in 1767 the British government introduced a new set of taxes on imported items, including glass, paper, paints, lead, and tea. As taxes on trade, the British government believed the colonists would accept these taxes more readily. Moreover, these taxes, known as the Townshend Duties after Grenville's successor, Charles Townshend, would be collected by new commissioners operating in the colonies and keeping a close watch on any merchants avoiding payment.

The Townshend Duties provoked fury throughout the colonies. A widespread campaign of non-importation—or boycotting of British goods—followed, severely impacting trade. The new local tax collectors merely provided a ready focus for radical anger. The Townshend Duties were clearly futile: by 1770 it was estimated that the revenue raised amounted to barely £21,000 ($5 million in current dollars), largely as a result of the boycotts of British imports, while that same boycott had cost the British economy perhaps £700,000 ($163 million today). Fearing that opposition to the taxes might spark greater political upheaval, in 1768 the British government sent four regiments of soldiers to Boston to enforce "passive obedience," as one colonial newspaper put it. The presence of British troops in Boston would lead to violence, most notably in March 1770, when troops fired on a crowd in an incident that became known as the Boston Massacre.

A succession of more rigorous British policies toward the colonies during the 1760s had created a growing divide between the British government and the American colonies. Few described this impasse more eloquently than Edmund Burke, speaking in the British Parliament in 1767: "The Americans have made a discovery that we mean to oppress them; we have made a discovery that they intend to raise a rebellion against us. We do not know how to advance; they know not how to retreat." While revolution was not a certainty, by 1770 few in the colonies could see how retreat was possible. Most colonists continued to seek better treatment *within* the British empire rather than separation from it. Yet opportunities for reconciliation were quickly running out.

AMERICAN ARCHIVE

# The Declaratory Act (1766)

The repeal of the Stamp Act in March 1766 in the face of fierce opposition within the American colonies represented a humiliating surrender by the British Parliament. In order to reassure its critics at home that the British government was not losing control of the colonies, Britain had to reassert control over its American possessions. As a result, the British Parliament passed the Declaratory Act the same day that it repealed the Stamp Act. The full title of the act made its real purpose clear: "for the better securing the dependency of his Majesty's dominions in America upon the Crown." The Act declared that the British Parliament had the same powers to make laws and approve taxes for the colonies as it did for Britain. There could be no doubt: the colonies remained fully under the authority of Parliament.

While the repeal of the Stamp Act temporarily silenced opposition within the colonies, the strong message of the Declaratory Act soon led to renewed unrest. Thomas Jefferson denounced the Act as "a basis broad enough whereon to erect a **despotism** of unlimited extent." In 1775 the Continental Congress would ask: "what is to defend us against so enormous, so unlimited a power?" The Declaratory Act represented Britain's attempt to assert its power over the empire; instead it would stir greater colonial resentment.

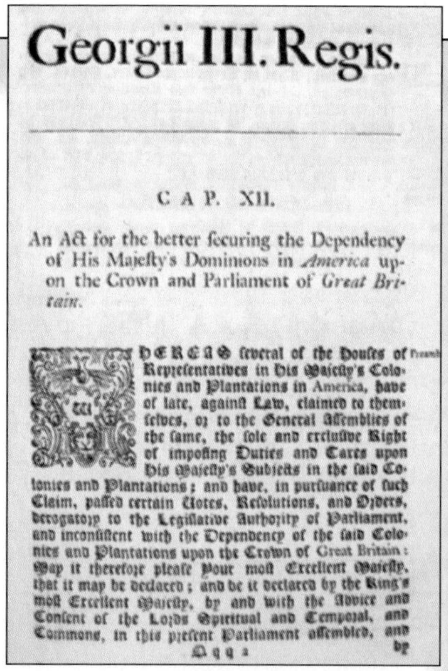

Georgii III. Regis.

C A P. XII.

An Act for the better ſecuring the Dependency of His Majeſty's Dominions in *America* upon the Crown and Parliament of *Great Britain.*

WHEREAS ſeveral of the Houſes of Repreſentatives in His Majeſty's Colonies and Plantations in America, have of late, againſt Law, claimed to themſelves, or to the General Aſſemblies of the ſame, the ſole and excluſive Right of impoſing Duties and Taxes upon His Majeſty's Subjects in the ſaid Colonies and Plantations; and have, in purſuance of ſuch Claim, paſſed certain Votes, Reſolutions, and Orders, derogatory to the Legiſlative Authority of Parliament, and inconſiſtent with the Dependency of the ſaid Colonies and Plantations upon the Crown of Great Britain: May it therefore pleaſe Your moſt Excellent Majeſty, that it may be declared; and be it declared by the King's moſt Excellent Majeſty, by and with the Advice and Conſent of the Lords Spiritual and Temporal, and Commons, in this preſent Parliament aſſembled, and by

Qqq 2

**Figure 2.18** The opening of the printed copy of the Declaratory Act. Note the prominent heading "Georgii III Regis"—Latin for "King George III." What political message might the printer have intended to communicate by the layout of this page?

An Act for the better securing the Dependency of His Majesty's Dominions in *America* upon the Crown and Parliament of *Great Britain*

Whereas several of the houses of representatives in His Majesty's colonies and plantations in America have of late, against law, claimed to themselves, or to the general assemblies of the same, the sole and exclusive right of imposing duties and taxes upon His Majesty's subjects in the said colonies and plantations; and have, in pursuance of such claim, passed certain votes, resolutions, and orders derogatory to the legislative authority of Parliament, and inconsistent with the dependency of the said colonies and plantations upon the crown of Great Britain: may it therefore please Your Most Excellent Majesty that it may be declared, and be it declared by the king's Most Excellent Majesty, by and with the advice and consent of the Lords Spiritual and Temporal, and Commons, in this present Parliament assembled, and by the authority of the same, That the said colonies and plantations in *America* have been, are, and of right ought to be, subordinate unto, and dependent upon the imperial crown and Parliament of *Great Britain*; and that the king's Majesty, by and with the advice and consent of the Lords Spiritual and Temporal, and Commons, of *Great Britain*, in Parliament assembled, had, hath, and of right ought to have, full power and authority to make laws and statutes of sufficient force and validity to bind the colonies and people of *America*, subjects of the crown of *Great Britain*, in all cases whatsoever.

And be it further declared and enacted by the authority aforesaid, That all resolutions, votes, orders, and proceedings, in any of the said colonies or plantations, whereby the power and authority of the Parliament of *Great Britain* to make laws and statutes as aforesaid is denied, or drawn into question, are, and are hereby declared to be, utterly null and void to all intents and purposes whatsoever.

## Think It Through

1. What was Britain's motivation for approving the Declaratory Act?
2. According to the Declaratory Act, what was the role of the British Parliament in the empire? How did it compare to the role of colonial assemblies?
3. Why might colonial leaders find the Declaratory Act offensive? Choose one passage that you think might especially anger them. Explain your choice to a classmate.

## PAST VOICES

# The Boston Massacre (1770)

The continual presence of British soldiers in Boston from 1768 inevitably led to conflict. Soldiers and artisans engaged in frequent brawls in taverns and alleys, and citizens of Boston regularly harassed the troops stationed in the city. On March 5, 1770 these tensions culminated in a violent confrontation that became known as the Boston Massacre. A group of young men taunted a sentry who, fearing for his safety, called for reinforcements. A small company of soldiers came to his aid, led by Captain Thomas Preston. Scuffles broke out as more citizens arrived. The crowd hurled snowballs and other projectiles at the soldiers, who eventually began shooting. Five Boston residents lay dead or dying by the time order was restored, and other citizens and soldiers were injured.

Preston and the soldiers were subsequently tried for murder but were acquitted, although two were convicted of manslaughter. Ironically, the soldiers were defended by John Adams, who later became president and who risked his reputation in Patriot circles to ensure a fair trial. At the urging of leading Boston citizens, the British authorities agreed to remove their troops from the city to reduce the risk of further violence.

The wider political significance that the events of March 5, 1770 acquired can be attributed to the efforts of the Boston engraver and Patriot sympathizer Paul Revere. Revere produced a vivid print showing the British soldiers firing upon a crowd of Boston citizens. *The Bloody Massacre* soon circulated throughout the colonies as an effective piece of anti-British propaganda. The following is a description of the event from the *Boston Gazette* of March 12, 1770:

> Thirty or forty persons, mostly lads, being by this means gathered in King Street, Capt. Preston with a party of men with charged bayonets, came from the main guard to the commissioner's house, the soldiers pushing their bayonets, crying, make way! They took place by the custom house and, continuing to push to drive the people off pricked some in several places, on which they were clamorous and, it is said, threw snow balls. On this, the Captain commanded them to fire; and more snowballs coming, he again said, damn you, fire, be the consequences what it will! One soldier then fired, and a townsman with a cudgel struck him over the hands with such force that he dropped his firelock; and, rushing forward, aimed a blow at the Captain's head which grazed his hat and fell pretty heavy upon his arm. However, the soldiers continued the fire successively till seven or eight or, as some say, eleven guns were discharged.
>
> By this fatal manoeuvre three men were laid dead on the spot and two more struggling for life; but what showed a degree of cruelty unknown to British troops … was an attempt to fire upon or push with their bayonets the persons who undertook to remove the slain and wounded!

**Figure 2.19** Paul Revere's print of the Boston Massacre.

The following verse from Revere's engraving clearly illustrates his political views:

> Unhappy Boston! See thy Sons deplore
> Thy hallow'd Walks besmear'd with guiltless Gore.
> While faithless P[resto]n and his savage Bands,
> With murd'rous Rancour stretch their bloody Hands;
> Like fierce Barbarians grinning o'er their Prey;
> Approve the Carnage, and enjoy the Day.

## Think It Through

1. How did the confrontation between soldiers and artisans in Boston become a focal point for opposition to the presence of the British military in the colony?
2. Compare the description of the events of March 5, 1770 from the *Boston Gazette* with the verses on Paul Revere's print. What differences in language or content can you identify?
3. What elements of Revere's image of the Boston Massacre would make it effective anti-British propaganda? Why?

### Calm before the Storm

In 1770 Britain repealed the Townshend Duties as a result of the damage to trade caused by the boycott of British goods following their imposition. However, the British prime minister, Lord North, was determined to assert his government's control over the American colonies. The tax on tea remained in order to save face. Having secured another victory, colonial opposition was muted for the next few years. The profitable trade with Britain resumed and collection of taxes on tea (as well as on molasses, from the earlier Sugar Act) proceeded. The colonists' apparent willingness to pay taxes that had previously stirred such anger puzzled contemporaries and, later, historians. Had the earlier opposition simply reflected an understandable dislike of new taxes? Were the American colonists sincere in their constitutional objections to "taxation without representation"? Was active involvement in the business of the British empire too profitable to be renounced for political protest? The answer would come soon.

## Reaction

For almost two years following the repeal of the Townshend Duties, opponents of British policy largely fell silent. Some may have believed that the crisis had passed. Yet Burke's 1767 warning about the impasse between Britain and its American colonies proved prophetic: retreat was impossible. In the summer of 1772 Governor Thomas Hutchinson of Massachusetts announced that from now on government officials would be paid by Britain rather by the colony's Assembly—a move that would free them from local control.

In response, a Committee of Correspondence was established in Boston to discuss with other towns the threat this decision posed to colonial liberties. In March 1773 the Virginia House of Burgesses created a similar committee to share information and opinions on how to address such challenges to colonial liberties; the other colonies followed. There were grounds for concern. In the summer of 1773 the Boston committee obtained confidential letters from Governor Hutchinson to the British government advocating "some further restraint of liberty, rather than the connection with the parent state should be broken."

# Culture Notes

## *Phillis Wheatley (1754–1784), Colonial Poet*

In 18th-century America the writing of serious literature was restricted to an educated elite, such as lawyers and clergy. It is astonishing, therefore, that the most famous poet in colonial America was a female African-American slave. Phillis Wheatley of Boston was the first African-American, the first slave, and only the third woman in America to publish a collection of poems, which she did in 1773.

Phillis Wheatley arrived in Boston in 1761 at the age of seven. She had been brought as a slave from West Africa and was purchased by John Wheatley as a servant for his wife. The young Phillis, named after the slave ship that brought her to America, soon mastered English. The Wheatleys were impressed by Phillis's intelligence and decided to provide her with an education, encouraging her to study theology and classical literature. Phillis's first poem appeared in print when she was 13; at 19 she published a collection of poetry entitled *Poems on Various Subjects, Religious and Moral.* Few believed that a slave (or woman) could write poetry, and Phillis was examined by a committee of Boston ministers to confirm that she was the author of the poems. She eventually travelled to London to promote her writing. Freed by her owners, Phillis married and began work on a second volume of poetry before her death in 1784.

In addition to the religious themes typical of 18th-century literature, Phillis Wheatley tackled politics in her poems. She was critical of the British government's treatment of the colonies, and celebrated those who fought and died for independence: "How the first martyr for the cause should bleed / To clear the country of the hated brood." She quickly earned the admiration of George Washington and others for her support of the Patriot cause. Wheatley's opposition to Britain's oppression of the colonies arose from her own experience of slavery: "and can I then but pray / Others may never feel tyrannic sway?" Other voices expressed similar doubts about slavery. The question of how colonial cries for "liberty" could be reconciled with the practice of slavery would endure throughout the American Revolution and after.

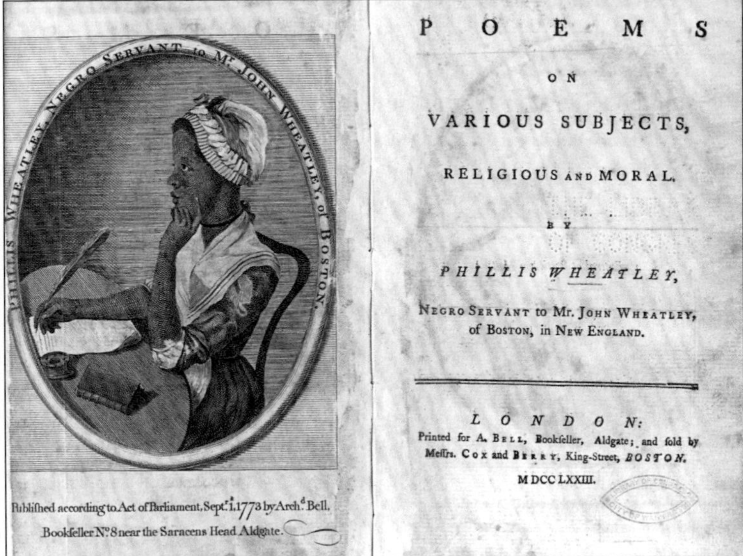


POEMS
ON
VARIOUS SUBJECTS,
RELIGIOUS AND MORAL.
BY
PHILLIS WHEATLEY,
NEGRO SERVANT to Mr. JOHN WHEATLEY, of BOSTON, in NEW ENGLAND.
LONDON:
Printed for A. BELL, Bookſeller, Aldgate; and ſold by Meſſrs. COX and BERRY, King-Street, BOSTON.
MDCCLXXIII.

**Figure 2.20** The title page of Phillis Wheatley's *Poems on Various Subjects, Religious and Moral* included a portrait of the author. Why might the publisher have chosen to prepare and print a portrait of Wheatley?

The following poem, addressed to King George III in 1768, praised the king for abolishing the hated Stamp Act and encouraged the British government to rule the colonies with peace and justice, for "a monarch's smile can set his subjects free." It offers a taste of Wheatley's poetry—and her keen interest in politics.

YOUR subjects hope, dread Sire—
The crown upon your brows may flourish long,
And that your arm may in your God be strong!
O may your sceptre num'rous nations sway,
And all with love and readiness obey!

But how shall we the British king reward!
Rule thou in peace, our father, and our lord!
Midst the remembrance of thy favours past,
The meanest peasants most admire the last*

May George, beloved by all the nations round,
Live with heav'ns choicest constant blessings
crown'd!

Great God, direct, and guard him from on high,
And from his head let ev'ry evil fly!
And may each clime with equal gladness see
A monarch's smile can set his subjects free!

* The repeal of the Stamp Act.

## Think It Through

1. What does Phillis Wheatley's experience reveal about contemporary attitudes toward women in colonial America?
2. Why might a slave who openly supported the cause of American independence present a challenge to colonial leaders?
3. Examine the poem by Wheatley addressed to King George III. How does it combine flattery with a call for better treatment of the colonies?

**Figure 2.21** Tarring and feathering was a traditional form of humiliation adopted by Patriots to punish prominent Loyalists, like this tax collector in Boston. Notice the men dumping tea off the ship in the background, and the teapot being emptied down the tax collector's throat.

## Boston Tea Party

The continuation of the tax on tea led to boycotts of British tea and considerable smuggling from other sources. While some colonial merchants continued to prosper, the East India Company, which controlled most of the legal trade, suffered. In May 1773 Parliament passed the Tea Act, allowing the East India Company to bypass colonial wholesale merchants and market its tea directly to shopkeepers in America. This cheaper tea would undercut local suppliers.

Radicals protested this new British attempt to control the colonial economy, and any merchant or shopkeeper prepared to accept the East India Company's tea was threatened with "tarring and feathering." In this violent act of public humiliation the accused was doused with hot tar and then covered with goose feathers. Local committees asked captains of ships carrying tea to sail away without delivering their cargo. When Governor Hutchinson refused to allow a ship to leave Boston before being unloaded, a mob of citizens led by Samuel Adams disguised themselves as Mohawk Indians. On December 16, 1773 they boarded the vessel and dumped the cargo into the harbour. The "Boston Tea Party" was followed by similar acts of vandalism in other ports, where cargos of tea were destroyed.

## Coercive Acts

The British response to the Boston Tea Party and the disturbances that followed was swift and harsh. In April 1774 Parliament passed a series of laws known as the Coercive Acts. The Acts were designed to subdue the rebellious colonists and restore British authority in Massachusetts. The first Act closed the port of Boston to all trade until compensation was paid for the cargos of tea destroyed. The second Act revoked self-government in Massachusetts, stripping the Assembly of the power to appoint colonial officials and forbidding most town meetings. The Coercive Acts again allowed troops to be stationed, or "quartered," in Boston. A military governor, General Thomas Gage, was appointed to enforce the new laws. The Coercive Acts were soon labelled the "Intolerable Acts" and provoked outrage throughout the American colonies.

Supplies and messages of support for the citizens of Boston flooded in from other colonies, whose citizens were alarmed at Britain's treatment of Massachusetts. Fears about whose liberties might be eliminated next proved well founded, for when the House of Burgesses in Virginia denounced the Coercive Acts as a hostile act the British governor dissolved the Assembly. In a demonstration of unity with Massachusetts, the members of the Virginia assembly then declared that "an attack made on one of our sister colonies, to compel submission to arbitrary taxes, is an attack made on all British America." British policy appeared to have succeeded where generations of colonial politicians had failed: in forging an alliance between colonies accustomed to viewing one another with suspicion. This was an ominous development.

**Figure 2.22** This British cartoon mocked Patriot women for boycotting British goods in the name of honour and liberty while behaving scandalously and relying on slaves to serve them. Why might this criticism be effective?

# WE THE PEOPLE

## Samuel Adams

1722–1803

"We have no other alternative than independence, or the most ignominious and galling servitude." Such was the stark choice the Boston delegate Samuel Adams laid before his colleagues in the Continental Congress assembled in Philadelphia in the summer of 1776. There were few more impassioned advocates of independence than the Massachusetts Patriot leader.

Samuel Adams was born into a prosperous Boston merchant family in 1722. He studied at Harvard College before entering the family business, in which he enjoyed little success. For nine years he also held the post of tax collector in Boston but his accounts quickly fell into arrears. In contrast to his lack of business or administrative acumen, Adams was a capable political organizer. In addition to being a member of the Boston political elite, where he gained a reputation for outspoken radicalism, he forged close ties with the city's working classes. In 1748 Adams launched the *Independent Advertiser*, a Patriot newspaper designed to appeal to Boston's labourers.

The imposition of the Stamp Act duties in 1765 coincided with Adams's election to the Massachusetts House of Representatives. In the legislature Adams proved to be an unwavering critic of British government policy, quickly developing a reputation as "obstinate and inflexible." As the radicals gained control of the legislature Adams became their spokesman, serving as clerk of the House (the leader of the Assembly). Adams again galvanized the opposition when the British government imposed the Townshend Duties, drafting a letter to other colonial assemblies that urged a joint response. In 1768 he denounced the arrival of British troops in the colony and wrote articles in colonial newspapers advocating resistance.

In December 1773 Adams was instrumental in organizing the Boston Tea Party, though he was careful to avoid being directly implicated. Reluctant to condone violence publicly, Adams nevertheless argued that "when the people are oppressed … they are not to be blamed." The British responded by suspending the Massachusetts legislature but Adams, as clerk, refused to obey the governor's orders until the legislature had met to choose delegates to the Continental Congress. Given his long-standing opposition to British colonial policies, it was only natural that Adams was included among the delegates.

**Figure 2.23**
This portrait of Samuel Adams was painted by John Singleton Copley in 1772. At the time Adams was the leader of the Patriot cause in Boston. He is pointing to the charters and documents guaranteeing the liberties of Massachusetts.

As a member of the Continental Congress, Samuel Adams was an outspoken advocate of independence. He scorned other delegates' calls for negotiation and compromise with Britain and urged his colleagues to stand firm: "Courage, then, my countrymen; our contest is not only whether we ourselves shall be free, but whether there shall be left to mankind an asylum on earth for civil and religious liberty." A signatory of the Declaration of Independence, Adams served in Congress until 1781 and then returned to Massachusetts, where he later served a term as governor. With less talent and enthusiasm for government administration than for political agitation, Adams eventually retired to Boston, where he died in 1803.

### Think It Through

1. What factors contributed to Samuel Adams's success as a leader of radical opposition to Britain?
2. Explain what Adams might have meant when he argued that "when the people are oppressed … they are not to be blamed."
3. Examine the portrait of Adams by John Copley showing Adams with the symbols of Massachusetts's history. What might the political significance of this portrait be?

## The Quebec Act

For many colonists resentful of restrictions on trade and settlement and outraged by Britain's stern response to colonial unrest and criticism, the final straw came with the Quebec Act of 1774. The Act was intended to ensure the loyalty of the French-Canadian population by protecting Roman Catholicism and the French civil law, both detested by many American colonists. It also appointed a council to govern Quebec—a move many colonists viewed as a dangerous precedent for reorganizing colonial governments in America. Most seriously, the Act also extended the boundaries of Quebec to include all lands north of the Ohio River.

While the Iroquois welcomed the Quebec Act's protection of their lands from encroaching settlers and **speculators**, American colonists were outraged. Many leading Virginians, including George Washington, Thomas Jefferson, and Patrick Henry, had made extensive land purchases and speculations. These were now worthless. Throughout the colonies the Quebec Act was seen as a repeat of the outrageous Proclamation of 1763, designed to frustrate the colonies' natural expansion and development.

## The Gathering Storm

In the decade since the end of the French and Indian War in 1763, Britain had strengthened its direct control of the American colonies. A succession of new taxes, restrictions on westward expansion, and less colonial autonomy in government angered colonial leaders. The increased British military presence in the colonies did nothing to reduce tensions. Fifty-five delegates from 12 colonies met in Philadelphia in September 1774 to consider responses to British policy. While few members of the Continental Congress advocated revolution, many delegates were convinced that a new relationship between the American colonies and Britain was essential.

**Figure 2.24** By 1770 Boston was the leading port in America. This engraving shows the arrival of British reinforcements following unrest in the town.

### CHECK YOUR UNDERSTANDING

1. Why did Britain impose taxes on the colonies?
2. What methods did colonists use to express their disapproval of the new taxes?
3. Who were the Sons of Liberty?
4. What was the significance of the Boston Tea Party?
5. How did the Coercive Acts help unite opposition in the Thirteen Colonies?

# THE HISTORIAN'S CRAFT

## Understanding the Nature of Primary Sources

The authors of this textbook have included evidence and information from a wide range of primary sources. Throughout the book there are many examples of written evidence, period illustrations, and even video and audio clips (via Internet links). In Chapter 2 alone there are official documents, poetry, speeches, a newspaper article, paintings, prints, and a cartoon.

Primary sources are attractive. Historians enjoy finding and researching primary sources—and so do many history students. Many members of the general public like learning about the mysteries and intrigues of history by reading books or watching TV programs based on primary evidence. The overall attraction of primary sources is their eyewitness quality. They allow you to read what people in history wrote or read, to see what they drew or painted, and to hear what they sang or shouted. Primary sources have a "you-are-there" quality that makes history seem alive, allowing you to enter the world of the participants. When you see the masthead of the Pennsylvania newspaper and read the opening lines of its feature story (Figure 2.17), you feel the anger of American colonists. When you speak the verses of Phillis Wheatley aloud (page 58), you feel the warning beneath her polite veneer of loyalty.

### Cautions about Primary Sources

Despite the benefits of primary sources, historians approach them with caution. Even though such sources are from the historical period and were produced by participants or eyewitnesses, they are still constructions. Samuel Adams chose the words of his speeches (page 60); the publisher of the Pennsylvania newspaper chose what to include and what to leave out of the story (Figure 2.17). These sources are useful but must be questioned to gauge their reliability and recognize bias or prejudice (see The Historian's Craft features in Chapters 3 and 4). For example, although the Declaratory Act presents the biased British view of colonial matters (page 54)—"That the said colonies and plantations in America have been, are, and of right ought to be, subordinate unto, and dependent upon the imperial crown and Parliament of Great Britain"—no secondary source in American history can better capture the uncompromising British position as to the subservient status of the colonists.

As you study this text, enjoy the appeal of primary sources while bringing the critical mind of the historian to bear on first-hand evidence.

### Try It!

1. Consult Figure 2.4. What inferences about farming methods and colonial life can you make based on this image? How can you find out if you inferences are correct?
2. See Figure 2.22. The British cartoonist reflects the contemporary prejudice against women taking an active role in politics. How does the cartoonist (a) portray an unflattering view of women generally? (b) mock the women's stand against the Stamp Act?
3. Choose one piece of primary evidence from this chapter that gives you a strong sense of "being there." Explain why it speaks strongly to you.

# STUDY HALL

## Thinking

1. Create a summary organizer to analyze the causes of the American Revolution. The chart should have column headings: Cause, British Purpose, American Reaction, Your Reaction. Use the following as Causes: Proclamation of 1763, Sugar Act, Stamp Act, Townshend Duties, Declaratory Act, Tea Act, Coercive Acts, Quebec Act.
2. From the point of view of the British government, the wars against France were a world war fought in America, the West Indies, India, and Europe. How might that point of view account for Britian's treatment of the colonies?
3. Religion is an important part of the American heritage. How is this fact demonstrated in the events before 1776?
4. Consider the Stamp Act and the Tea Act. Were the American responses to the new taxes appropriate to the grievance?
5. At what point do you think the growing crisis between the American colonies and Britain might have been defused, and how?
6. In 1728 the Quakers, an important religious group in England and in Pennsylvania, condemned slavery. In 1772 the High Court declared slavery illegal in Britain and 14,000 slaves in Britain were freed. Research the debate over slavery in Britain and the colonies. What role did religion play in opposing slavery? Why do you think slavery in the colonies was so widespread?

## Communication

7. The British, the American colonists, the French, and the Native Americans all had different points of view. Write a headline that each of these groups might have written to announce an event in the Seven Years War such as the Battle of Quebec, Washington's defeat at Fort Necessity, or Braddock's defeat.
8. Imagine a woman's point of view about working on a frontier farm in the northern colonies. Write a journal entry that shows a day in the life of a "deputy husband" or "yoke mate."
9. Write a speech for Pontiac to deliver that explains the reasons why he and his people waged war on Britain and the colonists. Be sure to demonstrate the Native American points of view about land, settlements, forts, and the French surrender. What phrases can you use to make Pontiac's points more forceful and passionate?

## Application

10. Imagine North America if France had won the Seven Years War and retained control of the Ohio Valley and the centre of the continent. What would a map look like today? What impact would such a victory likely have had on the development of the Thirteen Colonies?
11. As historians work, they know that the colonies eventually gained independence and can trace the events that divided the colonies from Britain. Yet the colonies were British. Which events united the colonists with Britain and showed a unity or belonging?
12. In a spiral of crisis, reaction, and consequence, one event leads to another in an unending progression toward disaster. Explain events from 1763 to 1774 in these terms. Use a diagram with labelled events to aid your description.

# UNIT II REVOLUTIONARY AMERICA

# 3 Revolution (1774–1791)

## KEY CONCEPTS

In this chapter you will consider:

- the causes and consequences of divisions between Patriots and Loyalists in American society
- the origins and significance of the Declaration of Independence
- the factors that led to American victory in the Revolutionary War
- the dispersal of Loyalists to Upper Canada and the Maritimes
- the political and economic challenges facing the United States after the American Revolution
- the creation and adoption of the United States Constitution

## The American Story

After years of mounting tension between Britain and its American colonies, disagreements over trade, taxes, and representation erupted into revolution. Out of this revolution, a new nation was created. Yet winning independence and building a viable and united nation required determination and negotiation. It also demanded a new government structure, one that could meet the many challenges facing the newly independent nation.

## TIMELINE

**1774**
- First Continental Congress

**1775**
- Skirmishes at Lexington and Concord

**1776**
- Declaration of Independence
- Thomas Paine publishes *Common Sense*

**1777**
- American victory at Saratoga

**1781**
- Articles of Confederation
- British surrender at Yorktown

## IMAGE ANALYSIS

**Figure 3.1** Following a public reading of the Declaration of Independence on July 7, 1776, a large group of Patriots gathered on the Bowling Green in New York City. Fired by the Declaration's denunciation of King George III, the members of the crowd acted decisively to demonstrate their independence. First, they toppled and destroyed an equestrian statue of their former king. Then they hauled the metal away to be melted down for ammunition to be used against British troops.

Many leaders of the American Revolution, including George Washington, felt uneasy about such spontaneous demonstrations, fearing they could encourage mob rule. This tension—between unruly popular protests and the desire to establish a new form of government through orderly change—would continue throughout the revolution. It would also help shape the debate on the Constitution that followed the end of the war in 1783.

▸ Treaty of Paris — **1783**

▸ Constitutional Convention — **1787**

▸ Washington inaugurated as president — **1789**

▸ Bill of Rights — **1791**

# INTRODUCTION

Look again at the painting of the Patriots pulling down the statue of King George in New York. What emotions seem to be animating these people—excitement, pride, relief, joy? Do you recall any photographs of similar demonstrations in modern times? Perhaps you remember pictures from Baghdad that showed crowds of Iraqis pulling down a statue of Saddam Hussein after the American invasion in 2003. Or maybe you have seen photos of joyful Berliners in 1989 dismantling the wall that had divided their city for decades. By the time the Berlin Wall fell, it had become much more than a barrier. Like the statues of King George and Saddam Hussein, it had attained the status of a symbol, a sign of oppression. Why are symbols so important in our lives? Why do people have such strong emotional responses to things like statues, flags, and uniforms?

As you read this chapter, examine the visual material it contains for symbols of the young country that was just beginning to take shape. What did these symbols mean to American people at the time? Are they still important today—that is, do they still have a powerful effect on the way Americans think of themselves? Jot down a list of symbols that are important in your own life. Try to explain why they affect you so deeply.

# DECLARING INDEPENDENCE

As you saw in Chapter 2, discontent within the American colonies over British imperial policy steadily mounted from the time of the Proclamation of 1763 to the passage of the Coercive Acts in 1774. Colonial leaders had employed strategies from petitions to boycotts to get the attention of the British authorities and win some form of redress for their grievances.

To learn more about the American Revolution, visit www.emp.ca/ah.

Even as colonial anger grew, few realized they were embarking on a road to revolution. This road began in Philadelphia in 1774 with a Continental Congress and led to battles in Massachusetts and beyond. This time the breach with Britain would be irreparable.

## The First Continental Congress

In a direct response to the Coercive Acts, which had become known in America as the Intolerable Acts, delegates from the Thirteen Colonies met in Philadelphia in September 1774 for a Continental Congress. Many of these delegates—such as Samuel Adams and his cousin John Adams from Massachusetts, and George Washington and Patrick Henry from Virginia—were already deeply involved in political agitation. Despite their unhappiness with British policies, however, most delegates still favoured increased economic sanctions against Britain over complete independence.

To make its case clear, the Congress issued a formal Declaration and Resolves charging that Parliament had violated colonial rights. The Congress also authorized the creation of local Committees of Observation and Safety to monitor colonists' loyalties (whether they were pro- or anti-British) and to take steps to defend the colonies. These committees formed the foundation of self-government in the colonies. Beyond the authority of royal governors, they marked the colonies' first steps toward political **autonomy**.

## Lexington and Concord

During the last months of 1774 General Thomas Gage, the British governor of Massachusetts, grew increasingly alarmed by the actions of the Committee of Safety in Boston. Committee leaders were organizing the local militias into units composed of minutemen—soldiers who would be available for duty on a moment's notice.

On the evening of April 18, 1775 Gage sent 700 **redcoats**, or British soldiers, to seize militia weapons stored at Concord, about 30 kilometres west of Boston. Paul Revere—a leading Boston Patriot and engraver of *The Bloody Massacre* (described in Chapter 2)—rode overnight from Boston to Lexington and on to Concord, warning the minutemen of the approaching force. When the British passed through Lexington on their way to Concord, they found a group of minutemen blocking their path. Shooting began and before long eight Americans lay dead with ten more wounded.

The British soldiers proceeded to Concord, where they destroyed a supply of gunpowder. By this time the alarm had been raised throughout the countryside, making the return march to Boston a disaster for the British. Minutemen lying in wait behind fences and trees ambushed the redcoats repeatedly, inflicting almost 300 casualties (73 killed and more than 200 wounded).

In Boston, Governor Gage and his soldiers now found themselves surrounded by an angry, hostile, and armed population. It was no longer safe for British soldiers to venture outside the city. The skirmishes at Lexington and Concord on April 19, 1775 had ignited a revolution.

"Gentlemen may cry peace, peace! But there is no peace ... I know not what course others may take, but as for me, give me liberty or give me death!"

—Virginia Patriot Patrick Henry, predicting in 1775 that rebellion would soon erupt in Massachusetts

**Figure 3.2** This engraving of the battle at Lexington was printed a few days after the battle and was based on eyewitness accounts. Examine the image carefully. What advantages did the British army enjoy on the open ground of this field outside Lexington? Why would the minutemen adjust their tactics after such an encounter?

## The Second Continental Congress

Even as an armed militia laid siege to British forces in Boston, delegates to the Second Continental Congress met in Philadelphia in May 1775. Most delegates were reluctant to defy the king, but a few saw little hope for a peaceful resolution. John Adams feared that "the cancer [of tyranny] is too deeply rooted and too far spread to be cured by anything short of cutting it out entire."

In light of the events at Lexington and Concord, the delegates realized they had to act quickly to provide direct aid to Massachusetts and strengthen the colonies' defences. To this end, they began recruiting soldiers from several colonies. They also appointed George Washington head of the new Army of the Continental Congress, which they arranged to finance by borrowing money from France.

At the same time, the Congress continued to seek a peaceful resolution with Britain. The delegates sent petitions to London urging the British government to restore colonial liberties; all were ignored. When the Congress sent a final appeal, known as the Olive Branch Petition, Britain responded by placing further restrictions on trade with the colonies. In August 1775 George III declared that the American colonies were in "open and avowed rebellion" and called on all loyal subjects to "bring the traitors to justice."

## No Turning Back

By the late spring of 1775 a military stalemate had developed around Boston. General Gage and several thousand British troops found themselves trapped in the city, besieged by around 10,000 colonial militiamen. On June 17 the British attempted to break out by attacking the American position on Breed's Hill overlooking the city.

This first major battle of the war, known as the Battle of Bunker Hill, proved to be a model for later encounters. The British charged the Americans three times. The first two attacks failed under withering fire from the colonial troops. When the British regrouped and charged a final time, the Americans ran out of ammunition and were swept from the hill. The redcoats had taken their objective, but at a terrible cost: British casualties (dead and wounded) numbered over 1,000, or approximately 40 percent of the force. Moreover, the fighting failed to lift the siege. When Washington arrived with reinforcements in early 1776, the British were forced to abandon Boston for the remainder of the war. The battle had given the colonial soldiers a psychological lift, proving they could stand against—and inflict heavy casualties on—the best of the British army.

## The Case for Independence

In the aftermath of Bunker Hill and George III's proclamation that the colonies were in rebellion, all hopes of a peaceful transatlantic reconciliation evaporated. In 1776 leaders in various colonies began to ask for a formal

# Culture Notes

## *"Yankee Doodle": Popular Songs of the Revolution*

The success of the American Revolution depended on the Patriots winning the psychological war against the British, especially by maintaining popular support for their cause. From taverns to battlefields, music proved to be a powerful tool for promoting revolutionary enthusiasm. Many songs summoned colonists to fight for their liberties against British oppression. Most are now forgotten but a few remain well known. Of these, none is more celebrated than "Yankee Doodle."

Despite the song's fame, its origins remain obscure. The song probably came from Britain and reached America well before the revolution, by the 1760s. Ironically, early versions of the song were meant to ridicule the upstart colonists. "Yankee" was a colloquial term for an American, while "doodle" was the British term for a fool or idiot. As British troops marched to Concord in 1775 they sang the song to mock the Patriot militiamen who stood in their path. By adapting the song for their own use, the Patriots transformed "Yankee Doodle" into a musical expression of the American Revolution.

As with most popular songs of the time, many variations of "Yankee Doodle" circulated. One version described the experiences of two recruits to the Patriot cause while offering a subtle criticism of General Washington's character:

Father and I went down to camp
Along with Captain Gooding,
And there we see the men and boys
As thick as hasty pudding.

**CHORUS**
Yankee doodle keep it up,
Yankee doodle dandy
mind the music and the step,
And with the girls be handy.

**Figure 3.3** What does this painting suggest about the importance of popular music during the American Revolution?

And there was Captain Washington,
And gentlefolks about him:
They say he's grown so tarnal proud,
He will not ride without 'em.

In an age of limited literacy, popular songs were an effective way to spread political ideas. Today, they offer us a glimpse into the attitudes and opinions of the common people whose support was crucial to the success of the American Revolution.

### Think It Through

1. Explain why songs would be effective propaganda tools for the American cause during the revolution.
2. Why is it ironic that "Yankee Doodle" became a musical symbol of the American Revolution?
3. Can you think of any popular songs today that convey a political message? Identify one and explain its message.

declaration of independence from Britain. In early June a Virginia delegate to the Continental Congress presented a motion declaring that "these united colonies are, and of right ought to be, free and independent states."

Following some debate the Congress created a committee to draft a more formal declaration of the delegates' vision for the colonies. Committee members, including Benjamin Franklin and John Adams, were impressed by the literary talents of a young Virginia delegate named Thomas Jefferson and assigned him the task of composing the declaration.

**APPENDIX**

**The Declaration of Independence is reproduced in the Appendix.**

On July 2, 1776 the Congress voted for independence. After some revisions to Jefferson's document, the Congress unanimously approved the Declaration of Independence two days later on July 4, 1776. Popular celebrations broke out in several states in the following weeks, including the one in New York City that destroyed the statue of the hated oppressor, George III.

## Did Equality Extend to All Men?

In an age of pervasive social, economic, and political inequalities, the Declaration of Independence shocked many people with its assertion that "all men are created equal." Some colonists wondered whether this natural equality really extended to everyone, including the slaves owned by so many Americans at the time.

Despite being a slave owner himself, Thomas Jefferson did include a clause in his first draft of the Declaration that condemned King George for enslaving Africans, arguing that this practice went "against human nature itself, violating its most sacred rights of life and liberty." This criticism, however, proved too much for the many slave-owning delegates who feared such rhetoric might lead to calls for **emancipation**, or the freeing of all slaves in America. In the end, the reference to the cruelty of the slave trade was omitted from the Declaration's final text. It was left to a later generation of Americans to extend the ideal of equality expressed in the Declaration to all the people of the country.

**Figure 3.4** The drafters of the Declaration of Independence present the document to the Continental Congress in June 1776. The chief author, Thomas Jefferson, wears a red waistcoat. How has the artist indicated that this is a significant moment in American history?

AMERICAN ARCHIVE

# The Declaration of Independence

**Figure 3.5** John Locke, the English political philosopher and author of the *Two Treatises of Government* (1690), profoundly influenced the writers of the Declaration of Independence.

The document that Thomas Jefferson penned in 1776 has attained a mythical status in the American consciousness. Perhaps no passage in the Declaration is dearer to Americans than the one in which Jefferson explains that all people have rights and liberties, and that it is the purpose of government to protect these:

> We hold these truths to be self-evident, that all men are created equal; that they are endowed by their Creator with certain inalienable rights; that among these are life, liberty, and the pursuit of happiness;
>
> That to secure these rights, governments are instituted among men, deriving their just powers from the consent of the governed.

Were these thoughts original to Jefferson, or did they reflect ideas he borrowed from others?

## The Social Contract

Actually, Jefferson's lines owed much to radical theories of government that came out of the European **Enlightenment**, a philosophical movement that emphasized the importance of human reason and individual rights. The idea of the "social contract" was developed by the English philosopher John Locke.

According to Locke, an agreement or "contract" exists between every government and its people. In exchange for the people's obedience, the government pledges to protect their rights and liberties. If a government violates the people's rights, the social contract is broken and it is lawful for the people to replace that government with another.

## Justifying Rebellion

This last point is crucial, since it gave Jefferson a *theoretical* justification for rebellion against the king. Once Jefferson had justified revolution in theory, his next step was to show that Britain under George III had violated its obligation to protect the colonists' liberties *in practice*. To this end Jefferson levelled a long and inflammatory list of personal charges against the king, whom he referred to merely as "he":

> He has refused his assent to laws, the most wholesome and necessary for the public good; ...
>
> He has plundered our seas, ravaged our coasts, burnt our towns, and destroyed the lives of our people.

Once Jefferson had established that the king had violated the social contract between the British government and the colonies, he could conclude that the American people were justified in replacing the British government with one of their own making. The document ends with a solemn declaration that dissolves all connections with Britain and establishes the United States as an independent country:

> We, therefore, the representatives of the United States of America ... declare, that these united colonies are, and of right ought to be, free and independent states, that they are absolved from all allegiance to the British Crown, and that all political connection between them and the state of Great Britain is, and ought to be, totally dissolved.

## Think It Through

1. Why did the delegates to the Second Continental Congress feel they needed a formal declaration of independence from Britain? Identify two reasons.
2. The terms "life" and "liberty" are easy to understand, but what did Jefferson mean by the phrase "the pursuit of happiness"? Did he mean that people just like to feel good, or that they should be free to seek a way of life they find fulfilling? Explain.

# PAST VOICES

## THOMAS PAINE'S *Common Sense*

**Figure 3.6** Thomas Paine, author of *Common Sense.*

If the American Revolution was to succeed, the common people—from farmers to merchants to soldiers—had to understand its causes. In January 1776 the Englishman Thomas Paine, a radical journalist who settled in Philadelphia in 1774, published *Common Sense.* The pamphlet provided an easy-to-understand defence of the revolution and sold more than 100,000 copies in the year of its publication. About 15 percent of the male population bought a copy, and many copies were eagerly passed from reader to reader. Paine's pamphlet helped forge a common revolutionary identity throughout the colonies.

Paine began by criticizing rulers who violated, rather than protected, the rights of their citizens. This led to his first principal theme, the evils of George III, whom Paine denounced as "the Royal Brute of Britain" and an "inveterate enemy to liberty." He charged that the British monarch was directly responsible for many of the injustices inflicted on the colonies, an argument Thomas Jefferson would develop further in the Declaration of Independence.

To colonists who feared the economic consequences of severing ties with Britain, Paine argued that America could handle its own affairs and avoid the dangers of European wars if freed from British control. While his politics were influenced by Enlightenment ideas about the importance of liberty, Paine was among the first to articulate the need for America to distance itself from Europe. This theme would grow increasingly more significant in American foreign policy.

> But the injuries and disadvantages which we sustain by that connection [to Britain], are without number; and our duty to mankind at large, as well as to ourselves, instructs us to renounce the alliance: because, any submission to, or dependence on, Great Britain, tends directly to involve this Continent in European wars and quarrels, and set us at variance with nations who would otherwise seek our friendship, and against whom we have neither anger nor complaint.

*Common Sense*, with its passionate language and straightforward arguments, stirred colonists to take up arms against the king.

### Think It Through

1. Explain the factors that made Paine's pamphlet a bestseller.
2. Identify one example of Paine's effective use of language in the excerpt above. Why would this phrasing appeal to a reader in colonial America in 1776?

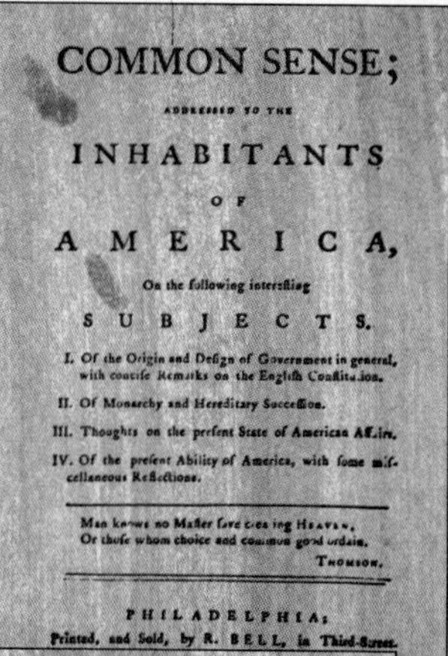

COMMON SENSE;

ADDRESSED TO THE

INHABITANTS

OF

AMERICA,

On the following interesting

SUBJECTS.

I. Of the Origin and Design of Government in general, with concise Remarks on the English Constitution.

II. Of Monarchy and Hereditary Succession.

III. Thoughts on the present State of American Affairs.

IV. Of the present Ability of America, with some miscellaneous Reflections.

Man knows no Master save creating HEAVEN,
Or those whom choice and common good ordain.
THOMSON.

PHILADELPHIA;
Printed, and Sold, by R. BELL, in Third-Street.

I. Of the Origin and Design of Government in general, with concise Remarks on the English Constitution.

II. Of Monarchy and Hereditary Succession.

III. Thoughts on the present State of American Affairs.

IV. Of the present Ability of America, with some miscellaneous Reflections.

**Figure 3.7** The title page of the first edition of Thomas Paine's *Common Sense*. Do you think that the idea of "common sense" politics still appeals to Americans today? Explain your position.

## CHECK YOUR UNDERSTANDING

1. List the steps taken by the First and Second Continental Congresses both to avoid and prepare for war.
2. Why did American efforts to reach a compromise with the British government in 1775 fail?
3. Why was the text condemning King George III for enslaving Africans removed from the Declaration of Independence?
4. What events caused the Congress to declare independence?

# WAGING WAR

The Americans clearly faced considerable obstacles in a war for independence. Britain's navy was the finest in the world, while its army was disciplined, well trained, and well equipped. Despite these advantages, Britain faced considerable challenges. It would be a long and costly project to crush the revolution and then use military might to keep the unwilling colonies under British rule.

By contrast, the colonists only had to resist the British army until the British government grew weary of war and agreed to recognize American independence. Yet as simple as this strategy seemed, the colonists' lack of funds or an organized army complicated the task, as did deep divisions within colonial society between supporters and opponents of the revolution.

## Revolution or Civil War?

The Revolutionary War was a conflict between the colonists and Britain, but it was also a civil war waged within America. Patriots saw independence as the only solution to oppressive British policies; **Loyalists** opposed such a solution. The war divided colonies, communities, and even families. Benjamin Franklin was one of the foremost leaders of the Patriot cause, while his son William was the royal governor of New Jersey and a committed Loyalist.

### Patriots

Patriots came from every rank in colonial society. Some were wealthy merchants and lawyers annoyed at Britain's control over trade. Many rich Virginia planters supported the Patriot cause for the same reason. Patriot leaders were drawn mainly from the wealthy and educated elites, but the majority of the movement's members came from the lower classes: artisans and poor farmers. One commentator reported in 1774 that "the gentleman and mechanic, those of high and low life, the learned and the illiterate" were discussing politics and demanding to have their opinions heard.

There were even some Patriot sympathizers in lands north of the Thirteen Colonies. In Montreal a group of radical English merchants led by Thomas Walker agitated against the Quebec Act and quarrelled with the governor. When the Continental Congress sent a petition to Quebec in 1774 asking for support, Walker circulated it throughout the colony. He and other merchants proposed sending delegates from Montreal to the Continental Congress in Philadelphia in 1775.

After an American force invaded Quebec, Walker and his associates were arrested as traitors. Walker escaped with the help of the American force and fled to Boston, a political choice that forced him to abandon his home and business. He had to devote considerable effort to securing compensation for his losses after the war.

## Loyalists

About one-fifth of the population of the American colonies—perhaps 500,000 individuals—remained loyal to the British Crown throughout the revolution. Who were these Loyalists, whom the Patriots called "Tories" in reference to English supporters of the king? Some were royal officials, such as tax collectors or governors. Others were members of the Anglican clergy, ministers of the Church of England. Still others were wealthy merchants and landowners who feared that social and economic upheaval would follow a successful revolution against Britain.

The majority of Loyalists, however, were poor farmers and artisans who opposed the colonial elites who led the revolution. They accused these leaders of being interested only in preserving their own wealth and power in colonial society. Many minority groups, such as German settlers in Pennsylvania, supported the Loyalists because they too felt marginalized in colonial society. **Tenant farmers** across the South chose Loyalism as a means of resisting their wealthy Patriot landlords and acquiring some land for themselves.

In refusing to support the Patriot cause, Loyalists took great risks. Local Committees of Safety pressed suspected Loyalists to swear oaths in support of the Continental Congress. Those who refused faced intimidation, violence, or imprisonment. Many were forced to flee their homes and seek refuge in areas controlled by the British.

## 49th PARALLEL Butler's Rangers and Joseph Brant

The American Revolution presented difficult choices for colonists and Aboriginal peoples alike. Many who chose to support Britain abandoned their homes in the colonies and sought safety in British territories. Some of these Loyalists formed militia bands to attack American settlements. Often, Native Americans who feared the westward expansion of settlements that would follow an American victory joined Loyalist bands.

John Butler was a Loyalist officer in the New York militia who lived in the Mohawk River Valley, working closely with the Iroquois as an **Indian agent**. He fled to Canada in 1777 and raised a company of about 500 rangers, men skilled in fighting and surviving in the wilderness. Butler's Rangers cooperated closely with the Iroquois to harass American settlements. From their base at Fort Niagara, the Rangers conducted bloody raids into the Mohawk River Valley, striking fear into colonists throughout New York State.

The same year that Butler fled to Canada, the Iroquois chief Joseph Brant travelled to London to offer his services. Brant was skilled at playing off one group of Europeans against another. In fact, his Iroquois name, *Thayendanegea*, meant "He Who Places Two Bets." Brant realized that the Iroquois future would be bleak if British influence in the interior came to an end.

Brant made a great impression on British officials and convincingly argued his case for an alliance between the Iroquois and the British. Upon his return to America, Iroquois warriors joined forces with Butler's Rangers in a series of raids. The attacks spread terror on the American frontier and diverted American soldiers from the main campaigns along the Atlantic seaboard.

Despite their efforts on behalf of Britain, the Iroquois did not merit a single mention in the Treaty of Paris, which ended the war. Brant was disillusioned, knowing that his people could never return to their traditional lands. In 1784 the Iroquois received a Loyalist land grant along the Grand River in Canada. Brant and his followers settled there, and today their descendants live on the Six Nations Reserve. John Butler and his supporters were given lands in the Niagara Peninsula; for a time, Niagara-on-the-Lake was known as Butlerburg.

When Butler died in 1796 his friend Joseph Brant lamented that "there are none remaining who understand our manners and customs as well as he did"—a warning for the future.

### Think It Through

1. How did Brant and the Iroquois contribute to the British war effort during the Revolutionary War?
2. Brant died in 1807 fearing for the future of Native Americans. In what ways might his experiences during and after the American Revolution have influenced his opinions?

**Figure 3.8** One of Butler's Rangers. The British thought of John Butler as a hero, but early American historians characterized him as "barbarous, treacherous, revengeful, ferocious, merciless, brutal, diabolically wicked, and cruel." How would you account for this difference in opinion?

**Figure 3.9** Chief Joseph Brant, painted during his visit to London to gain support for the Iroquois. Brant spoke English fluently and had even helped translate the Bible into the Iroquois language.

## The Continental Army

Initially the Continental Congress believed local militias could fight the war against the British. The lesson learned from early battles such as Bunker Hill was that the colonists needed a large, trained, and disciplined army to defeat professional British soldiers and their officers. Washington himself argued for a Continental Army under the direct control of officers appointed by the Congress. His suggestion was met by considerable opposition stemming from the fear of creating a standing army that might later threaten American liberties. In the end, however, Washington prevailed.

The Continental Army did not conform to the popular myth of citizen-soldiers ready to lay down their lives for their homes and farms. Most of the men who enlisted were poor and unmarried, without land or close ties to their communities. They had little to lose by enlisting and welcomed the promises of food, steady wages, and a grant of land following the war. Yet the biggest problem for the army in the early years of the war was **desertion**. In 1777 alone, 30 to 40 percent of soldiers deserted. Food and pay proved unreliable, and many soldiers lacked adequate clothing. The worst trial came in December 1777 when the army settled at Valley Forge near Philadelphia and was forced to endure an unusually bitter winter. Almost 3,000 men died of disease, exposure, and malnutrition.

**SOUND BITE**

"We had engaged in the defense of our injured country and were willing nay, we were determined, to persevere as long as such hardships were not altogether intolerable."

—Seventeen-year-old Joseph Martin of Connecticut recounts in his diary that, despite shortages of blankets, shoes, and food at Valley Forge, he and his fellow soldiers are determined to carry on.

**Figure 3.10** General Washington and Baron von Steuben review the ragged troops of the Continental Army at Valley Forge. A German officer, von Steuben accepted the assignment of drilling the raw recruits into a disciplined fighting force. By the spring, the men had new uniforms, knew how to march and fight in formation, and were eager to match themselves against the British.

In all, almost 100,000 men served under Washington. As well as ensuring the ultimate success of the revolution, the Continental Army brought together men from various colonies and, through trials and hardships, gave them a common identity—one that helped promote an urgently needed sense of national unity.

## What about the "Ladies"?

During the American Revolution, many women sought to contribute to the war effort in whatever ways they could. In some cases, this meant providing increased support at home. In others, it meant putting their lives on the line in battles. Still other women attempted to have a say in the drafting of the Constitution. In many cases, however—despite their efforts and regardless of their wealth or social status—women's voices were not heard and their contributions did not receive the recognition they deserved. The examples of two women from opposite ends of the social spectrum provide ample evidence of this fact.

Abigail Adams was the wife of the Patriot leader John Adams. In a famous letter written to her husband while he was attending the Continental Congress in March 1776, she urged him to "Remember the Ladies, and to be more generous and favourable to them than your ancestors." She went on to say, "Do not put such unlimited powers in the hands of the Husbands. Remember, all men would be tyrants if they could. If particular care and attention are not paid to the ladies, we are determined to foment [stir up] a rebellion, and will not hold ourselves bound to obey the laws in which we have no voice or representation." John Adams was not persuaded. He replied in part, "Depend upon it. We know better than to repeal our masculine systems." Women played no role in drafting the new state constitutions, either. Only New Jersey's constitution granted women the right to vote—a right it cancelled, along with the right of free blacks to vote, in 1807.

**Figure 3.11** This popular image from 1779 shows a woman armed as a Patriot soldier. What does this suggest about some of the radical consequences of the American Revolution, and the role that women played in it?

At the other end of the social scale, women played an important support role in the war. Many stayed at home to run businesses or manage households in their husbands' absence, while some accompanied their husbands to war. One of the most famous female warriors was Mary McCauley Hays, the wife of Private John Hays. During the exhausting summer heat of 1778 Mary brought water to her husband and his gun crew, earning the nickname Molly Pitcher. When her husband was wounded at the Battle of Monmouth, she took his place in the gun crew so that they could continue fighting. During the fight, a cannonball passed right between Molly's legs and tore away her petticoats. Molly became a scrubwoman after the war and the Pennsylvania Assembly later granted her an annual pension of $40 (about $900 in current dollars).

The advice of the "ladies" largely went unheeded and their heroic war acts were all but forgotten. But the actions of women during the revolution—of outspoken advocates like Abigail Adams, and brave fighters like Mary Hays—marked the beginning of a change that would eventually occur in attitudes toward women.

## The Military Campaigns

When the Revolutionary War began, the Patriots had no clear military strategy. Their leaders disagreed on whether they should fight a primarily offensive or defensive war. Early in the conflict, the Americans were willing to go on the attack, which led to a disastrous decision to invade Quebec.

### Quebec

Fearing a British attack from Quebec in the wake of the Declaration of Independence, the Americans determined to launch a pre-emptive strike on the colony. In late 1775 two American armies headed north. The first, commanded by General Richard Montgomery, left from upstate New York. At Montreal in November 1775 Montgomery's force defeated the British, who withdrew downriver to Quebec.

Pursuing the British to Quebec City, Montgomery was joined in late December by a second force, commanded by Benedict Arnold, which had marched overland from Massachusetts through bitter winter weather. The combined American forces attacked on New Year's Eve in the midst of a blinding snowstorm; the British troops forced the soldiers back and killed Montgomery. Arnold maintained a siege for several months, until spring arrived and British reinforcements forced him to retreat.

The American defeat owed much to the harsh weather; Arnold had lost one-third of his force to cold and hunger even before reaching Quebec. The reluctance of the French-Canadian population to support the invaders also doomed the American plan.

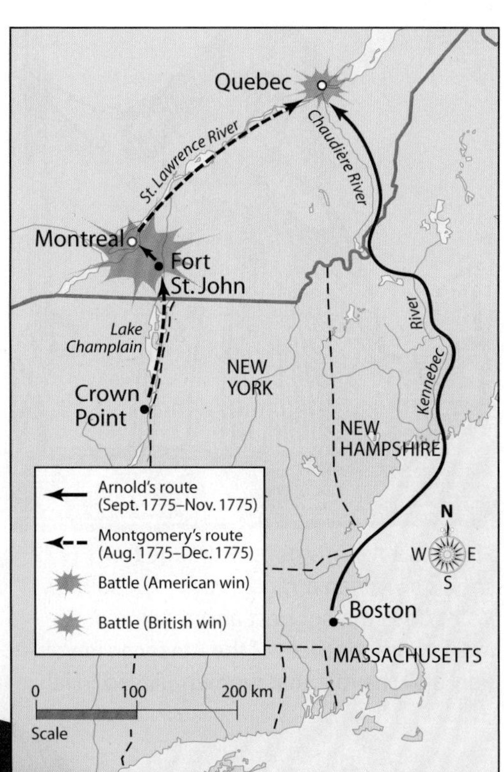


**Figure 3.12** The Quebec campaign, 1775–76. This map shows the two-pronged attack. One American force travelled up Lake Champlain toward Montreal before heading to Quebec, while a second army left Boston and travelled directly to Quebec. Why did the Americans wish to attack British troops in Canada?

## American Strategy

After Quebec, George Washington and other American leaders chose to adopt a defensive military strategy that was really quite simple: harass British forces wherever possible while at the same time avoiding a crushing defeat. Surrender by Washington would spell the end of the revolution, but the longer the Continental Army remained in the field, the greater the chance of victory.

Indeed, pressure on the British government to reach a settlement with the colonies mounted as the conflict dragged on. Even as General Washington complained about troop desertions and lack of funds, the British faced similar problems. The war's impact on colonial trade was devastating, and this stirred opposition from many British merchants. Many Englishmen refused to enlist for service in America despite enticements. This forced the British government to hire Hessian **mercenaries**, soldiers-of-fortune from the Hesse area in western Germany.

At sea, the Americans pursued a similar strategy to that on land. Instead of major naval engagements, American captains like John Paul Jones fought battles against single British ships and ran the blockade of American ports. Everywhere the strategy was the same: draw the war out until the British lost the will to fight and recognized American independence.

## British Strategy

While the Americans adopted a defensive strategy, the British went on the offensive. Their plan for crushing the rebellion was clear:

- the British navy would blockade American ports along the east coast,
- the Loyalists would work to undermine the revolution from within, and
- the British army would try to divide the northern and southern colonies in order to force their surrender.

The last point was the key to the whole campaign. The army had to succeed in its stated objectives for the overall strategy to work.

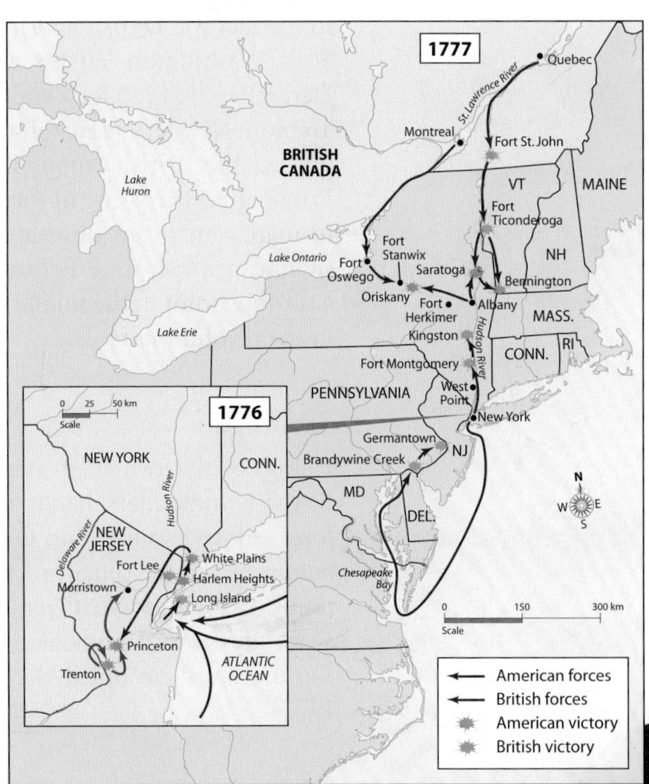


**Figure 3.13** British military strategy hinged on a three-pronged movement into upstate New York that would annihilate the Continental Army and divide the colonies in two. This map for the northern campaigns shows the British advances north from New York and south from Quebec, and the American victory at Saratoga.

**Figure 3.14** Although historically inaccurate (Washington could not have made the crossing standing up), this famous painting of Washington leading his army across the Delaware River clearly illustrates the determination of Washington and his men, struggling against considerable odds. How has the artist accomplished this?

In the late summer of 1776 General William Howe and more than 30,000 British troops occupied New York City in preparation for a march north along the Hudson River. Howe planned to meet a second British force moving south from Quebec and a third advancing from Lake Ontario in the West. The combined British force would then defeat any Patriot forces in the area and **pacify** New England before turning south.

Although outnumbered and demoralized, the Continental Army sought to distract the British and frustrate this plan. Before Howe could leave New York, Washington led his forces across the ice-bound Delaware River on December 25, 1776 for a successful surprise attack on Hessian mercenaries at Trenton, New Jersey. He followed up with another victory at Princeton, which pushed the British troops in New Jersey back to the safety of New York. Washington's crossing of the Delaware not only made Howe rethink his plan to march north into upstate New York; it also acquired a deeper symbolic significance over time. For many Patriots, this daring attack came to represent a turning point in the military struggle against Britain and renewed their faith in the revolutionary cause.

## Saratoga

Failure of the British strategy owed more to delays and poor decisions by British commanders than to the efforts of Washington's troops. Even as British forces moved south from Quebec, Howe remained stubbornly in New York before finally heading, not north, but south into Pennsylvania. Seeking to punish Washington for Trenton and Princeton, Howe defeated the Americans at the battles of Brandywine Creek and Germantown, Pennsylvania. He then captured and occupied the colonial capital of Philadelphia in September 1777.

Howe's failure to advance north from New York left the British force moving south from Quebec vulnerable to attack. After suffering several defeats, the British invaders, commanded by General John Burgoyne, surrendered at Saratoga on October 17, 1777. This brought an end to the British grand strategy.

One of the American heroes of Saratoga was Benedict Arnold, a leader of the Quebec campaign of 1775–76 who had also won strategic battles in upstate New York in 1775. Arnold was appointed commander of Philadelphia following the victory at Saratoga, but soon fell into shady business dealings in an effort to support his extravagant lifestyle. He was later court-martialled for these by the Continental Congress and rebuked by Washington. In 1780 Arnold devised a plan to surrender West Point, a New York military base, to the British for a reward of £20,000 (about $4.5 million today). The plot was discovered but Arnold managed to elude capture. He was awarded the rank of brigadier general in the British army and served in a number of campaigns against the Americans. Despite Arnold's contributions at Saratoga and other battles, his actions were overshadowed by his treason at West Point and his name became synonymous with traitor.

The American victory at Saratoga won much popular support for the Patriot cause. It also persuaded France to recognize American independence and enter the war on the American side. This was a tremendous boost for the Americans, as it provided them with funds and naval support they would otherwise have lacked. France's intervention also forced Britain to relocate some of its troops from America to the Caribbean to defend its West Indian colonies from French attack.

When the American ambassador to France, Benjamin Franklin, was told that the British had captured Philadelphia, he responded: "No, Philadelphia has captured the British."

What do you think Franklin meant by this reply?

## The War in the South

While many of the most famous battles of the Revolutionary War (from Lexington and Bunker Hill to Princeton and Saratoga) occurred in the northern colonies, much of the fiercest fighting took place in the South. In late 1778 General Henry Clinton led a British force to capture Savannah, Georgia before moving on to South Carolina, where Charleston surrendered in May 1780.

The British effort made extensive use of Loyalist militias and companies of former slaves, who were promised freedom in exchange for supporting Britain. On the American side, Colonel Francis Marion, known as the Swamp Fox, led a Patriot militia that successfully harassed the British. One American officer described the vicious fighting between these forces of "irregulars" as "little less than savage fury."

Although the British commander in the South, General Charles Cornwallis, enjoyed considerable military success, he knew that a final victory would require subjugating the Patriot strongholds of Virginia. As the first step in this campaign, Cornwallis led his forces north via Chesapeake Bay to Yorktown, Virginia. It was a fatal error.

### Yorktown

In the spring of 1781 with Cornwallis in Yorktown, Washington heard that a French fleet was due to arrive off the Virginia coast. Hurrying south, Washington brought the Continental Army and his French allies to encircle the British forces at Yorktown. For more than a month, the American and French forces, aided by the French fleet, besieged the British garrison. General Cornwallis realized that relief was impossible and surrendered to Washington's army on October 19, 1781. As the British soldiers marched out, their band played the popular song "The World Turned Upside Down."

Although the British still held New York, the surrender at Yorktown had a profound effect on their government's will to continue the war. Recognizing the strategic impact of the loss and the boost it gave to American confidence, the British prime minister, Lord North, tendered his resignation and a new government was installed that favoured granting the American colonies their independence. In July 1782 the American envoy, Benjamin Franklin, arrived in London to negotiate a peace treaty to recognize American independence.

### CHECK YOUR UNDERSTANDING

1. What reasons did most soldiers have for joining the Continental Army?
2. How did the Continental Army create a sense of national identity?
3. Why did the Americans fail to take Quebec?
4. Outline the British strategy to defeat the revolution. Why did it fail?

## THE RESULTS OF THE WAR

The results of the Revolutionary War were far reaching, not just for the United States but for Europe and Canada as well. The Americans achieved their independence under a form of ad hoc or temporary government that everyone recognized was too weak to sustain itself. The end of the war would force the United States to create a more viable and lasting form of government.

In Europe the end of the war deepened the old hostility between the colonial powers, Britain and France. To avoid major concessions to France in the peace negotiations that followed the war, Britain agreed to meet most of the Americans' territorial demands. The financial support that France had provided the Americans with during the war weakened France's own financial health, and would eventually play a role in hastening the French Revolution. In Canada, the influx of Loyalists during the war would affect the way this British territory developed for years to come, particularly in the area that would become Ontario.

# The Search for a Strong and Stable Government

During the war, while George Washington struggled to keep his army in the field, the Continental Congress faced challenges of its own. Prosecuting a war required money and an effective government administration. Despite this need, the Congress possessed few powers and many delegates opposed a strong central government. Having declared their independence from Britain, the colonies were reluctant to cede too much of their power to any new government, even one of their own making. The direct result was the Articles of Confederation. This created a weak central government and left many crucial powers with the individual states.

## The Articles of Confederation

The Continental Congress adopted the Articles of Confederation in November 1777 after considerable debate, and then sent them to the state legislatures for approval. The Articles created a national government headed by a Congress, in which each state's delegation held a single vote. Most questions were decided by a simple majority, although major decisions would require unanimous approval. The head of Congress was the president, who acted as chairman of its debates but held no executive powers.

### The Articles of Confederation and the United States Constitution

| | Articles of Confederation | US Constitution |
|---|---|---|
| **Army** | Congress has no power to raise an army. It must rely on individual states for soldiers. | Congress can raise an army in emergencies. |
| **Taxation** | Congress must rely on states for tax revenue. | Congress may tax individuals directly. |
| **President** | The president has no executive power. He simply presides over meetings of Congress. | The president has executive power as head of government administration. |
| **Representation** | Each state has one vote (regardless of population). | Each state has two votes in the Senate, and the number of seats in the House of Representatives is determined by population. |
| **Passing laws** | Laws require approval of 9 of 13 states. | Laws require approval of a majority in both the Senate and the House of Representatives, and the signature of the president. |
| **Authority** | States retain ultimate authority. | The Constitution (not the states) is considered the highest authority. |

**Figure 3.15** This chart compares key aspects of the Articles of Confederation (1777) and the United States Constitution (1789). How might the Constitution produce a stronger and more effective federal government?

The Articles assigned the Congress a range of responsibilities, including control of foreign affairs and the army, coinage and postal service, relations with Native Americans, and the settling of disputes between states. Crucially, however, the Congress did not have the power to tax. It merely divided its expenses among the states, which were responsible for raising the money. This left Congress dependent on the states for its revenues. Since the states were often slow or reluctant to deliver funds, Congress was often too short of cash to meet its financial obligations.

## A Military Coup?

The dangers of having a weak government that was often unable to pay its expenses soon became obvious. Throughout the war, Congress struggled to ensure that the soldiers of the Continental Army received regular pay, clothing, food, and other supplies. Some soldiers deserted as a result of these commitments not being met, and some citizens refused to serve in the army, afraid they would never be paid.

As the fighting against Britain ended, conditions only grew worse. At the end of the war more than 10,000 men camped at Newburgh, near New York, growing impatient as they waited to be paid and discharged. Their officers had been promised life pensions but feared these would never be paid. In a dramatic bid to avoid mutiny, George Washington called a meeting of his officers on March 15, 1783.

Washington appealed to his subordinates' patriotism and skillfully played on their sympathy, protesting: "I have grown gray in your service." By defusing the Newburgh unrest, he helped to ensure that the American Revolution would not end in a military **coup**. The United States had survived a serious test of its democracy, but could not continue under its present form of government.

## States' Rights

It is worth noting that when Congress passed the Articles of Confederation, most of the states had already adopted their own constitutions and jealously guarded their present powers. The Articles confirmed this, stating clearly that all powers not assigned to the Congress belonged to the states.

Approval of the Articles soon revealed a division among the states over the question of the western lands. Some states without these territories, such as Maryland, wanted the western lands to be administered by the Congress on behalf of all. States like Virginia, on the other hand, viewed these lands as their own. In 1781 Virginia agreed to give up its claim to these territories and the final state, Maryland, ratified the Articles of Confederation. However, debates over states' rights, the division of powers, and the political consequences of westward expansion would rage for years. Eventually they would lead to the divisions that caused the Civil War.

# Recognition and Growth of the United States

In 1782 representatives from the United States, Britain, and France met in Paris to negotiate the peace treaty that would officially mark the end of the war. The Americans' main aims in the negotiations were clear: to win recognition of their independence and the withdrawal of British forces from America. Some American politicians wanted the treaty to clarify their fishing and trading rights, and some went so far as to hope for the surrender of Canada.

The French were eager to acquire British colonies in the Caribbean and other territorial concessions, complicating America's negotiations with Britain. Recognizing its dependence on French military assistance in defeating the British, Congress instructed the American negotiators to follow the lead of the French diplomats in everything else once they had secured recognition of American independence. In Paris, the American negotiators Benjamin Franklin, John Jay, and John Adams chafed at the instructions to follow France's lead. The British diplomats recognized this and offered the Americans a deal so generous they could not refuse it, successfully driving a wedge between the Americans and the French.

## The Treaty of Paris

In November 1782 the British and Americans reached a tentative agreement without the knowledge or approval of the French. Britain recognized American independence and promised to withdraw its remaining troops from the Northwest "with all convenient speed." It also gave the Americans all the lands south of Canada and north of Spanish Florida, from the Atlantic Ocean to the Mississippi River, thus creating a country larger and richer in natural resources than any of the European powers.

**Figure 3.16** This 1782 American cartoon shows a smiling America (right) holding out an olive branch symbolizing peace, while Britannia (left) weeps at the loss of her colonies.

In exchange, the American government promised to stop seizures of Loyalist property and to provide compensation for previous Loyalist losses. While American negotiators gloated that this deal left "not much to desire," the French were appalled by the betrayal. In reality, though, France had little choice but to accept this *fait accompli*—particularly when the Americans hinted at the possibility of a British–American alliance against France. The Treaty of Paris was signed at Versailles on September 3, 1783.

## The Loyalist Legacy

Because the Revolutionary War ended with British defeat, those Americans who had remained loyal to the British Crown now faced painful choices. Could they remain in the new United States? If not, where would they go? Some Loyalists chose to remain in America and give their allegiance, however grudgingly, to the new government. Others fled.

Many former military officers and some wealthier Loyalists returned to Britain or settled in the West Indies. For most, however, this was not an option. The majority of Loyalists were poor farmers and labourers who lacked the resources to cross the Atlantic. Instead, they accepted offers of land in other British territories in North America. Almost 40,000 settled in the Maritime colonies, many along the north shore of the Bay of Fundy, where a new colony—New Brunswick—was created for them in 1784.

**Figure 3.17** Loyalist settlements were concentrated in two areas: Upper Canada (now Ontario) at Niagara and along the St. Lawrence, and in Nova Scotia and along the St. John River Valley (New Brunswick).

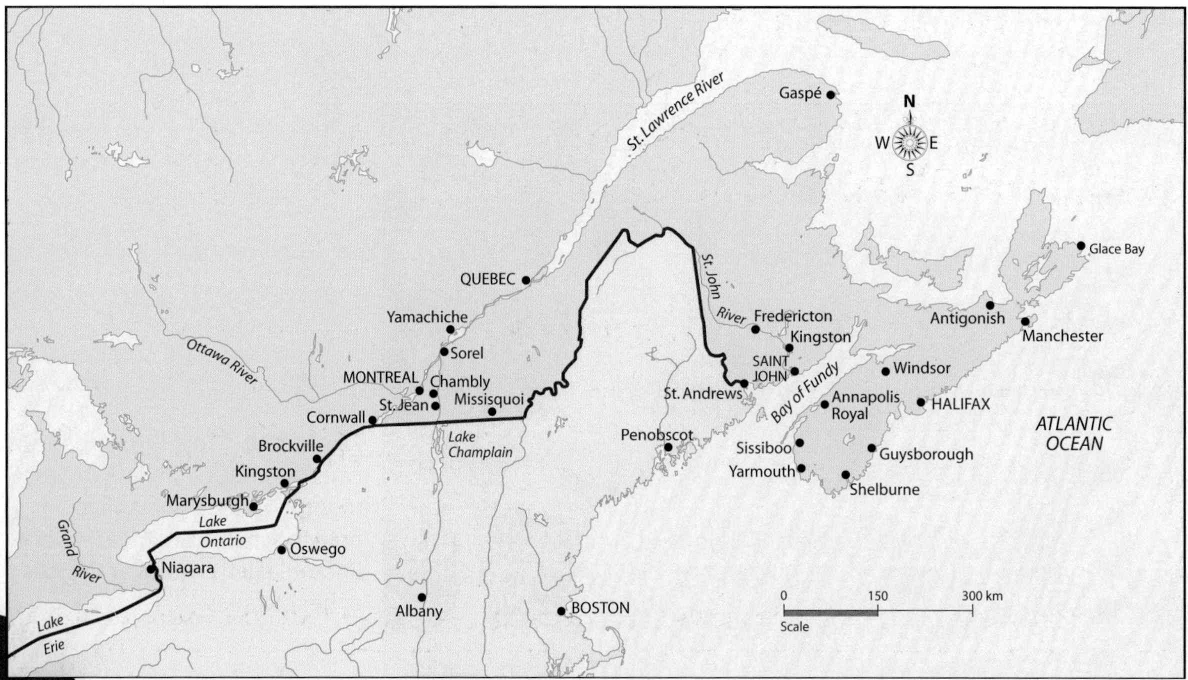

## The Black Loyalists

Among the groups of Loyalists who settled in Nova Scotia were 3,000 former African-American slaves, some of whom had fought in a British regiment called the Black Pioneers. Despite their support for the British cause, many of the black Loyalists were denied the land grants given to all other Loyalists. In 1792 about 1,200 black Loyalists accepted a British offer of free passage to Sierra Leone, in Africa. There they helped build the capital city of Freetown.

**WEB LINKS** 

To learn more about the black Loyalists, visit www.emp.ca/ah.

## Upper Canada

Other Loyalists settled in the colony of Quebec: a few in Montreal and Quebec City, but most on farms along the St. Lawrence River, particularly around Kingston and Prince Edward County. The arrival of an English-speaking population in the upper St. Lawrence Valley prompted the British government to divide the colony into two in 1791, creating Upper and Lower Canada. Upper Canada, which eventually became Ontario, was profoundly shaped by the Loyalist experience. Its people remained hostile to America and proud of their loyalty to the British Crown during the revolution. The motto of the modern Province of Ontario—"Loyal she remains"—reflects this heritage.

**Figure 3.18** As refugees from the American Revolution, Loyalists settled in camps like this one along the St. Lawrence at Johnstown (later Cornwall) before receiving land to farm. How might the Loyalists' plight be similar to that of refugees arriving in Canada today? How might it differ?

### CHECK YOUR UNDERSTANDING

1. How did the desire of each state to protect its rights create problems in governing the United States?
2. List the gains of the United States under the Treaty of Paris.
3. What options were open to Loyalists in the United States following the revolution?
4. How were black Loyalists treated differently from other Loyalists?

# THE CONSTITUTION

By the time the Treaty of Paris was signed in 1783 leaders in the United States feared that they would be overwhelmed by the challenges of the Articles of Confederation. The debts incurred during the war were so great that they threatened to destroy the new nation and drive the colonies back under the protection of Britain. If the new United States were to survive, the government needed radical change.

**APPENDIX**

**The US Constitution and its amendments are reproduced in the Appendix.**

The changes were expressed in the text of the Constitution. Formed by the ideas of liberty expressed in the Declaration of Independence, the Constitution gave the United States government its own unique identity.

## Economic Woes

The Continental Congress financed the Revolutionary War by issuing more than $190 million (about $6 billion in current dollars) in a paper currency called **Continentals**. This increase in circulating currency, combined with shortages of imported goods, produced severe **inflation**. By 1781 it took 146 Continental dollars to buy one Spanish dollar, where four years earlier it had cost only three!

By the end of the war, economic depression had replaced inflation. The American economy struggled to recover from the dislocation of its trading relationship with Britain. At the same time, the new national government faced crushing debts to its allies, France and Spain. The government passed this burden on to the states, which responded by raising taxes.

### Shays's Rebellion

The increase in taxes led directly to a revolt by farmers in Massachusetts. Already in debt from the loss of British markets, the farmers found themselves unable to pay the higher taxes. In response, the state began confiscating their farms and imprisoning them for debt.

The farmers organized themselves into armed bands, attacked courthouses, and freed the prisoners. The revolt in western Massachusetts, led by Daniel Shays, quickly spread to other states. The state militias eventually restored order, but the popular unrest shocked the country's leaders. As one leading conservative political figure observed, after Shays's Rebellion, "it was time to clip the wings of a mad democracy."

**Figure 3.19** Daniel Shays and his men take control of a Massachusetts courthouse. Why would such a popular uprising alarm the leaders of the newly independent United States?

## The Constitutional Convention

In May 1787, 12 of the 13 states sent delegates to a meeting in Philadelphia. (Rhode Island, always independent, refused to participate.) After selecting George Washington to preside over their discussions, the delegates to this Constitutional Convention began to debate changes to the Articles. They quickly realized that more than a modest reform of the Articles was required.

James Madison of the Virginia delegation advanced a plan that some delegates found too radical. The Virginia Plan, as it came to be known, called for greatly enhancing the powers of the central government. Madison planned to divide those powers between three branches: legislative (a bicameral, or two-chamber, congress), executive (a president), and judicial (a federal court system).

The Virginia Plan aroused much opposition, partly because Madison wanted representation in both houses of Congress to be based on population. This idea favoured larger states, such as Virginia and Pennsylvania, at the expense of smaller ones, such as Connecticut. A compromise plan, the New Jersey Plan, focused on congressional representation. Under the New Jersey Plan only representation in the lower chamber of the Congress (the House of Representatives) would be based on population, while in the upper chamber (the Senate) each state would have an equal representation of two members.

### The Question of Slavery

Next, the delegates had to reconcile the interests of states with and without slavery. Southern states wanted their slaves to be included in calculating their populations, even though slaves did not qualify as citizens. In this way, they hoped to increase the voices of their states in the new government. At the same time, however, they did not want slaves counted in calculating the taxes their citizens had to pay.

Eventually, delegates agreed on another compromise, by which five slaves were counted as three freemen. This became known as the **three-fifths rule.** Astonishing as the rule may seem today, it reflected the widespread view at the time that slaves were property rather than human beings.

Finally, the Constitution expressly protected the slave trade for a period of 20 years. Why did opponents of the slave trade from northern states (including Benjamin Franklin) accept this? Not for the last time, many believed that preserving the union was more important than eradicating slavery.

### The Electoral College

Selecting the chief executive was another area of contention. Although the revolution had been fought to escape from the British Crown, many of the delegates to the Convention, including Alexander Hamilton of New York, could see the benefits of a **constitutional monarchy**. Hamilton wanted the president to be chosen by Congress for life and to enjoy considerable power, including the right to veto legislation.

Once more the delegates were able to reach a compromise that the majority could accept. Rather than holding office for life, the president would be limited to a four-year term. He would not be appointed by Congress, but neither would the people elect him directly. Instead, **electors** chosen by state legislatures would assemble to select the president. Only if they failed to agree on a candidate would the choice fall to the Congress.

## Approving the Constitution

Many state politicians were furious when they learned that the Constitutional Convention was proposing a whole new form of government instead of merely revising the Articles of Confederation. They feared the Constitution would significantly weaken the power of the states by favouring a strong central government.

Since the passage of the Constitution required the approval of nine of the 13 states, vigorous efforts began to either encourage or block its passage. Generally, well-educated professionals (doctors, teachers, lawyers), merchants, and artisans favoured the Constitution, while farmers universally opposed it. The educated elites believed the country needed a strong government to promote trade and financial stability. The farmers feared the taxes that the government might impose.

**Figure 3.20** This 1787 cartoon from Connecticut vividly shows the divisions in that state over the new constitution. On the one side were opponents (mainly farmers), and on the other were supporters (chiefly merchants).

## WE THE PEOPLE

### Benjamin Franklin

### 1706–1790

In organizing the Constitutional Convention, congressional leaders knew they had to persuade certain people to attend if the meeting were to have the prestige necessary to impress the American people. Although he was 81 years old, frail, and retired from public office at the time, Benjamin Franklin was at the top of their list. Franklin's presence at the Convention—and his signature on the Constitution—were key factors in winning public acceptance for the new form of government.

Born the youngest of 15 children to a poor Boston family, Franklin was apprenticed to his brother, a printer, at the age of 12. By 16 he was writing for his brother's newspaper, *The New England Courant*, which openly criticized the British authorities.

Franklin left Boston for Philadelphia, where he opened his own print shop. In 1732 he launched his most successful publication, *Poor Richard's Almanac*, which was filled with practical information and a collection of popular proverbs such as "Early to bed, early to rise, makes a man healthy, wealthy and wise." It quickly became an annual bestseller.

**Figure 3.21** In 1754 Benjamin Franklin created one of the first political cartoons, arguing for a union of the colonies. What makes this cartoon such an effective image?

Franklin was also devoted to science and was particularly interested in electricity. He theorized that lightning was a form of electricity and conducted experiments that led to the invention of the lightning rod, used to protect buildings and ships from lightning strikes. He also formulated the law of conservation of charge, one of the basic principles of physical science. Franklin was hailed in Europe and America as one of the leading scientists of the time.

In Philadelphia, Franklin grew fascinated by politics. By 1757 he was in England as the Pennsylvania Assembly's agent to inform the British government about political conditions in the colony. Enjoying London society, Franklin remained there for 18 years before growing disillusioned with British policy. He returned to America in April 1775 and served as an outspoken and radical delegate to the Second Continental Congress, where he assisted in drafting the Declaration of Independence.

In late 1776 Franklin went to France as the Congress's envoy, and there he created an instant sensation. Dressed in plain clothes and wearing no powdered wig (it irritated his scalp), Franklin was idolized by the French nobility for his plainspoken wit and intellectual accomplishments. His social success helped him win loans from the French government for the United States and paved the way for the military alliance between the two countries.

When the Revolutionary War ended, Franklin joined the peace negotiations with Britain before returning to America in 1785, rejoicing that "I shall now be free of Politicks for the rest of my life." When he died in 1790 the National Assembly in

**Figure 3.22** In France, the king and court were captivated by Franklin's colonial simplicity.

France, but not the American Congress, observed three days of mourning.

In his lifetime Franklin wore many hats: publisher, philosopher, political agitator, scientist, and diplomat. His most significant contribution was to serve as a symbol of America for the world. His simple dress and habits, which hid a sophisticated character, helped create an image of America that was intriguing and sympathetic to Europeans. Franklin was the only person to sign the Declaration of Independence, the Treaty of Paris, and the Constitution of the United States, and was, according to Jefferson, "the ornament of our country, and I may say, of the world."

## Think It Through

1. Explain how Franklin succeeded in promoting American interests in France.
2. In addition to his work with electricity, Franklin developed many inventions. Why would his scientific work win him respect in Europe?
3. Do you think that the image Franklin cultivated—of the simply dressed, plainspoken colonial—still influences the way Americans think of themselves today? Explain.

### Federalists and Anti-Federalists

The supporters of the new constitution called themselves **Federalists.** The most articulate expression of their position appeared in the *Federalist Papers*, a series of 85 essays published in New York newspapers in 1787–88. Although intended to promote ratification of the Constitution in New York, these essays were read—and influenced public opinion—throughout the United States.

In the *Federalist Papers*, Alexander Hamilton, James Madison, and John Jay argued that the diversity of opinions present in a large **republic** would protect individual rights by preventing any one faction from dominating the nation's government. Contrary to what their opponents might argue, only a strong and effective central government could successfully defend individual liberties.

On the other hand, many stalwart supporters of the revolution rejected the new constitution. These opponents became known as **anti-Federalists.** Less organized than the Federalists and without the same access to the press, they opposed the new constitution for a variety of reasons. In general, their dissent focused on the fear that the new central government would undermine the autonomy of the individual states. Many of the early leaders of opposition to Britain, such as Samuel Adams of Massachusetts, viewed the new constitution as a betrayal of the idea of liberty that had inspired their revolutionary struggle.

"Extend the sphere [of government] and you take in a greater variety of parties and interest; you make it less probable that a majority will have a common motive to invade the rights of other citizens ... The influence of factious leaders may kindle a flame within their particular States, but will be unable to spread a general conflagration through the other States."

—James Madison in *The Federalist*, Number 10

## Ratification

On paper, the procedures for approving the Constitution were clear. In order to prevent any one state from blocking the process, the Constitution required the approval of only 9 of the 13 states for ratification. As well, to avoid interference from vested interests, voting in each state would be by a special meeting of delegates rather than by the existing state legislature. Even so, the process of **ratification** proved complex and controversial.

The process began smoothly, with Delaware ratifying the Constitution in December 1787, earning it the title of "the first state." It was not until June of the following year, however, that the ninth state, New Hampshire, gave its approval. With the Constitution now in effect, major states like Virginia and New York could not afford to be left out; they too ratified. In the end only North Carolina and Rhode Island voted against the Constitution, but both would eventually change their minds.

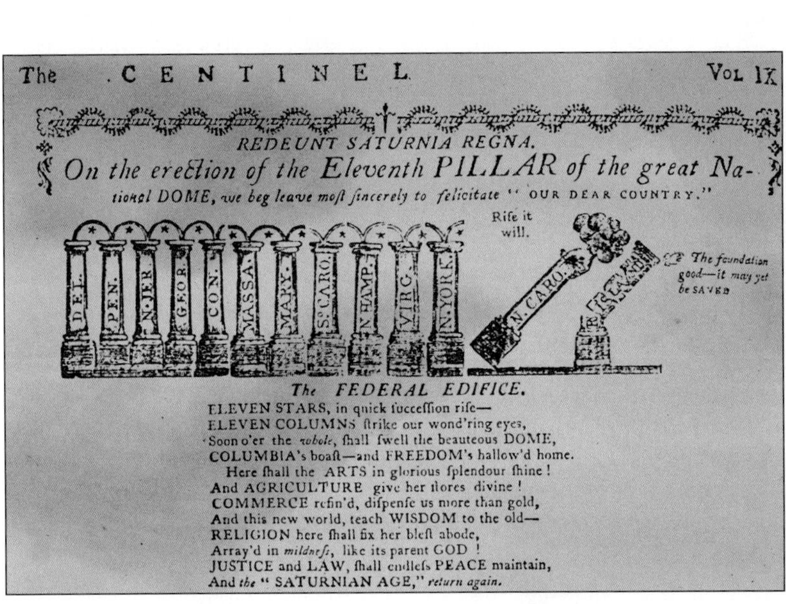


**Figure 3.23** This cartoon celebrated the ratification of the Constitution by New York, the 11th state, in July 1788. Only two states remained. North Carolina and Rhode Island had initially rejected the Constitution. Why might pillars have been chosen to represent each state?

## The Bill of Rights

One Federalist strategy to win over several initially reluctant states was a promise to amend the Constitution by including a bill of rights that would limit the powers of the federal government over individual people and states. In June 1789, Congress began considering 12 amendments, and by 1791 Congress and the states had ratified ten of these. The first ten amendments became known as the Bill of Rights.

The First Amendment guaranteed the rights of free speech and a free press, freedom of assembly, and the right to petition the government. It also formed the legal basis for the separation of church and state in the United States, declaring that "Congress shall make no law respecting an establishment

### The Bill of Rights (1791)

| | |
|---|---|
| **1** | Fundamental freedoms: freedom of religion, freedom of speech and of the press, freedom of assembly, and freedom to petition the government. |
| **2** | The right to "keep and bear arms" in order to ensure a "well regulated militia." |
| **3** | No quartering of soldiers in private homes. |
| **4** | Prohibits "unreasonable searches and seizures" of persons or their private property without warrants and "probable cause." |
| **5** | Legal rights, including the right not to be tried twice for the same serious offence, the right not to be imprisoned without due legal process, and the right not to be forced to testify against oneself in court. |
| **6** | The right of an accused individual to "a speedy and public trial" before an "impartial jury," to be informed of charges, to hear witnesses and evidence against him, and to have access to legal counsel. |
| **7** | The right to trial before a jury in civil cases is guaranteed. |
| **8** | Excessive bail, excessive fines, and "cruel and unusual punishments" prohibited. |
| **9** | Rights not mentioned in the Constitution are nevertheless not denied. |
| **10** | All powers not assigned to the federal government of the United States "are reserved to the States respectively, or to the people." |

**Figure 3.24** This chart summarizes the rights guaranteed in the first ten amendments of the US Constitution (known collectively as "The Bill of Rights"). They form the basis of the individual liberties enjoyed by Americans today. Can you think of specific reasons why the framers of the Constitution would have included these particular rights in their list?

of religion, or prohibiting the free exercise thereof." The Second Amendment protected the right "to keep and bear arms" in order to provide a militia for "the security of a free State."

Given the original motivation for the Bill of Rights, perhaps the most significant amendment was the Tenth Amendment, which stated that all powers not expressly granted to the federal government were reserved to the states, or the people. This helped allay the fears of many anti-Federalists about the threat posed by the new constitution to state rights or individual liberties.

## The Constitution of the United States

The goals of the Constitution were ambitious. In the words of its preamble, they were "to form a more perfect Union, establish Justice, insure domestic Tranquility, provide for the common Defence, promote the general Welfare, and secure the Blessing of Liberty."

As a result of recent experience under British rule, the drafters of the Constitution were determined to thwart any possibility of tyranny. To this end, they based the Constitution on two key principles: separation of powers, and checks and balances.

### Separation of Powers

The Constitution established three branches of government, each with clear responsibilities distinct from the other branches. This separation of powers helped ensure that no single branch could exercise complete control over the government.

Article 1 assigned all legislative powers, including the power to make laws and raise taxes, to a Congress composed of two chambers: a House of Representatives and a Senate. Article 2 vested executive power in a president, who would oversee the government administration and also serve as commander-in-chief of the armed forces. The term of office of the president was set at four years, subject to re-election.

Article 3 provided for a Supreme Court to serve as a court of appeal and to rule on constitutional and other significant cases. Article 4 guaranteed certain rights to the states, while the remaining articles set out procedures for amendment and ratification, and made clear that the new government would honour all previous debts and obligations.

### Checks and Balances

In addition to clearly dividing responsibilities between the three branches of government, the Constitution was carefully crafted to ensure that each branch of government was controlled by the others. This system of checks and balances was intended to prevent tyranny or abuses by any single branch. For example, the president could veto a law passed by Congress, but Congress

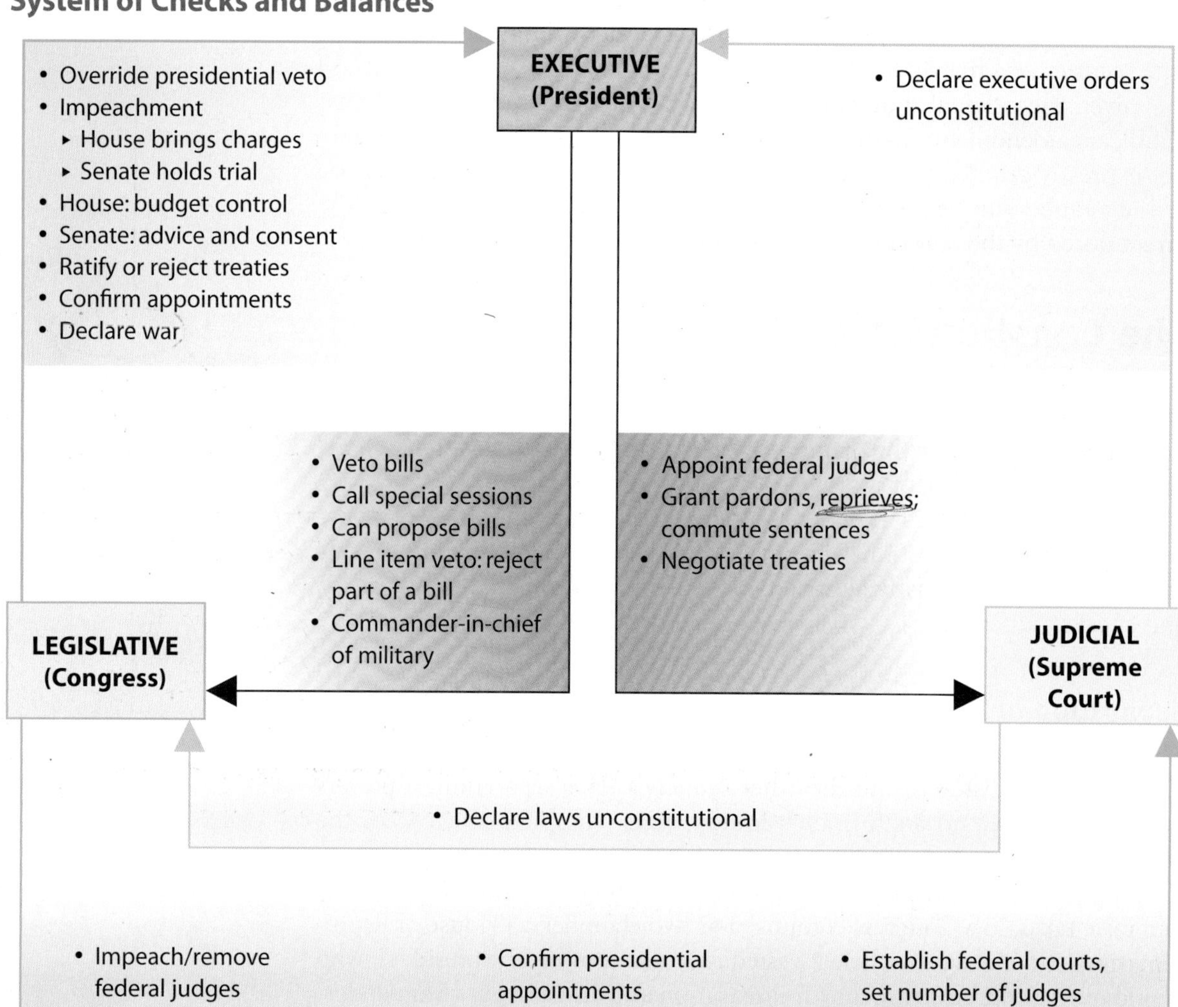


**Figure 3.25** The system of checks and balances that the Constitution set in place. These were intended to ensure that no single branch of the federal government became too powerful.

could override the veto by a two-thirds vote and also had the power to impeach the president for serious crimes.

Given the dangers the military might present to a democratic republic, control of the armed forces included several checks and balances. Congress had the power to levy troops and to declare war, but the president exercised control over the military as commander-in-chief. In foreign affairs, the president and his administration had the responsibility to negotiate treaties but the Senate had the power to reject those treaties.

Finally, the Supreme Court provided a vivid example of the system of checks and balances between all three branches. Justices of the Supreme Court were nominated by the president but required the approval of Congress. In turn, the Supreme Court had the duty and responsibility to ensure that the laws passed by Congress and the decisions made by the president did not violate the Constitution.

While this system added considerably to the complexity of government, its intention was to protect the republic and reduce the risk of tyranny. Having won American independence from Britain and successfully established a federal system of government, the new government of the United States still faced daunting challenges. In Chapter 4 you will examine several of these challenges and the leaders who confronted them.

## CHECK YOUR UNDERSTANDING

1. How did the Constitutional Convention compromise on the issue of slavery?
2. How, according to Madison, would a stronger central government protect individual rights?
3. Explain how the Bill of Rights helped alleviate the fears of anti-Federalists regarding the rights of individual people and states.
4. Explain how the separation of powers and the system of checks and balances were designed to prevent tyranny.

# THE HISTORIAN'S CRAFT

## Interpreting the Written Record

Many of the primary sources available to historians exist in the form of written records. These include both official documents as well as the words of ordinary people. Such sources provide information about the times but must be evaluated for perspective and bias.

### Looking for Meaning

When historians and history students study a written document, they usually read through it once to understand the general meaning and acquire an overall impression of the times. For example, as you read the Declaration of Independence you gain a general understanding of the freedoms claimed by the colonists as well as an impression of the writers' passion. Historians then use several devices to analyze a document in greater depth.

Historians may analyze a document to discover its two or three key points. Sometimes they identify general statements and supporting evidence, or main arguments and examples. For example, in the last verse of "Yankee Doodle" (page 69), the general statement is that Washington had grown very proud. The supporting evidence is that he surrounded himself with the upper class ("gentlefolk") and would not travel without them. Historians may also highlight a key sentence, phrase, or quotation. For example, in the excerpt from Thomas Paine's *Common Sense* (page 72), the words "any submission to, or dependence on, Great Britain, tends directly to involve this Continent in European wars and quarrels" illustrate the central meaning.

### Identifying Perspective and Bias

Primary sources may be the raw stuff of history and come directly from the times, but they have all been constructed or filtered by their authors. Accordingly, historians make every effort to assess their validity and reliability. They ask questions to determine if the document is genuine: "Is this document original or a copy?" "Is this document complete or incomplete?" They ask questions about reliability: "Was the author really there?" "Was the writer a participant or an observer?" They ask questions about perspective: "Is the writer expert enough to comment accurately?" "Does the author belong to one side or the other?" For example, historians reading the diary of Joseph Martin (page 76) would recognize his anti-British perspective but still welcome his first-hand observations as a combatant in the war.

After asking all these questions, historians—and history students—must determine if the author is biased (that is, prejudiced), discriminatory, or racist. If the answer is yes, then they must decide to what extent they can rely on the primary source. For example, historians would be reluctant to judge the character of Colonel John Butler based on writers who described him as "barbarous, treacherous, revengeful, ferocious, merciless, brutal, diabolically wicked, and cruel" (page 75).

When historians recognize bias they must consider the words of the authors with this bias in mind. Even writings that are clearly discriminatory or racist help us gain a picture of the past, reflecting less tolerant times. As well, historians recognize that they are reading sources through the lens of the present and interpreting the sources from their own perspectives. They try not to let modernisms (for example, current standards about equal rights) obscure the meaning of words from the past.

### Try It!

1. Choose one of the written documents in this chapter. Which sentence or phrase best captures the meaning of the whole excerpt?
2. Choose one of the clauses in the Declaration of Independence. What is the general statement in this clause? What evidence is provided to support or illustrate the statement?

# STUDY HALL

## Thinking

1. In what ways did the Declaration of Independence reflect the ideas and worldview of the political elites in the American colonies in 1776?
2. "Victory for the American colonies in the Revolution owed more to British military errors and political weakness than to American military success." Do you agree or disagree with this statement? Why?
3. Some historians consider the Revolutionary War only one major episode in the lengthy war between Britain and France that raged throughout the 18th century. Reflect on what you have learned in Chapters 2 and 3. What evidence exists to support this view?
4. In what sense could the American Revolution be considered a civil war? Explain.
5. Did the Constitution abandon the goals of the revolution? Compare the kind of government created by the Constitution with the goals and grievances stated in the Declaration of Independence.

## Communication

6. Imagine how a member of Lord North's government in London would respond to the grievances listed in the Declaration of Independence. Select five of the grievances and write a response to each from an English point of view.
7. Research the experience of the Army of the Continental Congress during the winter at Valley Forge, Pennsylvania. Compose a series of diary entries from the point of view of a common soldier describing the conditions endured that winter.
8. Imagine you are a Loyalist refugee fleeing to New Brunswick in 1784. Write a personal letter explaining your reasons for abandoning your home and the challenges you face moving north.
9. Read about the role of the president in Article II, Section 2 of the Constitution. Discuss what powers make the president important and whether you think the checks on the president's powers are enough to prevent tyranny.

## Application

10. Study the illustration showing the citizens of New York toppling the statue of George III on page 65. Research similar events, such as the destruction of Brock's monument at Queenston Heights or the toppling of Saddam Hussein's statue in Baghdad in March 2003. What do such acts reveal about the nature of revolutions and the symbolic importance of public monuments?
11. Now that you have studied the American Revolution, review the material in the Quebec Act in Chapter 2. What influence did this act have on the start of the war? Think about how things might have been different if Britain had *not* passed the Quebec Act. Consider the grievances of the colonists, and the response of the people of Canada to the American invasion.

# 4 Birth of the Republic (1789–1828)

## KEY CONCEPTS

In this chapter you will consider:

- The contribution of George Washington to the early development of American government
- The emergence and role of early political parties in the United States
- The significance of republican ideals in American society and government
- The impact of European politics and conflicts on the United States
- The causes and consequences of the War of 1812
- The expansion of the American economy in the early 19th century

## The American Story

By the end of the 18th century the United States had won its independence from Britain and was equipped with a stronger constitution. Nevertheless, the country faced a variety of challenges. Political factions, foreign entanglements, and crushing debts all threatened the survival of the young republic. Repeated disputes with Britain, which culminated in the War of 1812, showed that American independence may have been recognized but was not yet respected. At the same time, economic growth, territorial expansion, and military victories fostered a fresh sense of pride and optimism among Americans for the future of their nation.

## TIMELINE

- **1789** ▸ Washington inaugurated as president
- **1798** ▸ Alien and Sedition Acts
- **1800** ▸ Election of Thomas Jefferson as president
- **1803** ▸ Louisiana Purchase
- **1807** ▸ Embargo Act

## IMAGE ANALYSIS

**Figure 4.1** In the late summer of 1814 America's war with Britain was going badly. A British naval force sailed up the Potomac River and put Washington, DC to the torch, forcing President James Madison and his government to flee. The British then turned their attention to Baltimore, but there they encountered stronger American resistance. The determination of the defenders of Fort McHenry was a key factor in the defence of Baltimore. Despite a heavy bombardment on the night of September 13 the Americans refused to surrender.

Among those who witnessed the assault was Francis Scott Key, an American lawyer and prisoner aboard one of the British war ships. When Key saw the American flag still fluttering above the fort the next morning, he was so overcome with pride that he penned a patriotic poem "The Defense of Fort McHenry." Set to an old popular tune and renamed "The Star-Spangled Banner," the song was an instant hit. It identified America as "the land of the free and the home of the brave" and perfectly expressed the patriotism of the young republic still trying to establish itself on the world stage.

| ▸ Battle of Tippecanoe | ▸ War against Britain begins | ▸ Treaty of Ghent | ▸ Battle of New Orleans | ▸ Monroe Doctrine |
|---|---|---|---|---|
| 1811 | 1812 | 1814 | 1815 | 1823 |

# INTRODUCTION

Before you read this chapter, ask yourself the following question: How do the leaders of a young country win the respect of other nations? For the leaders of the United States in the early 19th century the answer seemed clear. They tried to win friends and overcome their enemies in three ways: through trade, through war, and through the expansion of their territory.

American activities in each of these areas had a direct and lasting impact on the developing relationship between the United States and your own country, Canada. As you learn more about the turmoil and conflict between these nations in the early 19th century, you may come to see their present relationship in a slightly different light. You may also gain a better understanding of why this relationship remains complicated—sometimes friendly, sometimes tense—even today, 200 years later.

# THE FEDERALIST ERA

When George Washington took the oath of office as president on April 30, 1789 in New York (then the federal capital), the government and nation were facing enormous challenges. America lacked an effective army and navy, possessed no government administration, and was deeply in debt. Yet in the succeeding decade, known as the Federalist era, these problems were addressed. By the end of the century the United States had established a strong political and administrative system and was ready to embark on a period of unparalleled economic and territorial expansion.

**Figure 4.2** New York City, the first capital of the United States, in the early 1790s.

| The Presidents: 1789–1825 | | |
|---|---|---|
| **George Washington** | No Party | April 30, 1789 – March 4, 1797 |
| **John Adams** | Federalist | March 4, 1797 – March 4, 1801 |
| **Thomas Jefferson** | Republican | March 4, 1801 – March 4, 1809 |
| **James Madison** | Republican | March 4, 1809 – March 4, 1817 |
| **James Monroe** | Republican | March 4, 1817 – March 4, 1825 |

## Washington's Presidency

As president, Washington faced challenges with no precedents to guide him; as he observed, "I walk on untrodden ground." How should the president behave? How should he be addressed? These questions were full of political significance. Some suggested "His Elective Majesty" or "His Mightiness," but these titles were dangerously reminiscent of the titles of kings (there had in fact been early campaigns by some in the army to make Washington king). In the end these regal titles were rejected in favour of the simpler "Mr. President" or "His Excellency."

At least in the beginning, Washington strove to remain above petty politics, allowing his ministers—talented and ambitious men like Thomas Jefferson and Alexander Hamilton—to argue and dispute policy while he presided over the government as head of state. A shy and reserved man, Washington successfully blended the formality of a monarch with the simplicity of a republican leader. Meanwhile, his government confronted serious problems that would have to be overcome if the new nation hoped to survive and prosper.

**Figure 4.3** George Washington taking the oath of office at the Federal Hall in New York.

### Fiscal Program

The first challenge facing Washington's administration was **fiscal** in nature. Lacking reliable revenues and burdened by the debts of the Revolutionary War, the new American government was essentially bankrupt. Washington entrusted this problem to Alexander Hamilton, the Secretary of the Treasury, who proposed a fiscal program in 1790 designed to solve the nation's financial troubles. Hamilton's plan called for the federal government to assume responsibility for all state debts and pay all outstanding debts in full. Some saw Hamilton's plan to honour all debts at face value as rewarding speculators, who had bought up many of the old debts at a discount and stood to make a substantial windfall profit. Hamilton, however, believed that this step was

**Figure 4.4** Alexander Hamilton in the early 1790s, when he served as America's first Secretary of the Treasury.

essential to preserving the new government's credit. In order to generate the revenue needed to pay off the national debt, Hamilton proposed an **excise tax** on distilled liquors, such as whiskey. The plan was met with considerable opposition, particularly from states (mostly in the South) that had already paid off their debts. Such states resented now having to take responsibility for the debts of other, less frugal states. With Washington's support, however, Congress approved the plan.

Next, Hamilton proposed a private Bank of the United States to manage the national debt and hold the government's funds. Some members of Washington's cabinet, including Thomas Jefferson, opposed this plan because the Constitution did not give the federal government the specific power to establish a national bank. Despite some misgivings, Washington again backed Hamilton's proposal and the Bank of the United States began operations in 1791. Finally, Hamilton proposed a **tariff**, or a tax on imports, to protect American industry from foreign competition and thereby encourage its development. Congress rejected this proposal, however. Farmers relied on export markets for their crops, and Congress feared that other nations would respond to the American tariff by imposing tariffs of their own.

## Rebellion and Opposition

Hamilton's introduction of an excise tax on distilled spirits caused a crisis in the summer of 1794. A popular revolt—the so-called Whiskey Rebellion—erupted in western Pennsylvania as a result of the tax. Alarmed by this display of unrestrained democracy and determined to preserve the power of the federal government in the face of the first major threat to its authority, Washington assembled an enormous military force of over 13,000 men and sent it to occupy the area around Pittsburgh. The show of force accomplished its goal; the rebels were swiftly defeated and order was restored. The government had survived its first significant challenge.

**SOUND BITE**

"All communities divide themselves into the few and the many. The first are the rich and the well-born; the other the mass of the people ... turbulent and changing, they seldom judge or determine right."

—Alexander Hamilton, addressing the Constitutional Convention in 1787

Despite eliciting popular resentment and anger from his political opponents, Hamilton's fiscal plan succeeded in restoring the health of the nation's finances. Much of the opposition to the plan resulted from the critics' disapproval of the influence it gave to the wealthy merchant and banking elites of cities like Boston and New York. Hamilton—himself a resident of New York—and the Federalists had already earned the hostility of those who resented the social and economic privileges of the elite. In 1789 the *New York Daily Advertiser* spoke for many when it condemned "the monarchial, aristocratical, oligarchical, tyrannical, diabolical system of slavery, the New Constitution." In order to pacify southern opponents of Hamilton's plan and secure their votes in Congress, an agreement was reached to relocate the new nation's capital from New York to Philadelphia. This would be a prelude to a new capital to be constructed on the banks of the Potomac in the District of Columbia, on the Virginia border. In 1800 the government was relocated to this new capital, which was later named Washington.

## WE THE PEOPLE
### Alexander Hamilton
## 1755–1804

It was "the most dramatic moment in the early politics of the Union." In the morning mist of July 11, 1804 on a riverbank at Weehauken, New Jersey, two prominent American politicians faced each other in a duel. Aaron Burr was a leading New York politician and vice-president of the United States. His opponent, Alexander Hamilton, was a former Treasury Secretary and a leader of the Federalist Party. Within minutes Hamilton lay mortally wounded—a dramatic conclusion to an extraordinary life that had seen Hamilton rise from poverty and obscurity to wealth and power.

**Figure 4.5** The fatal duel fought between Alexander Hamilton and Aaron Burr in 1804.

Alexander Hamilton began life as an illegitimate child on the island of Nevis in the West Indies. Orphaned at a young age, Hamilton was apprenticed to local merchants. He quickly demonstrated his intelligence and skill and eventually travelled to New York to study at King's College (now Columbia University) with the help of a local patron.

Hamilton's arrival in New York coincided with mounting popular protests against British policy in the colonies. He quickly became a passionate supporter of the Patriot cause, publishing essays in New York newspapers urging resistance to British rule. When war erupted in 1775 Hamilton eagerly joined the staff of General Washington, whom he served as **aide-de-camp**. Washington came to rely heavily on Hamilton's organizational skills and formed a high opinion of his abilities. Hamilton eventually received his own command, serving with distinction at Yorktown.

As a representative to the Continental Congress, Hamilton grew frustrated by the weakness of the government under the Articles of Confederation. He soon became convinced of the need for a stronger federal government that could grapple with the issues confronting the new nation. Together with James Madison and others, Hamilton composed a series of essays setting out a clear vision for a strong central government. The *Federalist Papers* served as a blueprint for the US Constitution.

In the early 1790s Washington recruited Hamilton to take on the greatest challenge to the new nation's survival—its finances. As America's first Secretary of the Treasury, Hamilton worked diligently to solve the financial problems facing Washington's government. His plan tackled the debt and created a national bank to manage the nation's finances. Hamilton became increasingly convinced of the dangers of popular democracy (as witnessed in the **French Revolution**) and the need to limit the powers of the states, and quarrelled repeatedly with Thomas Jefferson and James Madison over American foreign policy and the role of the federal government. Despite Hamilton's influence, his ambitions were frustrated by his Federalist colleague John Adams following Washington's retirement, leading to a bitter division within the Federalist Party. Even Hamilton's wife admitted that her

**Figure 4.6** Given Hamiton's central role in establishing the finances of the American government, it is fitting that his portrait appears on the US $10 bill.

husband displayed "a character perhaps too frank and independent for a democratic people."

Never allowed to forget his lowly origins, Hamilton was sensitive to assaults on his honour, whether real or imagined. Such assaults were unavoidable in the poisonous political climate at the end of the 18th century, for Hamilton's keen intellect and sharp pen made many enemies. Aggravated by perceived insults, Hamilton used his considerable political influence to thwart the ambitions of his Federalist enemy John Adams and the Republican Aaron Burr in the presidential election of 1800. This ignited a slow-burning feud with Burr, a rival in New York state politics, which culminated in the duel that ended Hamilton's life.

### Think It Through

1. In what ways did Hamilton's career illustrate the possibilities for social advancement open to young men during the revolutionary era?
2. Describe Hamilton's contributions to the development of American government.

For an in-depth discussion of the most famous duel in American History, visit www.emp.ca/ah.

## Foreign Policy

The second significant challenge that confronted Washington's administration arose in the area of foreign policy. In 1789 a revolution began in France that culminated in the **Terror** and the execution of King Louis XVI in 1793. The French Revolution soon led to war between Britain and France—and a dilemma for America. Opinion in the United States was sharply divided over which side America should support. Merchants and businessmen argued (through their spokesman, Hamilton) that America's economic and commercial interests made supporting Britain essential. They also feared the radicalism of the French Revolution.

Thomas Jefferson and many others supported the ideals of the French Revolution, such as the equality of citizens, and argued that the United States was morally obligated to repay the assistance that France had given America during its own revolution. In April 1793—acutely aware of the dangers of involvement in a war—Washington issued a proclamation of **neutrality**. The proclamation stated that the United States would be "friendly and impartial" in its dealings with both France and Britain. This marked the beginning of a general policy of neutrality that American governments would strive to follow in succeeding decades, with varying degrees of success.

Despite Washington's proclamation of neutrality, the new French ambassador Edmond Genêt began paying American agents to attack British property

**Figure 4.7** The execution of the French monarch, King Louis XVI, on January 21, 1793 attracted considerable support in America. One newspaper associated with Thomas Jefferson described it as "a great act of justice."

in the West. Encouraged by Jefferson and others, Genêt also licensed American vessels to seize British shipping on behalf of France. Genêt's meddling in American politics soon left him in disgrace, but not before he had demonstrated the danger that involvement in European affairs could pose for the United States.

## Jay's Treaty

Anxious to ensure that relations with Britain were not damaged by the Genêt affair, Washington sent John Jay to London to settle outstanding disagreements left over from the Revolutionary War. In November 1794 Jay and the British concluded a treaty, known as Jay's Treaty, which guaranteed that all remaining British troops in the Northwest would be withdrawn within two years and the United States would enjoy privileged trading status with Britain. Yet the treaty failed to address the issue of compensation for property—including slaves—seized by Britain during the war, and Britain reserved the right to continue searching American ships. This convinced critics of Washington's government, led by Jefferson, to denounce Jay's Treaty as too favourable toward Britain. Jay was burned in effigy across America and even the exalted Washington did not escape criticism. In reality, however, the treaty with Britain—a world power with sizable military might—represented a considerable achievement for the young republic. While many Americans were unhappy with some of the terms, Jay had likely secured the best deal possible.

The vehement attacks that followed the signing of Jay's Treaty, and the **partisan** hostility of Jefferson and others toward Washington's government, convinced a weary Washington to retire in 1796 and return to his estate at Mount Vernon, Virginia. In choosing not to seek a third term, Washington established a precedent that a president should normally serve no more than two terms. This precedent became law in 1951.

# PAST VOICES

## Washington's Farewell Address

In 1796, with his political career at an end, Washington looked to the future and saw many dangers. Determined to sound a warning to the American people and their leaders, he prepared a Farewell Address with the assistance of his friend and adviser Alexander Hamilton. Despite its title, the Farewell Address was not delivered as a speech but was instead widely published in the newspapers. With Hamilton's help, Washington hoped that it would be read and his counsel remembered in the years ahead.

In his Address, Washington identified several challenges for the new nation. The first was the need to ensure unity throughout the country, avoiding divisions between states or regions. Washington was one of the first to argue that there must be a common American identity. Each area of the country had different interests, but these had to be set aside for the common good. Washington's second concern was with the emergence of political parties, or factions. These had destabilized Washington's own government, and threatened to weaken presidents and undermine the nation's government in the future.

Washington's Farewell Address is best known for its powerful warning against alliances with other nations, particularly in Europe. America's geographic isolation was a blessing, Washington believed, whose advantages should not be overlooked. Due to its geographic location, America could keep out of foreign affairs and remain isolated from the wars and tensions that afflicted Europe.

While many of Washington's words were largely ignored (including his strong disapproval of political parties), his opposition to foreign involvement was embraced. In foreign policy, the United States generally pursued a policy of **isolationism**. Opponents of the League of Nations in 1919 or US involvement in the Second World War cited Washington's caution to "steer clear of permanent alliances with any portion of the foreign world," making the Farewell Address a key text for understanding the growth of the United States and its place in the world.

**Figure 4.8** George Washington in 1796, the year he retired as president.

"Our detached and distant situation invites and enables us to pursue a different course. If we remain one people under an efficient government, the period is not far off when we may defy material injury from external annoyance; when we may take such an attitude as will cause the neutrality we may at any time resolve on to be scrupulously respected; when belligerent nations, under the impossibility of making acquisitions on us, will not lightly hazard the giving us provocation; when we may choose peace or war, as our interest, guided by justice, shall counsel.

Why forego the advantages of so peculiar a situation? Why quit our own to stand on foreign ground? Why, by interweaving our destiny with that of any part of Europe, entangle our peace and prosperity in the toils of European ambition, rivalship, interest, humor or caprice?

It is our true policy to steer clear of permanent alliances with any portion of the foreign world ..."

### Think It Through

1. What were Washington's aims in publishing the Farewell Address?
2. Why did Washington believe the United States should avoid foreign entanglements?
3. Review The Historian's Craft in Chapter 3 (page 98). What one word or phrase in the Farewell Address best illustrates Washington's hopes or fears for the United States in the future? Explain your choice.

# Politics and Faction

Most early American leaders, including George Washington, believed that the growth of political factions and parties was damaging to the republic and would lead inevitably to corruption and civil strife. Others, like Thomas Jefferson, took a different view. Jefferson defended political parties and factions as natural and vital to democracy, for "in every free and deliberating society there must, from the nature of man, be opposite parties and violent dissensions and discords, and one of these, for the most part must prevail over the other for a longer or shorter time." The final years of the 18th century would indeed be marked by dissensions and discords, as two political parties vied for power.

## Federalists and Republicans

Despite Washington's efforts to maintain a fragile political unity, two organized political parties emerged in America in the early 1790s: Federalists and Republicans (also known as Democratic-Republicans). Each represented a radically different vision of the new nation. With a few exceptions, the Federalists—whose leaders included Alexander Hamilton, John Jay, and John Adams—drew their support from the northern states (particularly New England) and from the cities. The merchant elites of New York, Boston, and Philadelphia were largely Federalist; the party emphasized trade and commerce. As supporters of the Constitution, most Federalists also favoured a stronger central government.

The Republicans (not related to the modern Republican Party) were led by Thomas Jefferson and James Madison. Republican sympathies were strongest among farmers, and in the South and West. The party also enjoyed substantial support among the urban poor and among recent immigrants. Suspicious of the power of the central government, Republicans argued for strict limits on its powers and promoted the rights of states.

The divisions between Federalists and Republicans were most evident in the area of foreign policy. Federalists sought improved relations with Britain (for example, Jay's Treaty), in part to protect America's trading interests. Federalists were also openly hostile toward France. They feared that the radical ideas of the French Revolution might prove contagious, infecting American society and politics. By contrast, the Republicans were sympathetic toward revolutionary France and its ideal of democratic equality. They regarded the Federalists' pro-British policies as a betrayal of the principles of the American Revolution.

The election of 1796 clearly demonstrated the divisions between Federalists and Republicans. Both groups organized themselves as political parties, formulating policies, nominating local candidates, and publishing literature denouncing their opponents. Following a nasty campaign, the Federalist John Adams defeated the Republican Thomas Jefferson to become the second president of the United States.

**Figure 4.9** John Adams, the second president of the United States.

## John Adams and the XYZ Affair

President Adams successfully pursued the financial policies introduced by Alexander Hamilton. Even as these began to yield results, Adams had little cause for celebration. First, the election of 1796 had left his Republican nemesis, Thomas Jefferson, vice-president. Relations between the two men were tense. Moreover, shortly after becoming president, Adams faced a foreign policy crisis with France.

Despite Washington's proclamation of neutrality, the French were seizing American ships. They were also ignoring and insulting the American envoys dispatched to resolve the issue. Worse still, the corrupt French foreign minister, Charles Maurice de Talleyrand, was preventing the dispute from being resolved. Through anonymous agents known only as X, Y, and Z, Talleyrand was demanding a sizable personal bribe, payment of alleged damages, and a public apology from President Adams for previous anti-French remarks before negotiations to settle the dispute could begin.

The American representatives balked at the blatant corruption and calculated insult. When word of the XYZ Affair leaked out, a wave of anti-French sentiment swept through the country. Adams and the Federalists enjoyed a surge in popularity (they won control of Congress in 1798), while the pro-French Republicans temporarily lost much of their support. The United States teetered on the brink of war with France. Seeking to follow the advice Washington had given in his Farewell Address—and determined to avoid a costly and destructive war—Adams restrained the Federalists. Instead, he decided to dispatch another peace mission to France.

## Alien and Sedition Acts

Infuriated by continued attacks on Adams in the republican press, and concerned with the activities of French agents following the XYZ Affair, in 1798 the Federalists vowed to use their power in Congress to protect the nation from foreign political ideas and silence their Republican opponents. Their efforts produced two of the most controversial and allegedly undemocratic laws in the history of the United States: the Alien Act and the Sedition Act.

The Alien Act tackled the "danger" posed by immigrants to the United States. Most new immigrants tended to be Republican supporters, and many Federalists shared the **xenophobic** opinion expressed by President Adams's nephew William Shaw: "The grand cause of all our present difficulties may be traced ... to so many hordes of Foreigners immigrating to America ... Let us no longer pray that America may become an asylum to all nations." Federalists feared immigrants as importers of radicalism and as potential Republican voters. To neutralize this threat, the Alien Act raised the residence requirement for citizenship—as well as the **franchise**, or the right to vote—from 5 to 14 years. This effectively robbed the Republicans of many supporters.

In order to silence the attacks on the president and his administration that poured from the Republican press, the Sedition Act made it possible to prosecute editors and politicians for **sedition**, or criticizing the government in speech or print. Despite some modest safeguards, the Sedition Act was used extensively as a tool to stifle the Republican press. Judges sympathetic to the Federalists did not hesitate to pressure juries to convict editors. Jefferson and the Republicans denounced these two acts as an assault on the democratic principles expressed in the Declaration of Independence and the Constitution. A climate of fear and intimidation afflicted politics, and Federalist popular support began to decline.

## Election of 1800

As the election of 1800 approached, the Federalists were increasingly divided over the consequences of the XYZ Affair. Anxious to preserve peace, Adams quarrelled publicly with powerful Federalists including Alexander Hamilton, who demanded war. Jefferson's Republicans exploited such divisions, even gaining support in several northern states.

The election of 1800 was characterized by a negative tone and personal attacks. Adams was denounced as a warmonger and monarchist (and supporter of Britain), while the federalist press characterized Jefferson as an atheist and a Jacobin (a supporter of the Terror). The election was significant since, for the first time, four states allowed all white males to vote regardless of wealth or class—a major step toward greater democracy. In the end, the result was a tie between the two Republican candidates, Thomas Jefferson and Aaron Burr, forcing Congress to decide the outcome. A lengthy period of voting ensued during which the Federalists sought to frustrate Jefferson's election by voting for Burr as the "lesser evil." Jefferson was finally chosen as president on the 35th **ballot**, and Burr became vice-president. The Federalist era had come to an end.

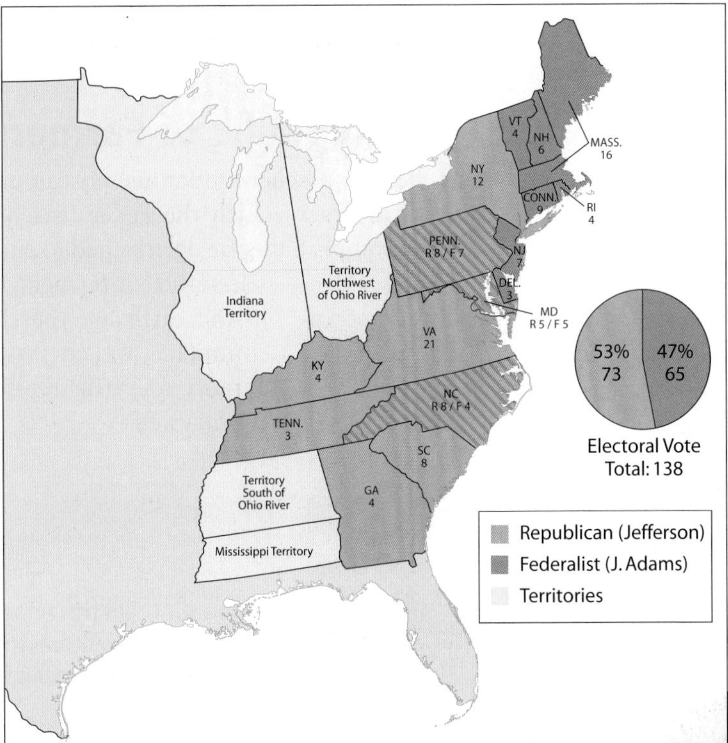


**Figure 4.10** In the election of 1800 Jefferson won in the southern states and in the farming areas of Pennsylvania and New York. The Federalists' strength was in New England.

## CHECK YOUR UNDERSTANDING

1. What significant challenges did Washington face as president?
2. In your own words, outline the key components of Hamilton's plan to revive America's finances.
3. What was Jay's Treaty and why was it so unpopular?
4. Use a two-column chart to compare the policies of the Federalist and Republican Parties in the following categories: Area of Support, Economic Views, Government, Foreign Policy, and Leadership.
5. What dilemma did the French Revolution pose for Americans?
6. How were the Alien and Sedition Acts designed to weaken the Republican Party?

# AGE OF JEFFERSON

The election of 1800 was truly revolutionary. Despite bitter political disagreements, power had passed peacefully from the Federalists to the Republicans. This established an important democratic precedent. The election also represented an ideological change. Although Jefferson was a wealthy Virginia landowner (and slaveholder), he presented himself as a simple farmer, in contrast to the Federalist business elite. Jefferson's inauguration in 1801 was symbolic of the change; the new Republican president chose to walk along the muddy streets from his lodgings to the Capitol to swear the oath rather than travel by carriage as his Federalist predecessor had done.

## A Republic of Farmers

Jefferson believed that his most important duty as president was to promote democracy, which the Federalists had repeatedly undermined. In order to accomplish this, he determined to encourage the growth of a nation of simple, self-sufficient farmers. According to Jefferson, "those who labor in the earth are the chosen people of God." Manufacturing, commerce, and cities were, in Jefferson's view, opposed to democracy; the true republican virtue was to be found in the countryside.

**Figure 4.11** In this image celebrating the Jeffersonian republican ideal of an agricultural society, Columbia (a female figure representing the United States) is shown with a farmer ploughing his field.

## Jeffersonian Government

In accordance with his simple republican ideals, Jefferson was determined to preside over a "wise and frugal government." This was not difficult, for in 1800 there were fewer than 150 employees in the entire federal civil service in Washington. Jefferson also firmly believed that the powers of the president and other branches of the federal government were closely circumscribed by the Constitution. This view of limited powers for each branch (executive, legislative, and judicial) did not go entirely unchallenged, however. In his 1803 decision *Marbury v. Madison*, the chief justice of the Supreme Court—the Federalist John Marshall—defended the power of the court to review decisions made by the president and his cabinet, and to interpret the Constitution.

**Figure 4.12** Thomas Jefferson, who served as the third president of the United States from 1801 to 1809.

## Culture Notes

### *Thomas Jefferson and Monticello: Republican Architecture*

In 1784, shortly after arriving in Paris to represent American interests, Thomas Jefferson wrote longingly to a friend: "I am savage enough to prefer the woods, the wilds, and the independence of Monticello, to all the brilliant pleasures of this gay capital [Paris] ... for tho' there is less wealth there, there is more freedom, more ease, and less misery." Even amid the delights of Paris, Jefferson clearly missed his country estate at Monticello, near Charlottesville, Virginia. Since the late 1760s Jefferson had worked to create a home there whose quality befitted a leading Virginia landowner and American politician.

As the author of the Declaration of Independence, Jefferson was a political philosopher. Far more than just a fine country house, Monticello was designed to express Jefferson's political ideas through architecture. Jefferson remained committed to the virtues of republicanism throughout his political career. These included simplicity and balance. Accordingly, in planning Monticello Jefferson

**Figure 4.13** Jefferson devoted many hours to planning his house at Monticello—even preparing architectural sketches like this one. Note the classical columns and simple domes characteristic of Palladian architecture.

was inspired by the theories and writings of the 16th-century Italian architect Andrea Palladio, who had tried to recreate the classical simplicity of the ancient Roman republic and its buildings in his own work. Monticello's regularly spaced pillars, combined with simple capitals and minimal ornamentation, reflected the republican virtue of simplicity. Balance was achieved by the building's symmetrical appearance—a central domed structure joined two equally proportioned wings.

Jefferson's political and aesthetic ideas were also profoundly influenced by the time he spent in France. He was a fervent supporter of the ideals of the French Revolution, and in 1796 began an ambitious plan to expand and renovate Monticello, inspired by the architecture he had seen while in Europe. The interior of the house was redesigned to conform to the most up-to-date French architectural plans. During the late 1790s Jefferson also incorporated many modern conveniences, including fireplaces designed to maximize heat while conserving fuel. These renovations continued throughout Jefferson's years as president.

Jefferson returned to Monticello upon his retirement and lived there for the remainder of his life. Financial woes, however, prevented him from continuing the development of "our own dear Monticello," as he once described his house. When he died at Monticello on July 4, 1826 (the fiftieth anniversary of the signing of the Declaration of Independence), Jefferson was heavily in debt. As a result, his daughter was forced to sell the house and its contents the following year.

Jefferson laboured over Monticello for more than 40 years, planning, building, and renovating. The result was a unique structure, which Jefferson aptly described as an "essay in architecture." Classical Roman, French, and American theories and models were blended into a house that reflected its resident and architect. Like Monticello, Jefferson was influenced by the virtues of the ancient Roman republic, the political ideas and writings of French philosophers, and his personal experience in American politics. When Jefferson's likeness was chosen for the current American five-cent coin, it was fitting that an image of Monticello was chosen for the reverse. Nothing could better symbolize Jefferson's political ideals.

## Think It Through

1. How did Jefferson's time in France influence his design for Monticello?
2. Jefferson once described Monticello as "an essay in architecture." What do you think he meant by this?
3. Search the Internet for examples of modern buildings—private or public—whose designs reflect political ideas. Use an image search in Google, with search terms such as "architecture democracy" or "architecture nazi."

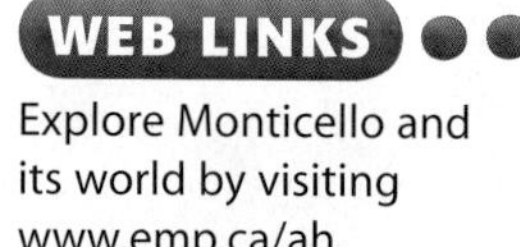


Explore Monticello and its world by visiting www.emp.ca/ah.

**Figure 4.14** Located away from the tumult of partisan politics, Monticello was a classical country refuge for Jefferson. What elements in its design remind you of Roman architecture?

## The Louisiana Purchase

In order to promote the **agrarian** republic that Jefferson desired, the United States had to continue to expand westward. Yet these plans faced a major obstacle: the lands west of the Mississippi and the mouth of the river at New Orleans were controlled by France, which had acquired them on a lease from Spain in 1800. For the United States, French control of this territory represented a grave threat to the future survival of the nation: it threatened to choke off westward expansion.

Determined to ensure American access to the interior without recourse to war, in 1803 Jefferson sent envoys to the French emperor, Napoleon Bonaparte, offering to purchase New Orleans at a price of $2 million (about $43 million in current dollars). To their surprise, Napoleon countered with an offer to sell the entire Louisiana territory for $15 million (about $320 million today). The American envoys did not possess the authority to make such a purchase, but hurried nevertheless to agree to this bargain. Questions were later raised about whether the Constitution gave Jefferson the power to acquire territory, and some wondered whether Napoleon had the right to sell territory that was only leased from Spain.

Despite these doubts, the result of the Louisiana Purchase was clear: with the stroke of a pen Jefferson had added more than 2 million square kilometres of territory to the United States, from the Mississippi River to the Rocky Mountains, doubling its size. He had also ensured American control over the Mississippi River, essential for economic development. Most significantly, Jefferson had succeeded in "enlarging the empire of liberty," for he believed that the survival of republican virtues depended on an expanding society of farmers on the new lands.

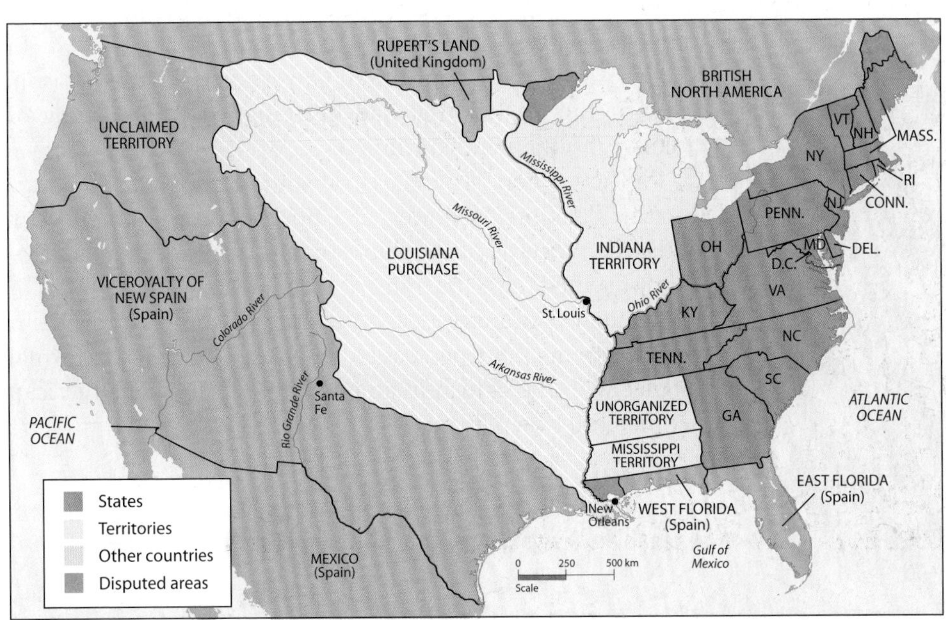


**Figure 4.15** The Louisiana Purchase enabled the United States to acquire a territory that extended westward from the Mississippi as far as the Rocky Mountains.

## Lewis and Clark

The Louisiana Purchase provided Jefferson—who was already interested in exploring the potential for westward expansion—with an excuse to dispatch his private secretary, Meriwether Lewis, and a colleague, William Clark, on a journey of discovery across the continent. Between 1803 and 1806 Lewis and Clark trekked from the Mississippi through the Great Plains and the Rocky Mountains to the Pacific Ocean and back, accompanied by a small group that included the young Shoshone (sha-SHOW-ni) woman Sacagawea, who served as a guide and interpreter. Over the course of their journey, which took two and a half years, Lewis and Clark gathered scientific data, prepared maps of the newly acquired territory, and made contacts with Native American peoples throughout the West. Their journey awakened Americans to the potential for settlement in the interior of the continent, and within a few years the first settlers arrived.

**WEB LINKS**

To learn more about the journeys and discoveries of Lewis and Clark, visit www.emp.ca/ah.

## Tecumseh and Tippecanoe

Jefferson was acutely aware of the impact of westward expansion on Native Americans, who were being pushed off their lands by the arrival of American settlers. Reflecting his belief in the virtues of an agrarian society, Jefferson believed that the solution lay in encouraging these peoples to abandon their traditional lifestyle and become farmers. Missionaries attempted to teach agricultural skills; while some Aboriginal peoples like the Cherokee tried to adapt, others rejected this approach. They preferred to follow the example of earlier Native American leaders like Pontiac, who had resisted American expansion (see Chapter 2).

The acknowledged leader of this resistance was the Shawnee warrior Tecumseh. Together with his brother-in-law Tenskwatawa, known as the Prophet, Tecumseh preached a powerful political and spiritual message. He urged Native Americans to sever contact with Americans (and their alcohol), place no faith in treaties, cease farming, and return to their traditional nomadic lifestyle. With clandestine support from the British, Tecumseh forged a Native American alliance across the Northwest. In Indiana Territory he confronted Governor William Harrison, rejecting the treaties that had been signed and warning of violence if settlement continued.

In November 1811 Harrison and his soldiers fought a force of Tecumseh's followers at Tippecanoe, or Prophetstown. While the outcome of the Battle of Tippecanoe was inconclusive, it resulted in the burning of Prophetstown and the loss of Tenskwatawa's near mystical influence, led to increased attacks on settlements, and persuaded Tecumseh to make a formal alliance with the British in an effort to halt further American advances into the Northwest.

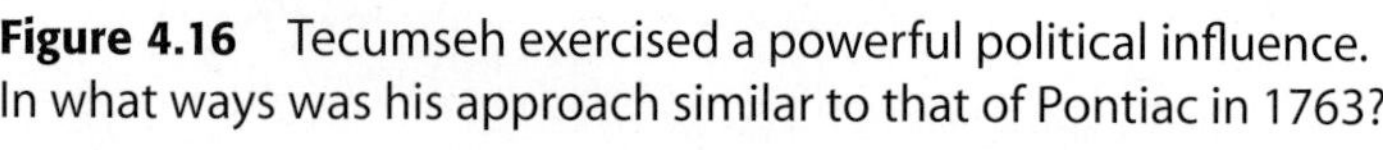

**Figure 4.16** Tecumseh exercised a powerful political influence. In what ways was his approach similar to that of Pontiac in 1763?

# Foreign Crises

Although Jefferson began his presidency by echoing Washington's view that America should remain neutral, trading with all nations and making alliances with none, the resumption of war in Europe between Britain and France soon challenged this neutrality. Foreign crises threatened to undermine Jefferson's government and destroy America's economy.

## Pirates and Impressments

As a producer of raw materials (from cotton and tobacco to grain and wood), America's dependence on trade with European nations left it vulnerable to a variety of threats. One of the first came from the Barbary pirates, privateers who operated from bases in North Africa to harass ships in the Mediterranean and the North Atlantic. The United States navy successfully fought against the pirates between 1801 and 1805. In one celebrated engagement, a force of marines rescued American captives from the Barbary base at Tripoli (now Libya), leading to a surge of American patriotism. As a sovereign nation, the United States had a right to free the captives.

The United States claimed another right as a neutral nation: the right to trade freely with any other nation. As the **Napoleonic Wars** raged in Europe, however, neither Britain nor France would permit the United States to trade with their opponent. American merchants attempted to carry on trade despite the war, but faced problems. American vessels carrying cargo from the French West Indies to Europe, for example, were confiscated by the British navy—a clear violation of neutral rights.

Even more serious was the British practice of impressments—seizing British and other sailors, including Americans, and forcing them to serve in the navy. Conditions in the British navy were harsh, prompting many sailors to desert

| American Exports, 1803 (by value, millions $) | | | |
|---|---|---|---|
| Wheat | 9.3 | Fish products | 2.6 |
| Cotton | 7.9 | Rice | 2.4 |
| Tobacco | 6.2 | Manufactured goods | 1.3 |
| Wood products | 4.2 | Other | 4.0 |
| Meat/dairy | 4.1 | TOTAL | 77.0 |

| American Exports, 1803 (% by destination) | |
|---|---|
| British empire | 28% |
| Dutch empire | 21% |
| French empire | 16% |
| Spanish empire | 9% |
| Others | 26% |

Source: American State Papers, 1803 (Library of Congress).

**Figure 4.17** As these charts illustrate, American exports during the early 1800s continued to be dominated by raw materials, and Britain remained America's most important trading partner.

and join American merchant ships; it was estimated that up to 25 percent of sailors on American ships were British deserters. In 1803 the British navy began stopping American vessels at sea and arresting escaped British sailors, ignoring American neutrality. Even worse, British commanders on the high seas often refused to acknowledge American citizenship, arguing that all Americans—as former British subjects—still owed allegiance to the Crown. If manpower was short, they seized American sailors along with British deserters, and thousands of Americans found themselves forced to serve in the Royal Navy.

Anger at this blatant disregard for American neutrality and nationhood erupted in June 1807. British warships attempted to stop and search an American vessel, the *Chesapeake*, within American waters. The captain of the *Chesapeake* refused and the British vessel opened fire. A number of American sailors died in the attack, while the British seized four—three of whom held American citizenship. Angered at the *Chesapeake* outrage, the American public demanded war.

## Embargo Act

In response to the continuing seizures of American ships and impressments of sailors, Jefferson's government sent diplomatic protests, demanded compensation, and insisted that Britain respect American neutrality. Jefferson was unwilling to risk war against Britain's superior naval force, and when the British government ignored American protests, Jefferson proposed a boycott of British goods to force Britain to halt impressments. This failed to have much effect, however, and in 1807 Jefferson imposed an **embargo**, prohibiting any trade between America and Britain (or France). By denying the European powers access to American raw materials such as lumber or cotton, Jefferson hoped to force them to respect American neutral rights.

The Embargo Act failed completely. While it took some time for Britain to feel the impact of the suspension of trade, the consequences for American trade and commerce were immediate and catastrophic. Exports dropped by 80 percent, agricultural prices collapsed, and an economic depression followed. Many merchants were driven into bankruptcy. It was clear that Jefferson had seriously miscalculated: the embargo had a far more severe impact on the United States than on Britain. While Britain could look elsewhere for at least some of the raw materials its factories required, the United States relied heavily on Britain as a market for its raw materials.

To make matters worse, smuggling blunted the intended pain for Britain. Many American merchants and ship owners continued to trade with Britain, weakening the impact of the embargo. Vessels were "blown off course" into British and foreign ports, and the Canadian border witnessed active smuggling. Even some state governors refused to cooperate. In New England the Federalists exploited the economic hardship to encourage opposition to Jefferson's government. The embargo cast a pall over Jefferson's final months in office and clouded the prospects for his Republican successor, James Madison.

## CHECK YOUR UNDERSTANDING

1. What values—for example, democracy—are represented by Jefferson's idea of an agrarian republic?
2. Why might the Louisiana Purchase have been illegal?
3. Describe Tecumseh's influence on relations between Native Americans and the American government.
4. What values did Tecumseh and Tenskwatawa represent?
5. What were impressments, and why did the practice anger Americans so much?
6. Why did the Embargo Act fail?

# THE WAR OF 1812

Continued disregard for American neutrality, and British support for Native American resistance to western expansion, suggested that America had not yet fully achieved independence. A generation after the revolution, the United States was still seeking full recognition from Britain. The result of American discontent over this fact would be a second war of independence—the War of 1812.

## Causes

James Madison had served as Secretary of State (foreign minister) before 1809. For this reason, he understood the demands for war in the face of British provocations—such as impressments and support for Tecumseh—as well as the American need for greater respect from Britain. As president, however, Madison followed Jefferson's lead in seeking to avoid hostilities as long as possible. Even as the Embargo Act began to have the desired impact on Britain's economy, pressure mounted on Madison to declare war. By 1812 that pressure would prove irresistible.

### Free Trade and Sailors' Rights

The official cause of war with Britain was summed up in the slogan "Free Trade and Sailors' Rights." The war was the direct result of British policies: seizure of American ships and impressments of American sailors. In his War Message—delivered to Congress on June 1, 1812—President Madison had denounced "the continued practice of violating the American flag on the great highway of nations, and of seizing and carrying off persons sailing under it." Madison maintained that it was British actions, in the face of American efforts to maintain peaceful relations, which had given rise to the conflict. Yet there were other factors that led directly to war, factors that had little to do with "Free Trade and Sailors' Rights."

SOUND BITE

"The acquisition of Canada this year, as far as the neighbourhood of Quebec, will be a mere matter of marching."
—Thomas Jefferson, 1812

### War Hawks

The strongest voices demanding war with Britain came from a group of young Republican politicians led by Henry Clay of Kentucky and John C. Calhoun of South Carolina. These "War Hawks" were angered by Britain's lack of respect for the United States. They also advocated expansion of the United States to incorporate Canada, and resented British support for Native Americans like Tecumseh who stood in the way of America's westward expansion. Ironically, a war that was officially waged to protect shipping and sailors instead focused on territorial expansion and was fought largely on American and Canadian soil, far from the Atlantic.

AMERICAN ARCHIVE

## President Madison's War Message, 1812

Under mounting pressure from various groups—including members of Congress demanding war, merchants opposed to British restrictions on American trade with Europe, and settlers on the western frontier alarmed by British support for Native Americans—President Madison felt he had little choice but to act. On June 1, 1812 Madison sent a lengthy statement to Congress outlining British offences against American ships and sailors, and detailing the American government's futile efforts to secure redress. In Madison's view, the repeated actions of the British represented "a series of acts hostile to the United States as an independent and neutral nation." Having received the president's War Message, Congress wasted little time in taking action. On June 18, 1812 the United States Congress, determined to oppose "force to force in defense of their national rights," declared war against Britain:

> In reviewing the conduct of Great Britain towards the United States our attention is necessarily drawn to the warfare just renewed by the savages on one of our extensive frontiers … It is difficult to account for the activity and combinations which have for some time been developing themselves among tribes in constant intercourse with British traders and garrisons without connecting their hostility with that influence …
>
> We behold our seafaring citizens still the daily victims of lawless violence, committed on the great common and highway of nations, even within sight of the country which owes them protection. We behold our vessels, freighted with the products of our soil and industry, or returning with the honest proceeds of them, wrested from their lawful destinations, confiscated by prize courts … and their unfortunate crews dispersed and lost, or forced or inveigled in British ports into British fleets …
>
> We behold, in fine, on the side of Great Britain a state of war against the United States, and on the side of the United States a state of peace towards Great Britain.
>
> Whether the United States shall continue passive under these progressive usurpations and these accumulating wrongs, or, opposing force to force in defense of their national rights, shall commit a just cause into the hands of the Almighty Disposer of Events … is a solemn question which the Constitution wisely confides in the legislative department of the Government. In recommending it to their early deliberations I am happy in the assurance that the decision will be worthy the enlightened and patriotic councils of a virtuous, a free, and a powerful nation.

### Think It Through

1. Why did Madison blame the British for Native American attacks?
2. Review The Historian's Craft in Chapter 3 (page 98). How did Madison use language to contrast the different attitudes and actions of Britain and the United States in the crisis?
3. The Constitution gives Congress the power to declare war (see Article I, section 8). How does Madison's War Message to Congress illustrate this power?

**Figure 4.18** This vivid 1813 cartoon shows President Madison scoring a blow in a boxing match against John Bull, the national personification of Britain (dressed here as King George III). How has the cartoonist attempted to contrast American and British character?

***A Boxing Match, or Another Bloody Nose for John Bull.***

**John Bull:**

"Stop, Stop Stop Brother Jonathan, or I shall fall with the loss of blood — I thought to have been too heavy for you — But I must acknowledge your superior skill — Two blows to my one! — And so well directed too! Mercy mercy on me, how does this happen?!!"

**President Madison:**

"Ha — Oh Johnny! you thought yourself a *Boxer* did you! — I'll let you know we are an *Enterprizeing Nation*, and ready to meet you with equal force any day."

### New England

Not everyone supported the rush to war. Every Federalist in Congress voted against the declaration of war—a sign of the divisions within the American nation. Opposition continued after the war began, and in New England there was active resistance throughout the conflict.

Encouraged by Madison's Federalist opponents and fearful of economic losses, many merchants continued to trade with British colonies despite the war, even supplying provisions to the British army. Boston merchants refused to contribute to loans for the war effort, while newspapers published editorials denouncing the war. State governors frustrated military planning by prohibiting their militiamen from serving beyond their state boundaries. Even as Madison prepared to confront the military might of Britain, his mind remained preoccupied with New England sedition.

## Combat

While the War Hawks and their supporters were eagerly determined "to teach Britain a lesson," the nation's military preparations did not match their patriotic fervour. The American army and navy had been greatly reduced in strength under Jefferson and Madison, leaving the nation ill equipped for the coming contest. As a result, military campaigns would prove disappointing.

### The Invasion of Canada

Apart from isolated naval battles fought along the Atlantic coast, the main clash between Britain and America occurred in Canada. The pattern of the conflict was set early on when a small force of British soldiers and their Native American allies captured Fort Detroit. The British commander, General Isaac Brock, played on the defenders' fears of Native American fighters to convince the Americans to surrender without a fight. While the American commander, William Hull, defended his actions as having "saved Detroit and the territory from the horrors of an Indian massacre," others were less charitable.

The surrender of Detroit was a bitter blow at the outset of the war, and one American politician denounced it as "the most weak, cowardly and imbecile [act] ever known." For their part, American armies made repeated attempts to invade Upper and Lower Canada (present-day Ontario and Quebec), but with a few notable exceptions these efforts met with failure. Still smarting from the loss of Detroit, in October 1812 the Americans attempted to invade the Niagara Peninsula but were driven back at Queenston Heights.

In 1813 a further invasion force advanced as far as Stoney Creek before being defeated. Later that year American armies moving toward Montreal were decisively beaten in battles at Chateauguay and Chrysler's Farm. A final futile invasion effort along the Niagara Peninsula ended in disaster at the Battle of Lundy's Lane on July 25, 1814, when an American force commanded by General Winfield Scott fought a bloody engagement in the darkness, resulting in almost 2,000 British and American casualties. One British officer described the scene on the battlefield at Lundy's Lane the next day as a "shocking spectacle."

American attempts to invade Canada failed for several reasons. The American military was insufficiently prepared and trained and, as at Fort

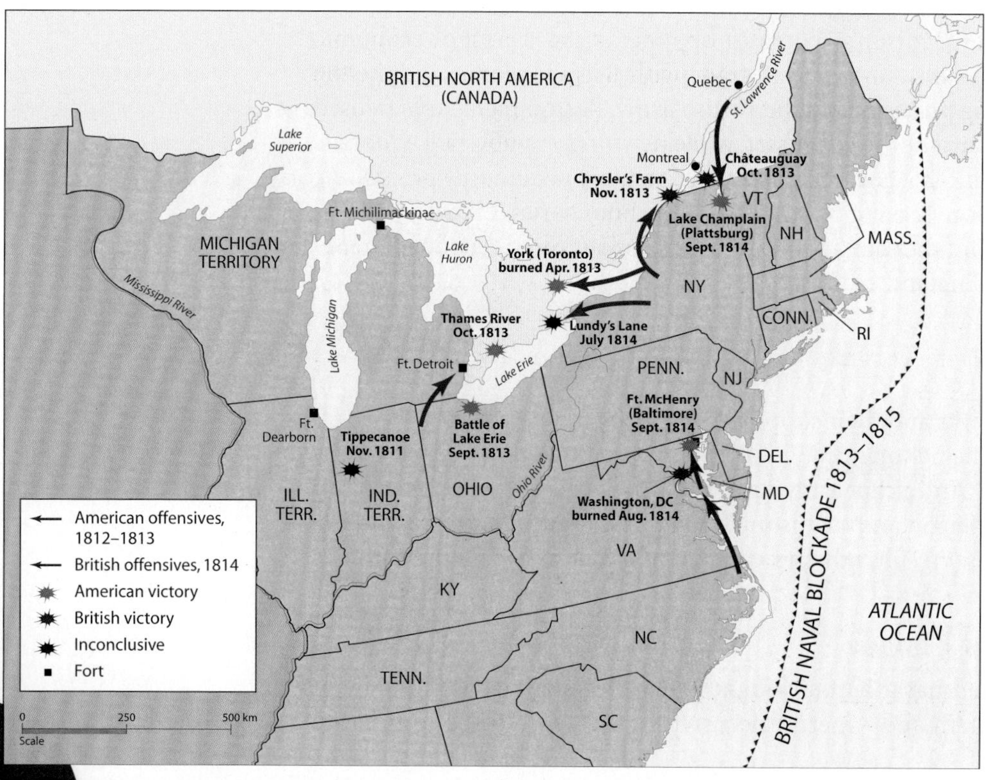


**Figure 4.19** The principal campaigns of the War of 1812 were conducted along the border with Upper Canada.

**Figure 4.20** An American soldier at Lundy's Lane described the confusion of the battlefield: "The darkness and smoke combined with the fitful light made the faces of those in the opposing ranks wear a blue sulphurous hue, and the men at each flash had the appearance of laughing."

Detroit, often led by incompetent commanders. As well, the military had been allowed to decline in strength. Desertions were common—particularly after it became clear that the war would not be concluded quickly—and some soldiers were openly critical of the conflict despite the mood of patriotism. One American officer privately ridiculed the war as "folly triumphant," lamenting that friends and neighbours with close ties along the frontier found themselves "coerced, by a hand unseen, to cut throats."

Indeed, the American invasion plans assumed active support from the population of Upper Canada, the majority of whom were recent immigrants from the United States. The British authorities in Canada shared the American view of the local population. British commanders like Brock doubted whether the Canadians would remain loyal, fearing that they would instead quickly flock to join the invading forces. Far more reliable, in the view of British commanders, were the Native American fighters, who played a vital role in most battles.

In the end, despite British fears, the majority of the residents of Upper Canada fought vigorously to defend their lands and farms against the invading army. Only a few Canadians acted as spies for the American forces—eight were tried and executed for treason at Burlington in 1814. It was clear that the conquest of Canada would be no easy task.

## Victories: Lake Erie and the Thames

Although the conquest of Canada proved impossible, there were notable American victories. In April 1813 the capital of Upper Canada, York (now Toronto), was attacked and briefly occupied by an American force. Further success came in September of that year when an American naval force commanded by Commodore Oliver Hazard Perry defeated a British fleet on Lake Erie. American control of the Great Lakes facilitated the recapture of Detroit.

## 49th PARALLEL

# The Raid on York, 1813

During the first year of the War of 1812 the Americans made little progress in their campaign to capture Upper Canada. By contrast, British forces had successfully seized several important American forts, including Fort Detroit and Fort Dearborn (site of Chicago). Initial American efforts to invade British territory had been repelled. Yet despite these setbacks, in the spring of 1813 the Americans made fresh plans to capture the British naval base at Kingston in order to cut off British communications between Montreal and Niagara. Rumours about the strength of the British garrison at Kingston, however, prompted a change of plans; the American force was diverted to attack York (now Toronto), the capital of Upper Canada.

Before dawn on April 27, 1813 the American forces landed west of the town. After encountering some resistance from British soldiers and their First Nations allies, the American troops began to advance on Fort York. The American commander, General Henry Dearborn, was unable to accompany his men ashore due to illness, leaving direction of the American forces to Brigadier General Zebulon Pike. With only 600 soldiers, the British commander decided to retreat to Kingston. This left the local militia the task of defending the capital of Upper Canada.

As the British retreated, they set fire to Fort York as well as to an unfinished warship in the harbour. The fire at Fort York led to the explosion of the **magazine**, which killed Pike as well as many American soldiers. Now lacking effective leadership, the American troops began to loot the town of York, setting fire to government buildings and destroying records. One resident described the results: "The appearance of the Town [York] & garrison were dismal. The latter shattered and rent by the balls & the explosion of the magazine ... The Town thronged with the Yankees, many busy getting off the public stores. The Council office with every window broke & pillaged of every thing that it contained. The Government building, the Block House and the building adjacent all burned to ashes." The Americans remained at York for six days before sailing away.

The raid on York came at a high cost. The American dead and wounded exceeded 20 percent of the force of 1,700 men. The attack also failed to bring the

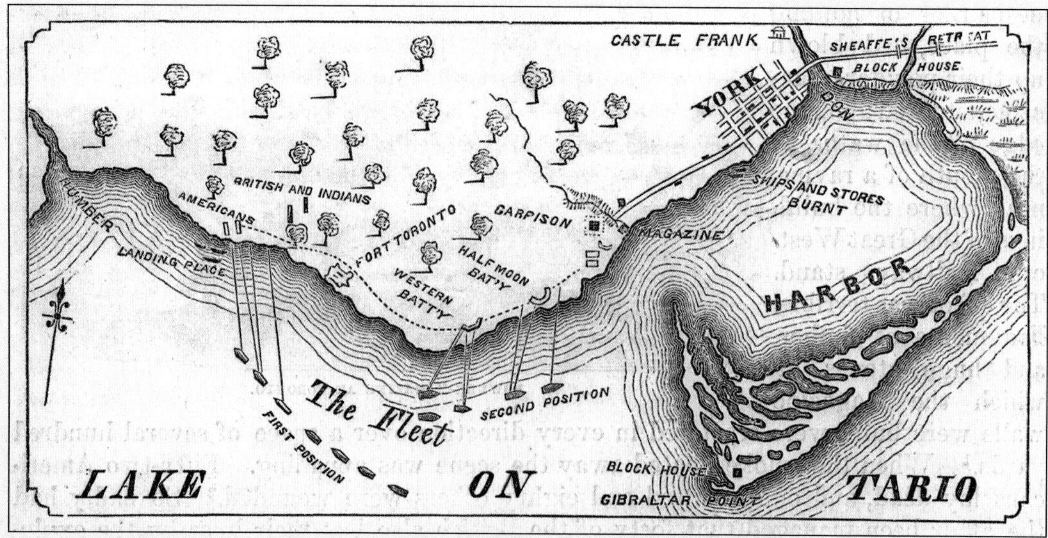


**Figure 4.21** A map showing the American attack on York. The American forces landed west of the town—between the Humber River and the fort, near the site now occupied by the CNE.

strategic advantage the Americans had hoped for; British communications remained intact. Furthermore, the events at York encouraged the British to attack Washington, DC the following summer, burning government buildings and forcing the capital's citizens (including President Madison) to flee. It was perhaps the lowest moment of the war for the United States. Finally, in York, memories of the attack endured. These served only to intensify the hostility of Upper Canada's leading residents toward the United States, leaving them suspicious of the republic's motives for decades to come.

## Think It Through

1. Why did the Americans attack York in April 1813?
2. Was the American attack on York a success or a failure? Explain.

Pursuing the advantage, in the fall of 1813 an American force led by General William Harrison (former governor of Indiana Territory) crossed the Detroit River and pursued a British force along the Thames River. A contingent of Native Americans, led by the charismatic Tecumseh, joined the British. When the American and British armies finally met at Moraviantown (near Chatham), the British fled after only a brief fight, leaving Tecumseh and his outnumbered warriors to continue the fight alone. In the fierce struggle that followed, Tecumseh was killed and his body mutilated. The killing of this feared Native American leader instantly made Harrison a popular hero (and helped him win the presidential election of 1840). The approach of winter prevented the Americans from exploiting their success, however, and Harrison and his army were forced to return to Detroit.

**Figure 4.22** This 1846 lithograph by American artist Nathaniel Currier depicted the death of Tecumseh at Moraviantown in 1813. Tecumseh's death was a blow to the British, who relied heavily on his effective leadership of their Native American allies.

## War in the South

While much of the fighting was concentrated along the border with Canada, war was also waged in the South against Native Americans, some of whom were allied with the British. Inspired by Tecumseh's resistance to American expansion, in August 1813 a group of Creeks, known as the Red Sticks, attacked Fort Mims in the Alabama territory and killed over 200 settlers.

In response, a force of militiamen (and some Native American allies) led by Andrew Jackson of Tennessee conducted a campaign against the Creeks, which culminated in the Battle of Horseshoe Bend in March 1814. In the battle, the Red Sticks were decisively defeated and many hundreds—including women and children—were slaughtered. Following this victory, Jackson forced the Creeks to surrender most of their lands to the government of the United States.

## Burning of Washington

In August 1814 the British launched a daring attack on Washington, DC, partly in retaliation for the earlier American attack on York. A contingent of British marines landed and marched on the capital. The assault spread panic through Washington's citizens. Members of the government, including Madison and his cabinet, fled before the approaching British force. In contrast, Madison's wife, Dolley, demonstrated considerable personal courage by calmly ignoring her husband's pleas to abandon the city. In delaying her escape, she managed to save a number of documents and valuables, among them a portrait of George Washington (shown in Figure 4.8). The British looted and burned government buildings, including the president's mansion, before retreating. The attack on Washington was a national humiliation, and Madison's flight prompted accusations of cowardice by his many political opponents. American pride was somewhat restored, however, when a subsequent British naval attack on Baltimore was thwarted.

Reconstruction of the city began the following year, and the president's mansion was rebuilt by 1817. People began referring to it as the White House because of the heavy coat of white paint that was used to cover up the remaining burn marks. The Capitol building, where Congress meets, was not completely restored until 1830.

## The Treaty of Ghent

Given Britain's continuing and consuming conflict with Napoleonic France, the war against America was merely a distraction for London. The demands of the European war also prevented Britain from devoting its full military strength to prosecuting the war against the United States.

In 1814 this global situation began to change. The collapse of France after Napoleon's defeat at Waterloo signalled to the American government that Britain might soon be able to give its full attention to the conflict in North America. At the same time, the British government was weary of war and anxious for peace. These considerations prompted the two sides to begin negotiations. After several months a treaty was signed at Ghent (Belgium), on

December 24, 1814. The Treaty of Ghent restored the boundaries that had existed prior to 1812 while ignoring the crucial issues of impressments and respect for American neutrality that had helped spark the conflict. The British did, however, agree to vacate their remaining forts in the West. They also abandoned their Native American allies, whose hopes for territory in the Northwest were ignored in the treaty. Most important was the treaty's symbolic significance—it represented a formal recognition by Britain of the full independence of the United States.

### New Orleans

Before word of the Treaty of Ghent had reached North America, a final battle was fought at New Orleans on January 8, 1815. A large and well-trained British force approached the city, which was defended mainly by militiamen from Kentucky and Tennessee together with a small number of professional soldiers led by Andrew Jackson. Despite being outnumbered, Jackson's force achieved a total victory; exposed to American fire as they advanced on the city, the British were slaughtered. British casualties (dead and wounded) numbered more than 2,000—including 700 killed—while American casualties numbered fewer than 20. The stunning victory at New Orleans transformed Jackson into a national hero and provided an appropriate patriotic conclusion to a war designed to demonstrate American nationhood.

## Consequences

The War of 1812 had a number of significant consequences for the United States. Most importantly, the war dispelled lingering doubts about American national "inferiority." The Americans had failed to capture Canada, but Andrew Jackson's triumph at New Orleans and Britain's agreement in the Treaty of Ghent to vacate its remaining forts in the Northwest gave Americans a sense of national pride. The United States had emerged victorious, finally earning the respect of the British. Indeed, some contemporaries began to refer to the War of 1812 as the Second War of Independence, completing the process of nation building that had begun at Lexington and Concord in 1775. Finally, the United States had fatally undermined the

**Figure 4.23** The American victory at New Orleans occurred two weeks after the Treaty of Ghent was signed.

Native American alliances—supported by the British—that had previously threatened westward expansion.

The War of 1812 highlighted the recurring problem of the rights of states within the federal system. Determined opposition to the war in New England led in late 1814 to the Hartford Convention, which drew up a declaration of the rights of individual states to oppose federal government policies with which they disagreed. The meeting was quickly forgotten with the end of the war, but the doctrine of **nullification** did not disappear. Instead, it would recur regularly and with growing significance in the decades ahead—on issues ranging from the tariff to slavery—and would eventually threaten the very survival of the American nation. Finally, the war made any future American efforts to persuade the rest of British North America to join the United States virtually impossible. In Canada, the Americans had left a legacy of suspicion of American expansionist plans.

### CHECK YOUR UNDERSTANDING

1. Who were the War Hawks, and why did they urge war against Britain?
2. Why were people in New England opposed to the War of 1812?
3. Why did repeated American invasions of Canada fail to achieve their goal?
4. List the terms of the Treaty of Ghent in point form.
5. What was the significance of the Battle of New Orleans?

# NATIONAL EXPANSION

Success against Britain in the War of 1812 had given the United States, in the words of one foreign observer, "a national character founded on a glory common to all." In the years following the war, this new national character translated into increased confidence in foreign affairs, and rapid economic and social development. Diplomatic and technological achievements signalled that the United States had come of age.

## Era of Good Feelings

The election of the Republican James Monroe of Virginia as president in 1816 marked a shift in the American political landscape. Support for the Federalists had been greatly undermined as a result of their opposition to the War of 1812, leaving the once powerful party of John Adams and Alexander Hamilton weakened and unable to effectively challenge the Republicans.

Indeed, by 1820 when Monroe sought re-election, the Federalists put forward no candidate and Monroe was re-elected unopposed. However, the Republicans did adopt many of the Federalists' ideas (including the need for a national bank), and Monroe included prominent former Federalists like John Quincy Adams in his cabinet. Celebrating the end of faction and a new political harmony, one Federalist newspaper proclaimed the beginning of an "Era of Good Feelings."

## Territories and Boundaries

American national pride remained strong during the following decade. Guided by Secretary of State John Quincy Adams, the United States secured recognition from European powers such as Britain and Spain, increased its territories, and confirmed its borders. For example, the 1817 Rush-Bagot Treaty with Britain fixed the 49th parallel as the northern boundary with British North America, between Lake of the Woods and the Rockies. In addition, the Convention of 1818 established joint British and American control over the Oregon territory in the Pacific Northwest. Greater success followed in 1819 when Adams concluded the Transcontinental Treaty with Spain, which ceded Florida to the United States. American soldiers had already occupied Florida, allegedly to end attacks by Native Americans launched from Spanish territory, and Spain had been powerless to halt these incursions. In exchange for renouncing claims to Texas (which some Americans believed was a mistake), Adams persuaded Spain to surrender Florida peacefully and give up any further claims to Louisiana.

## The Monroe Doctrine

The decline of the Spanish empire, which had enabled the United States to acquire Florida, led to revolutions in Spanish colonies across Central and

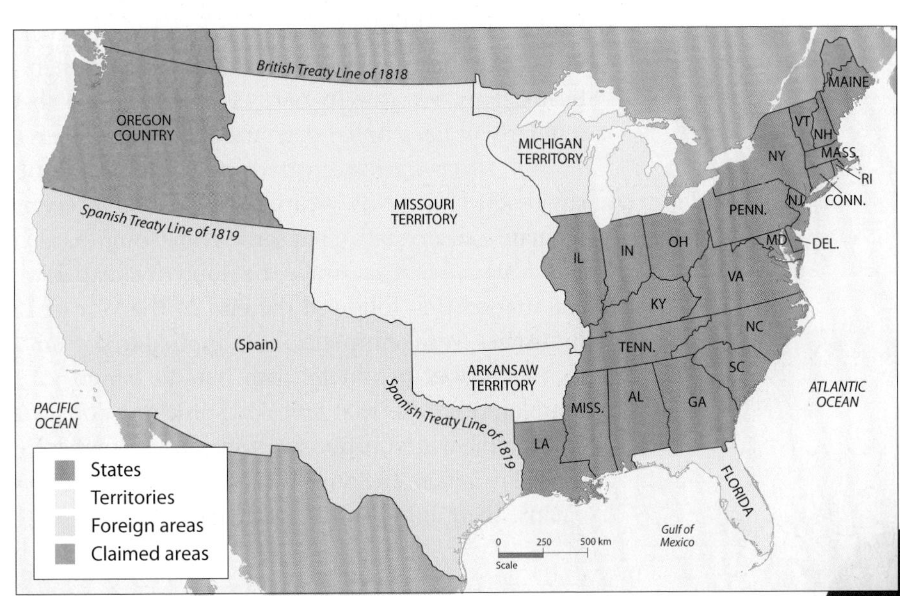


**Figure 4.24** By 1820 the territory and claims of the United States stretched from Florida to Maine, and from the Atlantic to the Pacific. How had the Louisiana Purchase transformed the United States into a North American nation?

South America, from Colombia to Mexico. In line with its own revolutionary history and republican ideals, the United States encouraged these new nations in their efforts to establish their independence. At the same time, European powers such as France and Britain were seeking to expand their influence in the Americas in order to fill the vacuum created by Spain's collapse.

In December 1823 the American government responded to this potential interference by issuing the Monroe Doctrine, a statement of foreign policy crafted by Secretary of State John Quincy Adams. The United States called on European nations to refrain from establishing new colonies in the Americas, and not to interfere in the affairs of newly independent nations. For its part, the United States vowed to defend the independence of these new republics and agreed not to intervene in European affairs (an echo of the sentiments expressed by Washington in his Farewell Address). Initially the Monroe Doctrine attracted little attention, but it set a significant precedent for future American involvement in Central and South America.

## The American System

In order to stimulate American economic growth following the War of 1812, the government pursued policies designed to foster industry and encourage **capitalism**. A group of politicians led by the congressional leader Henry Clay of Kentucky promoted these policies, which became known as the American System. They included a new national bank, a tariff to protect American industry from foreign competition, and a system of internal improvement—the construction of roads and canals to facilitate transportation.

### Banks and Tariffs

Sustained economic expansion required ready access to capital for investment in factories, roads, and canals; in the absence of a national bank, existing local banks were unable to meet this need. In 1811 the charter of the Bank of the United States, founded in 1791 by Alexander Hamilton, had lapsed under the Republicans. This was due in part to resentment of banks by farmers, who were regularly in debt to bankers and who were generally Republican supporters.

In 1816 Congress created the Second Bank of the United States, both to supply the large sums of capital needed to fuel economic expansion and to help regulate the currency. That same year, Congress also imposed a tariff. The tariff was designed to discourage the flood of cheap British imports into the American market that followed the end of the War of 1812, and protect American industries from competition. It applied to cotton and woolen cloth, as well as to a variety of products from hats to paper. While the tariff was generally popular, reactions to it revealed some divisions within the country. The tariff enjoyed the widest support among factory owners and merchants in the North, while farmers in the South feared that it might prompt the British to retaliate against their agricultural products.

## Factories and Technology

Largely protected from British competitors by the Embargo Act of 1807, the War of 1812, and then the tariff, American industry (unlike exporters of raw materials) thrived during the early 19th century. Perhaps the most powerful symbol of this new industrial capacity was the spread of cotton mills. While many industries still employed the "putting-out system," where scattered weavers or shoemakers worked in their own homes for a business owner, others began to create larger factories modelled on the British system.

The pioneer in this field was Francis Lowell, who visited England in 1810 to study textile mills. When Lowell returned to Massachusetts, he and his partners implemented what Lowell had seen abroad. Within a few years Lowell's firm had established an entire town—Lowell, Massachusetts—which boasted six textile mills and provided company housing and services for employees, many of whom were women who worked for a few years before returning home to marry. Under the influence of Lowell and other capitalists, New England became a centre for the textile industry. Part of Lowell's success came from his invention of the power loom, a new technology that greatly increased cloth production.

The growth of the textile industry depended on cotton from the American South, illustrating the regional economic interdependence that had developed by the early 19th century (that is, cotton from the South supplied mills in the North, and northern factory workers and southern slaves were fed by grain from the farms of Pennsylvania or New York). The growth of industry also demonstrates the degree to which the industrial economy of the North relied, however indirectly, on slavery for its prosperity.

Americans in the early 1800s were proud of developing another new manufacturing technique: interchangeable machine-made parts. The ability to replace a worn-out part with an exact duplicate meant that repairs were inexpensive and production could be standardized, resulting in lower costs.

**Figure 4.25** The mills at Lowell, Massachusetts symbolized the success of the new "American system of manufactures."

The principle was first employed in 1816 in gun manufacture and later spread to other industries. As commercial competitors, the British were very impressed. They soon named this new technique "the American system of manufactures."

## Roads and Canals

Improved transportation was the key to developing the American economy. Industrial growth required an effective transportation network linking factories to raw materials and providing ready access to markets. Existing roads were often impassable and, except by ship along the coast and major rivers, travel was slow. In 1800 a journey from New York to Baltimore took at least three days; a trip to Richmond, Virginia, was six or seven days long, while Detroit was four weeks away. Mud, dust, and snow made land journeys tedious and uncomfortable, and local efforts to improve roads—often through levying tolls—were limited.

Recognizing the need for improved long distance transportation to promote economic growth, the federal government embarked on a system of internal improvements. The first significant step was the construction of the National Road in 1808. The road ran from Baltimore west through the Appalachians, reaching Wheeling, Virginia by 1818. It was then extended through Ohio and Indiana, eventually stretching almost to the Mississippi near St. Louis.

While the construction of the National Road (and those that followed) dramatically improved personal travel and promoted settlement of the West, land transportation of bulk goods remained slow and costly. The foundation of the economy continued to be water transport. Most commercial trade within the United States still travelled along the Atlantic coast, and along the Mississippi and Ohio rivers; in order to improve this system, canals were

**Figure 4.26** John William Hill's 1830 watercolour *View of the Erie Canal.* At 586 kilometres long, the Erie Canal was 12 times the length of any existing American canal when it was completed in 1825.

needed to connect the Atlantic seaboard to the lakes and rivers of the interior. In 1817 Governor DeWitt Clinton of New York proposed a canal running from the Hudson River at Albany to Lake Erie at Buffalo. Despite the scorn of skeptics, the Erie Canal was completed by October 1825 at the staggering cost of $7 million (about $170 million today). Constructed largely by Irish immigrants, the Erie Canal was an engineering marvel that enabled cargo to be moved from the Atlantic to the interior in little more than a week. It became the centrepiece of a network of canals that linked the Atlantic coastal ports, the Great Lakes, and the Ohio and Mississippi rivers, spurring economic growth across the United States.

## Economic Growth

Under the American System, the economy of the United States grew dramatically during the decade following the signing of the Treaty of Ghent in 1814. Initially, however, the loss of overseas trade (which resulted as Britain resumed its pre-eminent economic position following the disruption of the Napoleonic Wars) led to an economic collapse. Yet even this so-called Panic of 1819, which witnessed bank failures, a sharp series of factory closures, and rising unemployment, proved to be only a temporary setback.

Despite the emphasis on industry and technology, agriculture remained at the heart of America's prosperity. The invention of the cotton gin in 1793 made separating cotton fibres and seeds far simpler, and by the early 19th century cotton cultivation dominated the South. Key to this was the expansion of cotton production into new areas like Alabama and Mississippi after 1816. The surge in cotton exports not only generated wealth in the South, it benefited the entire nation as much of the trade was diverted through ports such as New York and Boston. The profits of this trade were invested in New England factories like those at Lowell, which consumed yet more southern cotton. The capital also made possible the financing of roads and canals, and would be instrumental in the early development of railroads (the first railroad—the Baltimore and Ohio—opened in 1830) that would accelerate the pace of national expansion.

### CHECK YOUR UNDERSTANDING

1. Why was the period following the War of 1812 labelled the Era of Good Feelings?
2. Explain the Monroe Doctrine in your own words.
3. List the main components of the American System proposed by Henry Clay.
4. How did technological developments in the early 19th century promote the expansion of the American economy?
5. What was the significance of the completion of the Erie Canal?

# THE HISTORIAN'S CRAFT

## Interpreting Pictures from the Past

Like written documents, primary illustrated sources provide glimpses into history. Just like written sources, they too must be interpreted. Historians assess reliability, perspective, bias, and intolerance in historic visuals in order to construct an accurate picture of the past. This chapter reflects the range of illustrated evidence found throughout this textbook: cartoons, paintings, prints, sketches, and maps (to learn about the photograph as a primary source, see The Historian's Craft in Chapter 6).

### Looking for Meaning in Visuals

Historians first examine visual evidence for general meaning or overall impression—much as they do with written primary sources. For example, Figure 4.21 provides a view of the town of York, Upper Canada in 1813 when American forces raided the town. The map shows the location of the garrison in relation to the town. It also indicates where the Americans landed and the position of British troops and First Nations allies.

In Figure 4.22, *The Death of Tecumseh*, the artist shows the heat of the battle and illustrates the weapons used by both sides in the War of 1812. The artist portrays an American soldier as he personally slays Tecumseh. The overall subject is significant because Americans considered this war to be important, sometimes calling it the Second War of Independence.

In Figure 4.26, *View of the Erie Canal*, the artist provides a view of the canal soon after its completion (note the construction debris), with a commercial barge on the right and a packet boat with passengers on the roof on the left. The artist also illustrates the means of power—a team of horses on the towpath. Overall, the picturesque scene suggests that rural communities will benefit from this new marvel of technology.

### Looking More Deeply

Historians examining the map of York for deeper meaning note a critical detail: the location of the magazine at Fort York. When this munitions depot exploded the results were spectacular—heavy casualties among the Americans, damage to York, and the British retaliatory attack on Washington, DC in 1814.

When historians look more deeply at *The Death of Tecumseh*, they begin to question its reliability, noting that the print was made more than 30 years after the event. They know that the lithographer, Nathaniel Currier, was born during the war and therefore was not an eyewitness. Next, they remind themselves that Currier was a commercial artist interested in selling his work to patriotic Americans. He decided to depict the American soldier (possibly Colonel Richard M. Johnson or General Harrison) as a hero who personally killed Tecumseh, even though historians are unclear as to how Tecumseh died. Currier placed this American officer in the centre of the picture to heighten the focus on the "gallant" soldier. By placing Tecumseh at the side he minimized the emphasis on a Native American leader, thereby reflecting a prejudice of the time. Overall, this print tells us more about American tastes in the 1840s than it does about Tecumseh's death.

In looking at John William Hill's painting of the Erie Canal, historians might begin with the date: 1830. That was five years after the completion of the canal, so the building debris appears to be authentic. Further research reveals that Hill was a draftsman for the New York State Geological Survey. He painted this scene from first-hand observation. Additional research leads historians to other works by Hill that featured boats—a subject he was skilled at portraying. Overall, historians conclude that Hill's watercolour provides an accurate representation of the Erie Canal.

### Try It!

1. Choose one illustration from this chapter. What does it suggest to you about this period in history?
2. Choose one painting in this chapter or a historical map from an earlier chapter. Research the artist or map-maker. What does your research suggest about the reliability of the painting or map as a primary source?

# STUDY HALL

## Thinking

1. Who do you think had the greater impact on the development of the United States—George Washington or Thomas Jefferson? Support your opinion with specific facts from this chapter.
2. The United States barely survived the period from 1783 to 1815. What impact do you think the experiences of this struggle had on the national identity of Americans and on their worldview?
3. President Thomas Jefferson described his election as "the Revolution of 1800." In what ways could this election be described as a political or social "revolution"?
4. The War of 1812 has been called the Second War of Independence. Do you agree with this description? Why or why not?
5. In one of the *Federalist Papers* (discussed in Chapter 3), James Madison warned of the danger of political "factions"—that is, political parties. Did the contest between the Federalists and the Republicans prove that Madison was right?
6. In his Farewell Address, George Washington cautioned that the United States should remain neutral and free of foreign alliances. Was his advice followed? Do the events covered in this chapter prove that Washington was right?

## Communication

7. Imagine that you are the editor of a newspaper in Philadelphia in 1812. Compose an editorial articulating the key arguments in favour of war with Britain.
8. Some have said that Jefferson was a failure as president. Imagine you are President Jefferson and that you are preparing to retire. Make a defence of your time in office. Write and deliver a speech, or compose an excerpt from Jefferson's memoirs.

## Application

9. In the 1790s the Federalists responded to fears of foreign radicals and domestic criticism of the government by passing the Alien and Sedition Acts. Governments often react to external threats by restricting individual liberties. Research the reaction of the American government to foreigners during World War I, World War II, or following the terrorist attacks of September 11, 2001. Do you see similarities between the events of the 1790s and these later events? Explain.
10. How do you think Native Americans such as Tecumseh, or Native Americans living in the area of the Louisiana Purchase, might draw a map that showed the expansion of the United States from 1783 to 1815? What title would they give the map? What places of interest and events might they locate on the map? Draw the map and explain your choices.

# UNIT III NATIONALISM AND SECTIONALISM

# 5 Manifest Destiny (1828–1850)

### KEY CONCEPTS

In this chapter you will consider:

- The impact of greater democracy on American society and government
- Andrew Jackson's transformation of American politics and government
- The role of westward expansion in shaping American politics
- The significance of the doctrine of manifest destiny for American history
- The impact of individualism on American religion, philosophy, and literature
- The growth of social reform movements during the first half of the 19th century
- The continued tensions between the United States and British North America over territorial expansion

## The American Story

The early 19th century in America witnessed profound social and political changes. Few individuals illustrated this more clearly than Andrew Jackson. In 1828 Jackson was elected president as the "champion of the people" and the first leader from a frontier state, one west of the Appalachian Mountains. Behind these changes lay some fundamental ideas: a broader definition of democracy and a belief in America's manifest destiny. Manifest destiny was the powerful idea that America should expand to occupy the entire continent, from the Atlantic to the Pacific. That destiny would lead ultimately to economic and social development, but also to conflict with Native Americans as well as with Mexico and Britain.

### TIMELINE

| 1828 | 1830 | 1836 | 1838 | 1844 |
|---|---|---|---|---|
| ▸ Election of Andrew Jackson as president | ▸ Joseph Smith founds the Mormon Church<br>▸ First railroad engine begins service | ▸ Revolt in Texas—the Alamo<br>▸ Ralph Waldo Emerson publishes "Nature" | ▸ Trail of Tears | ▸ Election of James Polk as president |

## IMAGE ANALYSIS

**Figure 5.1** On March 4, 1829 an extraordinary scene took place in Washington, DC, the sober capital of the United States. Huge crowds of common people attended the inauguration of Andrew Jackson of Tennessee as president. Farmers and labourers surged through the streets on foot and pressed into the reception, tramping mud on the fine carpets and consuming free cakes and wine. This behaviour scandalized the social and political elites. One lady expressed their shock: "Ladies and gentlemen only had been expected at this levee, not the people *en masse*. But it was the people's day, and the people's President, and the people would rule. God grant that one day or other the people do not put down all rule and rulers." Jackson's inauguration clearly demonstrated that a new democratic system was emerging and that the "age of the common man" had arrived.

- ▸ John O'Sullivan coins the phrase "manifest destiny" — **1845**
- ▸ Mexican-American War begins — **1847**
- ▸ Women's Rights Convention at Seneca Falls — **1848**
- ▸ California gold rush — **1849**

# INTRODUCTION

In this chapter you will see that the second quarter of the 19th century in America was dominated by a belief in the possibility of "democratic" improvement. People began to think that politics, society, and the economy could be reshaped by ordinary men, independent of the elites who had previously directed the nation's affairs. Politicians, social reformers, writers, and philosophers all sought to instill in ordinary citizens the conviction that they could improve their own lives and, through participation in the political process, strengthen American democracy. This confidence in the power of the American people to prosper through democracy was the common refrain of the age—what the poet Walt Whitman called "the majesty and reality of the American people *en masse*."

# THE AGE OF JACKSON

During the two decades after the War of 1812 politics and society in America underwent a significant change. The established elites initially maintained their dominance over the government, but as the nation expanded westward the grip of old states like Virginia and Massachusetts began to loosen. The influence of the common people and the frontier grew dramatically.

## Democracy and the "Common Man"

As the right to vote was extended to all adult white males in the early 19th century, American politics became more broadly democratic. Politics was no longer the preserve of wealthy New England landholders and the aristocratic planters of Virginia. In place of elite parties such as the Federalists, new political parties appeared that found their base of support among farmers, labourers, and tradespeople. This popular interest in politics was spurred in part by the rapid growth in newspapers, whose numbers soared from fewer than 400 in 1810 to more than 1,200 in 1835.

Newspaper readers could be found everywhere in America. One foreign visitor remarked: "On board the steamer and on the rail, in the counting-house and the hotel, in the street and in the private dwelling, in the crowded thoroughfare and the remotest rural district, one is ever sure of finding the newspaper." The emergence of the popular "penny press" encouraged this dramatic growth in newspaper readership. Reflecting the rise of the "common man" in America, *The New York Sun* and its imitators enjoyed a wide circulation among the working classes due to their focus on reports of violent crime and other vices rather than elite politics. Although these new papers were still politically partisan, they succeeded in attracting many more readers.

The main beneficiary of this new democratic spirit was General Andrew Jackson, known to his friends and supporters as "Old Hickory" for his toughness in battle. Unlike previous political leaders, such as Washington and Jefferson,

Jackson came from a humble background. Born in a log cabin in South Carolina, he served as a courier in the Revolutionary War and was captured by the British. When he refused to clean the boots of a British officer, he was slashed with a sabre. This left him with physical scars he would carry for the rest of his life and an inveterate hatred of the British. After the war, Jackson studied law and made his way west to Tennessee, on what was then the frontier. There he entered politics, serving briefly as a member of Congress and attracting the attention and support of those anxious to rebalance American political life.

**Figure 5.2** Andrew Jackson was 62 years old by the time he entered the White House. Much of his fame rested on military exploits, especially his smashing victory at the Battle of New Orleans. Why do you think so many US presidents have been ex-soldiers?

Jackson's growing popularity was partly rooted in his powerful personality. He was strong willed and courageous, and several violent episodes from his youth contributed to his status as a legendary figure. He believed strongly in the Southern code of honour, which demanded revenge for even the slightest slur on one's character. Involved in several duels, he once shot a man dead for calling him a coward in print. He was renowned as an "Indian fighter," and the Native Americans called him "Sharp Knife" for his ruthlessness in battle. His strongly held beliefs and violent rages meant he could be a steadfast friend but an implacable enemy.

As the self-proclaimed champion of the common man, Jackson challenged John Quincy Adams (son of former president John Adams) and Henry Clay for the presidency in 1824. The election result was inconclusive; Jackson received the most votes, but no single candidate secured a majority in the Electoral College. As in 1800, Congress therefore decided the election. In return for an offer of an important government post, Clay threw his support to Adams, who then became president.

Jackson was incensed by this "treachery," and denounced the result as undemocratic. He vowed he would have revenge and defeat Adams four years later. In the interim, Jackson worked to discredit Adams and his administration while patiently organizing his supporters as the Democratic Party. On top of attacks by the Democrats, Adams struggled unsuccessfully to revive a weak economy. In the election of 1828 Jackson and his Democratic Party scored a significant victory, capturing 178 of 261 electoral votes. When Jackson took the oath of office in March 1829, witnessed by his exuberant supporters, it was clear that a new political age had dawned.

| The Presidents: 1828–1850 | | |
|---|---|---|
| **John Quincy Adams** | Republican | March 4, 1825 – March 4, 1829 |
| **Andrew Jackson** | Democratic | March 4, 1829 – March 4, 1837 |
| **Martin Van Buren** | Democratic | March 4, 1837 – March 4, 1841 |
| **William H. Harrison** | Whig | March 4, 1841 – April 4, 1841 |
| **John Tyler** | Whig | April 4, 1841 – March 4, 1845 |
| **James K. Polk** | Democratic | March 4, 1845 – March 4, 1849 |

# PAST VOICES

## Alexis de Tocqueville and *Democracy in America*

**Figure 5.3** Alexis de Tocqueville. What perspective did Tocqueville bring to his examination of American democracy?

In 1831 a French aristocrat, 25-year-old Alexis de Tocqueville (1805–1859), arrived in the United States. His mission was to study the American prison system and report his findings to the French government. Tocqueville spent months travelling across the United States, meeting civic leaders and ordinary people. He visited major cities, such as New York and Philadelphia, and frontier settlements, such as Buffalo and Cincinnati. At Detroit he was surprised to discover a keen interest in the latest Paris fashions on the edge of the wilderness. He also visited muddy Washington, DC, where he met many eminent men, including President Andrew Jackson.

In addition to carrying out his commission to study the prison system, Tocqueville proved a keen observer of American politics and society during the Age of Jackson—the first truly democratic era in American history. While critical of some of what he observed, he was deeply impressed by the American people and their democratic system of government. After his return to France, Tocqueville elaborated on his impressions in his book *Democracy in America*, which remains a key text for understanding the United States and its democratic character.

Several aspects of this character were particularly striking to a foreign visitor. Compared with European societies and their rigid class systems, American society seemed quite fluid, based as it was on the idea of equality. It was this "equality of condition" that Tocqueville believed formed "the fundamental fact" of American government and society.

> Among the novel objects that attracted my attention during my stay in the United States, nothing struck me more forcibly than the general equality of condition among the people. I readily discovered the prodigious influence that this primary fact exercises on the whole course of society; it gives a peculiar direction to public opinion and a peculiar tenor to the laws; it imparts new maxims to the governing authorities and peculiar habits to the governed …
>
> The more I advanced in the study of American society, the more I perceived that this equality of condition is the fundamental fact from which all others seem to be derived and the central point at which all my observations constantly terminated.

Tocqueville was a perceptive observer and critic of the new democratic American nation under Andrew Jackson, then in the midst of the Bank War. He warned of the dangers of democracy, which might easily justify unfair acts in the name of the people. His warning remains a powerful reminder of the potential dangers of a "tyranny of the majority"—as valid today as it was more than 150 years ago.

> In my opinion, the main evil of the present democratic institutions of the United States does not arise, as is often asserted in Europe, from their weakness, but from their irresistible strength. I am not so much alarmed at the excessive liberty which reigns in that country as at the inadequate securities which one finds there against tyranny. An individual or a party is wronged in the United States, to whom can he apply for redress? If to public opinion, public opinion constitutes the majority; if to the legislature, it represents the majority and implicitly obeys it; if to the executive power, it is appointed by the majority and serves as a passive tool in its hands. The public force consists of the majority under arms; the jury is the majority invested with the right of hearing judicial cases; and in certain states even the judges are elected by the majority. However iniquitous or absurd the measure of which you complain, you must submit to it as well as you can.

### Think It Through

1. In what ways, according to Tocqueville, did the concept of equality shape all aspects of American society in the 1830s?
2. Tocqueville argued that the "main evil" of American democracy was its "irresistible strength." Why was this so? Explain why you agree or disagree with his assessment.

### WEB LINKS

To learn more about Tocqueville's impressions of American society, politics, and culture, and trace his journey across the nation, visit www.emp.ca/ah.

## Political Crises

The foundation of Andrew Jackson's political creed was the **sovereignty**, or authority, of the people. In his words: "The people are the government, administering it by their agents; they are the government, the sovereign power." This was Jacksonian democracy: a movement dedicated to limiting the influence of elites and allowing the common man a clear voice in government. While this was in many respects a radical notion, it should be remembered that when Jackson argued for "majority rule" his political vision excluded many; women, blacks, and Native Americans were all denied a voice.

### The Bank War

As the representative of the common man against the elites, President Jackson did not hesitate to strike against those who opposed him. There were few more potent symbols of his elite opponents than the Second Bank of the United States, the BUS. As well as being an important commercial bank, the BUS served as chief banker to the American government, handling its transactions and holding the bulk of the nation's financial reserves. The bank also enjoyed close connections to members of Congress.

Echoing the views of the farmers who had elected him, Jackson viewed the bank as a representative of the urban financial elites. When the bank—led by its president, Nicholas Biddle, and assisted by Jackson's old foe Henry Clay—sought an early renewal of its federal charter, Jackson vigorously opposed the plans. When Congress approved the charter despite the president's opposition, Jackson vetoed it.

After the bank's powerful supporters failed in their attempt to defeat Jackson's re-election in 1832, the president determined to destroy the BUS forever. Jackson assured his supporters that "the Bank … is trying to kill me, but I will kill it." He ordered the US government to withdraw its funds from the bank and deposit them instead in a variety of smaller institutions. When his Treasury Secretary refused to carry out the order, arguing that it would destabilize the currency, Jackson fired him and appointed a more pliable man to the position.

In response to Jackson's actions, Congress sought to **censure** the president. Jackson defended himself by presenting a novel argument: since he was elected by the entire nation rather than by the voters

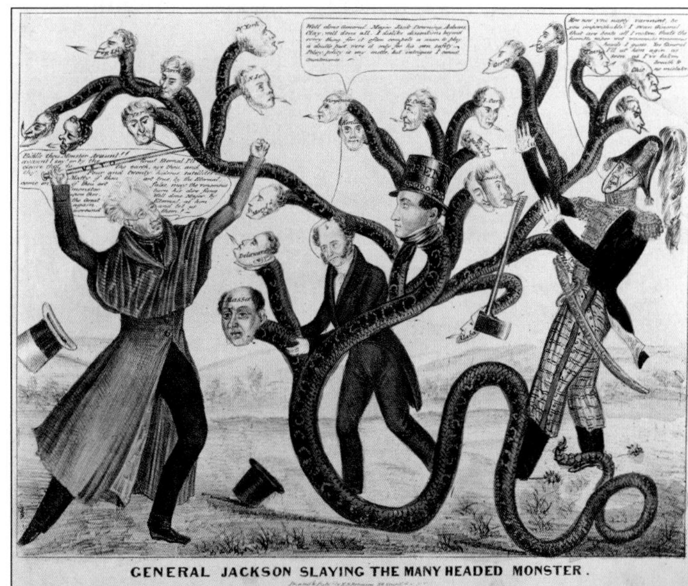


**Figure 5.4** A contemporary cartoon shows President Jackson trying to kill the "many-headed monster," the Bank of the United States. Why did Jackson set out to destroy the bank?

of a single state (as members of Congress were), he could speak for the whole country and overrule Congress if necessary. Following the withdrawal of government funds, Biddle and the BUS did not surrender easily. The bank limped along for a few years, but Jackson had fatally weakened its powerful position at the heart of the American financial system. Winning this battle, however, would later prove to be a costly victory.

## Nullification Crisis

In addition to his struggles with the BUS, Jackson fought to defend the power of the federal government against those who argued for the rights of states. The flashpoint came over the issue of the tariff, which had been introduced as part of the American System to encourage and protect manufacturing. While the businesspeople of the North supported the tariff, many Southerners who relied on exports (especially cotton) resented it. The tariff made imported luxury goods more expensive, and Southerners feared that it might lead other nations to retaliate, damaging their cotton trade.

The leader of the opposition to the tariff was John C. Calhoun of South Carolina, Jackson's vice-president. When his concerns were overlooked, Calhoun argued that states like South Carolina had the right to ignore those federal laws they strongly opposed, a principle known as nullification. Jackson denounced this idea as treason, and Calhoun was forced to resign. Jackson also threatened to use the army to collect the tax in South Carolina if state authorities refused to cooperate. In the end, the federal and state governments reached a compromise by which the tariff would continue but be gradually reduced.

The nullification crisis demonstrated Jackson's determination to defend the powers of the federal government against state interests, by force if necessary. It also revealed the divisions in the country between the economic interests of the North and the South—a growing sectionalism that would become more significant in the years to come. Finally, the crisis cost Jackson the support of the Southern elite, who now denounced his policy toward the South as "the mad ravings of a driveling dotard."

## The Trail of Tears

Because Jackson resided in the frontier state of Tennessee, his election reflected the shift in population and political power toward the West. Just as he appealed to the common men who elected him, so Jackson worked to address the concerns of settlers hungry for more land. Unfortunately, the Native American nations east of the Mississippi formed a major obstacle to westward expansion.

In order to limit conflicts between Native Americans and settlers and open more farmland to settlement, Jackson sponsored the **Indian Removal Act of 1830**—the only significant law he pushed through Congress in his eight years as president. The Removal Act in effect evicted all Native Americans from their hereditary lands in the East and sent them to lands west of the Mississippi in what are now the states of Oklahoma and Arkansas. Jackson argued that "removal" was in the Native Americans' own best interest since in their new lands they would be free to govern themselves without interference from the US military or white settlers. While some of the Native inhabitants went willingly, others had to be removed by force.

Among those who refused to move were the Cherokee, known as one of the five "Civilized Tribes" for the way they had adapted to white society. The Cherokee had developed a written language; lived in towns made up of wooden buildings; supported themselves as farmers; constructed roads and bridges; ran their own school system; and governed themselves by means of a constitution modelled on that of the United States. They defended their right to stay where they were by arguing that they held title to their lands in Georgia and that, as a separate nation, were not subject to the laws of the state. In a remarkable judgment, even the Supreme Court of the United States agreed.

But the Cherokee's efforts to preserve their independence fell victim to the American government's need for land, and Jackson was reluctant to force a confrontation with Georgia over Indian policy at the same time as he was dealing with the nullification crisis. In a direct and passionate appeal to Congress, the Cherokee Chief John Ross pleaded for the removal order to be rescinded:

> By the stipulations of this instrument [the removal order], we are despoiled of our private possessions, the indefeasible property of individuals. We are stripped of every attribute of freedom and eligibility for legal self-defence. Our property may be plundered before our eyes; violence may be committed on our persons; even our lives may be taken away, and there is none to regard our complaints ... We are overwhelmed! Our hearts are sickened ... when we reflect on the condition in which we are placed by the audacious practices of unprincipled men.

**Figure 5.5** The Cherokee nation on the Trail of Tears, as depicted in this 1942 painting by Robert Lindneux. Why did the Cherokee's journey west come to be known by this name?

**SOUND BITE**

"I fought through the Civil War and have seen men shot to pieces and slaughtered by thousands, but the Cherokee removal was the cruelest I ever saw."

—A Georgia militiaman who guarded the Cherokee on the Trail of Tears

Congress ignored Ross's appeal, and in 1838—the year after Jackson left office—federal troops removed more than 14,000 Cherokee from their ancestral lands and held them in squalid camps before sending them to Oklahoma.

White settlers anxious to occupy the vacant land looted and burned the Cherokee homes. The Cherokee were forced onto steamboats for the first part of their journey before being crowded into railroad boxcars. They made the final part of the journey on foot, over many hundreds of kilometres. More than 4,000 Cherokee died along what became known as the Trail of Tears. Scholars estimate that in 1824 there were more than 75,000 Native Americans living east of the Mississippi, yet by 1840 almost all had been pushed west. American settlers now occupied their former lands.

## The Second Seminole War, 1835–1842

While the Cherokee turned to the courts in an effort to halt their removal, other Native American nations chose to fight. Led by their chief, Osceola, the Seminole of Florida ignored government orders to move west. Osceola warned of war if the government attempted to relocate the Seminole, and threatened to kill any Seminole leaders who cooperated with the removal. War did in fact erupt late in 1835, and Osceola conducted a skillful campaign in the Florida swamps against a succession of American generals sent to defeat him.

In October 1837 Osceola was lured to a truce meeting, captured, and imprisoned. Despite his death a few months later, the Seminole War continued until 1842. By the time it ended, the war had cost the government more than $30 million (about $820 million in current dollars) and the lives of 1,500 soldiers, making it the most expensive "Indian War" in US history. Some Seminoles remained in Florida, living deep in the Everglades, but more than 3,000 eventually moved west and many others perished in the fighting. In the end, despite their different responses to the threat, the Cherokee and Seminole suffered the same fate: the loss of their traditional homelands and the decimation of their populations. This was the heavy price paid by all who stood in the path of **manifest destiny**.

**SOUND BITE**

"This is the only treaty I will make with the whites!"

—Words spoken by Osceola as he plunged his dagger into the Treaty of Payne's Landing, meant to remove the Seminole from Florida to Oklahoma

**Figure 5.6** Osceola was a ruthless and determined defender of the Seminole. Identify one reason why the Seminole lost their war against the US government.

## AMERICAN ARCHIVE

# *Worcester v. Georgia*

In 1830, to hasten the removal of the Cherokee, the government of Georgia passed a law preventing sympathetic outsiders from gaining access to Cherokee territory. The following year, a dozen missionaries who ignored this law were arrested and duly convicted. Led by Samuel Worcester, the missionaries appealed to the US Supreme Court. They argued that the law under which they had been convicted was unconstitutional because states did not have the authority to pass laws that concerned sovereign Indian nations.

Under Chief Justice John Marshall, the Supreme Court had already declared that the Cherokee and other Native American peoples, while lacking the powers of foreign nations, did enjoy a special status within America. Now the court confirmed that they were "distinct, independent political communities"—in fact, "nations"—and that sole responsibility for relations with them rested with the federal government, not those of the states.

> America, separated from Europe by a wide ocean, was inhabited by a distinct people, divided into separate nations, independent of each other and of the rest of the world, having institutions of their own, and governing themselves by their own laws. It is difficult to comprehend the proposition, that the inhabitants of either quarter of the globe could have rightful original claims of dominion over the inhabitants of the other … which annulled the pre-existing rights of its ancient possessors.

The State of Georgia, therefore, had no power to restrict entry into Cherokee territory.

> The Cherokee Nation, then, is a distinct community, occupying its own territory, with boundaries accurately described, in which the laws of Georgia can have no force, and which the citizens of Georgia have no right to enter but with the assent of the Cherokees themselves or in conformity with treaties, and with the acts of congress. The whole intercourse between the United States and this nation is, by our Constitution and laws, vested in the government of the United States.

Having rendered its judgment, however, the Supreme Court lacked the power to do anything about it.

**Figure 5.7** John Marshall, chief justice of the Supreme Court and author of the judgment in support of the Cherokee. Why was Marshall's judgment never enforced?

Determined to remove the Cherokee and seize their lands, authorities in Georgia chose to ignore the ruling; President Jackson refused to intervene. "Marshall has made his opinion," he reputedly declared, "now let him enforce it."

While these legal challenges ultimately failed to prevent the removal of the Cherokee from their traditional territory, the ruling in *Worcester v. Georgia* was a landmark in the relationship between Native Americans and the United States. It affirmed that Native American tribes were nations that enjoyed considerable legal autonomy, or independence, and that sole responsibility for their treatment rested with the federal government of the United States.

## Think It Through

1. In what ways did *Worcester v. Georgia* shape relations between the United States and Native American groups?
2. Why did the Supreme Court argue that the Cherokee enjoyed rights as a "nation"?

## King Andrew

The economic consequences of the Bank War, his harsh treatment of Native Americans, and his dictatorial methods of dealing with Congress made President Jackson many enemies. Taking their cue from the English critics of King George III in the late 18th century, the anti-Jackson groups formed a new political party: the Whigs. Pursuing the analogy to George III, the Whigs openly attacked Jackson as "King Andrew," a tyrant who trampled on the Constitution with his excessive use of the presidential veto to thwart Congress. While the Democrats continued to draw their traditional support from small farmers and from the South and West, the Whigs now attracted former Federalists, social reformers, and merchants from the North and Northwest.

## Van Buren and the Panic of 1837

Throughout his administration Andrew Jackson relied on his close political adviser and, from 1833, vice-president, Martin Van Buren of New York. (Van Buren was known as "Old Kinderhoek"—abbreviated to "OK"—the source of this colloquial phrase). Van Buren succeeded Jackson as president in 1837, the same year that the financial crisis resulting from the Bank War precipitated an economic collapse known as the Panic of 1837. Banks failed, businesses closed, and unemployment rose.

In cities such as New York more than a third of workers were without jobs and mobs rioted in protest. These economic problems lasted for almost six years. Van Buren could do little as misery spread, and his opponents ridiculed him as "Van Ruin." Given these difficulties, it is not surprising that the election of 1840 witnessed the defeat of Jackson's Democratic Party and the triumph of the Whigs, led by another military hero, William Harrison. Harrison died after only a month in office, allowing his vice-president, John Tyler—a defector from Jackson's Democrats—to enter the White House.

**Figure 5.8** A political cartoon from 1832 satirizing Andrew Jackson's belief in the need for a strong presidency to govern the United States. Why would it be considered an insult to refer to the president as "King"?

## 49th PARALLEL

# The *Caroline* Incident

Relations between the US and British North America seriously deteriorated during Martin Van Buren's presidency. On the night of December 29, 1837 the skies above Niagara Falls were illuminated by an American steamship, the *Caroline*, ablaze as it drifted downstream before plunging over the falls. Earlier that evening, a party of British sailors had boarded the vessel while it was docked on the American shore. After killing the night watchman, the raiders set fire to the *Caroline* and then cut her loose from her moorings. What provoked this attack?

Following his failed rebellion against the colonial government in Upper Canada (now Ontario) in December 1837, William Lyon Mackenzie fled with his supporters to the border with the United States. They established a base on Navy Island in the Niagara River and made plans to invade Upper Canada. Keen to promote republican values in the remaining British colonies, sympathizers in the United States used the steamship *Caroline* to ferry supplies to Navy Island and keep the base supplied. As the British had intended, the loss of the *Caroline* was a serious setback for Mackenzie: it soon forced him to abandon Navy Island and his plans for a future invasion.

The attack on the *Caroline* had immediate and grave repercussions. Relations between Britain and the United States reached their lowest ebb since the end of the War of 1812. All along the border, outraged Americans organized themselves into so-called patriot organizations, such as the Hunters' Lodges and the Patriot Army of the Northwest. They drilled and carried out raids against Upper Canada, pledging to "remember the *Caroline*" and demanding restitution for the unprovoked attack. For three years regular attacks occurred across the Niagara River and the Detroit River, and at Pelee Island in Lake Erie. The American government eventually moved to restrain the activities of the patriot organizations in order to preserve American neutrality. Although war was narrowly averted, the *Caroline* incident and the patriot raids demonstrated how fragile the peace was along the border more than 25 years after the Treaty of Ghent had ended the War of 1812.

**Figure 5.9** The *Caroline* going over Niagara Falls. Why did the attack on the *Caroline* result in armed confrontations between Americans and Canadians?

In March 2003 the *Caroline* incident re-emerged in a very different context. The British government had defended its sinking of the *Caroline* as a "pre-emptive act" designed to thwart Mackenzie's efforts to launch fresh attacks against Upper Canada. The British argued that their actions in December 1837 were justified under international law as a form of self-defence. When the United States declared war against Iraq in 2003—despite the fact that Iraq had not attacked the US or its allies—the American government argued that the war was justified as a pre-emptive strike to prevent future attacks. US government lawyers specifically cited the precedent of the *Caroline* to justify their country's right to act against such threats in advance.

## Think It Through

1. What impact did the *Caroline* incident have on relations between Britain and the United States?
2. The British government defended the sinking of the *Caroline* as a necessary act to prevent greater instability and destruction. Is the principle of pre-emptive action justified, in your view? Explain your position.

## CHECK YOUR UNDERSTANDING

1. In what ways did the election of 1828 demonstrate the new democratic spirit of American politics?
2. How did Andrew Jackson redefine the powers of the president?
3. How did the nullification crisis reveal the divisions that existed in American society?
4. List the causes of the Trail of Tears.
5. What factors led to the establishment of the Whig Party?

# WESTWARD EXPANSION

The spread of democracy in America during the early 19th century was related in part to the experience of the frontier. As the population pushed westward, traditional politics and society fragmented. Americans had long been conscious that one of the main forces shaping their society was this constant expansion. Thomas Jefferson had argued that it could lead eventually to possession of the entire continent, and later politicians and writers actively promoted this idea.

It became an article of American faith that the United States had a "manifest destiny" to occupy North America. As a result, territorial conflicts arose with Mexico in the South and with Britain in the West. In Texas and California American settlement led eventually to **annexation** by the United States. Throughout the course of this expansion, belief in the need to spread democracy and American civilization remained a powerful motivator for Americans and their leaders. One of the first clear applications of the idea of manifest destiny was in Texas.

**SOUND BITE**

"[It is] our manifest destiny to overspread the continent allotted by Providence for the free development of our yearly multiplying millions."

—Democratic journalist John O'Sullivan in 1845

**Figure 5.10** This painting by the American artist John Gast is called *American Progress*. Notice the Native Americans on the left. What does the image suggest about the fate of Native Americans under the policy of manifest destiny?

## Texas and Mexico

Mexico achieved independence from Spain in 1821. At the time, Mexico's Texas territory was home to a small Spanish population, known as Tejanos, and Native Americans, chiefly the Comanches. In order to populate Texas and control Comanche raids, the Mexican government invited American settlers into the province.

The American land agents Moses Austin and his son Stephen organized the first settlements. Despite now living in Mexico, the Austins and other groups of Americans who followed enjoyed considerable autonomy. Their chief business was cotton, cultivated with the aid of slaves brought from the United States. The number of Americans continued to grow as time passed, and by 1830 Americans outnumbered the Tejanos. Unlike the first settlers—some of whom had married into Tejano society—these new arrivals had scant respect for the Mexicans and no intention of living under their authority or laws. For many, hostility was sharpened by racism: the Mexicans were regarded as inferior.

### The Lone Star Republic

When the Mexican government tried to tighten control over its Texas territory in the early 1830s, many Americans living there grew alarmed and decided to escape from Mexican control. Some feared that the recent abolition of slavery in Mexico would be extended to Texas. When negotiations between the United States and Mexico over annexation collapsed and local attempts at mediation by the Austins proved fruitless, a revolt broke out in 1835.

A small army of American volunteers quickly captured the main Texas town of San Antonio. In response, Mexican President General Santa Anna led an army north into Texas. On March 6, 1836 Santa Anna captured the San Antonio stronghold of the Alamo, where a small group of Texans had refused to surrender. Despite the deaths of the 187 defenders—including frontier heroes Jim Bowie and Davy Crockett—the Texans transformed defeat at San Antonio into a symbol of their struggle for "freedom." "Remember the Alamo!" became their battle cry.

**WEB LINKS**

Explore the story of the Alamo by visiting www.emp.ca/ah.

**Figure 5.11** The Alamo in San Antonio, Texas has become a symbol of heroic resistance against overwhelming odds.

Santa Anna's success proved short lived. A force of Texans commanded by Sam Houston soon surprised and defeated the Mexican army beside the San Jacinto River. The Texans captured Santa Anna and forced him to sign a treaty granting Texas its independence from Mexico.

When the new provisional government of Texas asked to be admitted to the United States, the federal government in Washington rejected the idea. President Jackson was sympathetic, but many in Congress, including John Quincy Adams, feared upsetting the delicate balance between slave and non-slave states (the Texans used slaves on their cotton plantations). Instead, in 1837 the independent Republic of Texas—the "Lone Star Republic"—came into being, with Sam Houston as its first president.

The annexation of Texas remained a sensitive political issue, and in 1844 it became the focus of the presidential election. The Whigs were divided, first arguing for annexation and then repudiating their plans in response to protests from anti-slavery groups. The Democrats and their candidate, James Polk of Tennessee, campaigned for manifest destiny, which meant welcoming Texas into the United States. After Polk won a narrow victory, Texas became the 28th state in 1845.

## The Mexican-American War

US relations with Mexico deteriorated following the annexation of Texas. President Polk responded by sending American troops to the disputed Mexican border with Texas and the US navy to the Pacific coast of California, where a number of American settlers and armed agents staged a revolt against the Mexican authorities. The Mexican government flatly rejected Polk's offer to purchase these disputed territories, prompting the president to order troops into disputed territory along the Rio Grande River (now Texas and New Mexico). In April 1846 Polk used a minor incident between American and Mexican soldiers as a pretext to ask Congress for a declaration of war. Ignoring his own manoeuvring, Polk alleged falsely that war "exists by the act of Mexico herself."

The Mexican-American war that began in May 1846 was controversial. Some believed that Polk had misled Congress by misrepresenting Mexico's responsibility and hiding his own government' s involvement. Others saw the conflict as an attempt to expand Southern slave territory, further entrenching slavery in America. Protesting the president's prominent role in promoting and prosecuting the war, Polk's Whig opponents denounced the conflict as "Mr. Polk's War." The philosopher Henry David Thoreau was so disillusioned with the war that he went to prison briefly rather than pay taxes to support it. He also wrote the powerful essay "Civil Disobedience," which

**SOUND BITE**

"When a sixth of the population of a nation which has undertaken to be the refuge of liberty are slaves, and a whole country [Mexico] is unjustly overrun and conquered by a foreign army, and subjected to military law, I think that it is not too soon for honest men to rebel and revolutionize. What makes this duty the more urgent is the fact that the country so overrun is not our own, but ours is the invading army."

—Henry David Thoreau, "Civil Disobedience" (1849)

would later motivate Gandhi and Martin Luther King in their non-violent struggles for human rights.

Led by generals Zachary Taylor and Winfield Scott and directed by Polk, the American military campaign enjoyed early success, easily capturing most of northern Mexico (now California, Arizona, and New Mexico). When these losses did not encourage Mexico to sue for peace, American forces moved south toward Mexico City. Here they faced fierce opposition, and casualties quickly mounted on both sides.

**Figure 5.12** Newspapers informed ordinary Americans about the Mexican-American War, fostering patriotism and stimulating public discussion and criticism of American policy.

Ferocious fighting marked the campaign to capture Mexico City, with the Americans killing hundreds of Mexican civilians in retaliation for American losses; General Scott admitted that his troops had "committed atrocities to make Heaven weep." The fighting finally ended in September 1847 with the capture of Mexico City by Scott's army, and in February 1848 the Treaty of Guadalupe Hidalgo concluded the war. In exchange for a payment of $15 million (about $420 million today), Mexico ceded its provinces of California and New Mexico (which included Arizona, Utah, and Nevada) to the United States. While some, including Polk, pushed to seize all of Mexico, the mounting cost of the war for the US—13,000 casualties and $97 million (about $2.7 billion today)—and continued opposition from the Whigs made this impossible.

The Mexican-American War had a considerable impact on the United States. The country acquired substantial territory in the Southwest, promoting the cause of manifest destiny. The divisive issue of extending slavery into new territories emerged again. Questions were raised about the powers of the president in waging war. Finally, a growing popular press stirred up patriotic feelings by carrying regular reports of the exploits of Taylor, Scott, and their troops.

## Moving West

The fulfillment of manifest destiny required expanded transportation networks to permit settlers to reach the new territories in the West and to ship the products of their farms to markets in the East. It also demanded political stability and protection against foreign interference within the new territories.

### Early Railroads

The transportation revolution that made rapid westward expansion possible began along a 21-kilometre track outside Baltimore in 1830. The Baltimore and Ohio (B & O) Railroad was experimenting with new technology: a steam locomotive nicknamed Tom Thumb. Returning from its first run on August 28,

**Figure 5.13** The Tom Thumb locomotive may have lost the battle, but the railroads won the war. From 21 kilometres of track in 1830, the network would expand to more than 48,000 kilometres within 30 years. By 1850 the railroad network stretched as far as Chicago and Cincinnati, and would soon reach beyond the Mississippi.

Tom Thumb encountered a horse-drawn carriage; the two drivers agreed to a race in order to demonstrate which technology was more powerful and reliable. Although the advantage belonged initially to the horse (with its faster acceleration), it was not long before the steam locomotive caught up to and passed the horse and carriage. Then, just as the horse's driver was ready to concede defeat, a fan belt slipped and Tom Thumb rapidly lost traction. The horse surged ahead and held the lead until the end.

Despite this initial setback, the Tom Thumb locomotive had demonstrated the superior power of steam, and the future of railroads was assured. The American railroad system grew dramatically even though there would be other technological challenges, such as the need for heavier iron rails; strong ties; and standard gauges, or track widths.

## The Overland Trails

Following in the footsteps of early explorers and fur traders like the "Pathfinder" John Charles Frémont, a steady stream of settlers began moving westward in the 1840s. Before the extension of the railroad network across the continent in the 1860s, they went by way of the Overland Trails, which ran for more than 3,000 kilometres from Missouri across the Rockies to the Pacific. While some settlers sought adventure, others simply wanted a better life in the West—especially after losing money in the Panic of 1837.

Their journeys, which could last six months or more, were difficult and even dangerous. Harsh weather, disease, and accidents took their toll on the pioneers, as did occasional attacks by Native Americans who felt threatened by the arrival of these newcomers. Yet by 1860 almost 300,000 men, women, and children had travelled in the wagon trains along the Platte River and then through the Rocky Mountain passes, following the Overland Trails to Oregon and California.

## Pioneer Women

Thanks to the educational reforms mentioned later in this chapter, many of the pioneers on the Overland Trails came from the newly literate middle-class of American society. Women in particular were better educated than in the past, and they participated enthusiastically in what was becoming a national obsession by keeping a diary or journal of their experiences. Scholars estimate that about one in every 200 pioneers in the 1840s and 1850s set down a written record of their time on the Trails, which means that historians today have a wealth of primary sources dealing with the pioneer experience from this period in American history.

What did pioneer women write about in their diaries? Often, they reflected on the work they did every day—work that was still assigned according to very traditional ideas about a woman's role in society. As a pioneer named Helen Carpenter noted:

> In respect to women's work, the days are all the same, except when we stop … then there is washing to be done and light bread to make and all kinds of odd jobs. Some women have very little help about the camp, being obliged to get the wood and water … make camp fires, unpack at night and pack up in the morning—and if they are Missourians they have milking to do if they are fortunate enough to have cows. I am lucky in having a Yankee husband and so am well waited on.

Besides cooking and packing up, the women in a wagon train also cleaned and mended clothes, looked after the children, and nursed the sick. Because there were frequent epidemics of **cholera** and smallpox, and periods when food and water were in short supply, this could be a full-time job in itself.

At this time the husband was regarded as the head of the family. He held sole title to the family farm and house, and if he decided to sell the farm and emigrate to Oregon, his wife had to follow whether she wanted to or not. "I am going with him," wrote one such woman, "as there is no other alternative." Often, however, women were just as enthusiastic about heading west as their husbands. "I was possessed with a spirit of adventure," noted Miriam Thompson Tuller, "and a desire to see what was new and strange." It was partly this "spirit of adventure" that set hundreds of thousands of pioneers on the Overland Trails and helped settle the American West.

**SOUND BITE**

"The weary journey last night, the mooing of the cattle for water, their exhausted condition … the stopping of the train to unyoke the poor dying brute, to let him follow at will or stop by the wayside and die, and the weary, weary tramp of men and beasts, worn out with heat and famished for water, will never be erased from my memory."

—Excerpt from Sallie Hester's diary entry on crossing the Nevada desert to California

## Oregon

During the early 19th century the Pacific coast north of California was home to Native Americans as well as small groups of European and American sailors, fur traders, and missionaries. Although both Britain and the United States claimed the Oregon territory, a treaty between the two countries called the Convention of 1818 stipulated that they would share control of the territory for at least ten years. The Hudson

Bay Company, for example, established a major fur-trading post, Fort Vancouver, near the mouth of the Columbia River.

In the 1840s American settlers began to arrive in Oregon via the Overland Trails, attracted by the prospect of free land. By 1844 more than 5,000 American farmers had settled there. Their presence led to some tensions between the United States and Britain, who had previously shared jurisdiction amicably.

During his presidential campaign in 1844 James Polk exacerbated these tensions by adopting the election slogan "Fifty-four Forty or Fight!" (demanding the entire Pacific Northwest for the United States, as far north as Alaska, at latitude 54° 40'). Once elected, President Polk abandoned this demand in favour of a negotiated settlement with Britain that extended the border between the United States and Canada along the 49th parallel all the way to the Pacific Ocean.

## California

South of Oregon lay the Mexican territory of California. In the early 1840s California was populated by Native Americans, several thousand Spanish-speaking *Californios* living at missions along the coast, and a small number of American traders. Seeking to follow the example of Texas, a group of Americans led by John Frémont seized control of the colony in 1846 during the so-called Bear Flag Revolt. Under the Treaty of Guadalupe Hidalgo, which concluded the Mexican-American War, Mexico recognized American possession of California in 1848.

**Figure 5.14** Carefully examine this map of the Overland Trails and the points where they ended. Why would British officials be concerned about the influx of American settlers the Trail brought into the Oregon territory?

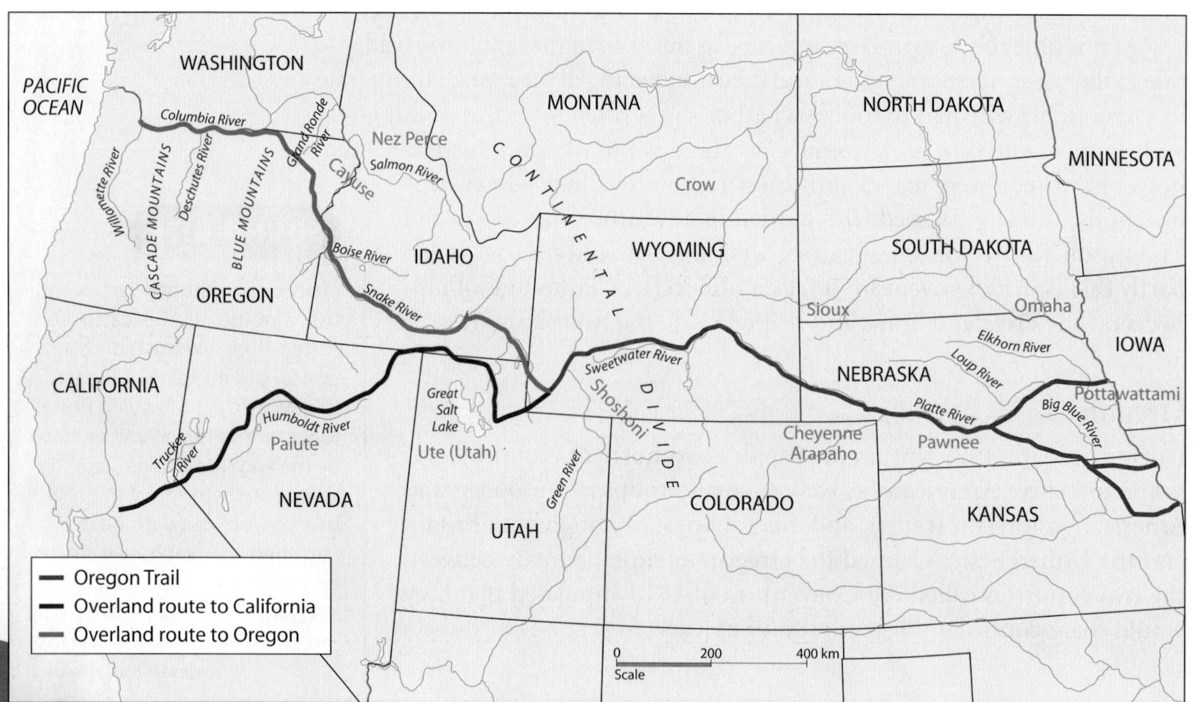

That same year, the chance discovery of gold in a stream at Sutter's Mill near present-day Sacramento transformed California from a thinly populated territory into a destination for thousands of people seeking to get rich quick. Word of the find spread like wildfire through the territory, and by late 1848 the news had reached the east coast.

The following year, thousands of **forty-niners** poured into California from large Eastern cities and as far away as Europe. The population of San Francisco—the arrival point for most of the miners who came by ship—grew from barely 1,000 in 1848 to an estimated 35,000 two years later. By 1852 California was home to more than 100,000 people—a figure ten times greater than before the discovery of gold.

Ordinary life during the gold rush was hard. Very few of the men who came to seek their fortune struck it rich in the streams of California. Instead, most became labourers for larger mines. Many of those who enjoyed the most success in California did so not by panning for gold but by selling supplies to miners. The German immigrant Levi Strauss grew wealthy through the sale of his tough denim work trousers.

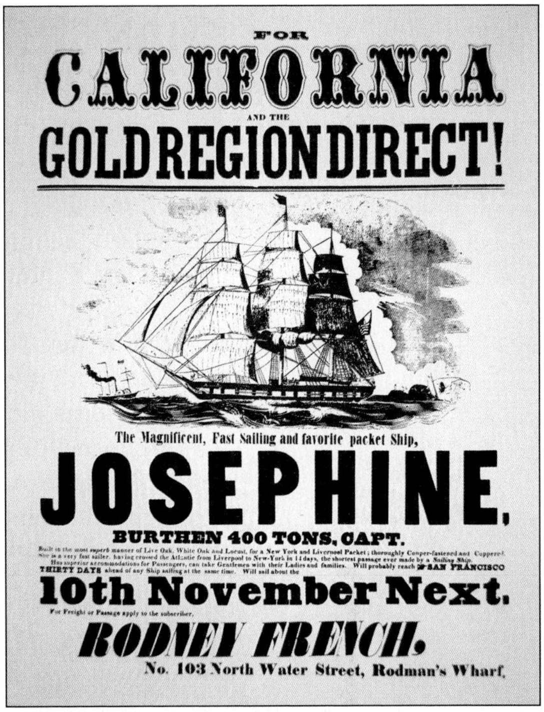

Many women joined the miners, operating boarding houses or working as prostitutes. Temporary mining camps seemed to spring up overnight and were just as quickly abandoned. The transient nature of these settlements meant that there was little social stability or sense of community, and the arrival of many Chinese and Mexican miners sparked considerable racism. As a result, violence was common in the camps, creating the image of the "Wild West" that would become a lasting part of the American identity.

**Figure 5.15** A poster advertising quick passage to the California gold fields in 1849. Trace the route a ship would have taken from New York to Sacramento at this time.

## CHECK YOUR UNDERSTANDING

1. Identify three ways in which the idea of manifest destiny influenced American society during the 1830s and 1840s.
2. Describe the causes of the revolt in Texas.
3. Explain why the Mexican-American War was so controversial.
4. Describe the role of the Overland Trails in the settlement of the West.
5. How did the discovery of gold transform California and its society?

# CHANGING CULTURE AND IDENTITY IN AMERICA

The early decades of the 19th century were a time of ferment in American society. In part, these changes reflected the influence of the new democratic politics and the impact of the frontier on American life. Both these trends emphasized the importance of **individualism**, the belief that people should live in a way that makes them independent and self-reliant.

A range of new religious groups appeared and new philosophical ideas emerged. Writers reflected the new American identity in their books. Similar to the democratic emphasis on the "common man" and rejection of elitism, these new ideas and beliefs stressed the importance of each ordinary individual's experience of nature and of the divine. Out of these ideas and influences grew a powerful commitment to a range of exciting social reforms, from promoting the rights of women and urban workers to improving public education and the plight of prisoners.

## Religious Revival

In religion, individualism played a key role in the Second Great Awakening, a religious revival that swept the American frontier over the first half of the 19th century. Its religious enthusiasm recalled the original Great Awakening that had transformed colonial society during the early 18th century (see Chapter 2). At the same time, its emphasis on basic religious education and simple preaching was designed to address the spiritual needs of the common man. The response to this religious enthusiasm was dramatic: church attendance soared, and people placed a renewed emphasis on public morality and hard work as the outward symbols of personal piety.

At many of the revival meetings, preachers stressed the need for each individual to repent, or ask forgiveness for his or her sins, and to develop a close and personal relationship with God. These revivals owed much of their success to the self-reliant nature of frontier life, where organized social structures and traditional churches had limited influence. The message of individual responsibility and personal faith made sense to many farmers and settlers, and by the mid-1820s sizable, enthusiastic crowds were attending the revival meetings.

Observers were struck by the range of individuals and families—rich and poor alike—who travelled to these meetings, with "coaches, chaises, wagons, carts, people on horseback, and multitudes traveling from a distance on foot." Many came seeking a personal religious experience where "the hardest hearts are melted into tenderness; the driest eyes overflow with tears, and the loftiest spirits bow down." Revival meetings could last for a week or more, and combined an opportunity to socialize with an intense religious experience.

### Shakers and Mormons

Some American reformers of the early 19th century were motivated by powerful religious visions of a new society—an American **utopia**, or ideal society.

Rapid social change and frontier expansion spawned groups such as the Millerites, who fervently prepared for the Second Coming of Christ, which they believed would occur on October 22, 1843. When it did not, the group eventually evolved into the Seventh-day Adventist Church.

Another utopian group, the Shakers, was founded by Ann Lee. Lee's followers regarded her as a female incarnation of God, balancing the male Jesus. The Shakers challenged accepted social norms by rejecting the traditional notion of family. All members of the Shaker community were considered equal and lived in celibacy, or without having sexual relations. They made their ideals visible in their buildings and crafts, which were marked above all by simplicity and usefulness. Music, and especially dance, played a crucial role in their worship. By the 1830s there were several dozen Shaker communities from Maine to Florida, with more than 8,000 members. The practice of celibacy, however, led to the slow but steady decline of this group.

Perhaps the best-known—and certainly the most successful—result of this religious ferment was the emergence of the Church of Jesus Christ of Latter-day Saints (or Mormon Church), whose members are known as **Mormons**. Founded by Joseph Smith in upstate New York in 1830, the Mormons formed a well-organized and close-knit community that was largely isolated from the wider society. After several moves, the Mormons settled in Nauvoo, Illinois. There, their practice of **polygamy**—by which a man was allowed to have more than one wife—led to violent disputes with their new neighbours that resulted in the murder of Smith.

To escape further persecution, Smith's successor, Brigham Young, led the Mormons westward in 1847 to the shores of the Great Salt Lake in Utah. Here

**Figure 5.16** Shakers dancing in their community hall in Lebanon, New York. One contemporary witness described the Shaker religious service as consisting of "dancing, singing, leaping, clapping their hands [and] fallling on their knees."

**Figure 5.17** A Mormon wagon train travelling through Echo Canyon on the way to the future site of Salt Lake City, Utah. What difficulties and dangers would the Mormons have faced on their journey?

they founded an isolated community on the frontier where they could practise their faith free from outside interference. Mormonism was in harmony with the idea of manifest destiny, as it was strongly tied to the idea of the frontier as a place where one could live in freedom and to a belief in divine providence toward America—the idea that God took a personal interest in the country's well-being.

## New Trends in Philosophy: Transcendentalism

In philosophy, individualism formed the basis of a popular movement called **Transcendentalism.** The New England poet Ralph Waldo Emerson gave the clearest explanation of this philosophy in his essay "Nature" (1836). Emerson believed that there was a spiritual reality beyond ordinary life and its troubles, and that people could best sense this reality by examining the wonders of the natural world, rather than through organized religion or society. Stressing the importance of each individual's personal discovery of transcendental, or higher, reality, Emerson wrote that all that mattered was "the integrity of your own mind."

In an attempt to live this transcendental life alone with nature, Emerson's friend Henry David Thoreau spent two years in a cabin

**Figure 5.18** The American poet and philosopher Ralph Waldo Emerson. In "Nature," Emerson summed up his Transcendental philosophy in his statement, "Every natural fact is a symbol of some spiritual fact." Explain in your own words what Emerson might have meant by this.

at Walden Pond, outside Concord, Massachusetts. Thoreau's radical rejection of the materialism of 19th-century America was exceptional, and represented a notable challenge to social and political norms. In a famous phrase, Thoreau described how most Americans—caught up in the struggle for survival or the pursuit of wealth—"lead lives of quiet desperation." Following the ideas of Emerson and Thoreau, Transcendentalists founded a number of communities, such as Fruitlands, in Massachusetts. These communities did not usually last, because they focused on philosophy at the expense of industry and thus ran out of money.

**SOUND BITE**

"I went to the woods because I wished to live deliberately, to front only the essential facts of life, and see if I could not learn what it had to teach, and not, when I came to die, discover that I had not lived."

—Henry David Thoreau, *Walden* (1854)

Transcendentalism and democratic individualism were also reflected in literary works such as Herman Melville's *Moby-Dick* (1851), a philosophical novel chronicling the pursuit of a white whale by the extraordinary Captain Ahab. The novel also offers lavish praise of Andrew Jackson, whom Melville believed had been chosen by the "great democratic God" as one of the "selectest champions from the kingly commons."

While Melville praised democracy and the individual, other writers criticized the Transcendental philosophy. Nathaniel Hawthorne, in pessimistic works such as *The Scarlet Letter* (1850), examined the Puritan legacy by focusing on the trials and suffering of people struggling against the forces of evil they discovered in their own souls.

## Reforming Society

The early 19th century was an age of optimism. The spread of religious ideas, the philosophy of Transcendentalism (with its emphasis on personal integrity), and democratic political movements all contributed to a conviction that the evils of society must be confronted and eliminated. In *Democracy in America*, Tocqueville declared that during the 1830s Americans fervently believed that "man is endowed with an indefinite faculty for improvement." This belief in the need for improvement sparked what the poet Emerson called "the demon of reform"—an optimistic desire to reshape American politics and society.

**Figure 5.19** Captain Ahab's mysterious obsession with the great white whale has become part of American folklore. What other 19th-century American novels can you identify?

# Culture Notes

## The Hudson River School

The American national identity that was emerging during the 1830s and 1840s was brilliantly reflected in the art of the time. Seeking to express this unique American character—one that differed sharply from the way Europeans viewed themselves—some painters began to look to wilderness landscapes for inspiration.

Thomas Cole was one of the first of these artists. He was attracted to the landscapes he discovered as he explored the Hudson River Valley in New York in 1825. His paintings of mysterious forests and mountains such as the Catskills and Adirondacks marked the birth of the first school of painting to originate in America: the Hudson River School. Cole produced a series of works depicting the wonders of nature, including the majesty of Niagara Falls.

By the 1840s the leadership of the school had passed from Cole to others, including Asher Durand and Fredric Edwin Church. Through his writing and art, Durand expressed the goals and objectives of the Hudson River School: to find artistic inspiration in American (not European) subjects and, like the Transcendentalists, to discover spiritual truth in the natural world. Durand summed up the goals of the school as follows: "The external appearance of this our dwelling-place, apart from its wondrous structure and functions that minister to our well-being, is fraught with lessons of high and holy meaning ... Go not abroad then in search of material for the exercise of your pencil, while the virgin charms of our native land have claims on your deepest affections." Durand paid tribute to the school's founder, Thomas Cole, in his 1849 painting *Kindred Spirits*, which showed Cole standing in the midst of an American forest scene.

The artists of the Hudson River School were clearly influenced by European romantic painters like John Constable and Joseph Mallord William Turner. At the same time, they deliberately set out to create a style that reflected the new democratic society emerging under Andrew Jackson. They were artists motivated above all by national pride, whose goal was to forge a national artistic identity. Critics responded to these ideas, one of them announcing: "Every American is bound to prove his love of country by admiring Cole."

**Figure 5.20** Thomas Cole's painting of Niagara Falls created a sensation when it was exhibited in 1829. Why would Cole choose Niagara Falls as a subject for his painting?

**Figure 5.21** In his painting *Kindred Spirits* Asher Durand showed the respect he had for Thomas Cole, both by including Cole in the painting and by imitating his artistic style.

In looking to the natural landscape to develop a national identity, the artists of the Hudson River School blazed a trail that Canada's Group of Seven would follow a century later. Although the Hudson River School fell out of favour in the United States by the later 19th century, the contributions of Cole, Durand, and others have not been forgotten. Indeed, their influence extends beyond the traditional art world. In 2005 the creators of a video game based on the popular Harry Potter books and films modelled their scenery on the art of Cole and Durand. With its dramatic landscapes and powerful contrasts of darkness and light, the art of the Hudson River School closely matched the themes of J.K. Rowling's novels.

### Think It Through

1. In what ways did the Hudson River School reflect the importance of the wilderness experience in America during the 1830s and 1840s?
2. How did artists like Cole and Durand contribute to the growth of the American national identity?

## Workers and Unions

Beginning in the 1830s traditional economic patterns of master, journeyman, and apprentice were disappearing. There were fewer independent craftsmen and more factory workers. Few journeymen could hope any longer to become masters in their trade.

The blend of economic discontent and the new spirit of popular democracy produced a growth in labour unions and working-class political parties. For example, the Workingmen's Party was founded in Philadelphia in 1827 to fight for a ten-hour workday, a public school system, and cheap land in the West. The party also criticized elite institutions like the Bank of the United States. Jackson's Democrats took up some of these causes and gained many working-class votes as a result.

The slow pace of economic and political change frustrated many journeyman workers. As a result, a wave of strikes swept through cities like New York during the mid-1830s, as skilled workers organized themselves to protect their interests. In New York, the General Trades Union (GTU) organized workers in a wide range of crafts and led more than 40 strikes. Hostile employers used the courts and police to stop these activities. The general unemployment and economic collapse that followed the Panic of 1837 doomed the GTU, making it impossible to push for higher wages or improved working conditions. Nevertheless, the 1830s represented the beginning of an organized labour movement in America that was dedicated to reforming living and working conditions.

These political changes reflected the dramatic growth in American cities during the first half of the 19th century. The populations of cities like Philadelphia, Baltimore, and Boston grew at a rate of at least 25 percent each decade. During the 1820s alone the population of New York City swelled by over 60 percent to more than 200,000, causing the city to emerge as the nation's largest. Two factors fuelled the growth of cities and urban society: the expansion of trade with the interior (via the Erie Canal and other routes) and the arrival of Irish and German immigrants (which began in the 1820s and accelerated in the 1830s and 1840s).

The arrival of immigrants changed the character of cities by establishing poor neighbourhoods marked by ethnic and class divisions. These new arrivals also stirred up much hostility when they did not immediately integrate into America. In Boston—an early centre for Irish settlement—one newspaper lamented in 1837 that "Our foreign population are too much in the habit of retaining their own national usages, of associating too exclusively with each other, and living in groups together." Immigration would continue to transform America throughout the 19th century and beyond.

**Figure 5.22** *New York from Brooklyn Heights,* drawn by William James Bennett in 1836, gives a good view of the busy harbour of New York City. On the basis of what you see in this illustration, identify at least one reason why New York became the largest city in the United States in the 1820s.

## Education

"In a republic, ignorance is a crime."

—American educator Horace Mann

For many reformers in the early 19th century, the key to transforming society was education. Two areas attracted particular attention: free elementary education and education for women. In Massachusetts, Horace Mann led the campaign for free public schooling, arguing that it would diminish poverty and promote economic prosperity. He fought for increased funding and instituted a number of educational reforms, including better training for teachers and a minimum six-month school year.

In 1836 William McGuffey published his *Eclectic Reader*, a new type of reading textbook that had several objectives. As well as developing literacy, its stories aimed to instill moral virtues and patriotism. Arguably the most-read book in America at the time, McGuffey's reader played a profound role in shaping social attitudes.

McGuffey was following in the footsteps of Noah Webster, who had laboured since the 1780s to gain recognition for a distinctly "American" language guided by what he called "republican principles" rather than the British elitism of "the King's English." Aiming for simplicity, Webster argued that spelling should be simplified (by changing "colour" and "labour" to "color" and "labor," for example). His publication of the *American Dictionary of the English Language* in 1828 represented the culmination of his efforts to infuse the English language with the same patriotic and democratic ideals that distinguished the United States.

The expansion of schooling required increased numbers of teachers, many of whom were young women. Even though female educators were paid a fraction of what male teachers were paid, women found that teaching represented one of the few avenues for employment open to them. A number of secondary schools were established, such as Mount Holyoke in Massachusetts, to train young women for their role as educators in schools and homes. As Catherine Beecher, founder of several schools for women, argued: "It is to mothers, and to teachers, that the world is to look for the character which is to be stamped on each succeeding generation, for it is to them that the great business of education is almost exclusively committed." Oberlin College in Ohio was the first co-educational college in the country and graduated its first female student in 1841.

While women made some strides in education during this period, schools remained shut to most African-Americans. In the South it was still illegal to educate blacks, and in the North only slightly more than 100 African-Americans had

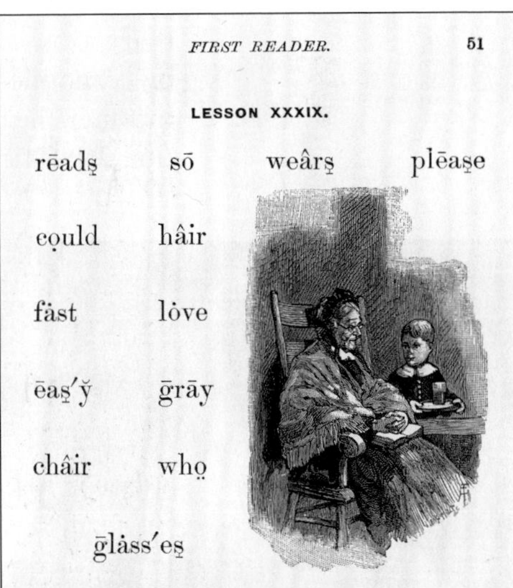
*FIRST READER.* 51

LESSON XXXIX.

rēads sō wêars plēase

could hâir

fȧst lȯve

ēas'y grāy

châir who

glȧss'es

See my dear, old grandma in her easy-chair! How gray her hair is! She wears glasses when she reads.

She is always kind, and takes such good care of me that I like to do what she tells me.

**Figure 5.23** McGuffey's reader was more than just an anthology, or collection of stories. What social purpose did it serve?

attended college by 1840. When Prudence Crandall began admitting blacks to her school in Connecticut, her white students went elsewhere, she was arrested, and the school building was vandalized. Crandall finally gave up in frustration, and it was not until after the Civil War that African-Americans as a group would experience any real gains in education.

## Social and Moral Reform

Women were at the forefront of a number of reform movements, including the **temperance movement**, which involved limiting the sale and consumption of alcohol. The American Temperance Union was founded in 1826 and within a decade its membership had swelled to more than 200,000. Temperance advocates, led by women and evangelical clergy, stressed the damaging effects of alcohol on the economy and family life, and sought to reinforce the middle-class virtues of sobriety and thrift.

Drinking was a common leisure activity in early 19th-century America—particularly for the working classes, who resented middle-class efforts to control their lives. At most social gatherings, from card games to political rallies, hard liquor like whiskey or rum was available in abundance. Annual liquor consumption rates—at more than 26 litres per capita in 1830—were more than double today's average.

Campaigners distributed lurid tracts depicting the evils of "demon drink." They adopted the techniques of religious revivalists, holding large public meetings and delivering powerful appeals to abandon alcohol. Working-class organizations also attacked drunkenness, arguing that sobriety offered labourers the best hope for escaping poverty. For their part, factory owners argued that excessive drinking led to more accidents and lower productivity. Assisted by economic shocks such as the Panic of 1837 (which decreased disposable income), the temperance campaigns succeeded in reducing alcohol consumption dramatically during the 1830s and 1840s, to a level similar to today.

Still other reformers focused on the state of American asylums and prisons. In the early 19th century there was often little or no distinction made between those who suffered from mental illness and those who had committed crimes. The mentally ill were regularly imprisoned—sometimes for life—rather than treated in hospitals or asylums. The leader of the crusade to improve society's treatment of the mentally ill was the evangelist Dorothea Dix of Massachusetts. During the 1840s Dix advocated for public facilities to care for these patients, denouncing the miserable conditions in which they often lived: "chained, naked, beaten with rods, and lashed into obedience."

**Figure 5.24** Dorothea Dix campaigned tirelessly for prison reform and better treatment of the mentally ill. Why were such reforms necessary at this time in America?

Similar concerns over prison conditions prompted reformers to demand prisons designed to reform criminals rather than merely punish them. These new penitentiaries attracted attention even from Europe, as when the young Frenchman Alexis de Tocqueville was sent to study American prison reforms.

## Women's Rights

The 1830s and 1840s in America are often referred to as the "age of the common man" for the democratic revolution that gave white men of all classes the right to vote and take a more active role in politics. As you have seen, the spread of popular democracy had begun to reshape American politics. Yet there were limits.

Despite their commitment to reforming society, for example, women found themselves largely excluded from the public realm. Still, there were a few notable exceptions. Sarah and Angelina Grimké became active anti-slavery campaigners, and Angelina won a measure of fame as the first woman to address the Massachusetts state legislature.

While many women worked behind the scenes for social reform causes, a few—like Lucretia Mott and Elizabeth Cady Stanton—pushed for a greater political voice for women. In 1848 a remarkable conference took place at Seneca Falls in upstate New York. The Women's Rights Convention marked the beginning of the long campaign for political, legal, and social equality for American women.

To discover more about the lives and accomplishments of Elizabeth Cady Stanton and Susan B. Anthony, visit www.emp.ca/ah.

## A Troubling Question

Even as they pushed for women's rights, temperance, or improvements to education or prisons, many reformers in the early 19th century believed there existed no greater moral offence in the United States than slavery. While some white American reformers remained blind to the plight of slaves, others advocated for the eradication of slavery in America on the grounds that slavery was an affront to the American ideal of liberty. Slavery had been a potent political issue for decades, but as Americans pushed westward into new territories a troubling question kept recurring: what was the future of slavery in the United States? Trying to resolve this question would divide the nation and ignite its greatest crisis.

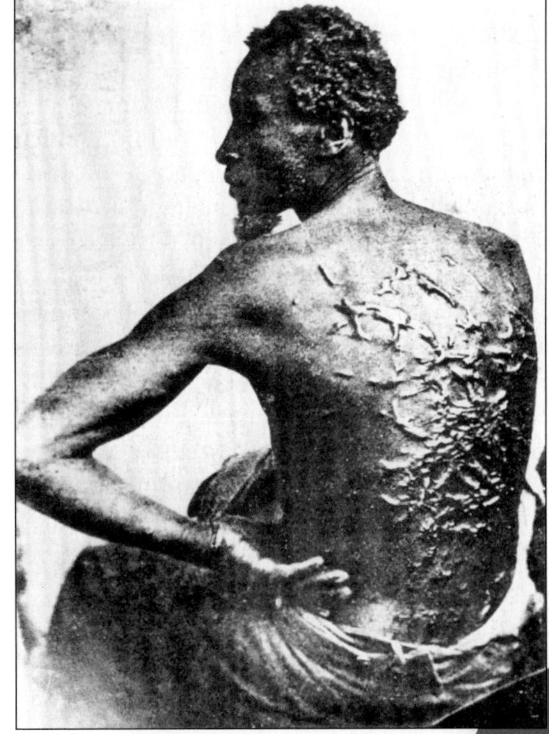

**Figure 5.25** A former slave with scars on his back from repeated beatings. The injustices of slavery on the one hand, and its economic importance to the South on the other, would divide the US for many years and lead eventually to the Civil War.

# WE THE PEOPLE

## Elizabeth Cady Stanton

1815–1902

"We hold these truths to be self-evident, that all men and women are created equal." These stirring words formed the opening of the Declaration of Sentiments, drawn up by the women's rights campaigners who met in Seneca Falls, New York in the summer of 1848. They intended this echo of the Declaration of Independence to suggest that the condition of women in mid-19th-century America—that is, their lack of most property and political rights (including the vote), and their lack of access to higher education—was as great an offence as Britain's abuse of the American colonies. They advocated for the same kind of radical response that the colonies had demanded, short of physical violence.

The convention was organized by a handful of committed women, one of the most radical of whom was Elizabeth Cady Stanton, a native of Boston. Coming from a family long associated with reform causes, Stanton married a noted abolitionist and was soon active in a number of reform campaigns, including those in support of temperance and abolition.

Moving from the comforts of Boston society to rural upstate New York opened Stanton's eyes to the daily hardships faced by the majority of women, and made her determined to fight to improve women's lives. Joining forces with the Quaker activist Lucretia Mott—who was already well known for her campaigns to improve prison conditions and the miserable treatment of Native Americans—Stanton mobilized support for the convention at Seneca Falls. The meeting passed a variety of resolutions demanding greater rights for women. Stanton was particularly adamant in arguing for female **suffrage**, or the right to vote, despite the fact that many women's rights campaigners thought this demand went too far.

**Figure 5.26** Elizabeth Cady Stanton. "Because man and woman are the complement of one another," wrote Stanton, "we need woman's thought in national affairs to make a safe and stable government."

In 1851 Stanton met the activist Susan B. Anthony, and over the following decades the women fought together to have the vote extended to women. Most American men (and many women) greeted this idea with derision, and even Stanton's friend and colleague Lucretia Mott had warned Stanton that her suffrage campaign would "make us look ridiculous." Undeterred, Stanton and Anthony continued their crusade, although success proved painfully slow. The vote was first granted to women in Wyoming in 1869, but it was not until 1920 that the passage of the 19th Amendment guaranteed all American women the right to vote.

Stanton became more radical as she grew older. In addition to her campaign for female suffrage, during the 1870s and 1880s Stanton threw her energy into the fight to allow women greater access to divorce and even advocated providing basic information on birth-control methods. She believed that Christianity prevented women from securing their rights, and as an outspoken campaigner did not hesitate to denounce it, declaring: "The Bible and the Church have been the greatest stumbling blocks in the way of women's emancipation." Such radical positions alienated many of her colleagues, but Stanton was undaunted.

Stanton's commitment to a variety of reforms was typical of the mid-19th century, when reform-minded women embraced a number of related causes—most notably the abolition of slavery and an improved status for women. Elizabeth Cady Stanton was convinced that "some active measures should be taken to remedy the wrongs of society in general, and of women in particular." From Seneca Falls until her death, Stanton devoted her energy to realizing the basic principle of the Declaration of Sentiments—"that all men and women are created equal."

### Think It Through

1. Why did the participants in the Women's Rights Convention at Seneca Falls draft a declaration modelled on the Declaration of Independence?
2. What does Elizabeth Cady Stanton's career demonstrate about the links between the campaign for women's rights and other causes, such as the abolition of slavery?
3. In what ways was Elizabeth Cady Stanton typical of female reformers of the mid-19th century?

## CHECK YOUR UNDERSTANDING

1. Describe the changes in American religious life during the early 19th century.
2. In what ways did the philosophy of Transcendentalism contribute to the growth of individualism in America?
3. What factors led to the emergence of a labour movement during the 1830s?
4. How did McGuffey's textbook help shape American society?
5. Describe the contribution of women to social reform movements.

# THE HISTORIAN'S CRAFT

## Researching History on the Internet

We usually think of historians examining faded documents and fragile artifacts from the past, but they—and you—can use the modern technology of the Internet to discover more about American history. With the click of a mouse, you can access pictures, videos, music, and texts.

Historical research always presents challenges. How do we search through all of the data for the key points? How will we know if a source we have found is accurate (true and free of error) or reliable (reflecting sound research and supported conclusions)? Such questions apply to any historical source, be it print, illustration, or virtual. Yet the sheer volume of material accessible on the Internet presents a special challenge. Moreover, the open accessibility of the Internet poses a problem of its own, since anyone can prepare web pages to reflect their interests or opinions. As with any historical source, you need a set of critical tools to use the Internet effectively.

### Critical Thinking Tools

Ask the following questions to ensure that the Internet sources you use are accurate and reliable:

- Are the authors of the website identified? What qualifications do they have?
- Do the authors have a particular bias?
- Was the site created by a university, archive, or museum?
- Is the information from a well-known online encyclopedia, such as Encarta.com or Britannica.com?

The information on websites is only as reliable as the individuals who create it. University, archive, or museum sites are prepared by experts, and their content is usually reviewed by editors. In many cases, the URL (Internet address) offers important clues about dependability. Look for university-created websites that include ".edu" in the URL (e.g., www.eagleton.rutgers.edu/e-gov/e-politicalarchive-Jackson.htm), or for addresses ending in ".org" for sites created by museums and other historical organizations (e.g., www.californiahistoricalsociety.org). URLs including ".gov" offer reliable information, too (e.g., the US Government Printing Office site at www.gpoaccess.gov/coredocs.html). Some online encyclopedias are also reliable (see above). Avoid personal websites and homepages when doing research. While they may provide interesting or entertaining information, they are not reviewed for accuracy or reliability.

For a list of some excellent Internet sites on American history, visit www.emp.ca/ah.

### Searching the Internet

How can you deal with the challenge of finding what you are looking for among hundreds of search results? There are two important Internet research tools: search engines and subject directories. To be a successful Internet researcher, you must use these tools correctly. The key is to ask: "How much do I already know?" If you know the specific topic you are looking for (e.g., Jacksonian democracy), a search engine like www.google.ca or www.yahoo.com is best to locate a particular web page quickly. If you know only the general subject (e.g., American democracy), a subject directory like www.vivisimo.com or a CNET search—www.search.com—will be more helpful. These directories group relevant web pages into helpful subject categories and subcategories. Often, you will discover pages and topics that you did not realize existed.

Finally, remember that many public and school libraries offer access to online databases that are never included by Internet search engines in their results. These are reliable and easy to use and most have been designed with students in mind.

### Try It!

1. Find two Internet sites providing information about the Trail of Tears. Evaluate each for accuracy and reliability using the critical thinking questions above.
2. Write a brief report comparing and contrasting the advantages and disadvantages of the two sites. Which would you recommend to a classmate? Why?

# STUDY HALL

## Thinking

1. John Quincy Adams said manifest destiny was "as much a law of nature as that the mighty Mississippi should flow to the sea." Explain how this analogy applies to the American idea of manifest destiny. Develop two analogies to show the meaning of manifest destiny. One should be positive and the other negative.
2. Summarize the impact of the idea of manifest destiny on Mexico, Canada, and Native Americans.
3. Are the news media important partners in a democracy? Explain in terms of the United States in the age of Jackson and in terms of Canada today.
4. Suggest an alternative solution to the eviction of the Cherokee and the Trail of Tears. Your solution should open land to settlers while protecting the rights of the Cherokee.
5. What questions would an investigative reporter want to ask about the Mexican-American War? Remember the 5Ws: who, what, when, where, and why. Consider moral questions raised by the war.
6. What values of the Second Great Awakening can still be found in American culture today?
7. Is a public education system an essential part of a democracy? Debate the need for public schools versus private schools.

## Communication

8. On a map of North America, illustrate the idea of manifest destiny and how the United States grew in the 1830s and 1840s. Use colours or symbols to show the difference between actual growth and the gains that believers in manifest destiny intended to make.
9. Look again at the excerpt from Thoreau's "Civil Disobedience" in the Sound Bite on page 150. Rewrite the excerpt in your own words. Now review the Declaration of Independence (in the Appendix). Do you think that the events of the Mexican-American War and the existence of slavery are just causes for civil disobedience?
10. Write a speech that Elizabeth Cady Stanton could have given in an attempt to persuade her fellow Americans to support women's rights. Include references to events, ideas, and people from American history up to 1850 that would help support her arguments.
11. Choose a figure from American history discussed in this chapter to research further (e.g., Andrew Jackson, Osceola, Elizabeth Cady Stanton). Make an oral presentation about that person's importance in shaping the United States.

## Application

12. "Dissent" is disagreement with majority opinions or widely held views. How important is dissent to a thriving democracy?
13. "Many Americans still see themselves as people of the frontier because…" Complete this sentence using a fact from this chapter. Share and compare your answers with other students in class.
14. Find examples of the president of the United States today speaking on behalf of the nation as a whole. What search terms might you use for an Internet search?
15. The United States is a complex society—it is hard or even impossible to make generalizations about the country. How is this complexity seen in the period covered in this chapter in terms of politics, culture, and economy?
16. If Jackson had not defeated nullification, what impact would it have had on governing at the federal level in the United States?

# 6 The Crisis of the Union

## (1850–1865)

### KEY CONCEPTS

In this chapter you will consider:

- The integral role slavery played in the 19th-century American economy and society
- The significance of slavery for American society and politics during the 1850s
- The factors that led to the dissolution of the Union and the outbreak of the Civil War
- The course of the Civil War and its impact on American society and politics
- The influence of the Civil War on the political development of Canada

## The American Story

By the midpoint of the 19th century an increasing number of Americans were condemning the institution of slavery as an affront to the ideal of liberty expressed in the Declaration of Independence. At the time, however, slavery was a key element of the American economy and society; the debate over it led to legal disputes, political divisions, and mounting violence that in 1860 culminated in the secession of the South and the dissolution of the Union. The resulting civil war devastated America, both North and South. It was only at an enormous economic, social, and personal cost that slavery was eliminated and the Union restored.

### TIMELINE

- **1820** ▸ Missouri Compromise
- **1850** ▸ Compromise of 1850 ▸ Passage of the Fugitive Slave Act
- **1851** ▸ *Uncle Tom's Cabin* published
- **1854** ▸ Republican Party is formed
- **1857** ▸ Dred Scott decision

## IMAGE ANALYSIS

**Figure 6.1** This illustration shows a recruitment poster aimed at recruiting African-American soldiers for the **Union** army during the Civil War. Faced with the constant need for fresh troops to sustain the Northern war effort, the Union army began recruiting former slaves in 1863. Before the war's end, some 180,000 black soldiers would fight against the **Confederacy**. Even in the Union army, though, racism was deeply ingrained. Black regiments were often restricted to menial labour, and officers were exclusively white.

Despite the horrors of war and continued racial discrimination, few experiences did more to encourage African-Americans to demand equal rights than military service. As the former slave and leading abolitionist Frederick Douglass observed about these new Union soldiers: "Once let the black man get upon his person the brass letters U.S., and there is no power on earth which can deny that he has earned the right to citizenship."

- **1859** ▸ John Brown's raid of Harper's Ferry
- **1860** ▸ Election of Abraham Lincoln as president
- **1861** ▸ Civil War begins
- **1863** ▸ Emancipation Proclamation ▸ Battle of Gettysburg
- **1865** ▸ Confederate General Robert E. Lee surrenders at Appomattox ▸ Assassination of President Lincoln

# INTRODUCTION

Living in Canada in the 21st century, it may be difficult for you to appreciate the ways in which slavery and the Civil War have seared themselves into the American national memory. Slavery denied a race of people the basic rights and freedoms that the rest of America took for granted, and its legacy endured for generations. The war devastated entire communities and killed or maimed hundreds of thousands of young men, many of them teenagers no older than yourself. People fought and lost their lives to resolve a fundamental question: Could a nation whose citizens disagreed over an issue as significant as slavery remain united? The failure of politicians and ordinary Americans to resolve their differences peacefully led directly to the greatest crisis faced by the United States in its history—one that threatened the nation's very survival.

# SLAVERY AND ABOLITION

Socially and politically, the United States was founded on several fundamental ideals. The first was freedom—"life, liberty, and the pursuit of happiness," in the words of the Declaration of Independence. The second ideal was the right to maintain property. The practice of slavery in America and the discussion surrounding its abolition brought these two ideals into conflict, both because some men were not free and because abolishing slavery would deprive certain free men (slaveholders) of their property (slaves). The inability to resolve this conflict of ideals would ultimately lead the Southern states to **secede** from the American Union and begin a devastating **civil war**.

## The Peculiar Institution

Slavery had been present in America almost since the arrival of the Europeans. The Spanish enslaved the Aboriginal peoples of the Caribbean islands to work in their gold and silver mines, and in 1619 the first African slaves arrived to work on the tobacco plantations in Virginia. Soon, slavery was widespread throughout colonial America.

While some colonists, such as the Quakers, were influenced by their religious beliefs to oppose slavery, the practice was still legal in most colonies on the eve of the American Revolution. The war, however, marked the beginning of the movement to end slavery, since many Patriots believed it was inconsistent with the ideal of liberty then circulating in America.

Although the authors of the Declaration of Independence were critical of the slave trade, negative references to slavery were dropped from the final text to win the support of Southern delegates (as you saw in Chapter 3). Thomas Jefferson, the main author of the Declaration and a slave owner himself, believed that emancipation would soon follow American

**SOUND BITE**

"The peculiar institution of the South—that, on the maintenance of which the very existence of the slaveholding States depends, is pronounced to be sinful and odious, in the sight of God and man; and this with a systematic design of rendering us hateful in the eyes of the world—with a view to a general crusade against us and our institutions."

—Senator John C. Calhoun of South Carolina (1837)

independence. Stirred by these ideas of liberty, the Northern states abolished slavery, and by the early 1790s almost all states had banned the importing of slaves. Complete abolition seemed imminent. For their part, Southern politicians often avoided using the word "slavery" altogether, and instead referred to it by the vague phrase "the peculiar institution." In their view the institution of slavery formed an essential element of the Southern way of life.

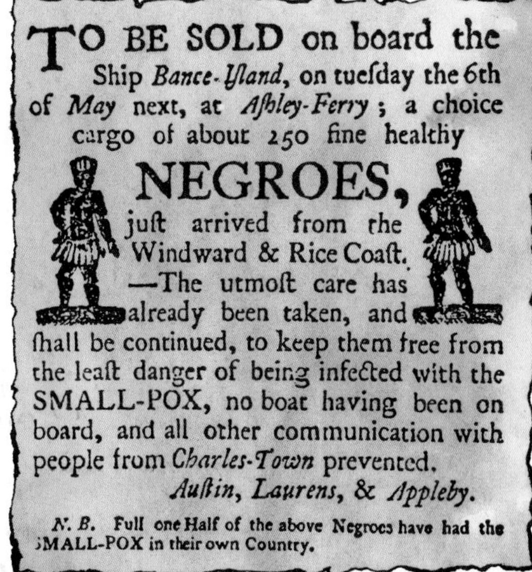


**Figure 6.2** Slaves were imported to America from the Caribbean, and sold in sales like this one in Charleston, South Carolina.

## King Cotton

The survival of slavery in America resulted primarily from economic developments and new technology. In 1793 the invention of the cotton gin—a machine that separates cottonseeds from the fibres, previously a slow and painstaking process—encouraged the large-scale cultivation and processing of cotton. This in turn required the large and productive labour force that only slaves could supply. As cotton exports grew dramatically in the early 19th century, so did the demand for slaves. After 1810 cotton production increased further as new agricultural lands opened up from Alabama to Texas. Settlers from Virginia and the Carolinas moved westward into these new lands, bringing with them the institution of slavery.

While intimately associated with Southern agriculture, slavery played a vital role in developing the economy of the entire nation. Northern merchants, ship owners, and bankers all profited from cotton cultivation and trade, so they too had a stake in maintaining slavery. Cotton mills like those in Lowell, Massachusetts (see page 131) drove the industrial expansion of the Northern states and depended on a cheap supply of the raw material to make a profit.

It is easy to argue that American prosperity in the first half of the 19th century was founded on cotton and the use of slavery to produce it. Whereas in 1800 cotton exports accounted for only 7 percent of total American exports, by 1820 that portion had risen to 32 percent; by 1860 it had reached an astounding 58 percent. There were sound economic reasons for Southerners to proclaim: "Cotton is King." Meanwhile, the profits to be made from cotton discouraged other investments, leading to a lack of diversified industries in the South. By 1860, fewer than 20 percent of the nation's factories were located south of the **Mason-Dixon Line**, which formed the border between Pennsylvania and Maryland.

**Figure 6.3** This image of a slave in chains was popular with British and American abolitionists and was frequently reprinted in their publications. Why might it make a powerful appeal?

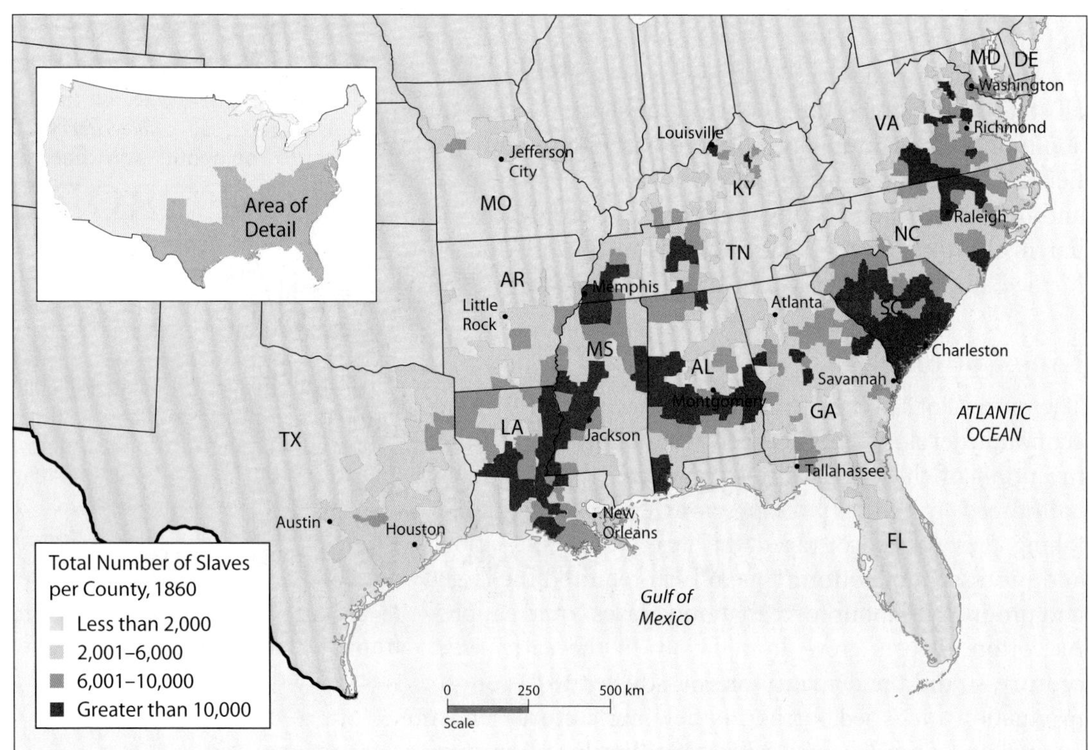


**Figure 6.4** On the eve of the Civil War, slaves were concentrated in the "black belt," named for its rich soil and large number of slaves. The region stretched from coastal Virginia through South Carolina and across Alabama to the Mississippi River.

The growth of the cotton economy had a direct impact on the spread of slavery in America. In 1790 the slave population of the United States was estimated at 700,000, but by 1860 it exceeded 4 million. The fact that the importation of slaves had been banned in 1808 made the increase all the more remarkable. Abolitionists waiting for a gradual extinction of slavery were waiting in vain; in the South the institution was simply growing stronger over time.

## Slave Life

While slaves brought great prosperity to the South, none possessed the legal rights of even the most poorly paid employees. Slaves—like livestock—were considered property, and as such were at the mercy of their masters. If they disobeyed or failed to work hard enough, they could be beaten without legal consequences (although their economic value discouraged such abuse). Most slaves on plantations were "field slaves," who typically laboured from dawn until dusk cultivating cotton, tobacco, sugar cane, or rice. A few "house slaves" worked as domestic servants.

Perhaps the cruellest aspect of slavery was the **slave trade**: the actual buying and selling of human beings. Although the importation of slaves had been

**Figure 6.5** Slave markets like this one were common across the southern United States during the 1850s. How has the artist emphasized the social and power divisions between slaves and planters?

prohibited in 1808, those slaves already in the country could still be bought and sold. Some traders attempted to avoid breaking up families, but most had no such scruples. Many masters would sell any slave who ran off and was recaptured, in the hope that the fear of being separated from their families would discourage others from running away.

The slave market was a common sight in many towns across the South. The demand for slaves and the high prices paid—a good farm worker sold for $1,000 or more (about $28,000 today)—demonstrated the value of slavery to the Southern economy. It also ensured that any attempt to limit or eliminate the "peculiar institution" would be met with fierce resistance.

## Abolition

Opposition to slavery took many forms. Since the early 1800s some campaigners had advocated the freeing of slaves and their resettlement in Africa. These plans met with limited success. A more active campaign for abolition, headed by the newspaper publisher William Lloyd Garrison, began in 1831. Garrison denounced slavery as immoral and demanded that it be eliminated from American society. Garrison and his associates were joined by free blacks, including Frederick Douglass and Sojourner Truth, who worked throughout the 1840s to help slaves escape and advance the cause of abolition.

**SOUND BITE**

"Urge me not to use moderation in a cause like the present. I am in earnest—I will not equivocate—I will not excuse—I will not retreat a single inch—AND I WILL BE HEARD."

—William Lloyd Garrison, from an editorial in the abolitionist newspaper *The Liberator* (1831)

### *Uncle Tom's Cabin*

The publication in 1851 of Harriet Beecher Stowe's bestselling novel *Uncle Tom's Cabin* galvanized Northern support for abolition. In a racist age, the book took the unusual approach of presenting a sympathetic portrait of black

# Culture Notes

## Spirituals and Slavery

Despite the inhumanity of slavery, a vibrant slave culture developed in the South, with a focus on music. The **spirituals**, or sacred songs, sung by slaves reflected both the strong influence of African musical forms such as "call and response" and the value of religious faith to people living in misery. Singing these songs helped forge a stronger community among slaves while motivating and inspiring them to endure their harsh lives. It also allowed them to express social and political protest, and even represented a means of coded communication, guiding slaves to freedom along the **Underground Railroad**.

Some spirituals spoke of heroes from the Hebrew Bible, like Moses ("Go Down, Moses") and Joshua ("Joshua Fit [fought] the Battle of Jericho"), who led the people of Israel out of slavery in Egypt to the Promised Land. Others protested the poverty endured by slaves and forecast a better world to come, one where "I got shoes, you got shoes, / All God's children got shoes. / When I get to Heav'n gonna put on my shoes, / Gonna walk all over God's Heav'n."

A few spirituals offered coded messages about the Underground Railroad, the route taken by escaped slaves to the North. References to the "Land of Canaan," for example, could refer to Canada. The African-American leader Frederick Douglass later revealed the significance of these songs: "A keen observer might have detected in our repeated singing of 'O Canaan, sweet Canaan / I am bound for the land of Canaan' something more than a hope of reaching heaven. We meant to reach the North, and the North was our Canaan."

The most famous spiritual was "Swing Low, Sweet Chariot." It spoke about deliverance from suffering, and also served as a code announcing the approach of **conductors**, or organizers, on the Underground Railroad:

Swing low, sweet chariot,
Coming for to carry me home.
Swing low, sweet chariot,
Coming for to carry me home.

**Figure 6.6** An illustration from Harriet Beecher Stowe's anti-slavery novel *Uncle Tom's Cabin* showing African-American slaves singing spirituals. "There were [songs]," wrote Stowe, "which made incessant mention of 'Jordan's banks,' and 'Canaan's fields,' and the 'New Jerusalem'... and, as [the slaves] sung, some laughed, and some cried, and some clapped hands, or shook hands rejoicing with each other, as if they had fairly gained the other side of the river."

I looked over Jordan, and what did I see,
Coming for to carry me home?
A band of angels coming after me,
Coming for to carry me home.

If you get there before I do,
Coming for to carry me home,
Tell all my friends I'm coming too,
Coming for to carry me home.

Spirituals like "Swing Low" were an expression—in song—of the determination of African-Americans to be freed from bondage and to maintain their self-respect despite the institution of slavery.

### Think It Through

1. What functions did spirituals serve among the slave population? Provide examples to illustrate each function.
2. Closely examine the text of "Swing Low, Sweet Chariot." In what ways might it be about escaping slavery? In what ways could it be an expression of religious faith and hope?

**WEB LINKS**  Learn more about spirituals by visiting www.emp.ca/ah.

slaves. Its sentimental story of a kind-hearted slave sold away from his family awakened many naive Northerners to the harsh injustices of slavery. By 1854 Stowe's novel had sold more than 1 million copies and had been adapted for the stage. Aware of the danger it posed, several Southern states banned the book, and men could be imprisoned just for possessing it.

President Lincoln later acknowledged the powerful influence of *Uncle Tom's Cabin* in rallying opposition to slavery. Meeting with Harriet Beecher Stowe at the height of the Civil War in 1863, Lincoln greeted her: "So you're the little woman who wrote the book that made this great war."

**WEB LINKS** 

To read *Uncle Tom's Cabin* and learn more about the impact of the book, visit www.emp.ca/ah.

## The Underground Railroad

The Underground Railroad—an informal network of individuals (both black and white, including many Quakers) who helped escaped slaves en route to the North or to Canada—was a major component of the abolitionists' efforts in the fight against slavery. The food and clothing, hiding places, and contacts that the Underground Railroad provided helped thousands of slaves flee to freedom. Committees in cities like Boston and Philadelphia raised funds to

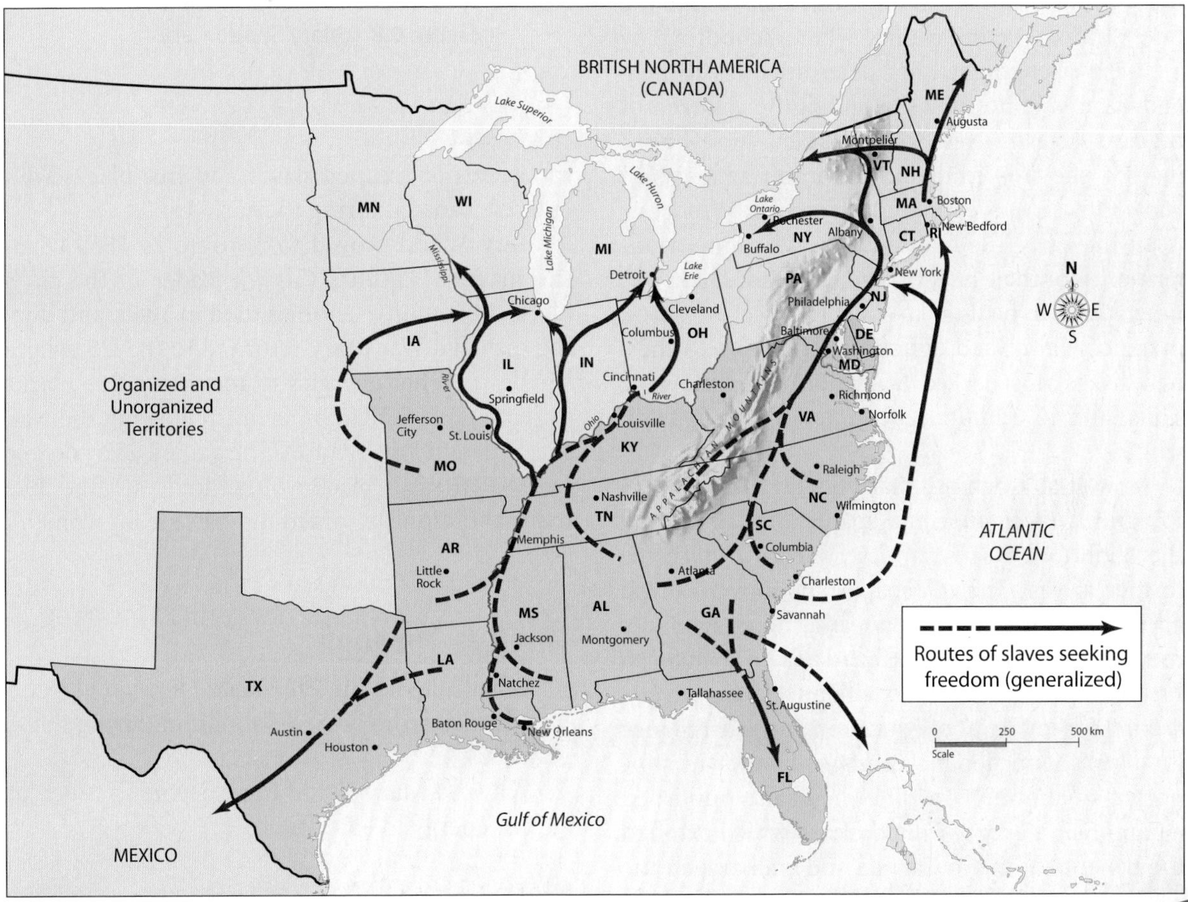

**Figure 6.7** While there was no single "official" Underground Railroad, slaves followed a variety of well-travelled routes from the Southern states to freedom in the Northern states, Canada, and even Mexico.

# WE THE PEOPLE
## Mary Shadd Cary
1823–1893

"Self-reliance is the fine road to independence." These words summed up the creed of the abolitionist and newspaper editor Mary Shadd Cary. Few leaders of the abolitionist cause were more determined to equip former slaves to help themselves. Born into a free black family in the **slave state** of Delaware in 1823, Shadd became an outspoken advocate of the rights of free blacks and former slaves, both in the United States and in Canada.

Mary Shadd's commitment to the cause of abolition began at an early age. Her parents were active in the Underground Railroad. As a child Mary moved with her family from Delaware to the free state of Pennsylvania, where schooling by Quakers strengthened her determination to help end slavery. For a time she taught the children of fugitive slaves in New York and New Jersey, until in 1851 she crossed the border into Canada West (now Ontario), eventually settling near Windsor.

In the early 1850s Windsor was an important terminus for the Underground Railroad. There was much work to be done to assist the escaped slaves, many of whom had difficulties adjusting to their new lives. Most lacked education or employable skills, and in addition encountered racism from whites.

As well as teaching, Mary Shadd founded the *Provincial Freeman*, a newspaper that promoted the abolitionist cause and served as a voice for former slaves. The newspaper supported radical abolitionists like John Brown and encouraged former slaves to come to Canada. The *Provincial Freeman* filled its columns with attacks on slavery, arguments in favour of education and self-reliance for blacks, and denunciations of lukewarm supporters of abolition. In 1852 Shadd also published a pamphlet, *Notes of Canada West*, which extolled the benefits of life in Canada and encouraged the thousands of escaped slaves and free blacks who entered Canada during the early 1850s.

**Figure 6.8** Mary Shadd Cary.

Mary Shadd moved to Toronto in 1855 when she married Thomas Cary, a leader in the city's black community. Thomas died in 1860, and during the Civil War Mary returned to the US, where she devoted her energies to recruiting free blacks to serve with the Union army. Following the war, she settled in Washington. She gained a law degree in 1883 (the first black woman to do so) and, like many abolitionists, joined the crusade for women's rights.

### Think It Through

1. What role did the *Provincial Freeman* play in advancing the cause of abolition during the 1850s?
2. Why did Mary Shadd Cary devote so much of her energy to education?

assist the fugitive slaves, while individual conductors performed much of the most dangerous work. The escaped slave Harriet Tubman made 19 trips south, leading more than 300 slaves to freedom.

When they reached freedom in Canada West (now Ontario), many former slaves settled in local communities. One centre of this settlement was at Chatham, where the arrival of large numbers of blacks created tensions in the community. By the early 1860s blacks made up almost one-third of the town's population. Facing racism, some opted instead to establish their own separate communities, such as Dawn, Ontario. Dawn was founded by the black clergyman Josiah Henson, who was reportedly the model for the title character in *Uncle Tom's Cabin.*

## Dred Scott

Abolitionists were enraged in March 1857 when the Supreme Court ruled on the case of Dred Scott, a slave from Missouri who had moved with his master to the **free state** of Illinois and then to the free Wisconsin Territory. When they returned to Missouri in 1846, Scott sued for his freedom on the grounds that his previous residence in free territory meant that he was now free.

Eleven years later the Supreme Court—which had a majority of justices from the South—rendered its judgment. Chief Justice Roger Taney (a Southerner) ruled that Scott, as a slave, was not a citizen and therefore could not bring his case before the court. Taney did not stop there. Instead, he attempted to resolve the question of slavery once and for all. He argued that since slaves were property and the Bill of Rights prohibited the government from unjustly depriving people of their property, the federal government had no right to ban slavery in the territories. According to Taney, the Missouri Compromise—which restricted the spread of slavery in the Western territories (see page 181)—was unconstitutional.

The impact of the Dred Scott ruling was enormous. In the South there was rejoicing. One Georgia newspaper declared that "Southern opinion upon the subject of southern slavery ... is now the law of the land." In the North politicians and journalists denounced Taney's decision and questioned the future role of the Supreme Court. Abolitionists grew alarmed at the increasing power of Southern slave owners in national politics.

## John Brown

The bloodshed in Kansas (see page 183) and disappointments like the Dred Scott ruling led a few abolitionists to conclude that only violence would succeed in eradicating slavery. After murdering several pro-slavery settlers in Kansas, the radical abolitionist John Brown went east to raise funds and gather weapons for an armed assault against slavery in the South. On October 16, 1859 Brown and 21 volunteers, including five blacks, seized the federal **arsenal** at Harper's Ferry, Virginia. After a brief battle against US forces led by Colonel Robert E. Lee, Brown was captured, tried, and executed.

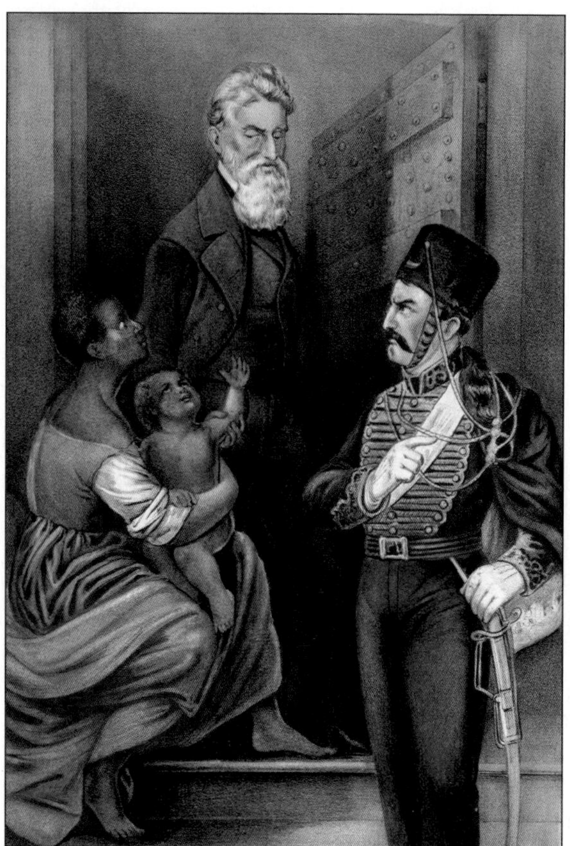

**Figure 6.9** John Brown quickly came to be viewed as a martyr for the abolitionist cause. In this popular print, a slave woman and her young child pay tribute to Brown as he is led to his execution. What elements of the print would make it effective propaganda for the abolitionist cause?

While many Northern abolitionists rejected Brown's violent tactics, others regarded him as a hero—a martyr in the fight to end slavery. In the South, by contrast, people saw the raid on Harper's Ferry as revealing the dangers posed by abolitionists, and as evidence of the hatred of Northerners for the South. Brown's final letter from prison offered a blunt warning for the future: "The crimes of this guilty land will never be purged away but with blood."

**SOUND BITE**

"John Brown's career for the last six weeks of his life was meteor-like, flashing through the darkness in which we live. I know of nothing so miraculous in our history."

—Henry David Thoreau, "The Last Days of John Brown" (1860)

## CHECK YOUR UNDERSTANDING

1. How did a new technology—the cotton gin—help spread slavery?
2. What were the consequences for the South of basing its economy on "King Cotton"?
3. Why was *Uncle Tom's Cabin* banned in the South?
4. a. What was Dred Scott's defence in his bid for freedom?

   b. On what grounds did the Supreme Court rule against Scott?
5. Why did Southerners feel threatened by John Brown's raid on Harper's Ferry?

# FROM COMPROMISE TO SECESSION

Throughout the first half of the 19th century the question of slavery dominated American politics. Federal politicians worked out a succession of political compromises to govern the slave trade and to decide in which new territories slavery would be legal. Through these compromises they were seeking to hold the United States together, despite the deep divisions slavery opened between the North and South.

## The Politics of Slavery

Between the 1820s and the 1850s the political crisis around the issue of slavery focused on one question: Should the nation permit the extension of slavery to new territories in the West? Since several of these territories would soon become states—and be represented in Congress—the outcome of this decision would determine the future of slavery not simply in the West, but in the entire nation.

Northern abolitionists argued that extending slavery to the new territories would not only spread an evil institution over a wider area, but would also give slaveholding states eventual control of Congress. Southern slaveholders argued passionately that slavery should be allowed to expand westward. They feared any weakening of their power in Congress and wanted to ensure at least a balance between slave and free states. Both sides realized that the debate about extension was really a debate that would ultimately determine whether the institution of slavery would continue to exist in the United States.

### The Missouri Compromise

The first effort to regulate the spread of slavery in the West came in 1820 when opponents of slavery objected to admitting Missouri to the Union as a slave state. At the time there were 22 states in the Union, perfectly balanced between 11 free and 11 slave states. This meant that each side had equal representation in the US Senate, and that neither side could pass laws to which the other would object.

Senator Henry Clay of Kentucky resolved the debate over Missouri by proposing the Missouri Compromise, which admitted Missouri as a slave state and Maine as a free state. In addition, no more slave states would be permitted north of the southern boundary of Missouri.

The Missouri Compromise was only a temporary solution, and slavery continued to influence the course of western settlement (as you saw in Chapter 5). Furthermore, the Compromise proved difficult to enforce, since settlers—some with slaves—kept moving into unorganized territory. In the face of this reality, politicians in Washington had to struggle to maintain the integrity of the Missouri Compromise.

In 1846 some anti-slavery politicians took the debate one step further by seeking to outlaw slavery in all the territories acquired from Mexico. The so-called Wilmot Proviso passed in the House of Representatives but was defeated

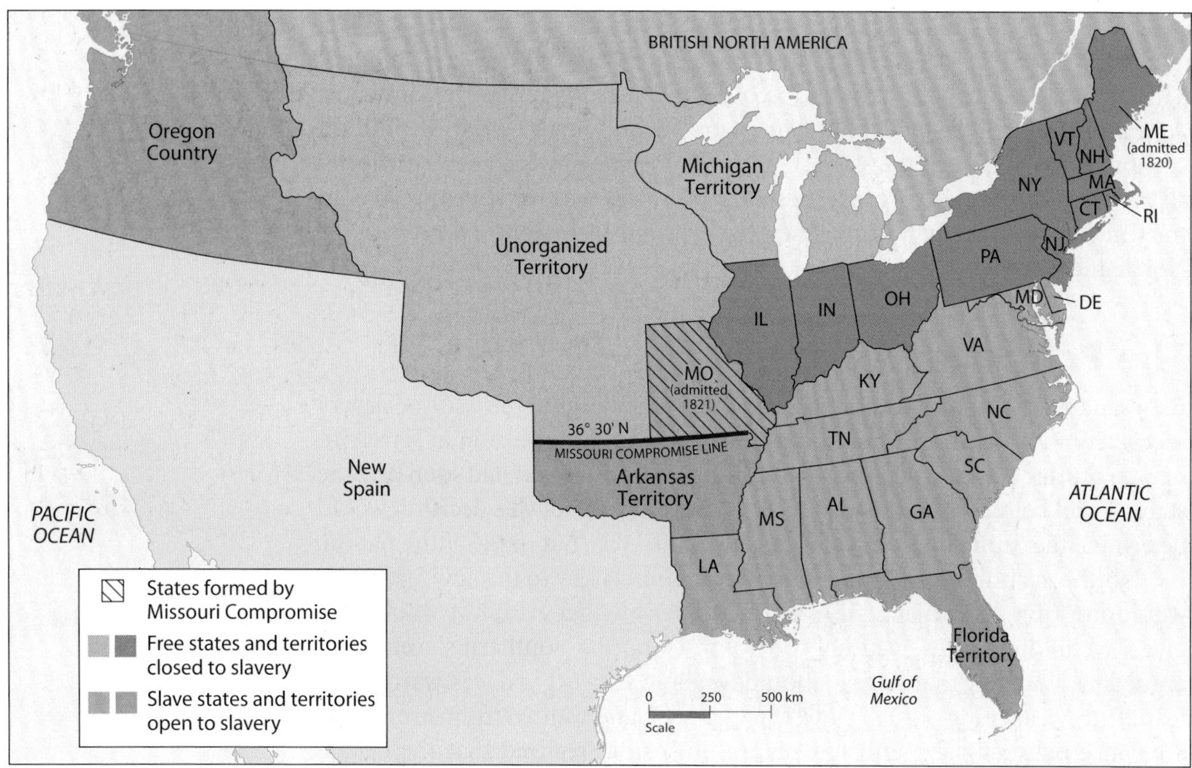


**Figure 6.10** The Missouri Compromise succeeded temporarily in maintaining a balance between free and slave states in Congress. Why was it only a matter of time before a new compromise would be necessary?

in the Senate and failed to become law. Southern politicians regarded the proviso as a direct attack on the future of slavery. For the first time, serious political divisions arose between North and South—divisions deep enough to cut across traditional political parties.

## The Compromise of 1850

By 1850 the Texas war of independence and the California gold rush caused many Americans to doubt whether the Missouri Compromise could continue. By creating several new American territories and then flooding these territories with waves of settlers from the East, the war and the gold rush raised questions about where slavery would be allowed to expand and how far political leaders could influence events in the West. Fearing for the future of the Union if the question of slavery was not resolved, three aging political titans—Daniel Webster of Massachusetts, John Calhoun of South Carolina, and Henry Clay of Kentucky—worked to fashion a new compromise.

The Compromise of 1850 contained several components. First, California was admitted as a free state, and in the other former Mexican territories the local populations would decide whether or not they wished to accept slavery. (Both of these provisions violated the Missouri Compromise.) In addition, while slavery remained legal in Washington, DC, the slave trade was banned there; public slave auctions in the streets of the capital had deeply offended many abolitionists.

In exchange for these concessions to abolitionists, the federal government assumed the debts of the recently admitted slave state of Texas. Congress also passed the Fugitive Slave Act, which required the federal government to use its power and authority to apprehend escaped slaves and return them to their masters. The Act also imposed penalties on anyone found to be assisting fugitive slaves. While many Americans rejoiced, believing that the Compromise of 1850 had preserved the Union, others were more pessimistic.

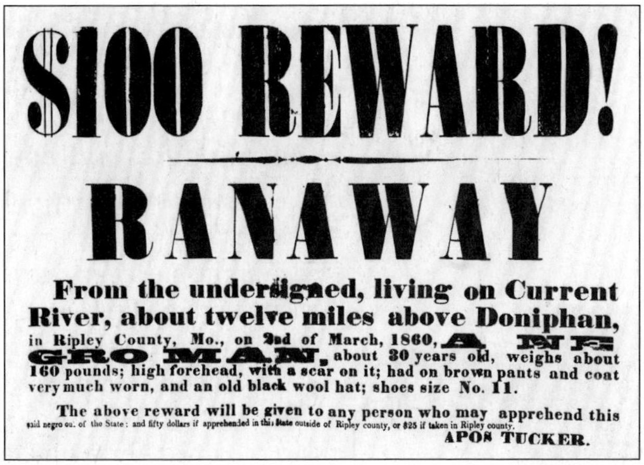

**$100 REWARD!**

**RANAWAY**

**From the undersigned, living on Current River, about twelve miles above Doniphan,** in Ripley County, Mo., on 2nd of March, 1860, **A NEGRO MAN,** about 30 years old, weighs about 160 pounds; high forehead, with a scar on it; had on brown pants and coat very much worn, and an old black wool hat; shoes size No. 11.

The above reward will be given to any person who may apprehend this said negro out of the State; and fifty dollars if apprehended in this State outside of Ripley county, or $25 if taken in Ripley county.

APOS TUCKER.

**Figure 6.11** Under the Fugitive Slave Act, slave owners looked for assistance to apprehend escaped slaves, like this male slave in Missouri.

Abolitionists were infuriated by the Fugitive Slave Act. In Northern cities like Boston, they openly harassed anyone pursuing escaped slaves, and crowds freed imprisoned slaves. Abolitionists also redoubled their efforts to help former slaves to flee to Canada, beyond the reach of the law. For their part, Southerners denounced this flouting of the law and grew disillusioned with the power of the US government to protect what they considered their property. The gulf between these two halves of the nation grew wider. One Ohio senator noted that "the question of slavery in the territories has been avoided. It has not been settled."

## Bleeding Kansas

Only four years after the Compromise of 1850, the pressures of westward expansion created a new crisis. Senator Stephen Douglas, a Northern Democrat and opponent of slavery, favoured the notion of popular sovereignty: the idea that local settlers should decide the issue of slavery in each territory. He proposed to organize two new territories, Kansas and Nebraska, which would stretch from the northern border of Texas to the 49th parallel.

Douglas believed slavery was unlikely to take root in either territory, but by allowing for the *possibility* of slavery in Kansas, his Kansas-Nebraska Act of 1854 essentially repealed the Missouri Compromise. Forgotten in this Act were the Native Americans in the territory, whose presence and land rights were almost entirely ignored.

In 1856 a struggle for control of Kansas erupted between supporters and opponents of slavery. As pro-slavery settlers from the neighbouring slave state of Missouri arrived in Kansas, "free-soil" settlers from New England also flooded in, determined that Kansas not accept slavery. Supporters in the East sent reinforcements and weapons to each side. Pro-slavery forces looted and burned the free-soil town of Lawrence, and opponents of slavery—led by John Brown—retaliated with raids of equal ferocity. Dozens of settlers were slaughtered. As the nation watched in horror, "Bleeding Kansas" offered a stark foreshadowing of the greater conflict to come.

### Lincoln and the Republican Party

The existing two-party political system of the Whigs and Democrats did not survive the strains of the slavery debate, as members of the two parties divided over the question. Between the passage of the Kansas-Nebraska Act in 1854 and the presidential election in 1856, many Northern Whigs and other abolitionists joined forces to create the Republican Party, which was dedicated to halting the spread of slavery.

"A house divided against itself cannot stand. I believe this government cannot endure, permanently half slave and half free."

—Abraham Lincoln, in debate with Stephen Douglas

Among the leading figures in the new party was an Illinois politician and lawyer named Abraham Lincoln. Although not an abolitionist himself, Lincoln regarded slavery as a "monstrous injustice" and opposed the Fugitive Slave Act. In 1858 he attracted national attention by challenging Stephen Douglas for election as senator from Illinois. Although Douglas opposed slavery, he did not advocate abolishing it in the South. In a series of celebrated debates with Douglas, Lincoln argued that slavery must ultimately be destroyed or it would destroy the Union. Although Lincoln lost the election, the debates established him as a leader of the Republican Party and a determined opponent of slavery.

## Secession

By 1860 tensions throughout America over the future of slavery would reach a breaking point, producing a grave political crisis and leading to the dissolution of the Union. The election of the Republican Abraham Lincoln to the presidency in 1860 prompted South Carolina to secede, and ten other Southern states eventually followed. Decades of political compromise had failed to save the nation.

### The Election of 1860

The division between supporters and opponents of slavery had already reshaped American politics during the 1850s (for example, by destroying the Whig party). In 1860 the question of slavery fractured the Democrats. The leading Democratic presidential candidate was Stephen Douglas of Illinois, who argued for popular sovereignty. At the national Democratic convention in Charleston, South Carolina (the heartland of the South) Douglas failed to gain sufficient support from delegates. He refused to endorse legal protection for slavery in all the territories, which was the price of Southern support.

With the convention delegates failing to agree on a candidate, the Democrats next assembled in Baltimore (in the "border state" of Maryland) and here they nominated Douglas. Southern Democrats were outraged; they met separately and selected the current vice-president, John Breckinridge, as their candidate. Concerned about national divisions over slavery, some former Whigs from border states formed the Constitutional Union Party, which favoured a

**Figure 6.12** This political cartoon vividly depicted the consequences of divisions in the Democratic Party between supporters and opponents of slavery.

further political compromise (similar to that of 1850) to defuse the mounting crisis; they nominated John Bell of Tennessee as their candidate. Rejecting radical abolitionists, the Republican Party selected the relatively moderate Abraham Lincoln of Illinois in order to appeal to as many Northern voters as possible.

The election of 1860 was perhaps the most momentous in American history. The key issue remained the extension of slavery in the territories. Breckinridge (Southern Democrat) favoured it, while Lincoln (Republican) opposed it, Douglas (Northern Democrat) argued for popular sovereignty, and Bell (Constitutional Union) advocated further political compromise. With the Democratic Party divided and the Constitutional Union new to the political scene, it was clear that Lincoln would win.

Although the outcome was not in doubt, the election still attracted enormous attention. In the South politicians and citizens spoke openly about the threat of secession, while in the North many refused to believe the danger was real. Political debate gripped the nation as never before. One Southerner observed that "little else was done this year, than discuss politics. Vast crowds would daily assemble at the places of popular resort, to canvass the questions

| The Presidents: 1850–1865 | | |
|---|---|---|
| **Millard Fillmore** | Whig | July 9, 1850 – March 4, 1853 |
| **Franklin Pierce** | Democratic | March 4, 1853 – March 4, 1857 |
| **James Buchanan** | Democratic | March 4, 1857 – March 4, 1861 |
| **Abraham Lincoln*** | Republican | March 4, 1861 – April 15, 1865 |

* assassinated

By the time of the 1860 election, the Democrats had been in power for eight years. Why did they fail to have their presidential candidate elected in 1860?

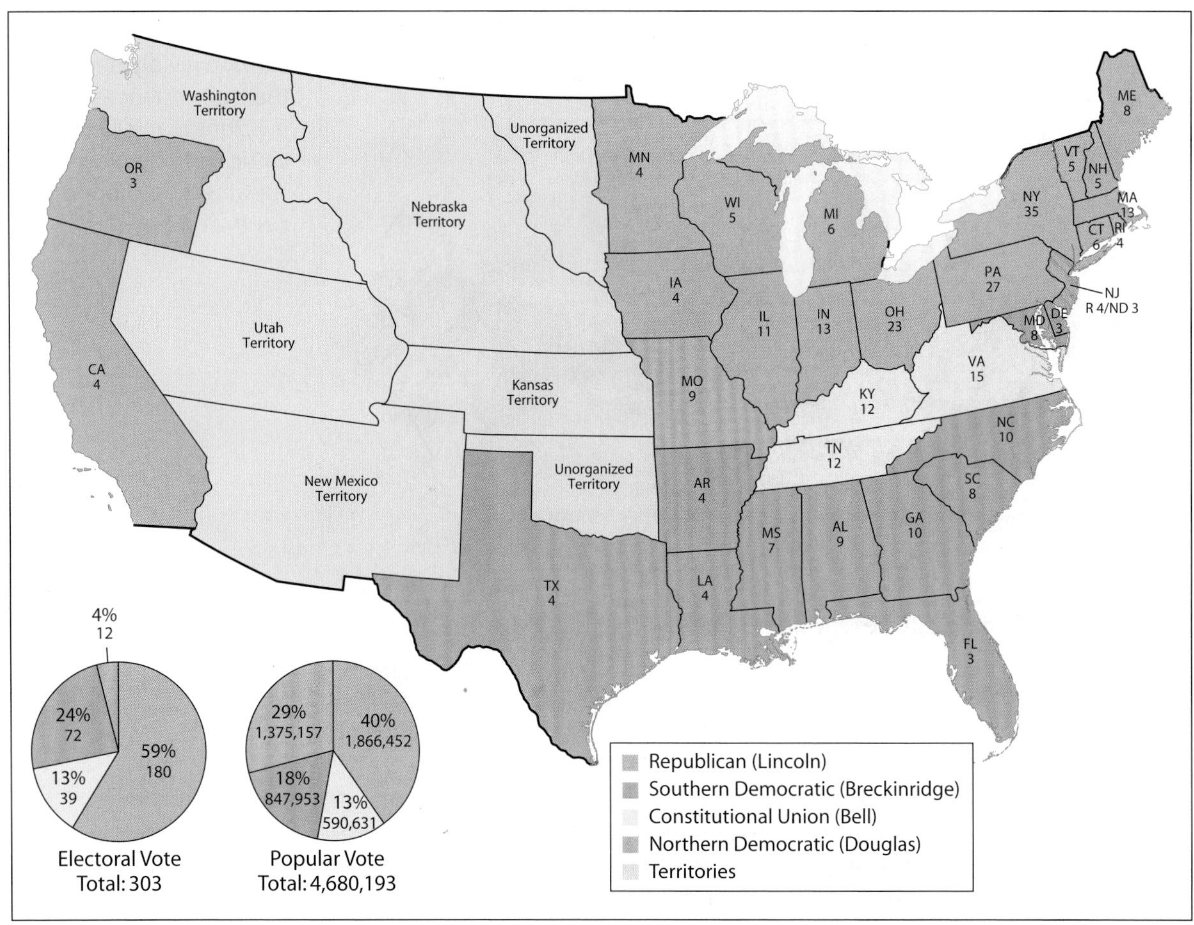


**Figure 6.13** This map clearly illustrates the division over slavery revealed by the presidential election of 1860.

at issue." Given such enthusiasm, it is scarcely surprising that voter turnout was 81.2 percent—the second highest turnout in American history, exceeded only by the 81.8 percent turnout in 1876.

The election of 1860 demonstrated the depths of sectionalism in America, with its two political contests: Lincoln versus Douglas in the North, and Breckinridge versus Bell in the South. Indeed, in ten Southern states Lincoln's name did not even appear on the ballot. In the Electoral College Lincoln won a clear mandate (180 of 303 votes), but received only 40 percent of the popular vote. Douglas secured only 12 electoral votes, although he garnered almost 30 percent of the popular vote. Breckinridge swept the Southern states, while Bell took three border states.

## The End of the Union

Southerners believed that the election of a president whose party was committed to abolition threatened the very survival of their society, based as it was on the institution of slavery. While some sought further compromise,

**Figure 6.14** This cartoon from *Harper's* depicts the outcome of the 1860 presidential election, with (from left to right) Lincoln, Douglas, and Breckinridge tearing portions of the map while Bell uses glue in an attempt to repair it.

many agreed with the South Carolina politician David Harris, who declared: "[S]ecession is a desperate remedy, but of the two evils [secession and abolition] I do think it is the lesser."

On December 20, 1860 South Carolina became the first state to secede; in the following weeks, six other states from Texas to Florida followed suit. In February 1861 delegates from these seven states assembled in Montgomery, Alabama to create the **Confederate States of America (CSA)**, which would eventually incorporate eleven states. The new country's constitution was modelled on that of the United States, except that it explicitly safeguarded slavery and emphasized the rights of individual states. The delegates chose Jefferson Davis of Mississippi, a US senator and former secretary of war, as president of the CSA.

In his inaugural address on February 18, 1861 Davis argued that secession was consistent with the ideas contained in the Declaration of Independence, for government required the consent of the governed. Since the South's independence posed no threat, Davis urged the North to allow the Confederacy to exist in peace. Lincoln's own address, given three weeks later, in part echoed Davis's words: "We are not enemies, but friends. We must not be enemies. Though passion may have strained, it must not break our bonds of affection." Such

**Figure 6.15** The austere Jefferson Davis, president of the Confederate States of America.

sentiments proved impossible to sustain, however, for Northern opinion overwhelmingly demanded that the Union be preserved.

### Fort Sumter

Despite their mutual desire for peace, both Lincoln and Davis began to prepare for war during the early months of 1861. The first flashpoint focused on government property in the seceded states: What would become of federal forts and naval bases there? In South Carolina Confederate forces besieged Fort Sumter, which guarded the harbour of Charleston.

The fort's commander appealed to the federal government for relief, but Lincoln hesitated. On the one hand, dispatching a naval force to relieve Fort Sumter would likely ignite a war. On the other, the Union must be defended. Lincoln eventually did send ships, but before they arrived Jefferson Davis ordered Confederate forces to capture the fort. On April 12, 1861 the assault on Fort Sumter began, and after two days of bombardment the fort capitulated. The Civil War had begun.

## Causes of the Civil War: A Summary

It is easy to see that the bombardment of Fort Sumter marked the beginning of the Civil War. It is not so easy to summarize the causes of the war, partly because the conflicts between North and South—or free and slave states—were so deeply rooted in American history. Some of the chief causes have been examined in this chapter, but others have been touched on in earlier chapters of this book. Following is a summary of what many historians consider the five main causes of the American Civil War. As you read the summary, see if you can think of any other factors that might have contributed to the start of the war. Try to decide which of the five causes listed below was the most important.

### States' Rights

Conflict over the question of states' rights had existed since the Revolutionary War (see Chapter 3). Thinkers like Thomas Jefferson believed in state sovereignty (the idea that each state had the right to decide what was best for itself), while Federalists like Alexander Hamilton believed in a strong central government (that the good of the whole country was more important than that of any individual state).

These ideas surfaced again when, during Andrew Jackson's presidency, John Calhoun pushed the idea of nullification—that each state had the right to disregard any federal law with which it disagreed. Jackson forced Calhoun to abandon nullification by declaring it treasonous. In the years leading up to the Civil War, states' rights became an issue once more, with the Southern states fearing that those in the North would force them to free their slaves. Since nullification was no longer an option, many Southern politicians decided that secession was the only way to preserve their traditional rights.

## Economic Differences

The stark economic differences between North and South also contributed to the start of the war. The North was evolving into an urban and industrial society. It absorbed most of the immigrants—many of whom were drawn to big cities where they could find steady work in factories—who were arriving in the US from Europe. These immigrants provided the North with a cheap source of labour, but they also made Northern society more diverse and less conservative than society in the South.

The Southern economy was mostly rural and agrarian, and centred on one crop, cotton, which was profitable partly due to the slave labour used to plant and harvest it. The year 1859 marked the first time in US history that the value of the industrial goods produced exceeded that of the agricultural goods produced. As the North adapted to the **Industrial Revolution**, the Southern economy stagnated in an outdated system. Those who profited most from it, however—the owners of large plantations—resisted any suggestion of change.

## Westward Expansion

The annexation of Texas, California, and the lands seized after the Mexican-American War forced the United States to decide whether the new territories and states should be slave or free. As you saw earlier in this chapter, a succession of compromises attempted to maintain a balance between slave and free states and give both sides equal representation in the US Senate. By 1860, however, the balance had shifted to 18 free and 15 slave states. Many Southerners feared that they were being outmanoeuvred, and that a Senate majority was giving the North the power to control the way people lived in the rest of the country.

## Slaveholders versus Abolitionists

The growing strength of the abolitionist movement caused grave concern in the South. Southerners knew that many abolitionists had at least tacitly supported John Brown's violent crusade to free the slaves. They also knew that abolitionists were making it impossible to enforce the Fugitive Slave Act in Northern cities. They pointed to Brown's use of violence and the abolitionists' willingness to break the law as evidence of the fact that the North would use any means available—even the most violent—to impose its will on the South.

**SOUND BITE**

"Let there be no compromise on the question of *extending* slavery ... If there be, all our labor is lost, and ere long must be done again ... On the territorial question, I am inflexible."

—Abraham Lincoln, December 1860

## Lincoln's Election

Abraham Lincoln's victory in the presidential election of 1860 was the immediate cause of Southern secession. Lincoln was a Republican, and one plank of his party's platform declared that "the normal condition of all the territory of the United States is that of freedom."

Ever since John Brown's raid on Harper's Ferry, some Southern politicians had threatened to secede if a Republican became president. Lincoln was not an abolitionist, but he strongly opposed extending slavery to the territories. Although he tried to keep out of sight after the election to avoid making tensions worse, by the time Lincoln took office on March 4, 1861 seven Southern states had already seceded. Now it was not a question of whether there would be a war—only of when it would begin.

### CHECK YOUR UNDERSTANDING

1. In your own words, summarize the argument used by Northerners against the spread of slavery into new territories.
2. What impact did the expansion of the US after 1820 have on the Missouri Compromise?
3. What were the unintended consequences of the Kansas-Nebraska Act?
4. List the causes of the Civil War in what you consider their order of importance, then justify your ranking.

# CIVIL WAR

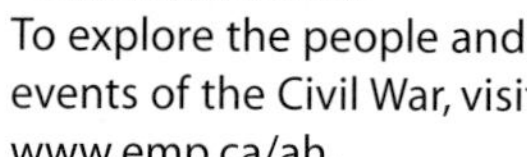


To explore the people and events of the Civil War, visit www.emp.ca/ah.

The four years that followed the breakup of the United States were among the most traumatic in the nation's history. The violence and political differences of the 1850s paled before the tragedy of the Civil War, as Americans paid the price for the political failure to resolve the question of slavery. Thousands of soldiers died in battle or from disease, much of the South was left in ruins, and shortly after the war ended Northerners lost the president who had led them through it.

## Union and Confederacy

In the frenzy following the attack on Fort Sumter, men on both sides of the sectional divide were eager to enlist. In the North they were determined to restore the Union fractured by secession. So many volunteers flooded recruitment offices that some had to be turned away. In the South men rushed to defend Southern honour and preserve slavery. The popular press egged them on. One circular urged the inhabitants of Tennessee: "To Arms! For our Southern soil must be defended."

Despite the equal rates of enthusiasm in both the North and South, at first glance it appeared that the two sides were unevenly matched. At 22 million, the population of the Northern states was four times greater than the non-slave population of the South, at 5.5 million. The Confederacy had only a single ironworks (at Richmond, Virginia), and one Northern state (New York) had more factories than the entire Confederacy combined.

## Confederate Hopes?

Despite the economic and numerical superiority of the North, the South enjoyed several advantages. The first was the supply of slave labour that could be used in agriculture and industry. This helped free up a greater proportion of the white population for military service. Another advantage was that—at least in theory—the Confederacy's war aims were more easily achieved than those of the North. Waging a successful defence required fewer soldiers than an offensive campaign.

For inspiration, Confederate leaders recalled the experience of the American Revolution, when the colonists' rebellion had succeeded against the greatest military power of the age. The Confederacy simply had to prolong the struggle until the North agreed to recognize its independence. By contrast, the North faced a far more difficult task: to conquer the South and reunite the nation by force.

**Figure 6.16** Confederate General Robert E. Lee and his officers. Lee's strategic brilliance on the battlefield was one of the factors that helped the South hold out for more than four years against the numerical superiority of the Union armies. What other advantages did the South enjoy?

Confederate hopes for victory hinged in part on support from Britain. Why did Confederates believe that Britain, with its vocal abolitionists, would support their cause? The answer was simple: British textile mills used American cotton. The economic costs of a prolonged disruption in the cotton supply could force Britain to intervene diplomatically, if only to pressure Lincoln to restore normal trade by recognizing Confederate independence

The British did have some sympathy for the Confederate cause, but hopes for British intervention were misplaced. It soon became apparent that Britain was less reliant on American cotton than some Southerners believed. Still, there was always the possibility that the international situation might change to the Confederacy's advantage—and thanks to an incident on the high seas, it nearly did.

## The *Trent* Incident

In November 1861 the Union navy stopped and searched a British vessel, the *Trent*, in the Caribbean. Two Confederate agents were on the *Trent* en route to Europe in hopes of gaining diplomatic recognition for the CSA from Great Britain and France. The Union officers seized them and took them to Boston. The British government vehemently objected to the seizure, threatened war if there was no redress, and readied troops and ships to send to Canada.

Neither Washington nor London really wanted war, and with the assistance of Queen Victoria's husband, Prince Albert, and the American Secretary of State, William Seward, the two countries found a diplomatic solution. The

US apologized and released the two men, claiming in its defence that the Union captain had acted on his own, without official permission. The two agents continued to Europe and the crisis passed.

## Battles and Generals

Several important factors shaped the course of the military campaigns of the Civil War. Battle casualties were particularly high. In large measure this reflected advances in technology, with new rifles like the American-made Springfield and the British-made Enfield, which were more accurate (and lethal) over greater distances. At the same time, commanders continued to rely on traditional strategies, especially massed infantry attacks, in which scores or hundreds of soldiers would rush the enemy line in successive waves. The result was carnage on an unprecedented scale, with thousands of casualties in a single battle like Shilah, Antietam, or Gettysburg.

Another factor that influenced the course of the military campaign was the relative quality of the commanders on each side. In this the Confederacy enjoyed a definite advantage. Many of the Southern commanders had trained at West Point and held high rank in the American army before accepting commissions in the Confederate army. Indeed, Lincoln offered General Robert E. Lee the overall command of the *Union* army at the beginning of the war. Lee seriously considered the offer before deciding that he owed a greater duty to his home state of Virginia.

### Bull Run to Antietam

At the beginning of the war, the Union strategy for defeating the Confederacy called for blockading Southern ports and seizing control of the Mississippi River. This so-called Anaconda Plan would slowly squeeze the South, starving it of resources and forcing Davis's government to sue for peace. The plan was the creation of Winfield Scott, the Union army's general-in-chief and a hero of the Mexican-American War. Scott was elderly, in poor physical condition, and frequently ill. While the plan of blockading the South would require time, Scott believed that it offered the best hope for success with the smallest number of casualties.

If the Union commanders were prepared to wait patiently, their commander-in-chief was not. Convinced of the need to achieve a quick victory in order to preserve the Union, Lincoln pressed his generals for decisive action in the summer of 1861. The Union army finally advanced on the Confederate capital of Richmond, but the anticipated easy victory proved a chimera. At the Battle of Bull Run on July 21, 1861 the Confederate army decisively beat the Union forces. The Northern soldiers fled back to Washington, DC, but the disorganized Confederates failed to follow and exploit their advantage.

Recognizing the need for better organization, Lincoln appointed George McClellan as commander of the Army of the Potomac, the main Union army.

**Figure 6.17** Union General Winfield Scott's plan to defeat the Confederacy was known as the Anaconda Plan, for its intention to strangle the Confederate war effort. Why was it given this name?

A capable administrator, McClellan immediately began to provision, train, and augment his army. Within months the Army of the Potomac numbered more than 100,000 men, but McClellan hesitated to embark on campaign.

Unhappy with these delays, Lincoln urged his commander to attack. In the spring of 1862 McClellan finally launched his eagerly anticipated invasion of Virginia, but he was soundly beaten by General Robert E. Lee during the Seven Days' Battles. The Army of the Potomac retreated to Washington once again. Then, news of a Union victory at Shiloh, Tennessee by a force commanded by General Ulysses S. Grant came from the west. The cost, however, was staggering: more than 20,000 Union and Confederate soldiers killed or wounded in two days of brutal fighting. But Shiloh was merely a hint of the greater bloodshed to come.

Anxious to exploit McClellan's timidity and encouraged by President Davis, Confederate General Lee now led his army north. He hoped to increase pressure on the Union government to sue for peace, perhaps even by capturing Washington, DC. Davis wanted to demonstrate that the Confederacy was winning and thereby persuade Britain to intervene. Incredibly, Union scouts found a copy of Lee's plans wrapped around a bundle of cigars. On September 17, 1862 at Antietam, Maryland, McClellan's army stopped Lee's advance. With almost 6,000 killed and three times that number wounded, Antietam was the bloodiest single day in American history. It was said that in places the dead lay piled three deep.

**SOUND BITE**

"I never realized the 'pomp and circumstance' of the thing called glorious war until I saw this ... Men lying in every conceivable position; the dead ... with their eyes wide open, the wounded begging piteously for help."

—A Confederate soldier, following the battle of Shiloh

**Figure 6.18** The Civil War was one of the first wars to be captured on film, as in the aftermath of the battle of Antietam, shown here. What message might the photographer have been attempting to convey? How might photographs such as this affect the Union war effort?

Lee retreated, but McClellan remained cautious and failed to exploit his advantage; a furious Lincoln relieved McClellan of his command. The fortunes of the Union armies, however, did not improve. In December 1862 an attack on Lee's army at Fredericksburg, Virginia failed utterly, and the Union army suffered 12,000 casualties. One Union soldier expressed his bitter frustration by observing: "It was not a fight, it was a massacre." At the close of almost two years of war, the Confederacy was holding its own on the battlefield. Union victory remained elusive.

**SOUND BITE**

"Victory has no charms for me when purchased at such a cost."

—General George McClellan, reflecting on Union casualties in 1862

**Figure 6.19** President Lincoln and General McClellan meet at the camp at Antietam in early October 1862. What might this photograph suggest about Lincoln's role in directing the Union war effort?

## PAST VOICES

# Walt Whitman: A Poet in the Civil War

> "The expression of American personality through this war is not to be looked for in the great campaign, and the battle-fights. It is to be looked for … in the hospitals, among the wounded."
>
> —Walt Whitman

While soldiers' letters and diaries vividly convey the carnage of the Civil War battlefield, few Americans more powerfully or poignantly recorded the painful impact of the Civil War on the nation's soul than the poet Walt Whitman. Too old for active service in the Union army, Whitman nevertheless came to Washington, DC determined to contribute to the war effort. He spent long hours assisting in the military hospitals, tending wounded and dying soldiers. Despite the staggering human cost of war, Whitman remained a fervent supporter of the Union cause and of President Lincoln, whom he encountered regularly during his time in Washington.

Whitman expressed his Civil War experiences in a collection of poems entitled *Drum Taps*, published in 1865. These poems address a range of subjects, from parents' anxiety for their sons' safety to the impact of the war on the lives of ordinary men—farmers and students—who suddenly find themselves fighting as soldiers. Perhaps the most powerful poem in the collection is "The Wound Dresser," in which Whitman evokes the plight of soldiers dying from their wounds in the hospitals and describes his own emotions as he struggles to comfort and care for them.

This struggle became a consuming passion for Whitman, who, in the words of a friend, believed "that these men, far from home, lonely, sick at heart, need more than anything some practical token that they are not forsaken." Whitman's poetry offers a moving reminder of the human cost of the conflict, a cost that was often paid far from the battlefields.

**Figure 6.20** Walt Whitman, around 1860.

**The Wound Dresser (excerpts)**

Bearing the bandages, water and sponge,
Straight and swift to my wounded I go,
Where they lie on the ground after the battle brought in,
Where their priceless blood reddens the grass, the ground,
Or to the rows of the hospital tent, or under the roof'd hospital,
To the long rows of cots up and down each side I return,
To each and all one after another I draw near, not one do I miss,
An attendant follows holding a tray, he carries a refuse pail,
Soon to be fill'd with clotted rags and blood, emptied, and fill'd again.

I onward go, I stop,
With hinged knees and steady hand to dress wounds,
I am firm with each, the pangs are sharp yet unavoidable,
One turns to me his appealing eyes—poor boy! I never knew you,
Yet I think I could not refuse this moment to die for you, if that would save you.

…

I am faithful, I do not give out,
The fractur'd thigh, the knee, the wound in the abdomen,
These and more I dress with impassive hand (yet deep in my breast a fire, a burning flame).

## Think It Through

1. Why did Whitman regard his work in the Washington hospitals as so important?
2. In "The Wound Dresser," how does Whitman attempt to convey the suffering of the wounded soldiers to his readers? Give an example.

## Gettysburg and Vicksburg

The climax of the military campaign came in July 1863, when General Lee led another invasion of the North—perhaps in a final effort to draw Britain into the war or to weaken Northern morale. At Gettysburg, Pennsylvania, Lee's army met a Union force led by General George Meade. With more than 160,000 soldiers involved, Gettysburg was the largest battle ever fought in North America.

The fighting raged for three days. Lee's army enjoyed some initial success, but was unable to push Union forces from their strong position. On the third day, Lee launched an assault across the open ground in front of Cemetery Ridge that proved suicidal. Of the 12,500 men involved in Pickett's Charge, fewer than half returned. The battle was lost. Confederate casualties numbered 28,000 killed or wounded—a third of Lee's total force—while Union forces lost 23,000 men.

Gettysburg represented the "high tide of the Confederacy," the final time that a Confederate army would invade the North. The day after Pickett's Charge, the South suffered another blow along the Mississippi. On July 4, 1863 General Grant captured the Confederate fortress of Vicksburg after a lengthy siege. The Union now controlled the entire Mississippi River, the main route into the heart of the Confederacy. One Confederate general lamented that "the Confederacy totters to its destruction," but despite these blows to the South, final victory for the Union was almost two years away.

**SOUND BITE**

"We here highly resolve that these dead shall not have died in vain—that this nation, under God, shall have a new birth of freedom—and that government of the people, by the people, for the people, shall not perish from the earth."

—Words spoken by Abraham Lincoln at the dedication of the Union war cemetery at Gettysburg, November 1863

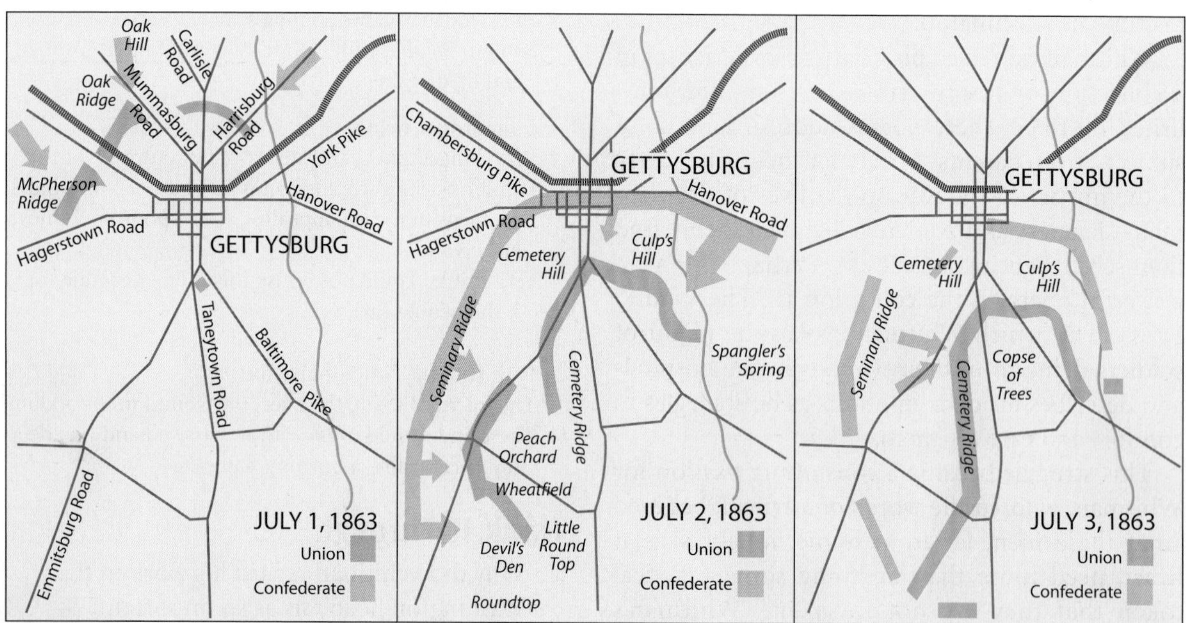


**Figure 6.21** The battle of Gettysburg lasted from July 1 to July 3, 1863. Use these maps to trace the action of the battle over the three days. Pinpoint the decisive engagement on July 3. Why do you think the Confederate attack failed? Why is Gettysburg called the "turning point of the Civil War"?

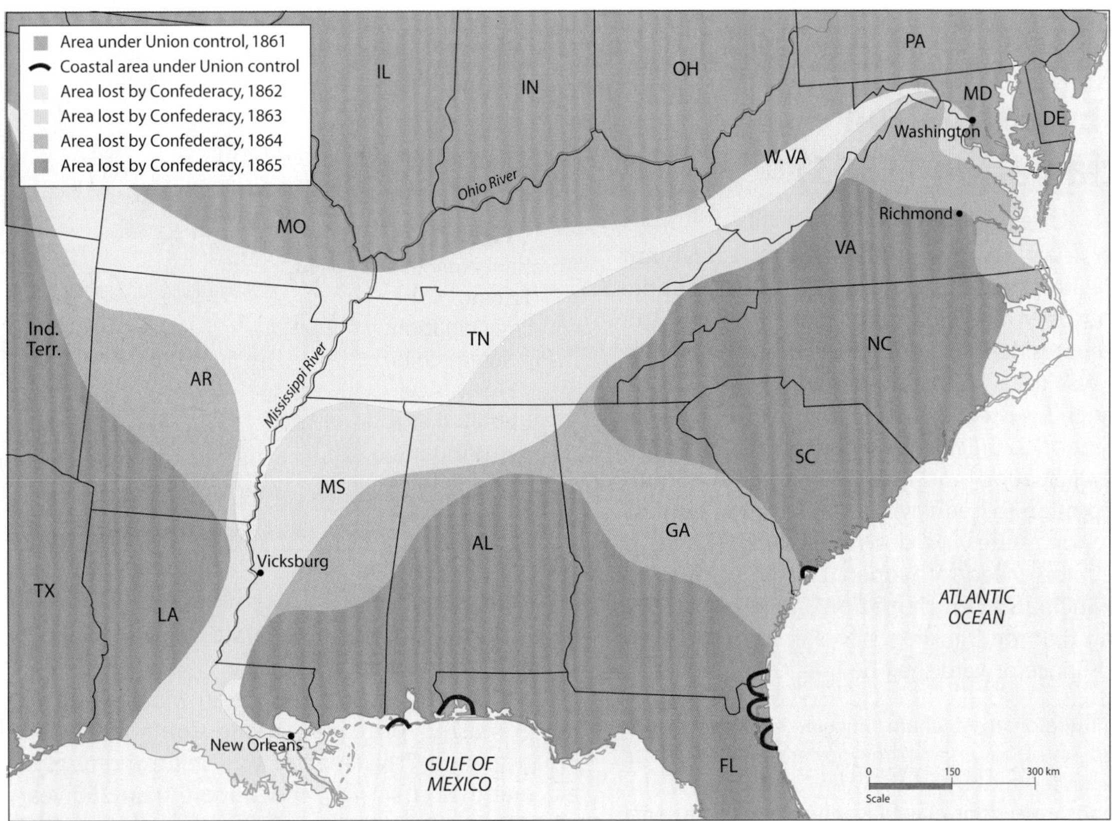


**Figure 6.22** This map illustrates the control that the Union soon gained over the Mississippi Valley, effectively severing the Confederacy in two.

# Emancipation

Although the North waged war to stop secession and preserve the Union, the underlying cause was the issue of slavery. Only fear of alienating those slave states that remained in the Union (Delaware, Maryland, Kentucky, and Missouri) or undermining support for the war in the North caused the government in Washington to avoid presenting the war as a fight to end slavery.

For their part, abolitionists loudly advocated emancipation as the primary purpose of the war. The New York newspaper editor Horace Greeley argued that fighting Southern secession while allowing the continuation of its cause—slavery—was "preposterous and futile." Having first announced that they had no intention of interfering with slavery (and even returning escaped slaves to their owners), the Union armies soon began keeping captured slaves as **contraband**, or illegal goods; freeing them from their masters; and employing them as labourers.

By 1862 the limited success of Union armies persuaded Lincoln that victory over the Confederacy required a bold step. As well as answering the criticisms of Northern abolitionists, announcing the emancipation of slaves would achieve several other purposes. It would encourage slaves to support

AMERICAN ARCHIVE

# The Emancipation Proclamation (1863)

**Figure 6.23** Abraham Lincoln's issuing of the Emancipation Proclamation in 1863 was celebrated as a transforming moment in American history.

One day in early January 1863 a young woman ran through the streets of London, England shouting: "Lincoln's been and gone and done it." What the American president had done, after months of deliberation, was to tackle the fundamental cause of the Civil War: the existence of slavery.

Four months earlier Lincoln had issued his preliminary emancipation proclamation, warning the South of his intention to free slaves in January 1863 unless the rebellious states laid down their arms. When, as expected, this failed to happen, Lincoln signed the final **Emancipation Proclamation** on January 1, 1863 declaring that the 3 million slaves across the South "are and henceforward shall be free."

> Now, therefore I, Abraham Lincoln, President of the United States, by virtue of the power in me vested as Commander-in-Chief of the Army and Navy of the United States in time of actual armed rebellion against the authority and government of the United States, and as a fit and necessary war measure for suppressing said rebellion, do, on this first day of January, in the year of our Lord one thousand eight hundred and sixty-three ... order and declare that all persons held as slaves within said designated States, and parts of States, are, and henceforward shall be free; and that the Executive government of the United States, including the military and naval authorities thereof, will recognize and maintain the freedom of said persons.

Within the United States, opinions of the Emancipation Proclamation varied widely. Lincoln's supporters within the abolitionist movement hailed it as "a great moral landmark" while his Democratic opponents in the North denounced it as "unnecessary, unwise and ill-timed, [and] impracticable." In the Confederacy people greeted Lincoln's act with derision.

Whatever others thought, with this single stroke Lincoln succeeded in transforming the war. It was no longer solely about restoring the Union, but had been fashioned into a crusade to end slavery. At the same time, the details of the Proclamation raised many questions and criticisms. The Proclamation applied only to slaves in territories currently in rebellion—that is, under Confederate control. Slaves in Union territory were not freed.

Designed to assist the Union in winning the war by increasing pressure on the Confederacy, the Emancipation Proclamation was still a momentous act, one that effectively ended more than 250 years of slavery in America. It signalled that Union victory would mean the end of the traditional slaveholding society. It also encouraged African-Americans to assist in the fight for emancipation by serving in the Union armies—an invitation that almost 200,000 would accept.

> And I hereby enjoin upon the people so declared to be free to abstain from all violence, unless in necessary self-defence; and I recommend to them that, in all cases when allowed, they labor faithfully for reasonable wages.
>
> And I further declare and make known, that such persons of suitable condition, will be received into the armed service of the United States to garrison forts, positions, stations, and other places, and to man vessels of all sorts in said service.

## Think It Through

1. Many leading abolitionists, including members of Lincoln's government, were initially skeptical about the value of the Emancipation Proclamation. Why?
2. According to the Proclamation, what role did Lincoln intend for freed slaves? Why might this prove controversial?

the Union war effort; stimulate support for the Union cause among abolitionists in Britain and elsewhere; and bring fresh energy to the North's flagging war effort, transforming the war into a moral crusade to end slavery.

The Union victory at Antietam in September 1862 offered Lincoln the ideal opportunity to announce his policy of emancipation. To be effective, it was essential that the move not be viewed as a sign of Union weakness.

### Tensions within the Union

While abolitionists and African-American leaders praised Lincoln's courage in finally tackling the existence of slavery, many of his supporters feared that emancipation would not be popular with the general public in the North, already weary of war. It did not take long for the negative consequences of the Proclamation to become apparent: many whites in the North were unwilling to fight and die in order to free slaves.

In July 1863 riots broke out in New York City to protest the controversial imposition of a **draft**, or compulsory military service. Hostility toward the war (newspapers had just printed casualty figures for Gettysburg) combined with racial and economic tensions to produce the worst rioting the United States had ever seen. Poor Irish and German immigrants believed—with some reason—that the burden of fighting and dying was falling disproportionately on them. Wealthier Americans could purchase exemptions from military service by paying someone else to serve in their place.

Much of the anger and violence was directed against African-Americans, and more than 100 were **lynched** by mobs before troops arrived to restore order. The popular hostility toward blacks was ironic, for the eagerness of blacks to enlist helped limit the wider impact of the draft. Many Union politicians, appalled by the violence of the riots, were quick to condemn them. Yet criticism of the war within the North did not disappear. Some Democrats had already begun to call for reconciliation with the South. A few of these so-called **copperheads**, named after a poisonous snake, even made contact with Confederate agents or encouraged desertion from the Union army—both acts that could be considered treasonable.

## Women and the War

During the Civil War, the absence of men at home meant that women had to shoulder greater responsibilities than usual. In the South they took over the running of farms and plantations, and some worked as nurses in military hospitals. Because there were few factories in the South, many households became "mini factories," turning out uniforms and other supplies for soldiers at the front.

In the North, besides running the farms, women also replaced men in factories, stores, government offices, and schools. Northern women distinguished themselves as nurses, organizing a system of field hospitals that was superior to anything that existed in the South.

## 49th PARALLEL

# Canadians and the Civil War

The American Civil War had a significant economic, political, and social impact in Canada. Northern demand for agricultural products led to an economic boom here, as exports soared. Canada also became a haven for Confederate agents, who came to the country to raise funds and purchase arms.

Just as Canada would serve as a refuge for American draft resisters during the Vietnam War in the 1960s and 1970s, so British North America became a destination for Americans avoiding military service during the Civil War. Many of these early **draft dodgers**, known as skedaddlers, settled in New Brunswick and elsewhere along the border.

The Civil War profoundly shaped politics in British North America. In the tense atmosphere that followed the *Trent* incident, Britain sent troops to Canada; however, as the crisis waned, these troops gradually went home. Anxious to transfer the burden of defence to the colonies, the British government increased pressure on colonial politicians to organize themselves to confront any future threat. Fears of invasion by a victorious Union army after 1865 encouraged discussion about colonial defence and the need for greater unity in British North America.

The Civil War also helped shape the Canadian confederation. Leaders like John A. Macdonald believed that the Civil War had been caused in part by the excessive power wielded by the states. As a result, the British North America Act would limit the powers of the provinces vis-à-vis the federal government.

Many young Canadians experienced the Civil War firsthand. Some estimates claim that as many as 40,000 Canadians fought in the conflict, although the exact number is difficult to verify. Most had settled in the United States before the war, but others were lured south by the promise of pay or adventure or were kidnapped by recruiters and drafted into the Union army. Canadians in the Union army included the young Calixa Lavalée, who was living in Rhode Island in the early 1860s and who later composed "O Canada."

As a teenager, Newton Wolverton of Canada West (Ontario) enlisted in the Union army and later worked as a clerk in Washington. The *Trent* incident and the threat of war with Great Britain understandably worried many soldiers from British North America serving in the Union army. Newton, aged 16, was chosen to present these concerns to President Lincoln, who was impressed with the young man's eloquence. Lincoln's response reassured Newton: "I want you to go back to your boys and tell them that … as long as Abraham Lincoln is President, the United States of America will not declare war on Great Britain."

**Figure 6.24** The most extraordinary Canadian Civil War experience involved Sarah Emma Edmonds of New Brunswick. Disguised as a man, she enlisted as a nurse in the Union army and served at Antietam. Edmonds then worked as a Union spy. After contracting **malaria**, she deserted—before admission to hospital could reveal her secret. She later recounted her adventures in the bestselling book *Nurse and Spy in the Union Army*.

## Think It Through

1. Evaluate the impact of the Civil War in British North America.
2. Research other cases of Canadians who served in American military campaigns—for example, in Vietnam. Why did they choose to enlist? How do their reasons compare with the examples from the Civil War?

## Northern Nurses

**Figure 6.25** Clara Barton, founder of the American Red Cross.

One of the reasons for the superiority of Northern hospitals was the fact that the North had greater financial resources than the South. But the North also benefited from the organizational abilities of two determined women: Dorothea Dix and Clara Barton.

As you read in Chapter 5, Dix spent much of her life working to improve conditions in mental hospitals and jails. At the start of the war, she was appointed Superintendent of the United States Army Nurses. Dix recruited and trained nurses (who had to be older than 30 and "of plain appearance"), organized supplies, and inspected camps.

Working in Washington when the war broke out, Clara Barton volunteered to care for critically ill soldiers and travelled to the sites of the bloodiest battles to set up field hospitals. In 1864 President Lincoln asked her to help trace the thousands of missing Union soldiers. The following year she went to the Confederate prison camp at Andersonville to document the dead and imprisoned soldiers there. In 1877 Barton founded the American branch of the International Red Cross.

The contribution of women to the Union war effort helped to strengthen the campaign to secure the vote for women, which was already being waged by campaigners like Elizabeth Cady Stanton and Susan B. Anthony (see Chapter 5, We the People, page 166).

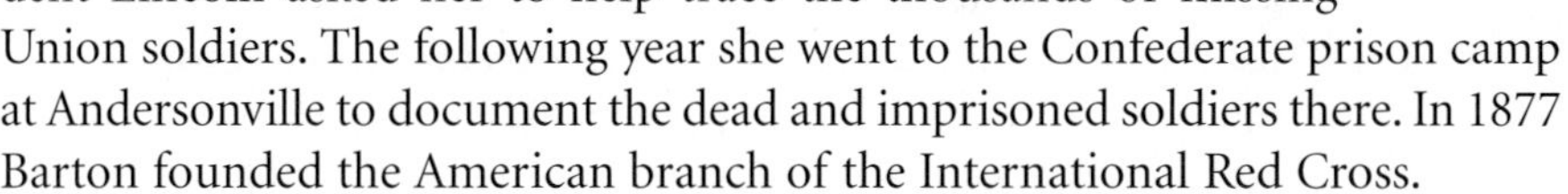

### CHECK YOUR UNDERSTANDING

1. What advantages did the North and South enjoy at the beginning of the war?
2. What difficult choice did Robert E. Lee face when the war began?
3. What was the impact of Union victories at Antietam and Gettysburg on the course of the war?
4. Why did Lincoln issue the Emancipation Proclamation?
5. What were the causes of the riots in New York in 1863?

# THE WAR'S END AND AFTERMATH

By 1864 the tide of Union victories left little doubt about what the final outcome of the war would be, yet still the suffering and bloodshed continued. At the same time, ordinary citizens and political leaders alike began to consider how they would rebuild the nation when peace finally arrived. How should the defeated Confederacy be treated? Would former slaves enjoy the same rights as other citizens?

## Atlanta to Appomattox

Frustration with the Union's failure to exploit the victory at Gettysburg prompted Lincoln to appoint Ulysses S. Grant, the victor of Vicksburg, as general-in-chief of the Union forces. Known as a "butcher of men," Grant had a reputation for ruthlessly waging total war. His soldiers claimed that Grant's initials—U.S.—stood for "unconditional surrender." When he invaded Virginia in 1864, Grant embarked on a campaign to destroy civilian property in an effort to terrorize the South and weaken the people's resolve.

In early September 1864 the Confederacy suffered a further disaster when General William Sherman's Union army captured Atlanta. After burning the city, Sherman's forces began a slow march along the 400-kilometre route to the Atlantic port of Savannah. Sherman's goal, in his own words, was "to whip the rebels, to humble their pride ... and make them fear and dread us."

During the final months of 1864 Sherman's men methodically destroyed the bridges and railroads, farms and plantations, and crops and livestock of Georgia. The total destruction was calculated to exceed $100 million (about $1.4 billion in current dollars). Sherman's strategy succeeded. One terrified Georgia resident reported that "they say no living thing is found in Sherman's track."

The successes of Sherman and Grant were timely, for in 1864 Lincoln was fighting his own desperate battle for re-election as president. In a bid to increase his support, Lincoln selected as his vice-presidential candidate the Tennessee Democrat Andrew Johnson, who had remained loyal to the Union. Lincoln's Democratic opponent was George McClellan, the former general with whom Lincoln had quarrelled repeatedly concerning the conduct of the war.

**Figure 6.26** Retreating Confederate troops burned Richmond, Virginia in April 1865, leaving total destruction. Does this image remind you of others you have seen?

McClellan favoured a negotiated settlement with the Confederacy. In the end, news of the fall of Atlanta stiffened Northern resolve and gave Lincoln a narrow victory over McClellan. Despite the high economic and personal costs of the conflict, a majority of the Union population was prepared to prosecute the war to the bitter end.

Grant's army was now closing in on Richmond, the Confederate capital. The prospect of imminent defeat persuaded President Davis and General Lee to propose the unthinkable: arming slaves to fight for the South in exchange for their freedom. But it was too late. At the beginning of April, Lee abandoned Richmond and the Confederate government fled, leaving the capital in flames.

Accepting the inevitable, Lee and his remaining troops surrendered to Grant at Appomattox Court House, Virginia on April 9. Now a fugitive, Jefferson Davis was captured a month later, having failed to re-establish the Confederate government in Texas. The war had ended after almost four years of fighting. One of the Union soldiers occupying Richmond eloquently summed up the feelings of the nation when he wrote: "I have seen enough of war."

**SOUND BITE**

"Officers and men [are to be paroled and they can] ... keep their side arms, and let all the men who claim to own a horse or mule take the animals home with them to work their little farms ... This will do much toward conciliating our people."

—General Ulysses S. Grant, outlining the terms of surrender at Appomattox Court House

## The Effects of the War

The Civil War was a tragedy for America. Although the North emerged victorious, it paid a heavy price, and the South was left in ruins. The very nature of civil war meant that there were no true victors—both sides had lost much. General Grant recognized this when, at Appomattox, he prohibited any celebrations. Instead, he reminded his men of the need for charity and sympathy, for "the rebels are now our countrymen again."

The human cost of the war was staggering. Of a total population of 31 million, more than 550,000 perished in battle or as a result of disease—more than the total number of those lost in all other wars ever fought by the United States. Casualties were almost evenly divided between North and South, although the burden on communities and families in the South was far greater. Large numbers of the dead, like Private Edwin Jemison of Louisiana, were only teenagers. Many communities had lost an entire generation of young men.

At the same time, the war transformed America. The scourge of slavery—which had divided the nation for generations and held the country's economy and politics ransom—was finally removed, although racism would

**Figure 6.28** Private Edwin Francis Jemison of Louisiana served in the Confederate army. He was killed fighting in Virginia in July 1862, aged 17.

### Civil War Casualties

| | Union | Confederacy | Total |
|---|---|---|---|
| **Combat deaths** | 110,070 | 74,524 | 184,595 |
| **Other deaths (disease, etc.)** | 249,175 | 124,000 | 373,458 |
| **Wounded** | 275,175 | 137,000 (est.) | 412,175 (est.) |

**Figure 6.27** This chart clearly illustrates the heavy toll suffered by both sides in the Civil War, while raising some questions. Why would disease have caused more deaths than battle wounds? Why might you argue that the Confederacy suffered more heavily than the Union?

endure. The war also strengthened the powers of the US government, particularly the role of the president. Finally, the struggle in the North to preserve the Union inspired a renewed nationalism. This nationalism would soon turn from military to other concerns, such as the completion of a transcontinental railroad and industrial and technological innovation. While in no way diminishing the human tragedy of the Civil War, the changes the conflict brought about would pave the way for the advances the US experienced over the remainder of the 19th century.

### Devastation of the South

As a result of the war, the Southern economy and society were devastated. Large parts of the South—particularly Virginia, South Carolina, and Georgia—were in ruins. Union armies had torn up railroads, destroyed ports, and reduced cities to ashes. Banks shut down, and the Confederate currency was worthless. In the agricultural heartland of the South plantations had been pillaged and abandoned, and slavery—the foundation of the Southern economy—had been abolished. The war brought about the total destruction of Southern life as it had existed before 1860. Few expressed the despair better than one Georgia woman who recorded in her diary: "We are going to be wiped off the face of the earth." The process of rebuilding the South would be lengthy and difficult.

### Resurgence of the North

While the North suffered many casualties, the Civil War helped strengthen its economy by encouraging industrial expansion to supply the war effort. This expansion only intensified the economic differences between the North and the South. Whereas prior to 1860 most of the wealthiest states had been in the South and their prosperity had been based on agriculture and slaves, after the Civil War the picture changed completely. The ten wealthiest states were now in the North, and their prosperity was derived from industry.

This growth in industry would accelerate in the years immediately following the war, with few developments revealing the change more clearly than the explosion in railroad construction that began in the mid-1860s. In turn, the growth of railroads encouraged a rapid westward expansion of the United States. Industrial development, railroads, and Western settlement were all consequences of the Civil War, and would become key characteristics of the succeeding decades.

### Lincoln's Second Inaugural Address

Lincoln set out a powerful vision for rebuilding the fractured nation when he took the oath of office for a second time. Delivered on March 4, 1865 as the Civil War's suffering drew to a close, his second inaugural address was barely 700 words in length. While some in the assembled crowd anticipated a forceful condemnation of the Confederacy and others expected lavish praise for

**Figure 6.29** The only known photograph of Lincoln speaking, delivering his second inaugural address on the steps of the US Capitol, on March 4, 1865.

Union armies, Lincoln offered neither. Instead, the president delivered a brief meditation on the causes of the war. He argued that the four years of suffering were a divine punishment for the sin of slavery, for which the entire nation was guilty. He ended by proclaiming in simple but stirring terms the need for reconciliation between North and South:

> With malice toward none, with charity for all, with firmness in the right as God gives us to see the right, let us strive on to finish the work we are in, to bind up the nation's wounds, to care for him who shall have borne the battle and for his widow and his orphan, to do all which may achieve and cherish a just and lasting peace among ourselves and with all nations.

## Proposals for Amnesty

As early as December 1863 Lincoln had begun the reconstruction of the South by pacifying those areas that had come under the control of the Union army, beginning in Louisiana. Lincoln's plan was a patient one, designed to offer incentives to rejoin the Union. As soon as 10 percent of the voters in a state swore an oath promising loyalty to the United States and accepting emancipation, they could elect a state government and look forward to readmission to the Union.

In contrast to this generally lenient approach, radical Republicans in Congress argued for stricter conditions. Despite mixed success in Louisiana—where voters resisted efforts to extend rights to blacks—Lincoln persevered in his plans. He urged his fellow Republicans to be patient, for, while "the new government is only to what it should be as the egg is to the fowl, we shall sooner have the fowl by hatching the egg than by smashing it." The end of the war and the bitterness that followed would sorely test this presidential plan "to bind up the nation's wounds."

## The Loss of Lincoln

There remained one final casualty of the war. On April 14, five days after Lee's surrender, President Lincoln was shot at Ford's Theater in Washington by a Confederate sympathizer named John Wilkes Booth. By murdering the president, Booth was determined to avenge the South's defeat. His act plunged the North into shock and grief, while former slaves across the South lamented the loss of the "great Emancipator." For the Southern states, Lincoln's death was a calamity, since he was the only person in the country who had accumulated the political capital to reconcile North and South. Lincoln's successor—Vice-President Andrew Johnson, a Democrat and native of Tennessee—would be unable to thwart Northern demands for revenge.

**Figure 6.30** The Union army discovered the Confederate prison camp at Andersonville, Georgia in May 1865, a month after Lincoln's assassination. Of the 49,500 Union soldiers held there, about 13,000 died of disease and starvation. The camp commander, Henry Wirz, was the only Confederate officer executed after the war. The abuse of Union prisoners hardened sentiment in the North against the South, and would mean that the terms of Reconstruction after the war were not as generous as Lincoln had wished.

## CHECK YOUR UNDERSTANDING

1. How did the appointment of General Ulysses S. Grant as commander of the Union armies change the direction of the Civil War?
2. What was the purpose of General Sherman's march through Georgia?
3. Identify three ways in which the Civil War transformed the United States.
4. Why was Lincoln's death a calamity for the South?

# THE HISTORIAN'S CRAFT
## Learning from Historical Photographs

### Photographs as Historical Sources

Photographs are a fairly recent source of historical evidence. The first American photographs were made in the late 1830s in the form of daguerreotypes—silver images on copper sheets. Daguerreotypes were expensive to make, and required the subject to remain completely still for minutes at a time. Accordingly, most early photographs were taken by professionals in studios. By the 1860s, however, journalists and documentary photographers began to enter the field. Popular interest in the Civil War encouraged early photographers to capture historic events with their cameras.

### Civil War Photographs

In the 1860s most pictures were still posed, as you can see from the photographs included in this chapter (for example, see the Web Links feature on the Civil War on page 190 and the photograph of Lincoln and McClellan at Antietam in Figure 6.19). These photographs provide us with a glimpse of people at war, their dress, and other aspects of their lives. The war photographers, however, wanted more. As the technology at the time would not allow them to take action shots of combat, they tried to capture the feel of war by taking pictures of battlefields in the aftermath of battles. Sometimes, photographers enhanced the drama in these photos. At other times, they used the photographs to engage in propaganda.

One of the best-known cases of such manipulation involved Alexander Gardner, publisher of a photo-book on the war. Gardner moved and posed a dead soldier in order to create a more romantic shot, adding a discarded rifle to the scene for better effect. He also published a photo of dead Confederate soldiers whom he described as having perished as traitors far from home. He then rearranged the same bodies to show what he now said were Union soldiers lying peacefully in death—apparently content in their loyalty. (See the link for these photos at www.emp.ca/ah.)

*(Concluded on the next page.)*

# THE HISTORIAN'S CRAFT (Concluded)

## Thinking Critically about Historical Photographs

Gardner's manipulations remind us to think critically about historical photographs:

- Who took the photograph, and why? (Was it an expert who could recognize the key events? Was the photographer biased or sensationalist?)
- What sort of equipment was used? (Was it an early camera that could take only posed photos? Was a telephoto lens used to zoom in on only one part of the scene?)
- Was the print altered in some other way? (Did the photographer crop the print to eliminate some figures or part of the scene? Did the photographer adjust the contrast or other features to influence our impression—a question all the more critical in our age of digital cameras and computers?)

Admittedly, these questions are difficult for viewers today to answer when looking at historical photographs. Yet it is valuable to think historically in this way as you interpret photographs that authors of historical sources have chosen to include.

## Interpreting Historical Photographs

As you look at a historical photograph, use questions such as these to find historical meaning:

- Who are the people? (name, age, sex, title, occupation)
- What is the setting? (buildings, landscape, surroundings)
- What activities are taking place? (work, warfare, family scenes)
- What inferences can you make about the people, the place, and the historic times?
- What effect was the photographer trying to create?
- What questions for further research does the photo raise?

## Try It!

1. Choose one photograph in this chapter and interpret it using the questions above.
2. Choose a different photograph and crop it by covering part of it. How is the meaning or impact of the photograph changed? What does this suggest about the common view that photographs are objective sources that capture events as they really happened?

# STUDY HALL

## Thinking

1. Most Southerners did not own slaves. In spite of this fact, why might they defend slavery and be willing to die to preserve the "peculiar institution"?
2. What evidence from this chapter could be used to support an argument that Lincoln was one of the greatest presidents in American history?
3. How valid is it to argue that the Civil War was really about states' rights, rather than slavery?
4. Debate the following issues:
   a. If the South had accepted confining slavery to the original slaveholding states, there would have been no Civil War.
   b. John Brown was not a hero but a common criminal.
   c. The Civil War was fought over the issue of secession, not slavery.
5. American historian Michael B. Oren points out that all Americans were outraged when the Barbary States of North Africa captured American ships in the early 1800s and made the crews and passengers slaves. Thus Americans objected to Africans holding Americans as slaves but not to Americans holding Africans as slaves. In what sense is this attitude an example of "moral relativism"?
6. Should people today who display the Confederate flag ("the Stars and Bars") be considered advocates of racial oppression and intolerance, or simply defenders of Southern history and tradition?

## Communication

7. Design a poster that abolitionists could use to recruit conductors for the Underground Railroad.
8. Investigate slave markets and sales in Southern states. Write a report on what happened at such sales from the point of view of an abolitionist and from the point of view of a slave.
9. What possible routes might an escaped slave in Georgia take to get to Canada? Start with a map of US geographic features. Consider the shortest route to the North and the Canadian border, physical barriers, etc. What might a suitable title for such a map made available to abolitionists be?
10. Lincoln is a revered figure in American history whose life and death have become symbols in the American dream and the American nightmare. Investigate Lincoln's position on the issue of slavery both before and after being elected president. Prepare a two-column organizer that summarizes "Myth" and "Reality" about Lincoln.

## Application

11. Slaves not only tried to escape to the North, they also rose up in rebellion. Use the Internet to find examples of slave rebellions—for example, Nat Turner's. Organizing a rebellion was difficult. Make a list of challenges that slaves would face both in escaping to the North and in rising in rebellion.
12. "What if … ?" There is a danger in seeing events in history as inevitable. What would have happened if Douglas had won the 1860 election? Select another event from this chapter where there could have been a different outcome and discuss what the results for the United States might have been.
13. Conduct a virtual tour of Civil War battlefields using Google Earth. Battlefields based on forts are still visible, so look for Fort Sumter and Fort Wagner. Also visit Antietam National Battlefield Park, Vicksburg National Battlefield, and Manassas National Battlefield. Use the layer features of Google Earth—such as populated places, roads, travel and tourism, and parks and recreation areas—and Google Earth Community to help you analyze the sites.

# 7 Reconstruction and Expansion (1865–1880)

## KEY CONCEPTS

In this chapter you will consider:

- The effort to reshape Southern economic, social, and political life following the Civil War
- The impact of Reconstruction on national politics
- The role of industry and new technology in transforming the American economy
- The consequences of urbanization and increased immigration for American society
- The influence of westward expansion and new technology on American agriculture
- The causes and consequences of conflict between Native Americans and settlers in the West

## The American Story

The years following the Civil War were marked by unprecedented industrial expansion, technological development, and population growth. These factors produced a dramatic transformation of American society and the national economy. This expansion came at a cost, however. As the population moved westward, once again the issue of relations with the Aboriginal peoples of America became critical. At the same time, Americans could not fully escape the recent past. National politics was dominated by the need to address the legacy of slavery and rebuild a fractured union: the process of Reconstruction.

## TIMELINE

**1865**
- 13th Amendment abolishes slavery

**1866**
- 14th Amendment protects civil rights for former slaves

**1867**
- Reconstruction Act

**1869**
- 15th Amendment grants blacks voting rights
- Transcontinental railroad completed

## IMAGE ANALYSIS

**Figure 7.1** In 1868 Americans were excited by the imminent completion of the transcontinental railroad. As well as linking California to the east, it would open up the American West to large-scale settlement. The railroad would also transform the West from a wilderness of lakes, rivers, and mountains inhabited by Native Americans into a "civilized" land of farms and towns. This would be the culmination of the dream of manifest destiny—the inexorable march of American power across the continent—which had inspired generations of American politicians, writers, and adventurers.

Few captured this national confidence better than Frances Flora Palmer, the creator of this popular print *Across the Continent: Westward the Course of Empire Takes Its Way*, which vividly illustrates the two parts of the American West, and the central role of the railroad in transforming the wilderness into settlement.

- Standard Oil founded — **1870**
- Financial panic — **1874**
- Reconstruction ends; Battle of Little Bighorn — **1876**
- Chief Joseph surrenders — **1877**

# INTRODUCTION

By 1865 the United States had endured almost five years of costly and bloody civil war. As you will discover in this chapter, over the ensuing two decades the nation would be reshaped by immigration and the settlement of the West, by massive capital investment, and by new technology. Before the full benefits of this new era could be realized, however, it was essential to address the legacy of the war. The nation needed to be restored to health, and to mend the wounds of slavery. This process of reconstruction would be painful.

As you read this chapter, consider how many of these issues still face modern North American society. How do immigration and new technology continue to shape our lives and communities today? Have attitudes toward minorities (including African-Americans and Aboriginal peoples) changed? Can you think of modern parallels to the corruption that afflicted politics and business during the later 19th century? Although more than a century separates us from the world described in this chapter, you may be surprised to discover that Americans then grappled with many of the same concerns that confront Americans today.

# RECONSTRUCTION

In his second inaugural address, Abraham Lincoln set out a vision for rebuilding the shattered nation after the Civil War: "With malice toward none, with charity for all, with firmness in the right as God gives us to see the right, let us strive on to finish the work we are in."

Yet resistance across the South and political divisions in the North would soon frustrate this ideal. Even as the lives of former slaves were transformed by freedom, **Reconstruction**, the program of social legislation that would grant new rights to blacks, was creating new divisions within the country. In the end, while the Union would be restored, the wider transformation of the South envisaged by some reformers would not last.

## Presidential Reconstruction

The primary goal of President Lincoln as the Civil War drew to a close was to restore the Union, reintegrating the former Confederate states into the United States as smoothly as possible. His successor, Vice-President Andrew Johnson, shared this goal. Johnson was a political anomaly—a Southerner who had remained loyal to the Union. He was against slavery chiefly because he saw it as a tool used by wealthy landowners to consolidate their control over the economy and politics of the South, thereby denying poorer whites a share of economic and political power. In fact, Johnson had little respect for African-Americans, and wished to see poor white farmers—not freed slaves—enjoy power and prosperity. In explaining his plans for restoring the South, President Johnson repeatedly stated: "White men alone must manage the South."

Initially, Johnson pardoned all former Confederates who swore an oath to the Union, and even military officers and wealthy landowners generally received presidential pardons. State conventions were held in each formerly Confederate state to draft new constitutions—a prerequisite to readmission to the Union. The main conditions imposed were to repudiate secession, and to accept the total abolition of slavery.

By the end of 1865 ten of the eleven states had met these requirements and looked forward to rejoining the Union in the near future. Johnson announced to the nation that the Union would soon be restored. In December 1865 the 13th Amendment was ratified, confirming the abolition of slavery. The main objectives of Johnson's plan, which became known as Presidential Reconstruction, were now fulfilled: the abolition of slavery and the reincorporation of the ex-Confederate states into the union.

| The Presidents: 1865–1880 | | |
|---|---|---|
| **Abraham Lincoln*** | Republican | March 4, 1861 - April 15, 1865 |
| **Andrew Johnson** | Democratic | April 15, 1865 - March 4, 1869 |
| **Ulysses S. Grant** | Republican | March 4, 1869 - March 4, 1877 |
| **Rutherford B. Hayes** | Republican | March 4, 1877 - March 4, 1881 |

* assassinated

## Radical Reconstruction

More radical Republicans in Congress resented President Johnson's leniency toward Southern states, who continued to limit the civil rights of former slaves. Most of these states passed so-called **Black Codes**: laws restricting the labour rights of blacks, preventing land ownership by former slaves, and prohibiting interracial marriages. To ensure that former slaves enjoyed all the rights of citizenship, Congress passed the 14th Amendment in 1866. It was intended to ensure that states could not deny former slaves their civil rights (such as the right to sue in court and the right to own property). The amendment also restricted the rights of former Confederate politicians to seek election to Congress. The Republicans saw this as a way to protect their majority, by preventing an influx of Southern Democrats.

Johnson's plan for Reconstruction faced its greatest challenge when the Republican Congress passed the Reconstruction Act in 1867, imposing harsher conditions on the South. This law divided the South into military districts that were occupied by soldiers and ruled by generals; it imposed martial law; and it ensured that Confederate sympathizers were removed from government posts. Before being readmitted to the Union, states had to draft new constitutions that guaranteed the vote to former male slaves. If the states refused, military authorities had the power to act on their behalf.

All this time, the struggle in Washington between Johnson and the Republican Congress grew more heated. Angered by Johnson's apparent unwillingness to deal harshly with the South, the House of Representatives in February 1868 voted to impeach or formally charge the president with "high crimes and misdemeanors." The case went to trial before the Senate, which required a two-thirds majority vote to remove Johnson from office. Ultimately, Johnson held onto his post by a single vote, but it was clear that Congress, rather than the president, was now in control of the government. This power shift led to a new phase in relations with the South, a phase often referred to as the period of Congressional, or Radical, Reconstruction.

**SOUND BITE**

"I have never desired bloody punishments to any extent, even for the sake of example. But there are punishments quite as appalling, and longer remembered, than death ... Strip the proud nobility of their bloated estates; reduce them to a level with plain republicans; send them forth to labor, and teach their children to enter the workshops or handle the plow, and you will thus humble the proud traitor."

—Republican Congressman Thaddeus Stevens, a leader of Radical Reconstruction

Determined to accelerate the process of Reconstruction in the wake of the attempted impeachment of Johnson, in 1868 the Republicans selected the popular former Union General Ulysses S. Grant as their candidate for president. Giving the vote to blacks in the South had a decisive effect on the outcome of the 1868 election in several states, for Grant received more than 500,000 of their votes. He beat his opponent, former New York governor Horatio Seymour, by just 300,000 votes.

In February 1869 the Republican Congress passed the 15th Amendment, guaranteeing that "the right of citizens of the United States to vote shall not be denied or abridged ... on account of race, color, or previous condition of servitude." This applied throughout the nation. Congress forced the final three unreconstructed Southern states (Mississippi, Texas, and Virginia) to accept the 14th and 15th Amendments before being readmitted to the Union. This they all did in early 1870, completing the process of reconstructing the Union, after almost five years of intense political struggle.

**Figure 7.2** (*Far left*) This 1867 illustration celebrated the new right of African-Americans to vote. Why might the artist have included a soldier as well as a farmer and tradesman?

**Figure 7.3** (*Left*) Considered a symbol of Reconstruction, Hiram Rhodes Revels (1827–1901) was the first African-American elected to the US Senate. He served as a Republican senator from Mississippi (1870–71). Ironically, he occupied the same Senate seat once held by Jefferson Davis, president of the Confederate States of America.

AMERICAN ARCHIVE

## The Fifteenth Amendment

The Republican victory in the presidential election of 1868 owed much to the votes of African-Americans. To ensure that these citizens continued to enjoy the right to vote and that the accomplishments of Reconstruction were not undermined, in February 1869 the Republican Congress passed the 15th Amendment to the Constitution. The 15th Amendment declared that no male citizen could be prevented from voting because of race. It also allowed the federal government to intervene in elections in the South—even sending soldiers if necessary to ensure that former slaves were free to vote.

While the 15th Amendment was an important statement of legal equality, it was not without flaws. Many politicians from the North remained uncomfortable with extending voting rights to African-Americans. To limit this political opposition and ensure its passage, the amendment did not rule out other grounds (besides race or status as former slaves) for limiting suffrage, or voting rights. As a result, it soon proved possible to circumvent the amendment and deny former slaves the right to vote on other grounds, such as education or property ownership.

For their part, some women's rights advocates, many of whom had campaigned actively to abolish slavery, argued that it was unjust to ban voting discrimination based on race, but allow discrimination based on sex. By ignoring their concerns, the amendment drove a wedge between some abolitionists and campaigners for women's rights (for more on this conflict, see the We the People feature in Chapter 5 on page 166).

**The 15th Amendment (ratified February 1870)**

**Article 1** The right of citizens of the United States to vote shall not be denied or abridged by the United States or by any State on account of race, color, or previous condition of servitude.

**Article 2** The Congress shall have power to enforce this article by appropriate legislation.

### Think It Through

1. Explain the political circumstances that led to the adoption of the 15th Amendment.
2. In some ways the 15th Amendment represented a compromise. Why was this the case?

**Figure 7.4** This cartoon celebrates the benefits of the new rights that African-Americans enjoyed following the passage of the 15th Amendment and the guarantee of the vote. Can you identify any specific rights?

## Transforming the South

To learn more about the Reconstruction era, visit www.emp.ca/ah.

Reconstruction extended far beyond politics, however. Radical Republicans like Thaddeus Stevens of Pennsylvania demanded a refashioning of Southern society, redistributing land from wealthy landowners to poorer white farmers and the newly freed blacks: "The whole fabric of southern society must be changed … [I]f the South is ever to be made a safe republic let her lands be cultivated by the toil of the owners." Only in this way, thought Stevens and other Radicals, would the effects of slavery be eradicated.

**Figure 7.5** Education was an important part of the work of Freedmen's Bureau. Textbooks like this one aimed to teach students moral virtues like punctuality and sobriety, as well as proper spelling.

### Freedmen's Bureaus

Congress quickly recognized that the newly freed slaves needed assistance if they were to survive. With the collapse of the plantation economy, many former slaves found themselves with no means of support and nowhere to live. The primary way to address this urgent need was through the Bureau of Refugees, Freedmen, and Abandoned Lands, popularly known as the Freedmen's Bureau, which distributed emergency food and clothing to poor Southerners, both black and white. The bureau negotiated wages and settled legal disputes between blacks and whites. It also supported more than 3,000 schools across the South, where former slaves could receive a basic education. To many blacks who were denied schooling during slavery, education was synonymous with freedom.

Much of the aid to former slaves in the South was administered by agents from the North. These men were responsible for putting the policies of Radical Reconstruction into practice, including operating offices of the Freedmen's Bureau. While some confined their activities to economic development, others became involved in politics, promoting the interests of the Republican Party. Those who used Reconstruction as an opportunity to seek and profit from political office in the South were denounced by Southerners as **carpetbaggers**.

In their work, Reconstruction workers encountered considerable resistance from many white Southerners, keen to thwart Reconstruction policies and preserve power over the former slaves. The **Ku Klux Klan**, a secretive organization that assaulted and murdered former slaves and the Northerners who had come to assist them, led resistance to Reconstruction. The Klan conducted violent campaigns designed to hinder the election of Republican governments across the South and to frustrate national elections. Their efforts were concentrated in those areas where blacks represented only a narrow majority of the population, and intimidation would be most effective in maintaining control.

Republican governors at first tried to ignore the resistance, fearing that an active response would simply intensify the violence. Some governors, however, such as William Holden of North Carolina, eventually resorted to military campaigns against the Klan. The violence that resulted left many Americans, in both the North and the South, with the impression that Reconstruction could only be accomplished through continued armed struggle—a cost that many viewed as too high.

**Figure 7.6** Members of the Ku Klux Klan. Founded in 1866 by veterans of the Confederate Army, the Klan opposed Reconstruction and terrorized freed slaves as well as Freedmen's agents.

### Sharecropping

Most former slaves hoped to be granted a portion of the land on which they had toiled for their masters, and in this way become independent farmers. Despite their belief that the government would assign them land confiscated from slave owners, it soon became clear that no significant redistribution of land was planned, and only a small proportion of former slaves, perhaps 15 percent, could afford to purchase their own farms.

Instead, some found work on plantations for cash wages or for a share of the profits. Others participated in **sharecropping**, a system in which families received a plot of land, which they were free to cultivate, in exchange for paying one-third to one-half of their crop to the landowner at harvest time. The drawbacks for the former slaves were clear: they could not leave the farm until the harvest had been completed, and they often became deeply indebted to the landowner, who advanced them seed and supplies on credit that was payable against next year's crop.

Many understandably came to view sharecropping as a form of economic bondage. For landowners anxious to find sufficient labour in the absence of slavery, sharecropping offered a reasonable solution, since it effectively tied the former slaves to the land and kept them from becoming financially independent.

## The End of Reconstruction

The continued success of Reconstruction depended on active support from the North. Without the dedicated financial, administrative, and military resources of the federal government, the Reconstruction program could not continue. In the early 1870s, however, political and economic developments would shift the government's focus away from the South, and lead the nation to gradually abandon Reconstruction.

### Crisis and Corruption

One factor that led to this shift in focus was economic. During the early 1870s the United States endured an economic depression so severe that it occupied most of the government's attention. The depression itself will be discussed in more detail later in the chapter. For now, it is important to note that one of its effects was to undermine electoral support for the governing Republican Party, the party of Reconstruction.

Over this same period, a succession of scandals involving bribery and corruption shook the Republican administration of President Grant. The Whiskey Scandal involved treasury agents and distillers, led by Grant's private secretary, who pocketed millions of dollars in excise taxes. The Credit Mobilier Scandal revealed that a number of prominent Republican politicians (including Vice-President Schuyler Colfax) had created a fictitious company in order to pocket government subsidies intended for the building of the Union Pacific Railroad. Although Grant himself was never directly implicated in these scandals, they engulfed senior Republicans and undermined public confidence in his administration. By contrast, the Democrats, who were determined to end Reconstruction, soared in popularity.

In 1876, political corruption climaxed in a disputed presidential election. Having served two terms, Grant retired, worn out by the scandals that had battered his administration. The Democratic Party candidate, Samuel Tilden, garnered 250,000 more votes than his Republican opponent, Rutherford B. Hayes. It appeared that Tilden had won, but Republicans were determined to hold on to power if possible. In three Southern states whose governments were still controlled by Republicans (Florida, South Carolina, and Louisiana), state officials reported victories by Hayes. Democrats in those three states also made returns, declaring Tilden victorious. Amidst serious accusations of fraud from each side, an electoral commission composed of senators, members of the House of Representatives, and Supreme Court justices was given responsibility to resolve the disputed election. With a Republican majority, the commission awarded the election to Hayes, who then received 185 Electoral College votes to Tilden's 184.

This did not end the crisis, however. Democrats, who controlled the House of Representatives, threatened to block Hayes's inauguration. Only a last-minute deal that handed control of state governments in the disputed states to Democrats (opposed to Reconstruction) avoided a constitutional crisis. In order to calm the political storm that followed, President Hayes promised to halt further federal government intervention in Southern states. The government withdrew federal troops and military governors, and without this armed support, Reconstruction was doomed. The contested election of 1876 thus marked the end of Reconstruction in the South.

## The Legacy of Reconstruction

"The slave went free; stood a brief moment in the sun; then moved back again toward slavery." It is not difficult to understand why the African-American historian W.E.B. Du Bois described the Reconstruction era this way. Despite new constitutional guarantees, African-Americans found their legal rights restricted by the Black Codes. They endured racial discrimination and violence from the Ku Klux Klan. Former slaves faced poverty and economic hardship, particularly because of the sharecropping system. By the mid-1870s, the heady optimism of the early years after the Civil War had evaporated. Perhaps the program had simply been too ambitious?

Yet the pessimism of Du Bois and others tended to overlook the lasting impact of Reconstruction, which sought to remake Southern society and reverse the damage wrought by centuries of slavery. It was a bold plan in which former slaves gained access to education, the right to vote, and above all freedom. For the first time, African-Americans served in government and were elected to the US Senate. Finally, Reconstruction, and particularly the participation of African-Americans within it, established a vision to be pursued throughout the following century, one that culminated in the civil rights movement of the mid-20th century (see Chapter 12).

**Figure 7.7** Born into slavery, Frederick Douglass escaped at the age of 19 and became a leading abolitionist. In 1876 he criticized the limited progress of Reconstruction by challenging white Americans: "Do you mean to make good to us the promises in your Constitution?" What did he mean? Was his criticism justified?

**SOUND BITE**

"The Yankees helped free us, so they say, but they let us be put back in slavery again."

—Former slave Thomas Hall, reflecting on the outcome of Reconstruction

**CHECK YOUR UNDERSTANDING**

1. Why did Congress impose a harsher reconstruction on the South than did President Andrew Johnson?
2. How did the Freedmen's Bureau help former slaves?
3. What was the purpose of the Ku Klux Klan and what methods did it use?
4. How did the Republicans prevent Samuel Tilden from becoming president?
5. In your own words, explain W.E.B. Du Bois's view of Reconstruction.

# GROWTH OF A NATION

During the last decades of the 19th century the United States emerged as one of the wealthiest nations in the world. How did this happen? The key was the convergence of several factors, including immigration and rapid population growth, advances in industry and transportation, and agricultural improvements. They laid the groundwork for a period of astounding national growth.

## Immigration and Urbanization

One of the most notable developments of the decades following the Civil War was a rapid expansion of the American population between 1870 and 1890, from fewer than 40 million to over 60 million. While rising birth rates were part of the explanation, much of the increase came from immigration. Between 1865 and 1890, over 10 million immigrants arrived in the United States, and in one year alone (1882) more than 1.2 million immigrants entered the country.

Most new arrivals settled in cities rather than in rural areas. Whereas in 1820 fewer than 5 percent of Americans lived in communities of 10,000 or more people, by the end of the 19th century this proportion had risen to over 20 percent. As immigrants arrived and rural populations migrated to urban areas, the major cities grew dramatically: between 1870 and 1900 Philadelphia doubled in size, New York's population tripled, and Chicago expanded to five times its original size.

### Population Growth of Ten Largest American Cities, 1870–1880

| City | 1870 Population | 1880 Population | % Increase |
|---|---|---|---|
| **New York City** | 942,292 | 1,206,299 | 28% |
| **Philadelphia** | 674,022 | 847,170 | 26% |
| **Brooklyn** | 396,099 | 566,663 | 43% |
| **St. Louis** | 310,864 | 350,518 | 13% |
| **Chicago** | 298,977 | 503,185 | 68% |
| **Baltimore** | 267,354 | 332,313 | 24% |
| **Boston** | 250,526 | 362,839 | 45% |
| **Cincinnati** | 216,239 | 255,139 | 18% |
| **New Orleans** | 191,418 | 216,090 | 13% |
| **San Francisco** | 149,473 | 233,959 | 57% |

**Figure 7.8** This table shows the population growth of the ten largest US cities between 1870 and 1880. During that same period, total US population grew by 26 percent. How did the growth of major cities compare with the overall population increase? Which cities grew the most during this decade? Why?

### Push and Pull Factors

Push and pull factors combined to encourage the surge in immigration in the decades following the end of the Civil War. **Push factors**, including economic and political upheavals in Europe, led many to leave their homes and seek a new life across the Atlantic. The growth of industrial cities in Europe, for example, had led to an agricultural revolution that saw many small family farms replaced by larger commercial operations. Many families now faced an uncertain future. A rise in population compounded the crisis caused by this shortage of farmland. Political upheavals in Germany and parts of eastern and central Europe prompted some to seek a more hospitable home in America. At the same time, demand for unskilled labour for America's growing industries and the availability of cheap farmland in the west were **pull factors** luring many European immigrants to the United States. In addition, improvements in transportation (particularly steamships and railroads) made immigration to America more efficient and affordable.

## Problems for Cities

Immigrants to cities faced many challenges—particularly finding lodging and employment. (You can read more about living and working conditions in cities in Chapter 8.) Their needs offered local politicians an opportunity to cement their own power, by providing assistance in return for political support. The result in many cases was rampant political corruption. In cities such as New York and Chicago, powerful political "machines" dominated municipal government. These "machines" were political organizations that provided practical assistance to city residents (particularly new immigrants seeking housing or jobs) in exchange for money and votes.

While municipal political machines no doubt helped many new immigrants to settle into the city and overcome the insecurities of urban life, they came to control politics and grew corrupt. The most famous political machine was New York's Tammany Hall, controlled by the Democrat William "Boss" Tweed. Through their control of the city administration, Tweed and his colleagues stole vast sums—estimated at more than $200 million between 1869 and 1871 (more than $3.3 billion today)—from the city government's coffers. Eventually exposed by the press, including the magazine *Harper's Weekly* and its political cartoonist Thomas Nast, Tweed was sent to prison. Despite the fall of Tweed, political machines, including Tammany Hall, continued to control political life in New York and elsewhere.

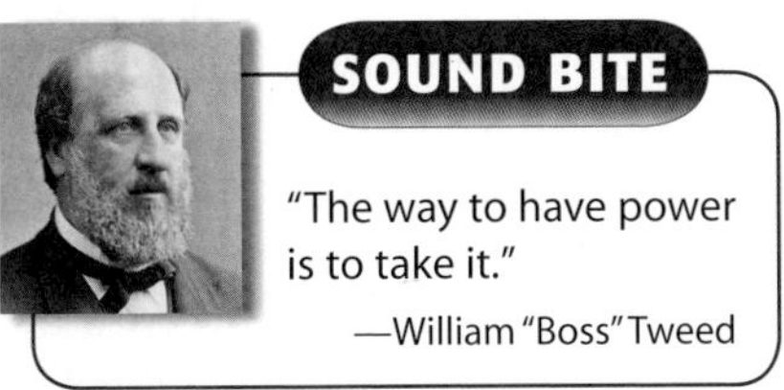

**SOUND BITE**

"The way to have power is to take it."

—William "Boss" Tweed

**Figure 7.9** The cartoonist Thomas Nast conducted a crusade to expose the corruption of New York City politics under "Boss" Tweed and Tammany Hall. What does this cartoon suggest about the reasons for Tweed's political power?

**Figure 7.10** The Great Fire of Chicago caused widespread panic as residents fled the flames. One observer described streets "choked with all manner of goods and people."

Nor was political corruption the only threat to American cities. The dangers of urban overcrowding were vividly illustrated in October 1871, when a fire that broke out among the barns and tenements of a crowded Chicago neighbourhood got out of control. The fire continued to burn for three days, laying waste to a vast area of the city. The editor of the *Chicago Tribune* compared the scale of the fire to the greatest battle of the Civil War: "Nobody could see it all—no more than one man could see the whole of the battle of Gettysburg. It was too vast, too swift, too full of smoke, too full of danger, for anybody to see it all." The Great Fire of Chicago took a tremendous toll: 250 killed and almost 100,000 left homeless, with 17,500 buildings destroyed. Yet the devastation would soon be erased and the city rapidly rebuilt. The spirit of the residents once the fire was extinguished was summed up by one Chicago journalist, who boldly proclaimed, "We can conquer everything else."

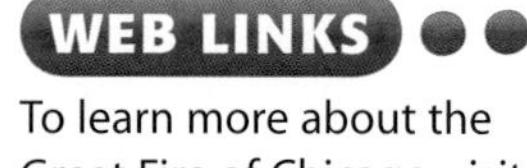


To learn more about the Great Fire of Chicago, visit www.emp.ca/ah.

## Improving City Life

Living conditions for new immigrants in the tenements of New York City, Pittsburgh, and Chicago were appalling, and various attempts were made to improve the quality of life in American cities. (See also Chapters 8 and 9.) Among the many plans, two merit particular mention. The first was the campaign to provide urban parks—an attempt to incorporate rural life into the heart of the cities. The leader of this campaign was Frederick Law Olmsted, who designed Central Park in New York (which was begun in 1859 and finally completed in 1873). In keeping with the popular democracy of America, these urban parks were designed to be public spaces, open to all.

Another expression of this popular democracy was the provision of public libraries, which could provide education and information to all citizens.

**Figure 7.11** Winter in Central Park in the 1860s. The park was (and remains) a popular location for ice skating in New York. How might this scene have changed in 150 years?

While a few public libraries existed in the 1870s, their number increased dramatically following the announcement by industrialist Andrew Carnegie that he would build a library for any community prepared to guarantee that it would be maintained. Between 1881 and 1907 Carnegie's largesse provided funds for more than 1,000 libraries, many of which are still in operation.

## Industrial Growth and Big Business

The decades after the Civil War witnessed an unprecedented expansion of the American economy. This growth was fuelled by a variety of factors, including the rapid increase in population, the creation of a vast national network of railroads, massive investment of capital, and the emergence of an industrial economy.

### Economic Resources

The rapid growth of the American economy following the Civil War was made possible by an abundance of natural resources. In particular, two raw materials were critical to this new industrial economy: iron and coal. Iron was used in the production of steel, which in turn was used to construct railroads and blast furnaces, both fuelled by coal. Coal was also the primary means of generating steam power, which drove the machinery of factories across America. The discovery of abundant iron ore deposits in the Mesabi Range in northern Minnesota and the development of coal fields in Pennsylvania, Ohio, and Kentucky were therefore key factors in the nation's economic growth. The symbol of this growth was the railroad.

## The Railroad Boom

On May 10, 1869 the president of the Central Pacific Railroad arrived at Promontory Point in the Utah Territory to hammer the last golden spike of the first transcontinental railroad, merging the Union Pacific and Central Pacific Railroads. Work had begun six years earlier from Omaha, Nebraska in the east and Sacramento, California in the west. Construction was challenging and costly, but two factors contributed to the successful completion of the project. The federal government provided substantial subsidies (ranging from $9,000 to $28,000 per kilometre—or about $150,000 to $480,000 in current dollars) to encourage construction. As well, the availability of cheap labour made large-scale construction possible. Irish immigrants and ex-slaves worked from the east, while in the west the Union Pacific imported more than 10,000 Chinese labourers to lay tracks through the treacherous mountains. Within a few years other transcontinental routes would follow, including the Southern Pacific from Los Angeles to New Orleans. Between 1870 and 1890 the distance covered by American railroads more than tripled, from barely 80,000 kilometres to over 250,000 kilometres. American railroads were soon among the nation's largest employers—the Pennsylvania Railroad alone had more than 20,000 employees.

**WEB LINKS** 

Explore the construction of the transcontinental railroad by visiting www.emp.ca/ah.

The impact of this railroad boom on the United States was enormous. It led to a rapid expansion in the population of the West. For example, the combined population of Minnesota, Kansas, Nebraska, and the Dakotas grew from barely 300,000 in 1860 to surpass 2,000,000 by 1880. By offering farmers and ranchers access to new lands, and enabling them to ship their cattle and grain easily to markets in the East, railroads promoted ranching and farming on the Great Plains to a degree not previously possible. The development of

**Figure 7.12** The Central Pacific and Union Pacific Railroads were joined at Promontory Point, Utah on May 10, 1869, marking the completion of the transcontinental railroad. Using a book or the Internet, find a photograph of the completion of the Canadian Pacific Railway at Craigellachie, BC on November 7, 1885. How do the two photographs compare?

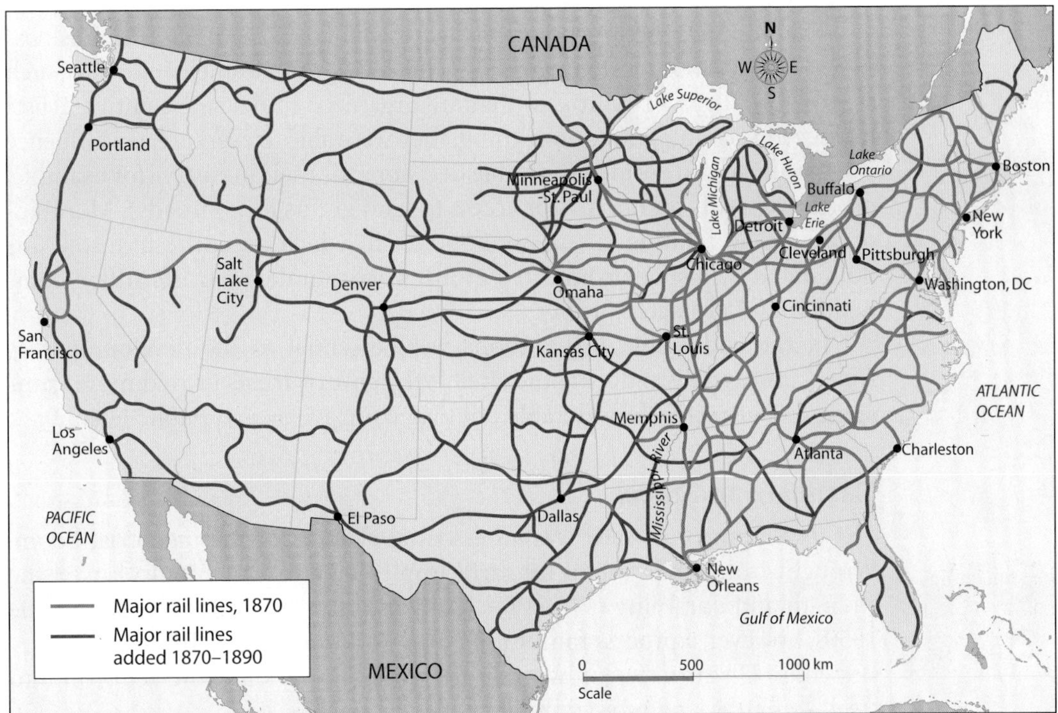


**Figure 7.13** Between 1870 and 1890 the railroad network extended to reach all areas of the United States, with most growth occurring west of the Mississippi River.

new technologies such as steel rails and the air brake made possible larger and heavier trains, which led to reduced transportation costs and, ultimately, lower consumer prices.

## Corporations and Trusts

New forms of financing and organization encouraged the railroad boom and revolutionized wider American business practices. For example, railroads aggressively sought capital to finance expansion by selling bonds to eager investors.

The foremost business change following the Civil War was the emergence of the **corporation**. Corporations are legal entities that allow many owners to act together as a single company, distinct from the individuals who own it. Each corporation is governed by a charter (a legal document setting out its structure and powers). In addition, corporations are "immortal"—they continue to exist beyond the life of individual owners or administrators.

Corporations were well suited to the needs of larger businesses such as railroads, whose assets and operations spanned many states. For one thing, they were governed by the principle of limited liability, which meant that investors were only responsible for debts up to the value of their investment in the company. This limited liability helped to encourage investment by minimizing risk.

The popularity of corporations led to the creation of another business model, the **trust**. A trust is a group of corporations in a single industry (such as steel, oil, sugar, or railroads) that are organized into a single entity. Trusts had several advantages. For one thing, they were able to exert greater influence over politicians to ensure favourable decisions for their industry (for example, protective tariffs on imports or access to land grants for railroads). More significantly, by creating virtual monopolies in which an entire industry was dominated by a single connected group of corporations, trusts stifled competition and protected profits.

In the end, while corporations were essential to the development of American capitalism during the later 19th century, trusts proved more damaging and attracted considerable political controversy and public hostility.

## Carnegie and Steel

The development of steel was an essential element of the industrial boom. Wrought iron, while useful for farm implements or small tools, lacked the strength and durability needed for heavy industry like railroads. During the 1850s, however, a process for refining iron was developed in Britain by Henry Bessemer. His furnace, known as a Bessemer converter, converted iron into steel—a harder and more durable metal.

**WEB LINKS**

To discover more about the career and accomplishments of Andrew Carnegie, visit www.emp.ca/ah.

American entrepreneur Andrew Carnegie was among the first to exploit Bessemer's invention. A former railroad manager, he quickly recognized the possibilities of large-scale steel production. Carnegie established his mills around Pittsburgh in western Pennsylvania, which soon became the centre of the American steel industry—an industry that now lay at the heart of the American industrial economy. As demand for steel grew, particularly from railroads, production increased and prices dropped. In 1867 only 2,500 tons of steel rails were produced, at a cost of $170 per ton (about $2,500 per ton today), compared with 460,000 tons of iron rails. By 1884 steel rail production exceeded 1.5 million tons, and the cost had fallen to only $32 per ton (about $715 per ton today). At the same time, iron rails had disappeared.

**Figure 7.14** The Edgar Thomson Works were the first steel mills opened by Andrew Carnegie, outside Pittsburgh in 1875. They became the basis of the steel industry in western Pennsylvania, and the foundation of Carnegie's wealth. What impact would these mills have had on the local environment?

Beyond lower costs, the technological impact of steel was dramatic: steel rails lasted up to ten years (compared with two years for iron), and could carry ten times the weight of iron rails. Carnegie himself profited enormously from the demand for steel, earning him the title "the richest man in the world." When he finally sold his company in 1901, he received $225 million (about $5.8 billion in current dollars).

# WE THE PEOPLE 1839–1937

## *John D. Rockefeller*

"If you want to succeed you should strike out on new paths, rather than travel the worn paths of accepted success." These were the words of John D. Rockefeller, who created the American oil industry and became a symbol of both the best and worst aspects of the new American approach to business.

**Figure 7.15** A cartoon of Rockefeller from 1901. How has the artist attempted to illustrate the power of Standard Oil? What opinion do you think the artist might have of Rockefeller? Why?

The son of a travelling peddler, Rockefeller began work as a clerk in Cleveland before the Civil War. When the oil boom hit Ohio in the early 1860s, he saw a new opportunity and joined friends in investing in the industry. By the age of 25 Rockefeller had bought out his partners, and soon operated the largest refinery in Cleveland. In 1870 he established the Standard Oil Company, which grew during the decade to control over 90 percent of US refineries, thereby making Rockefeller one of the wealthiest men in America—at the age of 40.

How had Rockefeller accomplished this astonishing success? It came from a combination of good fortune and ruthless determination. During the depression of 1873, Standard Oil bought up many bankrupt refineries. Rockefeller negotiated preferential treatment from railroads, promising large oil shipments in exchange for lower freight costs. He did whatever was necessary to eliminate competition: spying on his competitors to lure away their customers, or selling his product so cheaply that other refineries lost their customers and were driven out of business. To increase profits, he also made sure he controlled all aspects of the industry, from oil production and pipelines to refineries and retail gas stations.

Rockefeller was the first to hit upon the idea of forming trusts. To organize his business, in 1882 Rockefeller created the Standard Oil Trust—a group of companies that appeared to be separate entities but were in fact controlled by a single board of directors headed by Rockefeller himself. In this way he could control the entire oil industry as if it were a single company—in effect creating a monopoly. The practice of creating trusts quickly spread to other major industries, from steel to banking to railroads.

It was not long before politicians and critics began to attack Rockefeller for his business practices, his use of trusts, and his monopoly. Standard Oil became a symbol of all that was wrong with American capitalism. Eventually this public criticism forced the break-up of the Standard Oil Trust (in 1911). While Standard Oil itself has disappeared as a single company, its name survives in Canada as Esso (an abbreviation of Standard Oil—SO).

There is no doubt that Rockefeller was ruthless in his business dealings. However, like many other industrialists at the time, Rockefeller shifted his energies to philanthropy, donating considerable sums to educational institutions, hospitals, and other charities. In this, he shared the view of Andrew Carnegie that the rich should devote their wealth to the common good. He was also determined to rescue his reputation, which had been tarnished by accusations of greed. In this he was only partially successful.

With his creation of the Standard Oil model, Rockefeller boasted that he "revolutionized the way of doing business all over the world." Even the journalist Ida Tarbell, who frequently condemned Rockefeller's business practices as immoral, acknowledged that "his instinct for the money opportunity in things was amazing." Rockefeller's life embodied the contradictions of the American dream. On the one hand, he represented the ideal of the self-made man who rose from humble beginnings to great wealth through hard work. On the other, his greed and ruthlessness in business were seen as typical of the failings of late 19th-century American capitalism.

### Think It Through

1. How did Rockefeller gain control over the oil industry during the 1870s?
2. Why did Standard Oil and Rockefeller attract criticism? What were the consequences of this criticism?
3. What current corporations (or their founders and owners) have similar reputations to that of Rockefeller and Standard Oil? Explain.

## Robber Barons or Entrepreneurs?

Popular attitudes toward the leaders of American industry in the later 19th century varied widely. They were praised for their entrepreneurial spirit and determination to improve American life, but also condemned as "robber barons" who manipulated markets and conspired to create monopolies. Where does the truth lie? Some industrialists, like railroad magnate Jay Gould (perhaps the archetypal robber baron), clearly stopped at nothing to enrich themselves: bribing government officials, committing fraud, and using armed thugs to intimidate their competitors. Others, like John D. Rockefeller, pursued questionable business practices, including predatory pricing (reducing the price of their products in order to drive competitors out of business). Most, including Andrew Carnegie, did not hesitate to use force to prevent workers from organizing or striking in search of improved pay and working conditions.

At the same time, some of these industrial leaders devoted considerable effort and wealth to charitable causes. In addition, their entrepreneurial energy helped to create the dramatic industrial growth that transformed the American economy and society during the closing decades of the 19th century.

## The Depression of 1873

The frenzy of railroad expansion following the Civil War eventually triggered an economic collapse in 1873, when speculation in railroad bonds led to a financial crash. As investors' confidence evaporated, the crisis spread. Eventually over half the nation's railroads defaulted, unable to pay the interest on their bonds. Soon banks and even the New York Stock Exchange felt the blow. Within two years over 100 banks had collapsed, and many thousands of businesses had failed.

The impact of the depression fell most keenly upon workers, who often found themselves unemployed and penniless. The national unemployment rate reached 15 percent, and in New York City it surpassed 25 percent. Many unemployed labourers had no choice but to leave home in search of work or assistance elsewhere. These wandering unemployed were known as "tramps," as they went from town to town "on the tramp." The depression of the 1870s, with its high unemployment and homelessness, offered a foretaste of the American experience during the Great Depression of the 1930s (see Chapter 10).

Responses to the depression varied. Many workers began to organize, calling mass meetings to demand that governments organize and fund public works projects that would provide employment. At the same time, business and political leaders generally rejected calls for assistance, arguing that the depression was a natural part of the business cycle and that governments should not interfere. The depression of the 1870s lasted over five years, making it the most serious economic crisis yet experienced by the United States.

### The Great Railroad Strike of 1877

In 1877, a number of major railroads began cutting wages and hours in an effort to reduce operating costs. Workers, angered that their incomes were falling while living costs remained high, walked off the job in response. The strikes spread rapidly across the country, from Pittsburgh and Baltimore to Chicago and San Francisco, bringing the nation's railroad network to a standstill. To head off damage to the wider economy, state governors summoned local militias to reopen railroads and crush the strikes. Violent clashes ensued in several cities, with soldiers firing on crowds of civilians and strikers, leading to more than 100 deaths. Damage to railway property was extensive—over $4 million in Pittsburgh alone (more $80 million in current dollars). The Great Railroad Strike had a broad impact. Many Americans blamed immigrants who had brought radical political and economic ideas from Europe. At the same time, workers realized that stronger labour organizations were needed to protect their rights against powerful companies backed by government.

## Culture

Despite the sneers of contemporary European commentators, suggesting that America lacked any serious culture, the decades that followed the conclusion of the Civil War witnessed a transformation of American cultural life—from art and music to literature. By 1879 art museums had opened in Washington, New York, Boston, and Chicago, and the first symphony orchestras had formed in New York.

While novelists like Henry James presented an image of American society focused almost entirely on the upper classes, others aimed to capture the grittier realities of American life. The novelist William Dean Howells was typical of this trend. Initially, like Henry James, he argued for idealism in literature—a "genteel tradition" that depicted life as it should be, rather than how it was. He believed that literature should seek to improve American society. By the early 1880s, however, Howells had abandoned this approach, and instead began writing novels like *The Rise of Silas Lapham* (1885), which offered a realistic depiction of urban middle-class life.

# Culture Notes

## *Mark Twain (1835–1910) and Huckleberry Finn*

**Figure 7.16** The novelist Samuel Clemens (Mark Twain).

Few individuals more fully captured the transformation of American society during the decades after the Civil War than the writer Samuel Clemens, who wrote under the pen name Mark Twain. In his novels and newspaper columns, Mark Twain described life in the South after Reconstruction, the social changes occurring in American cities, and life on the frontier.

Twain's own experience mirrored the challenges of life on the American frontier. Leaving his native Missouri in 1861, he travelled west to the mining towns of Nevada, where he worked as a reporter. By 1864 he was employed as a newspaper columnist in San Francisco, the major city of the West. A keen observer of American life and morals, Twain critiqued the wealth and corruption of American society in his novel *The Gilded Age: A Tale of Today* (1873). A succession of popular novels followed, including *Tom Sawyer* (1876) and *The Prince and the Pauper* (1882).

Nowhere are the themes of the frontier, the legacy of slavery, and the importance of popular American culture more evident than in *The Adventures of Huckleberry Finn* (1884), the story of an impoverished young white boy growing up on the banks of the Mississippi in the years before the Civil War. As the novelist F. Scott Fitzgerald observed: "Huckleberry Finn took the first journey back. He was the first to look back at the republic from the perspective of the west."

In this excerpt, the young Huck Finn describes his struggle to balance his frontier freedom with the attempts of society to "sivilize" him:

> The Widow Douglas, she took me for her son, and allowed she would sivilize me; but it was rough living in the house all the time, considering how dismal

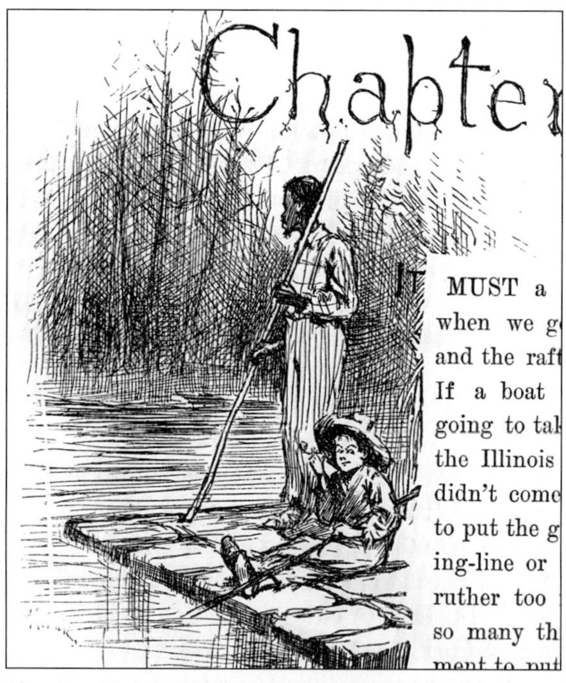

**Figure 7.17** Huckleberry Finn and his friend Jim, a runaway slave, spent time travelling the Mississippi on their raft. Huck describes what he loves about this idyllic life: "We said there warn't no home like a raft, after all. Other places do seem so cramped up and smothery, but a raft don't. You feel mighty free and easy and comfortable on a raft."

regular and decent the widow was in all her ways; and so when I couldn't stand it no longer, I lit out. I got into my old rags, and my sugar-hogshead [barrel] again, and was free and satisfied. But Tom Sawyer, he hunted me up and said he was going to start a band of robbers, and I might join if I would go back to the widow and be respectable. So I went back.

The widow she cried over me, and called me a poor lost lamb, and she called me a lot of other names, too, but she never meant no harm by it. She put me in them new clothes again, and I couldn't do nothing but sweat and sweat, and feel all cramped up. Well, then, the old thing commenced again. The widow rung a bell for supper, and you had to come to time. When you got to the table you couldn't go right to eating, but you had to wait for the widow to tuck down her head and grumble a little over the victuals, though there warn't really anything the matter with them. That is, nothing only everything was cooked by itself. In a barrel of odds and ends it is different; things get mixed up, and the juice kind of swaps around, and the things go better.

*Huckleberry Finn* had a deep impact on the development of American popular literature—particularly its use of colloquial language to illustrate ordinary life. The 20th-century American novelist Ernest Hemingway was unequivocal in his praise, claiming, "All modern American literature comes from one book by Mark Twain called 'Huckleberry Finn.'"

### Think It Through

1. From what you have read, in what ways could *Huckleberry Finn* be considered the first great American novel?
2. In the brief excerpt from *Huckleberry Finn*, how does the novelist use language to illustrate the young boy's character?

Explore the life and world of Mark Twain, and the characters he created, by visiting www.emp.ca/ah.

### CHECK YOUR UNDERSTANDING

1. What pull factors attracted immigrants to the United States?
2. How did Frederick Law Olmsted and Andrew Carnegie contribute to the movement to improve city life?
3. Why was coal an essential part of American economic success?
4. Draw a labelled diagram to explain the terms "corporation" and "trust."
5. What caused the depression of 1873?

## FARMING LIFE

The technological advances during the second half of the 19th century had a significant impact on farming in America, particularly in the West. Farm work benefited from a wide range of inventions that made production easier and more efficient; however, farmers themselves found little cause for celebration. Despite the demands of a swelling population, increased production ultimately led to steep declines in agricultural prices. The result was significant economic hardship in rural areas, as increased production failed to translate into greater prosperity.

## New Technologies

American farmers in the West benefited directly from a series of important new technologies throughout the mid and late 19th century. John Deere's steel plough (first developed in 1837) made it possible to break through the thick grasses and hard soil of the Great Plains, while McCormick's reaper (invented in 1831 and sold extensively from the mid-1850s) significantly reduced the labour of harvesting. The use of windmills to pump water from underground aquifers for irrigation was another essential technology in the semi-arid Great Plains. One of the most valuable but often overlooked developments of the era was the invention of barbed wire fencing (first sold in 1874), which enabled farmers to protect their crops from wandering animals.

The impact of these new technologies was dramatic. In 1870 it was estimated that a single farmer could plant and harvest eight acres of wheat in a season, but 20 years later, with the aid of new technologies, that same farmer could successfully farm more than 15 times as much land! Finally, through land grants the government actively encouraged the development of agricultural colleges to promote improvements in farming practices and research on crops and technology.

### Growth of Farming in the West: 1860–1880

| | Number of Farms (Average Hectares) | |
|---|---|---|
| | 1860 | 1880 |
| **Iowa** | 59,629 (25.7) | 185,351 (43.4) |
| **Kansas** | 10,108 (16.0) | 138,561 (31.4) |
| **Minnesota** | 17,999 (12.5) | 92,386 (31.8) |
| **Missouri** | 88,552 (28.6) | 215,575 (31.4) |
| **Nebraska** | 2,533 (19.1) | 63,387 (35.2) |

**Figure 7.18** This chart compares the number of farms and the average hectares being cultivated (planted with crops) in five Western states between 1860 and 1880. What do these numbers suggest about the impact of technology and new settlement on agriculture in the West?

**Figure 7.19** This Nebraska family in the mid-1880s is preparing to harvest their wheat crop. Notice the house built of sod. Can you identify examples of the impact of new technology on this farm?

## The Homestead Act

As well as improvements in technology, settlement of the West was also encouraged by passage of the Homestead Act in 1862. The Act offered prospective farmers a quarter section of land (64 hectares) at no cost—provided that they lived on it for five years and "improved" it by clearing the land and planting crops.

The success of the Homestead Act was limited, however. Many of the land grants were not suitable for farming, and even with determined effort they could not support a family. As a result, more than half of the grants were eventually forfeited by settlers, discouraged by the challenges of eking out a living on the Great Plains. Most other settlers purchased their lands directly from railroads or speculators, both of whom had reserved or bought up prime lands (with good soils, close to rivers for irrigation and railroads for transportation) for themselves. While the Homestead Act undoubtedly encouraged settlement of the West, only perhaps 10 percent of settlers benefited directly from its grants.

## Farmers, Tariffs, and Railroads

Despite the promises of cheap land and increased productivity, many farmers found prosperity elusive in the years after the Civil War. The tariff policy pursued by successive governments protected American manufacturers,

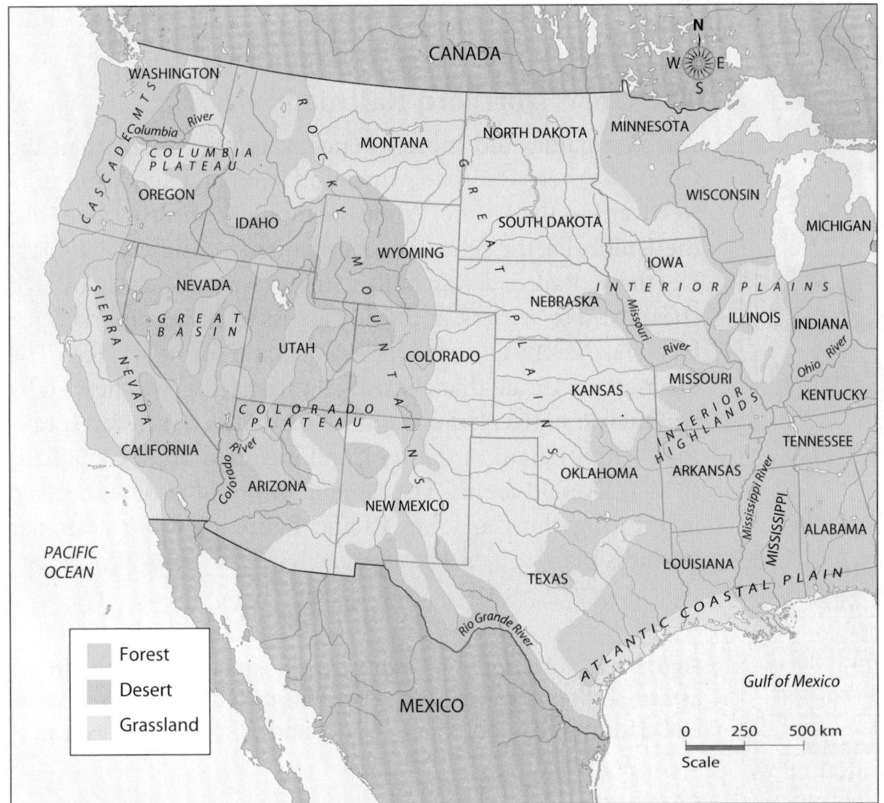


**Figure 7.20** The topography of the American West ranged from grasslands to desert, much of it inhospitable for settlement.

ensuring that prices for farm equipment remained high. At the same time, railroads could charge whatever they wanted for transporting grain and other commodities to market, for farmers had no other means of accessing markets. The result was growing discontent, and a belief that farmers' interests were being ignored.

## The Grange

In 1867 farmers formed the National Grange of the Patrons of Husbandry, a fraternal organization that became known as the Grange (a word for farm). The Grange tackled two main threats to farmers' livelihoods: railroads and grain merchants. Under their influence, laws were passed in many states to ensure fair prices for grain and to limit rail freight charges and fees for storing grain. The last of these was challenged in the courts, but in *Munn v. Illinois* (1877) the Supreme Court ruled that states had the power to regulate private businesses in the wider public interest. In some states the Grange organization established co-operative stores, where farmers could purchase supplies at reasonable cost. The Grange also operated many grain elevators, where farmers could be assured of a fair market price for their harvest.

The political activism of the Grange was not confined to agriculture. The organization also campaigned for an end to corruption among public officials, and the provision of free schooling in rural areas. As you will see in Chapter 8, the depression of the 1870s eventually eliminated many of the economic gains achieved by the Grange. However, the tradition of agricultural activism endured, and would provide the roots of the Populist movement that emerged in the 1890s.

To learn more about life in the American West, visit www.emp.ca/ah.

## The Great Northern Railroad

Few companies did more to encourage settlement than the Great Northern Railroad, which ran from St. Paul, Minnesota westward to the Pacific. While the builders of earlier lines like the Union Pacific relied on government subsidies, the Great Northern Railroad was built using private funds. It offered cheap land to settlers, and ready access to eastern markets for farmers, thereby ensuring itself a demand for its services. The business syndicate that controlled the railroad was headed by an Ontario native, James J. Hill (regarded as the cleverest railroad entrepreneur of the age), and included other Canadians such as Donald Smith. The same men would also be involved in creating the Canadian Pacific Railroad, using a similar business plan.

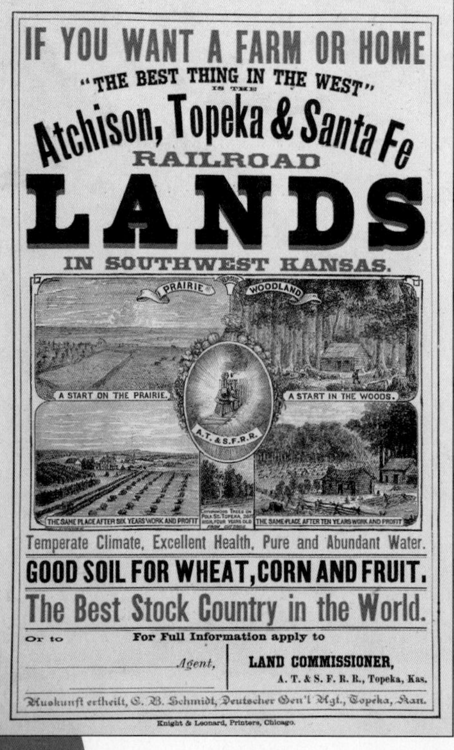


**Figure 7.21** American railroads used posters like this one to attract settlers, advertising the benefits of settling on the prairie. Railroads made huge profits selling land to settlers in this way.

## CHECK YOUR UNDERSTANDING

1. How did land grant agricultural colleges influence American agriculture?
2. Explain how each of the following contributed to the growth of the American economy: the steel plough, the reaper, wind-powered water pumps, barbed wire.
3. Why were more than half of all grants of land under the Homestead Act forfeited?
4. Describe how the Grange used the power of state governments to help farmers.

# CLAIMING THE WEST

Since the Louisiana Purchase in 1803 first gave America access to the lands beyond the Mississippi, westward expansion had been closely tied to the idea of manifest destiny (explored in Chapter 5). This process of westward expansion accelerated during the latter third of the 19th century, as increased immigration and a growing population produced a heightened demand for farmland. At the same time, technological improvements (particularly the extension of railroads) made the process of settling the West easier. Yet this process of westward settlement also reignited an old conflict with the Aboriginal peoples who occupied these lands.

## Purchase of Alaska, 1867

Following the disruption of the Civil War, the United States resumed its plans to extend its territory across North America, fulfilling what many saw as its manifest destiny. Secretary of State William Seward actively pursued this goal, seeking new territories and access to foreign markets. In 1867 Seward negotiated the purchase of Alaska from Russia at a cost of $7.2 million (about $106 million today). Many people dismissed this move as "Seward's Folly"—they regarded Alaska as a frozen wasteland without value. However, the purchase proved to

**Figure 7.22** This cheque was payable to the Russian ambassador to the United States, who accepted payment on behalf of his government for the purchase of Alaska.

be a shrewd one. It removed Russian influence from the Pacific coast of North America and gave the United States access to furs and other resources (including, eventually, gold as well as oil). With this acquisition Seward believed that the United States had moved a step closer to his dream: that all of North America—including Canada—would one day form part of the republic.

## Relations with Canada

As noted in Chapter 6, relations between the United States and Britain had been strained during the Civil War (as in the *Trent* Incident in 1861), and these tensions continued after 1865. Raids by a radical group called the Fenian Brotherhood prompted Britain to send troops to counter the threat to British North America emanating from the United States.

At the same time, Canadian politicians like John A. Macdonald strove to restore the reciprocity (free trade) that had existed during the 1850s between the United States and British North America. These efforts met with little success, however. With the tremendous economic growth produced by settlement of the West and the expansion of industry, American political leaders during the 1870s focused on boosting their own industry further through protective tariffs, rather than on encouraging free trade.

## Aboriginal Conflicts: Causes

Since the 1600s the Aboriginal peoples who inhabited America had been pushed steadily westward by the expansion of European settlement, leading to recurring conflict and the relentless destruction of Native American societies. The final major stage in this crisis came on the Great Plains during the 1860s and 1870s. What factors had prompted this renewed conflict?

### Settlement

The main factor that led to renewed conflict between Native Americans and the government was the expansion of settlement. The search for silver and gold and the thirst for farmland fuelled an influx of settlers, who often paid little heed to the territory or rights of Native Americans. Rumours of gold in the Black Hills of South Dakota, for example, encouraged outsiders to occupy land previously set aside for the Sioux under the Treaty of Fort Laramie. Similar tensions had followed the 1859 discovery of the Comstock Lode, an area rich in silver and gold deposits in Nevada. The westward extension of the railroad was viewed by Native Americans with deep suspicion, as the harbinger of further settlement.

### Decline of the Buffalo

For centuries the Great Plains had been dominated by the buffalo (bison), which roamed the continent in the millions. The buffalo were the basis of the Native American life on the Plains, providing food, clothing, and shelter. The

## 49th PARALLEL

# The Fenian Raids

Throughout the late spring of 1866, the border between British North America and the United States was alive with rumours of invasion. From Canada West (Ontario) to New Brunswick, fear of attack from the United States abounded. The source of the threat was not the United States government, but rather a small, revolutionary group of former Union soldiers.

During the Civil War some Irish immigrants serving in the Union Army had formed branches of the popular Irish nationalist organization the Fenian Brotherhood. Its goal was the end of British rule in Ireland. Immediately following the end of the war, some of these Fenians laid plans for an invasion of British North America. They intended to strike a symbolic blow against Britain on behalf of their compatriots in Ireland (under British rule), and perhaps even establish a republic in the colonies. With the end of the Civil War, many of the Fenian soldiers also sought fresh adventure. In the words of a popular Fenian song:

**Many a battle has been fought**
**Along with the boys in blue***
**So we will go and conquer Canada**
**For we've nothing else to do**

* the Union Army

Initially the Fenians intended an invasion of New Brunswick, but the arrival of the colonial militia, backed by the British navy and assisted by the American authorities, convinced the Fenians to abandon this plan. Instead, on May 31, 1866 a force of 1,500 Fenians, commanded by "General" John O'Neill, crossed the Niagara River and captured Fort Erie. Moving westward, the Fenians were met on June 2 at Ridgeway by a hastily assembled force of militiamen, supported by a few companies of British troops. Despite defeating the British and Canadians, the Fenian force soon withdrew. Learning that British and militia reinforcements were en route, the Fenians crossed back into the United States, where the authorities arrested their leaders. A few days later another Fenian force crossed from Vermont into

**Figure 7.23** This image depicts the Battle of Ridgeway, June 2, 1866. How did the Fenians use Irish national symbols to make clear their identity?

Canada East (Quebec), where they ransacked several towns before the American government's seizure of their supplies ended their military campaign. By mid-June the Fenian crisis had passed, although subsequent summers witnessed renewed panics and occasional minor skirmishes along the border.

While the military threat posed by the Fenians may have been slight, the fear their activities stirred across British North America empowered politicians like John A. Macdonald who argued for a union (Confederation) of British territories in North America to strengthen colonial defence. Among the most outspoken critics of the Fenians and vigorous advocates of Confederation was Thomas D'Arcy McGee, who urged that the only way to deal with the Fenian threat was "to cut it out by the roots." McGee was shot and killed on an Ottawa street one night in early April 1868. Many believed that the man convicted of murdering him—an Irishman named Patrick James Whelan—was a Fenian, but the connection was never proven.

## Think It Through

1. Why did the Fenians decide to attack British North America?
2. What impact did the Fenian raids have on Canadian politics during the mid-1860s?

**Figure 7.24** As a communal activity, buffalo hunting formed an integral element of the life of Native Americans on the Great Plains. The scale of these traditional hunts fascinated American visitors.

arrival of Europeans with their horses and guns led to a dramatic decline in the size of herds; by 1860 there were fewer than 12 million buffalo, a fraction of their former numbers. Consumer demand for buffalo robes and industrial demand for buffalo hides led to wholesale slaughters, further decimating the herds. The arrival of the railroads and the flood of settlers that followed accelerated this decline; just two decades later, only hundreds remained. For their part, government and military officials supported the slaughter, accurately foreseeing that the disappearance of the buffalo would fatally weaken the Native American societies, making them easier to conquer and control.

## Aboriginal Conflicts: Responses

As we have seen, the American government's policy toward Aboriginal people during this period was one of assimilation—the belief that the best long-term solution would be to break up Native American nations and absorb them into the settler population. This policy would prove catastrophic for Native American societies in the decades to come.

One step in achieving the goal of assimilation was establishing the reservation system. As early as the 1850s the American government, spurred on by missionaries and others, had begun to set aside areas called "reservations" for a number of Plains Indians. Through a combination of government pressure and military force, Native Americans were compelled to abandon their traditional hunting grounds and settle on these tracts of land. Once on the reservations, they were encouraged to adopt farming, a way of life that was alien to them. In many cases, however, the lands set aside for reservations were poor in quality, and farming proved difficult.

During the 1860s and 1870s, as more Aboriginal people were crowded onto reservations and as the reservations were repeatedly reduced in size, even basic survival became a challenge. Some people began to starve. At the same time, government funds earmarked for relief were regularly pocketed by corrupt officials, adding to the woes of those living on reservations. Despite the efforts of a few campaigners to address these injustices, there was little improvement. The efforts to use reservations as a stepping-stone toward eventual assimilation of Native Americans into American society were failing.

## Aboriginal Leaders and Resistance

Native American responses to the settlers' insatiable hunger for land varied. Some believed that the best course of action was to accept the treaties offered, and settle on the land set aside for them. Others decided to negotiate directly with the US government.

An example of the latter type of leader was the Sioux leader Chief Red Cloud. In 1865, Red Cloud led his people in a battle to halt the spread of miners and other settlers into what remained of the Sioux's traditional hunting grounds in Wyoming. The Sioux successfully fought the US military to a draw in what became known as the Great Sioux War. Believing his victories put him in a position of strength, in 1868 Red Cloud led a delegation to meet face-to-face with President Grant. As a result, the Treaty of Fort Laramie (1868) created the Great Sioux Reservation, an enormous tract of land that included the Black Hills of South Dakota.

Another leader who refused to accept quietly the miseries of life on reservation was the Apache chief Geronimo. After a brief time confined to a reservation, the Apache people determined to return to their traditional nomadic and raiding lifestyle. For almost a decade Geronimo led Apache warriors in a campaign against US authorities. The conflict did not end until, hounded by the army and weakened by starvation, Geronimo and his remaining band of warriors surrendered in September 1886.

**SOUND BITE**

"What treaty have the Sioux made with the white man that we have broken? Not one. What treaty have the white man ever made with us that they have kept? Not one. When I was a boy the Sioux owned the world; the sun rose and set on their land; they sent ten thousand men to battle. Where are the warriors today? Who slew them? Where are our lands? Who owns them?"

—Sioux leader Sitting Bull laments the US government's treatment of his people

## Little Bighorn

Nowhere had tensions over the reservation system been greater than in the Black Hills of South Dakota, where the Treaty of Fort Laramie guaranteed an extensive reservation to the Sioux and Cheyenne. Discovery of gold in the area in 1875, however, prompted the American authorities to attempt to seize the land and motivated the Sioux and Cheyenne to resist. Sporadic fighting broke out between the US Army and Native warriors.

As part of a wider effort to eliminate Native American resistance, a US cavalry force was sent to the area. Ignoring orders to await the arrival of reinforcements, one of its officers, Lieutenant Colonel George Armstrong

**Figure 7.25** Chief Red Cloud, leader of the Oglala Sioux.

Custer, advanced with a small force to the Little Bighorn River in Montana. There, on June 25, 1876, he was ambushed by a much larger force of Sioux and Cheyenne. In the ensuing battle, Custer's force of more than 200 men was wiped out. The Native victory proved short-lived, however. Over the following months, the US Army relentlessly pursued the Sioux and Cheyenne warriors until all had surrendered. The battle quickly became known as "Custer's Last Stand," and aroused popular hostility toward the Aboriginal people of the Plains.

With the passage of time, judgments about Little Bighorn have changed. Historians have increasingly viewed Custer as reckless rather than heroic, for ignoring orders and risking his men in pursuit of personal glory. Ironically, Custer himself understood the Sioux desire to live free, rather than confined to shrinking reservations: "If I were an Indian, I would certainly prefer to cast my lot … to the free open plains rather than submit to the confined limits of a reservation, there to be the recipient of the blessed benefits of civilization with its vices thrown in." Little Bighorn would come to symbolize both the folly of US military efforts against Native Americans, and the futility of Aboriginal resistance to American expansion.

**Figure 7.26** Examine these two illustrations of the Battle of Little Bighorn. The first was drawn by an eyewitness (and participant), the Sioux Chief Red Horse, while the second was a popular print of *Custer's Last Fight*. How are Native Americans presented in each? How has the artist of *Custer's Last Fight* attempted to portray the general as a heroic figure? What emotions would each image provoke in the viewer? Why?

## PAST VOICES

### Chief Joseph and the Nez Perce

"Give them all an even chance to live and grow. All men were created by the same Great Spirit Chief." With these words, Chief Joseph, the leader of the Nez Perce, appealed directly to the members of the American Congress to allow his people to return to the land in Oregon that had been forcibly taken from them. Despite his eloquence the pleas of Chief Joseph fell on deaf ears, and his people were sent to another reservation instead, where Chief Joseph would die, a broken man.

The Nez Perce traditionally lived in the area where Idaho, Washington, and Oregon meet. From their earliest contact with Americans in 1803, when they assisted the Lewis and Clark expedition, the Nez Perce had worked to accommodate themselves to the authorities. Many had converted to Christianity, and they helped maintain order among other tribes.

In 1855 the Nez Perce had ceded some land to the American government, but retained a reservation of over 3 million hectares. Despite this accommodation with the American authorities, the influx of settlers and prospectors into Nez Perce territory increased pressure to surrender more land. As gold was found on the reservation, disputes arose over what land had been ceded.

In 1877 the Nez Perce were ordered to leave their territory. Some of the younger members of the tribe responded with violence, attacking local settlers. American soldiers were sent to restore order, which provoked further fighting. Led by Chief Joseph and the warrior Looking Glass, a group of 450 Nez Perce set out for Canada, attempting to evade the soldiers pursuing them. For two months they wandered through the Northwest, fighting several battles en route, before being trapped barely 48 kilometres from the Canadian border.

With no hope of escape, in early October 1877 Chief Joseph urged his people to end their struggle

**Figure 7.27** Chief Joseph, leader of the Nez Perce.

against the US military and surrender. His words demonstrate his concern for the Nez Perce, and express the despair that Native Americans in general felt when confronted by the loss of their traditional lands and way of life. Chief Joseph spoke eloquently for all:

> I am tired of fighting. Our chiefs are killed. Looking Glass is dead. Toohoolhoolzote is dead. The old men are all dead. It is the young men who say "yes" or "no." He who led on the young men is dead. It is cold and we have no blankets. The little children are freezing to death. My people, some of them, have run away to the hills and have no blankets, no food; no one knows where they are—perhaps freezing to death. I want to have time to look for my children among the dead. Hear me, my chiefs! I am tired; my heart is sick and sad. From where the sun now stands I will fight no more forever.

#### Think It Through

1. Why might the Nez Perce have resented their treatment during the 1860s and 1870s?
2. According to Chief Joseph, how had the struggle with the Americans affected Nez Perce society?

## CELEBRATING THE CENTENNIAL

Word of the massacre at Little Bighorn reached the east on July 4, 1876, the very day that the United States was celebrating the centennial of the signing of the Declaration of Independence and the birth of the nation. Scarcely a decade had passed since Lee's surrender at Appomattox and the assassination of Lincoln, yet the nation was eager to celebrate and look forward. A lavish exhibition was held at Philadelphia, extolling the accomplishments of a century of American economic growth and technological achievement. In the words of one foreign visitor, the exhibition would offer "a vision of American production ... [for] from a thousand factories will come evidences of the wonders of American mechanical skill." Evidence of these wonders abounded among the more than 30,000 exhibits. (Many would later form the basis of the Smithsonian Institute, the first national museum.) In addition to a wide range of manufactured goods, visitors marvelled at locomotives, factory equipment, and the towering Corliss Engine, a massive steam engine that generated 1400 horsepower of energy to power the exhibition.

Brimming with optimism for the future, the Centennial Exhibition also betrayed the ongoing tensions created by American expansion. Native American artifacts occupied a prominent place in the exhibit halls, reflecting keen public interest—an interest the news of Little Bighorn served only to heighten. The organizers originally proposed to include live Native Americans as

**Figure 7.28** The Government Hall at the Centennial Exhibition included Native American artifacts like this teepee—ironically together with other exhibits celebrating the economic and territorial expansion of the United States over the previous century.

part of the exhibit ("Only the cleanest and finest looking"), but a failure to find suitable "specimens" and the unwillingness of Congress to pay for feeding and housing the participants meant that mannequins were used instead.

Within months of the exhibition, the election of Rutherford Hayes as president would signal the end of Reconstruction, and the cause of equality for African-Americans would rapidly recede from public view. Even as industrialization and territorial expansion accelerated in the late 19th century, issues of race and the fate of Aboriginal peoples would remain unresolved.

**WEB LINKS** 

Explore the world of the Philadelphia Centennial Exhibition (1876) by visiting www.emp.ca/ah.

## CHECK YOUR UNDERSTANDING

1. What ultimate goal was William Seward pursuing when he purchased Alaska from the Russians?
2. What policy did the US government adopt toward Aboriginal people? How did it put this policy into practice?
3. What factors explain the difficulties that the Aboriginal people of the Great Plains encountered in their attempts to farm on the reservations?
4. What did the Sioux nation achieve through armed resistance to the United States?
5. What caused Americans to violate the Treaty of Fort Laramie?
6. What was the purpose of the Centennial Exhibition in Philadelphia?

# THE HISTORIAN'S CRAFT

## Thinking Historically

### Thinking beyond the Facts

Historians know it is more important to understand the meaning and importance of facts than simply to list them. It is a fact that the Reconstruction Act was passed in 1867; but it is more valuable to grasp what Reconstruction was and understand that it embraced concepts of civil rights and reconciliation.

With that in mind, here is a guide for thinking beyond simple facts:

- Look for the broader concepts underlying individual facts. For example, how does the concept of manifest destiny underlie the Homestead Act of 1862?
- Focus on key facts. These are events, documents, or dates that relate to turning points that mark the beginning of something or the end of something, or that seem to symbolize a whole period.
- Identify how individual facts are related—was a particular event the *cause* of something else that happened? Or was it the *effect* of something that occurred previously?
- Understand the character of the period so that you have a scaffold for placing facts in context. For example, knowing the main features of the era of big business and robber barons allows you to understand the career of John D. Rockefeller.

### Organizing Your Thinking

Historians not only manage facts, they organize their understanding so that they can make meaning of it and communicate history to others. As a student you need to do the same thing when you prepare review notes, write an essay, or organize a presentation.

One way to organize is to think in big-picture terms. For example, you could organize your thinking about late 19th-century expansion into new territory under the heading *Westward Expansion*. Alternatively, you could zoom in to the micro-level and explore the features of this period through the life of one person—Chief Joseph of the Nez Perce.

Another way to organize your thinking is to think in terms of fields of history. Historians often specialize in and produce their work in fields such as economic history, social history, cultural history, political history, military history, and diplomatic history.

### Thinking about People from the Past

Another method for thinking about history is to empathize—to put yourself into the shoes of those who were there. For example, if you put yourself into the shoes of a former slave who became a sharecropper, you might feel the frustration and bitterness of that person. By empathizing with the sharecropper in this way, the history becomes alive and meaningful for you. Yet this approach to history is not easy to accomplish. We know a lot about the period but we can never know everything about that person's life and times. We try to immerse ourselves in the historic time, but we always bring our own modern perspectives to the situation. Here are some useful guidelines for empathizing with historical figures:

- Review your general knowledge of the historical period.
- Reconstruct the personal context of the person—his or her class, age, ethnicity, gender, and beliefs.
- Find the parallels and contrasts between your own experiences and that of the person.
- Reflect: What would you have done? Was the person typical or atypical of the times? What is universal and what is unique in this person's experiences?

### Try It!

1. Identify a key fact in the section on Reconstruction. Explain why it is a key fact—that is, did it mark the end of something or the beginning of something?
2. What topics in this chapter would fall under "diplomatic history"? "cultural history"?
3. Put yourself into the shoes of one of the people mentioned in this chapter. What new ideas or perspectives on the history of this period does this exercise provide you with? What questions arise from this empathetic approach?

# STUDY HALL

## Thinking

1. State, in the form of a question, the challenge faced by the United States at the end of the Civil War.
2. In what way could the 15th Amendment be seen as an act of hypocrisy on the part of the Republicans? What criteria do you think should be used to judge its fairness and effectiveness?
3. How to deal with defeated enemies and, especially, how to reunite a country after a civil war are challenges that have faced different cultures throughout history. Which approach do you think was the more appropriate way to deal with these challenges: the more lenient, conciliatory approach of Presidential Reconstruction, or the Radical Reconstruction later sought by Congress? Explain your reasoning.
4. Debate the following: The so-called robber barons such as Andrew Carnegie and John D. Rockefeller were in fact essential to the economic development of the United States.
5. In your view, should the United States today make restitution for its treatment of the Aboriginal people of the Plains in the 19th century? Why or why not?

## Communication

6. Design a poster that could be used to attract Europeans to emigrate to the United States in 1876. Be sure to combine push and pull factors and advertise the achievements of the United States.
7. Create a diagram to explain how new technologies could increase farm production but also fail to increase farm incomes.
8. Write a short journal entry describing how the centennial celebrations of 1876 might have been viewed from the perspective of:
   a. A Plains Indian
   b. A former slave
   c. An immigrant to Chicago
   d. A veteran of the Union Army

## Application

9. Investigate the election of 1876. What lessons does it teach about voting in a democracy? Based on what you have learned, suggest some electoral reforms you would introduce to make elections fairer in the United States today.
10. Use Google Earth to tour the route of the Union Pacific Railroad. What is revealed about the challenges of railroad construction and the job faced by those who actually built it?

# UNIT IV EMERGING POWER

# 8 The Gilded Age and Imperialism (1878–1901)

## KEY CONCEPTS

In this chapter you will consider:

- Examples of federal legislation designed to eliminate government corruption
- The contributions made by Canadian inventor Alexander Graham Bell to the birth of the electronic communications industry
- Patterns of immigration and causes of urban poverty
- The political response of farmers to their financial plight
- The labour movement's struggle to improve its members' working conditions
- The closing of the American frontier and the marginalization of Native Americans
- The roles played by women and African-Americans in reform movements
- The causes and long-term effects of the Spanish-American War

## The American Story

In the last quarter of the 19th century, modern America began taking shape, with developments that eventually changed the US from a primarily farming and rural society to a country dominated by industrial development in the major cities. Driven by great advances in technology, this shift brought fabulous wealth to industrialists and financiers, while poorer farmers and many of the working class lived in unimaginable squalor. Powerful newspapers and new political parties began to lobby, with mixed success, for governments to take a hand in social reform. At the end of the century the United States engaged in its first imperialist war, and through the colonies it acquired, began extending its influence around the globe.

## TIMELINE

**1879**
- Thomas Edison invents the first practical electric light

**1881**
- Booker T. Washington named first principal of Tuskegee Institute

**1882**
- Standard Oil Trust is formed

**1883**
- Joseph Pulitzer buys the *New York World*

**1886**
- Haymarket Square riot
- Statue of Liberty dedicated in New York City

## IMAGE ANALYSIS

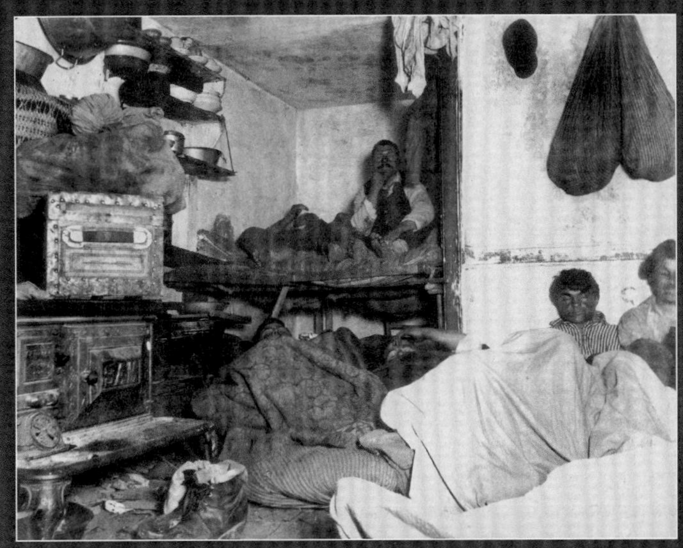

**Figure 8.1** The top photo shows the Breakers, the summer retreat of the railroad and steamship tycoon Cornelius Vanderbilt II. This mansion contained 70 rooms and sat on a 5-hectare estate facing the Atlantic Ocean by Newport, Rhode Island. It was completed in 1895 at the incredible cost of $7 million (about $186 million today). Vanderbilt imported hundreds of European workers to finish the building in two years. He filled it with Italian marble flooring, alabaster columns, and gold panelling. Entire rooms were built in European workshops, dismantled and shipped to Newport, and reassembled in the mansion.

The bottom photo is from a book by the journalist Jacob Riis called *How the Other Half Lives*, published around the time that construction began on the Breakers. The photo shows a working-class family living, like many thousands of such families, in a New York City tenement. "It is not unusual," wrote Riis, "to find a dozen persons—men, women, and children—at work in a single room." The inequalities illustrated by these two photographs defined the Gilded Age and would encourage reformers to begin a search for solutions to the ills that plagued American society.

- ▸ Jane Addams founds Hull House in Chicago — **1889**
- ▸ Massacre at Wounded Knee — **1890**
- ▸ Populist Party is formed — **1892**
- ▸ Spanish-American War — **1898**
- ▸ Assassination of President William McKinley — **1901**

**Figure 8.2** In his novels, Horatio Alger portrayed the United States as a land of opportunity. He implied that anyone who was honest and willing to work hard could achieve success and financial security. Do you think this formula would work for everyone in American society at the time? Explain.

# INTRODUCTION

If you were a young person from a middle-class American family in the 1880s, you would probably be familiar with the books of Horatio Alger. Alger wrote dozens of novels on the same theme: a hard-working boy of good moral character escapes poverty through the assistance of a wealthy businessman who hears about his thrift, honesty, and courage. Typically, Alger's heroes do not achieve immense wealth but do gain respect and a comfortable, middle-class standard of living. While these are not exactly "rags-to-riches" stories, they do reflect the premise of the **American dream**.

Mark Twain, best known today for *The Adventures of Tom Sawyer* and *The Adventures of Huckleberry Finn*, had a different view of American society. In 1873 Twain and Charles Dudley Warner published *The Gilded Age*, which dealt with the corruption of the Grant administration (covered in Chapter 7). The term "Gilded Age" came to be associated with the period from 1878 to 1901, referring to an America where injustice and abuse of power abounded and where a favoured few achieved great wealth at the expense of the many.

# FEDERAL REFORMS: ELIMINATING CORRUPTION

The scandals and corruption that marked President Grant's administration outraged the American public and led to calls for reform. Despite the fraud and corruption associated with his election (discussed in Chapter 7), when Rutherford B. Hayes took office as president in 1877 he resolved to begin the long process of cleaning up corruption in the federal government.

| The Presidents: 1877–1901 | | |
|---|---|---|
| **Rutherford B. Hayes** | Republican | March 4, 1877 – March 4, 1881 |
| **James Garfield*** | Republican | March 4, 1881 – September 19, 1881 |
| **Chester A. Arthur** | Republican | September 19, 1881 – March 4, 1885 |
| **Grover Cleveland** | Democratic | March 4, 1885 – March 4, 1889 |
| **Benjamin Harrison** | Republican | March 4, 1889 – March 4, 1893 |
| **Grover Cleveland** | Democratic | March 4, 1893 – March 4, 1897 |
| **William McKinley*** | Republican | March 4, 1897 – September 14, 1901 |

* assassinated

## Hayes versus Patronage

Hayes first targeted **patronage,** the practice of appointing friends and political supporters to public office. He prohibited federal civil servants from taking an active part in politics and blocked key appointments made by members of Congress. For example, he fired Chester A. Arthur—a future Republican president—from a top position in the New York customs house because this was a patronage appointment.

Hayes also made strides in eliminating patronage from the Department of the Interior, one of the worst offenders in this regard. He called for the use of competitive exams to ensure that civil servants would be selected and promoted on the basis of merit rather than as a result of their connections. Hayes believed that reform was urgent both because patronage threatened government stability and because rapid population growth in the United States was producing a dramatic growth in the federal civil service.

Hayes's decision not to run in the 1880 presidential election led to a split in the Republican Party. A group of conservative Republicans known as Stalwarts wanted to nominate Grant for a third term, but after a long, drawn-out party convention a former Union general named James A. Garfield won the nomination. Five months after he was elected president, Garfield was assassinated by James Guiteau, a Stalwart supporter and a frustrated seeker of a patronage appointment.

**SOUND BITE**

"There can be no complete and permanent reform of the civil service until public opinion emancipates congressmen from all control and influence over government patronage ... No proper legislation is to be expected as long as members of Congress are engaged in procuring offices for their constituents."

—President Rutherford B. Hayes

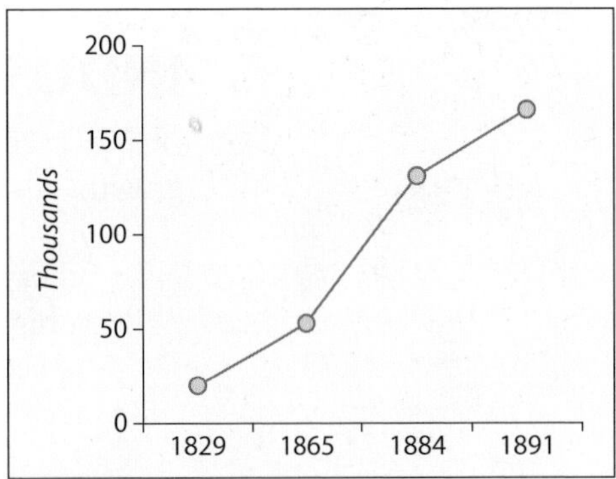


**Figure 8.3** Growth of the federal civil service. By 1891 the federal civil service was eight times larger than it had been 60 years earlier. In what ways could this explosive growth encourage corruption among government officials?

## The Pendleton Act

Following Garfield's assassination, Vice-President Chester A. Arthur was sworn in as president. Many in politics hoped for a return to the more easygoing style of government under Grant, but Arthur became a reformer.

In 1883 Congress passed the Pendleton Act. Signed into law by President Arthur, the Act took three steps to wipe out patronage and other forms of corruption. First, it instituted the system of competitive exams that presidents Grant and Hayes had called for, which ensured that only well-qualified people would be hired for government posts. It also included measures to protect civil servants from political interference, and prohibited them from using their office for political or personal advantage. Finally, it discouraged **nepotism**, or the hiring of relatives, by limiting the number of people from any one family who could be employed as civil servants.

While these were necessary reforms, the Pendleton Act covered only 10 percent of federal civil servants at the time it was passed. Furthermore, it did little to address other serious problems that had emerged in a society undergoing rapid industrialization and massive change.

## CHECK YOUR UNDERSTANDING

1. How did President Rutherford B. Hayes reform the federal government?
2. Find the dictionary meanings of the term "gilded." How do these help give additional meaning to the term "Gilded Age"?
3. Explain how patronage would interfere with the passage of just laws by Congress and with honest government.
4. In your own words, explain how each of the three parts of the Pendleton Act would improve government.

# INDUSTRIAL GROWTH

In the 1880s and 1890s three important factors influenced US industrial growth:

- cheap energy and abundant natural resources,
- a high birth rate and a steep rise in immigration that swelled the workforce and provided a broad consumer base, and
- technological advances that greatly expanded efficiency and output.

One of the chief technological advances during the period was in the spread of railroad tracks across the nation, making the transportation of people and goods faster, cheaper, and more efficient. In 1870 there were just 84,000 kilometres of railroad track in the United States. Problems occurred because these tracks varied in gauge, or width, and so could not be connected to each other. At this time, most tracks were made of iron. Unlike steel, iron is brittle and tends to warp, break, and rust.

Lower steel costs allowed companies to replace old iron tracks with tracks made of steel. This—combined with government subsidies, the adoption of a standard gauge, and the consolidation of hundreds of small rail lines under the control of a few large companies—greatly boosted railroad construction. By 1900 more than 270,000 kilometres of railroad track criss-crossed America.

This industrial expansion helped improve the living standards of most Americans. The real **gross national product (GNP)**—the *quantity* of goods and services produced per person—increased by 29 percent between 1881 and 1893. Labour-saving products, including the sewing machine, telephone, typewriter, and electric stove, became available at reasonable prices. The user-friendly Kodak camera turned thousands of Americans into amateur photographers.

## Technological Advances

The explosion of new discoveries and inventions was spearheaded by home-grown innovators and entrepreneurs such as Thomas Edison, George Westinghouse, and Gustavus Swift.

### Thomas Edison

Born in rural Ohio, Thomas Edison overcame partial deafness and a lack of formal schooling to become the greatest inventor in American history. His development of a reliable, low-cost electric light bulb in 1879 meant that factories could operate 24 hours a day (so Edison can be blamed, indirectly, for the night shift). Some of his other inventions include the phonograph, the dictating machine, the movie camera, and Portland cement. Edison's genius is best revealed in his founding of the first modern research laboratory, at Menlo Park, New Jersey. He believed in a team approach, and employed dozens of assistants and technicians to create more than 1,000 patented inventions.

**Figure 8.4** A canny businessman, Thomas Edison forged ties with powerful industrialists such as Cornelius Vanderbilt and J.P. Morgan to market his inventions.

### George Westinghouse

After designing the railroad air brake, which allowed for longer and more efficient trains, George Westinghouse turned his attention to the new field of electrical power transmission. Here, Westinghouse found himself in competition with Thomas Edison, who was promoting a distribution system based on low-voltage DC (direct current). Westinghouse bought the patents for a more efficient and cost-effective system based on AC (alternating current), developed by Nikola Tesla. Edison tried to persuade the public that AC transmission was dangerous by having a professor, Harold Brown, electrocute animals on stage. After the Westinghouse Corporation won the bid to provide electrical power for the Chicago World's Fair, however, AC power quickly became the standard for electrical distribution systems around the world.

**Figure 8.5** George Westinghouse.

### Gustavus Swift

No longer willing to endure the difficulties and expense of delivering his livestock to slaughterhouses in the eastern United States, Gustavus Swift decided on an innovative but risky solution. He hired Andrew Chase to come up with a practical design for a refrigerated railcar. Chase succeeded, and soon Swift was slaughtering cattle in Chicago and shipping low-cost, high-quality dressed meat to his customers in eastern cities. By 1885 Swift had established the first national meat-packing company in the United States and was selling his products internationally. By the time of his death in 1903, slaughtering and meat-packing had become the single biggest industry in the United States, and Swift's plants were processing a total of 8 million cattle, hogs, and sheep each year.

**Figure 8.6** Gustavus Swift.

## 49th PARALLEL

# Alexander Graham Bell Invents the Telephone

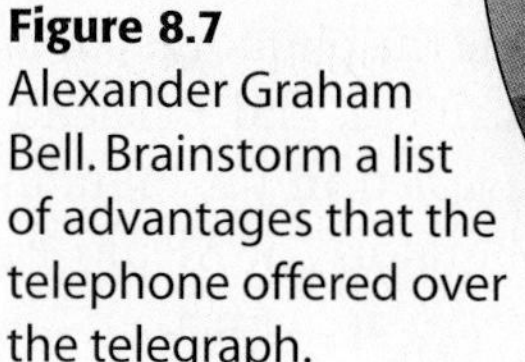

**Figure 8.7**
Alexander Graham Bell. Brainstorm a list of advantages that the telephone offered over the telegraph.

By the mid-19th century the means of communication had remained virtually unchanged since the dawn of civilization. People spoke to each other face-to-face or they sent written messages by foot, horseback, or boat. There was a direct correlation between space and time—sending a message over a certain distance took a certain amount of time, no matter what.

All that changed virtually overnight when Samuel Morse invented the telegraph in 1844. Suddenly, information could travel at the speed of an electric current. Once telegraph wires had been strung across the North American continent, messages that would otherwise have taken months to reach their destination could be delivered in seconds. Before long, a search began for the means of taking the next step in the communications revolution.

If it was possible to turn electrical impulses into sounds that could be decoded into words, shouldn't it also be possible to electronically transfer the sounds of the human voice? Several inventors worked on this problem. The one who succeeded first was Alexander Graham Bell, a driven teacher who was fascinated all his life by the sound of the human voice, perhaps partly because his beloved mother was deaf.

Bell was born in 1847 in Edinburgh, Scotland. A brilliant student, he worked with his two brothers on the construction of different kinds of "speaking machines" that could imitate the sound of the human voice. When both his brothers died of tuberculosis, Bell's parents took him to Brantford, Ontario, in the hope that the drier climate would improve his health.

In 1872 Bell opened a school for the deaf in Boston, Massachusetts. At this time, he suffered so severely from stress headaches that he sometimes had to retreat to the family's estate at Brantford to recover. It was here, in what he called his "dreaming place," that Bell first worked out the idea for a "harmonic telegraph." Bell theorized that if sound waves could be transformed into an "undulating" (or varying) electrical current, then the current could be turned back into the original sound waves at the other end of the circuit.

Working with the technician James Watson in Boston, Bell managed to construct a model of a telephone in 1876. He quickly patented the device, and with some improvements it was showcased at the Philadelphia Centennial Exposition, where it created a sensation. Although Bell marketed the telephone as a business machine, by 1886 more than 150,000 Americans owned a phone. Bell became a millionaire.

## Think It Through

1. "Leave the beaten track behind occasionally and dive into the woods," said Bell. "You will be certain to find something you have never seen before." Explain the role of the imagination in Bell's work.
2. Keep track of the different electronic communications devices you use over the course of one week. Explain how your life would be different without access to these devices.

# The Concentration of Wealth

The Gilded Age saw an unprecedented concentration of wealth in the hands of a few. This peaked around 1900, when the richest 1 percent of the population held 45 percent of the national wealth. Powerful bankers and financiers amassed huge personal fortunes by acquiring ownership of rapidly growing industries.

## The Spread of Trusts and Holding Companies

As you learned in Chapter 7, trusts were a form of corporation pioneered by John D. Rockefeller to avoid local anti-monopoly laws. Wealthy financiers used this legal device to take control of entire industries, which also gave them control over prices and labour costs. The **holding company** was another form of corporation that developed after trusts were declared illegal. Holding companies operate by buying enough stock in a variety of companies to give them a controlling interest in each.

The New York financier J.P. Morgan staunchly supported trusts and holding companies because he saw them as a way to bring order, stability, and efficiency to different industries. He believed that larger business enterprises would produce economies of scale—that is, that the high volume of production would result in lower per-unit costs.

By the early 1890s about 300 trusts had been created, including giants like the Sugar Trust, the Distillers and Cattle Feed Trust, and the American Tobacco Trust. Alexander Graham Bell's company, American Telephone and Telegraph, held a monopoly in the burgeoning telephone industry, while American Harvester manufactured more than 80 percent of all farm machinery. The existence of such huge enterprises created a lack of competition, which allowed the trust owners to keep prices high and wages low. This ensured the concentration of wealth at the top of society.

## Conspicuous Consumption

At the time, those who were very rich had no qualms about flaunting their wealth. They built huge mansions and summer homes that they decorated lavishly. Vanderbilt, Morgan, and their friends tried to outdo each other by buying the biggest yachts, the best racehorses, and the largest art collections. Their wives hosted grand balls and banquets. At one dinner party, the hostess gave her favourite dog a

**Figure 8.8** J.P. Morgan made his first fortune in the railroad industry, and led efforts to reorganize and consolidate railroads in the United States. By 1900 Morgan's banking firm had a controlling interest in more than 160,000 kilometres of railroad track—half the total in the United States.

**SOUND BITE**

"No man in this land suffers from poverty unless it be more than his fault, unless it be his sin … [I]f men have not enough, it is owing to the want of provident care, and foresight, and industry, and frugality, and wise saving."

—Protestant clergyman Henry Ward Beecher

$15,000 diamond collar (almost $400,000 in current dollars), while at another the owners transformed their supper room into a tropical forest.

In his book *Theory of the Leisure Class* (1899), the sociologist Thorstein Veblen coined the term **conspicuous consumption** to explain the behaviour of the rich. Veblen argued that they were behaving like the barbarians of old, who engaged in wasteful competitions to prove their higher status. Some of the rich justified their wealth by twisting Charles Darwin's theory of natural selection to argue that they had risen to the top because they were the fittest and strongest, and therefore had a God-given right to their power and privileges. This offshoot theory was called **social Darwinism**, and it excused poverty in society by identifying it as the result of moral vice.

## The Urban Poor

Rapid population growth in the United States was accompanied by a marked shift of people to the cities. During the Gilded Age, the US population grew from 50 million to 75 million, while the urban population rose by 15 million.

The new city dwellers came mainly from Europe and rural America, attracted by job opportunities for unskilled labour in rapidly growing industries. The most popular destinations were New York City and Chicago. In New York, many Jewish immigrants found work in the "needle" trades as sweatshop labour. By 1913 the clothing industry was the largest in the city, employing more than 300,000 people, most of whom lived in the crowded Lower East Side.

In Chicago, workers found employment in the rail yards, factories, and meat-packing plants. There were so many meat packers that the poet Carl Sandburg later hailed Chicago as "Hog Butcher for the World." Everywhere,

**Figure 8.9** The Lower East Side in New York City was one of the first and most crowded urban ghettos in the country. Here, Jewish immigrants from eastern Europe lived segregated (for the most part) from the rest of the city, and developed a close-knit community based on a shared culture, language, and religion. Why would immigrants from a similar place and background tend to settle in the same quarter rather than spread out over the whole city?

labourers worked long hours at jobs that were often unsafe and poorly paid. By 1914 New York's population had reached 4 million and Chicago's had reached 2 million. Of these city dwellers, 8 out of 10 were immigrants or the children of immigrants.

There were a number of private responses to urban poverty and the problems it created. In 1889, at age 29, Jane Addams founded Hull House, modelled on a **settlement house** she had seen in London, England. Addams's refuge for immigrants would inspire other reformers to open similar houses in cities throughout the United States. Another attempt at social reform came from the Woman's Christian Temperance Union (WCTU), founded in 1874. The WCTU sought to eliminate the consumption of alcohol, which members saw as the root of many social ills, including poverty, unemployment, and spousal and child abuse.

**SOUND BITE**

"America's future will be determined by the home and the school. The child becomes largely what he is taught; hence we must watch what we teach, and how we live."

—Jane Addams

## Immigration

From the end of the Civil War in 1865 to 1890, 10 million immigrants arrived in the United States. Among them were large numbers from Scandinavia, who established farms in the Midwest, and Chinese labourers brought in to work on the railroads and gold mines of the West.

From 1890 to the outbreak of World War I, another 15 million immigrants arrived. Most came from poor, rural areas in southern and eastern Europe. The massive migration left the United States more ethnically diverse, but also created a backlash among longer-term residents. In California in 1885 a mob of whites attacked Chinese miners, killing more than 20 of them.

**Figure 8.10** In 1892 the US government established Ellis Island to process the thousands of immigrants who were arriving every month. Located in New York Harbor, close to the newly dedicated Statue of Liberty, Ellis Island became the largest point of entry for immigrants. Eventually, nearly 12 million landed on the island for screening by immigration officials.

**WEB LINKS** 

To take a virtual tour of Ellis Island and learn more about the Statue of Liberty, visit www.emp.ca/ah.

# WE THE PEOPLE

## Jane Addams

1860–1935

Jane Addams was a radical thinker and writer who devoted her life to three causes: feminism; social reform; and **pacifism**, or the anti-war movement. Born to a prominent Illinois family in 1860, Addams lived an unconventional life for a woman of her time. She never married, never had children, and never accepted the precept that her place was in the home. Immersing herself in work she considered vitally important, Addams would be hailed as a saviour and vilified as a traitor. She was also the first woman in America to receive a Nobel Prize.

Addams's father convinced her that, as a member of the privileged class, she owed a debt to society. After graduating from the Rockford College for Women, Jane decided to pay that debt by becoming a doctor. Before she could finish her medical studies, however, back problems forced her to undergo a painful operation and then spend several months strapped to a wooden board. This gave her much time to think about what she should do with her life.

In search of an answer, Jane toured Europe, where she visited a group of Christian reformers at a London settlement house called Toynbee Hall. Inspired, she returned to Chicago in 1889. There, she found an old mansion that she renovated and opened to the neighbourhood immigrants—Poles, Irish, Germans, Russians, Italians, and Greeks, all struggling to establish themselves in their new country.

Staffed by sympathetic, well-educated young women, Hull House tried to improve conditions for the poor in two ways. The first was through education: Addams offered kindergarten, language, nutrition, and art classes. The second was by agitating for social justice: Addams involved her students in neighbourhood improvement projects, health clinics, and labour organizations. Soon, 2,000 people were coming to Hull House each week. Addams and her co-workers eventually succeeded in having laws passed that limited working hours for women, abolished child labour, and made school attendance compulsory.

**Figure 8.11** Jane Addams was often criticized for her attempts to involve the government in social reform. In her time, people took the Protestant work ethic seriously, believing that every person had an obligation to improve his or her own living conditions through hard work.

In 1898, when the US caught "war fever" in the run-up to the Spanish-American War, Addams took a firm pacifist stance. She outraged many by drawing a link between newspaper publicity about the war and increased murder rates in Chicago. Nevertheless, she kept writing and speaking out against all forms of war, and in 1931 received the Nobel Peace Prize.

### Think It Through

1. Explain why settlement houses were necessary in large American cities during the Gilded Age.
2. Do you think the government should take an active role in improving living conditions for the poor? Explain.

Many other examples of violence against recent immigrants occurred elsewhere.

As a result of popular concern regarding immigration, Congress passed the Exclusion Act in 1882 barring entry to criminals, the mentally ill, and the destitute. In 1885 the Contract Labor Act clamped down on Chinese immigrants, essentially barring all immigration from China for the following ten years.

Still, a poem by Emma Lazarus, inscribed on the base of the Statue of Liberty, reflected the way the majority of Americans thought of their country—that is, as a haven for the poor and oppressed from around the world:

> "Keep ancient lands, your storied pomp!" cries she
> With silent lips. "Give me your tired, your poor,
> Your huddled masses yearning to breathe free,
> The wretched refuse of your teeming shore.
> Send these, the homeless, tempest-tost to me,
> I lift my lamp beside the golden door!"

## Tenement Life

Once they passed through Ellis Island, most new immigrants settled in cities, concentrating in ethnic neighborhoods with names like Little Italy and Chinatown. They were attracted partly by job opportunities, and partly by the chance to converse in their native language and live in affordable housing. Unfortunately, the housing was often substandard and overcrowded.

The most crowded residences were called dumbbell **tenements** because of their shape. These buildings were generally six stories high, with four tiny apartments of three rooms on each floor; none of the apartments had running water or electricity. Air shafts were supposed to provide light and ventilation, but they were so narrow that light seldom penetrated and little ventilation occurred. Typically, the shafts filled with garbage that attracted rats and spread disease. One of the few city regulations applying to these tenements required that they have fire escapes, and it was there that many residents slept in the summer to escape the suffocating heat of their apartments.

Even though government intervention was clearly needed to make the tenements safer, these ethnic enclaves had little political clout. In New York changes occurred only after the journalist Jacob Riis published

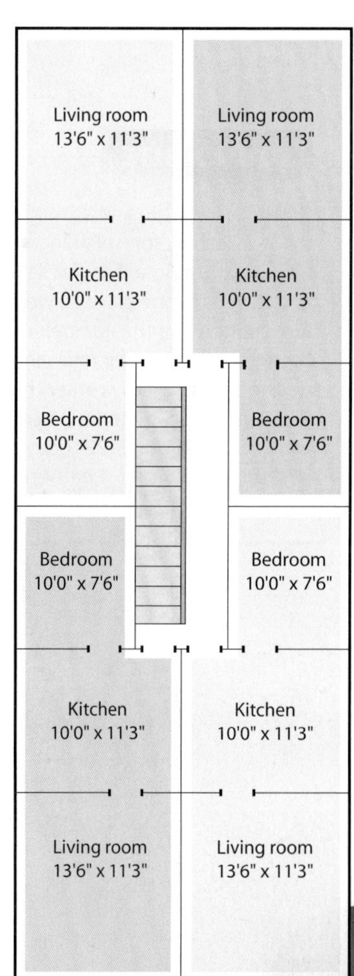


**Figure 8.12** A diagram of a typical dumbbell tenement. In 1898, 74,000 people lived in the Tenth Ward on the Lower East Side in New York. They lived in 1,196 tenement buildings like this one, crammed into an area of six blocks. The population density was 184,000 per square kilometre—the highest ever recorded anywhere.

**WEB LINKS**

To learn more about Jacob Riis and the effect of his photography on social reform movements, visit www.emp.ca/ah.

**Figure 8.13** As a photojournalist for the *New York Tribune*, Jacob Riis was among the first to use flash powder with his camera. This new technology allowed him to reveal the squalid interiors of the tenements, shops, and restaurants of the Tenth Ward.

a sensational exposé on tenement life in *Scribner's Magazine* in 1889. In 1901 New York City finally passed the Tenement House Act, which outlawed new construction of tenements on narrow lots and required landlords to improve sanitary conditions and light access in existing buildings.

**SOUND BITE**

"[For factory girls in Philadelphia] there is a fine for speaking to your next neighbour, a fine for laughing; and ... girls in one place ... were fined ten cents a minute for being late, though many of them had to come for miles in winter storms ... [O]ne poor girl who really worked hard one week ... made $3.50 [about $80 today]; but the fines against her were $5.25 [about $122 today]. That seems ridiculous; it is ridiculous, but it is pathetic and it is shameful."

—Henry George, *The Crime of Poverty* (1885)

## Working Conditions

The large numbers of workers desperate for jobs led to the sort of exploitation that characterized the Gilded Age. Workers laboured for bosses who drove them hard for 10 to 14 hours a day, six days a week. Railroad work was one of the most dangerous occupations. Each year, 30,000 railroad workers were injured on the job; about 2,000 were killed.

Female immigrants were an important part of the workforce, with many finding employment in the textile mills. Others worked in the garment industry performing piece work, and were paid according to the number of items they produced in crowded sweatshops or in their own homes. Child labour was also prevalent. In 1880 one child in six under the age of 16 worked. Children as young as six worked alongside their mothers in factories that were noisy, unsafe, and uncomfortably hot.

## Prejudice and Segregation

During the Gilded Age, blacks in the South remained an economic underclass and were increasingly terrorized by the Ku Klux Klan. Meanwhile, blacks in the industrial North endured poverty and discrimination.

By the turn of the century Booker T. Washington had become a nationally recognized leader of African-Americans. Born a slave, Washington proved to be a talented student and a brilliant orator. In 1881 he was named the first principal of the Tuskegee Institute in Alabama. There, he developed a curriculum for young men and women that emphasized vocational training, good citizenship, self-help, and the value of hard work.

Washington sought accommodation, rather than confrontation, with whites. He argued that agitating for complete political and economic equality would provoke a backlash from whites. At the Cotton States and International Exhibition in Atlanta in 1895, Washington outlined his views in a speech that became known as the "Atlanta Compromise." Critics of Washington today view his approach as a sellout of black interests, while others argue that it was the best of several poor options.

**Figure 8.14** Booker T. Washington at the Tuskegee Institute. In what way did the Tuskegee curriculum embody the American dream?

**SOUND BITE**

"To those of my race who depend on bettering their condition in a foreign land, or who underestimate the importance of preserving friendly relations with the southern white man who is their next door neighbor, I would say: 'Cast down your bucket where you are.' Cast it down, making friends in every manly way of the people of all races, by whom you are surrounded."

—Words spoken by Booker T. Washington in the "Atlanta Compromise," 1895

## Separate but Equal?

In 1896 the US Supreme Court delivered a decision in *Plessy v. Ferguson* that echoed the Dred Scott case. (Recall that in 1857 the Supreme Court ruled that no black person could be, or ever was, a citizen of the United States.) Plessy, who was one-eighth black, was arrested under a Louisiana law for sitting in a railroad car reserved for whites. The Supreme Court ruled that states could legally segregate whites and blacks in public facilities, reasoning that enforced separation of the two races did not "stamp the colored race with a badge of inferiority."

This doctrine of "separate but equal" had an immediate and devastating effect on African-Americans. State governments throughout the South passed **Jim Crow laws** ("Jim Crow" was a euphemism for "black") to create—among other things—separate waiting rooms, separate factory entrances, separate dining areas, separate seating on buses, and—most damaging of all—separate schools. All this ensured that Southern blacks had little chance of sharing in the prosperity of the Gilded Age.

## CHECK YOUR UNDERSTANDING

1. Select three statistics you would use to show the growth of the American economy from 1878 to 1901.
2. In your own words, explain how a holding company works. Make up an example based on the music or grocery business to illustrate your understanding of the term.
3. Explain the concept of social Darwinism. In what sense did the corrupt business practices and income disparities of the Gilded Age show flaws in this idea?
4. List the problems faced by workers in growing American cities.
5. What role did immigration play in creating the new American economy?

# TROUBLE ON THE FARM

Farmers continued to make up a large part of the population of the United States during the Gilded Age. Although their proportion of the population declined by 11 percent, their numbers rose by almost 8 million. The number of farms and hectares under cultivation increased as the railroads opened the Midwest for settlement. Farm productivity rose thanks to scientific advancements and the development of improved farming equipment, including plows, harrows, and planters made from steel, and steam-powered harvesting machines and threshers.

| | 1870 | 1880 | 1890 | 1900 |
|---|---|---|---|---|
| **Total population (in millions)** | 38,558 | 50,116 | 62,941 | 75,994 |
| **Farm population (estimated)** | 18,373 | 22,981 | 29,414 | 29,414 |
| **% of labour force who were farmers** | 53 | 49 | 43 | 38 |

**Figure 8.15** Farm statistics, 1870–1900. It is interesting to compare these figures with those for 1990, when the total population of the United States was 246 million and the farm population was 4.6 million—only 2.6 percent of the labour force. Brainstorm three reasons to account for the decline in the number of farmers over the course of the 20th century.

The rapid rise in farm output contributed to decreases in the prices of agricultural commodities. In a sense, farmers were falling victim to their own success. Consider the prices of wheat and corn in Kansas from 1870 to 1900, as illustrated in Figure 8.16.

Contributing to this **deflation**, or decline in prices, was competition from other grain producers (such as Canada) and a general weakening of the US economy that culminated in a severe depression beginning in 1893.

| Year | Wheat | | Corn | |
|---|---|---|---|---|
| | *Yield** | *Price* | *Yield** | *Price* |
| **1870** | 15.5 | $1.07 | 31.3 | $0.48 |
| **1880** | 14.1 | 0.86 | 29.7 | 0.29 |
| **1890** | 14.1 | 0.69 | 28.6 | 0.30 |
| **1900** | 13.3 | 0.57 | 21.2 | 0.30 |

* bushels per acre

**Figure 8.16** Wheat and corn prices, 1870–1900. Prices for these commodities kept declining, even as production fell, partly because of the large surpluses kept in storage from previous years. What were some of the factors that affected production over this period?

## Natural Disasters

Farmers have always depended on favourable conditions for success: fertile soil, sufficient moisture, pest-free conditions, and a long enough growing season. Unfortunately, nature doesn't always cooperate. In the 1890s the boll weevil, an insect that lays its eggs in cotton balls, entered the United States and devastated cotton fields throughout the South. On the prairies, swarms of grasshoppers destroyed grain crops. The worst disaster was a drought in the early 1890s that damaged wheat and corn production.

For many farmers, the drought came as a surprise. Although moist weather had prevailed in the Midwest for 20 years, these conditions were in fact unusual for a region that historically was dry. The railroads and the government capitalized on pseudo-science to lure settlers to the Great Plains; "rain follows the plow" became a popular slogan that had no basis in fact. Large numbers of farmers arrived who relied on methods best suited to the moist climate along the east coast. When the drought hit, they could do nothing but watch helplessly as their crops withered.

## Business Policies

The drought magnified the effects of a general economic downturn. Hoping that crop prices would remain high, farmers had taken out long-term loans to finance the purchase of land and farm machinery. They had to pay premium interest rates because the bankers knew that the climate in the Midwest made lending riskier.

When crop prices fell even as crops failed, farmers found themselves with huge debts and few dollars with which to pay them off. In Kansas alone, banks foreclosed on about 150,000 farm mortgages between 1880 and 1890. This forced thousands of families off the land, and left many with a deep distrust of banks.

**SOUND BITE**

"There are three great crops raised in Nebraska. One is a crop of corn, one is a crop of freight rates, and one a crop of interest. One is produced by farmers, who sweat and toil, from the land. The other two are produced by men who sit in their offices and behind their bank counters and farm the farmers."

—Editorial in a Nebraska newspaper, 1890

Farmers were also incensed at having to pay the railroads more to ship their goods than industrial shippers did to send equivalent quantities over longer distances. The railroad companies argued that they needed the volume business from big customers to generate enough cash flow to cover their expenses, and that the higher rates they charged farmers gave them a modest profit in a competitive industry.

## The Demise of the Grange

In Chapter 7, you saw how farmers organized a national association known as the Grange to address their grievances. Grange-controlled state legislatures passed laws designed to lower freight rates, which angered railroad owners. The conflicts between the Grange and railroad companies came to a head in 1877 when the US Supreme Court ruled in favour of the Grange in *Munn v. Illinois.*

The success of the Grange was short-lived. Rail owners found ways around the laws or simply cut services to regions populated by troublesome farmers. The failure of businesses financed by the Grange reduced membership as well as the political power of the organization.

The final blow for the Grange came in 1886 with the Supreme Court's decision in *Wabash v. Illinois.* The court ruled that a state law governing rail rates had no force, since even that portion of the railroad that fell within the state's boundaries was part of interstate commerce and was therefore under the jurisdiction of the federal government. Courts overturned dozens of other state laws regulating railroads within a year; by this time, the Grange had become little more than a social organization. Farmers would found a new organization—the Farmers' Alliance—to pursue their grievances.

### CHECK YOUR UNDERSTANDING

1. Explain the meaning of the phrase: "farmers were falling victim to their own success."
2. List the economic and natural challenges faced by American farmers.
3. Why did farmers dislike banks and railroads?
4. Why did the Supreme Court decision in *Wabash v. Illinois* help destroy the Grange movement?

# ATTEMPTS AT REFORM

The reforms sought by the Farmers' Alliance and a new political party called the Populist Party would run into strong opposition, both from big business and from the US Supreme Court. Although many reform efforts failed in the short term, they would lay the foundation for more successful attempts in the early part of the 20th century.

# Populism

The Farmers' Alliance had two main branches: the Northern Alliance (centred in the Midwest) and the Southern Alliance (which operated in Louisiana, Texas, and Arkansas). The Southern Alliance was affiliated with an African-American organization called the Colored Farmers National Alliance. Worsening economic conditions boosted membership in the alliances, and by 1888 the Southern Alliance alone had 250,000 members. Two issues divided the membership, however.

First, "conservatives" (those who wanted to focus on local *economic* initiatives, such as persuading merchants to lower their prices) opposed "activists" (those who wanted to promote a national *political* agenda). Second, members disagreed on the issue of race. Some wanted African-Americans to have full membership rights, while others wanted to exclude blacks from the alliance's national committees and leave it to state organizations to determine whether blacks could join.

Ultimately, the alliance broke down under boycotts organized by the railroad owners and commodities brokers, the agents who sold the farmers' grain and livestock. The farmers refused to give up. They joined forces with union members belonging to the Knights of Labor to establish the Populist Party. The Populists held their first national convention in Omaha, Nebraska in 1892, adopting a political platform that favoured the rights of the people against the interests of "big business." Thus the Populists offered the first organized political challenge to the privileged classes of the Gilded Age.

**SOUND BITE**

"Raise less corn and more hell."

—Mary E. Lease, Populist supporter

## Free Silver

One "plank" in the Populist platform was the free coinage of silver. Why was this an issue for farmers and labourers at the time?

Populists saw "free silver" as a remedy for declining crop prices, blaming the Coinage Act of 1873 for the deflationary spiral. Prior to 1873 the federal government backed the American dollar through a combination of gold reserves and silver coins. The Coinage Act ended the minting of silver and pegged the dollar to a **gold standard**. This tightened the money supply because the government could only print as much money as it had gold, and gold was much rarer than silver.

Bankers supported the gold standard because it discouraged inflation and kept borrowing costs steady. Populists supported "free silver" because it would increase the flow of money in circulation, boosting crop prices while bringing down the cost of borrowing.

In the presidential election of 1892 the Populists nominated James B. Weaver—a former Civil War general—as their candidate. By running a third-party candidate rather than trying to persuade the Democrats or Republicans to support free silver, the Populists were taking a big gamble. Weaver would have to pry enough voters away from the two main candidates to win a majority

AMERICAN ARCHIVE

# The Populist Platform of 1892

When the Populists convened to write a **platform**, or statement of principles, in Omaha for their first convention in 1892, their intentions were twofold. First, to summarize the major problems facing the nation; second, to offer practical solutions to these problems that would appeal to their working-class base.

The first problem identified by the Populists was the two-class system that divided the country's population into a small number of rich individuals at the top and the masses of the poor below:

> The fruits of the toil of millions are badly stolen to build up colossal fortunes for a few, unprecedented in the history of mankind; and the possessors of these, in turn, despise the Republic and endanger liberty. From the same prolific womb of governmental injustice we breed the two great classes—tramps and millionaires.

The second problem was that the super-rich had corrupted the political system, denying the common people a voice and reducing the government to a **plutocracy**, or rule by the wealthy:

> We have witnessed for more than a quarter of a century the struggles of the two great political parties for power and plunder, while grievous wrongs have been inflicted upon the suffering people ... They propose ... to destroy the multitude in order to secure corruption funds from the millionaires.

Since the Populists felt the existing system no longer served the needs of the people, they believed the solution began with forming a third political party—one that had no tie to the wealthy class. The Populists recommended expanding the government's powers to correct injustices created by the rapid expansion of wealth and industry:

> We believe that the power of government—in other words, of the people—should be expanded (as in the case of the postal service) as rapidly and as far as the good sense of an intelligent people and the teaching of experience shall justify, to the end that oppression, injustice, and poverty shall eventually cease in the land.

The platform also proposed the following reforms, all tied to increased government powers:

- unlimited coinage of silver and gold,
- government ownership and operation of the railroads,
- the use of the secret ballot system for all elections, and
- the adoption of a graduated income tax to tax the wealthy at higher rates than the poor.

Although the Populist Party would effectively disappear by the end of the century, it would pass the torch of government reform to the new Progressive Party, which enjoyed greater success in redefining the role of government. During the Progressive Era in the early 20th century most state governments would adopt referendums and the secret ballot. Additionally, the federal government would adopt Populist programs by passing the Hepburn Railroad Regulation Act of 1906 (which gave more power to the Interstate Commerce Commission) and the 16th Amendment in 1913 (which made the income tax constitutional).

## Think It Through

1. According to the Populist platform, what were the main problems facing the country in 1892?
2. What solutions did the platform offer for solving these problems?
3. Speculate as to why the United States has never developed a viable three-party political system.

of votes in the Electoral College. The danger was that he would merely act as a spoiler, taking away enough votes from the candidate closest to his platform to allow the one most opposed to his ideas to win.

## Federal Reforms: Regulating Trusts and Railroads

Ultimately, Weaver's bid for power fell far short. He won only 22 electoral votes, while the Republican candidate, Benjamin Harrison, received 145. With 277 votes, the Democrat Grover Cleveland won his second term as president.

Born in 1837, Cleveland won his first term as president in 1884. He remains the only president in US history to serve two non-consecutive terms, and was the only Democratic president during a half-century of Republican domination that began with Abraham Lincoln's election in 1860.

Cleveland's admirers praise him for his honesty and single-mindedness. A cautious reformer, he believed his main duty as president was to block "bad bills" passed by Congress. In all, he vetoed 413 bills, or two-thirds of those passed by Congress during his term. In blocking a bill to fund aid to drought-stricken farmers, Cleveland summarized arguments against governmental social assistance that would hold sway until the time of the Great Depression in the 1930s:

**Figure 8.17** By percentage, the popular votes for Weaver, Harrison, and Cleveland in the 1892 election were 8.5%, 43%, and 46%, respectively. A prohibition candidate, John Bidwell, won 2.2%. In what part of the country did Weaver do best? Explain the reasons for his success in that area.

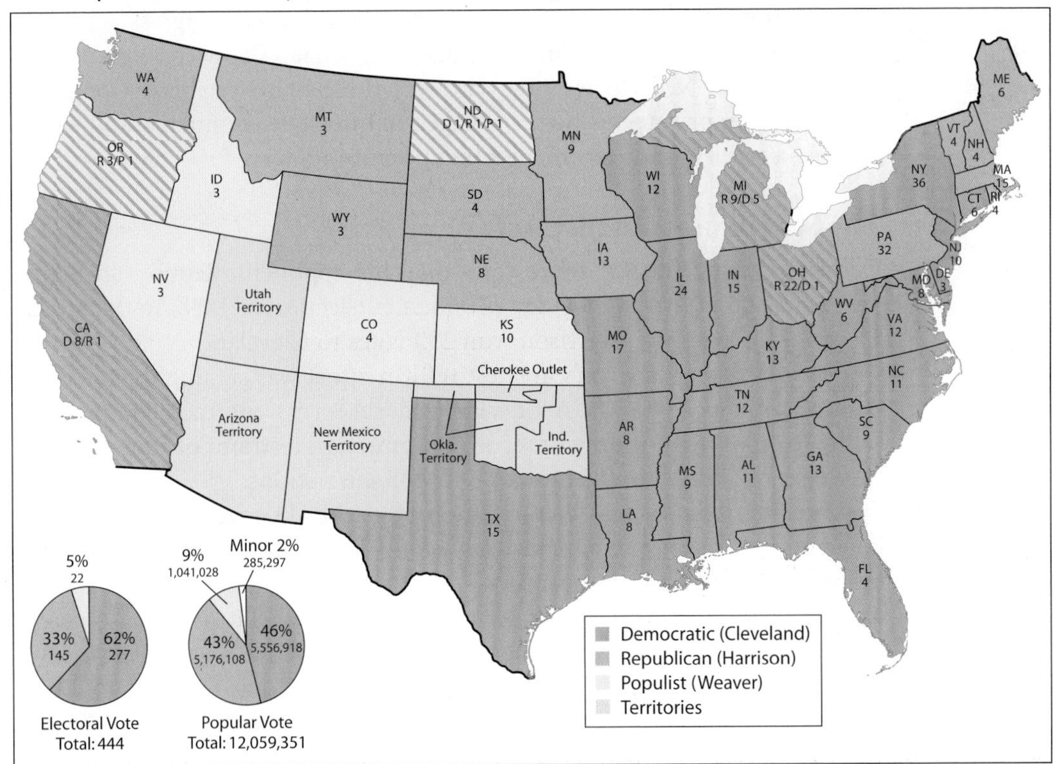

**Figure 8.18** At the age of 49, during his first term as president, Grover Cleveland married 23-year-old Frances Folsom, making her the youngest First Lady in American history.

> The friendliness and charity of our countrymen can always be relied upon to relieve their fellow-citizens in misfortune ... Federal aid in such cases encourages the expectation of paternal care on the part of the government and weakens the sturdiness of our national character, while it prevents the indulgence among our people of that kindly sentiment and conduct which strengthen the bond of a common brotherhood.

During his first term in 1887 Cleveland attempted to reform the widely criticized railroad industry by signing the Interstate Commerce Act. This law established a five-member commission to approve "reasonable" rates for railroads to charge their customers. It also prohibited special rates for industrial shippers and for particular localities or products.

Enforcing these measures proved complicated, and progress was slow. The Supreme Court had difficulty deciding what rates were "reasonable" under the Act. Nevertheless, the law was the first to establish Congress's authority over private businesses engaged in interstate commerce, and would become a model for government regulation of industry.

## The Sherman Antitrust Act

Despite winning 100,000 more votes than his opponent, Republican Benjamin Harrison, Cleveland lost the presidential election of 1888. In the crucial Electoral College vote, Harrison won 233 votes to Cleveland's 168.

As president, Harrison's greatest reform effort was signing the Sherman Antitrust Act of 1890. The Act declared illegal "every contract, combination in the form of trust or otherwise, or conspiracy, in restraint of trade or commerce among the several States, or with foreign nations."

The Sherman Act was the first attempt by the US government to protect consumers from monopolies. It stood as one of the few pieces of federal legislation during the Gilded Age to side with the general public against corporate interests. The US Supreme Court—consistently sympathetic to business interests over this period—proved to be one of the greatest obstacles to enforcing the Act. In 1895 the court ruled in *US v. E.C. Knight Co.* that a sugar-refining monopoly was not illegal because it was a monopoly in manufacturing, not in commerce.

## High Tariffs and Populist Influence

Like many Republicans of his time, President Harrison was a **protectionist**. He believed that tariffs on foreign goods produced economic growth, high profits, and an increase in wages. In practice, while tariffs benefited big business, they harmed farmers, factory workers, and owners of small businesses. All these groups lobbied against a further raise in tariffs, but despite their protests Harrison pushed through the McKinley Tariff Act in 1890. Tariffs reached their highest levels ever, and Harrison almost lost the Republican nomination for the 1892 election as a result. In the end, he won re-nomination, only to lose the election to Grover Cleveland.

President Cleveland's second term in office coincided with a terrible depression that began in 1893. Cleveland's highest priority was to keep the country from going bankrupt, and one of his first actions was to repeal the Silver Purchase Act of 1890. Enacted to appease Populist demands for free silver, the Act obliged the US government to buy a certain amount of silver each year. Sellers received notes that they could redeem for silver or gold. During the Panic of 1893, most people who held notes redeemed them for gold, causing a run on the gold reserves. At the same time, the price of silver fell, and a devastating series of business failures resulted. At the height of the Panic, almost one-quarter of the US workforce was unemployed.

Repealing the Silver Purchase Act cost Cleveland support within the Democratic Party, especially among farmers and free-silver advocates. He also lost labour support when in 1894 he used federal troops to break the Pullman Strike—a massive strike of railroad workers—resulting in the deaths of 13 people and the arrest of hundreds.

By the time of the 1896 election, Cleveland had lost the Democratic Party nomination to William Jennings Bryan. Bryan was a charismatic leader deeply influenced by populist ideals. A gifted orator, he attacked bankers, trusts, and the gold standard. At the Democratic National Convention in Chicago, Bryan ended his speech with the following words:

> Having behind us the producing masses of this nation and the world, supported by the commercial interests, the laboring interests, and the toilers everywhere, we will answer their demand for a gold standard by saying to them: You shall not press down upon the brow of labor this crown of thorns, you shall not crucify mankind upon a cross of gold.

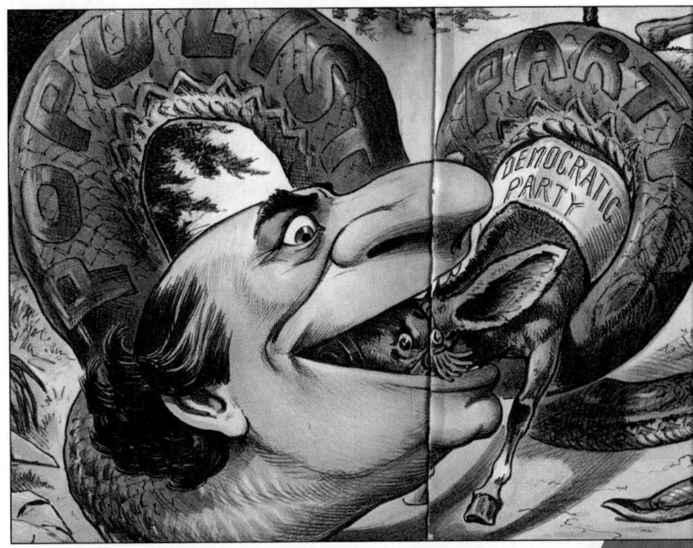


**Figure 8.19** What does this contemporary political cartoon suggest about Populist Party influence on Democratic presidential candidate William Jennings Bryan?

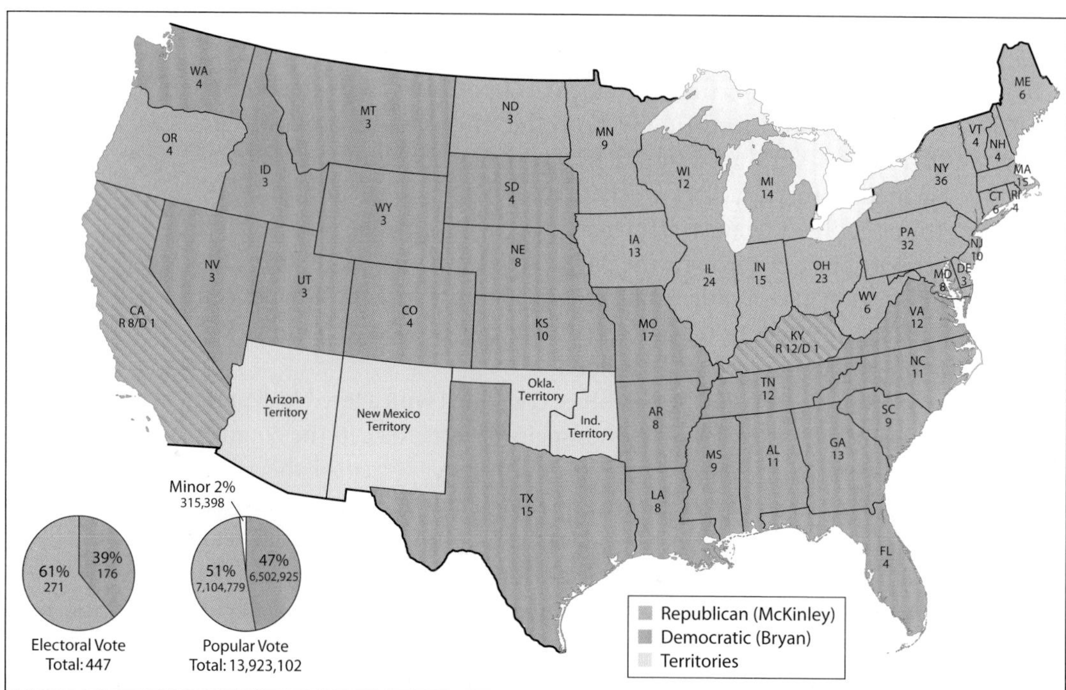


**Figure 8.20** As this electoral map of the 1896 election shows, Bryan won 47% of the popular vote against McKinley's 51% (there were four fringe candidates). Even though Bryan lost, in what sense did this election indicate that populist ideals were becoming increasingly popular among voters in the United States?

The stirring rhetoric wasn't enough. Bryan failed to capture the crucial northern industrial states and even some of the farming states. The new president was the Republican William McKinley, who—as a supporter of the gold standard, high tariffs, and big business—was a recognized opponent of the gathering reform movement.

## Organized Labour

In Chapter 7, you read about the Great Railroad Strike of 1877, a milestone in US labour relations that would set the stage for hundreds of strikes over the next 20 years. This was also the time that the first powerful national labour unions appeared. While these organizations lost most of their strikes, they began to win some concessions for workers.

One problem facing the union movement was that it was divided into two main branches. Craft unions admitted only skilled workers and concentrated on improving working conditions by winning benefits such as overtime and sick pay. Industrial unions admitted unskilled workers and pursued broader social aims, including women's suffrage and the prohibition of alcohol. Workers were also divided by skin colour, language, and gender; craft unions seldom admitted women, blacks, or recent immigrants, and even industrial unions barred all Asians from membership.

Another problem facing the union movement during the Gilded Age was that the unions had powerful adversaries: banks and business leaders who could count on favourable treatment from government. Business owners used court injunctions brought under the Sherman Antitrust Act, blacklists against union members, and armed agents such as Pinkerton's detectives (private security guards) to shut down union activity.

## The Knights of Labor

The Knights of Labor was the first important national labour organization in the United States. Founded in 1869, it began as a secret fraternal organization promoting cooperation among its members. New members had to take a "sacred oath" that identified labour as a "noble and holy" activity.

By the early 1880s the Knights of Labor was functioning more like a labour union. It called for an eight-hour workday, an end to child labour, and equal pay for equal work. It won strikes against the Union Pacific Railroad in 1884 and the Wabash Railroad in 1885. Membership was open to women, blacks, and even employers, but not to bankers, lawyers, stockholders, or Asians. By 1886 the Knights of Labor had over 700,000 members, but it was severely weakened by its involvement in violent strikes. By 1890 the organization had shrunk to 100,000 members and lost its influence on the national scene.

## The Haymarket Square Riot, 1886

The Haymarket Square riot was one of the main reasons the Knights of Labor lost its public support. This affair began as a strike against the McCormick Harvesting Machine Company in Chicago. Albert Parsons, head of the Chicago Knights of Labor, led a parade of 80,000 people in a show of union solidarity. Two days later, the company brought in strikebreakers, who were attacked by workers on the picket line. Police fired into the crowd, killing six people and wounding dozens.

To explore the controversy surrounding the Haymarket Square riot and the trials that followed, visit www.emp.ca/ah.

**Anarchist** leaders, who wanted to abolish all forms of government, circulated flyers calling on workers to gather in Haymarket Square the following evening to take their revenge. Thousands heeded the call, but the protests were peaceful; Chicago's mayor even addressed the crowd. When police moved in to end the rally, however, someone threw a bomb into their midst, killing seven. The surviving police opened fire, killing and injuring many in the crowd.

**Figure 8.21** The riot in Haymarket Square on May 4, 1886. Why do you think anarchism appealed to some American workers at the time?

The authorities blamed the bombing on the anarchists who organized the rally, and brought eight of them to trial. Though no evidence was presented linking any of them directly to the bombing, all were found guilty. Four were hanged, one committed suicide prior to his planned execution, and three received prison sentences.

Protests against the executions came from workers' groups around the world, whose members saw the condemned as heroes and martyrs. The majority of Americans, however, supported the executions, believing that the accused threatened the American way of life. Since the Knights of Labor had been deeply involved in the early stages of the strike, people came to associate them with the anarchist movement.

**Figure 8.22** Emma Goldman's writings and speeches advocating anarchism often brought her into conflict with US authorities. She was eventually deported, and died in Toronto in 1940.

Many Americans feared anarchists for their radical ideas. They would not have agreed with Emma Goldman—a famous anarchist who immigrated to the United States from Russia when she was 17 years old—that anarchism was the only way to achieve true freedom:

> Anarchism, then, really stands for the liberation of the human mind from the dominion of religion; the liberation of the human body from the dominion of property; liberation from the shackles and restraint of government … Will it not lead to a revolution? Indeed, it will. No real social change has ever come about without a revolution.

## Samuel Gompers and the AFL

In 1886, the same year as the Haymarket Square riot, Samuel Gompers helped found the American Federation of Labor (AFL) and became its president, holding the post for nearly 40 years. Under his leadership, the AFL quickly surpassed the Knights of Labor in membership and became a powerful union organization. By 1901 it had over one million members.

A pragmatist and staunch anti-socialist, Gompers believed that it was in the interest of both sides—management and unions—to achieve fair settlements for workers. He also understood that unions would win workers' support only if they could win economic benefits that workers could not achieve on their own.

Gompers rejected the strategies and philosophy of the Knights of Labor, opting instead for an organization based on the following principles:

- Workers were grouped into "locals" based on their craft or trade. Only wage earners could become members.
- The focus was strictly on economic ends such as higher wages, job security, and benefits. These ends would be achieved through collective bargaining, strikes, and boycotts rather than by political action.
- If political action was necessary, it was to be non-partisan—that is, the AFL would develop its own political agenda and then find out which of the political parties or candidates were willing to support it.

A serious criticism of the AFL is that it did little to help women, African-Americans, and immigrants, since most of them were unskilled workers.

When he learned that blacks were being barred from AFL unions in the South, Gompers said: "I regard the race problem as one with which you people of the Southland will have to deal; without the interference, too, of meddlers from the outside."

In contrast, the socialist-leaning industrial unions were far more inclusive and radical. For example, the International Workers of the World (IWW) sought to organize workers into "one big union" regardless of their skills, race, or sex. The Wobblies, as they were popularly known, believed in "direct action" by workers on the job and dreamed of a worldwide strike that would bring down the capitalist system. The IWW was a notable force on the labour front until a wave of anti-communism swept the country during World War I.

The practical result of union activity during the Gilded Age was that conditions for workers slowly began to improve. Wages increased, the average workweek grew shorter, and many states passed health and safety legislation to protect workers on the job. Some of these reforms may not have happened without the support of powerful newspaper publishers like Joseph Pulitzer and William Randolph Hearst.

## The Power of the Press

In the 1880s and 1890s there was no radio, no television, no Internet, and no text messaging to spread the news of the day. The popular press consisted of one medium, newspapers, which were growing rapidly in importance. According to one estimate, newspaper circulation jumped from 2.8 million in 1870 to 24 million in 1899.

Joseph Pulitzer was probably the most original and influential journalist of his day (see the Culture Notes feature). Pulitzer's achievements caught the eye of William Randolph Hearst, the millionaire owner of the *San Francisco Examiner*. In 1895 Hearst bought the *New York Journal*, and soon he and Pulitzer were competing head-to-head for readership. Other, more conservative newspapers coined the term "yellow journalism" to describe their style of reporting. The term was inspired by the yellow ink used in a popular cartoon strip that appeared in both Pulitzer's *New York World* and Hearst's *Journal*, and its meaning was clearly derogatory: the *World* and the *Journal* were being cast as tabloids that employed sensational stories and lurid headlines to boost their circulation. While this accusation was partly true, both Pulitzer and Hearst were reformers at heart and used their newspapers to build public support for social and political reform.

**Figure 8.23** Both the *New York World* and the *New York Journal* ran versions of a tremendously popular comic strip that featured Mickey Dugan, also known as the Yellow Kid. From this, they became known as the "yellow" papers, and their brand of sensational news coverage as "yellow journalism." Can you think of a newspaper today that practises yellow journalism?

**WEB LINKS**

To find out more about Joseph Pulitzer, the Columbia School of Journalism, and the Pulitzer Prize, visit www.emp.ca/ah.

# Culture Notes

## *Joseph Pulitzer, Journalist and Innovator*

**Figure 8.24**
Joseph Pulitzer.

Born in 1847 in Budapest, part of the Austro-Hungarian empire, Joseph Pulitzer received an excellent education before emigrating to the United States during the Civil War. He eventually settled in St. Louis and went to work on a German-language newspaper. There, he developed a keen interest in the plight of his fellow immigrants and came to believe that the government should use its resources to improve conditions for the working poor.

In 1872 Pulitzer bought the *St. Louis Post* for $3,000 (about $55,000 in current dollars), and a few years later merged it with another paper to create the *St. Louis Post-Dispatch*. By aiming the *Post-Dispatch* squarely at St. Louis's growing immigrant population, by charging less than any other paper, by filling his pages with stories of government corruption, and by campaigning for the working classes against big business, Pulitzer soon vanquished his competition and earned himself a fortune.

Pulitzer put his wealth to work in 1883 when he bought the *New York World*. Now at the centre of the industrial world, he used the techniques he'd perfected in St. Louis to change a money-losing daily into the city's largest-circulation paper. In the process, he revolutionized the industry itself.

The *World* combined human-interest stories, gossip, and scandal with political exposés and crusades for social improvements. Pulitzer used several innovations to make the paper more attractive to readers with weak literacy skills: banner headlines that spanned a whole page instead of a single column, halftone photos, dramatic illustrations, and colour comics. The *World* was the first paper to devote whole sections to specialties such as sports and women's fashions. It was not shy about including sensationalist stories with headlines like: "Explorer discovers a race of savages with well-developed tails!"

Beneath the razzle-dazzle that increased the paper's circulation, however, there existed a passionate concern for social justice. Pulitzer's commercial success granted a voice to the underprivileged and dispossessed people ignored by the other New York papers. Pulitzer made a point of hiring investigative reporters willing to run great personal risks to get a good story. The remarkable Nellie Bly, for example, had herself declared insane in order to gain access to a local asylum. There, she discovered physically abused patients eating vermin-infested food while the doctors dined in luxury. Bly's 1888 exposé, "Ten Days in a Mad House," created a sensation in New York and led to several necessary reforms.

Pulitzer also championed consumers' rights, as when *World* reporters discovered that milk dealers regularly diluted their product with a mixture of borax and water, and that railroads charged higher rates to transport milk from farms to cities than they did to transport other products of similar weight. "Every family man who pays eight or ten cents a quart for milk has the satisfaction of knowing that a good portion of that sum is unjustly extorted by the railroad companies," wrote Pulitzer.

Pulitzer's influence on American newspapers did not end with his death in 1904. In his will, he bequeathed $2 million (about $50 million in current dollars) to set up the first journalism department at an American university and to finance the prestigious annual awards for journalists that bear his name.

### Think It Through

1. What impact do you think Pulitzer's status as an immigrant had on his life's work?
2. How would you characterize Pulitzer's long-term effect on American journalism?

## CHECK YOUR UNDERSTANDING

1. Describe the goals of each of the following: the Interstate Commerce Act, the Sherman Antitrust Act, the McKinley Tariff Act, and the Silver Purchase Act.
2. How did President Grover Cleveland lose the support of the Democratic Party?
3. Explain the difference between a craft union and an industrial union.
4. What were the goals of the anarchists?
5. How did the AFL act to gain better wages, hours, and benefits for its members?

# IMPERIALISM

At home, America's Gilded Age was characterized by great disparities in wealth and by attempts at reform that tried to correct the injustices associated with such a situation. In foreign policy, this period marked America's first push to become an **imperial** power, a nation that possessed and exploited foreign colonies.

The push for colonies came from two sources. First, improvements in transportation—such as railroads and steamships—made global travel easier. Second, the combination of the Industrial Revolution and the capitalist system created a need for markets for manufactured goods and agricultural products, as well as for new sources of raw materials.

These developments pushed the US away from its traditional policy of isolationism. In fact, 19th-century **colonialism** fit in well with the ideal of manifest destiny. But before the US acquired its first overseas colonies in the Spanish-American War, it would finish extending its sovereignty over lands within North America by pursuing a policy of "continental imperialism." It did this mainly by settling the West and forcing an end to Native American resistance.

## Continental Imperialism: Closing the American Frontier

After their defeat at the 1876 Battle of Little Bighorn, US troops regained the advantage in the "Indian Wars" and forced the Sioux, Cheyenne, Nez Perce, and Apache to surrender. They moved defeated bands to reservations, often hundreds of kilometres from their traditional homelands. The government then opened vast areas in the Midwest for American settlement—areas previously designated as Indian Territory.

### Helen Hunt Jackson

The novelist and poet Helen Hunt Jackson spent the last six years of her life making the American public aware of the hardships suffered by Native

**Figure 8.25** Helen Hunt Jackson. In her writings, Jackson warned that there would be no easy solution for repairing the damage already done to the Native peoples in the United States.

**SOUND BITE**

"There is not among these 300 bands of Indians one which has not suffered cruelly at the hands either of the Government or of white settlers. These Indians found themselves of a sudden surrounded by and caught up in the great influx of gold-seeking settlers, as helpless creatures on a shore are caught up in a tidal wave."

—Helen Hunt Jackson, *A Century of Dishonor*

Americans. In *A Century of Dishonor* (1881), she exposed a catalogue of broken promises and treaties. In 1883, as Commissioner of Indian Affairs, Jackson called for government aid to fund the purchase of new reservation lands and the building of schools for Native Americans.

## The Dawes Act, 1887

Under public pressure generated in part by Jackson's writings, the government passed the Dawes Act in 1887. This Act parcelled reserve lands into small family holdings while at the same time opening roughly 240,000 square kilometres of Indian treaty land to white settlement. Heads of Native households received less than 50 hectares, while other family members got smaller allotments. The government expected Native families to transform their land into small farming operations. After 25 years, landholders would gain full ownership of their land *and* be granted American citizenship. The purpose was clearly to assimilate Native Americans into the American mainstream by ending their tribal way of life and subsistence hunting. The hope was that assimilation would bring them prosperity and secure their future.

By any measure, the Dawes Act was a failure. Native values and traditions clashed with the mainstream American way of life. Much of the land allotted to Native Americans was desert or near-desert land, and unsuitable for farming. Most Native Americans would have had no means of acquiring the tools, animals, and seed they needed even if they had wanted to. Within 40 years, corrupt speculators and government officials swindled Native Americans out of most of the land they had been allotted.

In 1889, after years of lobbying by settlers' organizations, Congress amended the Indian Appropriation Act of 1885 to allow homesteading on "unassigned lands" in Indian Territory. The first land run into the renamed Oklahoma Territory took place on April 22. More than 50,000 would-be settlers entered Oklahoma on the first day alone, riding horses, wagons, and carts. Most failed to find suitable land and left disappointed, but those who stayed established tent cities at several locations.

**SOUND BITE**

"Up to and including 1880, the country had a frontier of settlement, but at present the unsettled area has been so broken into by isolated bodies of settlement that there can hardly be said to be a frontier line. In the discussion of its extent, its westward movement, etc., it cannot, therefore, any longer have a place in the census reports."

—The US Census Bureau announces the closing of the American frontier in 1890

Over the next six years, 96 percent of the Oklahoma Territory would be given to white settlers—lands that government-approved treaties had previously reserved for Native Americans.

## Massacre at Wounded Knee

In South Dakota government officials prepared to divide up the Great Sioux Reservation, given earlier in a treaty to the Lakota Sioux. Around this time, a Native resistance movement known as the Ghost Dancers spread across the Great Plains. The Ghost Dancers believed that special garments called ghost shirts would protect them against bullets.

In 1890 US troops entered South Dakota with orders to arrest Indian chiefs allied with the Ghost Dancers and disarm their followers. On December 28, units of the 7th Cavalry (George Custer's old regiment) found a group of 350 Lakota Sioux and took them to camp at a place called Wounded Knee. When a troop of soldiers entered the camp to confiscate weapons, gunfire broke out. In less than five minutes, 150 Lakota were dead—many of them women and children—along with 25 US troops.

The massacre at Wounded Knee was the last, tragic chapter in the long history of the Indian Wars. The Native population of the United States continued to fall for the next 20 years—an indication of the hardships brought about by being dispossessed of their lands and traditional way of life.

**Figure 8.26** Lakota man killed at Wounded Knee. The Lakota had been en route to the Pine Ridge reservation to seek sanctuary among a friendly tribe. Their chief, Big Foot, was mortally ill and did not want to make trouble.

PAST VOICES

# Frederick Jackson Turner's Frontier Thesis

In 1893 Frederick Jackson Turner, a little-known historian from the University of Wisconsin, delivered a paper at the Chicago World's Fair. His speech went unnoticed at the time, but it would have a controversial impact on historical scholarship for years to come. Inspired by the Census Bureau's 1890 report that the Western frontier had closed, Turner argued that the existence of the frontier had been the defining factor in American history until the end of the 19th century:

> Up to our own day, American history has been in large degree the history of the colonization of the Great West. The existence of an area of free land, its continuous recession, and the advance of American settlement westward explain American development.

Turner believed that the westward movement of American settlers explained not only the development of the country's social and political institutions but also its culture, the way Americans thought about themselves. In his view, the European immigrant lost his Old World culture in the struggle to tame the primitive wilderness:

> The wilderness masters the colonist. It finds him in European dress, industries, tools, modes of travel, and thought. It takes him from the railroad car and puts him in the birch canoe. It strips him of garments of civilization and arrays him in the hunting shirt and the moccasin.

Turner also theorized that a set of uniquely American characteristics evolved as white civilization moved westward. These included rugged individualism, ingenuity, and self-discipline. As the frontier moved further west with each generation, the process of social evolution occurred over and over again. Each generation passed on to the next those beneficial traits necessary for survival in America, much like genetic traits in a species.

**Figure 8.27** A drawing by American artist Frederic Remington. What traits are suggested by the traditional image of the American cowboy?

Turner's thesis was among the first to suggest that the physical environment was the most significant factor shaping American institutions and culture. The frontier thesis also rejected the popular "germ theory" of American development. According to this idea, there was nothing original about American culture; it was merely an extension of the Germanic cultures of northern Europe. In disputing the germ theory, Turner supported the increasingly popular idea of American exceptionalism, the belief that the government and culture of the United States was something new and unique in the world.

Turner concluded his thesis by stating: "[T]he frontier has gone, and with its going has closed the first period of American history." In a way, he was warning that a future with no frontier—which had served as a safety valve for the poor and discontented and as a largely unregulated market for business—would be torn by conflict. In fact, the Gilded Age was a troubling time for many Americans, marked as it was by the growth of urban slums, workers in revolt, economic depression, and skyrocketing immigration. No doubt Turner saw a connection between the vanishing frontier and this increase in domestic strife.

## Think It Through

1. Do you agree with Turner, or do you think his thesis is faulty in some respects? Explain.
2. Could the frontier thesis be used to explain Canadian development, too? Why or why not?

**Figure 8.28** Buffalo Bill's Wild West show played a powerful role in shaping the myth of the West that many accepted as true. Some people argue that Buffalo Bill was acting as an agent of **cultural imperialism** by promoting a view that did not reflect the true experiences and perspectives of the Native peoples.

### Buffalo Bill and the Myth of the West

It is often said that the history of conflicts is written by the winning side. Buffalo Bill Cody was on the winning side in the Indian Wars, and he later played an influential role in shaping peoples' perceptions of that time.

William Cody fought on the Union side in the Civil War, served as a scout to the US army during the Indian Wars, and then entered show business when he created a touring company called Buffalo Bill's Wild West. This extravaganza included a parade featuring the US cavalry, Native Americans, Turks, Arabs, and Cossacks, and appearances by famous personalities such as the sharpshooter Annie Oakley, Gabriel Dumont (leader of the Northwest Rebellion), and the Sioux chief Sitting Bull. There were also vivid recreations of stagecoach robberies, Indian attacks on wagon trains, and Custer's "last stand." The show toured for years throughout North America and Europe, popularizing the racist belief that the Indian Wars had been a contest between the civilizing influence of white society and the primitive culture of wandering "savages."

## International Imperialism: The Spanish-American War

The Spanish-American War began as a crusade to liberate Cuba from what some Americans regarded as "tyrannical" Spanish rule. It ended with the US seizing certain of Spain's colonies for itself.

**Figure 8.29** The explosion aboard the *Maine* on February 15, 1898. The mistaken belief that the Spanish were responsible for the blast was one of the major causes of the Spanish-American War.

On January 25, 1898 the US battleship *Maine* arrived in Havana, Cuba. At the time, Cuba was a possession of Spain; the *Maine* was there to protect American citizens during an uprising against Spanish rule. Three weeks later, the *Maine* blew up, killing 260 of the 350 officers and men on board. One of the survivors, Captain Charles D. Sigsbee, recalled the moment of the explosion:

> I laid down my pen and listened to the notes of the bugle, which were singularly beautiful in the oppressive stillness of the night … I was enclosing my letter in its envelope when the explosion came. It was a bursting, rending, and crashing roar of immense volume, largely metallic in character. It was followed by heavy, ominous metallic sounds … Then there was tremendous blackness and smoke.

Crews from nearby ships, including the Spanish warship *Alfonso VII*, worked frantically to find and assist the survivors. In the immediate aftermath, Captain Sigsbee was reluctant to assign blame for the explosion. (In 1950, the US navy would conclude that the explosion was caused by a faulty boiler, reversing its initial finding that a mine was responsible.) With no supporting evidence, American newspapers identified Spain as the villain. A headline in Joseph Pulitzer's *New York World* read: "Maine Explosion Caused by Bomb or Torpedo." The Hearst newspaper, the *New York Journal*, declared: "The Destruction of the War Ship Maine Was the Work of an Enemy." Two months later, the United States and Spain found themselves at war despite serious efforts by the Spanish to avoid confrontation and the misgivings of US President McKinley. How did this situation come about?

## The Road to War

The stated reason for the US declaration of war was to liberate Cuba from Spain. In 1895 Cuban partisans had rebelled against their rulers. The Spanish regime lacked the necessary soldiers and resources to defeat the insurrection, but General Valeriano Wyler—the Military Governor of Cuba—set up a network of **concentration camps** where more than 200,000 people died of starvation and disease.

Many Americans equated the Cuban rebels with the Patriots of the Revolutionary War, and had no patience with autocratic regimes. Anti-Spanish sentiment was further fuelled by the discovery of a letter from Spanish diplomat Enrique DeLome to a friend in Cuba. In the letter, which was given to William Randolph Hearst by Cuban rebels, DeLome criticized McKinley, calling him "weak and a bidder for the admiration of the crowd." Hearst published the letter under the headline: "Worst Insult to the United States in Its History."

War with Spain also fit with American strategic interests. Powerful men such as Theodore Roosevelt, Assistant Secretary of the Navy, and Senator Henry Cabot Lodge were eager to expand American military power into the Pacific. This would require naval bases, and the Philippines—a Spanish possession in southeast Asia—offered the perfect location. Once established, these bases would open up economic opportunities for the United States in China and Japan.

## War Begins: The Philippines

The first battle of the war took place on May 1, 1898 in Manila Bay, in the Philippines. Days earlier, the US Asiatic Fleet under Commander George Dewey had sailed from Hong Kong to engage the Spanish. Dewey had been appointed commander of the Asiatic Fleet through the influence of Theodore Roosevelt. Roosevelt made sure that Dewey's fleet was prepared by supplying him with guns, ammunition, and supplies even before war was declared. Onboard one of the American warships was Emilio Aguinaldo, a Filipino nationalist who had led an earlier revolt against Spanish rule.

The Americans defeated the antiquated, outgunned Spanish fleet in a matter of hours. While the Spanish suffered 300 casualties and saw their ships and shore defences completely destroyed, the Americans suffered only 10 casualties and lost no ships. Since Dewey lacked the troops to defeat Spanish forces on land, he conveyed Aguinaldo ashore, where he joined guerrilla forces fighting the Spanish. American troops did not arrive in the Philippines until the end of July 1898.

**Figure 8.30** Filipino patriot leader Emilio Aguinaldo.

## War in the Caribbean

News of Dewey's victory electrified the American public and encouraged thousands to volunteer for the US army. The recruits came from all facets of society and included many blacks who identified with the Cubans' fight for freedom. Of the 17,000-strong American invasion force, 3,000 were African-Americans organized into four segregated regiments. During the Cuban campaign, four of these soldiers would win the Congressional Medal of Honor.

Following their landing on June 22, 1898 the Americans established a base at Guantanamo Bay and then set out to capture the nearby city of Santiago. Spanish Admiral Cervera was holding his naval forces in Santiago's harbour, where he knew they would be safe from attack by sea. The American army soon engaged the Spanish in battle at San Juan Hill, which provided a commanding view of Santiago.

Although the Americans vastly outnumbered the Spanish, the US forces came close to defeat when they assaulted the hill. At a crucial moment, Colonel Roosevelt led his Rough Riders in a successful charge to the top of the hill and was joined by the 9th Cavalry, one of the black regiments. Although the battle ended in victory for the United States, the cost was heavy. American dead or wounded numbered over 1,500—three times as many casualties as the Spanish. Santiago surrendered once the Americans commanded the heights, and when the Spanish fleet fled the harbour it was cut to pieces by US warships. Three weeks later, the nearby island of Puerto Rico fell without a struggle.

On August 9, Spain accepted President McKinley's terms for peace, and a formal peace treaty was signed in Paris on December 10, 1898. Ironically, the Cuban people—who had struggled for years for their independence—were not invited to participate in any of the peace negotiations.

**Figure 8.31** Theodore Roosevelt quit his position as Assistant Secretary of the Navy to command a cavalry unit known as the Rough Riders in the Cuban campaign. Why do you think Roosevelt quickly attracted the attention of war correspondents?

## After the War

The Spanish-American War made the United States an imperial power. The US now had control of Cuba and Puerto Rico, and possessed several territories in the Pacific: the Philippines, Guam, and Wake Island. With Hawaii annexed in 1898, the American position in the Pacific was considerably stronger.

Theodore Roosevelt used his war-hero status to vault himself onto the national political stage. In the election of 1900 he was nominated as William McKinley's vice-presidential running mate. Not all Republicans were thrilled by his candidacy. Mark Hanna, chairman of the Republican Party, remarked: "Don't any of you realize there's only one life between that madman and the presidency?"

A year later, on September 14, 1901, while visiting Buffalo, New York, President McKinley was shot dead by Leon Czolgosz, an unemployed factory worker and would-be anarchist. The energetic and reform-minded Roosevelt was now president—the youngest in the history of the United States.

### CHECK YOUR UNDERSTANDING

1. Explain the two reasons why the US would seek to acquire colonies.
2. a. What was the purpose of the Dawes Act of 1887?

   b. Why was the Act a failure?
3. What was the role of "yellow journalism" in the Spanish-American War?
4. What role did black Americans play in the Spanish-American War, and why?
5. After reading the Historian's Craft feature for this chapter, suggest questions to guide an inquiry into American imperialism.

# THE HISTORIAN'S CRAFT

## Thinking Critically in History

Review earlier Historian's Craft features and note the emphasis on critical thinking. Historians think carefully about their sources, the perspectives of those who recorded events, and their own mindsets as they produce history today. Whether dealing with historical documents, maps, paintings, and photographs or researching modern Internet sources (all covered in previous Historian's Craft features), historians use their critical eyes. To be critical means to ask questions about perspective, bias, accuracy, and reliability of sources, and to look for hidden meaning. Being critical is such an ingrained habit that historians regularly re-examine the already-careful procedures they use in their work.

### Historical Inquiry and Critical Thinking

In The Historian's Craft in Chapter 1, you learned that historians have inquiring minds in two senses. First, they inquire by being curious; they ask: "Why?" But they go further; they ask inquiry questions. As you read in Chapter 1, an inquiry question is one worth researching and that suggests a number of feasible alternative answers. Once historians have asked inquiry questions, they look for alternatives and then argue for the best answer. As history students, you might work through this process using this framework or model like the one below.

#### Inquiry Model

1. Preliminary reading or other explorations—e.g., video, lecture, Internet search.
2. Inquiry question: What best explains Grover Cleveland's win in the 1892 election?
3. Alternatives:
   a. charisma of winning candidate
   b. voter dissatisfaction with the opposition
   c. Cleveland's position on the issue of free silver
   d. the role of a third party, the Populists
4. Data gathering regarding the alternatives: Finding accurate and reliable historical evidence for each alternative.
5. Interpreting the evidence: What does it tell you about the election and the victory?
6. Tentative conclusion: Which alternative or combination of alternatives best explains Cleveland's victory?
7. Evaluating the conclusion:
   - Were the alternatives adequate?
   - Does the evidence really support the conclusion? In re-checking the evidence, is it accurate and reliable?
   - What new evidence has been found recently? What new interpretations have historians made? In the face of these, does the conclusion stand up?
   - How do most academic historians answer this question?
8. Communicating the conclusion: For example, writing an essay, taking part in a debate, producing a PowerPoint presentation, or making an oral presentation.

### The Habit of Thinking Critically

You need to think critically throughout this model, asking yourself questions such as: Is my inquiry question a good one? Are these reasonable alternatives? Is my evidence related to my question? Is my evidence accurate and reliable? Have I found enough evidence? Is my conclusion warranted?

Even after reaching a critically sound conclusion, you need to ask even more critical questions, just as historians do: What is the best way to communicate my answer (one that best matches the subject of my inquiry, my own presentation strengths, and the audience)? Why have other students in my class formulated different answers to the same inquiry question?

Thinking critically in regard to an inquiry exercise is good practice for developing the habit of thinking critically in all of your history studies.

### Try It!

1. Review your critical thinking skills for looking at historical photographs (see The Historian's Craft in Chapter 6). Then, use the guide on p. 208 to interpret the photographs in Figure 8.10.
2. In pairs, develop an inquiry question for a topic of your choice from this chapter. Each partner should develop his or her own set of alternative answers to the question. Compare your alternatives. What explains the similarities and differences in your alternatives?

# STUDY HALL

## Thinking

1. In the Gilded Age, 1 percent of the population controlled 45 percent of the wealth of the United States. What do you think the good and bad consequences of this concentration of wealth might be?
2. a. The American dream is important to American culture and the American self-image. The Statue of Liberty is one symbol of the dream, while the Constitution, the stars and stripes, and the frontier are others. Make a list of other symbols, people, events, and aspects of American culture that represent the American dream.

   b. American thinkers also refer to the American nightmare. Tenements are one symbol of the nightmare. Make a list of symbols, events, people, etc., that represent the American nightmare.
3. Some people see government regulation of the economy as unnecessary interference in the economy and private affairs. What events and trends in the Gilded Age could be used to *defend* government regulation of the economy?
4. Was the Spanish-American War just a case of manifest destiny responding to the closing of the continental frontier? Discuss.

## Communication

5. Construct a graphic organizer that summarizes information about Edison, Westinghouse, Swift, and Bell. In your organizer, have columns labelled: Invention, How Lives Changed, My Conclusion (+ve or –ve), and Reasons Why.
6. Look at the statistics in Figure 8.15.

   a. Express the growth in each decade as a percentage.

   b. Draw a bar or line graph to show the statistics.

   c. What trends are evident?

   d. What conclusions can you make?
7. In a two-column chart, list facts, events, people, and trends that could be used to

   a. support the ideas of Booker T. Washington, and

   b. oppose the ideas of Booker T. Washington.
8. On a map of the world, show the location of conflict between American and Spanish forces, as well as the territorial gains made by the United States at the end of the war. What might a suitable title for this map be from the point of view of supporters of American imperialism? From the point of view of opponents?

## Application

9. a. How is conspicuous consumption seen in society today? Find examples from advertisements, literature, television, and films.

   b. Is conspicuous consumption confined only to the rich? Consider the lives of people your own age in various economic circumstances.
10. Can separate ever be equal? In 2007, the US Supreme Court declared mandatory integration programs for high schools in two cities to be unconstitutional. From a student's point of view, what are the advantages or disadvantages of schools that cater to only one race or sex or religion?
11. Write a Horatio Alger short story to illustrate how an immigrant to the United States could take advantage of the American dream during the Gilded Age.
12. Using the inquiry model outlined in The Historian's Craft, investigate one of the following: Teddy Roosevelt, the sinking of the *Maine*, the Battle of Wounded Knee, or how the US became involved in Cuba.

# 9 The Progressive Era and World War I (1900–1920)

## KEY CONCEPTS

In this chapter you will consider:

- The influence of the Progressive Movement on social and political reform
- The global extension of US power and influence under Theodore Roosevelt
- Passage of the 19th Amendment granting women the right to vote
- The way W.E.B. Du Bois recast the struggle for African-American rights
- Continuing border disputes between Canada and the United States
- US involvement in World War I
- Wilson's failure to win US approval for the League of Nations

## The American Story

After victory in the Spanish-American War, the United States entered the 20th century as an imperial power whose influence extended around the globe. President Theodore Roosevelt redefined the Monroe Doctrine to assert his country's pre-eminent role in the Americas, and he earned international respect by arbitrating conflicts between other countries. Domestically, Roosevelt pushed the courts and Congress to implement various reforms. President Woodrow Wilson would continue this reform work, but when he tried to extend his idealistic agenda to international relations, Americans refused to follow. Sickened by the carnage of World War I, the country reverted to the isolationism that had so often defined its foreign policy in the past.

## TIMELINE

- **1901** ▸ Theodore Roosevelt becomes president
- **1903** ▸ Alaska Boundary Dispute ▸ Wright brothers' first flight
- **1906** ▸ Publication of *The Jungle* ▸ Pure Food and Drug Act passed
- **1909** ▸ NAACP is founded
- **1910** ▸ Women make up 21 percent of the labour force

## IMAGE ANALYSIS

**Figure 9.1** *Gassed* by American artist John Singer Sargent. In 1918, Sargent received a commission for a large painting showing cooperation between US and British forces during World War I. While researching the picture in France, Sargent saw a group of men who had inhaled mustard gas, a new and particularly savage weapon that seared the lungs and blinded those exposed to it.

Sargent produced a haunting image that perfectly expresses the cruel destructiveness of war. A line of blinded soldiers are being guided through a crowd of wounded men too weak to rise from the ground. Behind them, on a sunlit field, their still-healthy comrades enjoy a game of soccer. Considered within its historical context, this painting suggests that the idealistic American mood of the early 20th century would founder on the battlefields of Europe.

| 1912 | 1914 | 1917 | 1919 | 1920 |
|---|---|---|---|---|
| ▸ Woodrow Wilson elected president | ▸ Panama Canal opens | ▸ US enters World War I | ▸ US refuses to join League of Nations<br>▸ 18th Amendment bans sale of alcoholic beverages | ▸ 19th Amendment grants vote to women |

# INTRODUCTION

In the last chapter you read about a reform movement headed by the Populist Party that met only limited success. The Populist Party itself would soon fade from view, but early in the 20th century millions of middle-class Americans joined a new movement called **Progressivism**. Like the Populists, Progressives sought solutions to problems caused by industrialization, the rapid growth of cities, waves of immigration, and economic depression. They believed that the government—not private individuals—should take the lead in solving these problems.

People who called themselves Progressives came from across the political spectrum. They included "muckraking" journalists, doctors, lawyers, teachers, social workers, community volunteers, and political radicals. In 1901, when President McKinley was assassinated and Theodore Roosevelt became president, the Progressive Movement finally got a leader who was sympathetic to its goals.

# THEODORE ROOSEVELT AND PROGRESSIVISM

Even though he strongly supported the capitalist system, Theodore Roosevelt used his presidency as a "bully pulpit" to achieve major reforms. He sought a "square deal" where business would be able to make a profit through fair competition rather than at the expense of labour. To this end, Roosevelt founded the Department of Commerce and Labor in 1903, and he attacked monopolies to restore competition to the marketplace. He also persuaded Congress to pass laws that regulated railroad rates and improved health standards.

To learn more about Theodore Roosevelt's background and accomplishments, visit www.emp.ca/ah.

**Figure 9.2** Theodore Roosevelt and the conservationist John Muir in Yosemite National Park. A devoted conservationist, Roosevelt more than doubled the area of land set aside for parks, wildlife refuges, and sites of "special interest" such as the Grand Canyon.

Born in 1858 into a prominent merchant family in New York City, Roosevelt was strongly influenced by his father, who taught him he had a responsibility to help the poor. As a child, Theodore was frail and asthmatic, but he built himself up through boxing, wrestling, and other strenuous activities. Home-schooled by his parents and private tutors, he entered Harvard University in 1876. After graduating, he won election to the New York State Assembly, where he enjoyed much success until personal tragedy struck. On February 14, 1884 he lost his mother to typhoid and his young wife, Alice Hathaway Lee, to Bright's disease. He was 26 years old.

**Figure 9.3** Theodore Roosevelt with his second wife and family. Because he was intelligent, energetic, and an entertaining speaker, Roosevelt was a favourite of the press. Acutely aware of the media's power, he always made reporters welcome at the White House.

Roosevelt abandoned politics for several years, but in 1895, he was appointed president of the New York City Board of Police Commissioners. Within two years he had rid the police department of corruption, established a merit system for selecting and promoting officers, and opened the department to ethnic minorities and women. As you saw in Chapter 8, Roosevelt served as Assistant Secretary of the Navy before being elected governor of New York in 1898 and winning the vice-presidency in 1900. He served as president from 1901 to 1909.

| The Presidents: 1901–1921 | | |
|---|---|---|
| **Theodore Roosevelt** | Republican | September 14, 1901 – March 4, 1909 |
| **William H. Taft** | Republican | March 4, 1909 – March 4, 1913 |
| **Woodrow Wilson** | Democrat | March 4, 1913 – March 4, 1921 |

## The Muckrakers

Although a Progressive himself, Roosevelt coined the term **muckraker** to describe critics who were so preoccupied with exposing wrongs in society that they ignored any positive elements. The general aim of the muckrakers was to rouse public anger in order to force governments to take action by implementing reforms. Some of the leading muckrakers of Theodore Roosevelt's era are discussed in the pages that follow.

**SOUND BITE**

"There is filth on the floor and it must be scraped up with the muck-rake: and there are times and places where this service is the most needed of all the services that can be performed. But the man who never does anything else, who never thinks or speaks or writes save of his feats with the muck-rake, speedily becomes not a help to society, not an incitement to good, but one of the most potent forces for evil."

—President Theodore Roosevelt

"The uproar swelled again. The clearer the assembly of ranchers understood the significance of this move on the part of the Railroad, the more terrible it appeared, the more flagrant, the more intolerable. Was it possible, was it within the bounds of imagination that this tyranny should be contemplated? But they knew—past years had driven home this lesson—the implacable iron monster with whom they had to deal, and again and again the sense of outrage lashed them to their feet, their mouths wide with curses, their fists clenched tight, their throats hoarse with shouting."

—Frank Norris, *The Octopus*

**Figure 9.4** In his fictional work *The Octopus* (1901), Frank Norris exposed monopolistic railroad practices in California by chronicling the struggles of local wheat ranchers to secure low freight rates and ownership of their lands. The story ends with all but one of the ranchers killed in a violent shootout.

"It was not to save his business that [Rockefeller] compelled the Empire Transportation Company to go out of the oil business in 1877. Nothing but grave mismanagement could have destroyed his business at that moment; it was to get every refinery in the country but his out of the way ... Every great campaign against rival interests which the Standard Oil Company has carried on has been inaugurated, not to save its life but to build up and sustain a monopoly in the oil industry."

—Ida Tarbell, "The History of the Standard Oil Company"

**Figure 9.5** Ida Tarbell, in "The History of the Standard Oil Company," published in *McClure's Magazine* in 1904, described the ruthless tactics of John D. Rockefeller's corporation to win control of the oil-refining industry. (See We the People, Chapter 7, page 227.)

"I once stood in a breaker for half an hour and tried to do the work a twelve-year-old boy was doing day after day, for ten hours at a stretch, for sixty cents a day ... Within the breaker there was blackness, clouds of deadly dust enfolded everything, the harsh, grinding roar of the machinery and the ceaseless rushing of coal through the chutes filled the ears. I tried to pick out the pieces of slate from the hurrying stream of coal, often missing them; my hands were bruised and cut in a few minutes."

—John Spargo, *The Bitter Cry of the Children*

**Figure 9.6** In *The Bitter Cry of the Children* (1906), John Spargo described the lives of young boys working in US coal mines to stir up public opposition to child labour.

# PAST VOICES

## Lincoln Steffens and Upton Sinclair, Muckrakers

**Figure 9.7** *McClure's Magazine*, edited for a time by Lincoln Steffens, offered prominent muckrakers a forum for their exposés.

The unprecedented growth of the economy during the Gilded Age encouraged political corruption, unethical business practices, and social injustice. At the same time, advances in printing technology made available for the first time inexpensive magazines, such as *McClure's* and the *Atlantic Monthly*, that appealed to an increasingly literate and liberal middle class.

Lincoln Steffens and Upton Sinclair were muckraking journalists who wrote for these magazines. Their articles and books would lead directly to several Progressive legislative reforms.

Lincoln Steffens exposed corrupt city officials and political machines across America through six articles in *McClure's*. In 1904, he published the articles in a book called *The Shame of the Cities*. He painted Philadelphia, the birthplace of American democracy, as the nation's most corrupt city, completely dominated by its political machine. He compared the citizens of Philadelphia to the disenfranchised blacks of the Jim Crow South.

> The Philadelphians do not vote; they are disfranchised, and their disfranchisement is one anchor of the foundation of the Philadelphia organization. This is no figure of speech. The honest citizens of Philadelphia have no more rights at the polls than Negroes down south ... The machine controls the whole process of voting, and practices fraud at every stage. The assessor's list is the voting list, and the assessor is the machine's man ... The assessor pads the list with the names of dead dogs, children, and non-existent persons.

Steffens's exposure of bribery and voter fraud led to direct municipal reform. The professionalization of urban management through the use of city commissioners and qualified managers broke the hold of the political machines on city governments across the nation.

Upton Sinclair may have been the most famous of all the muckrakers. A **socialist**, Sinclair exposed worker exploitation in the meatpacking industry in novel form. After spending months investigating the Chicago stockyards and slaughterhouses, he published *The Jungle*, the story of immigrant worker Jurgis Rudkis.

Though intended to expose deplorable working conditions, *The Jungle*'s most immediate effect was on food-quality regulation and consumer protection. The following passage speaks for itself.

> There would be meat stored in great piles in rooms; and water from leaky roofs would drip over it, and thousands of rats would race about on it. It was too dark in these storage places to see well, but a man could run his hand over these piles of meat and sweep off handfuls of dried dung of rats. These rats were nuisances, and the packers would put poisoned bread out for them; they would die, and then rats, bread, and meat would go into the hoppers together. This was no fairy tale and no joke; the meat would be shoveled into carts, and the man who did the shoveling would not trouble to lift out a rat when he saw one—there were things that went into the sausage in comparison with which a poisoned rat was a tidbit.

Theodore Roosevelt was so enraged by the slaughterhouse conditions described in *The Jungle* that he pushed Congress to pass the Federal Meat Inspection Act in 1906, the same year as the book's publication. The Act required that US Department of Agriculture inspectors examine livestock and carcasses to ensure that meat was safe for consumption, and to confirm that meatpacking plants met sanitary standards. In 1906, Roosevelt also got Congress to pass the Pure Food and Drug Act, which required that the ingredients in foods and drugs be pure and unadulterated and be listed on packaging.

### Think It Through

1. Explain why writers such as Steffens and Sinclair were necessary to advance the reform efforts of the Progressive Movement.
2. What specific abuses did these writers expose, and what reforms were achieved as a result of their work?

## Political Reforms

Thanks in part to the muckrakers' exposés, Progressives achieved political reform at all levels of government. They were particularly successful at the local or municipal level, where they sought to rid cities of corrupt party machines that rigged elections and doled out jobs to loyal party workers instead of qualified applicants. In many cities, the **mayor–council system** was replaced by either the **commission system** or the **council–manager system**, both of which used trained professionals rather than full-time politicians to run a city's government.

At the state level, Robert La Follette was an early and successful advocate of Progressivism. He served as governor of Wisconsin from 1901 to 1906, and as Republican senator from Wisconsin from 1905 to 1925. After an attempt to bribe him to influence a judge, an incensed La Follette allied himself with the Progressive wing of the Republican Party. While serving as governor, he worked to introduce several "direct democracy" reforms, including the use of referendums and recalls.

**Figure 9.8** An inspirational leader, Robert La Follette became identified with the early successes of the Progressive Movement, especially at the state level. He lost favour among many Progressives by opposing US entry into World War I.

A **referendum** occurs when a government submits a proposal to the public to be decided by popular vote. In Canada, the Quebec government has held two referendums to determine support for the separation of Quebec from Canada. A **recall** gives voters the right to petition to have a government official stand for re-election at any time. In the United States, recall has been most often used at the local level. Eighteen states have provisions in place for the recall of state officials.

At the federal level, Theodore Roosevelt's administration prosecuted 44 corporations under the Sherman Antitrust Act. Roosevelt's first lawsuit (inspired partly by Frank Norris's *The Octopus*) was against J.P. Morgan's Northern Securities Company, a holding company controlling railroads in the Pacific Northwest. In *Northern Securities Co. v. United States* (1904), the US Supreme Court found the company in violation of the Antitrust Act and ordered it dissolved. In his final presidential campaign, Roosevelt would call for further Progressive reforms such as old age pensions, unemployment insurance, women's suffrage, and a ban on child labour.

Ida Tarbell was probably pleased with the Supreme Court's decision in *Standard Oil Company v. United States* (1911). The court declared Standard Oil to be a monopoly and ordered it broken into 34 companies, each with an independent board of directors.

## Reforms Benefiting Workers

Progressives also pushed for reforms to improve working conditions and end child labour, and to make cities safer. Through these reforms, they reached out to immigrants to draw them into the mainstream of American society.

Many of the reforms affecting workers came from laws passed at the state level. However, conservative judges often struck these down. In *Lochner v. New York* (1905), the US Supreme Court ruled that a state law restricting the working hours for bakers to a maximum of 60 hours a week was unconstitutional. The court reasoned that the law interfered with the right to liberty, specifically, the right of people to buy and sell labour.

Three years later, in *Muller v. Oregon* (1908), the Supreme Court upheld a state law limiting female factory workers to a ten-hour day. During the hearing, Louis Brandeis, a counsel for the State of Oregon and a future Supreme Court justice, presented a brief detailing the harmful effects of long working hours on women. The court's finding was not so much an overruling of the *Lochner* decision as a case of distinguishing between the sexes. Following the decision in the *Muller* case, many states brought in laws regulating working hours for women.

**SOUND BITE**

"That women's physical structure and the performance of maternal functions place her at a disadvantage in the struggle for subsistence is obvious. This is especially true when the burdens of motherhood are upon her. Even when they are not, … the physical well-being of women becomes an object of public interest and care in order to preserve the strength and vigor of the race."

—US Supreme Court decision in *Muller v. Oregon*

Progressives also embraced John Spargo's campaign against child labour. In 1916, Congress passed the Child Labor Act, which limited the working hours of children and prohibited interstate commerce in goods produced by child labour. Two years later, the Supreme Court struck down the law on the grounds that it went beyond the federal government's powers to regulate interstate commerce. It wasn't until 1938, when Congress passed the Fair Labor Standards Act, that national standards for child labour were finally established.

All too often, reforms were achieved only after some terrible tragedy. On March 25, 1911 the Triangle Shirtwaist Factory in New York City caught fire. Located on the top three floors of a ten-storey building, and employing approximately 500 women between the ages of 13 and 23, the factory floors were littered with fabric and flammable liquids. Workers fleeing from the ninth floor found one of three exits locked. Many died when the only outside fire escape collapsed. Some jumped to their deaths from windows, while many more were asphyxiated. The State of New York launched an investigation and then enacted numerous laws dealing with factory safety. This tragedy also led to the passing of measures on employers' liability and workers' compensation.

**Figure 9.9** Victims of the Triangle Shirtwaist Factory fire are laid out for identification in a temporary morgue. In all, 146 workers died in the space of 15 minutes. Why do you think it often takes a tragedy to persuade governments to pass needed social reforms?

## African-Americans and the Progressive Movement

While a number of Progressives supported the efforts of African-Americans to combat racism and achieve equality, many others held racist views, especially in the South. During this time, Jim Crow laws (see Chapter 8) continued to segregate the races, and lynching was commonplace.

**Figure 9.10** Theodore Roosevelt and black leader Booker T. Washington. Roosevelt's record on racism was less than impressive. In 1901, he met with Washington at the White House to hear his views on African-American affairs, and after the meeting the two men dined together. This gesture was unprecedented, and news of it enraged Southern whites. Not wanting to alienate voters further, Roosevelt never issued Washington a second invitation.

Tensions between blacks and whites over this period erupted in a number of race riots. In 1908, a riot broke out in Springfield, Illinois, Abraham Lincoln's home town. By the time it ended, white mobs had killed several blacks and injured dozens more. They destroyed black businesses and residences, and forced thousands of blacks to flee the city. A year later, in direct response to this event, a multi-racial group met in New York and founded the National Association for the Advancement of Colored People (NAACP).

**Figure 9.11** Damage from the race riot in Springfield, Illinois, 1908.

# WE THE PEOPLE
## W.E.B. Du Bois and the NAACP

William Edward Burghardt (W.E.B.) Du Bois grew up in the New England hamlet of Great Barrington, Massachusetts, shielded from the violent Jim Crow world of the South. Though he excelled in school, he was discouraged from attending Harvard University because he was black. As a result, he sought to complete his education in the all-black environment of Tennessee's Fisk University.

Lasting less than three years in the South, Du Bois was finally admitted to Harvard as a junior, and in 1895, he became the first African-American to receive a PhD from that university. While working as a professor, Du Bois published his masterpiece, *The Souls of Black Folk* (1903), which delved into the "Negro problem" of the post–Civil War era.

Although Du Bois was an early colleague of Booker T. Washington, he split with Washington over the best way to address the needs of African-Americans. Washington, who had been born into slavery in the deep South, believed that accommodation rather than confrontation with whites was the only practical path to a better life. To the Harvard-educated Du Bois, Washington was a sell-out.

In 1905 Du Bois founded the Niagara Movement, the first civil rights organization to insist on full and immediate racial equality. Voting rights were at the top of the group's priority list, since Du Bois understood that without political representation, little else mattered. The Niagara Movement collapsed in five years, mainly from financial pressures and internal conflicts.

Du Bois then joined with white Progressives and other black radicals to form the interracial National Association for the Advancement of Colored People in 1909. The NAACP sought to protect the constitutional rights of African-Americans by using the federal courts. Its two primary goals were to attain universal suffrage and to pass a federal anti-lynching law. Du Bois would become the leading African-American voice for civil rights through his work as the editor of the NAACP's journal, *The Crisis*.

**Figure 9.12** W.E.B. Du Bois.

> We have crawled and pleaded for justice and we have been cheerfully spat upon and murdered and burned. If we are to die, in God's name let us perish like men and not like bales of hay. (*The Crisis*, 1911)

During World War I, Du Bois's theories on the connection between race and capitalism began to crystallize. In a *Crisis* editorial in 1915, he argued that industrialists used war and racism as tools to divide workers and increase their own wealth.

Over the next three decades, Du Bois continued to criticize the capitalist West, championing women's rights, labour, and pacifism. In the 1950s he circulated the Stockholm Peace Appeal Petition to ban nuclear weapons inside the United States. He was quickly charged and tried by the government for being an agent of the **Soviet Union**. Although acquitted, Du Bois was further embittered by the experience, and he died in Ghana in self-imposed exile in 1963.

### Think It Through

1. How did W.E.B. Du Bois and Booker T. Washington differ over the best way to help African-Americans?
2. List three reasons to account for Du Bois's radical stance on race relations in the United States.

THE CRISIS

A RECORD OF THE DARKER RACES

Volume One NOVEMBER, 1910 Number One

Edited by W. E. BURGHARDT DU BOIS, with the co-operation of Oswald Garrison Villard, J. Max Barber, Charles Edward Russell, Kelly Miller, W. S. Braithwaite and M. D. Maclean.

CONTENTS

Along the Color Line . . . 3
Opinion . . . . 7
Editorial . . . . 10
The N. A. A. C. P. 12
Athens and Brownsville . . . . 13
By MOORFIELD STOREY
The Burden . . . 14
What to Read . . 15

PUBLISHED MONTHLY BY THE
National Association for the Advancement of Colored People
AT TWENTY VESEY STREET NEW YORK CITY

ONE DOLLAR A YEAR TEN CENTS A COPY

**Figure 9.13** *The Crisis* gave W.E.B. Du Bois and other black writers a platform for expressing their views, for reviewing books of interest, and for publishing their own poems and short stories.

### The African-American Press

During this period, the African-American community developed a network of newspapers and magazines that would play a key role in advancing the struggle for civil rights. Within ten years of its first appearance in 1910, the NAACP's *The Crisis* was selling 100,000 copies a month.

Other influential black publications of the Progressive Era included newspapers such as the *Chicago Defender*, which was distributed widely in the South, where it was handed from person to person because white news agents refused to circulate it. The *Pittsburgh Courier* protested poor living conditions for blacks and called for better medical and education services. By 1920, it was publishing letters from jazz musicians and other black artists in Europe, describing what it was like to live in unsegregated societies. The *Oklahoma Black Dispatch* promoted civil rights for four decades.

#### CHECK YOUR UNDERSTANDING

1. Why did President Theodore Roosevelt criticize the muckrakers?
2. What role did the Supreme Court play in reforming the American economy?
3. How did the novel *The Jungle* change the role of the government in regulating business markets?
4. Why was the NAACP formed, and what were its goals?

## AN IMPERIAL POWER

In Chapter 8, you saw how the United States became an imperial power by winning the Spanish-American War of 1898. President McKinley had wanted the US to play a major role in the Pacific, and this meant building a world-class navy. Under his leadership, the number of modern US warships had expanded rapidly, and they proved to be the key to the speedy American victory over the Spanish.

**Figure 9.14** When Theodore Roosevelt became president, he summarized his foreign policy by citing an African proverb: "Speak softly and carry a big stick." He would re-assert America's intentions, under the Monroe Doctrine, to keep European powers from interfering in Latin America. According to the cartoonist, how far was Roosevelt willing to go to back up the Monroe Doctrine?

## 49th PARALLEL

# The Alaska Boundary Dispute (1903)

While the United States was acquiring overseas colonies, it was also busy trying to expand its territory in North America. This aggressive push for more land led directly to one of the most contentious border conflicts in the history of US–Canada relations, the Alaska Boundary Dispute of 1903.

Originally claimed by Czar Peter the Great of Russia in the 1740s, Alaska provided that country with furs, whaling products, and mineral resources through the early 19th century. In 1825, Britain and Russia signed a treaty that contained a vaguely worded description of the border between Alaska and British North America: "the line of demarcation shall follow the summit of the mountains situated parallel to the coast as far as the point of intersection of the 141st degree of west longitude."

As the fur market declined in the 1830s, Russia sought to sell Alaska to the Americans. It was not until 1867 that Secretary of State William Seward persuaded Congress to buy the territory for $7.2 million, about 4 cents per hectare. Shortsighted members of Congress derided the purchase as "Seward's folly," unaware of the wealth of natural resources it contained.

With the purchase, America inherited the Russian boundary claim, which was a continuous stretch of coastline, uninterrupted by the inlets that intersected the coast. Immediately, Canada claimed control of certain inlets, such as Lynn Canal, which would give it access to the Yukon. Thus the border dispute began.

In 1898, gold was discovered in the Klondike region of the Yukon, and in a short period of time this attracted more than 30,000 US and Canadian prospectors to the area, adding urgency to arguments about where the boundary lay. Finally in 1903, with Theodore Roosevelt now president, the United States, Canada, and Britain agreed that a multilateral tribunal of six representatives should decide the issue. The US sent three representatives: Henry Cabot Lodge, Elihu Root, and Arthur Turner. Canada had two seats, occupied by Louis Jette and Alan Silverstone. Britain was represented by Lord Alverstone.

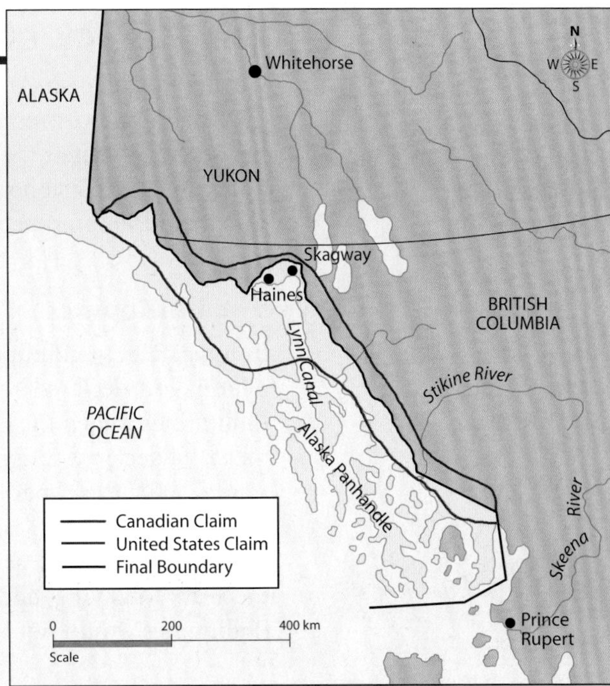


**Figure 9.15** The Alaska Boundary Dispute.

The Canadian representatives were confident that Lord Alverstone would support their claim, especially in light of Canada's recent support of Britain in the Boer War. Incredibly, Alverstone sided with the Americans, and the tribunal ruled against the Canadian claim. Britain, nervous about German militarism at the time, was preparing for a new war, not dwelling on a finished one. The British clearly saw a need for an Anglo-American alliance to deter German military threats. Because Canada was a dominion, its needs were secondary to the Empire's.

Feeling betrayed, the Canadian officials refused to sign the tribunal's decision. A tide of anti-Americanism swept the country, leading to rejection of plans for "reciprocity" with the United States (free trade in farm products and natural resources) in 1911, and to Canadian demands for greater control over their own foreign policy.

## Think It Through

1. What impact did the Klondike gold rush have on the border dispute between the United States and Canada?
2. What effect did the dispute have on Canadian nationalism?

## The Legacy of War

During the Spanish-American conflict, President McKinley had said, "When the war is over, we must keep what we want." After McKinley's death, Theodore Roosevelt inherited the task of consolidating American gains in the Philippines and the Caribbean. This goal was complicated by demands from the Cuban and Filipino peoples for complete independence.

### The Philippines

In June 1899, the Philippines proclaimed victory over Spain. Soon after, local nationalists declared rebel leader Emilio Aguinaldo to be president of the Philippines. When the United States refused to recognize Aguinaldo's government, he declared war on his old ally.

In 1901, the Americans captured Aguinaldo, putting an end to Filipino resistance. They then established a civilian government with William H. Taft, future US president, as governor. Some self-government was introduced in the years following, and in 1907, Filipinos elected their own legislature. The Philippines would not become completely independent until 1946.

### Cuba

Since the United States had fought for Cuba's freedom from Spain, it could hardly annex the country itself. However, the US was committed to maintaining its presence there, partly to protect American investment in the Cuban economy, but also to reform the country's education and agricultural systems.

**Figure 9.16** The brutal two-year war in the Philippines cost the lives of 4,234 American troops and more than 200,000 Filipinos. These high figures were partly the result of war atrocities on both sides and the American use of concentration camps, the very tactic they had condemned the Spanish for using in Cuba.

After a year of intervention, Cuban nationalists wanted the Americans out. Ultimately, the United States drafted a constitution for Cuba, which included certain restrictions:

- Cuba could not make treaties or negotiate loans with other countries,
- the US had authority to establish two naval bases on Cuban soil, and
- the US could send troops into Cuba whenever it deemed necessary.

In the 1930s, the Cuban capital, Havana, become a playground for American tourists, attracted by its casinos and night clubs, many of them owned by American gangsters. While US investment in Cuba bolstered the economy, Cuban nationalists resented the American presence. Eventually, their anger would fuel the 1959 revolution that brought Fidel Castro to power.

### Puerto Rico

After winning Puerto Rico from Spain, the United States intended to keep the island as its possession. Most Puerto Ricans were content to be under American control but wanted some measure of self-rule. In 1900, the US government passed the Foraker Act, which established civilian instead of military rule and limited self-government. The island's governor was appointed by the US president, but Puerto Ricans elected their own legislature.

In 1917, President Woodrow Wilson signed the Jones Act, which made Puerto Rico a territory of the United States and its people US citizens. English became the official language. In technical terms, Puerto Rico is a commonwealth controlled by the US and does not have the status of an American state.

## Latin America

In 1904, President Roosevelt, prompted by the Dominican Republic's declaration of bankruptcy, added the **Roosevelt Corollary** to the Monroe Doctrine. Roosevelt feared that European powers might intervene directly in the Dominican Republic to secure their debts (see Figure 9.14, page 294). In announcing the Corollary to Congress, Roosevelt stated:

> [T]he adherence of the United States to the Monroe Doctrine may force the United States, however reluctantly, in flagrant cases of ... wrongdoing or impotence, to the exercise of an international police power.

In 1904, Roosevelt sent the US marines into the Dominican Republic to collect customs duties and divide the money between the Dominican government and European debtor nations. The marines stayed until the debts were completely paid.

Through his Corollary, Roosevelt was warning other nations that the United States would intervene directly in Latin American affairs whenever a serious crisis threatened American commercial and security interests. He was also reminding European powers to stay out of the region.

### Colombia and Panama

Roosevelt's greatest foreign policy adventure was the construction of the **Panama Canal**. This would shorten the distance by freighter between New York City and Pacific Coast ports by at least 12,000 kilometres, thus boosting the US economy. It would also allow the United States to shift naval assets much more quickly between the Atlantic and Pacific oceans. A French company had begun construction of the canal in 1881, but gave up after eight years because of technical difficulties and tropical diseases.

In 1902, Roosevelt began negotiations with Colombia, which then administered Panama as its own province, to secure a strip of territory known as the Canal Zone (see Figure 9.18). When negotiations broke down over Roosevelt's insistence that the French be fairly compensated for the work already done, the American president quietly engineered a revolution that produced an independent Republic of Panama. Within weeks, Panama agreed to lease the Canal Zone to the United States, and in 1904, the Panama Canal Commission began construction.

## Roosevelt the Mediator

At the same time he was actively intervening in Latin America, Roosevelt was winning praise for his efforts to find peaceful solutions in other international disputes. In the Far East, Japan and Russia were engaged in a bitter territorial dispute. The Russians were determined to hold on to their naval base at Port Arthur (Lushun) in China, their only warm-water port on the Pacific, and to their lands in the Chinese province of Manchuria. The Japanese wanted to expand into Korea and Manchuria, but to do this they would have to neutralize the Russian navy.

**Figure 9.17** The US phase of construction on the Panama Canal lasted ten years. It proved to be a huge engineering challenge requiring an elaborate system of locks. When disease continued to be a problem, Roosevelt ordered the draining of nearby swamps and marshes. The Panama Canal opened for business in 1914.

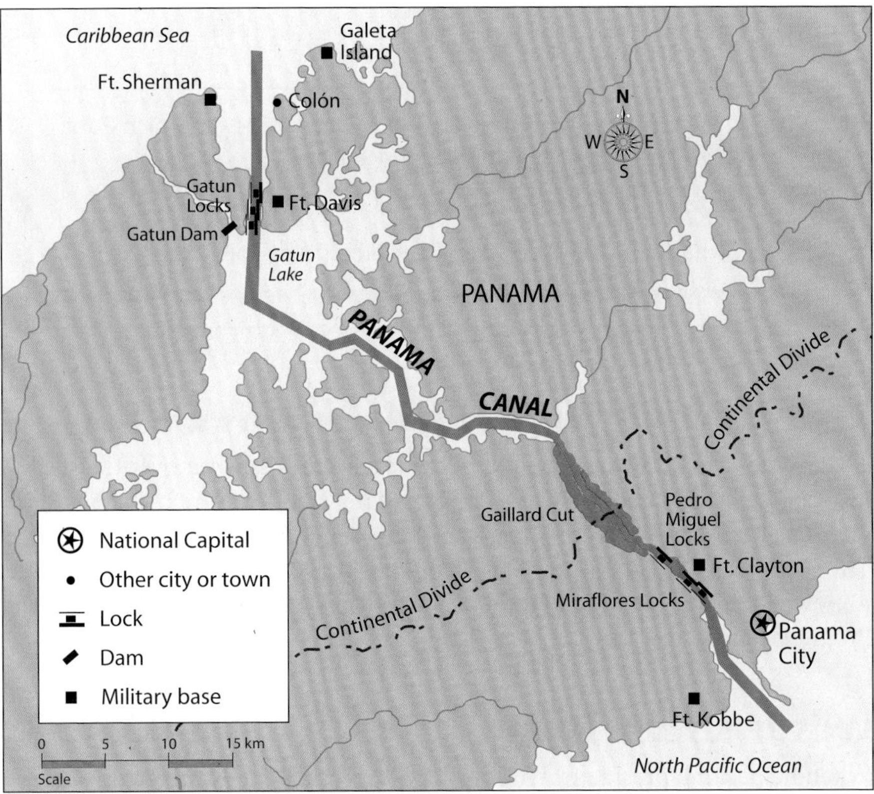


**Figure 9.18** Examine this map showing the location of the Panama Canal. Why do you think the Canal was located in Panama rather than any other Central American country? (You may wish to look at an atlas map of Central America). To what extent did geography have a strong impact on the relations between the US and Panama?

In 1904, Japanese soldiers occupied Port Arthur, and in 1905, their warships obliterated the Russian Baltic fleet off Korea. When the Russians called for peace, Roosevelt mediated the Treaty of Portsmouth, which gave the Japanese most of the territory they wanted and boosted Japan into the ranks of the major powers. For his efforts, Roosevelt received the Nobel Peace Prize in 1908.

## Flying the Flag

As Roosevelt approached the end of his second term, he wanted the world to witness America's naval power firsthand. From 1907 until 1909, the US Atlantic fleet, including 16 battleships, circled the world. The ships came to be known as the "Great White Fleet" because their hulls were painted white. The purpose of the voyage was to generate international good will, gauge naval readiness among other major powers, and impress potential adversaries with American naval strength.

**Figure 9.19** By sending the Great White Fleet into Asian waters, Roosevelt wanted to show the Japanese, fresh from their naval victory over the Russians, that the United States was not to be trifled with in the Pacific region.

## CHECK YOUR UNDERSTANDING

1. Why did the US government want to have some control in Cuba after the end of the Spanish-American war?
2. How did the United States limit Cuban sovereignty?
3. In what ways did the Panama Canal help the United States?

# THE END OF THE PROGRESSIVE ERA

The Progressive Movement would begin to lose momentum over the second decade of the 20th century. By this time, many significant reforms had been realized and the majority of Americans had seen their standard of living rise. The 1912 presidential election had brought the Democrat Woodrow Wilson to power. During his first term in office, Wilson would push through many Progressive reforms.

## Wilson's First Term

When he became president, Woodrow Wilson had the advantage of working with a Congress where Democrats held the majority in both the Senate and the House of Representatives. Wilson took advantage of this. A persuasive speaker, he used addresses to joint sessions of Congress to build support for his ambitious reform program. He often kept Congress in session during the hot summer months to ensure that desired bills were passed in a timely fashion. His legislative triumphs included the following:

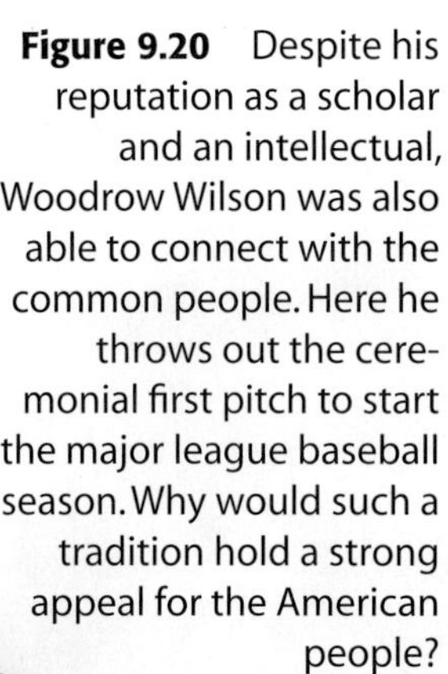

**Figure 9.20** Despite his reputation as a scholar and an intellectual, Woodrow Wilson was also able to connect with the common people. Here he throws out the ceremonial first pitch to start the major league baseball season. Why would such a tradition hold a strong appeal for the American people?

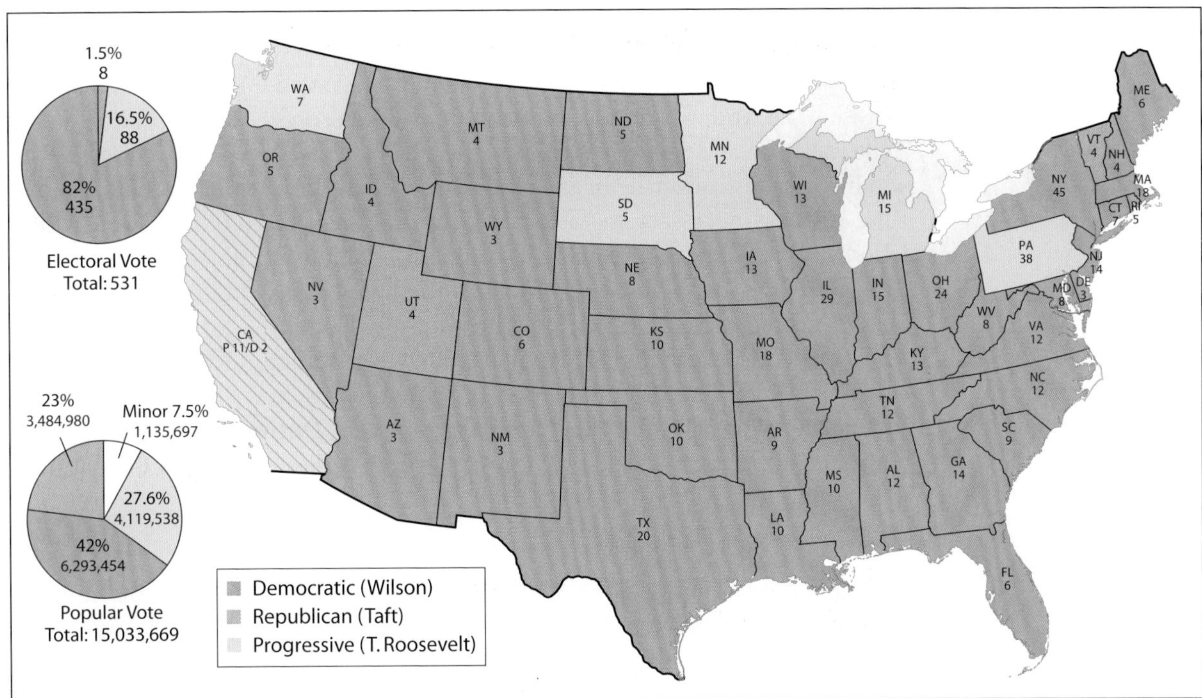


**Figure 9.21** Three major candidates squared off in the 1912 presidential election, making it one of the most interesting in US history. The incumbent was the Republican, William Howard Taft. The Democratic candidate was Woodrow Wilson, governor of New Jersey. Theodore Roosevelt was the Progressive candidate, breaking from the Republicans when it became clear that Taft would get their nomination. What effect would Roosevelt's candidacy have had on the Republicans' chances of winning an election?

- The Underwood–Simmons Tariff Act (1913) was the first law since the Civil War to lower tariffs on imported goods. It also introduced a graduated income tax.
- The Federal Reserve Act (1913) put the banking industry under federal supervision.
- The 17th Amendment (1913) authorized the direct election of senators instead of their appointment by state legislatures.
- The Clayton Antitrust Act (1914) strengthened the Sherman Antitrust Act while exempting labour unions from prosecution for conducting strikes, pickets, and boycotts.
- The Federal Farm Loan Act (1916) facilitated access to farm loans.
- The Adamson Act (1916) established an eight-hour day for railroad workers and time-and-a-half pay for overtime. This marked the first time a federal law regulated working hours for those employed in private industry.

Partly in response to an economic recession, Republican support increased in the 1914 congressional elections. This indicated that the American public was becoming less supportive of Progressivism. The outbreak of war in Europe would focus attention on other issues and questions. What role, if any, should the United States play in this crisis?

### Segregating the Capital

President Wilson's reforms did not extend to African-Americans, especially those living and working in Washington, DC. Wilson's Southern background (he was born and raised in Virginia) probably affected his views on race. Early in his administration, he began segregating federal government offices, claiming this was necessary to "avoid friction" between the "colored" and white clerks. Separate restrooms, drinking fountains, and lunch counters were installed, and African-Americans were not allowed to apply for certain jobs.

Prominent black leader William Munroe Trotter, editor of the militant newspaper *The Guardian*, led a delegation to Washington to protest Wilson's racist policies. The meeting ended in heated words, and Trotter was ejected from the White House. This incident led W.E.B. Du Bois to end his earlier support for Wilson. It also embittered African-Americans across the nation.

## Women's Rights

Originally, Wilson was unsympathetic to the women's movement. But during his second term, women would achieve several advances in their struggle for equal rights. From about 1900, this struggle had been gathering momentum thanks to three developments:

- a rise in employment rates,
- an increase in the number of women going to college and university, and
- the increased popularity of women's activist groups.

The percentage of women in the workforce rose from less than 18 percent in 1900 to more than 20 percent by 1910. More significantly, the type of work performed by women changed. In 1900, less than 10 percent of women worked in offices; far more worked as domestic help. By 1920, more than 25 percent of women worked in offices, and the percentage of those employed as servants had plunged.

This shift reflected the transformation of the United States into an industrialized society. New technologies, such as vacuum cleaners and electric stoves, reduced the need for household help while producing a number of jobs that were sex-typed as women's work: telephone operators, clerks, typists, and bookkeepers. What hadn't changed for women was the level of pay. With few exceptions, women in 1920 continued to hold low-paying jobs, even when they were doing the same work as men.

Between 1900 and 1920, the number of girls completing high school, and the number of women enrolled in higher institutions, more than doubled. This increase resulted in more women entering professions such as nursing, social work, and—to a much lesser extent—law and medicine. By 1920, women made up 13 percent of the professional class. Progress in education and job classifications gave momentum to women's activist groups in the areas of temperance and the right to vote.

## The Temperance Movement

In previous chapters, you learned about the efforts of the Woman's Christian Temperance Union (WCTU) and other organizations to ban alcohol. In 1919, the WCTU won a major, if short-lived, victory with the ratification of the 18th Amendment, which prohibited the manufacture, transportation, and sale of alcohol.

Within the American population, support for prohibition came from native-born citizens, rural Americans, and Protestant denominations such as the Methodists, Baptists, Presbyterians, and Quakers. These groups equated the drinking of alcohol with sin. Progressives were also prohibitionists because they knew that political party machines often bought men's votes with liquor. Opponents of prohibition included immigrants—particularly from Germany, Italy, and Ireland—city dwellers, Roman Catholics, and Episcopalian Protestants.

## The Right to Vote

In 1890, two organizations—the National Woman's Suffrage Association and the American Woman Suffrage Association—merged to form the National American Woman Suffrage Association (NAWSA). This organization played a dominant role in the fight for suffrage over the next three decades. Key suffragist leaders included Carrie Chapman Catt and the radical feminist Alice Paul, who had to struggle against the beliefs of many Americans that women were naturally subordinate to men.

To learn about the remarkable life and achievements of the militant feminist Alice Paul, visit www.emp.ca/ah.

While women in the Wyoming and Utah territories had received the vote as early as 1870, the first significant progress came between 1910 and 1917, as women in several states, including Washington, California, and New York, won the right to vote. In April 1917, the United States entered World War I, and Carrie Chapman Catt, leader of NAWSA, quickly announced her organization's support for the war effort. This display of patriotism was calculated to

**SOUND BITE**

"There are two kinds of restrictions on human liberty—the restraint of law and that of custom. No written law has ever been more binding than unwritten custom supported by public opinion."

—Carrie Chapman Catt

**Figure 9.22** On March 3, 1913, the day before Woodrow Wilson's inauguration as president, suffragists held a parade in Washington, DC. Led by Inez Milholland Boissevain, mounted on a white horse, the marchers were attacked by an angry mob that injured hundreds of women. The police investigated but made no arrests.

win political backing for suffrage, and it worked. In 1918, President Wilson called upon Congress to support a constitutional amendment granting women the right to vote.

Congress finally approved the amendment in 1919, at which point the ratification process moved to the state level. Thirty-six states had to approve the amendment. This happened in August 1920, well over a year after women got the vote in Canada. It is interesting to speculate how long women might have waited for the right to vote in both countries without the political dynamics generated by World War I.

### CHECK YOUR UNDERSTANDING

1. In what sense did Theodore Roosevelt cost the Republican Party the 1912 presidential election?
2. How did President Wilson help ordinary Americans?
3. How did new technologies affect the role of women?
4. Who supported the 18th Amendment and why?
5. What problems did women face in their campaign to get the vote?

# WORLD WAR I

In 1914 a war broke out in Europe that was to consume millions of lives and alter the world political order. The United States remained neutral until 1917, but played a decisive combat role in the closing months of the conflict. Already the foremost industrial country in the world, the US transformed itself from a debtor nation into the leading creditor nation by the end of the war in 1918.

## Europe at War

At the beginning of the 20th century, Europe was beset by forces that threatened to end a century of relative peace. Nationalism had unified two new states, Germany and Italy, while it undermined the old empires of Russia and Austria–Hungary, both of which ruled over diverse national groups.

Economic imperialism was producing a scramble for colonies in Africa. This imperial rivalry in turn fuelled militarism, as European countries raced to expand their armed forces and devise secret military plans. These developments drew Europe's major powers into competing alliances. Germany, Austria–Hungary, and Italy formed the Triple Alliance (also known as the Central Powers), while France, Britain, and Russia made up the Triple Entente. As these two alliances manoeuvred for pre-eminence, a single spark would be all it took to set off a terrible chain reaction. This happened on June 28, 1914 when a Serbian nationalist assassinated Archduke Ferdinand of Austria–Hungary in Sarajevo. (Serbia was an ally of Russia.) Within six weeks, the two sides were at war.

## Stalemate

Germany's failure to smash the Allied lines in 1914 at the Battle of the Marne, near Paris, produced a stalemate on the Western Front. The two sides built lines of trenches stretching from Switzerland to the North Sea coast. For more than three years, millions of men fought and died in those trenches trying to break the stalemate, while many millions more were wounded.

Despite terrible sacrifices on both sides, the battle lines barely moved. Machine guns and massed artillery barrages, aided by poison gas, accounted for much of the carnage. New weapons such as aircraft and tanks made their appearance but did not break the deadlock. On the Eastern Front, the battle lines were more fluid. There, Russia's advantage in numbers was more than offset by Germany's greater industrial capacity and superior military leadership.

**Figure 9.23** A front-line trench in France, 1918. The trenches were cut in straight lines from a parapet (lower right) and contained dugouts at intervals for the lookout guards.

# America Debates

In the United States, intense debates broke out over what stance the country should take. President Wilson wanted to maintain neutrality, which meant the US would continue to trade with both sides. The majority of Americans supported this position. Many felt a kinship with Britain because of the common language and culture, and sympathy toward France for its support of the

| Countries | Population (millions) | Military Deaths | Military Wounded | Total Casualties | Casualties as % of Population |
|---|---|---|---|---|---|
| **Allied Powers** | | | | | |
| France | 39.6 | 1,397,800 | 4,266,000 | 5,663,800 | 14.3 |
| Britain | 45.4 | 885,138 | 1,663,435 | 2,548,573 | 5.6 |
| Italy | 35.6 | 651,010 | 953,886 | 1,604,896 | 4.5 |
| Russia | 158.9 | 1,811,000 | 4,950,000 | 6,761,000 | 4.3 |
| Canada | 7.2 | 64,944 | 149,732 | 214,676 | 3.0 |
| United States | 92.0 | 116,708 | 205,690 | 322,398 | 0.4 |
| **Central Powers** | | | | | |
| Germany | 64.9 | 2,036,897 | 4,247,143 | 6,284,040 | 9.7 |
| Austria–Hungary | 51.4 | 1,100,000 | 3,620,000 | 4,720,000 | 9.2 |
| Turkey | 21.3 | 800,000 | 400,000 | 1,200,000 | 5.6 |
| Bulgaria | 5.5 | 87,500 | 152,390 | 239,890 | 4.4 |

**Figure 9.24** Casualties of selected countries in World War I. What effects would such casualty rates have on long-term relations between the warring nations, even after peace was declared?

American Revolution. These feelings weren't enough by themselves to overcome anti-war sentiment.

Other Americans were openly hostile to the Allies. Irish immigrants opposed Britain because of its oppression of Irish nationalists, while immigrants from Germany naturally sympathized with the Central Powers. American socialists such as Emma Goldman and Eugene Debs disparaged the war as a fight among capitalists for power and wealth at the expense of workers.

## Economic Considerations

Certainly, the war gave a boost to the US economy, since it created a demand for industrial and agricultural products. Farmers and business owners stood to make great profits as long as the war lasted.

In Europe, both sides placed orders with American companies, but Britain thwarted trade with the Central Powers by imposing a naval blockade on all goods of strategic value, including food. British warships intercepted freighters bound for Germany and seized their cargos.

When President Wilson protested these actions, the British ignored him. Despite this, the United States agreed to lend Britain and France large sums to help them finance their orders from American firms. This meant the US now had a vested interest in an Allied victory. If the Central Powers won, Britain and France would likely default on their loans.

## The U-Boat Threat

The Germans responded to the British blockade by turning to their submarine fleet. At first, German submarines, or **U-boats**, followed the "prize rules" of war. They would surface and order a cargo ship to stop, search it to confirm contraband, and allow the ship's crew to evacuate before sinking the vessel with their deck gun. When experience showed that this method put their U-boats at risk, the Germans declared the waters around Britain a war zone, and their submarines began torpedoing ships without warning.

On May 7, 1915 a German submarine fired one torpedo at the 27,000-tonne British passenger liner *Lusitania* as it was approaching the coast of Ireland en route to England. The *Lusitania* sank in 18 minutes, killing more than 1,200 people, including 128 Americans. Public

**Figure 9.25** A German U-boat sank the British liner *Lusitania*, which was flying an American flag in an attempt to deceive the Germans. Although the British denied it at the time, the *Lusitania* was carrying explosives and other contraband cargo. Do you think this fact made the ship a legitimate target in a war zone?

reaction in America was immediate, and President Wilson issued a stern note of protest. Germany promised to stop torpedoing passenger ships, but on March 16, 1916 a German U-boat mistakenly torpedoed the *Sussex*, a French ferry, killing 50 people, including several Americans. Wilson then issued the following warning:

> I have deemed it my duty, therefore, to say to the Imperial German Government, that if it is still its purpose to prosecute relentless and indiscriminate warfare against vessels of commerce by the use of submarines … the Government of the United States … can have no choice but to sever diplomatic relations with the Government of the German Empire altogether.

Five days later, Germany halted unrestricted warfare and reinstated the "prize rules."

## The Election of 1916

The election campaign of 1916 pitted Wilson against his Republican opponent, Charles Evans Hughes. Wilson promised to maintain US neutrality and pointed to Germany's abandonment of unrestricted submarine warfare as evidence of his persuasive powers. His campaign slogan was "He kept us out of the war."

Hughes declared he would take steps to prepare the United States for mobilization. His militant stance won him the endorsement of Theodore Roosevelt, but he still lost the election. Wilson picked up 49 percent of the popular vote and 277 Electoral College votes to Hughes's 46 percent and 254 Electoral College votes. Within months of being elected, Wilson would face a situation that put his election promise to the test.

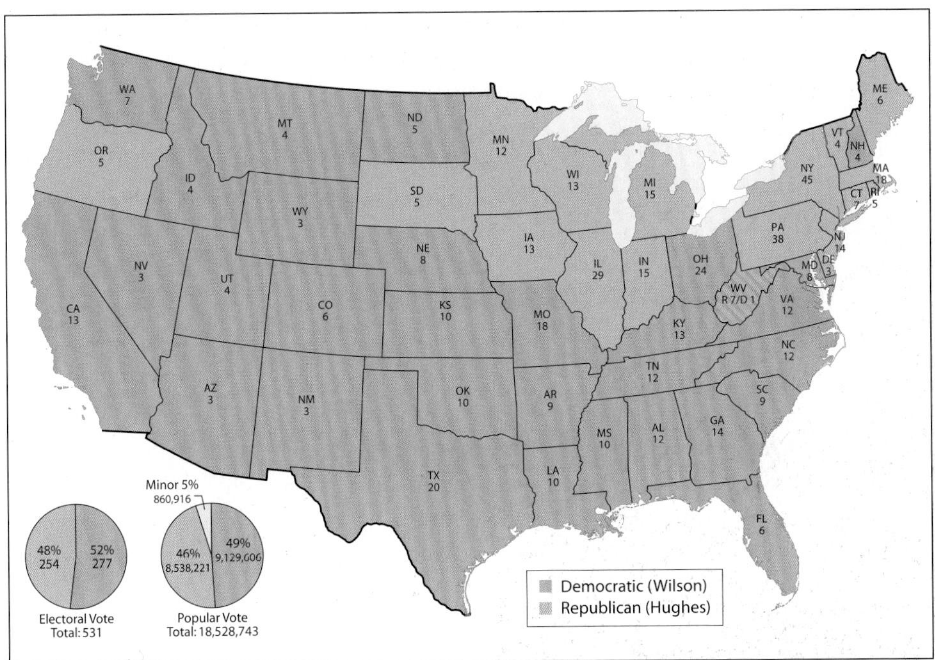


**Figure 9.26** Results of the presidential election of 1916. Wilson's share of the popular vote was greater than what he received in the 1912 election, but his share of Electoral College votes was less. How would you explain this?

### Unrestricted Submarine Warfare

On February 1, 1917 Germany took a calculated gamble and resumed unrestricted submarine warfare. The German high command knew this decision would provoke an American declaration of war, but they also understood the US army would need months to be ready for action. By that time, the Germans hoped their submarine campaign would have starved the British into submission. This would deny the United States the most practical landing zone for its troops in Europe.

German U-boats enjoyed immediate success. In February, the volume of shipping sunk in British waters jumped from an average of 270,000 tonnes per month to over 450,000 tonnes. In March, the tally was 508,000 tonnes; in April, 780,000 tonnes. By then, the United States was at war with Germany.

President Wilson declared war on April 6, partly in response to the U-boat campaign and partly because of the interception of a telegram that showed Germany was trying to ally itself with Mexico in the event of war with the United States, an incident that became known as the Zimmerman Telegram.

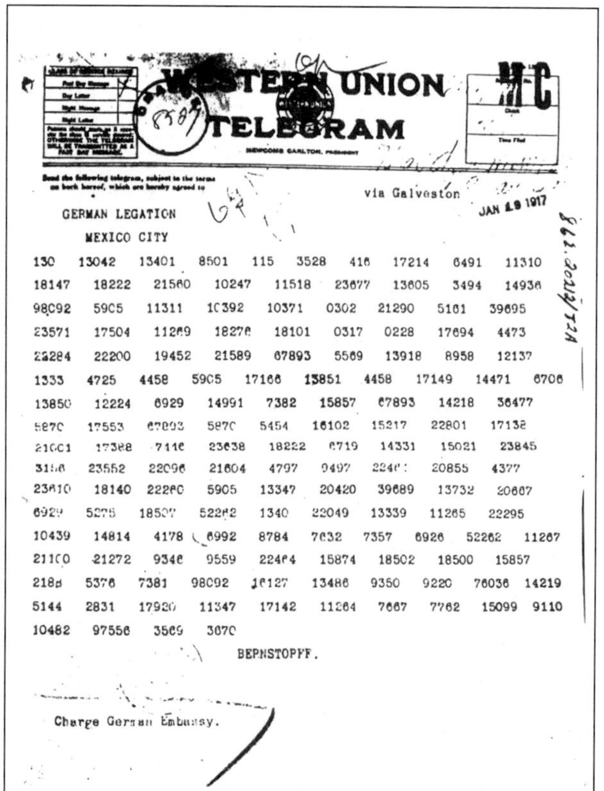

WESTERN UNION TELEGRAM

NEWCOMB CARLTON, PRESIDENT

Send the following telegram, subject to the terms on back hereof, which are hereby agreed to

via Galveston

JAN 19 1917

GERMAN LEGATION

MEXICO CITY

130 13042 13401 8501 115 3528 416 17214 6491 11310
18147 18222 21560 10247 11518 23677 13605 3494 14936
98092 5905 11311 10392 10371 0302 21290 5161 39695
23571 17504 11269 18276 18101 0317 0228 17694 4473
22284 22200 19452 21589 67893 5569 13918 8958 12137
1333 4725 4458 5905 17166 13851 4458 17149 14471 6706
13850 12224 6929 14991 7382 15857 67893 14218 36477
5870 17553 67893 5870 5454 16102 15217 22801 17138
21001 17388 7446 23638 18222 6719 14331 15021 23845
3156 23552 22096 21604 4797 9497 22464 20855 4377
23610 18140 22260 5905 13347 20420 39689 13732 20667
6929 5275 18507 52262 1340 22049 13339 11265 22295
10439 14814 4178 6992 8784 7632 7357 6926 52262 11267
21100 21272 9346 9559 22464 15874 18502 18500 15857
2188 5376 7381 98092 16127 13486 9350 9220 76036 14219
5144 2831 17920 11347 17142 11264 7667 7762 15099 9110
10482 97556 3569 3670

BERNSTORFF.

Charge German Embassy.

**Figure 9.27** The Zimmerman Telegram in code form. Deciphered, the telegram read in part: "We [Germany] propose an alliance with Mexico. ... We shall give general financial support, and it is understood that Mexico is to re-conquer the lost territory in New Mexico, Texas, and Arizona." Why would such a communication enrage the American public?

## America Joins the War

For an in-depth exploration of the reasons why the United States entered World War I, visit www.emp.ca/ah.

The United States' declaration of war against Germany came when its army numbered about 110,000 soldiers, far fewer than needed. Britain, France, and the other Allies were exhausted after almost three years of warfare. They had suffered millions of casualties and desperately needed fresh troops.

President Wilson wanted only volunteers for the fighting in Europe, but when recruitment levels proved disappointing, he asked Congress to pass the Selective Service Act of 1917. This gave the US government authority to conscript, or draft, soldiers.

## AMERICAN ARCHIVE

# Woodrow Wilson's War Message: April 2, 1917

Presidents George Washington and James Monroe had established a tradition of keeping the United States free from entanglements in European wars. From the time World War I started in 1914, a majority of Americans had favoured maintaining this neutrality, and President Wilson won re-election in 1916 based on his promise to keep America out of the conflict.

After Germany resumed unrestricted submarine warfare in February 1917, public opinion in the United States shifted. On April 2, 1917, Wilson went before a joint session of Congress to ask for a declaration of war. In an eloquent speech, the president made the case for war by characterizing Germany as a barbaric nation that threatened not only the US, but the world at large.

> Vessels of every kind, whatever their flag, their character, their cargo, their destination, their errand, have been ruthlessly sent to the bottom without warning and without thought of help or mercy for those on board, the vessels of friendly neutrals along with those of belligerents ... The present German submarine warfare against commerce is a warfare against mankind. It is a war against all nations.

Wilson was careful not to target the German people, but the autocratic government that had dragged them into war. In a sense, his goal was not just victory in battle, but a change of regime in the name of a democratic world order.

> We have no quarrel with the German people. We have no feeling toward them but one of sympathy and friendship. It was not upon their impulse that their government acted in entering this war ... A steadfast concern for peace can never be maintained except by a partnership of democratic nations.

Unlike Britain and France, who were fighting in part to win control of Germany's colonies, the United States, according to Wilson, would wage war to guide the world into a more democratic age:

> The world must be made safe for democracy. Its peace must be planted upon the tested foundations of political liberty. We have no selfish ends to serve. We desire no conquest, no dominion. We seek no indemnities for ourselves, no material compensation for the sacrifices we shall freely make. We are but one of the champions of the rights of mankind.

"All the News That's Fit to Print."

The New York Times.

THE WEATHER

PRESIDENT CALLS FOR WAR DECLARATION, STRONGER NAVY, NEW ARMY OF 500,000 MEN, FULL CO-OPERATION WITH GERMANY'S FOES

ARMED AMERICAN STEAMSHIP SUNK; 11 MEN MISSING

SURPRISE ATTACK AT NIGHT

11 IN A LIFEBOAT THAT SANK

Text of the President's Address

MUST EXERT ALL OUR POWER

To Bring a "Government That Is Running Amuck to Terms."

WANTS LIBERAL CREDITS

A TUMULTUOUS GREETING

The War Resolution Now Before Congress

**Figure 9.28** Front page of the *New York Times*, April 3, 1917.

Having established both the immediate threat posed by the German government and the goal of a democratic world order as reasons for going to war, Wilson ended his speech by warning that in spite of the horrors of war, the country must remain steadfast in its commitment to freedom and justice:

> There are, it may be, many months of fiery trial and sacrifice ahead of us. It is a fearful thing to lead this great peaceful people into war, into the most terrible and disastrous of all wars, civilization itself seeming to be in the balance. But the right is more precious than peace.

Congress erupted into applause as the president finished his speech, and two days later voted overwhelmingly in favour of war.

## Think It Through

1. According to Wilson, what were the two main reasons for the United States declaring war against Germany?
2. In what ways did Wilson's broader, philosophical arguments for war parallel his reformist, Progressive ideology?

**Figure 9.29** The United States financed its war effort by raising taxes and borrowing from the public, conducting three "Liberty Bond" drives. Hollywood movie stars such as (from left) Douglas Fairbanks Jr., Mary Pickford (who was born in Toronto), and Charlie Chaplin (born in London, England) spoke at huge rallies, urging their fans to buy these bonds.

Conscription came into force on May 18, 1917. In just over a year, 24 million men between the ages of 18 and 45 registered with their local draft boards. Of these, 2.8 million were drafted for military duty. Wilson appointed General John Pershing to lead these men. Training and transporting such a large force to the front lines in Europe would take more than a year.

## Turning the Tide

The first contingent of 17,000 American troops arrived in France in July 1917. By June 1918, over one million US troops were there. Of the two million soldiers in the American Expeditionary Force (AEF) who eventually reached France, about 1.4 million saw combat. Their involvement would prove decisive in bringing about the defeat of Germany and the other Central Powers.

In March 1918, Germany had launched a massive offensive on the Western Front, breaking the Allied front lines and advancing deep into France. Desperate fighting by British, French, and Canadian troops slowed the attack, and on August 8, the "Black Day of the German Army," they began a counter-offensive, aided by 130,000 US troops. On September 12, half a million American troops under General Pershing's command joined the push. This was followed by the Meuse-Argonne offensive, where Pershing commanded one million American and French troops.

Allied forces advanced steadily, winning back much French territory. On October 9, Kaiser Wilhelm, the German head of state, abdicated, and within a month German commanders persuaded their government to sue for peace. An **armistice**, or end of hostilities, was proclaimed on November 11, 1918, before any Allied troops had entered Germany.

During its relatively short time in battle, the American Expeditionary Force sustained over 320,000 casualties, including 117,000 dead. Half were killed in action; the rest were victims of disease and accidents.

## American Heroes: A Selection

### *Captain Eddie Rickenbacker*

Only 11 years after the Wright brothers' first airplane flight at Kitty Hawk, North Carolina, planes were being used in World War I as fighters, bombers, and reconnaissance craft. Before becoming a fighter pilot in March 1918, Eddie Rickenbacker enjoyed a lucrative career as a racing car driver. When the United States entered World War I, Rickenbacker, 27, quickly became the top American **ace** of the war by shooting down 26 German planes. After the war, he was named president of Eastern Airlines.

**Figure 9.30** Eddie Rickenbacker received the Congressional Medal of Honor, the United States' highest military award, for his accomplishments as a fighter pilot.

### *Helen Fairchild*

Weeks after America's declaration of war against Germany, Helen Fairchild and 63 other nurses volunteered to serve in Europe. On July 22, 1917, she joined a Casualty Clearing Station at Passchendaele on the Western Front. In November, she was exposed to mustard gas and began suffering abdominal pains. Despite this, she continued serving until undergoing surgery on January 13, 1918. She died five days later and was buried in a military cemetery in France.

**Figure 9.31** Helen Fairchild wrote to her family from the front: "I am with an operating team about 100 miles from our own Base Hospital, closer to the fighting lines ... We all live in tents and wade through mud to and from the operating room where we stand in mud higher than our ankles."

**Figure 9.32** Some of the men who formed the Harlem Hellfighters. By the end of the war, the 369th had been in action for 191 days, longer than any other American unit.

### *The 369th "Harlem Hellfighters" Regiment*

About 350,000 African-Americans served in World War I. They were trained in segregated camps and often mistreated, but despite this, most African-Americans still supported the war. The majority of black soldiers were organized into labour battalions, where they unloaded ships or worked in rear-area camps.

The regiments that saw the most action were the four that General Pershing lent to the 16th Division of the French Army. Of these, the most notable was the 369th Infantry, popularly known as the "Harlem Hellfighters." In France, the 369th fought alongside French units at Chateau-Thierry and Belleau Wood. Two of its soldiers were the first Americans to be awarded the **Croix de Guerre**.

## The War at Home

The US government mounted a relentless propaganda campaign to maintain public support for the war. President Wilson established the Committee for Public Information to organize the production of patriotic posters and pamphlets, and Hollywood filmmakers were encouraged to produce films on war themes.

During the war, the federal government passed two laws aimed at improving national security, both of which curtailed freedom of speech. The **Espionage Act** of 1917 made it a crime to convey information that would interfere with the "operation or success" of US armed forces or "promote the success of the enemy." Publications judged to be in violation of the Act could lose their mailing privileges.

The **Sedition Act** of 1918 extended the powers of the Espionage Act. Under the new provisions, Americans could be punished for

- speaking against the draft and military recruiting,
- encouraging soldiers to disobey orders or defect,
- discouraging the public from buying Liberty Bonds, or
- encouraging resistance to the United States or promoting the success of its enemies.

Under these laws, dozens of socialist publications were denied use of the US postal system. Anti-war demonstrators were arrested by the hundreds. Eugene Debs, the former presidential candidate and union leader, received a ten-year prison sentence for speaking out against recruiting. Over a hundred members of the socialist union, the IWW, were arrested and convicted of anti-war activities.

## Women and the War

Employment opportunities for women increased as men went into military service. Women took on new occupations: bank clerks, street car conductors, chauffeurs, locomotive dispatchers, telegraphers, and machine operators.

Typically, women were paid half the wages received by men, and this earned them the wrath of labour unions. The Women's Land Army helped women take over farm work normally done by men. Women who joined the Red Cross rolled bandages, knitted socks, and worked in military hospitals. At home, women had to contend with shortages of food, clothing, and fuel.

**Figure 9.33** One of the most vital roles for women was producing munitions. This was particularly dangerous work because of the threat of explosions and the use of chemicals that damaged workers' lungs and turned their skin yellow.

## African-Americans and the Great Migration

During the war, hundreds of thousands of African-Americans abandoned the South to move north in search of jobs in industrial centres desperate for workers. Detroit's black population grew by over 600 percent. Cleveland's black population increased by 300 percent, and Chicago's by almost 150 percent.

While the migrants found jobs, they also encountered racism. Whites used restrictions on real estate sales and other means to keep blacks out of their neighbourhoods. The result was that African-Americans began to concentrate in poor inner-city neighbourhoods. In the Harlem district in New York, the black population grew from almost nothing to 200,000 in less than two decades.

These rapid population shifts sometimes raised racial tensions to the boiling point. In 1917, a riot erupted in East St. Louis, where many blacks had moved to take jobs in local factories. Thousands of whites attacked black neighbourhoods, clubbing and lynching African-Americans and setting fire to their homes. Clearly, racial equality remained a distant dream in both the North and the South.

**Figure 9.34** Forty-eight blacks and eight whites died during the race riot in East St. Louis. In commenting on the riot, this editorial cartoon makes a devastating reference to President Wilson's War Message. What point is the cartoonist making?

## CHECK YOUR UNDERSTANDING

1. What American groups were opposed to the Allied cause and why?
2. How did loans to Britain and France help lead to the United States' entrance into the war?
3. Why was the Selective Service Act passed?
4. Why did African-Americans migrate to Northern cities?
5. How did both African-Americans and women contribute to the war effort?

# AFTER THE WAR: A TROUBLED PEACE

In his War Message to Congress, President Wilson had pledged to fight for freedom and to spread democracy around the world. In January 1918, Wilson outlined his plans for the peace that would follow the war before another joint session of Congress. The **Fourteen Points**, as they became known, were the first clear declaration of war aims by any Allied leader. Perhaps mistakenly, Wilson formulated them before consulting with any of his fellow leaders. Among other things, he called for

- open agreements openly arrived at—no secret deals,
- international free trade,
- reduction of armaments to the lowest possible level,

| | |
|---|---|
| **United States:** Wanted to implement Wilson's Fourteen Points, including the League of Nations, which would be a "general association of nations … affording mutual guarantees of political independence and territorial integrity to great and small states alike." | **France:** As leader of the country most heavily damaged by the war, Clemenceau wanted territory from Germany, the permanent weakening of its army, and reparations so large they would keep Germany in a state of poverty. |
| **Britain:** Lloyd George knew that the British public, many of whom lost loved ones in the war, wanted Germany punished. He also thought it important to maintain Britain's naval supremacy. | **Germany:** Favoured the US position but after surrendering its weapons had no negotiating power. Once the peace conference began, Germany found itself banished from the negotiating table and still subject to the wartime blockade of foodstuffs and other essentials. |

**Figure 9.35** The negotiating positions of the major powers at the Paris Peace Conference in 1919. The idealism of Wilson's Fourteen Points may have seemed natural to an American Progressive, but it struck many Europeans as foolishly naive.

- peaceful resolution of colonial claims, taking into account the wishes of subject peoples, and
- the creation of a "general association of nations" to promote world peace and security, which became known as the **League of Nations**.

Wilson wanted nothing less than a new world order based on his own Progressive beliefs. German leaders agreed to the November armistice partly because they trusted that the Fourteen Points would form the foundation of a permanent peace treaty.

The terms of the armistice required Germany to surrender most of its weapons as well as thousands of locomotives, railroad cars, and trucks. It was only when the armistice was being implemented that two Allied leaders, Prime Minister Clemenceau of France and Prime Minister Lloyd George of Britain, told Wilson they wanted punitive terms included in any permanent treaty with Germany. Privately, Clemenceau dismissed Wilson's peace plan with a quip: "President Wilson and his Fourteen Points bore me. Even God Almighty has only ten!"

**SOUND BITE**

"The Allied governments affirm, and Germany accepts, the responsibility of Germany and her allies for causing all the loss and damage to which the Allied governments and their peoples have been subjected as a result of the war."

—Article 233, the so-called War Guilt Clause in the Treaty of Versailles

## The Treaty of Versailles

The negotiations at Versailles, outside Paris, began on January 18, 1919 and lasted six months. In the end, Wilson agreed to abandon several of his points in order to win support for his major goal, the establishment of the League of Nations.

Signed in the Hall of Mirrors on June 28, 1919, the Treaty officially ended hostilities between Germany and the Allied Powers. (Separate treaties were

**Figure 9.36** The signing of the Treaty of Versailles in the Hall of Mirrors. Officials of the new German democratic government had no choice but to sign the treaty, but the German people felt humiliated. Fourteen years later, an Austrian war veteran named Adolf Hitler came to power in Germany partly by promising to overturn the treaty.

concluded with each of the other Central Powers.) The first 26 articles, known as the Covenant of Nations, described how the League of Nations was to operate. The remaining articles spelled out the settlement of war claims. In part, the treaty required that Germany

- accept blame for the war,
- give up its overseas colonies to Britain and France,
- turn over its coal fields in the Saar region to France for 15 years, and
- make reparations of $15 billion (about $175 billion today), to be paid over 65 years.

As well, Germany was forbidden to unite with Austria or to have an air force or submarines. It was also denied membership in the League of Nations.

## The League of Nations

The purpose of the League of Nations was to resolve international disputes peacefully, to achieve disarmament, to guarantee the independence and territory of its members, and to promote global welfare. The underlying assumption was that member nations would be willing to "consult together" to thwart aggression by outside powers. Collective action might include moral condemnation, economic sanctions, and even military action.

On January 10, 1920 ratification of the Treaty of Versailles brought the League into formal existence. Ten months later, the League held its first full assembly in Geneva, Switzerland. Although 41 nations sent delegates, the United States did not because the US Senate refused to ratify the treaty. The League of Nations, which had been the brainchild of an American president, was undermined at its inception by his own country's decision not to take part.

## Wilson's Defeat

Why had the Senate refused to ratify the Treaty of Versailles? In the mid-term elections of 1918, the Republicans won control of both houses of Congress. Despite this warning sign, President Wilson set out for the Versailles Conference without appointing a single Republican to the American delegation. When he returned home in July 1919 to seek Senate ratification of the treaty, he found considerable opposition to it.

Many Republicans believed that article 10 of the treaty would legally oblige the United States to commit military force to protect the security of member nations. They saw this as posing a direct threat to US sovereignty. Wilson thought the obligation was a moral commitment, not a legal one.

Wilson needed a two-thirds majority in the Senate to secure ratification. In September, he began a cross-country speaking tour to drum up public support for the treaty, but on October 2 he suffered a serious stroke. For almost a month, Wilson's wife, Edith Bolling Galt, acted for him secretly on presidential matters. After recovering, Wilson continued to oppose any compromise on the treaty despite mounting opposition from Democrats as well as Republicans. On November 19, 1919 the Senate voted 53–38 against the treaty.

President Wilson died on March 21, 1924 at age 67. It is likely that his growing unpopularity before his death arose from his focus on international issues while the US was experiencing serious domestic problems after the war.

## Domestic Problems

The Senate's rejection of the Treaty of Versailles reflected a general shift in the American mood from Progressivism toward more conservative values, and from internationalism to isolationism. The American people now wanted to focus on problems that were developing at home.

### Economic Turmoil

As soon as peace was declared, President Wilson ended wartime wage and price controls, and prices skyrocketed. At the same time, rapid reductions in arms manufacturing caused unemployment to soar. Even though most women willingly gave up their wartime jobs to returning soldiers, there was still not enough work to absorb the available labour force.

The government also ended guarantees on agricultural commodities. Farmers who had taken advantage of high wartime crop prices and expanded their farms now faced bankruptcy. Labour unrest spread as unions fought for better wages, improved working conditions, and more members. In September 1919, Boston's police force went on strike for better wages, and this led to widespread looting. In the same month, a nationwide strike of steelworkers broke out.

**SOUND BITE**

"There is no right to strike against the public safety by anybody, anywhere, any time."

—Massachusetts Governor Calvin Coolidge after hiring strikebreakers to end the Boston police strike

### Red Scare

Many Americans linked labour unrest to the rise of **communism**. In the Bolshevik Revolution of November 1917, communists had come to power in Russia. Inspired by their example, socialist workers in many countries, including the United States, formed communist parties.

In response, the federal government appointed a young J. Edgar Hoover as head of the Department of Justice's new General Intelligence Division. Hoover immediately began arresting suspected communists and other radicals. In January 1920, Attorney-General Mitchell Palmer initiated a series of raids after a bomb blew up outside his house. The **Palmer Raids**, as they became known, resulted in about 6,000 arrests, mostly of recent immigrants, and 600 deportations.

**Figure 9.37** On December 21, 1919 government officials rounded up more than 248 foreign-born radicals, including Emma Goldman. Those arrested were placed aboard a ship called the *Buford* and deported.

## Racism

The migration of Southern blacks into northern cities continued after the war. As white soldiers returned from the war and found themselves competing with urban blacks for jobs and housing, an already tense situation grew worse. In the summer of 1919, a wave of lynchings and race riots swept the country. A riot in Chicago began when white youths stoned to death a young black

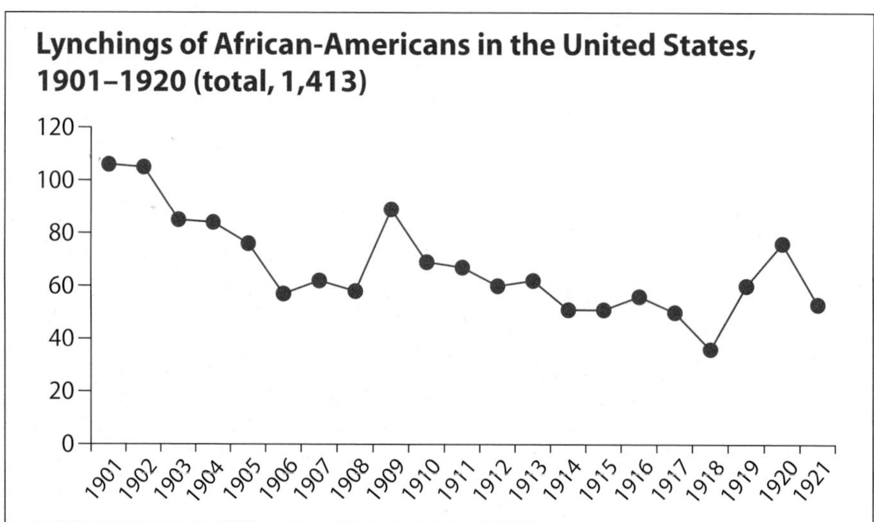


**Figure 9.38** Despite the positive achievements of the Progressive Era, the first 20 years of the 20th century were one of the worst periods in US history for the lynching of African-Americans. Although some members of Congress proposed anti-lynching laws during this period, none of the bills passed.

who had wandered into a so-called whites-only beach area. Twenty-three blacks and 15 whites died, and almost 1,000 people were left homeless.

## The Effect of the War on American Consciousness

Some of the American soldiers who served in World War I were talented writers who would draw on their experiences to produce accounts of the war and its aftermath that would change the way Americans viewed themselves. These included Ernest Hemingway, John Dos Passos, F. Scott Fitzgerald, William Faulkner, and e.e. cummings.

Many of the so-called **Lost Generation** came to feel disillusioned and cynical about traditional American values such as patriotism, conformity, hard work, frugality, temperance, and respect for elders. Their questioning attitude would be one of the factors that set the stage for the decade known as the Roaring Twenties.

**Figure 9.39** Allied graves at Passchendaele in Belgium, where the Allies and Germans together suffered more than half a million casualties. The unprecedented slaughter of World War I left an entire generation wounded in spirit.

# Culture Notes

## Ernest Hemingway and the Lost Generation

"You are all a lost generation."

—Gertrude Stein to Ernest Hemingway in conversation

Gertrude Stein's description of American **expatriates** in Paris during the 1920s came to characterize a whole generation of writers and artists who wrestled with the effects of the Great War. They included F. Scott Fitzgerald, T.S. Eliot, John Dos Passos, and Faye Boyle.

No one person, however, has come to represent the Lost Generation better than Hemingway himself. Through his real-life adventures as well as his tersely written, violent fiction, he embodied a generation of people disillusioned by the war's failure to "make the world safe for democracy." One of the great themes Hemingway treated in his books was the individual person's loss of faith—in religion, in patriotism, and in civilization itself.

He developed an **existential** outlook, a belief that each person is free to act but isolated in a world that is beyond his or her ability to control. Hemingway communicates this view of life in short stories and novels marked by concrete descriptions, a deceptively simple prose style, and realistic dialogue. It was his style, along with his focus on the era's major events, that made him the most influential American writer of the 20th century.

Raised in a suburb of Chicago, Hemingway began his professional career as a reporter on the *Kansas City Star*. In 1917, he joined the Red Cross ambulance corps and was severely wounded on the Italian front. In 1921, as a correspondent for the *Toronto Star*, he moved to Paris and immersed himself in the expatriate community there.

In 1929, Hemingway published *A Farewell to Arms*, the story of American ambulance driver Frederick Henry, who is wounded in Italy and falls in love with a nurse at the hospital where he recovers. The two decide to escape the war by fleeing to Switzerland, where she dies in childbirth. Hemingway's bleak view of the world is conveyed through the words of his characters:

**Figure 9.40** Hemingway's first novel, *The Sun Also Rises* (1926), established his reputation as a major American writer.

> The world breaks everyone and afterward many are strong at the broken places. But those that will not break it kills. It kills the very good and the very gentle and the very brave impartially. If you are none of these you can be sure it will kill you too but there will be no special hurry.

To artists like Hemingway, the idealism of the pre-war years had given way to a pessimistic view of the future. The war shattered all hopes of a better world through scientific advancements and social improvements, and the literature of the Lost Generation bore witness to the disappointment that followed.

### Think It Through

1. Explain why Gertrude Stein referred to Hemingway and his friends as a "lost generation."
2. Explain how the excerpt above illustrates Hemingway's existential outlook on life.

# CONCLUSION

The period 1900–1920 saw the rise and decline of Progressive reform in America. Government expanded to play a major role in bringing about political, social, and economic changes. Critics used a free press to raise public awareness of serious social problems. After a long battle, women won the right to vote, but not full equality with men. African-Americans gained a stronger voice through the NAACP and writers such as W.E.B. Du Bois, but racism continued to be a dominant feature of American society.

World War I transformed the United States into a world financial leader and industrial giant. However, disillusionment about the war, and President Wilson's failure to win American support for the League of Nations, resulted in the United States' retreat into isolationism. Nevertheless, as the US moved into the 1920s, the country was positioned to enjoy a period of unprecedented prosperity, one that would obscure the serious problems that still needed to be solved.

## CHECK YOUR UNDERSTANDING

1. How did Wilson's Fourteen Points influence the war?
2. What was the purpose of the League of Nations?
3. What domestic problems did postwar America face?
4. How did the US government respond to the rise of communism?
5. What was the general attitude of writers in the Lost Generation?

# THE HISTORIAN'S CRAFT

## Thinking Creatively in History

Like scientists, historians think critically and use formal procedures (like the inquiry model) and systematic approaches to interpreting evidence. Yet, there is an artistic side to history as historians imagine themselves in the shoes of people in the past. As well, they may purposely set aside scientific thinking in search of creative ideas.

### Rejecting Traditional Approaches

Sometimes we can't think creatively because we are trapped within the limits of tradition and logic. One way to break through such limits is to consciously reject the traditional. For example, historians traditionally describe US foreign policy in terms of isolationism (for example, hesitancy in entering World War I and rejection of the League of Nations) and involvement (fighting in the Spanish-American War and World War I).

What about looking at foreign policy from the viewpoint that the United States has always been imperialistic? This view is based on such considerations as manifest destiny, the Monroe Doctrine, the Roosevelt Corollary, American business and diplomatic involvement worldwide, and a history of military interventions. You might re-examine American foreign policy by holding up traditional thinking against this "contrary view."

### Creative Imagining in History

Sometimes, we need to be even more imaginative. Here are some possible approaches.

- *Unknown factors.* After studying a historical figure, we usually review what we know and don't know. We often know surprisingly little about such people's health, personal habits, hobbies, family life, and so on. Yet, these unknown factors might have affected that person's actions. You could search for evidence about such "unknown" details and reconsider your assessment of the figure. You could speculate as to how historical personalities might have acted differently had they been able to pursue that hobby or play that sport. For example, what if Theodore Roosevelt had fully pursued his interest in conservation?
- *"What if?"* Historians ask this question often. What if the United States had joined the League of Nations? What if women had been given the vote in 1890? Raising such questions is sometimes described as counter-factual history. "What ifs" could include the possibilities if a different leader had been elected, a bullet had followed a different trajectory, a vote in Congress had gone differently, and so on.
- *Impossible meetings.* Suppose that Booker T. Washington met Nat Turner, or that Woodrow Wilson had tea with Andrew Jackson. Such meetings could never have happened, but that is the fun of the exercise! In your classroom, you might bring the historical figures in this chapter together at a "history convention." Watching Emma Goldman meet George W. Bush could be exciting!

You might object that it is hard enough to learn what actually happened without thinking about what did not. But imagine the depth of thought that goes into speculating "What if?" Consider how much you have to know about a historical person to realize what you don't know. Think about how much you would learn about your historical figure in order to take part in an imaginary meeting. Finally, imagine the creative ideas you could get about the history in this chapter—and about the nature of history itself—through such techniques.

### Try It!

1. Re-examine US foreign policy described in this chapter from the perspective that the United States has always been imperialistic. What new ideas do you get?
2. Choose a historical figure from this chapter. Whom would you like him or her to meet at an "impossible meeting"? Write a brief dialogue between them.

# STUDY HALL

## Thinking

1. What criteria would you use to measure the success of Roosevelt's "square deal" and the reforms of the Progressives?
2. Compare President Theodore Roosevelt the Reformer with President Theodore Roosevelt the Imperialist and World Leader. Consider such categories as "long-term benefits for the country" and "fairness to others." Suggest other categories to use in the comparison.
3. The term "Ugly American" first appeared as the title of an American novel. It has come to be used for any American traveller who ignores other cultures and judges everything by American criteria. Do you believe Theodore Roosevelt deserves this title? Why or why not?
4. Describe, in your own words, the foreign policy challenge that President Wilson faced at the beginning of his second term.
5. Debate the following:
   a. The more involvement people have in their government, the better the government.
   b. The Sedition Act of 1918 was essential in a time of war.
   c. The Treaty of Versailles may have ended World War I, but it ensured that there would be a future world war.
   d. The United States was right to stay out of the League of Nations.

## Communication

6. Use graphs to show the changes in the roles of women in the workforce, changes in types of work for women, and changes in education for women.
7. Look at the table in Figure 9.24 (page 305). Show the data in the form of two graphs, one for the Allied Powers and one for the Central Powers.
8. Imagine how different people around the world would react to President Theodore Roosevelt's winning the Nobel Prize for Peace. Consider how headlines for the award might appear in newspapers in Cuba, the Philippines, Panama, and Colombia.
9. Design a sign for a woman to carry in the suffragist parade the day before Wilson's inauguration. What would be a good slogan and symbol for the sign?
10. Given the attitudes of Clemenceau and Lloyd George at the Paris peace talks in 1919, imagine how President Wilson might address them to persuade them to accept his Fourteen Points. Write a speech or letter to express his ideas.
11. Write a letter in which an African-American who has migrated to Pittsburgh, Pennsylvania and has a job in a steel factory persuades his friends to follow him there from the South.
12. Write a description of postwar America that would reflect the attitudes of the writers of the Lost Generation.

## Application

13. For each excerpt from the muckrakers (page 288), provide a short title that attracts readers and expresses the main idea of the reading. For each of the excerpts, state one powerful question that is raised for the thinking reader.
14. What features of American society and history would contribute to the United States' denial of equality, liberty, and independence to Cuba, Puerto Rico, and the Philippines after the Spanish-American War?
15. What criteria—such as long-term benefits for the United States—could be used to judge the effectiveness of presidents Roosevelt and Wilson? Identify which of the two you think was the more successful president, and explain why.

# 10 Between the Wars (1920–1940)

## KEY CONCEPTS

In this chapter you will consider:

- The federal government's attempts to deal with postwar economic problems
- Innovations in the transportation and entertainment industries
- The accomplishments of the Harlem Renaissance
- The persistence of racism and intolerance in the United States
- Radical changes in the roles of women in American society
- Causes of the Great Depression and Herbert Hoover's attempts to control it
- President Roosevelt's New Deal for the American people

## The American Story

The two decades of peace that followed World War I were anything but tranquil. The United States emerged from the war as the wealthiest nation in the world, and for several years its economy grew at an unprecedented rate before crashing abruptly in 1929. The **Great Depression** that followed brought with it hardships so severe and widespread that the very survival of the American dream seemed in doubt. The **New Deal** that President Franklin D. Roosevelt introduced to pull America out of its slump would lay the foundations of the modern welfare state, a move that continues to fuel heated debate today.

## TIMELINE

- **1920**
  - Warren Harding elected president
  - First commercial radio broadcast
- **1923**
  - Teapot Dome Scandal
- **1927**
  - First motion picture "talkie"
- **1929**
  - The Great Stock Market Crash
- **1930**
  - Passage of the Hawley–Smoot tariff

## IMAGE ANALYSIS

**Figure 10.1** *Dempsey and Firpo* by American painter George Bellows (1882–1925). This painting captures the most dramatic moment in American sports in the first half of the 20th century. It is 1925, the height of the Roaring Twenties, and the Argentinean boxer Luis Firpo has just knocked US champ Jack Dempsey through the ropes at New York City's Polo Grounds. Dempsey would climb back into the ring to defeat Firpo in four rounds, but for one stunning moment, a great champion had been humbled by a virtual unknown.

Bellows's painting evokes the raw excitement of the 1920s in the United States, when radio, motion pictures, sports spectacles, and jazz music all combined to create a popular culture that celebrated national prosperity. This prosperity was built on a weak foundation, however, and would come to a sudden end with the stock market crash in 1929. How would the United States find the resilience it required to recover from such a devastating blow?

- **1932**
  - ▸ Bonus Army marches on Washington, DC
  - ▸ Franklin D. Roosevelt elected president
- **1933**
  - ▸ Repeal of Prohibition
- **1934**
  - ▸ Passage of the Indian Reorganization Act
- **1935**
  - ▸ Passage of the Social Security Act
- **1939**
  - ▸ World War II begins

## INTRODUCTION

If you were living in New York City in 1925, you didn't have to see the Dempsey–Firpo fight live to enjoy the immediacy of the boxing match. Like millions of others, you could have followed the fight on the radio. The room you sat in would have been illuminated by electric lights, and you would have enjoyed the luxury of running water in the kitchen and bathroom.

If you were living in the rural South in 1925, you were probably too poor to own a radio, and the clapboard house you lived in would have had neither running water nor electricity. Your parents likely worked as sharecroppers on another person's land, which meant you didn't go to high school. Instead, you worked in the fields from dawn to dusk helping your family make ends meet.

The interwar period in the United States was a time that witnessed major social changes, even while old problems remained. For the first time, city dwellers outnumbered those living in rural areas, and the migration of Southern blacks to the North continued. The production of low-priced automobiles and the rise of commercial aviation gave many Americans unprecedented mobility. Women, who had won suffrage in 1920, consolidated their gains as a vital element of the workforce. Their new confidence was reflected in their fashions and their willingness to test traditional values and expectations.

## RETURNING TO "NORMALCY"

In the 1920 presidential election, the Republican candidate, Warren Harding, won by a landslide, taking 60 percent of the popular vote. The Republicans also took control of the Senate and the House of Representatives.

Republican success in 1920 came partly from the public's doubts about whether the United States should join the League of Nations, as well as from

| The Presidents: 1921–1940 | | |
|---|---|---|
| **Warren Harding** | Republican | March 4, 1921 – August 2, 1923 |
| **Calvin Coolidge** | Republican | August 2, 1923 – March 4, 1929 |
| **Herbert Hoover** | Republican | March 4, 1929 – March 4, 1933 |
| **Franklin Roosevelt** | Democrat | March 4, 1933 – April 12, 1945 |

**Figure 10.2** Warren Harding's outgoing nature and handsome appearance may have helped him win the 1920 election. Voters often described him as looking more "presidential" than the Democratic candidate, James M. Cox.

**Congress Party Divisions, 1921–1933 (minority parties not shown)**

| | House of Representatives | | Senate | |
|---|---|---|---|---|
| | Democrats | Republicans | Democrats | Republicans |
| 1921–1923 | 131 | 302 | 37 | 59 |
| 1923–1925 | 207 | 225 | 42 | 53 |
| 1925–1927 | 183 | 247 | 41 | 54 |
| 1927–1929 | 194 | 238 | 46 | 48 |
| 1929–1931 | 164 | 270 | 39 | 56 |
| 1931–1933 | 216 | 218 | 47 | 48 |

**Figure 10.3** Republicans kept control of the White House and Congress for 12 years. What can happen to the system of checks and balances (see Chapter 3) when the same party controls the executive and legislative branches of government?

a general weariness with Progressivism at home. The anger that many Irish Americans and German Americans felt toward President Wilson for his wartime policies was also a factor.

While Harding is remembered as a good public speaker, he often indulged in flowery rhetoric, as in this campaign speech:

> America's present need is not heroics, but healing; not nostrums, but normalcy; not revolution, but restoration; not agitation, but adjustment.

The word "normalcy" was Harding's own invention—he claimed he liked the sound of it. (The more usual term would have been "normality.") Whatever the word's origin, it captured the public's imagination. In effect, Harding was promising voters stability and a return to the days when government played a smaller role in the nation's affairs.

While the Democrats' Cox and his vice-presidential running mate, Franklin Roosevelt, barnstormed around the country, Harding campaigned from the front porch of his home in Marion, Ohio. Movie stars and business magnates came to Ohio to declare their support, and newsreel coverage was extensive. Harding's wife, Florence, proved to be a master campaigner by cultivating a favourable relationship with the press.

The 1920 presidential election was the first in which women in every state had the right to vote. It was also the first election where voting returns were broadcast by radio. Harding himself scored a couple of personal firsts: he was the first American president to ride to his inauguration in an automobile, and the first to speak on the radio.

## Postwar Economic Policies

As noted in Chapter 9, the end of the war brought a host of economic problems: wage cuts and unemployment as war production ended, plummeting prices for farm goods, and widespread labour unrest. Harding and the Republican-controlled Congress responded with a series of measures to reduce the size of government and free private enterprise from government regulation. To accomplish these goals, they

- eliminated wartime controls on the economy,
- cut corporate and income taxes,
- reduced government spending,
- paid down the national debt, and
- restored high tariffs to protect local industry.

The architect of many of these measures was the banker Andrew Mellon, whom Harding appointed as Secretary of the Treasury. Mellon followed a **laissez-faire**, or "hands off," approach to the economy. He remained Treasury secretary until 1932. Liberal Democrats and Progressives despised him, and even some fellow Republicans disagreed with his ultra-conservative economic measures.

Despite Mellon's tax cuts, marginal income tax rates (the rate paid on the top level of one's income) for high-income earners remained above their prewar levels. The resulting tax revenue allowed the US government to run up a series of budget surpluses during the 1920s. Mellon used a portion of this surplus to lower government debt from $26 billion ($293 billion today) in 1921 to $16 billion ($193 billion today) in 1930. It is worth noting that this was the last period of sustained debt reduction right down to the present.

Under the Ford–McCumber Tariff Act of 1922, Harding returned to the long-standing Republican policy of raising tariffs on imported goods. He won praise from US industry leaders when he raised tariffs on manufactured goods to 35 percent, the highest rate to date. America's trading partners, however, deeply resented the tariffs because the high rates made it harder to sell their products in the US, and therefore to pay off their war debts. In retaliation, they raised their own tariffs against American goods, and international trade suffered.

Even with the slump in trade, the US economy developed at a rate never seen before. Harding's contemporaries credited him with helping to launch this period of growth, but he didn't live long enough to witness much of it. He died suddenly on August 2, 1923, of a stroke or heart attack, while travelling from Alaska to San Francisco. After Harding's death, scandals emerged that left a permanent stain on his legacy.

## Harding's Scandals

At the beginning of his presidency, Harding appointed a cabinet that included men with impeccable credentials. In addition to Andrew Mellon, he recruited Herbert Hoover, who had led US efforts to feed millions of starving Europeans at the end of the war. Harding also appointed a former president, William Taft, as chief justice of the Supreme Court. Harding made some bad choices, too, and several of his appointees proved to be corrupt. The two most notorious examples were Charles Forbes and Albert B. Fall.

Harding chose Charles Forbes to head the newly created Veterans' Bureau. In 1923, Forbes resigned his post after one of his assistants committed suicide when news surfaced of widespread corruption at the bureau. In 1924, a Senate committee established that Forbes had taken bribes resulting from the operation of hospitals and the sale of government property. At trial, he was found guilty, fined $10,000 ($117,890 today), and sentenced to two years in federal prison.

As Harding's Secretary of the Interior, Albert Fall was put in charge of public lands and made responsible for oil reserve lands at Teapot Dome in Wyoming. In 1922, newspapers reported that Fall had leased land at Teapot Dome and elsewhere to friends of his in the oil business, in one case in return for a "loan" of $100,000 ($1,200,000 today). The Senate passed a motion declaring that the leases "were executed under circumstances indicating fraud and corruption." Fall was forced to resign, and in 1927 a court found him guilty of accepting a bribe. He received a one-year prison sentence.

Because of these scandals, Harding is considered one of the worst presidents in US history. Yet, to his credit, he reversed President Wilson's policy of excluding blacks from many federal government jobs and had the courage to speak about racial equality while visiting Birmingham, Alabama. Months before his death, he called for the United States to join the recently established World Court. It may be that his greatest shortcoming was poor judgment of character in his later appointments.

## Keeping Cool with Coolidge

After Harding's death, Vice-President Calvin Coolidge assumed the presidency. A former governor of Massachusetts, he had gained national notice for his forceful intervention in a police strike in Boston. As vice-president, Coolidge earned the nickname "Silent Cal" for his reluctance to make small talk at social functions.

A possibly apocryphal story from the time has the writer Dorothy Parker saying, "Mr. Coolidge, I've made a bet against a fellow who said it was impossible to get more than two words from you." Coolidge replied, "You lose." He was fortunate that his outgoing and good-humoured wife, Grace Anna Goodhue, was able to soften the unfavourable impression he often made.

During the 14 months between Harding's death and the 1924 election, Coolidge set out his political agenda and worked to maintain public faith in the presidency, now tainted by scandal. Like Harding, he believed that capitalism was the best system to achieve economic growth and should be left alone as much as possible. He failed in an attempt to veto the Soldiers' Bonus Act of 1924. This measure gave veterans some compensation for the lower pay they received while in military service compared to what they would have made in civilian life. Coolidge saw it as an unnecessary expenditure.

**Figure 10.4** Two of the slogans from the 1924 presidential election were "Keep Cool with Coolidge" and "Deeds—Not Words." Why might Americans find such slogans reassuring?

**SOUND BITE**

"They hired the money, didn't they?"

—President Coolidge's response when advisers suggested the best solution to the European debt crisis would be for the US to cancel all war debts

In the 1924 election, Coolidge won an impressive victory even though he conducted a lacklustre campaign, and despite fellow Republican Robert La Follette's (see Chapter 9) desertion of the party to run as a Progressive candidate. Coolidge won 54 percent of the popular vote. John W. Davis, the Democratic candidate, won 28.8 percent, while La Follette took 16.6 percent.

During the next four years, Coolidge kept a low profile, initiating little new legislation. He twice vetoed a farm relief bill that would have authorized the government to buy up crop surpluses, telling farmers that they should become more competitive by modernizing their operations.

In foreign affairs, the most pressing issue involved reparation payments and war debts. In 1923, following an inflation crisis, Germany defaulted on its payments. This put immediate pressure on Britain and France, who were using German reparation payments to pay their war debts to the United States.

In 1924, US Vice-President Charles Dawes led an international committee to resolve the crisis. The solution: Germany's payment schedule was adjusted and the United States agreed to make loans to Germany so it could recommence its payments to Britain and France, who then returned the money to the US as payment of their war debts. With the onset of the Great Depression in the 1930s, payment of reparations and war debts stopped permanently.

## CHECK YOUR UNDERSTANDING

1. Using Figure 10.3 (page 327), calculate the percentage change in representation in the House and the Senate for the Republicans and the Democrats from 1921 to 1933.
2. Identify four "firsts" associated with the 1920 presidential election.
3. What were the unintended consequences of the Ford–McCumber Tariff Act?
4. Explain the purpose of the Soldiers' Bonus Act.

# THE ROARING TWENTIES

The "Roaring Twenties" refers to the period of economic growth and social transformation that lasted in the United States from about 1922 to 1929. Thanks to steady increases in the production of manufactured goods, such as cars and radios, the growth in real gross national product (GNP) per capita was strong over this period. Unemployment jumped briefly in 1921, then dropped to 5 percent, where it stayed for the next eight years. In the manufacturing sector, real average wages for all workers rose about 5 percent between 1923 and 1929. This gave people more money to spend on luxuries and new electric conveniences.

Unfortunately, prosperity did not reach everybody. While upper-income and middle-class city dwellers thrived, farmers struggled after losing the overseas markets they had enjoyed during World War I. Through the 1920s, the rate of farm mortgage foreclosures climbed while farm employment fell.

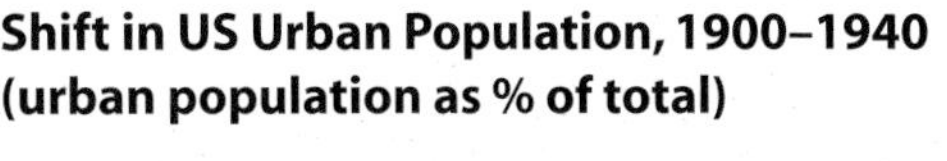


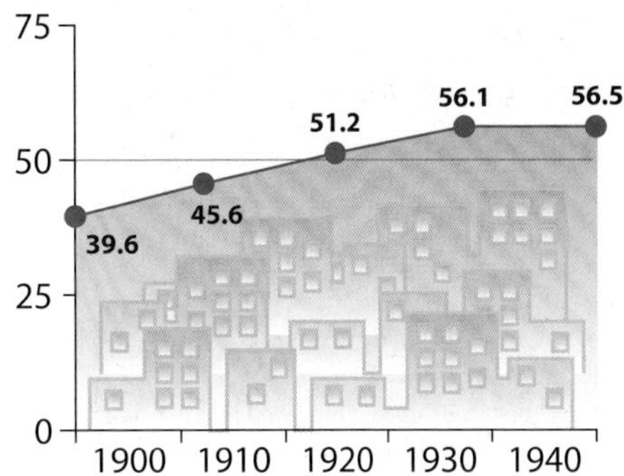


**Figure 10.5** The census year 1920 marked the first time in US history that more people lived in cities than in the country. Identify one reason to account for this population shift.

## Prohibition

The banning of liquor under the 18th Amendment enjoyed widespread support among rural residents, but it was very unpopular in the larger cities. Its unpopularity grew as the United States changed from a rural to an urban society, as rural residents and immigrants moved to cities to find jobs.

For many, the Roaring Twenties are symbolized by images of federal Prohibition agents destroying illegal stills and dumping confiscated liquor, while crowds danced to jazz and defiantly broke the law by consuming alcohol in big-city night clubs. There may be some truth in this picture, but far more potent forces of social change were also at work, including advances in transportation and communication technologies.

## Transportation Innovations

### The Car

Henry Ford, a self-made businessman from rural Michigan, refashioned the automobile from an expensive hobby into an affordable means of transportation. In the process, he enriched his country and transformed the physical form of its cities. Ford produced a simply designed car he called the Model T, and then drew on methods from meatpacking plants to devise a mass-production system based on four principles:

- A moving assembly line brought the partially assembled auto to the worker.
- Labour was divided into simple steps arranged in a fixed sequence.
- The speed of the assembly line and motions of workers were set to maximize efficiency.
- All auto parts were interchangeable; for example, any door or steering wheel would fit any chassis, or frame.

**Figure 10.6** Henry Ford and an early version of the Model T. While Ford paid his workers well for the time, he himself was pocketing $25,000 ($288,000 today) a day during the 1920s. Do you think such a great difference between the pay of an average worker and that of a company's chief executive can be justified? Explain.

**SOUND BITE**

"History is more or less bunk."

—Auto manufacturer Henry Ford

Ford began production of the Model T in 1908, but didn't get his assembly line into full operation until 1914. Once he did, the result was dramatic. The cost of Model Ts dropped from $950 ($19,800 today) to $280 ($5,800 today); the production time, from 728 minutes to 93 minutes. By the time production of the Model T ended in 1927, the Ford Motor Company had manufactured over 15 million cars.

The rise of the automobile touched every corner of US society. It stimulated the oil, steel, and rubber industries. It extended the 1920s housing boom into the suburbs, and it triggered the spread of new businesses such as service stations, roadside diners, and motels. Highway construction poured public funds into the economy. The combination of inexpensive cars and a network of new roads gave Americans greater mobility and a new sense of freedom. By 1928, more than 20 million cars were on the road, one for every six people.

## The Airplane

World War I speeded up the development of airplane technology. After the war, commercial aviation got off to a modest start when former military pilots known as "barnstormers" travelled across the country performing stunts and offering thrill rides to the public. A major boost came when the Airmail Act of 1925 authorized the government to contract out airmail service to private carriers. These fledgling companies later became the giants of commercial aviation: TWA, American Airlines, and United Airlines.

One of the early airmail pilots, Charles Lindbergh, achieved fame after he became the first person to fly solo non-stop across the Atlantic Ocean in his plane, the *Spirit of St. Louis.* He took off from Long Island, New York on May 21, 1927 and arrived in Paris 33 hours and 30 minutes later.

**Figure 10.7** Henry Ford was also involved in manufacturing aircraft. Most of the early airlines used the Ford Trimotor, which could carry 15 passengers and a crew of three. The Trimotors were noisy, uninsulated, unpressurized, and smelly. The aircraft's top speed was about 225 kilometres an hour. It had a ceiling of 2,000 metres, and had to land for fuel every 900 kilometres.

Lindbergh's success unleashed a flood of investment into aviation and boosted the development of passenger services. The number of airline passengers jumped from fewer than 6,000 in 1926 to 173,000 in 1929. Still, the cost of air travel made it too expensive for most people, who continued to rely on ships and trains for long-distance travel.

## Entertainment Innovations

### The Radio

In the 1920s, two recent inventions—radio and motion pictures—evolved rapidly to become the first of the electronic mass media. The radio allowed millions of people to experience events as they happened. It gave them the sense of being personally connected to those they listened to, a feeling that advertisers and politicians were quick to exploit. It influenced how people talked and thought and what they spent their money on. It bonded them together in ways never seen before, creating instant fads and overnight celebrities. During the hard times of the Great Depression, the radio would offer ordinary people a means of escape and the opportunity for a president to reach out and offer them hope.

**SOUND BITE**

"I live in a strictly rural community, and people here speak of 'The Radio' in the large sense with an over meaning. When they say 'The Radio' they don't mean a cabinet, an electrical phenomenon, or a man in a studio, they refer to a pervading and somewhat godlike presence which has come into their lives and homes."

—Writer and editor E.B. White

**Figure 10.8** The first commercially owned radio station, KDKA in Pittsburgh, began operation on November 2, 1920. By 1929, over 45 percent of American households had radios, and many families considered the radio their most prized possession. The medium created a mass culture in America that weakened regional identities, but helped to build a new national consciousness. How might the radio have affected political campaigns?

"My brother, Auguste, and I looked upon our invention as a novelty, capable of offering distraction for a few moments only ... The Americans have taken a toy and made it into a trade."

—Louis Lumière, inventor of the cinematograph

### Motion Pictures

During the 1920s, the fledgling American motion picture industry expanded rapidly to become the fourth-largest industry in the United States. Thousands of movie theatres sprang up to show the hundreds of new movies produced each year. Over half the population attended films once a week or more. Between 1922 and 1929, attendance at theatres rose from 50 million a week to 90 million a week.

Several factors contributed to this spectacular growth. Since the purpose of most films was to make money, they were designed as popular entertainment. They included romances, adventures, cowboy films, and comedies. The "studio system" brought the film industry under the control of a few major companies. The studios, in turn, created the "star system," which made celebrities out of their leading actors and actresses. This had the effect of generating greater ticket sales.

The industry started in New York but quickly relocated to Hollywood, which offered lower labour costs and a climate suited to year-round filming. Americans had more leisure time to attend movies, and automobiles made it easier for them to get to the theatres. In fact, Hollywood movies attracted a global audience. In 1926, they enjoyed a 90 percent market share in Britain and a 70 percent share in France. Hollywood was already helping to export American culture around the world.

## Sports and Music

During the 1920s and 1930s, professional sports and popular music attracted national audiences of radio listeners.

### Boxing

Before 1920, boxing was illegal in many states, but in that year, the state of New York passed a law legalizing boxing, and other states soon followed suit. Professional prize fights attracted thousand of spectators, while millions more listened to coverage of fights broadcast from ringside.

The most famous boxer of the period was Jack Dempsey, who reigned as world heavyweight champion from 1919 to 1926. Dempsey's championship fight with Georges Carpentier on July 2, 1921 was the first to be covered live by radio. In 1927, more than 100,000 people watched him fight Gene Tunney in an unsuccessful attempt to win back his crown. The first black heavyweight champion, Joe Louis, held the title from 1937 to 1949.

### Baseball

Baseball was the leading spectator sport during the 1920s. Total annual attendance at games averaged more than eight million during this period. The most famous baseball player was Babe Ruth. Although he spent his childhood in poverty, his talent as a ball player was quickly recognized. In 1914, at age 19, he began his major league career as a pitcher for the Boston Red Sox, where he also posted an impressive record as a batter. In 1920, he switched to the New York Yankees and began playing as an outfielder, which allowed him to bat in every game.

Until Jackie Robinson broke the colour bar in 1947, black baseball players did not play on major league teams. (In a blatantly racist act, they had been banned from playing major league baseball in 1887.) In 1920, the Negro National League was established, followed in 1923 by the Eastern Colored League. In 1924, teams from these leagues played the first Negro League series. Despite financial ups and downs, Negro leagues in various forms continued until 1960. The level of play was equal to that in any league, and major games attracted spectators in the tens of thousands.

**Figure 10.9** Over 15 years with the Yankees, Babe Ruth set several records and helped lead his team to four World Series championships. In 1998, he was ranked the best baseball player of all time.

## Jazz

The defining music of the time was jazz, a uniquely American musical form that originated in the African-American community in New Orleans and was brought north to Chicago and New York by travelling musicians. Radio broadcasts and the recording industry then succeeded in popularizing jazz nationwide. The American writer F. Scott Fitzgerald coined the term "the Jazz Age" to describe a time when privileged youth, disillusioned and disconnected from traditional values, recklessly pursued fun and pleasure.

**Figure 10.10** Bessie Smith, the most popular blues singer of the 1920s, grew up in Chattanooga, Tennessee. She gained fame as a live performer and through her recordings with many top jazz musicians, including Louis Armstrong and Fletcher Henderson, the most successful African-American jazz band leader of the 1920s.

**Figure 10.11** Benny Goodman was born in Chicago to Jewish immigrant parents. A gifted clarinet player, he was band leader on the *Let's Dance* radio show in the 1930s, and soon earned the title "The King of Swing." Goodman was the first white band leader to break the colour barrier and hire black musicians.

**Figure 10.12** Louis Armstrong grew up in New Orleans. He was famous for his virtuosity on the cornet, his brilliant improvising, and his mastery of scat singing, or singing in nonsense syllables.

# Culture Notes

## *The Harlem Renaissance*

The Harlem Renaissance was an African-American cultural awakening centred in the Harlem district of New York City during the 1920s. Historians often wonder why such an awakening occurs in a particular place and time. As with other Northern cities, New York's African-American population swelled as a result of the Great Migration during and after World War I. Southern blacks seeking greater freedom and economic opportunity came to New York and were attracted to Harlem by low rents and an abundance of housing.

**Figure 10.13** Harlem produced several gifted painters during the 1920s, including William H. Johnson, who moved there from South Carolina in 1918. In *Street Life, Harlem*, Johnson used bright colours and a "primitive" drawing style to evoke the feeling of a Harlem street on a Saturday night.

Harlem is situated in the hilly area north of Central Park. In the 1920s, it had wide, tree-lined streets, an active entertainment industry, and a growing number of book and periodical publishers, which made it ripe for an artistic explosion. The Harlem Renaissance found its philosophical roots in the intellectual movement led by W.E.B. Du Bois, James Weldon Johnson, and Alain Locke. In *The New Negro: An Interpretation*, Locke argued that artistic achievements would uplift the race and redefine black identity in America.

Two magazines provided early outlets for the writers of the Harlem Renaissance: the Urban League's *Opportunity* and the NAACP's *The Crisis* (see Chapter 9). Poets like Langston Hughes sought to break new ground by declaring their pride in their African heritage. In 1926, Hughes wrote:

> We younger Negro artists now intend to express our individual dark-skinned selves without fear or shame. If white people are pleased we are glad. If they aren't, it doesn't matter. We know we are beautiful. And ugly too.

Hughes's poetry showcased African-American identity and pride while raising questions that often made white readers uncomfortable.

**Merry-Go-Round**
Where is the Jim Crow section
On this merry-go-round,
Mister, cause I want to ride?
Down South where I come from
White and colored
Can't sit side by side.
Down South on the train
There's a Jim Crow car.
On the bus we're put in the back—
But there ain't no back
To a merry-go-round!
Where's the horse
For a kid that's black?

Hughes's contemporary, fiction writer Zora Neale Hurston, captured the black spirit by using African-American narrative patterns and dialect in her most famous novel, *Their Eyes Were Watching God.*

While the spotlight on Harlem faded with the Great Depression, the Harlem Renaissance stands as a turning point in African-American history and served as a springboard for future black artists such as Ralph Ellison and Toni Morrison. It did this by convincing African-Americans that they had a right to be proud of themselves.

### Think It Through

1. What role did the Great Migration play in the Harlem Renaissance?
2. In what ways did the art and literature of the Harlem Renaissance reflect pride in the artists' African heritage?

**WEB LINKS** 

To learn more about the Harlem Renaissance, visit the site for the Schomburg Center for Research in Black Culture at www.emp.ca/ah.

## Changing Roles for Women

Young women known as flappers personified youthful rebellion during the Roaring Twenties. Flappers were both a reflection of a younger generation left morally adrift after a terrible war, and the creation of the mass media. According to F. Scott Fitzgerald, the ideal flapper was "lovely, expensive, and about nineteen." John Held Jr., an artist and illustrator who helped create the flapper look, often portrayed them wearing loose galoshes that made a flapping noise when they walked.

Flappers broke with tradition by cutting short or "bobbing" their hair and by making up their faces with eye liner, powder, and bright lipstick. They had a distinct image and attitude. They smoked, drank, danced, drove their own cars, and flaunted their sexuality. This was the extreme version, portrayed in magazines and films. Most women, young and old, adopted more restrained versions of the flapper style.

For some women, it wasn't the image that was important but the notion that they were as capable as men and deserved the same opportunities. This was the belief of Amelia Earhart, who achieved world renown as a pilot. In 1931, she was the first woman to fly solo across the Atlantic. Other firsts followed: a solo crossing of the Pacific from Oakland, California to Honolulu and a solo flight from Mexico City to Newark, New Jersey. In 1937, her luck ran out during the last stage of a round-the-world flight. She and her navigator, Fred Noonan, disappeared somewhere over the Pacific Ocean after failing to locate their destination, Howland Island.

**Figure 10.14** Dorothy Parker, the legendary writer and social commentator, exemplified many of the qualities of the flapper. A member of the New York literary circle known as the Algonquin Round Table, she was famous for her savage wit, once remarking that a well-known film actress "runs the gamut of emotions from A to B."

**SOUND BITE**

"The most difficult thing is the decision to act, the rest is mere tenacity ... You can act to change and control your life; and the procedure, the process is its own reward."

—Amelia Earhart

**CHECK YOUR UNDERSTANDING**

1. What impact did urbanization have on the Prohibition movement?
2. Economically, why did the Twenties "roar"?
3. How did Henry Ford's use of the assembly line affect auto production?
4. What did Amelia Earhart do to show that women were as capable as men?

# THE FLIP SIDE OF THE TWENTIES

The glamour and exuberance that make this period so fascinating also had a dark side. **Bootleggers** reaped huge profits from the importation and sale of illegal liquor, and the 1920s were also marked by intolerance, narrow-mindedness, and bigotry.

## Organized Crime

The Bureau of Prohibition, set up in 1920 to enforce the Volstead Act (the popular name for the National Prohibition Act), was soon battling organized crime rings with international connections. Among the gangsters they opposed were Al Capone and his Chicago mob; Owen Madden, a New York bootlegger and owner of the famous Cotton Club; and members of Detroit's Purple Gang. Many of the mobsters had colourful nicknames: Ma Barker, Baby Face Nelson, Dutch Schultz, Lucky Luciano, and Pretty Boy Floyd.

These criminals used extortion, hijackings, armed robbery, and murder to expand their operations. They bribed police officers and judges and fought vicious gang wars to eliminate competition. The St. Valentine's Day Massacre on February 14, 1929 involved the machine-gunning of six members of George "Bugs" Moran's gang (and one innocent victim) on Al Capone's orders. Some mobsters achieved the status of public heroes. Recognizing an opportunity, Hollywood began producing gangster films, a genre that soon overtook Westerns in popularity.

## Intolerance

Racism and fear of radical political ideas remained strong during the 1920s. In 1921, a race riot in Tulsa, Oklahoma was sparked by rumours that a black man had sexually assaulted a white woman. More than 1,000 homes were burned, and as many as 300 people were killed. In 1923, a white mob invaded the small, mostly black community of Rosewood, Florida after a white woman claimed she had been raped by a black man. Officially, six blacks and two whites were killed, but other estimates set the death toll at more than 100.

### Revival of the Ku Klux Klan

In this racially charged atmosphere, the Ku Klux Klan enjoyed a revival. It began in 1915, with the release of D.W. Griffith's silent film epic, *The Birth of a Nation*. Griffith's popular but racist film portrayed the Klan as heroes and black males as sexual predators. By 1922, the KKK had six million members, drawn from all walks of white, Protestant society. This new version of the Klan targeted Jews, Catholics, communists, and immigrants as well as blacks.

With its popularity surging, the Klan extended its influence into the North and Midwest, and also into the highest levels of government. In 1926, thousands of Klan members marched through the streets of Washington, DC dressed in their distinctive robes. By 1930, however, and after a series of scandals, including the conviction of a prominent Klan leader for rape and murder, membership had dropped to fewer than 30,000.

## 49th PARALLEL

# Rum Running

With the onset of prohibition in the United States there developed an underground network of bootleggers or "rum runners," many of whom operated from Canada. Alcohol may have been illegal, but Americans had not lost their taste for it. In Chicago, Al Capone's gangsters celebrated the start of Prohibition by stealing $100,000 ($1 million today) worth of whisky from railroad cars and selling it all within hours.

The US government had foreseen the problem of bootlegging and would eventually employ more than 2,300 federal agents to stop it. The agents' paltry salaries, however, encouraged many of them to accept bribes from the rum runners. Even those who were "on the level" found it impossible to patrol the 6,400-kilometre border effectively.

Although some liquor crossed the border in trucks and cars, the bulk of it arrived on boats. The centre of the illegal trade was the border between Windsor, Ontario and Detroit, Michigan. The Hiram Walker distillery, for instance, loaded Canadian Club whisky that had been legally cleared for Cuba into small rowboats that were supposedly bound for Cuba (a long trip in a rowboat!) but wound up in Detroit an hour after embarking. There, the whisky would often be picked up by gang members and transported to distribution centres across the Midwest.

Another shipping route ran through Nova Scotia and the islands of St. Pierre–Miquelon. There it was not organized criminal gangs but Canadian fishermen who ran the rum past the US Coast Guard. The fishermen used old US navy submarine chasers, which were painted grey and cruised low to the water, making them difficult to spot. Once past the Coast Guard, they would hug the coast until they hit "Rum Row," vast collections of schooners and motor launches that waited for the final quick run into a safe harbour.

Perhaps the Canadian who profited most from bootlegging was Sam Bronfman, the owner of Seagrams Distillery. Some reports estimate that half the illegal liquor crossing the border from Canada came from Seagrams, and by the time Prohibition ended, Bronfman already had a well-established US distribution network for his products.

Despite the intention of US lawmakers and temperance advocates, Prohibition did little to curb alcohol consumption. In fact, it actually ushered in a national drinking spree that coincided with the advent of the Jazz Age. Prohibition would not be repealed until 1933.

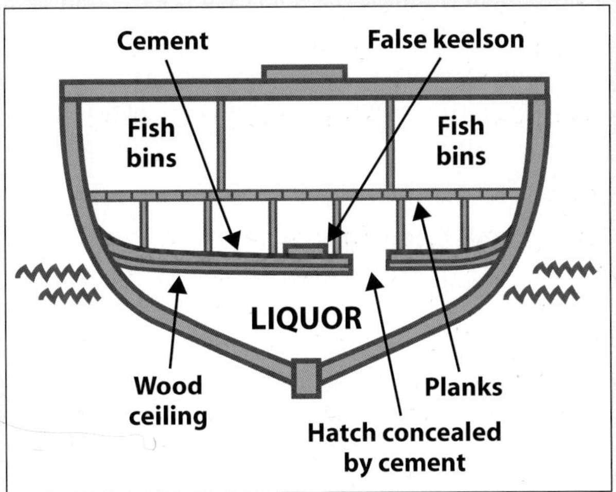

**Figure 10.15** Diagram of a rum-running boat from the Prohibition era.

## Think It Through

1. Describe the methods used by Canadian rum runners to smuggle their liquor across the border.
2. Would you characterize people like Al Capone as criminals or smart entrepreneurs who fulfilled a demand for a particular product? Explain your answer.

# WE THE PEOPLE

## *Marcus Garvey and Negro Nationalism*

> "Up you mighty race, you can accomplish what you will!"
>
> —*Marcus Garvey*

**Figure 10.16** Marcus Garvey's Universal Negro Improvement Association promoted the kinship of all black people and a "back-to-Africa" movement.

Born into a rural family on the north coast of Jamaica in 1887, Marcus Garvey would lead the first mass movement of African-Americans based on racial pride, self-help, and separatism. After working and studying in Central America and England, Garvey returned to Jamaica in 1914 and founded the Universal Negro Improvement Association (UNIA). Its goals were to instill racial pride in people of African descent, create economic opportunities, and recognize Africa as the homeland of all black people.

In 1916, Garvey moved to New York, where he opened a UNIA office in Harlem. He found little success until he began publishing the weekly newsletter *Negro World*. His message of racial pride appealed to African-Americans who felt ignored by both major political parties and bitter about the United States' failure to live up to the democratic rhetoric of World War I. How could the world be made safe for democracy when black people couldn't even vote in the South? By 1919, *Negro World* had a US circulation of over 50,000.

In 1920, Garvey staged a rally at New York's Madison Square Garden. There, the UNIA published the *Declaration of the Rights of the Negro Peoples of the World*, which called for the liberation of Africa from European colonialism and a back-to-Africa movement for blacks everywhere. By 1921, the UNIA had one million members in the US and four million internationally. These numbers far surpassed those for any other African-American organization, including the NAACP.

Not surprisingly, black leaders who fought for assimilation into white society, such as W.E.B. Du Bois and A. Phillip Randolph, attacked Garvey for his separatist goal of establishing a Negro homeland in Africa. Randolph even called Garvey the "Negro leader" of the KKK after an ill-advised meeting between Garvey and the Klan's Imperial Grand Wizard to discuss their common dream of returning US blacks to Africa.

To help connect African-Americans with their heritage continent, Garvey founded the Black Star Line, the first steamship company owned and operated by African-Americans. Financed solely by the sale of shares, the line collapsed in 1922 largely as a result of poor management. The next year, Garvey was convicted of mail fraud and sent to prison for two years. On his release, President Coolidge ordered him deported to Jamaica. The UNIA collapsed, and Garvey died in London, England in 1940.

Although he lacked a coherent program for ending racial oppression, Garvey's focus on black pride and respect for his people's African roots would echo throughout the 20th century. In 1964, the black leader Malcolm X testified to Garvey's lasting importance: "All the freedom movement that is taking place right here in America today was initiated by the philosophy and teachings of Garvey."

### Think It Through

1. Briefly describe the ideals and goals of Marcus Garvey and the Universal Negro Improvement Association.
2. Explain why mainstream African-American leaders opposed Marcus Garvey.

**WEB LINKS**

To explore the tumultuous career of Marcus Garvey, visit www.emp.ca/ah.

## Sacco and Vanzetti

Recent immigrants were also targets of intolerance during this time. In 1920, two Italian-born Americans—Nicola Sacco and Bartolomeo Vanzetti—were charged with robbing and murdering a security guard at a factory in South Braintree, Massachusetts. Both were found guilty of murder and sentenced to death. Several years passed while their lawyers appealed, but these efforts came to nothing. On August 23, 1927 Sacco and Vanzetti were electrocuted.

Their case attracted international attention as an example of people who were persecuted more for their ideas than their deeds. Sacco and Vanzetti were both anarchists with close ties to a radical group that advocated violence. Officials believed they were responsible for a series of bombings and other terrorist acts. Evidence indicates that the prosecutor and presiding judge in their case were strongly influenced by the popular fear of political radicals. This bias against the beliefs of the accused may well have denied them a fair trial.

**Figure 10.17** Vanzetti (l) and Sacco (r). Many intellectuals and artists of the 1920s supported Sacco and Vanzetti and believed they had been denied a fair trial. Ballistics tests conducted by the FBI in 1983 on the pistols used in the shooting indicated that Sacco was probably guilty and Vanzetti probably innocent.

**SOUND BITE**

"My conviction is that I have suffered for things that I am guilty of. I am suffering because I am a radical, and indeed I am a radical; I have suffered because I am an Italian, and indeed I am an Italian ... But I am so convinced to be right that if you could execute me two times, and if I could be reborn two other times, I would live again to do what I have done."

—Bartolomeo Vanzetti, speaking to the court upon being sentenced to death

## Anti-Immigration Legislation

The growing intolerance toward immigrants from southern Europe and China was reflected in federal legislation meant to back up Warren Harding's 1920 campaign promise that "this country will remain American." Starting in 1921, the US government introduced a series of measures that drastically cut immigration to America.

The Quota Act of 1921 set a ceiling of 350,000 immigrants a year and restricted quotas for each nationality to 3 percent of their share of the 1910 census. The National Origins Act of 1924 cut total annual immigration to

165,000 and cut quotas to 2 percent of the 1890 census. In the same year, the Oriental Exclusion Act virtually eliminated immigration from Asia. Then in 1927, the National Origins Act set a permanent immigration figure of 150,000 annually and limited immigration from southern and eastern Europe to 30 percent of that total.

The results were dramatic. While 4,107,209 immigrants arrived in the United States between 1921 and 1930, only 532,421 immigrants arrived between 1931 and 1940. Whereas 14.8 percent of the US population were foreign-born in 1920, by 1950, that figure had bottomed out at 6.9 percent.

## Hidden Weaknesses in the Economy

Although the 1920s was a period of great prosperity for the United States, there were many weak points in the economy. First, income growth was unevenly distributed. The top 0.1 percent of the population enjoyed a combined income equal to that of the bottom 42 percent. This tiny minority of the wealthy also possessed 34 percent of total savings, while 80 percent of the population had no savings at all.

In manufacturing, productivity increased 32 percent between 1923 and 1929; corporate profits rose 62 percent, but average wages rose only 8 percent. One result of this **economic disparity** was that more and more Americans couldn't afford the products they were being urged to buy: cars, radios, and home appliances. Many solved the problem by buying on credit. By the late 1920s, 60 percent of cars and 80 percent of radios were purchased this way. Not surprisingly, total consumer debt more than doubled between 1925 and 1929.

Another problem was the "multiplier effect" that a few large industries had on the economy as a whole. For example, the automotive industry created much of the demand for steel, textiles, glass, leather, and rubber. Cars also consumed large volumes of oil and gasoline and set off a wave of road construction and growth in travel-related industries. Any decline in auto manufacturing would have an immediate ripple effect across the entire economy.

Perhaps the most important economic weakness was psychological. America's boom had been sustained in part by the confidence of its people. Once they stopped believing that the good times would continue, they would also stop buying manufactured goods and investing their money. Then the fundamental weaknesses in the economy would assert themselves with a vengeance.

### CHECK YOUR UNDERSTANDING

1. State, in the form of a question, the problem faced by the Bureau of Prohibition.
2. What groups of people were the targets of KKK hatred?
3. How is the term "economic disparity" illustrated by the economy of the 1920s?
4. Why would a lack of consumer confidence hurt the US economy?

# HERBERT HOOVER AND THE GREAT DEPRESSION

When President Coolidge decided not to seek re-election in 1928, his able Secretary of Commerce, Herbert Hoover, stepped forward and won the Republican nomination. Hoover was an uninspiring public speaker, but he came with impressive credentials. From a modest background, he earned a degree in geology from Stanford University and spent the next 20 years travelling the world and making his fortune as an engineer. When World War I ended, he coordinated relief efforts that supplied food to millions of starving Europeans.

As Secretary of Commerce for presidents Harding and Coolidge, Hoover sought a more cooperative relationship between government, business, and labour. In short, he was a progressive who believed that government should play an active role in society. His supporters nicknamed him "the Great Engineer" for his celebrated managerial skills, but Coolidge, who disliked Hoover's wide-ranging involvements, called him "Wonder Boy."

During the 1928 presidential campaign, Hoover's Democrat opponent, Al Smith, lost support among certain voters because he was a Catholic. In the end, Hoover won an impressive victory, earning 58 percent of the popular vote. At the time of his inauguration, in March 1929, he was confident that America would continue to prosper. Events on Wall Street would soon prove him terribly wrong.

**SOUND BITE**

"We in America today are nearer to the final triumph over poverty than ever before in the history of this land ... We shall soon with the help of God be in sight of the day when poverty will be banished from this land."

—Herbert Hoover, in his acceptance speech at the Republican National Convention, 1928

## The Stock Market Crash of 1929

The booming economy of the 1920s fuelled a spectacular rise in the US stock market and sustained the confidence of investors. In 1921, the **Dow Jones Industrial Average**, an index measuring the average level of share prices on the New York Stock Exchange, stood at 60. By 1928, it had grown to 190. By September 1929, it soared to just over 380.

Along the way, more and more Americans began speculating in stocks. Many sought to leverage their investments by buying on margin—that is, they made a small cash payment, perhaps 10 percent of their total investment, and financed the rest through loans or mortgages on their homes. Banks also invested in the market. All this activity produced a speculative "bubble," an expansion so rapid that it cannot possibly be sustained and ends with a catastrophic burst.

In early 1929, the **Federal Reserve Board** began raising interest rates in an attempt to slow the heated economy.

**Figure 10.18** Wall Street, the heart of America's financial district, on Black Tuesday, October 29, 1929.

This made borrowing more expensive. Demand for consumer goods fell as people stopped buying on credit. Corporate investors pulled their funds from the market, and this triggered a general rush to sell. On Thursday, October 24, 1929, stock values plunged, and the Dow Jones Industrial Average declined 9 percent as almost 13 million shares were traded.

The next day, prices recovered somewhat as Wall Street bankers invested in the market in an attempt to restore confidence. Stockbrokers, however, continued calling in loans, and this produced further panic. On Monday, October 28, stock prices fell 13 percent, and on Tuesday (the press quickly dubbed it **Black Tuesday**), the Dow dropped another 12 percent as 16 million shares were sold. Thousands of investors saw their assets completely wiped out. Some investors were so distressed that they committed suicide.

## A Growing Economic Crisis

The US stock market crash marked the beginning of a worldwide economic depression, but it was not the cause of it. The Great Depression was actually rooted in the growing income disparity between rich and poor and in the overproduction and underconsumption of goods. Americans had overspent for years and now owed debt beyond their ability to pay. Many who had lost heavily in the stock market could no longer meet their day-to-day expenses, let alone consider major purchases. This meant that people cut back sharply on their spending, which reduced the demand for manufactured goods such as cars and radios.

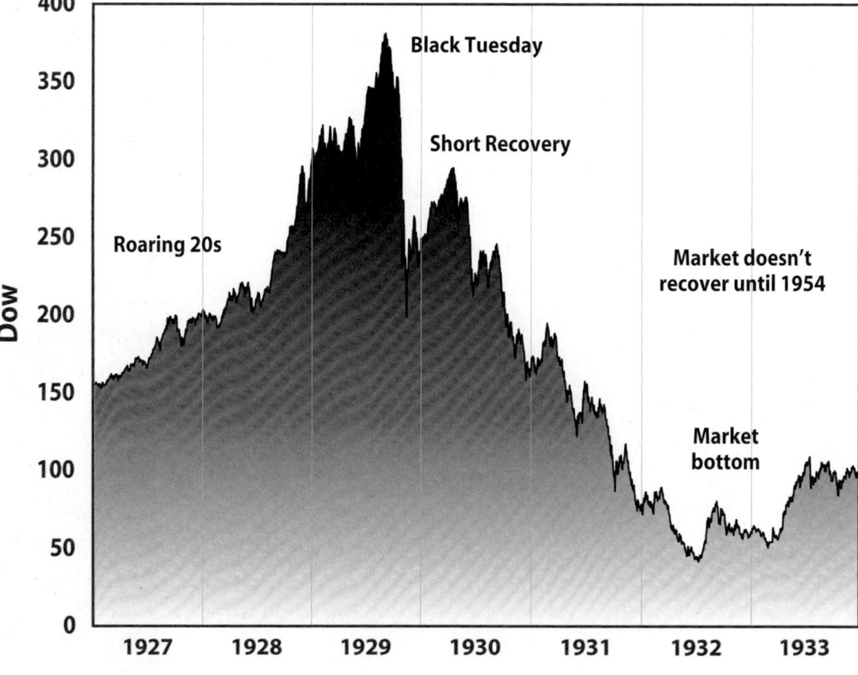


**Figure 10.19** This graph illustrates the collapse of the stock market in 1929 by tracking the decline in the Dow Jones Industrial Average. According to the graph, when did the Dow hit its lowest point? What does this tell you about the US economy in the years immediately following the crash?

Faced with plummeting sales, hundreds of factories and mills closed their doors. From 1929 to 1932, the declared unemployment rate rose from less than 4 percent to 25 percent, and unofficial estimates place this figure much higher. The rise in unemployment depressed the economy further, leading to more business failures.

### The Banking Crisis

The collapse of the stock market also destabilized the banking system, which in a sense was the cornerstone of the US economy. Fearing that banks no longer had the reserves to cover deposits, patrons rushed to withdraw all their savings.

The resulting panic produced what is known as a run on the banks. There were good reasons for worry, as many banks had lost heavily in the stock market and were accumulating unpaid business loans and mortgages. Bank runs occurred in 1930, 1931, and 1933. Thousands of banks failed—about 35 percent of all the banks in the United States—and $2 billion ($31 billion today) in deposits was lost. By 1933, the whole economy was grinding to a halt.

## Life during the Depression

The Great Depression touched people at every level of society. Millionaires and middle-class families alike found themselves suddenly destitute. In cities and towns, desperate men stood on street corners selling apples or pencils. Hundreds lined up outside mills and factories hoping for any kind of work, and at soup kitchens to receive free meals.

The loss of security made people feel anxious and depressed. This was especially true for those who experienced long-term unemployment: the unskilled, the young, and those over 55. African-Americans generally experienced higher unemployment rates than other groups, and there were many instances of blacks being laid off so that whites could be hired.

Parents felt ashamed that they could not provide for their families, and rates climbed for deficiency-related disorders such as rickets, skin ailments, and stunted physical growth. Every family had its own story of loss and suffering and of somehow trying to persevere.

According to US journalist Lindsey Williams:

> I was a nine-year-old boy at Flint [Michigan], when the Depression was heralded by the stock market crash of 1929. It is with great pain that I recall those days. My father abandoned my mother, me, and two younger sisters. Once in awhile we got a $5 bill in a letter from him without message or return address …
>
> We lost our home, moved to cheap rent places, then attic apartments. Mother gave up her possessions for back rent. She would not "go on welfare." That was a disgrace. Finally, … [w]e moved our beds into the basement of an uncle's home, and his family set us at their own meager table. My mother, maternal grandmother and three aunts pooled

resources. Our rented house was crowded—but home. Our meals were sparse, yet we all laughed when we read in a discarded newspaper the menu for prisoners at the county jail. They had the same meal that day—not much—as we were eating. A morning ritual was everyone assembling to make cardboard inserts for shoes whose soles had worn through. By the end of the day the inserts would be worn through also.

The point of this depressing tale is that it was not unusual back then. Today's generation cannot comprehend the demoralizing impact that a deep, economic depression has on a nation—thank God.

## Riding the Rails

Many people, like Lindsey Williams's father, left home in search of jobs elsewhere, sometimes jumping freight trains to travel across the continent. They were known as hobos. An estimated 2 million men and 8,000 women "rode the rails" jumping freight trains, which was illegal and dangerous. Railroad owners hired guards known as bulls to keep hobos off the trains. To avoid the bulls, many hobos would run alongside a train as it gained speed out of a train yard and then clamber into a boxcar. As many as 6,500 people died doing this—crushed between cars or cut to pieces under the wheels. Once on the train, the hobos would ride until it neared the next stop, then jump off to avoid the bulls again.

## Hoovervilles

People who could not pay their mortgages or rent lost their homes. Some were fortunate enough to find relatives to take them in, while others ended up homeless. Many took shelter in shantytowns known as **Hoovervilles**,

**Figure 10.20** Some of the Hoovervilles, like this one outside Seattle, were reasonably well organized. An unemployed lumberjack named Jesse Jackson acted as unofficial mayor. A census taken in 1934 of this community counted 632 men and 7 women living in 479 shanties of wood and tin construction.

named contemptuously after President Hoover. "Hoover blankets" were old newspapers the homeless used to keep warm at night. "Hoover wagons" were cars and trucks pulled by horses or mules for lack of money to buy gasoline.

### Life on the Farm: The Dust Bowl

A bumper wheat harvest in 1926 encouraged Midwestern farmers to expand their planting into dry, marginal lands. Wheat production increased, but the abundant harvests brought prices down. In 1931 a severe drought began, which lasted for years and turned parts of Kansas, Oklahoma, Colorado, and New Mexico into a vast "dust bowl." By 1934, the drought had destroyed more than 100 million hectares of farmland.

These severe conditions produced the largest migration in US history. Thousands of families abandoned the land, piling their few possessions into cars and trucks. By the end of the decade, 2.5 million people had fled the Midwest. Of these, about 200,000 moved to California where they sought migrant farm work, living all the while in tents and shacks. The local inhabitants called them "Okies" because the majority came from Oklahoma.

**Figure 10.21** The photographer Dorothea Lange took this photo of a 32-year-old mother of seven in a California migrant worker's camp. The family, said Lange, "had been living for weeks on frozen vegetables from the surrounding fields, and birds that the children killed. She had just sold the tires from her car to buy food."

**SOUND BITE**

"[O]nce in a while, it'd go all day and all night and maybe blow for a week before it was really no dust storm. And, of course, our parents had to turn the plates upside-down on the tables and cover 'em with a sheet or whatever, and we slept with them, the babies especially. They slept with wet sheets over their cribs so that they wouldn't breathe all that dirt."

—Imogene Glover, Oklahoma native and Dust Bowl survivor

**WEB LINKS**

To learn about John Steinbeck's stirring fictional account of Dust Bowl migrants to California, *The Grapes of Wrath* (1939), visit www.emp.ca/ah.

## Hoover Responds

What actions did President Hoover take to end the Great Depression? Were they effective? Some people have claimed, falsely, that he favoured laissez-faire economics and essentially did nothing. Others argue that while his intentions were good, he did too little, too late. Still others say he did too much. Hoover himself believed that his most urgent task was to restore public confidence in the economy, and that he could succeed in this through direct government intervention.

In 1929, at the height of the stock market crisis, Hoover directed the Federal Reserve Board to release hundreds of millions of dollars in credit. He

## PAST VOICES

# Woody Guthrie and Protest Music

This land is your land
This land is my land
From California
To the New York Island
From the redwood forest
To the Gulf Stream waters
This land was made for you and me.

Generations of American school children have sung this chorus of Woody Guthrie's most popular song, often to express strong feelings of patriotism. Upon deeper inspection, the song reveals a more radical message. Outraged by Irving Berlin's "God Bless America" and its aggressively patriotic overtones, Guthrie wrote "This Land Is Your Land" as a social protest song about class struggle. A later verse clearly reveals his intentions:

In the squares of the city,
in the shadow of the steeple,
By the relief office, I'd seen my people;
As they stood there hungry, I stood there asking,
Is this land made for you and me?

Guthrie's use of song as a form of protest was part of a larger folk music movement in the 1930s that had its roots in the slave spirituals (see Chapter 6) and in the union songs at the turn of the 20th century.

During the 1930s, miners, factory workers, and farmers gathered at town centres, churches, and union halls to listen to songwriters like Aunt Molly Jackson, Woody Guthrie, and Leadbelly sing about the oppressed, the people whom capitalism and industry had pushed aside and forgotten. Socialists and communists looked on folk music as the art of the **proletariat** or working class. After the stock market crash, bank failures, high unemployment, and widespread hunger, the popularity of protest songs reflected a growing unrest among the common people.

Woody Guthrie in particular became the nationally recognized voice of protest music during this period.

**Figure 10.22** Woody Guthrie's compositions and guitar style have had an enormous influence on modern popular music.

Originally from Oklahoma, Guthrie deliberately used his music to effect political change and stir up protests against government and big business. His album *Dust Bowl Ballads*, with tracks titled "Pretty Boy Floyd," "I Ain't Got No Home," and "So Long, It's Been Good to Know You," caught the imagination of the public and made him famous.

Soon Guthrie was recording songs in New York City, where he would influence another generation of folk artists, including Pete Seeger and Bob Dylan, both of whom idolized him. Today, protest music lives on through the voices and pens of singers like Bruce Springsteen and John Mellencamp and bands such as U2 and Rage against the Machine.

## Think It Through

1. What role did folk music play for those affected by the hardships of the Great Depression?
2. Explain why a songwriter like Woody Guthrie would be popular with communists, socialists, and other radical thinkers.

pressured business leaders to maintain current wages and increase capital spending. To create jobs for the unemployed, he committed federal funds to such construction projects as the Boulder Dam (later renamed the Hoover Dam) and the San Francisco Bay Bridge. He also set up a federal agency to coordinate relief efforts, and he created the Reconstruction Finance Corporation, which provided billions of dollars in aid to banks, farmers, and private industry. All the time, Hoover continually assured Americans that the Depression would soon be over.

The problem was that nothing Hoover did seemed to work, and the public grew tired of his promises. After a year of holding wages at 1929 levels, business leaders began cutting salaries and laying off workers. Many state governments ignored the president's request to increase spending on public works. Consumers, afraid of losing their jobs, continued to hold back on their spending. As the Depression deepened, Hoover would make controversial decisions on farm policies, international trade, and relief for the poor.

**US Government Income and Spending in Millions of Dollars, 1929–1932**

| Year | Federal Income | Federal Spending |
|---|---|---|
| **1929** | $4,058 | $3,320 |
| **1930** | $3,116 | $3,577 |
| **1931** | $1,924 | $4,659 |
| **1932** | $1,997 | $4,598 |

**Figure 10.23** As this table shows, federal government spending increased substantially during the Hoover administration, even while revenue plummeted. In what ways did President Hoover try to stimulate the economy?

## Farm Policies

In 1929, Hoover created the Federal Farm Board and gave it a budget of $500 million ($6 billion today) to "establish for our farmers an income equal to those of other occupations." The Farm Board's first priority was to raise wheat prices. It attempted to do this by stockpiling wheat harvests, thus reducing the supply.

The plan backfired badly. Other wheat-producing countries, including Canada and Argentina, jumped in and sold their wheat on the open market. Eventually, the United States had to sell its stockpiles, and this caused wheat prices to plummet. The Farm Board had spent hundreds of millions of dollars buying up surplus wheat and only made matters worse for American farmers.

## Hawley–Smoot Tariff, 1930

Ignoring the advice of leading economists, Hoover took a protectionist stance on international trade. In 1930, Congress passed the Hawley–Smoot Tariff Act, which effectively raised import duties on thousands of foreign goods to the highest levels in US history. Several of the United States' chief trading partners, including Canada and Britain, immediately responded with retaliatory tariffs. As a result, the US experienced a significant decline in exports over the next three years. Economists have calculated that between 1930 and 1932, the decline in exports amounted to 18 percent of the decline in total US GNP.

## Relief Efforts

While Hoover brought in several costly programs to end the Depression, he balked at approving direct relief payments to the growing legions of the poor and unemployed. He was convinced that if Americans began receiving federal welfare, they would lose the motivation to improve their situation. Eventually, the cries for relief from around the country would lead to one of the sorriest episodes of the Depression.

As you saw earlier, Congress passed the Soldiers' Bonus Act in 1924 over President Coolidge's veto. This Act gave veterans $1.25 ($14.74 today) for every day served overseas, and $1 ($11.79 today) for every day served at home, but payments would not start until 1945. In May 1932, about 15,000 veterans gathered in Washington, DC to demand immediate payment of their bonuses. This "Bonus Army" set up camps around the capital, the largest at a place called Anacostia Flats.

On July 28, President Hoover ordered the army to move in and clear out the protesters. The soldiers were commanded by General Douglas MacArthur, assisted by Major Dwight D. Eisenhower and Major George Patton, three capable officers who would go on to play prominent roles in World War II. The veterans didn't stand a chance. The soldiers advanced on Anacostia Flats with fixed bayonets and wearing gas masks. In a matter of hours, they had cleared the area and burned the camp to the ground.

Less than four months after this incident, Hoover was soundly defeated in the 1932 presidential election. Franklin D. Roosevelt claimed victory with 57.4 percent of the popular vote against Hoover's 39.7 percent. Roosevelt would be the first Democrat president since Woodrow Wilson, and the election also gave the Democratic Party control of both the House of Representatives and the Senate. Promising a New Deal to the American people, Roosevelt

**Figure 10.24** The burning of Anacostia Flats. Many Americans were dismayed to see war veterans, men who had risked their lives on behalf of their country, attacked and mistreated by their own armed forces. The event seemed to confirm President Hoover's status as an ineffectual and unsympathetic leader.

**Figure 10.25** A photograph of Herbert Hoover and Franklin Roosevelt on the way to Roosevelt's inauguration in March 1933. Compare this photo with a cartoonist's impression of the same scene. How has the cartoonist exaggerated the features of the two men to convey a message? What do you think this message is?

forged a coalition among urban residents, Southern whites, ethnic minorities, organized labour, and the poor.

The question on everyone's mind was whether Roosevelt could deliver on his promise and succeed where Hoover had failed. The stakes could not have been higher: the survival of the existing political and economic order and the American way of life.

### CHECK YOUR UNDERSTANDING

1. What is meant by the term "overproduction"?
2. What groups of people experienced long-term unemployment during the Great Depression?
3. What steps did President Hoover take to revive the US economy?
4. Why was the Farm Board a failure?

## ROOSEVELT'S NEW DEAL

As Franklin Roosevelt prepared to take office on March 4, 1933, the Great Depression hit rock bottom with a final run on the banks that threatened to shut down the entire US economy. In his inaugural speech, Roosevelt identified his "primary task" as putting America back to work, but the first problem he attacked was the banking crisis.

## Fixing the Banks

Two days after his inauguration, Roosevelt ordered a "bank holiday," which closed all the nation's banks. Three days later, he sent to Congress the Emergency Banking Act, which was passed and signed into law the same day. The new law allowed banks to reopen only once they had passed inspection by officials from the Treasury Department. By March 12, the majority of banks were back in operation.

In June, Congress passed the Glass–Steagall Act creating the Federal Deposit Insurance Corporation, which guaranteed bank deposits up to $5,000 ($78,000 today). These quick actions bolstered public confidence and put an end to bank runs. They also demonstrated the major strategy that Roosevelt would follow to combat the Great Depression: direct government intervention in the economy.

### The Brain Trust

Beginning with his governorship of New York (1928–1932), Roosevelt surrounded himself with a group of policy advisers that included academics from Columbia University as well as lawyers and politicians. The press soon nicknamed this group the "brain trust," and Roosevelt continued seeking their advice after he became president.

Among his top advisers were Raymond Moley, a professor of law and political science, and unofficial leader of the brain trust; Rexford Guy Tugwell, a professor of economics; and Adolf A. Berle Jr., a law professor. All three rejected laissez-faire economics as a solution to the Depression in favour of government management of the economy. In 1938, a young Canadian economist named John Kenneth Galbraith (see Chapter 11) joined the group, sharing their belief that governments could regulate economic forces to achieve prosperity for all.

**Figure 10.26** The adviser whom Roosevelt trusted most was his wife, Eleanor, shown here speaking into a radio microphone in 1934. Eleanor Roosevelt dedicated herself to furthering her husband's career and political agenda and became a political figurehead in her own right. She gave lectures, made radio broadcasts, and travelled widely. An astute observer of the political scene, she regularly reported her impressions back to Franklin.

AMERICAN ARCHIVE

# Franklin Roosevelt's First Inaugural Address

In preparing his inaugural address, Roosevelt wanted to accomplish three goals: to offer hope to the American people, to identify the roots of the problem that confronted the country, and to present his solution for overcoming that problem.

In stating that there was good cause for hope in spite of what he called "the dark realities of the moment," Roosevelt began with words that gripped his listeners and have echoed ever since in the country's collective consciousness:

> This is pre-eminently the time to speak the truth, the whole truth, frankly and boldly. Nor need we shrink from honestly facing conditions in our country today. This great Nation will endure as it has endured, will revive and prosper. So, first of all, let me assert my firm belief that the only thing we have to fear is fear itself—nameless, unreasoning, unjustified terror which paralyzes needed efforts to convert retreat into advance.

Roosevelt was suggesting to the people that they themselves possessed the necessary resources—psychological and material—to overcome the worst effects of the Depression.

Next, he identified the cause of the Depression as failures in the banking and financial systems, failures rooted in the simple greed for profits:

> Plenty is at our doorstep, but a generous use of it languishes in the very sight of the supply. Primarily this is because the rulers of the exchange of mankind's goods have failed ... Practices of the unscrupulous money changers stand indicted in the court of public opinion ... They know only the rules of a generation of self-seekers.

Where the free market system had failed, Roosevelt planned to use the federal government to succeed. Accordingly, he identified the first step in recovery as eliminating unemployment. He proposed having the government intervene to accomplish this, the same kind of vigorous intervention that might be used in time of war:

> Our greatest primary task is to put people back to work. This is no unsolvable problem if we face it wisely and courageously. It can be accomplished in part by direct recruiting by the Government itself, treating the task as we would treat the emergency of a war ... We must act and act quickly.

While focusing on employment, Roosevelt also proposed rules for the "strict supervision" of the banking and investment industries to avoid past abuses.

The confidence, determination, and optimism expressed in this speech had an immediate calming effect on the American public. The course of action outlined in it—direct government intervention through economic and social programs—would become a hallmark of the New Deal and permanently change the relationship between the American people and their government.

## Think It Through

1. Whom did Roosevelt blame for the Great Depression? Why?
2. Do you think Roosevelt was justified in his move to expand the powers of the federal government? Explain.

**Figure 10.27** President Roosevelt delivering his first inaugural address, March 4, 1933.

## The First New Deal, 1933–34

Roosevelt's New Deal was based on an ambitious legislative program that he and Congress implemented over a period of several years. It was organized around the **Three R's** of *relief* (immediate help for the unemployed), *recovery* (restoring the economy to a healthy state), and *reform* (finding and implementing permanent fixes to the economy's ills).

Roosevelt had no master economic plan at the time he became president, but he knew he had to act quickly and forcefully to restore public confidence. A year earlier, while addressing students at Oglethorpe University, he had described the challenge facing America and indicated the approach he intended to take:

> The country ... demands bold, persistent experimentation. It is common sense to take a method and try it: If it fails, admit it frankly, and try another. But above all, try something. The millions who are in want will not stand by silently forever while the things to satisfy their needs are within easy reach.

So Roosevelt founded his New Deal on an empirical (experimental; based on observation or experience) approach to repairing the nation's economy.

**SOUND BITE**

"The first days of the Roosevelt Administration charged the air with the snap and zigzag of electricity. I felt it. We all felt it. It seemed as if you could hold out your hand and close it over the piece of excitement you ripped away. It was the return of hope."

—US Congressman Emanuel Celler, *You Never Leave Brooklyn*, 1953

### Programs of the First New Deal

Roosevelt proved good on his word. From March 9 until June 16, 1933, in a special session of Congress later dubbed the **Hundred Days**, he persuaded Democratic majorities in the Senate and House to approve more than a dozen new laws. In addition to bringing in the financial reforms mentioned earlier, this legislation created numerous federal agencies, including those listed below. (The dates indicate when these programs were launched.)

Figure 10.28 A poster for the CCC, one of the most popular and successful of the New Deal programs.

#### *CCC (Civilian Conservation Corps), March 1933*

This popular work relief program offered unemployed young men rural construction work for six months at $1 ($15.56 today) per day. Participants lived in camps of 200 run by reserve army officers. This program operated from 1933 to 1942 and assisted more than three million youths.

### *AAA (Agricultural Adjustment Administration), May 1933*

The AAA persuaded farmers to destroy crops and livestock by paying them subsidies. The hope was that the resulting artificial scarcity would raise prices of farm products. In 1933 alone, millions of pigs and over 200,000 cows were slaughtered. Three years later, gross farm income had risen by 50 percent, but farm commodity prices remained stagnant. The AAA was unpopular among the general public, who were disgusted by the thought of crops and livestock being destroyed at a time of poverty and hunger.

### *TVA (Tennessee Valley Authority), May 1933*

The TVA aimed at reform and long-term recovery. It revitalized the economy of the Tennessee Valley by providing low-cost electrical power, flood control, safe river navigation, and regional economic planning. Under its direction, dozens of dams and electrical power-generating stations were built, providing employment to thousands of construction workers.

### *NRA (National Recovery Administration), June 1933*

The goals of the NRA were to reverse the slide in prices of industrial products by achieving "fair competition" through the regulation of wages, prices, working conditions, and output. The NRA enjoyed some initial success in raising wages, but rising prices soon curtailed consumer demand.

Roosevelt sold the New Deal by using the radio to talk directly to the American people. He was a brilliant communicator who spoke in a confident, reassuring tone. His broadcasts, known as "fireside chats," garnered huge audiences and had a calming effect on the public. Though real recovery was slow, Roosevelt managed to plant the seeds of hope early in his administration.

## The New Deal and Native Americans

One law passed in 1934 extended the New Deal's reforms to Native Americans. The Indian Reorganization Act (IRA) overturned the land distribution arrangements under the Dawes Act (see Chapter 8) that divided reservations into individually held plots and allowed speculators to sell off thousands of hectares of Native lands. The IRA also reversed many long-standing policies of the Bureau of Indian Affairs that discouraged Native cultural practices and removed children from their families to spend years in distant boarding schools. The main aims of the Act were

- to decrease the federal government's control over Native affairs,
- to grant local government powers to the individual tribes,
- to restore responsibility to Native Americans for managing their own lands, and
- to establish a sound and sustainable economy on the reservations.

Thanks to the IRA's focus on reversing the loss of Native lands, within 20 years of the Act's passage more than 8,000 square kilometres of land were returned to tribes across the country.

The IRA also encouraged Native peoples to revive their ancient traditions and beliefs. For example, it arranged for Native shamans to help deliver federal health care to their people. Coincidentally, in 1932, two years before passage of the IRA, a book called *Black Elk Speaks* was published. This book contained the observations of the Oglala medicine man Black Elk, who had fought at Little Bighorn and Wounded Knee. In the book, Black Elk describes his own visions and the Sioux religious beliefs that had sustained his people for hundreds of years. *Black Elk Speaks* would have a profound influence on the next generation of Native activists and inspire the founders of the American Indian Movement (see Chapter 12).

**SOUND BITE**

"The most important aspect of [*Black Elk Speaks*] is ... upon the contemporary generation of young Indians who have been aggressively searching for roots of their own in the structure of universal reality. To them the book has become a North American bible of all tribes. They look to it for spiritual guidance, for sociological identity, for political insight, and for affirmation of the continuing substance of Indian tribal life, now being badly eroded by the same electronic media which are dissolving other American communities."

—Vine Deloria Jr., author of *Custer Died for Your Sins: An Indian Manifesto* (1988)

### Successes and Failures

The programs of the first New Deal achieved some success. Between 1933 and 1934, the GNP went on an upswing, while unemployment fell to 16 percent. This was a substantial drop from the dark days of 1932, but still three times higher than rates seen during most of the 1920s.

On the downside, there was growing criticism in Congress and from the general public about waste and red tape in some New Deal programs. Then the Supreme Court ruled unanimously that the National Recovery Act, under which the NRA had been created, was unconstitutional. These developments frustrated Roosevelt, but he was not deterred. From 1935 to 1936, he introduced a series of initiatives known as the Second New Deal.

## The Second New Deal

The programs of the Second New Deal emphasized social reform. They tended to be more radical and pro-labour than the earlier programs. Roosevelt moved to the left to counter popular reformers such as Huey Long, Father Coughlin, and Dr. Francis Townsend.

Huey Long, a US senator and former governor of Louisiana, made provocative speeches calling for a radical redistribution of wealth from the very rich to the poor and middle class. Coughlin, a Catholic priest originally from Ontario, used his Detroit radio program to attack Wall Street, international bankers, communism, and the New Deal. Townsend was proposing a universal pension plan for people who had turned 65. Roosevelt's Second New Deal programs reflected his own belief that poverty was most often due to circumstances beyond one's control rather than one's moral failures.

## The Works Progress Administration (WPA), 1935

The WPA employed millions of men and women to work on projects such as highways and bridges, public buildings, airports, and the arts. In 1935 alone, this program received \$4 billion (\$59 billion today) in funding. It quickly became the largest employer in the country and operated until 1943. Lyndon Johnson, a future president of the United States, directed the National Youth Administration, the youth wing of the WPA.

## The Wagner Act, 1935

The Wagner Act created the National Labor Relations Board (NLRB), whose main function was to strengthen and protect collective bargaining by unionized workers. This goal reflected Roosevelt's belief that higher wages for workers were crucial to economic growth. It also assured the Democrats of continuing political support from organized labour. As result of the NLRB's efforts, membership in union organizations such as the American Federation of Labor grew dramatically.

**Figure 10.29** Although the Wagner Act was a boon to unions, it did not bring peace to labour relations in the United States. Here, police fire on union demonstrators at the Republic Steel Plant in Chicago in 1937, killing ten.

### The Social Security Act, 1935

Perhaps the most lasting legacy of the New Deal was the Social Security Act, which created an unemployment insurance program, a welfare program for poor families and the handicapped, and a universal system of retirement pensions. The original program did not provide funds for farm workers or domestic help.

From the beginning, this vast and costly program has been financed by payroll taxes, and it has always been controversial. Two legal challenges ended in 1937 with the US Supreme Court affirming that the Act was constitutional. In terms of the dollars involved, it is now the largest government program in the world.

## The Election of 1936

Despite grumblings from business groups and other laissez-faire advocates about the New Deal, Roosevelt won the 1936 presidential election with the second-largest popular-vote majority in US history. The Democrats also increased their majorities in the Senate and the House of Representatives.

This strong endorsement by voters emboldened Roosevelt to take action to counter the Supreme Court, which had struck down several pieces of New Deal legislation. He devised a plan for expanding the number of Supreme Court judges, a move that would allow him to pack the court with those

**Figure 10.30** Roosevelt's attempt to pack the Supreme Court with sympathetic judges cost him a good deal of political support. Why has the cartoonist included a donkey, the symbol of the Democratic Party, in this cartoon?

sympathetic to the New Deal. The uproar that followed forced Roosevelt to abandon the scheme, but not before it caused him lasting political damage.

The 1938 mid-term elections saw a surge in Republican representation in Congress, which reduced Roosevelt's ability to push forward any new programs. By then, he was turning his attention more and more to international affairs, as war clouds gathered in Europe and Asia.

## Significance of the New Deal

The New Deal transformed the relationship the American people had with their government. Some historians even credit it with saving democracy in America. They argue that without Roosevelt's interventions, the hard times of the Depression might have resulted in revolution and dictatorship. Others condemn the New Deal as an expensive failure that prolonged the Great Depression. They argue that market forces should have been allowed to operate freely, a strategy that might have produced short-term pain but a swifter recovery.

As the 1930s came to a close, most Americans still held to the promise of the American dream: people could achieve great success if they only had faith in themselves and worked hard. The 1920s had shown what could be achieved, while the 1930s had tested the dream. The 1940s were to put the United States, and all that it stood for, to its greatest test yet.

### CHECK YOUR UNDERSTANDING

1. What was the purpose of the bank holiday President Roosevelt declared and the Emergency Banking Act?
2. How did President Roosevelt use the then-modern technology of radio to fight the Great Depression?
3. What was the purpose of founding the New Deal on an empirical approach to the economy?
4. Why was there opposition to President Roosevelt's court-packing plan?

# THE HISTORIAN'S CRAFT

## Ways of Presenting History

### The Traditional Approach

One of the traditional ways to present history in high school classes is the formal essay. This approach involves declaring a thesis, presenting evidence to support it, and providing a conclusion.

For example, in this chapter you might declare that Calvin Coolidge was a president who outlived his time. To support this thesis, you could refer to his early career in restoring and maintaining "normalcy" and respect for the presidency after war and scandal. You might describe how his business mentality matched the boom of the early Twenties. Then you could contrast "Silent Cal's" image to the excesses of the Roaring Twenties. Next, you would show how Coolidge's non-interventionist policies were inappropriate for the late Twenties in the face of wild speculation and rural poverty. Finally, you would conclude by summarizing your supporting evidence and adding emphasis by quoting Coolidge in retirement: "I feel I no longer fit in with these times."

This approach is an excellent way to present your research and thinking in other products, too—for example, in a video using archival photographs.

### Approaches Based on Thinking Historically

There are many other ways to present your information. You might decide to use one of the approaches dealt with in The Historian's Craft features in Chapters 7, 8, and 9:

- an essay highlighting key turning points in a historical period (e.g., the Wagner Act of 1935),
- a presentation analyzing events in terms of how they reflect historical concepts (e.g., the New Deal as an example of the concept of social welfare),
- a computer image presentation using the inquiry model to explain the 1929 stock market crash, or
- a dramatized "improbable meeting" between Calvin Coolidge and John Kenneth Galbraith on how to deal with economic collapse.

### From the Extremes to Deeper Understanding

Another way to analyze history is a "pros and cons" study. You could do this for the topic of Prohibition. Your product could be a chart, an essay, or a class presentation. Whatever the product, you could go beyond the simple listing of pros and cons (something you have been doing since elementary school). Make a judgment about the overall positive or negative impact. Find parallels in proposals for modern prohibitions (e.g., of handguns or marijuana). Make the case that much of history is not black and white but more complex shades of grey.

### Putting the Personal into History Products

You might choose to organize and present your material in a way that reflects your strong personal interest. For example, you might find a personal hero to research—such as Marcus Garvey—and present a biography to your classmates based on your findings. If you have strong musical interests, you might write a formal essay based on this thesis: *Jazz is the most significant cultural gift made by the US to the rest of the world.* On the other hand, you might focus on an ordinary historical person and base your product on that person's life. For example, you might write an in-their-shoes account of Imogene Glover (see page 347) as if you were with her in the Dust Bowl in the 1930s (see The Historian's Craft in Chapter 7, page 244).

### Try It!

1. Prepare an outline for a formal essay on the New Deal. Write out your tentative thesis and list, in point form, the supporting evidence found in Chapter 10. Now undertake more research to test your thesis.
2. Put yourself in the shoes of a resident of a Hooverville. Describe the Great Depression from your empathetic perspective in a series of diary entries.

# STUDY HALL

## Thinking

1. American political scientist Clinton Rossiter once rated President Warren Harding as among the four worst presidents (along with Pierce, Buchanan, and Grant). What criteria would you use to judge a president? Does Harding deserve this reputation? Explain.
2. To what extent was President Calvin Coolidge a follower of the saying, "The best government is the least government"?
3. The trial of Sacco and Vanzetti raises comparisons with the worries of some immigrants today in a time of terrorism. What can individual citizens and governments do to ensure fair treatment for all in times of fear?
4. Was President Herbert Hoover's administration a failure? What criteria should be used to judge his attempts to fight the Great Depression?
5. Debate the following:
   a. The flapper was the first liberated woman.
   b. Limits on immigration in the 1920s were racist acts based on fear, not on economic necessity.
   c. The stock market crash of 1929 was caused by greed.

## Communication

6. In a diagram, show the flows of loans and reparations among Germany, France, Britain, and the United States.
7. American writer Ernest Hemingway (see Culture Notes, Chapter 9, page 320) believed that simple words and sentences could be used to express complex ideas and feelings. He worked hard to cut words from his writing and avoided adjectives whenever possible. Try using this spare style to describe an event in the social history of the interwar period.
8. Produce a jazz music radio program that will create interest in jazz from the 1920s and 1930s. Decide on criteria you will use to select three artists and one piece of music for each. Find recordings, write an introduction and conclusion for each of your selections, and "broadcast" them to your class.
9. Show the downward decline of the US economy in a spiral or circular diagram, connecting loss of confidence, overproduction, disparities of income and savings, and unemployment.

## Application

10. Canadian technology guru Marshall McLuhan taught that technologies extend human abilities. The hammer is an extension of the arm; the telephone is an extension of the ear and the voice. How did radio, motion pictures, airplanes, and cars extend human abilities? How did they change life for people?
11. Do a pro-and-con analysis of Franklin Roosevelt's plan to pack the Supreme Court with judges sympathetic to the New Deal.
12. In parts of Canada today, where there is high unemployment, should the government spend money on large construction projects in order to inject money into the local economy and create local jobs? Explain your views, referring to the American experience in the 1930s.

# UNIT V WORLD POWER

# 11 World War II and the Cold War (1941–1960)

## KEY CONCEPTS

In this chapter you will consider:

- The debate in America between isolationism and involvement in world affairs
- Factors that led to America's involvement in World War II
- The role of the United States in World War II
- The impact of the war on the American people and economy
- The origins, development, and effects of the Cold War
- The emergence of the American military-industrial complex
- Cultural changes in postwar America
- The evolution of a closer military relationship between Canada and the United States

## The American Story

The United States officially abandoned its isolationist policy by entering World War II in 1941, after Japan attacked its naval base at Pearl Harbor. Victory in World War II left the United States and its wartime ally, the Soviet Union, as the two global superpowers. But events in the immediate postwar period led Americans to believe that their one-time ally had become their greatest adversary. A cold war soon emerged between the capitalist West and the communist East for global influence and control. This conflict would shape the economic and political landscape of America for the next 40 years.

## TIMELINE

| 1935 | 1939 | 1941 | 1945 | 1948 |
|---|---|---|---|---|
| ▸ Roosevelt signs first Neutrality Act | ▸ World War II begins | ▸ Japan attacks Pearl Harbor | ▸ America drops atomic bombs on Japan<br>▸ World War II ends | ▸ Marshall Plan |

## IMAGE ANALYSIS

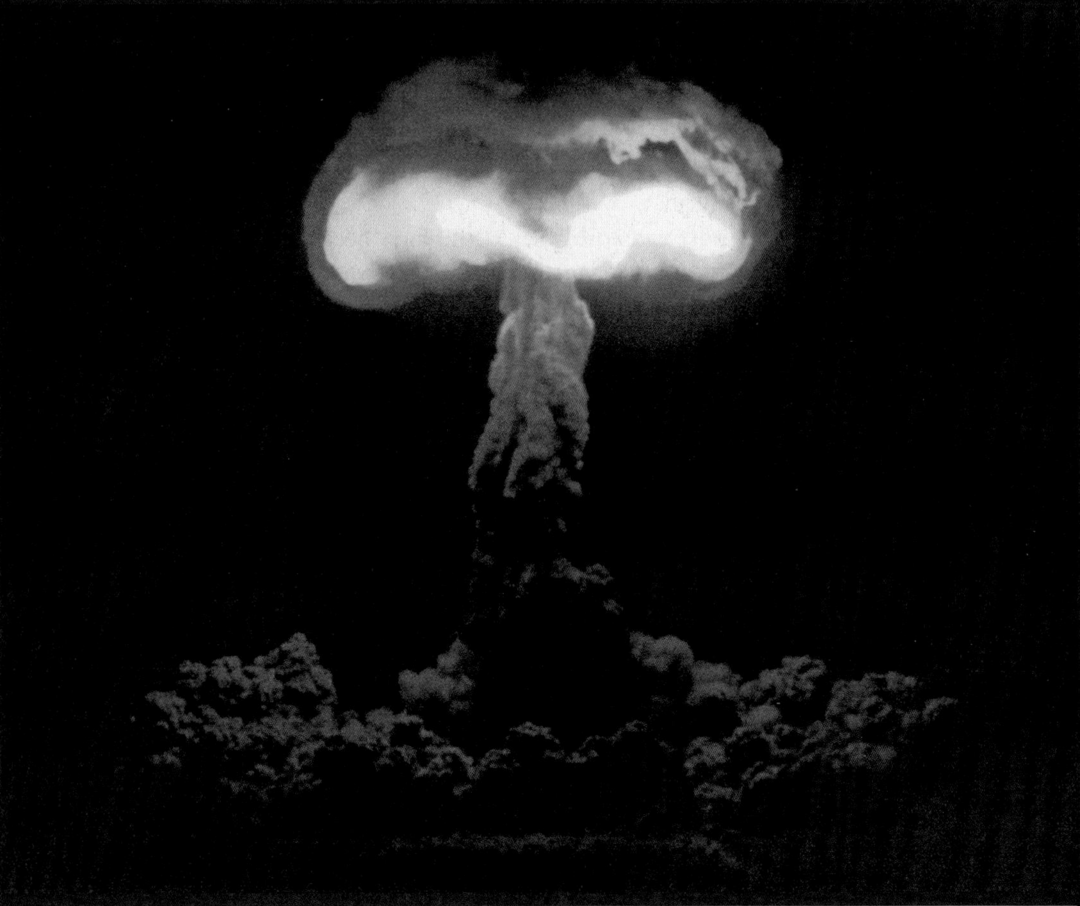

**Figure 11.1** This photograph shows an atomic bomb exploding at a test site in Nevada in 1957. The design, manufacture, and testing of nuclear weapons became a focus of the American military during the Cold War. President Harry S. Truman, who authorized the military use of atomic bombs against Japan in 1945, called the creation of these weapons "the greatest achievement of organized science in history." What other American scientific achievements might qualify as great but also devastating?

| 1949 | 1950 | 1953 | 1958 | 1960 |
|---|---|---|---|---|
| ▸ NATO established | ▸ Korean War begins<br>▸ McCarthy's investigations begin | ▸ Korean War ends | ▸ Canada and US sign NORAD agreement | ▸ U2 incident |

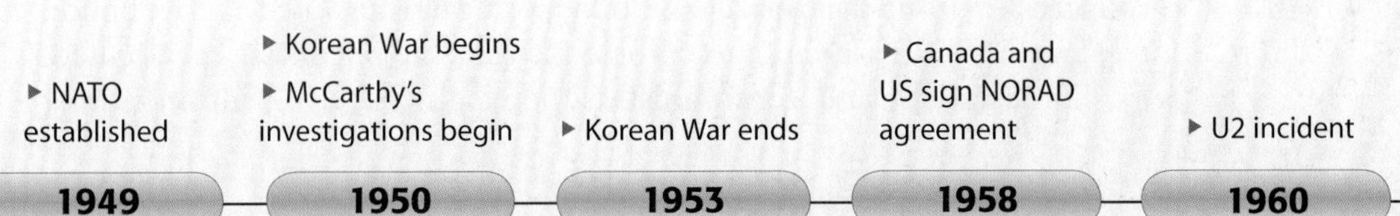

# INTRODUCTION

If you were a young American during the 1940s you would have witnessed the most devastating war in human history. Your friends and family might have gone abroad to fight—possibly to die. Every night you would have listened to war news on the radio; every day you would have checked the newspapers for lists of the dead, hoping not to find a familiar name there. The war would eventually end in victory for your country, but it would leave over 400,000 Americans dead.

In the postwar world you would have been among the first people ever to live with the knowledge that a nuclear war could obliterate life on earth. Bomb drills at school would be constant reminders of the peril. A lot of talk would be circulating about how dangerous communists were, and you would have been aware that the Cold War could turn "hot" at any time.

If you were from the middle class, you would also notice that life was becoming more prosperous. Your family would probably buy a television set and perhaps a new car. Your mother might quit her job and have another baby. You would be among the first group of young people ever to be called "teenagers," and you would probably listen to rock and roll. Your family and friends might move to the suburbs, where the hardships of the war years would gradually fade away.

Cold War America was a contradictory place: at home there was prosperity, **consumerism**, and suburban comforts, while outside the world seemed at times to teeter on the brink of nuclear war.

# WORLD WAR II

After World War I the United States returned to a policy of isolationism. Economic disaster in the 1930s had focused the country's attention inward, as people struggled to combat the hardships of the Great Depression. However, the growth of **fascist** regimes in Europe reopened the debate in America over isolation or involvement in global affairs. The United States gradually abandoned its policy of neutrality as World War II spread throughout Europe.

## The Road to War in Europe

In January 1933 Adolf Hitler, the leader of the National Socialist German Workers' Party (Nazis), became chancellor of Germany. Nazi **ideology** was rooted in Hitler's **anti-Semitism** and his belief that the German "master race" was superior to all others and should dominate Europe.

During his rise to power, Hitler used propaganda and corrupt political practices—including burning the German Parliament and blaming it on his adversaries—to secure the leadership of Germany. Once in office, he quickly eliminated any group that was capable of opposing him and used a secret police force, known as the Gestapo, to enforce his rule. He relentlessly persecuted Jews, homosexuals, and communists, among others, using intimidation,

**Figure 11.2** A scene from *Triumph of the Will*, a propaganda documentary commissioned by Hitler and directed by Leni Riefenstahl in 1934. What image of itself is the Nazi party attempting to convey to Germany and the world?

imprisonment, and murder. On November 9 and 10, 1938—in an event that has become known as Kristallnacht, or the "night of broken glass"—Nazis destroyed Jewish property in many German cities and sent approximately 30,000 Jews to concentration camps. Over the course of the war, the Nazis would kill 6 million Jews.

As the plight of German Jews grew more desperate, 937 refugees boarded a ship called the *St. Louis* bound for Cuba; most of the refugees had applied for US visas and intended to settle in the United States. On June 4, 1939, however, America refused them entry. Canada too refused, and Cuba allowed only a handful of those on board to disembark. The ship was forced to return to Europe, where the majority of its passengers subsequently died in Nazi concentration camps.

At the time, the United States had strict immigration quotas, which were favoured by the majority of Americans (see Chapter 10). Earlier, in February 1939, the Wagner–Rogers bill had been put before Congress to allow the admission of an additional 20,000 German Jewish children over a two-year period; the bill died in committee.

In 1936 Hitler signed a "treaty of friendship" with Benito Mussolini, Italy's fascist dictator, and began a military campaign to expand German territory. Knowing that England and France were determined to avoid reliving the horrors of World War I, Hitler pushed these countries to accept his bold moves in an effort to appease him. For example, in 1938 British Prime Minister Neville Chamberlain avoided direct confrontation with Hitler—and thereby avoided war—after Hitler's takeover of the Sudetenland, a part of Czechoslovakia. The non-aggression pact between England and Germany, Chamberlain

**Figure 11.3** Germany's expansion between March 1936 and March 1939. Why were European countries concerned about this expansion?

said, ensured "peace in our time." Figure 11.3 shows Hitler's conquests between March 1936 and March 1939.

In August 1939, sensing that war was imminent, Hitler signed a secret non-aggression pact with Soviet leader Joseph Stalin. Both sides agreed not to attack each other if war began. The pact was strategically important for Hitler because it freed him from the military disadvantage of fighting a war on two fronts at the same time. Before the US joined the Allied forces in 1941, Hitler had expanded across and occupied much of Europe.

## American Action and Inaction

As tensions in Europe increased, Congress passed neutrality acts in 1935, 1936, and 1937 forbidding the trade of munitions with any belligerent nation. An officially neutral stance, however, did not stop certain American industries from pursuing business opportunities abroad, nor did it produce a politically neutral effect. For example, when Italy invaded Ethiopia in 1935 the United States agreed to a League of Nations embargo on arms, ammunition, and implements of war; however, America increased its exports to Italy of scrap metal, scrap iron, and oil. While technically not in violation of the embargo, the American exports had obvious military uses.

President Franklin D. Roosevelt, who had been re-elected in a landslide victory in 1936, was torn as to how America should respond to events in Europe. He did not want war, but he was opposed to the spread of fascism. In 1937 Roosevelt had voiced his concern that "the epidemic of world lawlessness is spreading." He spoke approvingly of containing the epidemic by means of "quarantine," and repeated his commitment to pursuing "a policy of peace" and adopting "every practicable measure to avoid involvement in war." Despite repeated assurances from Hitler that Germany was not interested in war, Roosevelt suspected that war in Europe was inevitable. On Roosevelt's orders, the US military quietly began a rearmament program.

| The Presidents: 1941–1960 | | |
|---|---|---|
| **Franklin D. Roosevelt** | Democratic | March 4, 1933 – April 12, 1945 |
| **Harry S. Truman** | Democratic | April 12, 1945 – January 20, 1953 |
| **Dwight D. Eisenhower** | Republican | January 20, 1953 – January 20, 1961 |

## War in Europe Begins

On September 1, 1939 Germany attacked Poland. Two days later Britain and France—which had mutual defence treaties with Poland—declared war; Canada entered the war seven days later. In the spring of 1940 the German army and air force devastated western Europe, defeating Denmark, Norway, Holland, Belgium, Luxembourg, and France.

By the summer of 1940 Britain and the **Commonwealth** countries, including Canada, stood alone against Germany and Italy; all summer long Britain's civilian population endured nightly bombing raids. In an air war known as the Battle of Britain, which raged between the British Royal Air Force and the German Luftwaffe (air force), German forces bombed London and other British cities mercilessly. This campaign, known as the Blitz, reduced many British cities to rubble. By the fall of 1940, however, Britain rallied and was able to repel the German air attack, thus eliminating Hitler's opportunity to invade the island by sea.

When Hitler was unsuccessful in defeating Britain, he turned his attention to the Soviet Union. Ignoring the pact he had signed with Stalin in 1939, in June 1941 Hitler invaded the Soviet Union in a campaign called Operation Barbarossa. The ruthless dictator Joseph Stalin was now an ally of Britain in the war against Germany; he soon became known as "Uncle Joe" in the Western media.

In the spring of 1940 Germany built the Auschwitz concentration camp in occupied Poland. By the end of 1940 the Nazis created the Warsaw ghetto, which **segregated** Jews from the rest of the population in cramped living conditions; more than 13,000 Jews died of starvation in the ghetto in the first six months of 1941. In 1941 Hitler began to focus on how to eliminate Jews from Europe—a scheme he called his "final solution"—and by 1942 systematic murder began in Nazi death and concentration camps.

## America Offers Trade and Aid

With the fall of western Europe to the Nazis, Roosevelt's view of the war began to shift. Clearly, the United States supported the aims and principles of Europe's democratic countries and opposed Nazi aggression. Although still unwilling to send troops, Roosevelt contributed 50 old American **destroyers** to Britain's war effort; in exchange, he demanded that British leader Winston Churchill provide the United States with 99-year leases on land to be used for American military bases in the Caribbean and Newfoundland. Roosevelt knew that in the postwar world these bases would provide the United States with strategic power positions.

In September 1940 Congress passed its first peacetime draft, the Selective Training and Service Act. The Act increased the size of the American army to over one million soldiers, with almost as many in reserve. Neutrality, however, remained official American policy. Roosevelt faced significant opposition in Congress, where isolationist voices were strong.

**Figure 11.4** The war in Europe and North Africa.

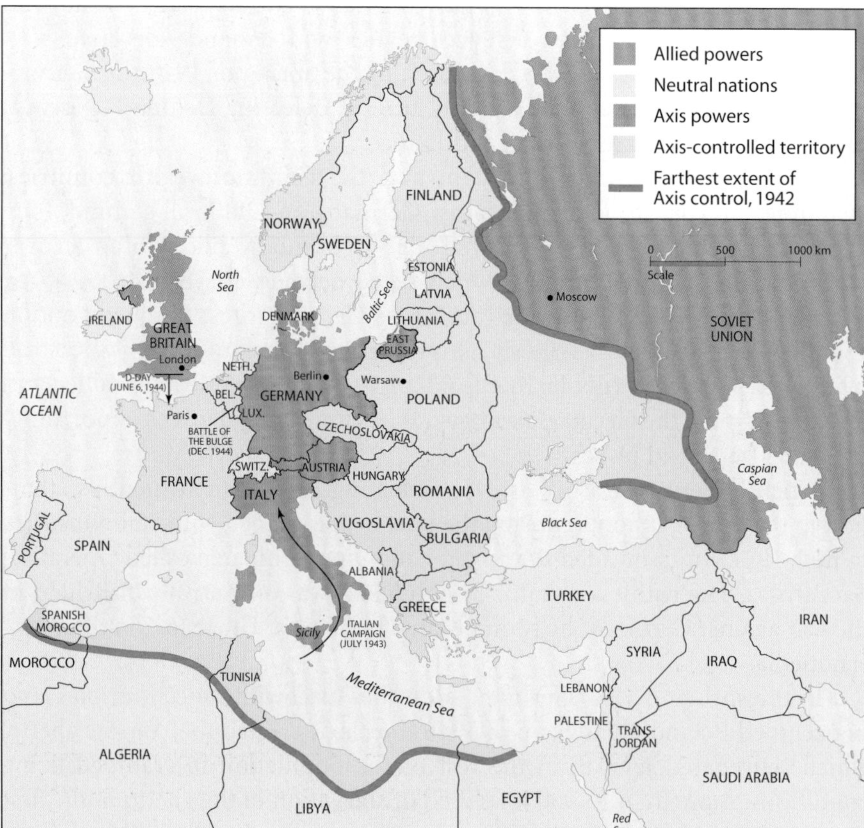

In the 1940 presidential election Roosevelt won an unprecedented third term in office on the promise that America would not enter the war. Shortly after the election, Roosevelt began to increase support for the **Allies**. By 1940, however, Britain's economy faced ruin. Bombed relentlessly and dependent on a Commonwealth and foreign-aid lifeline that was threatened by German submarines in the Atlantic, Britain endured its darkest period both militarily and economically.

Roosevelt proposed the Lend-Lease Act, under which America would lend Britain military supplies and Britain would pay America back at the end of the war. The Lend-Lease Act moved quickly through Congress, and by March 1941 supplies worth billions of dollars were heading to Britain. Shortly after Germany invaded the Soviet Union, the United States offered lend-leases to the Soviets as well.

In July 1941 Roosevelt and British Prime Minister Winston Churchill met in Argentia Bay, Newfoundland, where they drafted the Atlantic Charter. The document was both a statement of war aims—"the final destruction of the Nazi tyranny"—and a vision of a postwar world in which all nations would have the right to self-determination. The charter expressed the possibility that nations could govern their interactions through democratic processes rather than through military alliances, and advocated for an international organization to arbitrate disputes.

Even as the Allies fought against Hitler and racist Nazi policy in Europe, racial and ethnic discrimination continued in the United States. Rather than relax its immigration policies to assist the victims of Nazi persecution, the American State Department tightened its admission requirements. Otto Frank, the father of Anne Frank (the German Jewish teenager whose diary, published in 1947, recounts her family's experiences while living in hiding during the Nazi occupation of Amsterdam), was among the many who were unable to secure visas despite desperate and persistent attempts beginning in 1941. In 1943, 400 rabbis marched to the US Capitol to draw attention to the suffering in Europe; they were met by a mere handful of politicians.

## CHECK YOUR UNDERSTANDING

1. What was the purpose of the non-aggression pact between Germany and the Soviet Union?
2. Describe the *St. Louis* incident.
3. How did the United States help Britain after the war began?
4. What was the purpose of the Atlantic Charter?

## America Enters the War

The formation of the German–Italian–Japanese alliance in the fall of 1940 alarmed America, whose relationship with Japan was already tense. Japan's pursuit of an expansionist policy during the 1930s had threatened American economic interests in Asia. In 1931 Japan had invaded Manchuria, a northern region of China, and in 1937 it had invaded China itself, but neither the League of Nations nor the United States had acted decisively. In any case, Japan had quit the League in 1931.

By 1940 America was Japan's chief supplier of oil and scrap metal. Roosevelt attempted to dissuade Japan from participating in an alliance with Germany and Italy by placing an embargo on these commodities, but it was widely recognized in Washington that such an embargo increased the risk of war.

In July 1941 Japan occupied French Indochina (modern Cambodia, Laos, and Vietnam). America froze all Japanese assets and placed a total embargo on the country. Negotiations continued through the fall of 1941, with both sides demanding that the other abandon China and Indochina. (The US had already established a presence in China and Indochina prior to World War II.) Neither Japan nor America was willing to make any concessions. Representatives met in Washington in late November without success.

On December 7, 1941 Japan launched a surprise attack on the American naval base at Pearl Harbor, Hawaii, where most of the Pacific fleet was housed. This incident was part of a larger offensive in which Japan attacked Hong Kong, Malaysia, Thailand, and Singapore, as well as a number of strategic Pacific islands including Guam and Wake. The American government had suspected that Japan was planning to attack American territory but was unaware of the intended time or place.

Learn more about the attack on Pearl Harbor by visiting www.emp.ca/ah.

The assault on Pearl Harbor lasted two hours and resulted in the deaths of 2,400 Americans. Twenty-one ships were sunk or badly damaged, and 150 planes were destroyed. The Japanese lost fewer than 100 pilots and 30 planes. Roosevelt referred to December 7, 1941 as a "date which will live in infamy." Fortunately, American aircraft carriers were not in harbour on December 7, so they were ready for immediate military use. Moreover, the Americans were able to repair 18 of the 21 ships and use them in the war.

**Figure 11.5** Pearl Harbor, December 7, 1941. Isoroku Yamamoto, the Japanese admiral who had planned the attack, said: "I'm afraid we have awakened a sleeping giant and filled it with terrible resolve." What did he mean?

On December 8 the United States declared war on Japan, as did Britain. Due to an earlier Japanese–German alliance, America was also at war with Germany, and was now fully involved in World War II.

## Americans at War in Europe

Once the United States entered the war, American troops fought both in Europe and in the Pacific. The United States contributed soldiers, ships, tanks, and planes to the Allied war effort. Americans conducted daily bombing raids over Germany and over occupied France. In order to penetrate Europe, Allied leaders decided that the best strategy was to gain control of North Africa and, as Churchill stated, expose Europe's "soft underbelly" (Italy). In North Africa America bolstered the British forces led by General Bernard Montgomery with tanks and personnel under the direction of generals Dwight D. Eisenhower and George Patton. By the spring of 1943 the German Afrika Korps in North Africa had been defeated.

In July 1943 the Italian campaign began. American, British, and Canadian troops invaded Italy. By the end of that month, Mussolini had been overthrown and the local population welcomed the Allied troops. Hitler, however, hastily moved troops into Italy. The Allies advanced but the fighting was bloody and fierce. The German soldiers knew that the fall of Italy would hasten an Allied invasion of Europe and provide the Allies with further air bases from which to strike at Germany. They defended their position from fortified lines and refused to surrender to the combined British, American, and Canadian forces. Eventually, however, they were forced to retreat northward; the Allies liberated Italy by the end of 1944.

On the eastern front, the Soviets were on the offensive by the spring of 1943, fighting their way into Poland and reaching the Balkans by the fall of 1944. The war also intensified on the western front after the Allies landed in Normandy, France on June 6, 1944 (popularly known as D-Day). In a last, desperate attempt to arrest the Allies' offensive, German soldiers waged the Battle of the Bulge in Belgium in December of 1944.

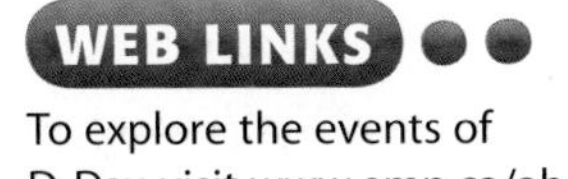


To explore the events of D-Day, visit www.emp.ca/ah.

Throughout the fall and winter of 1944–45 Allied forces liberated occupied Italy, France, Belgium, the Netherlands, and Luxembourg. Finally, in March 1945, Allied troops entered Germany.

**Figure 11.6** On D-Day, American General Dwight D. Eisenhower led 176,000 American, British, and Canadian troops across the English Channel to the beaches of Normandy, France in an assault known as Operation Overlord. This operation marked the beginning of the final phase in the liberation of Europe from Nazi occupation. Why was it a key event of the war?

**Figure 11.7** In response to an order from American General George Patton, US troops rounded up 2,000 German citizens to witness the horrors uncovered at Buchenwald labour camp in 1945. This photograph by Margaret Bourke-White depicts some of the many who could not look.

There, in April, they met Soviet forces, which had invaded Germany in 1944. Hitler committed suicide in his underground bunker at the end of April, and on May 7, 1945 Germany surrendered. The war in Europe was over. Over 40 million people had died; countless others had been injured, and the European countryside had been ravaged by war. As Allied troops entered Germany and Poland, the extent of Nazi atrocities in death and forced-labour camps became apparent to the world: 12 million people—6 million of whom were Jewish—had perished in camps such as Auschwitz, Dachau, and Buchenwald.

## Americans at War in the Pacific

By the spring of 1942 Japan was in control of the Pacific basin. Intensely loyal to Japanese Emperor Hirohito, the army pursued a ruthless and efficient military campaign. Japanese forces drove the Americans out of the Philippines, where they had been maintaining bases since the Spanish-American War, and threatened Australia. In air, land, and sea attacks Japan conquered Thailand, Guam, Wake Island, Hong Kong, the Philippines, Burma, and Singapore. Military success was sometimes followed by the brutal treatment of prisoners of war. In Hong Kong, for example, Japanese soldiers subjected Canadian prisoners of war to such abuses that many died.

Japanese domination did not last. After recovering from the shock of Pearl Harbor, America quickly rebuilt its military capacity and engaged Japan in a series of battles that raged across the Pacific. In May and June 1942 the United States prevailed in two strategically significant conflicts: the Battle of Coral Sea and the Battle of Midway. America's use of aircraft carriers and planes in the Battle of Coral Sea changed the nature of naval warfare in the

Pacific. The Battle of Midway marked the beginning of US military ascendancy and demonstrated the success of the US decision to combine air and sea power in an effort to unseat Japan from its strategic position.

The American strategy in the Pacific was called "island hopping." The US command focused on wresting from the Japanese only those islands that it considered vital, "hopping" over the ones that it considered less important. This strategy allowed the Americans to concentrate their resources in areas where they could achieve the greatest military advantage. It also moved them, step by step, closer to the Japanese home islands, allowed them to establish important supply lines across the Pacific, and gave them air bases closer to Japan that they could use for bombing raids. Between August 1942 and February 1943 US forces fought and won a brutal battle for the control of Guadalcanal. In 1944, after the deaths of many more American and Japanese soldiers, the Americans gained control of Guam. By 1945 they controlled the Philippines.

From Guam, the Americans launched a firebombing campaign against Japan itself. The firebombing of Tokyo on March 10, 1945 alone killed 130,000 people. General Curtis E. LeMay, who directed the campaign, stated that the United States "had two or three weeks of work left on the cities, a bit more to do on precision targets, and were just getting started on transportation. Another six months and Japan would have been beaten back into the dark ages." Author and military historian Martin Caidin estimated that in the six months of firebombing, "civilian casualties were more than twice as great as [the] total Japanese military casualties in forty-five months of war."

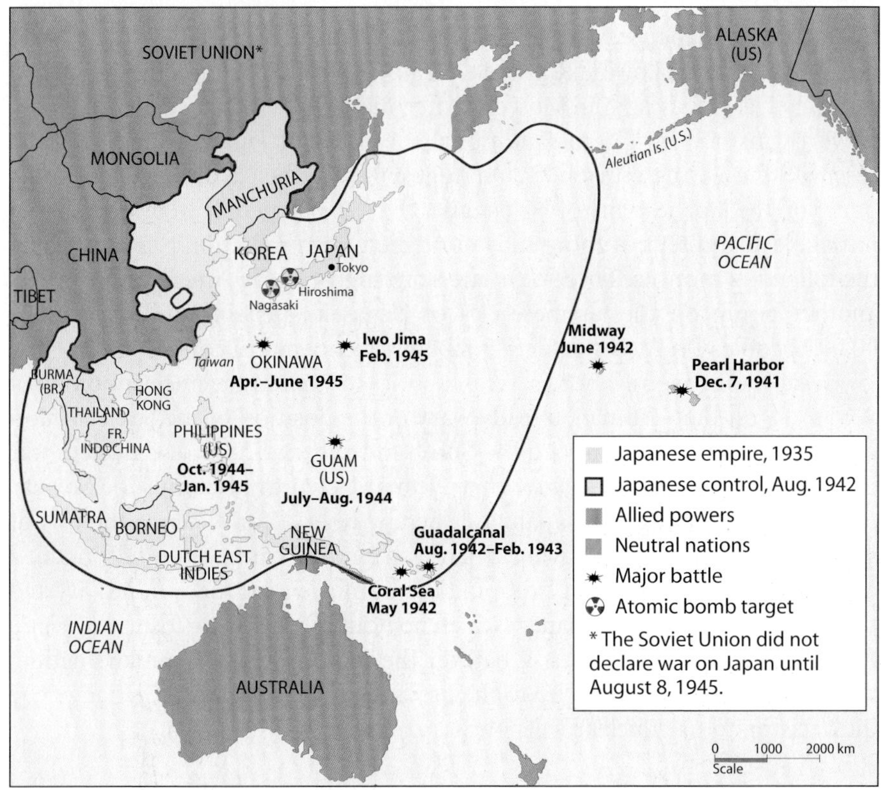


**Figure 11.8**
The war in the Pacific.

**Figure 11.9** The raising of the American flag over Mount Suribachi, on Iwo Jima. This image won the Pulitzer Prize and represented, for many Americans, the sacrifices made by ordinary soldiers during the war in the Pacific. What elements of the photograph make it visually effective?

In the spring of 1945 the Americans captured Iwo Jima and Okinawa, two islands considered part of the Japanese home islands. The soldiers who defended them fought to the death, and many chose suicide over capture by the Americans. Of the approximately 22,000 Japanese troops who defended Iwo Jima, fewer than 1,000 survived. American casualties in these battles were also very high, which proved to some American military leaders that an invasion of Japan itself would result in untold casualties. The closer American soldiers came to the Japanese home islands, the fiercer the fighting became. Throughout the war, **kamikaze** pilots had flown planes loaded with explosives into American ships, but in the spring of 1945 kamikaze attacks became frequent occurrences. Rumours circulated that Japanese civilians were being trained to counteract an **amphibious** invasion such as the one Eisenhower had led in Normandy. The US needed a new strategy.

## Dawn of the Nuclear Age

By August 1945 Japan was in a hopeless military position. Harry S. Truman, who became president following Roosevelt's death in April 1945, knew that Japan had instructed its ambassador in Moscow to negotiate peace with the Allies. Truman, however, insisted on the unconditional surrender of Japan, as had been the case with the German surrender. On August 6, 1945 the US dropped an atomic bomb on the Japanese city of Hiroshima. Over 70,000 people were killed in the initial blast, and tens of thousands more died from radiation poisoning over the following months. Three days later, on August 9, the Americans dropped another bomb on the Japanese city of Nagasaki, instantly killing another 40,000 people. On August 14, 1945 Japan surrendered unconditionally.

Historians have advanced several theories to explain the nuclear bombing. Some suggest that Truman, already wary of the position of the Soviet Union in the postwar world, dropped the bomb to frighten Stalin, and declare war on communism. Others suggest that Truman acted to pre-empt the Soviets' entry into the war against Japan and thereby reserve for America the role of sole occupying power following Japan's surrender. Truman himself justified his decision by arguing that dropping the bombs ended the war and averted the need for an invasion of Japan, which no doubt would have cost many more American and Japanese lives. Whatever the reason behind Truman's action, international affairs—right up to the present—were dramatically changed by the decision to use nuclear weapons.

## Wartime America

Because Americans fought World War II overseas, America's ability to produce munitions and supplies was unimpeded by bombings and ground fighting. Accordingly, during the war years an intensely profitable relationship developed between business and the military. Wartime production also brought about various social changes that affected the lives of many ordinary Americans.

### Business, Government, and the Wartime Economy

The implementation of the New Deal in the 1930s had centralized and strengthened the American federal government, and this centralization proved essential in organizing wartime production. Roosevelt established the War Production Board to coordinate food and labour, and to mobilize American industry to keep goods flowing steadily to Europe. Gasoline was rationed, as were other essential products and certain foods, such as eggs and flour. Scrap metal, rubber, paper, and other materials that could be of military use were collected. Production of bicycles, typewriters, and other goods that had no military use was restricted or prohibited in favour of production of arms and other instruments of war. To finance the war, the federal government raised taxes and sold **war bonds** similar to those sold in Canada.

Government spending grew from \$13.3 billion in 1941 (about \$191 billion today) to \$98.4 billion in 1945 (about \$1.2 trillion today). In 1943 alone the United States spent \$37.5 billion (about \$460 billion in current dollars) on armaments. Detroit, which shifted from automobile production to the manufacture of arms, became known as "the arsenal of democracy." Enormous production costs meant that only a small number of large corporations could compete for government contracts. As a result, wealth became concentrated in these few companies.

During the war, oil became a primary concern for the United States. The war required oil both for factories producing munitions and for the planes, trucks, and tanks used by the Allies. Countries such as Saudi Arabia—traditionally under the British sphere of influence—were wooed by American diplomats and businessmen as Britain's influence declined. Roosevelt was not just concerned with oil production during the war; he was also preparing for America's postwar role in the oil-rich Middle East.

The high employment rates of wartime America were a welcome change after the economic devastation of the Depression. However, government-controlled

**Figure 11.10** Despite all the many New Deal programs, it was World War II that finally pulled the United States out of the Depression, largely by eliminating unemployment.

**SOUND BITE**

"As things are now going, the peace we will make, the peace we seem to be making, will be a peace of oil, a peace of gold, a peace of shipping, a peace … without moral purpose or human interest."

—Archibald MacLeish, poet and Assistant Secretary of State

wages did not keep up with rising costs, and workers frequently went on strike to rectify the imbalance. Despite the generally patriotic atmosphere of wartime America, 6,770,000 workers were involved in an unprecedented 14,000 strikes.

## The War and Minorities

Many African-Americans remained relatively indifferent to lofty statements about the spreading of democracy and the liberation of subjugated people abroad. The American army was segregated—that is, black and white Americans fought in separate units—and black soldiers served under the command of white officers. Pressure from the National Association for the Advancement of Colored People (NAACP), however, resulted in the creation of an all-black squadron known as the Tuskegee Airmen. African-American soldiers were forced to bear many humiliations during World War II, such as the segregation of black blood plasma and being refused service even in restaurants that served German prisoners of war. The American army was not officially desegregated until 1948.

The war did provide some new job opportunities, as the demand for labour forced many companies outside of the South to hire new workers. However, the influx of thousands of African-Americans into the factories of industrial America created controversy. For example, police were called in when protesters in Detroit tried to prevent the newcomers from moving into public housing. Growing resentment of discrimination on the part of African-American labour leaders prompted Roosevelt to create the Fair Employment Practices Commission to promote minority hiring. Segregation continued in the South, however, and the commission did little to ease racial tensions.

Blacks were not the only ethnic group to face discrimination during the war. Americans of Italian and German descent were harassed, and suffered discrimination when seeking employment and housing. People of Japanese ancestry, however, endured particularly harsh treatment. In February 1942 Roosevelt authorized the **internment** of 120,000 men, women, and children of Japanese origin.

**WEB LINKS**

Learn about the internment of Japanese Americans and their later fight for redress by visiting www.emp.ca/ah.

**Figure 11.11** The Tuskegee Airmen flew over 15,000 missions. They sank a German destroyer and received 150 Distinguished Flying Crosses, yet 103 of them were arrested for entering the officers' club at Freeman Airfield in Indiana.

# PAST VOICES

## Internment of People of Japanese Origin

**Figure 11.12** The War Relocation Authority of the US army hired Dorothea Lange to photograph the internment of Japanese Americans during World War II. Most of her photographs were suppressed by US authorities.

On February 19, 1942 Roosevelt signed Executive Order 9066, which resulted in the forcible internment of 120,000 people of Japanese ancestry. On February 24, 1942 the Canadian government also relocated and interned more than 22,000 Japanese Canadians from the west coast, especially fishermen who they felt might be giving strategic information to the Japanese navy or acting as spies.

Like the Japanese Canadians who were placed in internment camps in the interior of British Columbia during the same period, more than two-thirds of those interned in the United States were native citizens and had never shown any disloyalty. Many Americans agreed with the internment, however, out of fear that the war might spread to the American continent.

In *Nisei Daughter*, Monica Itoi Sone offers some reflections about life in Camp Harmony, where she and her family—known as Family #10710—were interned in April 1942.

As the bus carrying the Itoi family arrived at Puyallup, Washington, someone commented, "Just look at those chicken houses. They sure go in for poultry in a big way here." The oversized chicken farm was the internment camp. The Itoi family's new home was a 5.5- by 6-metre room, with one small window; it was completely bare except for a tiny wood-burning stove and dandelions pushing their way up through cracks in the dirt floor.

When visitors arrived, they met the residents in a reception room just inside the wire gates. It was difficult for both residents and visitors. As a family friend left after visiting Monica's father, he glanced at the high wire fence and shook his head: "I don't like it, to see you in here. I don't understand it. I know you all my life. You're my friend."

Hope was sometimes in short supply, and many found solace in religion. One Sunday, the Reverend Everett Thompson asked the camp congregation to read parts of the Book of Psalms in unison. Monica remembers:

> We had begun to read more slowly and conscientiously as if we were finding new meaning and comfort from the Bible ... As we finished with the lines ... the room seemed filled with peace and awe, as if walls had been pushed back and we were free. I was convinced that this was not the end of our lives here in camp, but just the beginning; and gradually it dawned on me that we had not been physically mistreated nor would we be harmed in the future. I knew that the greatest trial ahead of us would be of a spiritual nature. I had been tense and angry all my life about prejudice, real and imaginary. The evacuation had been the biggest blow, but there was little to be gained in bitterness and cynicism ... The time had come to examine our own souls ... and help to build that way of life which we so desired.

These words were written by a woman whose mother's Bible had been confiscated because it was printed in Japanese, and whose father had been deprived of the few tools he had used to make furniture for their one-room apartment because they were contraband.

In 1945, at the end of the internment, the Itois returned to their home in Seattle.

### Think It Through

1. How do you know that the Itois were part of American society and culture before their internment?
2. What lessons can be learned from their internment?

## War Resisters

Although patriotic sentiment in white America was generally high, not everyone approved of the war; indeed, there were groups who strongly vocalized their opposition. **Conscientious objectors** accounted for only 43,000 of America's 10 million draftees, but that was three times the number who had refused military service in World War I. The Socialist Workers Party was unequivocally opposed to the war, while the Women's International League for Peace and Freedom argued that "war between nations or classes or races cannot permanently settle conflicts or heal the wounds that brought them into being."

## War and American Women

**Figure 11.13** Rosie the Riveter was a propaganda symbol designed to promote women's participation in wartime production. She appeared in many different forms and contexts. What image and message does this Rosie convey?

The transformative effect of the war on American life produced much temporary—but little permanent—change for women. Images such as those of Rosie the Riveter depicted the wartime role of many women who took jobs traditionally considered to be within the exclusive domain of men. With so many American men serving in the armed forces, women became not only factory workers but also bus, taxi, and truck drivers, train conductors, and ship and construction workers. Literally millions of women broke new ground, both in terms of employment and status during the war.

Perhaps the most obvious way in which women changed their status was through military participation, either in the Women's Army Corps (WAC)—where over 150,000 women served—or in other military positions, such as nursing. Non-traditional military jobs, however, were restricted in many ways. Women were expected to "act as women," according to the standards of the day. WACs, for example, were at first outfitted in skirts—hardly effective military dress for people performing rigorous physical work. Unlike their male counterparts, women were not allowed to serve overseas. And women in the military, like women in non-traditional civilian jobs, were expected to return to sex-segregated employment once the war ended. This gender discrimination was to last for much of the period that followed: the Cold War.

**Figure 11.14** Women in the Women's Army Corps relax in their quarters.

## CHECK YOUR UNDERSTANDING

1. Why did the US government seize Japanese assets and embargo all trade with Japan?
2. What facts support the argument that the Japanese attack on Pearl Harbor was a failure?
3. How did African-Americans contribute to the war effort?
4. What was the purpose of wartime propaganda?
5. What caused 14,000 strikes during wartime?

# THE COLD WAR

Once Germany and Japan surrendered and World War II ended, an uneasy peace settled over the world. The term "Cold War" was popularized by American journalist Walter Lippman to describe the 40-year conflict between the United States and the Soviet Union that followed the open warfare of World War II. Although the Cold War sometimes became "hot" and involved bloodshed (as it did in Korea), the United States and the Soviet Union never actually declared war against each other. For the **superpowers**, the Cold War represented a struggle for global control between communism and capitalism.

As the close relationship between business and the military continued, the wartime economy of World War II evolved into the wartime economy of the Cold War. This phenomenon, known as the **military-industrial complex**, provided massive profits for American munitions makers. The Soviet Union, which established satellite states and supported communist leaders in eastern Europe, also spent billions of dollars in its battle against the West.

**WEB LINKS** 

For an in-depth look at the events and personalities of the Cold War, visit www.emp.ca/ah.

## The Postwar World

Even before the end of the war, the United States was beginning to distrust the intentions of its wartime ally, Stalin. The US was already preparing for a struggle against the Soviet Union.

### Yalta

In February 1945 Churchill, Roosevelt, and Stalin met at Yalta, on the Crimean peninsula (Ukraine), to discuss their vision of the postwar world. Neither Roosevelt nor Churchill trusted Stalin, and their strategy was to use the meeting to limit postwar Soviet power. Both Churchill and Roosevelt wanted to preserve democracy in Europe, and Roosevelt needed Soviet support against Japan because the war in the Pacific was still raging. Stalin wanted a buffer zone in eastern Europe that would protect the Soviet Union from the West.

In partial exchange for help against Japan, Roosevelt and Churchill granted Stalin his buffer zone. Much of eastern Europe would remain under

**Figure 11.15** Seated from left to right, Churchill, Roosevelt, and Stalin pose for photographers at Yalta.

Soviet control, as Soviet regimes were established in countries such as Poland, Hungary, Bulgaria, Estonia, Latvia, and Lithuania. The three leaders also decided to divide postwar Germany into four zones, each occupied by either the United States, the Soviet Union, Britain, or France. Berlin, Germany's capital, would also be divided into four zones—even though the city lay in what would become the Soviet zone and, eventually, East Germany.

## Creation of the United Nations

To ensure a stable postwar world, Roosevelt supported the movement to create a new body for international cooperation, the **United Nations (UN)**. It was crucial to his plan that the institution be dominated by Western powers—that is, the United States, Britain, and France—but it was also important that the Soviet Union be included. At Yalta, Stalin had agreed to membership in the United Nations in order to obtain his buffer zone in eastern Europe.

In June 1945 further meetings in San Francisco established the Charter of the United Nations, which sought "to save succeeding generations from the scourge of war, to reaffirm faith in fundamental human rights, in the dignity and worth of the human person, in the equal rights of men and women and of nations large and small." According to the Charter, member states were "to practice tolerance and live together in peace with one another as good neighbours, and to unite [their] strength to maintain international peace and security." In the event of aggressive action by any nation, the Charter authorized member states to vote for one of three options: condemnation of the aggressor, imposition of economic sanctions against it, or military intervention. Unlike it had after World War I with the League of Nations, the United States did not hesitate to join the United Nations. In July 1945 the US became the UN's first member country, officially confirming its internationalist and interventionist policy.

The five permanent members of the United Nations Security Council—the United States, the Soviet Union, Britain, France, and China—constitute the main decision-making body, and each country has the right to veto any Security Council decision that goes against its interests. The Security Council, with its five permanent and ten temporary members, differs from the General Assembly of the United Nations in that it makes policy on all security matters, such as war. The General Assembly, on the other hand, is the largest body of the United Nations, and makes general policies.

In 1948 the United Nations adopted and proclaimed the Universal Declaration of Human Rights, a document which affirms that "recognition of the inherent dignity and of the equal and inalienable rights of all members of the human family is the foundation of freedom, justice and peace in the world." Eleanor Roosevelt, wartime First Lady of the United States, chaired the committee that drafted the declaration.

## The Soviet Union's Position after the War

During World War II, 20 million Soviets died. The Soviet countryside and cities were ravaged by the German invasion, and the economy fell into ruins. Reclamation of industrial and military strength was the Soviet Union's chief goal after the war. The United States was wary of the Soviet Union's increased influence in eastern Europe as well as of its atomic ambitions. The Soviets would soon isolate countries in their sphere of influence from the West.

## The Iron Curtain

Although Stalin had promised at Yalta to try to establish democracies in eastern Europe, he soon set up communist governments in territories under Soviet control. In some countries, such as Poland, communist governments were brought to power in elections conducted under the close watch of the Soviet military. In other countries, such as Albania, communist governments came to power in unopposed elections. Eastern Europe's communist countries became known in the West as "Soviet satellite nations."

In March 1946 Churchill made a speech in the United States warning that "From Stettin in the Baltic to Trieste in the Adriatic an **iron curtain** has descended across the Continent. Behind that line lie all the capitals of the ancient states of Central and Eastern Europe." The American government came to view all communist activity—even independent revolutionary movements—as examples of Soviet expansionism.

# WE THE PEOPLE 1884–1962
## *Eleanor Roosevelt*

Throughout her life, Eleanor Roosevelt worked to achieve social and political equality for all people. Through her efforts to instill self-respect in the forgotten classes of America, she personified the progressive ideals of the early 20th century. In 1945 she carried her beliefs onto the international stage by accepting an appointment as a delegate to the United Nations.

Eleanor Roosevelt was soon elected chair of the United Nations' Commission on Human Rights. There, she deliberated with the representatives of many nations and sought consensus for the words that would express their mutually held beliefs. Her work was instrumental in bringing about the Universal Declaration of Human Rights. In "In Your Hands," a speech delivered in 1958, she expressed her ideas about the origin and evolution of these rights:

> Where, after all, do universal human rights begin? In small places, close to home—so close and so small that they cannot be seen on any map of the world. Yet they *are* the world of the individual person: the neighborhood he lives in; the school or college he attends; the factory, farm or office where he works. Such are the places where every man, woman, and child seeks equal justice, equal opportunity, equal dignity without discrimination. Unless these rights have meaning there, they have little meaning anywhere. Without concerted citizen action to uphold them close to home, we shall look in vain for progress in the larger world.

A natural diplomat, Roosevelt had a talent for quieting occasional outbursts from fellow delegates. A *New York Times* reporter observed that "The Russians seem to have met their match in Mrs. Roosevelt. The proceedings sometimes turn into a long vitriolic attack on the US when she is not present. These attacks, however, generally denigrate into flurries in the face of her calm and undisturbed but often pointed replies."

Although born into the upper classes and a niece of Theodore Roosevelt, Eleanor was sensitive to the plight of people who did not share her privileges. Her childhood was troubled, as were aspects of her marriage to her sixth cousin Franklin Delano Roosevelt, the future president. During World War I, Eleanor immersed herself in public service as an official of the Red Cross. During the 1920s she became active in the League of Women Voters, the Women's Trade Union, and the Democratic Party. She used her considerable energy to tackle such issues as child labour, maternity rights, equitable pay, and women's education. In 1928 she served as the head of the women's division of the Democratic Party, organizing efforts to support social legislation.

**Figure 11.16** Eleanor Roosevelt believed that her work in forging the Universal Declaration of Human Rights was her greatest achievement.

After her husband was elected president, Eleanor Roosevelt travelled the country, listening to the concerns of the American people and serving as her husband's "eyes and ears." She also wrote a daily syndicated column called "My Day," which she continued throughout her life. She served at the United Nations until 1952, when she resigned after Eisenhower's election. She was reappointed by John F. Kennedy in 1961, and remained active in the Democratic Party until her death in 1962.

### Think It Through

1. How did Eleanor Roosevelt envision the role of the United Nations in global politics?
2. How did her career in the United States prepare her for her role at the United Nations?

# The Cold War Begins

Truman believed that the sort of economic decline that occurred in western Europe after World War I would provide an opportunity for communism to gain a foothold there. Accordingly, the United States took action to ensure that Europe would recover quickly from the devastation of war.

## The Truman Doctrine

Truman's policy for dealing with communism was containment—that is, refusing to allow communism to spread by supporting anti-communist movements around the world in an attempt to hinder Soviet influence.

In 1946 the United States supported Turkey against Soviet demands for control over the straits between the Black Sea and the Mediterranean. In 1947 Britain told the United States that it could no longer afford to support the government of Greece, where a civil war raged between the right-wing government and communist **insurgents**. Truman responded with a speech to Congress that has become known as the Truman Doctrine. In the speech, he stated that the United States must be "willing to help free peoples to maintain their free institutions and their national integrity against aggressive movements that seek to impose upon them totalitarian regimes." Believing that if Greece and Turkey did not receive US help they would fall to communism, Congress voted to provide \$400 million (about \$3.8 billion today) in military and economic aid.

## The Marshall Plan

In accordance with the Truman Doctrine and to ensure postwar stability, American Secretary of State George C. Marshall formulated a program composed of loans and aid to rebuild European countries and their economies. The United States offered the program to the Soviet Union and its satellites as well. While communist countries—under the close watch of the **Kremlin**—rejected it, Austria, Belgium, Denmark, France, Greece, Iceland, Ireland, Italy, Luxembourg, the Netherlands, Norway, Portugal, Sweden, Switzerland, Turkey, West Germany, and Britain accepted funds from the program, which became known as the Marshall Plan.

The United States advanced over \$13 billion (about \$123 billion in current dollars) in loans. These funds relieved widespread poverty and starvation, and assisted European countries in moving into two decades of unprecedented economic growth. The funds also

**Figure 11.17** Funds from the Marshall Plan financed the repair of West Berlin's largest concert hall and cultural centre, the Titania Palace, in 1950.

increased many Europeans' standard of living and helped bring social and political stability to many countries. The United States benefited as well, since European countries used the borrowed funds principally to buy American products.

Economic influence gave rise to American political influence in Europe. Of particular concern to the United States was the rise of communist parties in both France and Italy. In France, for example, the Communist Party had the support of approximately one-quarter of the population, but the infusion of American capital swayed the French people away from the utopian appeal of communism. The Marshall Plan undoubtedly helped weaken communism in western Europe; it also fuelled the ever-growing tensions between the two superpowers.

## Growing Tensions

During this period, activity in Berlin was also of concern. While the original plan at Yalta involved the division and occupation of Berlin by the four major powers, the talks by France, Britain, and the United States to merge their sections of Germany into one country prompted the Soviets to respond in protest. The Soviets felt that a rebuilt Germany, supported by the West, was a threat because Germany had twice before invaded their territory. As a result, in June 1948 the Soviets cut off land access to the West German part of Berlin, deep within East Germany. For over ten months, the United States and Britain airlifted supplies into the city. In May 1949 the Soviets—seeing the failure of their efforts to isolate West Berlin and not wishing to provoke further conflict—lifted their blockade.

Relief in the West, however, was short-lived. In August 1949 the Soviets detonated an atomic bomb for the first time. The world now had two atomic superpowers, and the **arms race** began. Over the next 40 years the United States and the Soviet Union would spend billions of dollars building their nuclear arsenals and developing new military technologies.

While America focused on containing communism in Europe, a communist government came to power in China in 1949 after a peasant army led by Mao Zedong defeated the right-wing forces of Chiang Kai-shek. Mao pushed Chiang out of mainland China onto the island of Taiwan. The United States continued to recognize Chiang as the Chinese leader and blocked any effort by Mao to gain a seat at the United Nations. In response, the Soviet Union walked out of the Security Council.

The postwar era also witnessed an upsurge of people around the world who sought independence from colonial rulers: the French in Indochina (Vietnam), the Dutch in Indonesia, and the Americans in the Philippines. Some of these independence movements, such as the one in Vietnam, were led by communists. From a US point of view, independence movements were worrisome because they created unstable political and economic conditions that encouraged the growth of communism. In 1946 the United States consented to Philippine independence on the condition that it be allowed to retain American naval and air force bases there.

# Cold War Alliances

The division between the communist and non-communist worlds, figuratively defined by Churchill's "Iron Curtain," became formalized with the establishment of Cold War alliances.

## NATO and the Warsaw Pact

A formal Western alliance was established in 1949 with the creation of the North Atlantic Treaty Organization (NATO). NATO, whose membership included both Canada and the United States, was based on the idea of collective security: if one member nation were attacked, the other member nations would defend it. By 1955 the Soviet Union and its satellites had developed their own alliance, known as the Warsaw Pact.

Eastern and Western factions were now firmly entrenched and the Cold War was in full swing. Hesitant to engage in war with one another (knowing too well the devastating consequences), the superpowers instead fought a series of **proxy wars**.

**Figure 11.18** Cold War Europe in 1955.

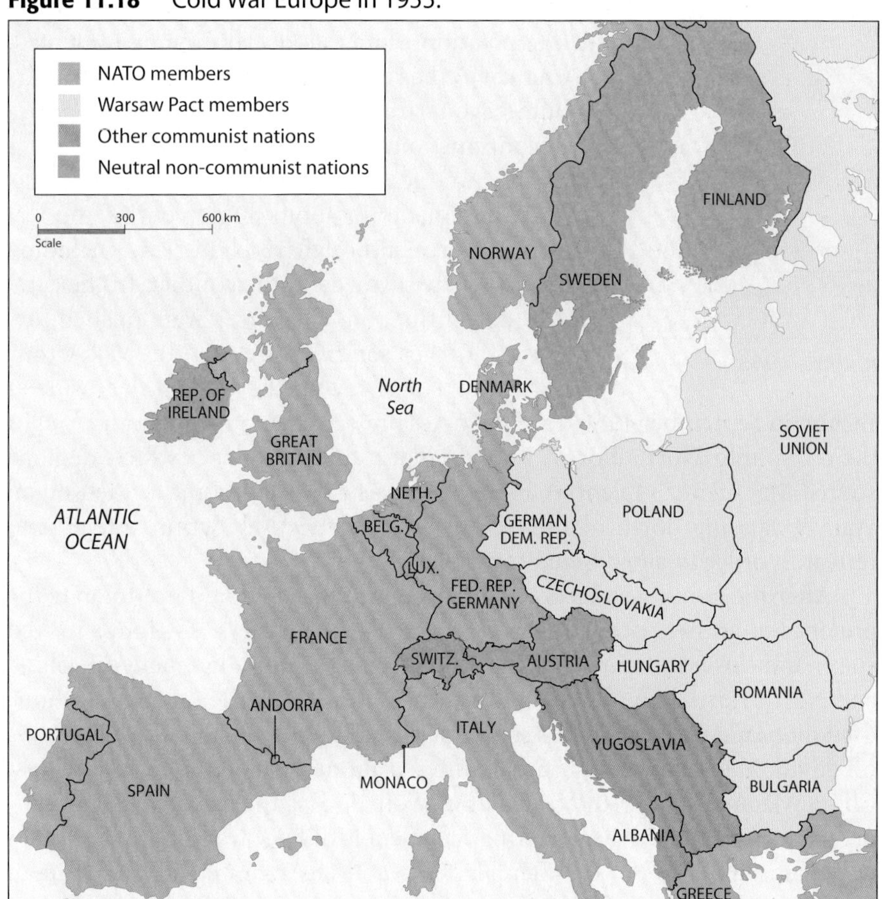

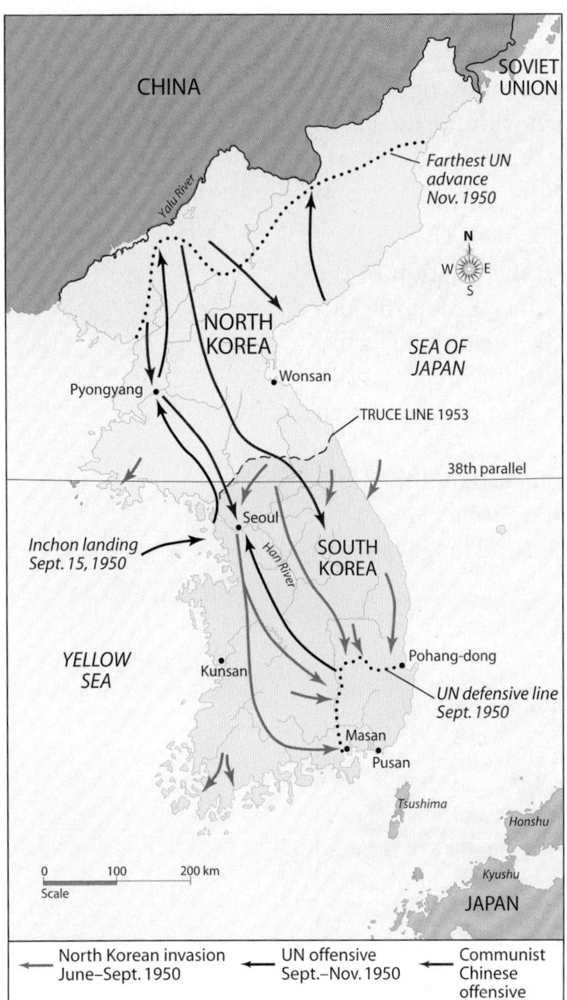


**Figure 11.19** The Korean War, 1950–1953.

## The Korean War

One armed conflict that raised tensions during the Cold War took place in Korea. The Japanese had occupied Korea in 1910, and after World War II the Soviets had liberated the northern part of the Korean peninsula while the Americans had liberated the South. Korea was thus divided along the 38th parallel, with a Soviet-influenced communist dictatorship in North Korea and an American-influenced dictatorship in South Korea. By the summer of 1949 both the Soviets and the Americans had withdrawn their troops from the region.

In June 1950 North Korea invaded South Korea. The United Nations immediately condemned the action. The Security Council (minus the Soviet Union, which had walked out because of the council's refusal to recognize communist China) called on member states to aid the South. Truman, who had already readied forces to send into Korea on the day that the United Nations made its declaration, commented: "A return to the rule of force in international affairs would have far-reaching effects. The United States will continue to uphold the rule of law."

The American army under General Douglas MacArthur made up about 80 percent of the UN forces in Korea, although 16 countries—including Canada—were involved in the conflict. In the early stages of fighting, the UN forces were pushed further and further south. However, after MacArthur landed troops partway up the Korean peninsula at Inchon in September 1950, the UN forces pressed their advantage and fought their way into North Korea. This dramatic military tactic, which demonstrated MacArthur's talent as a strategist, was a turning point in the Korean War. By landing north of the North Korean army, MacArthur forced it to retreat in order to avoid being trapped.

After the landing at Inchon, China warned that it would not tolerate the presence of an American-led force so close to its borders. As troops moved closer and closer to the Yalu River, which forms the boundary between China and North Korea, Chinese planes began bombing the UN forces. Two hundred thousand Chinese troops subsequently attacked, catching the UN troops off guard. MacArthur and Truman differed about what action to take against China. MacArthur advocated all-out war—including the use of nuclear weapons—but Truman felt that the American people did not want to wage another war against a major power. After a letter from MacArthur criticizing Truman was released, Truman fired the general. In the meantime, with the aid of

Chinese forces, the North Koreans were forcing the American-led forces to retreat to the 38th parallel.

President Eisenhower, elected in 1952 on a pledge to "go to Korea" to resolve the crisis, began to work toward peace. In July 1953 an official ceasefire was signed. The border between the two Koreas remained as it had been before the conflict began. During the three-year period of the war, an estimated 2 million Koreans, 54,000 Americans, and 132,000 Chinese had perished.

To a conservative America, the war was justified by the well-publicized threat of communism, and critics of the war were in danger of being labelled communist sympathizers. The willingness to characterize all dissent as communist-inspired would open the door to one of the more repressive episodes in 1950s America.

**Figure 11.20** A Korean wife, mother, and grandmother mourn the death of a young man who was killed outside his home in 1952 by a guerrilla fighter. This photograph was taken by Margaret Bourke-White, the same photographer who captured the image in Figure 11.7. How would you describe her work?

## Eisenhower, McCarthy, and the Anti-Communist Frenzy

After 27 years of Democratic leadership, the Republicans were optimistic that they would see their fortunes restored in the election of 1952. They knew that Americans were worried about the Cold War, the continuing conflict in Korea, charges of communist infiltration in the government, and news reports that suggested President Truman's officials had accepted bribes. The Republicans adopted the slogan: "Korea, communism, and corruption," and nominated war hero Dwight D. Eisenhower to lead the party. Eisenhower won a landslide victory over his Democratic opponent, Adlai Stevenson, and became the first career soldier since Ulysses S. Grant to be elected president (see Chapter 7).

Eisenhower's presidency was characterized by policies designed to achieve stability and consistency at home and abroad. During his time in office, the United States experienced phenomenal economic growth. Low-cost housing and a booming economy meant that most Americans enjoyed a life of great abundance. A new house in the suburbs, a larger television in the living room, and the newest car in the garage represented the fulfillment of the American dream. Most of the domestic conflicts that had rattled America in earlier decades were suppressed, or neglected, during this time. A generation scarred by war had set its sights on a quieter way of life.

Yet Americans remained uneasy, not sure that peace and prosperity would last. A fear of communist subversion hung over the country. Foreign events and espionage scandals were having a profound effect on the way Americans viewed their world, and contributed to strong anti-communist feelings.

Anti-communist rhetoric reached a peak when Joseph McCarthy, a junior senator from Wisconsin, announced in 1950 that over 200 communists had infiltrated the State Department. McCarthy's accusations were groundless, but

**Figure 11.21** A rally held in Washington on November 11, 1954 by supporters of McCarthy. Why did McCarthy's politics appeal to so many Americans?

they fed the "Red Scare," an anti-communist fervour that was taking hold of America. Between 1950 and 1954 McCarthy investigated the State Department's information program and overseas libraries, from which he removed such subversive texts as *The Selected Works of Thomas Jefferson.* He also investigated Voice of America, the official international broadcasting service of the American government. Libraries were encouraged to ban books by so-called communists and communist sympathizers, and widely circulated magazines contained articles with titles such as "Communists Are After Your Child."

The House Un-American Activities Committee (HUAC) interrogated Americans about their communist connections. A mere accusation of being a communist or communist sympathizer could ruin a person's career and personal life. Many Americans carried on bravely in the face of such persecution. For example, Paul Robeson, a singer and labour activist who was critical of government policy, was labelled a communist by HUAC. Over 80 of his concerts were cancelled, and in 1950 his passport was revoked. Despite the near collapse of his career, Robeson performed concerts at the Peace Arch Park on the US–Canada border in 1952 and 1953 to protest his travel ban; between 30,000 and 40,000 people attended.

By 1954 hundreds of groups were on the Department of Justice's list of organizations that were "totalitarian, fascist, communist or subversive" or were "seeking to alter the form of government of the United States by unconstitutional means." Such groups included the Chopin Cultural Center, the Committee for the Negro in the Arts, the League of American Writers, and the Yugoslav Seaman's Club. From Hollywood to Washington, any hint of criticism of McCarthy could be turned into an accusation of communism.

One celebrity who fell afoul of McCarthy was Arthur Miller, an author and playwright who famously stood up to "McCarthyism" by refusing to give evidence before HUAC in the 1950s. Miller's 1953 play *The Crucible* implicitly compared McCarthy's investigations to the Salem witch trials (see Chapter 1, pages 29 and 30). Over time, many Americans grew uneasy about McCarthy's fanaticism, and in 1954 broadcaster and World War II correspondent Edward R. Murrow used the television program *See It Now* to launch an intensive campaign against McCarthy before a wide audience.

President Eisenhower was privately critical of McCarthy's tactics but was aware that the majority of Americans supported the senator. Rather than risk a public confrontation, Eisenhower supported congressional bills that extended the powers of the FBI to hunt for communists. When McCarthy set out to expose generals in the American army for being insufficiently tough on communists,

**SOUND BITE**

"We will not walk in fear, one of another. We will not be driven by fear into an age of unreason if we dig deep in our history and doctrine and remember that we are not descended from fearful men, not from men who feared to write, to speak, to associate and to defend causes which were for the moment unpopular."

—Broadcaster Edward R. Murrow, May 9, 1954

however, Eisenhower pressured the Senate to condemn McCarthy for conduct unbecoming a senator. In December 1954 the Senate voted 67 to 22 to censure McCarthy, and popular enthusiasm for the senator plummeted.

## American Foreign Policy after 1953

American military intervention around the world increased dramatically during the Cold War, as did America's annual defence budget. The military-industrial complex grew so strong that Eisenhower warned Americans about its dangers in his Farewell Address to the nation in 1961 (see the American Archive feature later in this chapter). Canada, geographically positioned between the two nuclear powers, found itself more closely aligned militarily to the United States than ever before.

### Rearmament

Eisenhower's Secretary of State was John Foster Dulles, a man who influenced American foreign policy until 1962. An enthusiastic Cold Warrior, Dulles advocated the policy of **brinkmanship**, or, in his own words, a belief that in foreign policy, "if you are afraid to go to the brink [of war], you are lost." Eisenhower introduced a concept known as the **domino theory** in 1954. According to this theory, if one country fell to communism, others would respond like a row of dominos: "you knock over the first one, and what will happen to the last one is the certainty that it will go over very quickly."

Brinkmanship and the domino theory provided the theoretical underpinning for America's massive buildup of armaments in the 1950s and accounted for the establishment of a permanent wartime economy. Defence spending more than doubled from over $125 billion in 1950 to approximately $319 billion in 1960 (see also Figure 14.4 on page 481).

### Foreign Intervention

Through media broadcasts, Dulles informed eastern Europeans that the United States would come to their aid in overthrowing communist leaders. However, when East Germans and Hungarians tried to effect change in 1953 and 1956, respectively, the uprisings were crushed by the Soviets while the United States chose not to intervene. Ousting a Soviet government in a country deep within communist territory, such as Hungary, or one with such strategic importance for the Soviets as East Germany would have been a dangerous proposition for America, which lacked the necessary support for such a move among its NATO allies.

At the same time, American military interventions in other parts of the world increased. For example, in 1953 the CIA helped overthrow the government of Iran after it **nationalized** oil production. The US also intervened in Guatemala in 1954 after the socialist government there expropriated land owned by United Fruit, a large American corporation. Although the Guatemalan government had compensated United Fruit, the United States organized a coup that replaced the existing government with a new regime. The pretext for the US invasion of Guatemala was the prevention of a communist takeover of the country. The US feared a communist stronghold in the Americas as well as an eventual attack on the American continent.

## NORAD

As the Cold War progressed, American and Soviet scientists developed ever more devastating instruments of nuclear war, such as long-range bombers and intercontinental ballistic missiles, which could reach their targets in as little as half an hour. Fear of a Soviet attack prompted Canada and the United States to begin construction of three radar lines across Canada's North in 1949 that would provide an early warning system.

The collaborative effort became official in 1958 when Canada and the US signed the North American Aerospace Defense Command (NORAD) agreement. The Canadian government decided that it was preferable to allow an American military presence in Canada than to do without American radar.

## Interactions with the Soviet Union

Fighting a cold war did not prevent the United States from engaging in diplomatic discussions with the Soviet Union during the 1950s. In 1956 Nikita Khrushchev, the new leader of the Soviet Union, denounced many of the policies and practices of his predecessor, Joseph Stalin. Eisenhower and Khrushchev began to meet to discuss their interests and differences. When Vice-President Richard Nixon toured the Soviet Union in 1959, it appeared that relations between the two superpowers were improving.

Any such hope came to an abrupt end in May 1960, when an American U2 spy plane was shot down over the Soviet Union. At first, the United States denied that it was spying; when the Soviets revealed pictures of the aircraft, however, Eisenhower was forced to admit the truth. At the next summit meeting in Paris, Khrushchev demanded that Eisenhower apologize. Eisenhower refused and Khrushchev stormed out of the meeting.

**Figure 11.22** In the aftermath of the U2 incident, and faced with thousands fleeing East Berlin, Khrushchev ordered the building of the Berlin Wall. The wall, an Iron Curtain in concrete form, became the symbol of the struggle between the East and the West.

AMERICAN ARCHIVE

## Eisenhower's Farewell Address

By the end of his administration, Dwight D. Eisenhower had spent nearly his entire life in public service, mostly in the military. As the architect of D-Day, he was America's greatest war hero. Although he avoided direct military confrontation with the Soviets throughout his presidency, one of Eisenhower's biggest disappointments was his failure to make strides in disarmament.

Ironically, Eisenhower had reasoned that disarmament would be the result of negotiations with the Soviet Union, provided that the United States negotiated from a position of power.

Eisenhower believed that military and nuclear buildup was the only way to avert war by deterring a potential Soviet first strike, yet he also understood the dangerous implications of such a policy. On January 17, 1961 he chose to highlight these issues in his Farewell Address, which was broadcast throughout America on radio and television:

> Until the latest of our world conflicts, the United States had no armaments industry ... But now ... we are compelled to create a permanent armaments industry of vast proportions ... The conjunction of an immense military establishment and a large arms industry is new in the American experience ... we recognize the imperative need for this development. Yet we must not fail to comprehend its grave implications.

Eisenhower understood that the arms industry must not be allowed to drive foreign policy in Washington. The question he raised was whether the relationship between the armed forces and the industries that provided them with weapons was a safeguard from Soviet attack or a threat to democracy and American ideals:

> In the councils of government, we must guard against the acquisition of unwarranted influence, either sought or unsought, by the military-industrial complex. The potential for the disastrous rise of misplaced power exists and will persist.

**Figure 11.23** Eisenhower delivering his Farewell Address as president.

Finally, Eisenhower foresaw the potential for an erosion of civil liberties by the military-industrial complex as a result of the population's collective fear and its desire for protection. In other words, if Americans feared communism more than they cherished the Constitution, they might be willing to sacrifice their rights and freedoms in return for the security offered by the defence establishment:

> We must never let the weight of this combination endanger our liberties or democratic processes ... only an alert and knowledgeable citizenry can compel the proper meshing of the huge industrial and military machinery of defense with our peaceful methods and goals.

### Think It Through

1. Why did Eisenhower believe that a permanent military-industrial complex was necessary, and what were his two major warnings about it?
2. Why did Eisenhower put the onus of responsibility on American citizens? How can citizens act as watchdogs of their government?

## CHECK YOUR UNDERSTANDING

1. What was Roosevelt's vision for a postwar world?
2. What did the Marshall Plan offer Europe, and what did it accomplish?
3. List actions by the Soviet Union and other communist countries that produced fear in the United States.
4. In which countries did the United States support dictatorships?

# Everyday Life and Popular Culture during the Cold War

After World War II and the Korean War, Americans were eager for stable, peaceful times. Domesticity, marriage, children, and the comforts of suburban living became the desirable norms of the American middle class. Along with these peaceful ideals, however, loomed a sense of anxiety fostered principally by the news media. Ordinary people were encouraged to build backyard air-raid shelters, and schools conducted bomb drills—reminders that communism and its misguided enthusiasts were America's potentially lethal enemies. Thus, many Americans were enjoying new-found affluence knowing full well that it might not last.

## Consumerism and the Automobile Culture

Americans bought over 60 million cars during the 1950s. Increased car ownership resulted in the proliferation of motels, gas stations, fast-food restaurants, and other services eager to cater to an automobile-obsessed public. Cars enabled people to live relatively large distances away from their workplaces, which encouraged the rapid growth of suburbs around cities. To accommodate the nation's increased dependence on cars, the interstate highway system was built during the 1950s.

**Figure 11.24** Cars in the 1950s were designed with better starters, heaters, and radios than in the 1940s. Together with flashy designs, these features made cars more comfortable, stylish, and fun. Their fuel efficiency, however, was poor.

## 49th PARALLEL

# John Kenneth Galbraith (1908–2006)

John Kenneth Galbraith was an influential economist of the Cold War era. A bestselling author, he was also an active adviser to Roosevelt, Truman, Kennedy, and Johnson. Galbraith was born in Elgin County, Ontario in 1908 and grew up on a small farm. His father was a farmer, schoolteacher, and politician who instilled in Galbraith a love of education, a capacity for hard work, and a keen wit; from his mother—a political activist—Galbraith gained a sense of fairness and compassion.

After graduating from the Ontario Agricultural College (now the University of Guelph), Galbraith went to study, teach, and serve in the US, most notably under President Roosevelt—where his job was to control prices, and thus check inflation during World War II—and then under President Kennedy (1961–1963). As a Kennedy adviser, he was one of the very few to counsel the president against becoming militarily involved in South Vietnam.

Galbraith was one of America's most influential economists in the 1950s and 1960s, and wrote a popular trilogy of texts on economics: *American Capitalism* (1952), *The Affluent Society* (1958), and *The New Industrial State* (1967). *The Affluent Society* was a stinging rebuke of America's infatuation with materialism during the Eisenhower period. In a famous passage Galbraith describes a family which takes "its mauve and cerise, air conditioned, power-steered, power-braked automobile out for a tour ... through cities that are badly paved, made hideous by litter, blighted buildings, billboards ... into a countryside that has been rendered largely invisible by commercial art."

Galbraith argued that as America moved from an age of poverty to an age of affluence, a new economic theory was needed to curb the excesses of materialism and encourage investment in public goods and services, such as roads and schools. He claimed that without such a policy, business would respond to growing American affluence by simply creating more consumer desires through advertising. With the success of that advertising, Galbraith believed, Americans would acquire more and more luxury items, ultimately at the expense of parks, schools, and the environment.

Galbraith's solution to this problem was for governments to reduce consumption through consumption taxes (similar to Canada's provincial sales tax, PST, and federal goods and services tax, GST) and then invest the tax revenue in large-scale education programs. Galbraith's ideas provoked spirited debate and much criticism, especially from traditional economists. They claimed that Galbraith was an "aristocrat" who believed that consumers should not have free choice but instead have their choices determined by the "higher minds" of a paternalistic government. Galbraith responded that "The modern conservative [Galbraith's critics] is engaged in one of man's oldest exercises in moral philosophy; that is, the search for superior moral justification for selfishness."

**Figure 11.25** John Kenneth Galbraith. In what ways did he bring a Canadian perspective to solving American economic problems?

Galbraith died in 2006 at the age of 97, having written more than 40 books and having received the Presidential Medal of Freedom twice (from President Truman in 1946 and from President Clinton in 2000). In 1997 Galbraith, who often spoke and wrote of his Canadian upbringing, was made an officer of the Order of Canada.

## Think It Through

1. How did Galbraith's ideas about consumer society in the US accurately predict some of the socio-economic problems that exist today?
2. Think about Galbraith's proposal for US consumption taxes equivalent to the PST and GST that exist in Canada today. Do some research, and compare the taxation system in both countries. How has the US evolved historically in ways that demonstrate the difference in taxation philosophy (e.g., universal health care)?

The suburbs offered clean, child-friendly, homogeneous environments that served the American dream of upward mobility. Suburban growth, which increased by 46 percent in the 1950s, made home ownership affordable for millions. Many middle-class families left the city, which resulted in a larger concentration of poorer people—including minority groups—in urban areas. Businesses relocated to make consumption convenient for their more affluent customers. Supermarkets and shopping centres with parking lots were constructed to serve the suburban population.

## Television

Television overtook radio as the dominant form of mass communication during the 1950s. The number of homes with television sets rose from 8 million in 1950 to 42 million in 1960. Owning a television set was a symbol of prosperity, and by the end of the 1950s those Americans who were very prosperous owned colour televisions. In 1960 the first televised debate between presidential candidates Richard Nixon and John F. Kennedy would reveal that politicians must hone their media presence in order to win the approval of their living-room audiences.

Television also broadcast messages about conformity and consumerism. Idealized American families were presented on shows such as *Leave It to Beaver*, *Ozzie and Harriet*, and *Father Knows Best*, which also reinforced gender and racial stereotypes. Advertising was a crucial component of television programming. It bombarded Americans with reminders that consumption of a certain brand of cleaning product, fruit juice, or car was essential to their well-being.

## A Woman's Place

By 1946, 2.25 million women had quit their jobs and 1 million more had been laid off. Many American women felt the renewed social pressure to stay at home and focus on their families, accepting traditional roles as wives and mothers, and remaining financially and emotionally dependent on their husbands. Newspapers, magazines, and television programs extolled the virtues of cooking, cleaning, and complying.

Although the number of women employed outside the home rose during the Cold War, sex-segregated jobs were the norm; in the words of historian Cynthia Harrison, the era turned "Rosie the Riveter" into "Rosie the File Clerk." Many middle-class mothers took jobs after their children started school, but most were still expected to perform all the traditional wifely and motherly duties, single-handedly, after work. The prosperity of postwar America was accompanied by a massive growth in the birth rate known as the **baby boom**; the population grew by about 30 million during the 1950s alone. In an era dominated by families, the child—and eventually the teenager—became a centrepiece of American consumer and cultural life.

## Rock and Roll

Rock and roll emerged as the definitive popular musical style of the 1950s. Influenced by the blues, country, and rockabilly music, rock and roll was typified by strong rhythms, a quick beat, and amplified electric guitars. Some parents feared that rock and roll would lead their children into a life of indulgence and corruption, but teenagers fell in love with the music and called it their own. Hits like Bill Haley's "Rock Around the Clock" sold 17 million copies; *American Bandstand*, a popular television showcase, featured top-40 singers and ordinary teenagers who danced live before the cameras.

The fact that rock and roll evolved in large part from the blues—an African-American art form—accounted for some of the controversy that surrounded it. Some parents and critics objected to white teenagers enthusiastically embracing "black music." Racism was also endemic in the music trade itself in the 1950s. White and black musicians received radically different treatment in terms of radio play, top-40 rankings, tour arrangements, and television appearances.

**Figure 11.26** Singer Elvis Presley was known as "the king of rock and roll." His sexually provocative dance movements, which some considered obscene, were censored on his first television appearance in 1956. Nevertheless, Presley's performance—photographed from the waist up—was viewed by one of the largest television audiences in history.

## American Fine Arts

During the pre-war and war years, the American art scene—particularly in New York—was enlivened by the presence of many European masters who had escaped the Nazis, including Marc Chagall and Max Ernst. One immigrant artist who exercised a profound influence in America was the German-born painter Hans Hofmann. Hofmann inspired students with his ideas that art is connected to the laws of nature and should be an expression of an artist's deepest spiritual and emotional self.

**Figure 11.27** Abstract expressionist Hans Hofmann's painting *Land of Bliss and Wonder, California*, from 1960. The work illustrates one of Hofmann's aims as an artist: "I want the fullness of myself realized through color."

# Culture Notes

## The Beats

> The only people for me are the mad ones, the ones who are mad to live, mad to talk, mad to be saved, desirous of everything at the same time, the ones who never yawn or say a commonplace thing, but burn, burn, burn, like fabulous roman candles exploding like spiders across the stars and in the middle you see the blue centerlight pop and everybody goes, "Awww!"
>
> —Jack Kerouac, *On the Road*

**Figure 11.28** Beats William S. Burroughs and Jack Kerouac, photographed by Allen Ginsberg in 1953 in New York.

The mad people that Jack Kerouac wrote about were the Beats: an intellectual circle of literary rebels who rejected mainstream postwar American values, such as materialism and conformity. Originally a small group of close friends, the Beats spawned a cultural movement that emphasized adventure, spirituality, and the need to search for the meaning of life. Their words screamed out against injustice. They celebrated the experience of the moment, jazz, philosophy, and sexual—including homosexual—liberation.

The core Beats were Jack Kerouac, Allen Ginsberg, Neal Cassady, and William S. Burroughs, who met in Manhattan in the mid-1940s while attending Columbia University. The struggling writers eventually relocated to San Francisco, where Lawrence Ferlinghetti, a publisher and owner of the City Lights bookstore, heard Allen Ginsberg perform his poem "Howl" for the first time:

> I saw the best minds of my generation destroyed by madness, starving hysterical naked,
> dragging themselves through the negro streets at dawn looking for an angry fix,
> angelheaded hipsters burning for the ancient heavenly connection to the starry dynamo in the machinery of night,
> who poverty and tatters and hollow-eyed and high sat up smoking in the supernatural darkness of cold-water flats floating across the tops of cities contemplating jazz …

Soon after Ferlinghetti published *Howl and Other Poems*, the book was seized by customs officials and Ferlinghetti was arrested for breaking obscenity laws. The charges were dropped, but the case shone a spotlight on the Beat movement. Mainstream America was clearly not ready to hear what the Beats had to say, and critics too were wary. As the Beat movement grew, the media coined the term **beatnik**, which came to represent anyone devoted to the countercultural lifestyle espoused by the Beats.

The women of the Beat movement were often sidelined. Although the Beats' bohemian lifestyle allowed them to break free from suburban America, it kept their art in a world of subtle **misogyny**. Those women who did affect the Beat scene—such as Anne Waldman, Diane DiPrima, and Brenda Frazer—were influential mostly in the 1960s.

The Beats are generally considered to be the forerunners of the hippies of the 1960s. More importantly, they were the torchbearers of anti-establishment literature during the Cold War.

### Think It Through

1. How would you characterize the significance of the Beat movement?
2. After reading the excerpts above, how would you describe Beat literature?

Hofmann was a member of a group of postwar visual artists known as abstract expressionists. These artists refused to conform to traditional styles in the visual arts and instead demanded freedom of individual expression. The abstract expressionist movement became so popular, and its American artists so inventive in the 1940s and 1950s, that the world's centre of avant-garde art shifted from Paris to New York.

If Hofmann was the most influential teacher of the abstract expressionist movement, Jackson Pollock was perhaps its most original artist. In many complex and innovative paintings, Pollock expressed himself in a unique visual language: a combination of splashes, swirls, and drips of acrylic paint on unprimed canvas that he had nailed to his studio floor. His work reflected no formal patterns. It was unprecedented in its spontaneity and in the physical freedom that went into its creation. It was, in Pollock's own words, "energy made visible."

Many artists gravitated to New York in the 1950s because of its stimulating cultural atmosphere. The Cedar Bar was a popular gathering place where the abstract expressionists mingled with others, such as the Beat poets. Like the painters, the Beats were, in the words of publisher and poet Lawrence Ferlinghetti, "portraying the disintegration of the Old World."

**Figure 11.29** Not everyone enjoyed Jackson Pollock's work, and some of his critics referred to him as "Jack the Dripper." Pollock, however, continued to maintain that "Every good artist paints what he is."

**WEB LINKS**

To explore the life and art of Jackson Pollock, visit www.emp.ca/ah.

## CHECK YOUR UNDERSTANDING

1. How did television change American culture and politics?
2. What unique pressures did American women face in the 1950s?
3. From which musical styles did rock and roll originate?
4. Describe Jackson Pollock's painting style.

# THE HISTORIAN'S CRAFT

## Speaking with a Purpose in History

The Historian's Craft feature in Chapter 10 dealt with written presentations in history—for example, the formal essay, biography, and "in role" writing. These are the kinds of products that professional historians present to the public, but historians also make oral presentations—lectures, speeches, and narrated television programs. When they do, they think through and organize their ideas using the methods you studied in The Historian's Craft features in Chapters 7 to 9. In addition, they take into account the characteristics of effective oral presentations, and you can too.

### Preparing for Effective Oral Presentations

You have completed your historical thinking, your research, and the organization of your findings. What do you need to take into account before making an oral presentation? Here are some suggestions:

- *Who is my audience?* Is it my class? (They know me and have studied the same history.) Are they strangers? (I'll need to introduce myself and the historical context.)
- *What form will the presentation take?* Is there a time limit? How much time should I reserve for questions? When will I ask or answer questions?
- *What are my main points?* Can I focus on three or four? What should I open with? Should I recap? What should I conclude with?
- *How will I emphasize my main points?* Should I use visuals? Might I ask an audience member to read a quotation? How will I make my conclusion powerful?

### Effective Debating in History

In some ways history is all about debates. Historians debate key questions: Should the United States have joined the League of Nations? They debate traditional views versus revisionist ones: the view that Truman had to drop atomic bombs to end the war versus later views that he had choices. At times, historians—and history students, too—take part in formal debates. When they do so, they debate a proposition such as: Resolved that the United States faced a genuine threat in the 1950s from communist spies. There are two sides in a debate—the affirmative side (supporting the resolution), and the negative side (opposing it). There are also various debate formats depending on whether individuals or teams are involved and on other factors, such as time limitations and class size. In all cases, the following tips are useful:

- *Have sufficient relevant evidence to make your case.* Evidence of one communist agent is relevant but not sufficient to support the resolution. Evidence of one false claim by Senator McCarthy is relevant, but evidence of dozens is conclusive.
- *Ensure that the evidence is credible and has impact.* Quote an expert. Quote another who backs up the first. Use a few dramatic statistics: McCarthy claimed that there were 205 Red infiltrators in the State Department one day, 81 the next, and 57 soon after. Use a dramatic example: Actress Lucille Ball of the popular television comedy series *I Love Lucy* was a target.
- *Think about points in your argument that your opponent will attack.* Have responses ready.
- *Prepare your side of the argument as above and then do the same for the other side.* By anticipating the opposite argument, you can prepare rebuttals.
- *Listen to your opponent carefully.* Note inconsistencies in the argument and weak evidence. Bring forward evidence you kept aside to counter your opponent's argument.
- *Conclude with your best point.*

### Try It!

1. You are making an oral presentation to your class on the impact of rock and roll on American society in the 1950s. What are your three key points? How will you present them so that they have maximum impact on your audience?
2. Debate the following resolution: Canada was right to accept a US military presence on its soil in exchange for American protection under NORAD.

# STUDY HALL

## Thinking

1. Roosevelt called December 7, 1941 "a day which will live in infamy." Do you agree? Why?
2. Examine each of the theories as to why the United States dropped atomic bombs on Japan. What historical evidence supports each? Do you believe one theory over another? Why?
3. Debate the following issues:
   a. Resolved that the fear of communism led America to abandon its traditional values.
   b. Resolved that the Truman Doctrine advanced world peace.
4. Why do art forms such as abstract expressionism sometimes thrive in times characterized by relatively conservative values?

## Communication

5. Use an organizer to assess the positive and negative influences that the United States and the Soviet Union had in Europe after World War II.
6. In their careers as First Ladies of America, both Eleanor Roosevelt (see page 352 in Chapter 10) and Edith Bolling Galt Wilson (see page 316 in Chapter 9) acted on behalf of their disabled husbands. Research their achievements as First Ladies. Imagine that these women were able to communicate with each other about their experiences. Compose a short play or an extended dialogue to illustrate their encounter.

## Application

7. Research the war photography of Margaret Bourke-White. Imagine that you are present at one of the scenes she captured. Write a first-person account of it.
8. Draw a diagram that depicts the military-industrial complex.
9. The United States often intervened in the affairs of other countries, but it did not intervene in the Hungarian uprising against communism in 1956. Was this the right decision?
   a. Research the events that took place in Hungary in 1956.
   b. List facts about the Cold War that might affect your decision.
   c. Decide what you would have done and why.
10. Draw a web diagram or mind map that shows the origins of rock and roll, and the music styles that have evolved from rock and roll music.

# 12 A Time of Hope, Disillusionment, and Protest (1960–1975)

## KEY CONCEPTS

In this chapter you will consider:

- The Cuban Revolution as a trigger event that brought the United States and the Soviet Union to the brink of nuclear war
- The goals, methods, and accomplishments of the civil rights movement
- The reasons the United States became involved in the Vietnam War and the factors that led to its defeat
- The women's movement and the fight for gender equality
- The efforts of lesbians and gays, Native Americans, and Hispanic Americans to win respect and recognition of their rights
- The values and lifestyle of the hippie counterculture
- The rise of the environmental movement

## The American Story

The 15-year period that began with the election of the charismatic President John F. Kennedy saw millions of "baby boomers" come of age in America. Many members of this generation would grow up in affluence and develop a sense of entitlement to material wealth. In spite of the healthy economy, the period had its share of crises: the Cuban Missile Crisis in 1962 pushed the US and the Soviet Union to the brink of nuclear war; and in 1963, President Kennedy himself was assassinated. While some baby boomers grew up to struggle for the elimination of racism, sexism, poverty, and pollution at home, others went on to fight in the war in Vietnam, a conflict that would divide public opinion in America for years to come.

## TIMELINE

**1960**
- John F. Kennedy elected president

**1961**
- Bay of Pigs invasion

**1962**
- Cuban Missile Crisis
- Publication of Rachel Carson's *Silent Spring*

**1963**
- Assassination of President Kennedy

**1964**
- Gulf of Tonkin incident
- Civil Rights Act

## IMAGE ANALYSIS

**Figure 12.1** On July 20, 1969, as an estimated half a billion people worldwide watched on television, American astronaut Neil Armstrong climbed down from the Apollo 11 lunar module and onto the surface of the moon. "That's one small step for a man, one giant leap for mankind," Armstrong said.

Throughout American history, there have been several "where were you?" moments. During the 1960s there were at least three such moments: the Cuban Missile Crisis in 1962, the assassination of President John F. Kennedy in 1963, and Armstrong's walk on the moon in 1969. The moon landing—the first in human history—was the culmination of a goal set by President Kennedy in 1961 and one of the defining moments of the 20th century. The mission captured the public's imagination, representing both a pinnacle of human achievement and its further potential.

**1965**
- Civil rights march in Selma, Alabama
- Voting Rights Act

**1968**
- Tet Offensive in Vietnam
- Martin Luther King and Robert Kennedy assassinated

**1969**
- First manned moon landing
- Woodstock festival

**1972**
- Richard Nixon elected president

**1973**
- *Roe v. Wade* decision defines abortion rights
- US troop withdrawal from Vietnam

# INTRODUCTION

If you were a teenager in the 1960s, you might have watched a live television broadcast of President John F. Kennedy's inauguration on January 20, 1961 and been moved by the challenge the young president issued to his fellow Americans:

> Let the word go forth from this time and place, to friend and foe alike, that the torch has been passed to a new generation of Americans—born in this century, tempered by war, disciplined by a hard and bitter peace, proud of our ancient heritage—and unwilling to witness or permit the slow undoing of those human rights to which this Nation has always been committed, and to which we are committed today at home and around the world ...
>
> Now the trumpet summons us again—not as a call to bear arms, though arms we need; not as a call to battle, though embattled we are—but a call to bear the burden of a long twilight struggle, year in and year out, "rejoicing in hope, patient in tribulation"—a struggle against the common enemies of man: tyranny, poverty, disease, and war itself ...
>
> And so, my fellow Americans: ask not what your country can do for you—ask what you can do for your country.

What is your personal reaction to these words today? Do they bore you, anger you, bring out the cynic in you? Or do they inspire you? At the time, many baby boomers found Kennedy's words inspiring.

As you read this chapter, think about this speech and the way it relates to the chapter title: A Time of Hope, Disillusionment, and Protest. President Kennedy is remembered today for his idealism, eloquence, and courage and for the hope he inspired in the American people. At the same time, we cannot forget that he authorized a failed attempt to overthrow Cuba's communist government and that he sponsored a violent coup in South Vietnam that escalated America's involvement in that country's civil war, a war that would end in disaster for the US. At home, he was caught between segregationists in the South and the persistent campaign for civil rights for America's black community. As you read, think of how Kennedy's remarks in his inaugural speech relate to foreign relations and domestic policies during his term and later.

# THE KENNEDY YEARS

Kennedy won the 1960 presidential election by the slimmest of margins. Running as the Democratic candidate, he received 49.7 percent of the popular vote while his Republican opponent, Richard M. Nixon, who had served as vice-president in the Eisenhower administration, won 49.5 percent.

Some political observers argue that one of the deciding factors in the race was Kennedy's performance in four televised debates, the first in the history of US presidential campaigns.

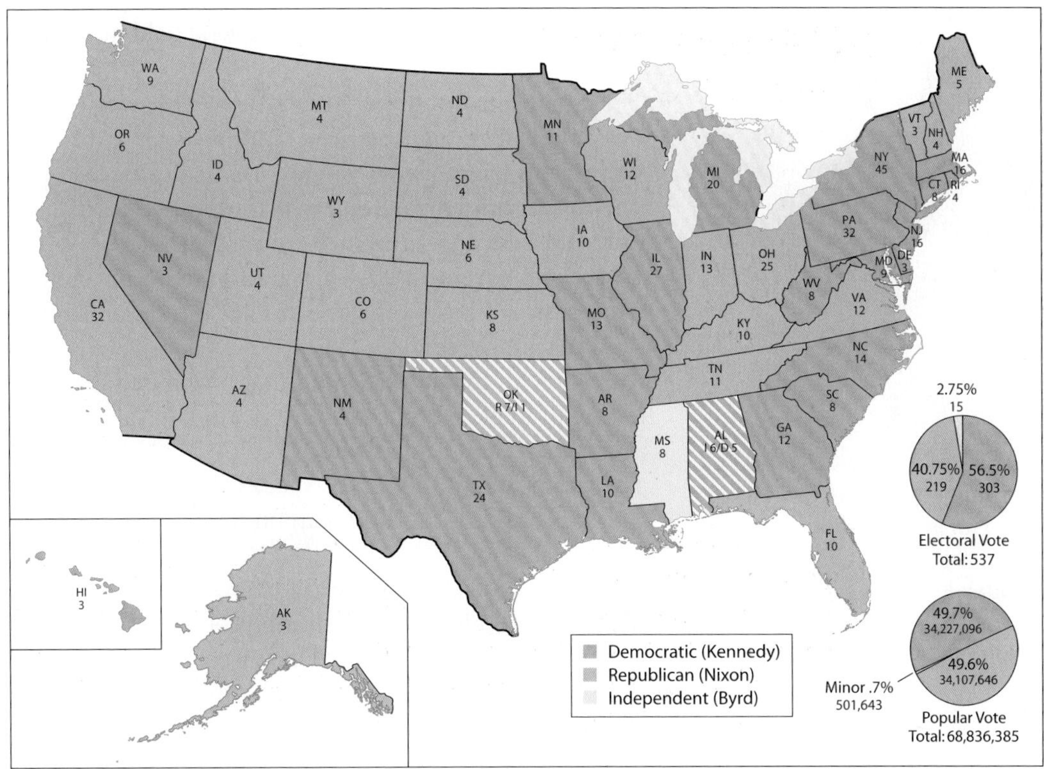


**Figure 12.2** Kennedy's margin of victory in the popular vote in 1960 was one of the closest ever in American history.

## Camelot

Following his election, Kennedy fostered his image as a dynamic and intelligent young president. The fact that his wife, Jacqueline, was both beautiful and fashionable helped to contribute to this image. They had two young children, John Jr. and Carolyn. Photographers were invited into the White House and to the Kennedy's summer home at Hyannisport, Massachusetts to record the family's activities, and Jacqueline transformed the White House into a showcase for the performing arts. For many Americans, a magical aura seemed to surround the Kennedy presidency, which became known as "Camelot" after the mythical kingdom of King Arthur and the knights of the Round Table.

| The Presidents: 1961–1974 | | |
|---|---|---|
| **John F. Kennedy*** | Democrat | January 20, 1961 – November 22, 1963 |
| **Lyndon B. Johnson** | Democrat | November 22, 1963 – January 20, 1969 |
| **Richard M. Nixon** | Republican | January 20, 1969 – August 9, 1974 |

* assassinated

**Figure 12.3** The Kennedys leave their Georgetown home for inauguration ceremonies on January 20, 1961. The election of the young Kennedy reflected the optimism that many Americans felt regarding their country.

President Kennedy's legacy includes several bold initiatives:

- The establishment of the Peace Corps, which sent thousands of young American volunteers to Third World countries to work on development projects
- The New Frontier program, which promised federal funds for education and medical care for seniors
- A proposal to reform US immigration policy by ending the practice of basing the selection of immigrants on their country of origin
- A treaty with the Soviet Union that prohibited the testing of nuclear bombs on the ground, in the atmosphere, and under water
- The commitment to win the space race with the Soviet Union by landing an American on the moon

Beneath the glowing public image, however, was a darker reality. Kennedy was plagued with health problems: severe back pain, Addison's disease, and colitis. There were rumours that he engaged in several extramarital affairs with other women, including film star Marilyn Monroe. In August 1963 he and Jacqueline suffered the death of a newborn son.

Kennedy is also remembered for his failed attempt to overthrow Fidel Castro's communist regime in Cuba and for his confrontation with the Soviet Union over the stationing of Soviet nuclear-tipped missiles in Cuba. At home, he was reluctantly drawn into the growing struggle between segregationists in the South and civil rights activists. And his sending of American advisers and other military aid to South Vietnam set the stage for a major expansion of that conflict.

## Cuba, Castro, and the Cold War

During the 1950s Cuba, an island nation 140 kilometres southwest of Florida, was very important to certain large American businesses, such as the United Fruit Company, a powerful US corporation that operated throughout Latin America. These businesses controlled over 80 percent of Cuba's utilities, mines, cattle, and oil refineries; 40 percent of its sugar; and 50 percent of its public railroads. In 1959, when Dwight Eisenhower was still president, rebel leader Fidel Castro overthrew Fulgencio Batista, the pro-American dictator who had dominated Cuba during this period.

After seizing power, Castro initiated a series of land reforms. He took land back from American owners, such as United Fruit, and instituted a nationwide housing and land distribution program. When the US-dominated **International Monetary Fund (IMF)** refused to lend Cuba money and the United States cut its sugar purchases, Castro turned to the Soviet Union for aid.

## Bay of Pigs Invasion

Concerned with the developments in Cuba, Eisenhower and the CIA took action. With the president's blessing, CIA operatives began training anti-Castro Cuban exiles in Guatemala to invade Cuba and overthrow Castro's government. Initially, the United States expected that its invasion would prompt a local uprising; however, Castro was a popular leader.

**Figure 12.4** Fidel Castro in "Rebels of the Sierra Maestra," a 1950s CBS News report that presented Castro in a sympathetic light.

Eisenhower left office before the invasion of Cuba was carried out. Newly elected President John F. Kennedy approved the CIA invasion plan, even though it violated the Charter of the Organization of American States (OAS). The OAS, an organization whose membership included both Cuba and the United States, was founded to strengthen peace and security in the region. In early January 1961 the United States severed diplomatic relations with Cuba but retained its naval base at Guantanamo Bay, which it had leased from Cuba since the Spanish-American War (see Chapter 8). On April 17, contrary to Kennedy's public statement that no invasion of Cuba would be launched, the United States assisted in landing a force of about 1,500 Cuban exiles at the Bay of Pigs. The Cuban military was ready for them, and captured about 1,200 soldiers. The invasion was a military disaster that both highlighted the dangers of the theory of brinkmanship (see Chapter 11) and tarnished the image of the United States and its new president.

## Cuban Missile Crisis

During the summer of 1962 the United States became aware that the Soviet Union was landing technicians and equipment in Cuba, and that military construction was under way. On October 14 an American spy plane photographed sites that had the potential to launch missiles toward North America. These weapons could strike American targets within 15 minutes—much more quickly than Soviet-based missiles, which could take up to an hour to reach the US. From a Soviet point of view, the missile sites probably provided a reasonable counterbalance to US missile sites close to the Soviet border in Turkey; from an American point of view, they constituted an act of aggression against the United States.

On October 22 Kennedy ordered a naval and air blockade around Cuba, and announced to the world that it was on the brink of nuclear war: "It shall be the policy of this nation to regard any nuclear missile launched from Cuba against any nation in the Western Hemisphere as an attack by the Soviet Union on the United States, requiring a full retaliatory response upon the Soviet Union." On October 26, as the United States prepared to launch an air attack on the missile sites, Soviet leader Nikita Khrushchev sent a message to Kennedy implying that the Soviet Union would remove the sites if the United States agreed not to invade Cuba. Kennedy's agreement brought the crisis to an end. It also marked the end of the policy of brinkmanship.

## 49th PARALLEL

# The Cuban Missile Crisis and Its Canadian Aftermath

Throughout the Cuban Missile Crisis, John Diefenbaker was prime minister of Canada. He had been on mutually respectful terms with former president Eisenhower, but his relationship with John F. Kennedy was less congenial. Kennedy's aggressive stance toward communism and his expectation that Canada would follow America's lead offended Diefenbaker's vision of Canadian autonomy. Diefenbaker resisted Kennedy's efforts to have Canada join the Organization of American States, and he resented Kennedy's apparent lack of respect for him. The fact that Kennedy was immensely popular in Canada did not improve Diefenbaker's feelings toward the American leader.

Kennedy chose not to inform Diefenbaker of the Cuban Missile Crisis until two hours before he warned the world of the possibility of impending nuclear war on October 22, 1962. The fact that Kennedy did not disclose the situation immediately to the Canadian government was a breach of protocol, as NATO and NORAD decisions are not to be made unilaterally. Kennedy asked Diefenbaker to put Canada on defence readiness condition (DEFCON) 2—one step away from nuclear war. Diefenbaker refused.

Diefenbaker infuriated Kennedy by publicly doubting that missile sites existed in Cuba and calling for verification by UN inspectors. Douglas Harkness, the Canadian minister of defence, bypassed Diefenbaker's authority and secretly ordered the military's chief of staff to put his forces on full alert. Meanwhile, Canada's chief naval officer ordered the Atlantic fleet to sea. In Diefenbaker's view, this situation undermined Canadian sovereignty because Canada's military had followed the orders of an American president instead of the orders of the Canadian prime minister. Diefenbaker's critics, however, claimed that he had acted indecisively at a time of crisis when Canada was duty-bound to honour its NORAD and NATO commitments. After the crisis subsided, Diefenbaker refused to allow the United States to house its nuclear missiles permanently on Canadian soil.

In January 1963 the Kennedy administration took action to undermine Diefenbaker with the assistance of the US State Department, the Pentagon, and

**Figure 12.5** An aerial photograph taken October 24, 1962 showing a medium-range ballistic missile site in Cuba.

Canadian opposition leader Lester B. Pearson. A retired US Air Force general held a press conference in Ottawa, condemning Diefenbaker's anti-nuclear stance. Shortly thereafter, Pearson held a press conference announcing that he was reversing his anti-nuclear position and that, if elected prime minister, he would accept American nuclear missiles in Canada. The US State Department then issued a press release supporting Pearson and implying that Diefenbaker had misled the Canadian people.

Diefenbaker accused the United States of meddling in Canadian domestic affairs and recalled his ambassador from Washington. As tensions heightened, the Canadian cabinet split on the nuclear weapons issue, and Defence Minister Harkness resigned in protest. Pearson and the opposition won a no-confidence vote in Parliament, and Diefenbaker's government fell on February 5, 1963. The subsequent election saw Pearson emerge victorious. As the new prime minister, Pearson re-established good relations with Washington, accepting virtually all of America's military demands.

Pierre Elliott Trudeau, who later served as minister of justice in Pearson's cabinet and succeeded him as prime minister, questioned US interference in Canadian internal affairs. He later asked: "Do you believe it was a coincidence? Why should the United States treat Canada any differently than Guatemala if reasons of state require it and circumstances permit?"

## Think It Through

1. Assess the extent to which the personal relationships between the Canadian and American leaders affected the actions taken by their governments during the Cuban Missile Crisis.
2. Do you believe that Kennedy's desire to have a compliant military ally on America's northern border justified American intervention in Canadian politics? Explain.

Listen to Diefenbaker and Pearson discussing Canada's response to the Cuban Missile Crisis at www.emp.ca/ah.

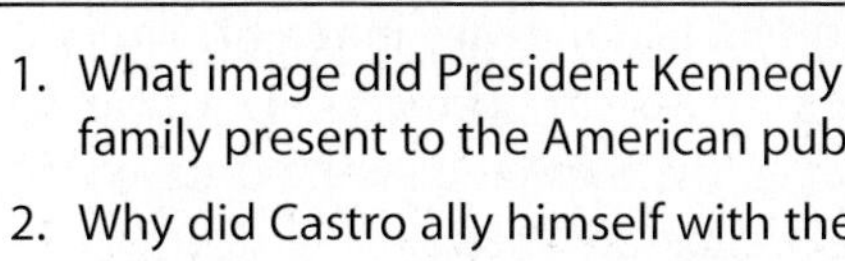


1. What image did President Kennedy and his family present to the American public?
2. Why did Castro ally himself with the Soviet Union?
3. Why did the Bay of Pigs invasion tarnish the reputation of the United States?
4. What threat did Soviet missiles in Cuba pose to the United States?

# THE CIVIL RIGHTS MOVEMENT

President Kennedy was to face another important crisis during his presidency, this time at home. In 1961 Kennedy enacted a presidential decree to require affirmative action in the public sector, but this step was overshadowed by a growing crisis in civil rights across the US. The prosperity of the 1960s did not reach all social groups: black Americans were denied opportunities that white Americans took for granted.

This inequality provoked a vigorous backlash. Actions taken by the National Association for the Advancement of Colored People (NAACP), grassroots organizations, church leaders, and the US Supreme Court combined to form a powerful civil rights movement that began in the 1950s and gathered strength during the 1960s.

## A Climate of Injustice

In 1950 African-Americans numbered 15.9 million and comprised 10.6 percent of the population. By the mid-1960s 46 percent of African-Americans were living outside of the South, but the North was not free of racism. Employers in the North, like those in the South, denied blacks equal treatment in hiring, promotion, and pay. Discriminatory real estate practices helped concentrate black populations in inner-city housing projects, and most black children attended poorly financed all-black schools. This pattern of limited housing and educational opportunities has been described as de facto segregation.

In the South segregation was institutionalized by law. Local ordinances required that blacks and whites attend separate schools and churches; eat in separate establishments; use separate washrooms, water fountains, and recreational facilities; and sit in separate areas on buses.

The civil rights movement that would transform America in the 1960s grew out of the grassroots activism of African-American political organizations and churches throughout the 1950s. The first area that these groups targeted was education. A major breakthrough in educational rights took place in 1954 with one of the most significant Supreme Court decisions of the 20th century.

## Segregation and Education

**WEB LINKS**

For a detailed account of the Supreme Court decision in *Brown v. Board of Education*, see www.emp.ca/ah.

In 1954, in the case of *Brown v. Board of Education*, the US Supreme Court determined that "separate educational facilities are inherently unequal." The decision effectively denied the legal basis for segregation. A year later, in a follow-up ruling known as *Brown II*, the Supreme Court ordered that states desegregate their schools "with all deliberate speed."

With no set deadlines, progress on school desegregation through the 1950s and 1960s varied widely across the country. In the North integration proceeded slowly, and sometimes reluctantly, but it did proceed. In the South, however, little progress was made.

The Southern resistance to school integration was vividly demonstrated in 1957 at Little Rock, Arkansas. Angry white mobs prevented nine black students from entering Central High School. The state governor refused to enforce the court order that authorized the students' entrance. Only after President Eisenhower sent in federal troops to protect the students were they able to attend classes.

**SOUND BITE**

"To separate them from others of similar age and qualifications solely because of their race generates a feeling of inferiority as to their status in the community that may affect their hearts and minds in a way unlikely to ever be undone … [I]n the field of public education the doctrine of 'separate but equal' has no place."

—Chief Justice Earl Warren, *Brown v. Board of Education*

By 1965 more than 75 percent of schools in the South remained segregated, but the pace of desegregation throughout America accelerated in 1971 when the US Supreme Court ruled in *Swann v. Charlotte-Mecklenburg Board of Education* that school officials could bus students to schools outside their neighbourhoods to achieve racial diversity. The practice of busing in children of different races was often met with outright hostility. Parents in Boston challenged the idea of busing to accommodate integration. In *Milliken v. Bradley* (1975) the Supreme Court held that there was no need to bus children between rich and poor school districts. This decision modified *Swann*, and reflected the court's position that integration should not be forced on school districts.

**Figure 12.6** *The Ordeal of Alice* by Jacob Lawrence (1963). How has the artist attempted to illustrate the damaging effect of school segregation on children?

## Rosa Parks and the Montgomery Bus Boycott

A year and a half after *Brown*, the fight for civil rights entered a new phase when African-American residents of Montgomery, Alabama used a non-violent protest to end the segregation of local buses.

On December 1, 1955 Rosa Parks was riding a city bus on her way home from work and Christmas shopping. Although Parks was sitting in the section reserved for blacks, the bus driver ordered her and three other African-Americans to move in order to make room for white passengers. When Parks refused, she was arrested by the police. At her trial, Parks was found guilty of disorderly conduct and of violating a segregation law, and was fined.

In response to Rosa Parks's arrest, a boycott of Montgomery's bus system was quickly organized. On the first day of the boycott, the Montgomery Improvement Association (MIA) was formed to coordinate efforts. Martin Luther King, a charismatic 26-year-old Baptist pastor, was elected as its president.

**SOUND BITE**

"I did not get on the bus to get arrested; I got on the bus to go home ... I had no idea that history was being made. I was just tired of giving in. Somehow, I felt that what I did was right by standing up to that bus driver. I did not think about the consequences."

—Rosa Parks

**Figure 12.7** Montgomery, Alabama bus boycott, 1956.

For over a year the town's black residents held to the boycott, despite efforts to break it. King's house was firebombed, and he and 88 other African-Americans were arrested for breaking a local law prohibiting boycotts. King and his supporters fought back by challenging the segregation law in court. On November 13, 1956 the US Supreme Court ruled that the segregation of buses was unconstitutional. The bus boycott was declared over on December 21.

The integration of Montgomery's buses showed the power of black churches and the effectiveness of non-violent protest. It resulted in the formation of the Southern Christian Leadership Conference (SCLC), which coordinated anti-segregation protests across the South. It also vaulted Martin Luther King into the leadership of the civil rights movement.

## The Struggle Expands

After ending bus segregation in Montgomery, civil rights activists broadened their activities to fight segregation in all areas of life throughout the South and succeeded in putting civil rights on the national agenda.

The wider civil rights campaign began on February 1, 1960 with a sit-in by black college students at a Woolworth's lunch counter in Greensboro, North Carolina. Students would occupy seats and ask to be served; when refused service, they remained seated until local authorities removed them. Other students would then take their places. Similar sit-ins soon spread throughout the South. To coordinate their efforts, the protesters formed the Student Non-violent Coordinating Committee (SNCC). The sit-ins were costly to business owners, who began desegregating their premises. This success prompted the use of sit-ins to integrate beaches, parks, and other public areas.

In 1961 the SNCC began sending interracial groups on "freedom rides" into the Southern states to end the segregation of bus terminals. In places like Anniston, Birmingham and Montgomery, Alabama, freedom riders were harassed, beaten, and jailed. Appalled at the mistreatment of protesters, Robert Kennedy—US attorney general and brother of President Kennedy—intervened to help curb the violence.

In 1963 the SCLC began a campaign to desegregate Birmingham's business centre using marches and sit-ins. The City of Birmingham obtained a court injunction to stop the protests, and several demonstrators, including King, were arrested. When the SCLC called on high school students to join the protest, more than a thousand showed up. Birmingham's Public Safety Commissioner, Eugene "Bull" Conner, ordered his men to unleash police dogs on the students and direct high-pressure hoses at them. The mayhem was caught on national television and the resulting public outcry brought President Kennedy into negotiations to stop the confrontation. On May 10, city officials agreed to desegregate Birmingham's businesses and end discriminatory hiring practices.

**Civil Rights Organizations: 1950s and 1960s**

| | |
|---|---|
| **CORE** | Congress of Racial Equality |
| **MIA** | Montgomery Improvement Association |
| **NAACP** | National Association for the Advancement of Colored People |
| **SCLC** | Southern Christian Leadership Conference |
| **SNCC** | Student Non-violent Coordinating Committee |

# WE THE PEOPLE
## Martin Luther King
## 1929–1968

**Figure 12.8** Martin Luther King speaking in Washington, DC, August 28, 1963.

In the American mind, no one is as closely associated with non-violent protest as Dr. Martin Luther King. Born into a family of ministers in Georgia in 1929 and educated at Morehouse College in Atlanta, King received his PhD in theology from Boston University in 1955. While at Morehouse, King discovered the writings of Henry David Thoreau and Mahatma Gandhi.

Thoreau believed that there are both just and unjust laws, and that every citizen has a moral obligation to disobey unjust laws. As this idea was resonating deeply with King, he watched Gandhi win independence for India from Great Britain through a peaceful revolution based on boycotts, sit-ins, and marches.

King applied Thoreau's philosophy and Gandhi's methods to the problem of racism in America. In his "Letter from a Birmingham Jail," he explained why he urged African-Americans to knowingly break the Jim Crow laws of the South and risk confrontation and jail: "There is a type of constructive, non-violent tension which is necessary for growth. The purpose of our direct-action program is to create a situation so crisis-packed that it will inevitably open the door to negotiation."

The philosophy of non-violent confrontation served as the underpinning for the civil rights movement, from King's leadership in the Montgomery bus boycott in 1955 to his campaigns in Atlanta, Birmingham, and Selma. In 1963 *Time* magazine named King Man of the Year. The following year Congress passed the Civil Rights Act of 1964 and King won the Nobel Peace Prize.

King decided to use his fame to tackle two issues he saw as closely related to the struggle for civil rights: poverty and Vietnam. In 1967 the SCLC began planning a "Poor People's Campaign" that was meant to culminate with a march on Washington in April 1968. As early as 1965 King had spoken out against the US-led war in Vietnam, but decided not to press the issue for fear of alienating President Johnson. After Johnson announced he would divert funds from his "War on Poverty" to the war in Vietnam, however, King returned to the issue:

> Vietnam is taking the young black men who have been crippled by our society and sending them 8,000 miles away to guarantee liberties in Southeast Asia which they had not found in southeast Georgia and East Harlem.

As part of his Poor People's Campaign King was visiting Memphis, Tennessee to support a strike of sanitary public works employees. In a speech on April 3, 1968 he said:

> I've been to the mountaintop. And I've seen the promised land. I may not get there with you. But I want you to know that we, as a people, will get to the promised land.

The next day, while standing on his motel balcony, King was shot and killed.

### Think It Through

1. Which two philosophers influenced Dr. King, and why did their works apply so effectively to the civil rights movement?
2. Think of Dr. King's lifelong devotion to achieving justice for African-Americans. Would you be willing to sacrifice yourself in the same way for any cause?

## March on Washington, 1963

**WEB LINKS**

For more in-depth information on the civil rights movement, including a timeline, visit www.emp.ca/ah.

On August 28, 1963 King and other civil rights leaders organized the March on Washington for Rights and Freedom. Their aim was to urge action on racial problems and show support for the new civil rights bill that President Kennedy had promised. The march succeeded beyond expectations, drawing more than 250,000 people from all parts of the United States. King delivered the closing address in front of the Lincoln Memorial:

> I have a dream that one day this nation will rise up and live out the true meaning of its creed: "We hold these truths to be self-evident, that all men are created equal" ... And when this happens, when we allow freedom to ring, when we let it ring from every village and every hamlet, from every state and every city, we will be able to speed up that day when all of God's children, black men and white men, Jews and Gentiles, Protestants and Catholics, will be able to join hands and sing in the words of the old Negro spiritual: Free at last! Free at last! Thank God Almighty, we are free at last!

King's speech is considered a masterpiece and, in its call for equality and freedom for all, one of the most eloquent expressions of the American dream ever uttered.

On September 15, 1963, less than three weeks after the March on Washington, a terrorist bomb blew up in a Birmingham church, killing four young black girls and injuring 22 others. The bomb was intended to intimidate and defeat those campaigning for civil rights. Instead, it provoked public outrage and re-energized the civil rights movement.

## Death of a President

Two months after the Birmingham bombing, on November 22, President Kennedy was assassinated in Dallas, Texas. Lee Harvey Oswald, a former Marine who had defected to the Soviet Union in 1959 and later returned, was arrested for the murder but was never tried in court. Two days after his arrest, while being moved under police custody, Oswald was gunned down by Dallas bar-owner Jack Ruby on live television.

Kennedy's violent death shocked millions of people around the world. His state funeral on November 25, a national day of mourning, was broadcast live to a grieving America. The assassination came to be seen as a portent that

**Figure 12.9** Minutes after this photograph was taken, on November 22, 1963 in Dallas, Texas, President John F. Kennedy was shot.

the decade that began with such hope and optimism was fated to end in violence and disillusionment. This trend would be aggravated in 1968 with the assassinations of Martin Luther King and Robert Kennedy.

## Voting Rights

After Kennedy's assassination, Vice-President Lyndon B. Johnson was sworn in as president aboard Air Force One, the presidential jet. Johnson, a Southerner from Texas, would prove to be more proactive than Kennedy on civil rights issues, especially in the area of voting rights.

Although the Civil Rights Act of 1957 had created some protections for eligible voters, by 1960 only about 10 percent of Southern blacks of voting age were registered. Whites used threats and intimidation to openly discourage blacks from registering. In 1964, spurred on by a new Civil Rights Act passed that same year, the SCLC sent hundreds of white and African-American volunteers into the South as part of a "Freedom Summer" campaign to register black voters. This proved to be dangerous work. Civil rights workers were harassed and bullied, and a number were murdered. Even after the passage of the Civil Rights Act of 1964, voting abuses continued.

In 1965 the SCLC decided to focus attention on Selma, Alabama because so few of its large black population were registered to vote. Selma police beat and arrested hundreds of protestors and killed Jimmie Lee Jackson, a black Vietnam veteran. The SCLC organized a march from Selma to Montgomery, 90 kilometres away, to protest Jackson's death.

On Sunday, March 7 the marchers were attacked on the outskirts of Selma by police using clubs, tear gas, and whips; 17 protesters were hospitalized. Again, television coverage was extensive and created sympathy for the marchers—not only in the US, but around the world.

Partly in response to the events of "Bloody Sunday," President Johnson signed the Voting Rights Act on August 6, 1965. The new law ended the practices that had held up the registration of black voters, and changed America's political landscape. By 1969 black voter registration had risen from 23 percent to 61 percent.

## The Movement Switches Gears

Following the passage of the Voting Rights Act, civil rights leaders shifted their attention from the South to pursue a broader, national agenda: the elimination of discrimination in employment, housing, and education throughout the country—both North and South. In 1965 the national unemployment rate among blacks was still twice that of whites. Many urban blacks lived in poor, crime-ridden areas known as ghettos.

African-American leaders generally agreed that the poverty, violence, and drug addiction afflicting many black communities were rooted in racism. However, they were divided on what strategy to pursue. Leaders like Martin Luther King wanted to hold to the philosophy of non-violence. Younger leaders tended to be more militant—a few demanded radical, even violent action. The fight over strategy would continue even as black ghettos erupted into violence.

## Riots

From 1964 to 1970 a wave of race riots tore apart cities across the United States. In total, about 750 riots occurred. More than 200 people were killed and thousands were injured and arrested. Property damage ran into the hundreds of millions of dollars (billions of dollars today).

The National Advisory Commission on Civil Disorder (NACCD), created by President Johnson in 1967, pointed to the "discrimination and segregation that have long permeated much of American life" as one of the underlying causes of the riots. It concluded that the United States was "moving toward two societies, one white, one black—separate and unequal," and warned that "to pursue our present course will involve the continuing polarization of the American community and, ultimately, the destruction of basic democratic values."

Although Johnson rejected many of the commission's findings and recommendations, he did sign the Civil Rights Act of 1968, which banned discrimination in the sale and rental of housing and prohibited retaliation against those promoting fair housing rights.

## Black Power

As the 1960s progressed many of the younger black leaders focused on developing an attitude of self-esteem, racial pride, and resistance to racism. The new movement was called "black power." Pride in black identity found expression in appearance and language: young blacks abandoned the conservative suits and dresses of the older generation and adopted the Afro hairstyle. They stopped referring to themselves as "Negroes" and demanded instead that they be called "blacks" or "African-Americans." Prominent black power advocates included Malcolm X, Huey Newton, and Angela Davis.

The black power movement sought cooperation and unity among blacks, both within America and throughout the world. It brought into sharper relief a question facing modern-day African-Americans: Where should they find their identity—in the promise of the American dream or in their racial heritage?

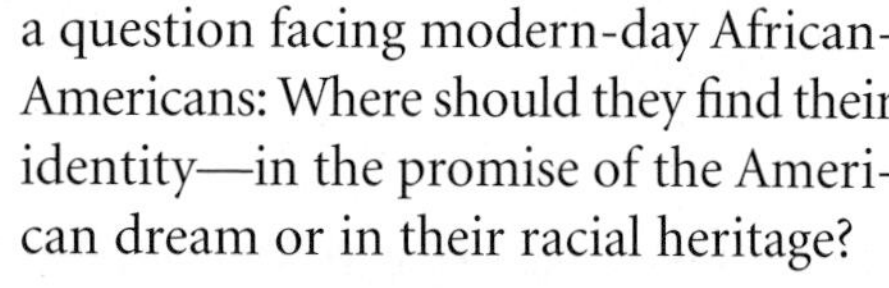

**Figure 12.10** Civil rights marchers in Martin Luther King's Poor People's Campaign, 1968. How did King's philosophy of non-violence translate to the civil rights movement? How was it opposed by some activists?

**Figure 12.11** Malcolm X (born Malcolm Little) was a Black Muslim minister and a member of the Nation of Islam sect. A charismatic orator, he opposed integration and embraced the black power movement. In 1964, after founding his own religious organization (the Organization of Afro-American Unity), he reversed his thinking and began advocating universal brotherhood. In 1965 Malcolm X was assassinated by Black Muslims while giving a speech in Harlem.

**Figure 12.12** In 1966, Huey Newton co-founded the Black Panther Party in Oakland, California. The Black Panthers originally focused on racism and police brutality, but then evolved into a Marxist political organization. After a series of shootouts with police that left 24 Black Panthers dead and Newton in prison for voluntary manslaughter, he renounced violence. The Black Panthers organized community programs offering free medical clinics and breakfasts for children. In 1989 Newton was shot and killed by a drug dealer in Oakland.

**Figure 12.13** A socialist philosopher and community activist, Angela Davis was active in the SNCC and the Black Panther Party. She was also an influential writer and thinker in the women's movement. She gained national notoriety when she was tried and acquitted on charges of conspiracy, kidnapping, and homicide related to the murder of Harold Haley, a California judge. As a university professor, Davis has remained active promoting racial and gender equality.

## CHECK YOUR UNDERSTANDING

1. What was meant by "de facto segregation" in the North?
2. What role did President Eisenhower play in school desegregation?
3. What forced the City of Montgomery to end racial segregation on city buses?
4. In what way did sit-ins at lunch counters and other public facilities advance the cause of civil rights?
5. What role did the media—especially television—play in ending segregation in Birmingham, Alabama?

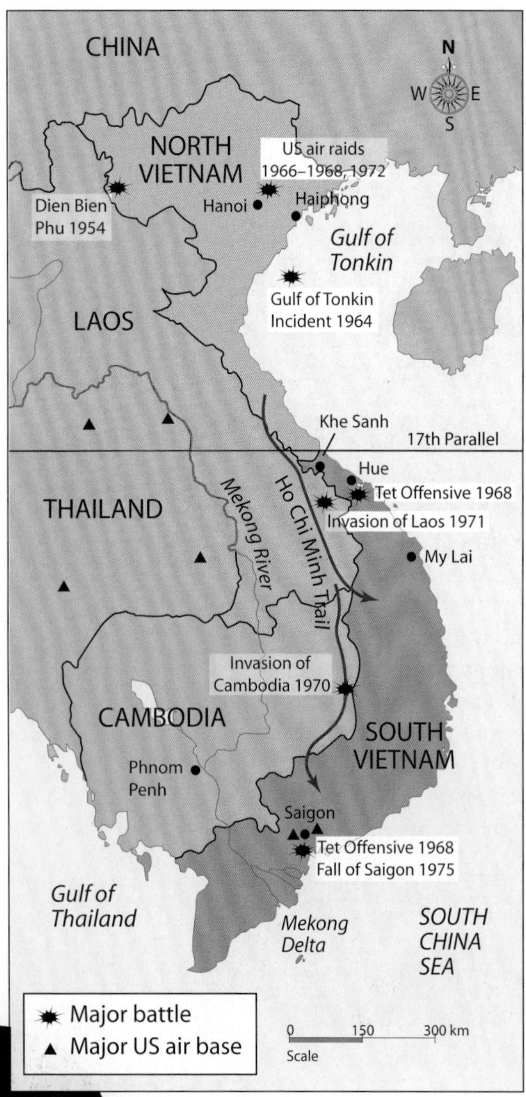


**Figure 12.14** Vietnam has a land area of 330,000 km$^2$, making it smaller than Newfoundland, but its population is more than two and a half times that of Canada.

# THE VIETNAM WAR

From 1955 to 1975, Vietnam in southeast Asia was divided by a civil war, one in which the United States was deeply involved. The conflict has also been characterized as a proxy war among competing superpowers: the United States, the Soviet Union, and China. The United States lost 58,000 military personnel and 153,000 more were wounded. Estimates of Vietnamese casualties are disputed, but certainly were many times higher than US casualties. The Vietnam War also had long-term effects on the American consciousness, aggravating the generation gap in the US and leading to violent political protests. It was the longest war in American history, and America's first military defeat.

By the time the Americans became involved in Vietnam, the country was no stranger to war and foreign interference. In the 19th century France had seized Vietnam as part of its empire. During World War II, Japan occupied Vietnam. To fight the Japanese, the communist Ho Chi Minh founded a national liberation movement called the Viet Minh. France reoccupied Vietnam following the war, and within months was in open conflict with the Viet Minh. The Chinese and the Soviet Union sent military aid to the Viet Minh, while the US supplied France with weapons and advisers. Ho Chi Minh's victory over the French in 1954 inspired other communist-led liberation movements around the world, including Fidel Castro's in Cuba.

At a 1954 peace conference in Geneva, Vietnam was partitioned into two zones. The Viet Minh were given control of the zone north of the 17th parallel, while the French retained temporary possession of the area to the south. Elections were scheduled for July 1956 to select a national government for a united Vietnam.

To learn more about the war in Vietnam, visit www.emp.ca/ah.

## The Diem Period (1955–1963)

In the North Ho Chi Minh consolidated power in the Democratic Republic of Vietnam, while in the South President Ngo Dinh Diem formed an anti-communist government.

Diem and US President Eisenhower were opposed to the elections required under the Geneva agreement. By US calculations, 80 percent of the Vietnamese population would elect Ho and the communists. Eisenhower's resistance to the elections reflected a broader American desire to prevent the spread of communism in Southeast Asia, based on the domino theory that you read about in Chapter 11.

In 1957 South Vietnamese insurgents killed more than 400 government officials to weaken the Diem regime. In 1959 North Vietnam began sending advisers and military equipment into South Vietnam via the Ho Chi Minh Trail.

In 1961, after attacks against Diem's government escalated, Kennedy ordered more US advisers and aid to South Vietnam. By the end of 1962 there were more than 12,000 US advisers in the country, and the value of US aid exceeded half a billion dollars ($3.5 billion today). Despite this show of support, Kennedy came to believe that Diem lacked the ability to defeat the Vietnamese communists, or Viet Cong. On November 2, 1963 South Vietnamese generals, with the encouragement of the CIA, killed Diem and took control of the government. Less than three weeks later, Kennedy himself was assassinated.

**Figure 12.15** Diem also faced opposition from Buddhist monks, a few of whom protested his efforts to quell their influence by burning themselves alive.

## The American War (1964–1968)

President Lyndon Johnson came into office with one overriding ambition: to extend Kennedy's legacy and to achieve a "Great Society" by implementing a broad domestic program emphasizing civil rights, urban renewal, and the reduction of poverty and crime. Johnson's landslide victory in the 1964 election over the ultra-conservative Republican Barry Goldwater demonstrated the American people's support for his liberal domestic policies. Like Eisenhower, however, Johnson was a firm believer in the domino theory; the

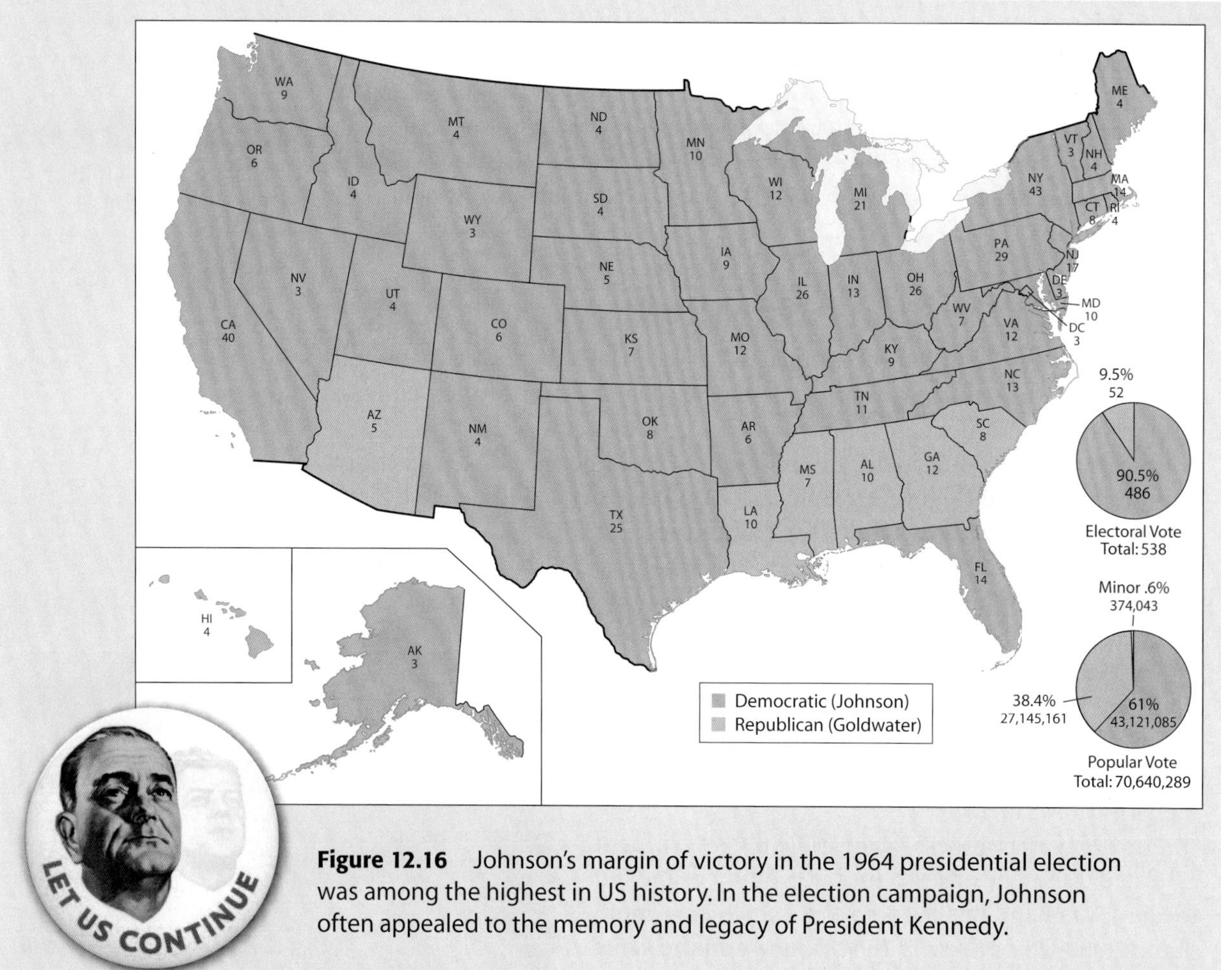


**Figure 12.16** Johnson's margin of victory in the 1964 presidential election was among the highest in US history. In the election campaign, Johnson often appealed to the memory and legacy of President Kennedy.

increasing conflict in South Vietnam led him to launch a massive American military campaign there to defeat the Viet Cong and the North Vietnamese Army (NVA).

## The Gulf of Tonkin Incident

On August 4, 1964 Johnson appeared on national television to announce that he had ordered US air attacks against North Vietnamese gunboats and shore facilities in response to unprovoked naval attacks on the destroyer *USS Maddox*, which had been patrolling in the Gulf of Tonkin. He called on Congress to approve a resolution that gave him authority to carry out "all necessary action to protect our Armed Forces." Newspapers across America accepted the official description of events and endorsed the air attacks. On August 7 Congress passed the Gulf of Tonkin resolution, giving Johnson wide-ranging authority to conduct military operations against the North Vietnamese without declaring war.

In 1967, after doubts were raised about Johnson's account of the Gulf of Tonkin incident, a Senate investigation determined that the North Vietnamese vessels had not launched torpedo attacks against the *Maddox*. The investigation also revealed that the *Maddox* had been on an intelligence-gathering mission, and may have been assisting South Vietnamese naval craft in carrying out raids on islands held by the North Vietnamese.

In early 1965 Johnson escalated American involvement in Vietnam by increasing the bombing of North Vietnam and areas of the South where the Viet Cong were strong. In March 1965, after Viet Cong units attacked US airfields, Johnson ordered 3,500 Marines to South Vietnam. By the end of the year there were almost 200,000 US soldiers there.

## Waging War

As it is today, in 1965 the United States was the leading military power in the world. It possessed the largest nuclear arsenal; its navy and air force were unequalled in technology and firepower; it had a large, highly trained army equipped with the most modern weapons. It also possessed a network of bases and a logistical system that allowed it to protect US interests throughout the world.

The North Vietnamese Army and the Viet Cong, by contrast, used the guerrilla warfare techniques that Mao Zedong had pioneered in China. They organized the peasants to provide food and support for combat troops, act as guides and gather intelligence, and set land mines and booby traps. Lightly armed militia units hit American patrols and positions without warning and then faded away into the jungle. They constructed a vast network of tunnels to escape detection and set ambushes.

Since Vietnam was a war without a front or a clearly defined line between friend and foe, it evolved into a particularly brutal conflict in which both sides committed atrocities. The NVA tortured American prisoners of war (POWs) and paraded them on television to give forced "confessions." There are documented instances of both sides killing prisoners in cold blood. Both sides also used unconventional weapons. The Viet Cong were adept at building "punji" traps, deep pits filled with sharpened stakes that would impale victims. US forces used napalm bombs and spread the defoliant Agent Orange over jungle areas to expose the trails and camps beneath the canopy. The toxic chemicals in Agent Orange left a terrible legacy, both for Vietnamese villagers and for the US soldiers who

**Figure 12.17** While some villages welcomed the Viet Cong and North Vietnamese Army, others were occupied under threat. American soldiers often found it difficult to distinguish noncombatants from combatants, in part because of the language barrier, and because villagers and guerrillas tended to wear similar clothing.

marched through the affected areas. Local inhabitants subsequently suffered high incidences of birth defects such as cleft palates, cataracts, and disfiguring skin disorders, and ex-GIs experienced higher-than-average rates of cancer.

On the US side, the most notorious incident was the massacre that took place on March 18, 1968 at the village of My Lai. American soldiers killed approximately 500 unarmed inhabitants, including 119 children and 27 seniors. After *New York Times* reporter Seymour Hersh exposed the incident, a formal army investigation was carried out. The army charged 26 soldiers with participating in or helping to cover up the massacre, but only Lieutenant William Calley was convicted. He received a life sentence but was released after less than four years of house arrest.

## Anti-War Sentiment in America

Vietnam was the first war in US history to be covered on television. News of atrocities like the My Lai massacre began to weaken public support for the war, as did the growing skepticism of news reporters over the press releases and briefings from the US military. Reporters began referring to the disparity between what they witnessed in the field and what the US military was claiming happened as a "credibility gap." The result was a sharp decline in the number of Americans who backed the US presence in Vietnam.

**Figure 12.18** The US anti-war movement received a major boost in 1967, especially among African-Americans, when world heavyweight champion Muhammad Ali refused induction into the military on the grounds of religious belief. Ali was tried and convicted of draft evasion, stripped of his title, and banned from boxing until 1970. Why might Ali's resistance to the war have had a wide influence?

**WEB LINKS**

To learn more on Muhammad Ali and his refusal to serve in the military, visit www.emp.ca/ah.

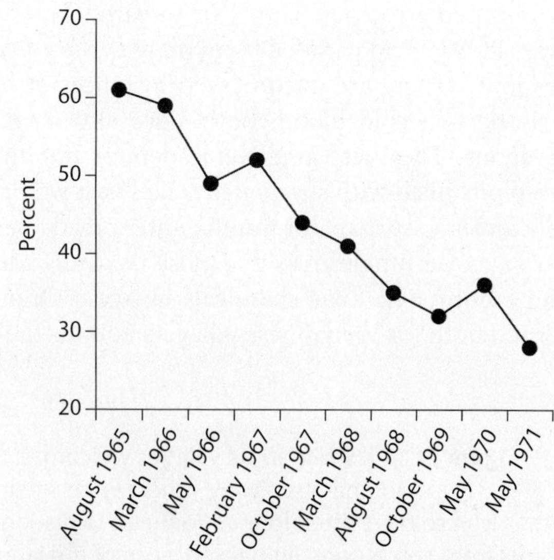


**Figure 12.19** Percentage of Americans who supported the US-led war in Vietnam, 1965–1971.

## Protests

The decline in public support for the war led to a rise in anti-war protests. Many of the protestors were baby boomers attending college, but the protest movement grew to include a cross-section of American society: working class and middle class, women and men of all faiths and cultures. Much of this anti-war sentiment was fuelled by the draft, which many Americans saw as unjust. Not everyone, however, was against the war. Millions of Americans continued to support it six years after the Gulf of Tonkin resolution in 1964. The war grew into an issue that created deep divisions in American society.

**SOUND BITE**

"I think [viewers] saw American troops acting in a way people had never seen American troops act before, and couldn't imagine ... To see young GIs ... lighting up thatched roofs, and women holding babies running away, wailing—this was a new sight to everyone, including the military."

—CBS correspondent Morley Safer

**Figure 12.20** The year 1968 was marked by the assassinations of Martin Luther King and Senator Robert Kennedy, and continuing protests against the Vietnam War, such as this one at the 1968 National Democratic Convention in Chicago. What different reactions would pro- and anti-war Americans have to Chicago police actions against the protesters?

## Draft Dodgers

As the United States became more immersed in the Vietnam War, the government increased the draft. Many men attempted to avoid service in Vietnam by enlisting in the Coast Guard or by joining the National Guard. Others protested the draft on moral grounds as conscientious objectors. Some 12,000 were army deserters. For an estimated 100,000 Americans, the best option was to seek refuge in Canada. Officially a non-participant in the Vietnam War, Canada willingly opened its doors to Americans avoiding the draft or deserting the army.

The draft was discontinued in 1973, and a day after he was inaugurated in 1977, President Jimmy Carter followed through on a campaign pledge and pardoned all draft dodgers who had left the United States. While many returned home, an estimated 50,000 settled in Canada. As many as 25,000 former draft dodgers remain in Canada today.

## The Tet Offensive

At the end of January 1968, on the eve of Tet (the Vietnamese New Year), Viet Cong and North Vietnamese forces launched a major offensive on the cities of the South and the main Marine base at Khe Sanh. An attack on Khe Sanh had been expected for weeks, but the assault on Saigon and other urban areas took the Americans by surprise. Viet Cong commandos were able to penetrate the grounds of the heavily fortified American embassy in Saigon, and regiments of the North Vietnamese Army occupied most of Hue province. After fierce fighting, the attackers were forced to retreat with the loss of about 45,000 troops.

Although the Tet Offensive was a technical defeat for North Vietnam, it shocked Americans and forced Johnson to reassess the progress of the war. After consulting with advisers, he concluded that even sending another 200,000 troops to Vietnam would not improve American chances for victory. In light of this and his own low standings in public opinion polls, Johnson decided not to seek re-election in 1968. His vice-president, Hubert Humphrey, lost the presidential election in November to the Republican candidate, Richard Nixon. Nixon had campaigned on a "law and order" platform, and said little about his position on the Vietnam War except that he wanted "peace with honor."

## Vietnamization: America Withdraws (1969–1973)

During his first term in office, President Nixon implemented a new Vietnam strategy with the assistance of his foreign policy adviser, Henry Kissinger. Nixon tried to reduce opposition to the war by introducing a lottery system for the draft. He adopted a policy of "Vietnamization," whereby the burden of fighting would gradually be shifted to the South Vietnamese army. He also began withdrawing US troops from South Vietnam; their numbers fell from 470,000 in 1969 to 156,800 in 1971.

To help prepare the South Vietnamese for their combat role, Nixon sent weapons, munitions, and other supplies. He also approved a secret invasion and bombing campaign of Cambodia, the country on Vietnam's western border and through which part of the Ho Chi Minh Trail ran.

When the invasion of Cambodia was made public, a new wave of anti-war protests swept across America. The publication of the "Pentagon Papers" in the *New York Times* in 1971 added momentum to the anti-war movement. These documents, prepared for the Department of Defense, revealed a long history of public deception by the US government.

**Figure 12.21** On May 4, 1970 an anti-war demonstration at Kent State University ended with four protesters shot dead by the Ohio National Guard.

## AMERICAN ARCHIVE

# The "Pentagon Papers"

> To see the conflict and our part in it as a tragedy without villains, war crimes without criminals, lies without liars, espouses and promulgates a view of process, roles and motives that is not only grossly mistaken but which underwrites deceits that have served a succession of Presidents.
>
> —Daniel Ellsberg

By leaking the classified "Pentagon Papers" to the *New York Times* in 1971, Daniel Ellsberg did everything in his power to expose the "villains, criminals, and liars" that he thought had misled Americans in an unwinnable war. Educated at Harvard and Cambridge, a veteran of the Marine Corps, and a brilliant military strategist, Ellsberg had been a "hawk" (or war supporter) until he joined other researchers to compile an official history of the war in Vietnam in 1967. After reading hundreds of documents, Ellsberg "believed that the pattern of secret threats and escalation needed to be exposed because it was being repeated under a new president [Nixon]."

The "Pentagon Papers" revealed that presidents Kennedy and Johnson had both authorized huge military buildups in Vietnam while they were publicly promising to scale back the number of troops. They also revealed that politicians had not been honest with the American public about the nature of the South Vietnamese government, the strength of the Viet Cong, the causes for America's entry into the war, and the degree of US covert military actions.

In 1964 President Johnson told the American people that South Vietnam was being attacked by a "communist conspiracy" directed by China. That same year, according to the "Pentagon Papers," the CIA, the State Department, and the Defense Intelligence Agency reported that communism's strength in South Vietnam was "indigenous"—the result of a popular homegrown movement.

Early in 1964 the American people were told that US involvement amounted to nothing more than sending money, military advisers, and logistical support. The "Pentagon Papers" revealed that the CIA had been using US civilian pilots to bomb the Ho Chi Minh Trail in Operation Barrel Roll. By the end of the year, US air force and navy pilots were secretly bombing Laos.

**Figure 12.22** Daniel Ellsberg.

Richard Nixon won the 1968 election with the promise of a "secret plan" to end the war. The plan proved to involve dropping more bombs on Southeast Asia in three years than had been dropped on Japan during World War II. When Nixon learned of the *Times*'s publication of the "Pentagon Papers," he obtained an injunction barring further installments (though the *Washington Post* was also publishing the papers by this time). In 1971, however, the US Supreme Court ruled that the *Times* had a constitutional right to publish the documents under the First Amendment.

Publication of the "Pentagon Papers" added momentum to the anti-war movement but did not really change the course of the war itself. The more significant effect of Ellsberg's disclosure was Nixon's attempt to stop such leaks of classified information. As you will learn in Chapter 13, publication of the "Pentagon Papers" led eventually to the Watergate scandal and Nixon's resignation in 1974.

## Think It Through

1. Why did Daniel Ellsberg deem it necessary to leak his research to the *New York Times*? Do you think this was ethical while his nation was at war?
2. What lies did the "Pentagon Papers" reveal to the American people?

By 1972 Henry Kissinger and Le Duc Tho of North Vietnam were well into secret peace talks (see the We the People feature on Henry Kissinger in Chapter 13). In October they reached an agreement, only to see the North and South Vietnamese leaders demand changes to the terms. Nixon brought the two sides back to the bargaining table through a massive bombing of North Vietnam, and on January 27, 1973 peace accords were signed. US military involvement in Vietnam was officially over, and the North Vietnamese released the American POWs they were holding.

## Collapse of the Republic of South Vietnam (1974–75)

Following the American pullout, the South Vietnamese regime survived for less than 16 months. The Army of the Republic of South Vietnam collapsed under a military offensive launched by the NVA on March 10, 1975. On April 29–30, the Americans evacuated more than 1,000 US citizens and more than 5,000 Vietnamese and other citizens from the US embassy by helicopter, and on April 30 an NVA tank broke through the gates of the presidential palace in Saigon.

The war in Vietnam was finally over. Fearing reprisals, thousands of South Vietnamese fled their homeland by sea. Eventually, many of these "boat people" made their way to the United States, Canada, and other countries to begin new lives. In the United States, a long period of healing began.

### CHECK YOUR UNDERSTANDING

1. Why was Vietnam divided into North and South at the 1954 Geneva Conference?
2. What was the importance of the Gulf of Tonkin resolution?
3. Why did the world's greatest military power have trouble fighting in Vietnam?
4. Why did President Johnson decide against running for re-election in 1968?
5. Refer to Figures 12.20 and 12.21. How could photographs such as these have affected both public and government support for the Vietnam War?

# OTHER SIGNS OF CHANGING TIMES

The turmoil that gripped America during the 1960s and early 1970s went far beyond the struggle for civil rights and protests against the Vietnam War. Feminist thinkers, gay and lesbian activists, and Native and Hispanic leaders alike also demanded an end to prejudicial attitudes and practices. Environmentalists campaigned to raise awareness about the harm that modern industry and unchecked consumerism were doing to the global ecosystem. It was a time when baby boomers questioned traditional moral values, experimented with new lifestyles and social relationships, and tested the limits of personal freedom.

## The Women's Movement

During the 1960s the women's movement unified in opposition to entrenched sexual discrimination in America. Its driving force was feminism, the belief that women and men should be treated equally in all aspects of life—legal, economic, political, cultural, and social. The movement had many antecedents, including the temperance and right-to-vote movements discussed in earlier chapters.

The year 1963 was a pivotal year for American women. The labour activist and social commentator Betty Friedan published the bestselling book *The Feminine Mystique*, in which she challenged the traditional view that a woman's place was in the home. Friedan argued that the roles of wife and mother robbed women of their identity because they defined women in relation to their husbands and children, and said that it was important for women to be financially independent and have careers outside of the home.

**SOUND BITE**

"The feminine mystique has succeeded in burying millions of American women alive."

—Betty Friedan (1921–2006)

The Equal Pay Act of 1963, passed by Congress in June, made it illegal for employers to pay women less than men for doing the same, or equal, work. The Act defined equal work as jobs requiring "equal skill, effort, and responsibility and which are performed under similar working conditions." The Civil Rights Act of 1964 extended protection against discrimination in the workplace. Employers could no longer retaliate against women who took legal action against them for unlawful discrimination.

In October 1963 the President's Commission on the Status of Women (PCSW), chaired by Eleanor Roosevelt, issued a report documenting gender discrimination in the workplace and making recommendations for equal employment opportunities, paid maternity leave, and affordable child care. State governments and other public agencies soon established their own "status of women" commissions. The government-sponsored Citizens' Advisory Council on the Status of Women (CACSW) was created to follow up on the recommendations of the PCSW.

In 1966, in response to the lack of progress in eliminating sex-segregated job advertising, former members of the PCSW and the CACSW founded the National Organization for Women (NOW). Betty Friedan and Dr. Pauli Murray co-authored its statement of purpose:

> We believe … the time has come to confront, with concrete action, the conditions that now prevent women from enjoying the equality of opportunity and freedom of choice which is their right as individual Americans and as human beings.

To learn more about the women's movement, visit www.emp.ca/ah.

During its early years NOW used petitions, demonstrations, marches, and court action to promote such causes as publicly funded child care, the repeal of abortion laws, equal treatment of women in facilities such as bars and restaurants, and an end to discriminatory hiring and promotion practices.

In 1971 the women's movement gained a new voice when the feminist activist Gloria Steinem published the first issue of *Ms. Magazine.* (The title "Ms." was created in 1961 by Sheila Michaels, a feminist and civil rights worker, who preferred it to "Miss" or "Mrs." because it did not define her by her marital status.) During the 1970s *Ms. Magazine* provided a forum for such feminist writers as Alice Walker, Angela Davis, and Susan Faludi.

### Abortion and *Roe v. Wade*

Feminists have generally supported abortion as part of a woman's right to make decisions regarding her own body. Those who oppose abortion believe that human life begins at conception and that fetuses are entitled to the same constitutional rights as other human beings.

In 1973 the US Supreme Court ruled 7–2 in *Roe v. Wade* that existing laws against abortion violated a woman's constitutional right to privacy. The majority opinion found that the right to privacy was "broad enough to encompass a woman's decision whether or not to terminate her pregnancy." According to the judgment, a woman's right to an abortion is determined by how far along in the pregnancy she is. The women's movement considered *Roe v. Wade* an important victory and continues to defend it against recent legal challenges.

### Equal Rights Amendment

Beginning in 1972 the women's movement engaged in another controversial campaign: ratification of an amendment to the Constitution guaranteeing equal rights for women. In 1923 Alice Paul of the National Women's Party had proposed a constitutional amendment that read: "Men and women shall have equal rights throughout the United States and every place subject to its jurisdiction." In 1971 the House of Representatives adopted a modified version of this amendment, and the Senate approved the measure the following year. By law, the amendment had to be ratified by 38 of 50 states; it failed, however, stalling at 35 ratifications.

"The law cannot do it for us. We must do it for ourselves. Women in this country must become revolutionaries."

—US Congresswoman Shirley Chisholm

The amendment's failure has been attributed both to a general shift toward more conservative values in the US at the time and to the fact that by this time women had achieved many of the rights and reforms they had sought to achieve for years. By 1980 the efforts of the women's rights movement meant that women enjoyed higher rates of educational attainment, better salaries and job opportunities, and higher positions in the corporate and political worlds than ever before.

## Lesbian and Gay Rights

During the 1960s and 1970s gays and lesbians joined the struggle for recognition of fundamental rights. Until the 1960s they had existed largely as an invisible minority because revealing their sexual orientation brought serious consequences. Gays and lesbians faced social ostracism from their families and neighbours, discrimination at work, and criminal prosecution. The federal government, for example, denied employment in military and security services to those who were openly gay.

The emergence of the lesbian and gay rights movement goes back to the 1940s, when gay communities formed in major urban centres such as New York and San Francisco. The event that transformed the campaign for lesbian and gay rights into a national movement—and gained worldwide attention—was the Stonewall riots in late June 1969. A protest erupted after police raided the Stonewall Inn, an unlicensed gay bar in Greenwich Village, New York. The situation escalated into violence, with police beating demonstrators and many in the crowd throwing rocks and bottles at police. Over the next few nights, gay men gathered outside the Stonewall Inn to protest police discrimination.

The riots had an immediate and far-reaching impact, as dozens of new gay rights groups formed across America. Annual rallies commemorating the riots were first held in 1970. In the 1980s the original emphasis on protesting discrimination shifted to celebrating diversity, and "pride parades" are now held each year across America and around the world.

## The Native American Civil Rights Movement

Earlier in this book you saw how European settlement and the westward expansion of the United States resulted in the occupation of Native American lands and the displacement of their populations. Government assimilation policies stripped Native Americans of their language and culture through English-only schooling and bans on traditional ceremonies. During the first half of the 20th century large numbers of Native Americans lived in poverty with little chance of finding work. Health and education standards were low, and bitterness and despair drove many to alcoholism and suicide. Meanwhile, other Americans based their image of Native peoples on stereotypes shown in movies and on television.

In the 1960s a Native American civil rights movement emerged. Inspiration came from the successes of the African-American civil rights campaign and from growing numbers of young, educated Native Americans who were less tied to life on reserves. As part of their strategy, Native activists sought to draw public attention to their cause.

In 1961 more than 500 representatives from 64 tribes gathered in Chicago. They issued a Declaration of Indian Purpose, which included the following statement: "We believe in the inherent right of all peoples to retain spiritual and cultural values, and that the free exercise of these values is necessary to the normal development of any people."

In 1968 Native activists met in Minneapolis and founded the American Indian Movement (AIM). Modelled on the Black Panthers, AIM originally sought to protect Native Americans living in inner-city ghettos from police abuse but its focus soon included action on educational reform, self-determination, redress for broken treaties, and settlement of land claims. AIM's adoption of aggressive tactics to capture media attention brought it into conflict with law enforcement agencies.

In November 1969 AIM protesters began a 19-month occupation of Alcatraz Island in San Francisco Bay, the site of a former maximum-security federal prison. The occupation captured international attention and gave AIM a leadership role in the fight for Native American rights. On Thanksgiving Day the following year, during the 350th anniversary year of the Pilgrims' landing in North America, AIM members painted Plymouth Rock red and occupied a replica of the Mayflower as part of a Day of Mourning protest.

Other acts of protest included the July 4, 1971 occupation of Mount Rushmore in South Dakota—where AIM protesters demanded the return of Lakota lands in the Black Hills—and the 1972 collaboration between AIM and other Native groups that resulted in the Trail of Broken Treaties March. Demonstrators travelled from the west coast to Washington, DC, and by the time they arrived they had been joined by thousands of supporters. When government officials refused to meet with them, they occupied the Bureau of Indian Affairs headquarters for six days.

In February 1973 hundreds of AIM members and local supporters began a 71-day occupation of the village of Wounded Knee on the Pine Ridge reservation in South Dakota, at the site of the Wounded Knee massacre of 1890 (see Chapter 8). AIM intervened after conflict arose between tribal traditionalists and the pro–US government council. Armed clashes resulted in the killing of two AIM supporters, and many involved in the occupation were subsequently arrested and imprisoned. Seven weeks after the occupation ended, a gun battle on the reservation between AIM members and law enforcement officials ended with the deaths of two FBI agents and one Native American.

Although the confrontational style of AIM activists alienated many in the United States, including some Native Americans, Native activism in the 1960s

**Figure 12.23** AIM members block a road during the occupation of Wounded Knee. Compare the methods used by Native Americans and African-Americans in their respective struggles for civil rights.

and 1970s did produce positive results. The Indian Civil Rights Act of 1968 guaranteed Native Americans on reservations many of the rights accorded to other Americans under the US Bill of Rights, while also giving weight to local tribal laws and customs. In 1972 Congress passed the Indian Education Act, which recognized that Native Americans have unique educational needs, including the preservation of their languages and cultures. Another sign of progress was a greater willingness on the part of government officials to discuss ways of achieving Native self-determination.

## Rights for Hispanic Americans

In 1970 Hispanic Americans made up 4.7 percent of the US population. Most traced their origins to Mexico, though in Florida there was a sizable population of Cubans and in New York City of Puerto Ricans. During the 1960s and 1970s many Hispanics participated in protests. Unlike other groups, they focused their energies on winning higher wages and benefits for farm workers. One individual stands out in this struggle: César Estrada Chávez, a child of migrant farm labourers and—like Martin Luther King—a believer in non-violent protest.

**SOUND BITE**

"We shall strike. We shall organize boycotts. We shall demonstrate and have political campaigns. We shall pursue the revolution we have proposed. We are the sons and daughters of the farm workers' revolution, a revolution of the poor seeking bread and justice."

—Union leader César Chávez (1927–1993)

In 1966 Chávez led a march of striking California grape pickers to Sacramento, the state capital. Eventually the various strike leaders formed the United Farm Workers (UFW), whose members included Mexicans, Chicanos (Mexican Americans), Filipinos, and Filipino Americans. The strike lasted for five years. At one point, to persuade workers and their supporters to remain dedicated to the principles of non-violence, Chávez fasted for 25 days. He also organized a successful boycott

**WEB LINKS** 

To learn more about Chávez and his involvement with migrant workers, visit www.emp.ca/ah.

**Figure 12.24** Influenced by César Chávez and the social struggles of the early 1970s, Judy Baca's "Great Wall" in Los Angeles depicts the importance of the Hispanic community in LA's multi-ethnic history. Why are street murals a powerful medium for commenting on social history?

of grapes across North America. In the end the UFW won union recognition and the right to make contracts with California growers. In 1975 Congress passed the Agricultural Relations Act, which granted farm workers collective bargaining rights and the right to hold union elections.

## The Baby Boom and the American Economy

By virtue of their numbers alone, Americans who came of age in the 1960s and 1970s were destined to have an enormous impact on society. Between 1946 and 1964, 76 million babies were born in the United States, accounting for 40 percent of the population. Unlike their parents, the majority of these children—especially white middle-class Americans—grew up in prosperity.

The economic vitality of the 1960s had its roots in many industries. With the creation of the National Aeronautics and Space Administration (NASA) in 1958, the US aerospace industry soared in the 1960s. The pinnacle of the US space program was the Apollo moon landing in 1969. Air travel increased through the decade, and in 1967 Boeing's 747, the world's first jumbo jet, was introduced. The Canada–US Automotive Agreement of 1965, commonly known as the Auto Pact, removed tariffs on cars, trucks, buses, tires, and automotive parts between the United States and Canada, and was a boon to the auto industry (especially General Motors, Ford, and Chrysler) in both countries.

The social legislative agenda that was initiated by President Kennedy did not end with his death; indeed, his assassination spurred Congress to enact many of his proposals. President Johnson sought to build a "Great Society" by spreading the benefits of America's successful economy to more citizens. In the summer of 1964, as part of his "War on Poverty," President Johnson established a federal jobs program for impoverished young people and cut personal and corporate income taxes. A variety of new programs followed, including Medicare (health care for the elderly), Food Stamps (food assistance for the poor), and numerous education initiatives (assistance to students as well as grants to schools and colleges). In 1967 Johnson extended the coverage of minimum wage and increased it to $1.40 per hour (about $8.90 per hour today).

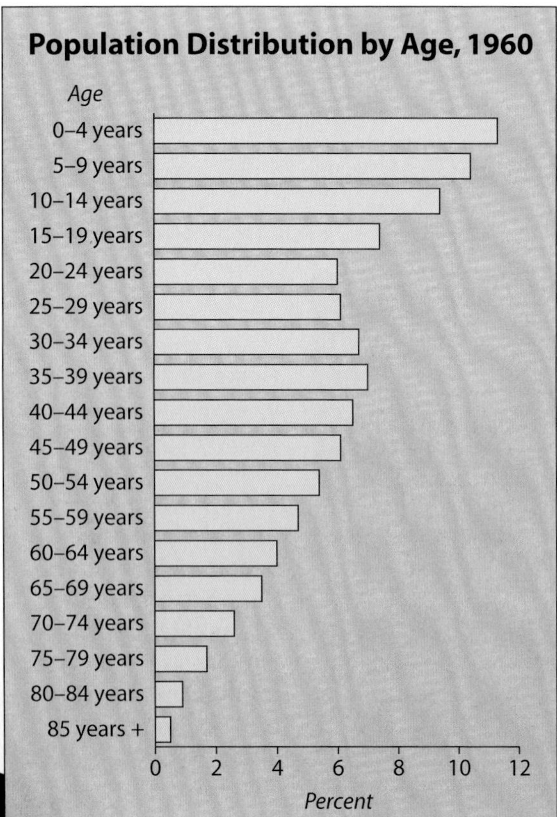


**Figure 12.25** As a result of the baby boom, in the 1960s almost half of the population was under the age of 25.

Johnson's tax cuts in his War on Poverty contributed to a short-term rise in prosperity, as did increased military spending on the war in Vietnam. In 1967 Johnson approved $70 billion appropriation for defence (almost $450 billion in current dollars). However, the defence budget grew by way of deficit, and Johnson's failure to raise taxes to fund the war effort resulted in higher inflation, eventually eroding this prosperity.

## Youth and Popular Culture

Confident and idealistic, many baby boomers rejected the materialism and conservative social values of their parents. Many took part in, or sympathized with, the major protest movements of the time. The introduction of the birth control pill in the mid-1960s liberalized their attitudes about sex. Many young people also became part of the **hippie** movement, rejecting conservative values and aesthetics and exploring alternative lifestyles and new forms of art, music, and literature. The hippie counterculture had far-reaching influence on the baby-boomer generation, and on wider American society.

In general, the hippies believed in cooperation rather than competition. They often lived together in communes, where chores were shared. Some communes included "free love"—that is, open sexual relationships. Although hippies rarely attended places of worship, many placed a high value on spirituality. They were attracted to the teachings of Eastern religions, such as Buddhism and Hinduism, and Native American beliefs about nature.

Hippies were also at the forefront of the back-to-the-land movement, which put a high value on self-sufficiency. Using local materials, many of these young people built their own homes and produced their own food. They favoured organic farming and avoided the use of harmful pesticides. By the mid-1970s the hippie counterculture was in decline, but some of its values are echoed in the environmental movement today.

**Figure 12.26** In 1967 tens of thousands of young people, attracted by media stories glamourizing the hippie subculture and psychedelic music scene, descended on San Francisco to participate in what was billed as the "Summer of Love."

# Culture Notes

## Music of Hope

By the time we got to Woodstock
We were half a million strong
And everywhere there was song and celebration
—Joni Mitchell, "Woodstock"

The Woodstock Music and Art Fair in the summer of 1969 drew more than 450,000 people to a small, muddy field near the town of Woodstock in central New York State. For four days, from August 15 to 18, the site became a kind of counterculture mini-nation in which the hippie ideals of peace, love, and music reigned; drugs were all but legal; and love was considered "free." Depending on one's point of view, Woodstock was either the defining moment of a generation or four long days of self-indulgence, noise, promiscuity, and illegal drug use.

Gathered that weekend was an eclectic assortment of folk and rock music performers including some of the leading musicians of the time, such as Neil Young and The Who. The diverse lineup reflected the monumental social changes that were taking place in the 1960s. Whether they were connected to such movements or not, the presence of performers like Jimi Hendrix, Janis Joplin, and Joan Baez was a reminder of the black civil rights movement, the women's movement, and the anti-war movement, and their impact on the values and attitudes of young people in America. Youth—or at least a significant proportion of American youth—were embracing movements for social change and new ways of thinking that challenged the conservatism represented by their parents' generation.

Despite rain, two deaths, several arrests, widespread drug use, and a serious lack of food, water, and sanitary facilities, the concert went on successfully and is considered a landmark event in music history.

Woodstock vividly captured the reciprocal relationship between music and social change that was characteristic of the 1960s. An artist might look to the anti–Vietnam War movement and be inspired to write, just as Dennis Lambert and Brian Potter were when they penned their famous peace song "One Tin Soldier." In turn, there was a good chance that their music would influence their listeners' ideas and draw them to the movement that originally inspired them to write.

**Figure 12.27** Woodstock was originally planned for 150,000 concertgoers. Organizers were overwhelmed when more than 450,000 people showed up.

Today, Woodstock—like only a handful of other historical events—is part of America's cultural lexicon. If "Watergate" is a code word for political corruption (see Chapter 13), "Woodstock" is shorthand for the '60s youthful hedonism and idealized hope for the future. Arnold Skolnick, the artist who designed Woodstock's distinctive dove-and-guitar poster, described it this way: "Something was tapped, a nerve, in this country. And everybody just came."

### Think It Through

1. Why is Woodstock so fondly remembered by the baby-boomer generation?
2. Is music today still a catalyst for social change? Provide two examples and explain how they are catalysts.

# The Environmental Movement

By the 1960s the nature conservation movement had been active in America for more than a century. In the late 1800s they formed societies such as the Sierra Club and the National Audubon Society to preserve the natural environment and protect wildlife. In the early 1900s President Theodore Roosevelt more than doubled the area of land set aside for national parks and wildlife refuges (see Chapter 9). The beginning of the modern environmental movement is generally dated to 1962, with the publication of Rachel Carson's book *Silent Spring* (see the Past Voices feature on page 434).

In the early 1960s environmentalists had focused on cleaning up litter and upgrading sewage treatment facilities for large cities. By the late 1960s they were drawing links between industrial pollution and harm done to the natural environment and human health. In the early 1970s grassroots organizations such as Greenpeace drew international attention to such issues as the hunting of whales and seals, the cutting of old-growth forests, destructive fishing methods, and the dangers of nuclear power generation. Greenpeace's global approach recognized that environmental problems cannot be solved by countries acting independently but rather require international cooperation.

## Action on the Environment

On January 28, 1969 a blowout at a drilling platform off the coast of California triggered a release of crude oil that lasted for days. Shorelines along the California coast were fouled and thousands of seabirds died. The incident highlighted the risks that accompany offshore drilling and led to calls for moratoriums on further drilling. Other spills also underlined the environmental risks of transporting oil by sea. Faced with mounting public pressure to protect the environment, America's political leaders began to take action:

- **1969** Congress passes the National Environmental Policy Act, requiring federal agencies to consider the environmental impact of any major actions that they undertake.
- **1970** Richard Nixon creates the Environmental Protection Agency (EPA) to develop and enforce government regulations under existing environmental laws.
- **1972** The US government bans the use of DDT within its borders.
- **1972** Congress passes the Water Pollution Control Act, surmounting a veto attempted by Nixon.

**Figure 12.28** In December 1968 the crew of Apollo 8 took the first photographs of Earth rising above the lunar horizon. This image, known as "Earthrise," was a dramatic reminder that all of humanity lives together on a tiny planet—"Spaceship Earth"—with limited room and resources, and that if we do not protect our environment we risk putting ourselves, and other living things, at risk.

# PAST VOICES

## Rachael Carson's *Silent Spring*

Figure 12.29 Rachel Carson.

> The "control of nature" is a phrase conceived in arrogance, born of the Neanderthal age of biology and philosophy, when it was supposed that nature exists for the convenience of man.
>
> —Rachel Carson

In her landmark book *Silent Spring* (1962), Rachel Carson demonstrated that human beings in the industrially and chemically obsessed 20th century were destroying the ecological system that supported them. In the tradition of the muckrakers from the early 20th century, she exposed the hazards of the insecticide DDT and questioned the public's blind faith in scientific and technological progress:

> Intoxicated with a sense of his own power, mankind seems to be going farther and farther into more experiments for the destruction of himself and the world.

Indirectly, she changed the way many Americans thought about nature.

After several failed attempts to find a publisher, Carson's *Silent Spring* was serialized in *The New Yorker* magazine in 1962 and then released as a book. The title alludes to a spring with no birdsong because all the songbirds have died from pesticide poisoning. Carson's thesis was that humanity was killing itself slowly through the misuse of chemical pesticides that polluted the environment. "We are subjugating whole populations to exposure to chemicals which animal experiments have proved to be extremely poisonous and in many cases cumulative in their effects," she wrote.

In *Silent Spring* Carson meticulously documented how DDT enters the food chain through birds that eat poisoned insects; how the poison is subsequently accumulated in the fatty tissues of animals, including humans; and how it thereby causes cancer and genetic damage. Moreover, Carson found evidence that marine life was also being harmed when soil laden with DDT drained into rivers and the sea.

> Can anyone believe it is possible to lay down such a barrage of poisons on the surface of the earth without making it unfit for all life? They should not be called "pesticides," but "biocides."

*Silent Spring* placed the blame for DDT pollution not only on farmers who overused pesticides, but also—and more importantly—on the government that failed to regulate its use and the chemical companies that profited from the public's ignorance. The book produced an immediate effect. On reading it, John F. Kennedy appointed a committee to study the use of pesticides that eventually called for a decrease in the use of toxic chemicals in the environment. *Silent Spring* is also credited with prompting the creation of the Environmental Protection Agency, the ban on general use of DDT in 1972, and the launch of the modern environmental movement.

### Think It Through

1. How did the public's perception of modern science pose a challenge to Carson?
2. Why do you think *Silent Spring* has had such a lasting impact on the way people view the relationship between themselves and nature?

**Figure 12.30** This monumental earthwork by Robert Smithson entitled *Spiral Jetty* (1970) is located on the Great Salt Lake in Utah. Built of mud, salt crystals, basalt, rocks, and earth, the sculpture is a tribute to nature. By the mid-1970s Americans had begun to appreciate that environmental degradation posed a serious problem for their country. However, few grasped the magnitude of the problem and the need for global action.

In the 1960s and 1970s Americans came to recognize that material prosperity did not prevent the widening of rifts in American society: racial, gender, and generational. The challenges to the status quo that were posed by protesters in the 1960s and early 1970s touched all aspects of life and produced a distrust of government, religion, business, and educational institutions. Growing awareness of the environmental cost of a consumer lifestyle raised doubts about the moral soundness of the American dream. Television exposed mass audiences to events happening in real time—in America, around the world, and beyond—magnifying their impact and creating a sense of immediacy and personal connection.

## CHECK YOUR UNDERSTANDING

1. How did the Equal Pay Act of 1963 define "equal work"?
2. Upon what constitutional right was *Roe v. Wade* decided?
3. Why did the Equal Rights Amendment fail?
4. What were four tactics used by AIM to capture media and public attention?
5. How was the hippie lifestyle related to the environmental movement?

# THE HISTORIAN'S CRAFT

## Dealing with Truth and Myth in History

### Historical Truth

Some historical facts are absolutely true: "The 88th Congress passed the Civil Rights Act of 1964." When the historical truth involves a judgment, however, the facts are not always absolute. Truth in history is based on careful interpretation of the available evidence. If new historical evidence appears or if existing evidence is proven unreliable, then historians must reassess the historical interpretation.

You can see an example of this process in the Gulf of Tonkin resolution (see pages 418–419). Historians writing in 1966 might simply have referenced the resolution as a statement of policy, while historians writing after the Senate investigation would have challenged Johnson's story and pointed to it as a misrepresentation. Historians writing today, however, have access to the president's telephone conversations with his secretary of defence; this evidence confirms that *USS Maddox* was not an "innocent bystander" and that Johnson sanctioned South Vietnamese naval attacks. Today's historian would confidently conclude that the president knowingly misled Congress and the nation.

### Truth and Myth in History

The matter of historical truth becomes complicated when dealing with historical figures who have taken on mythical status. Myths focus on the stories of gods and larger-than-life heroes who engage in monumental tasks. One American president was seen by many Americans—and other people around the world—as such a mythical hero.

John F. Kennedy captured people's imagination because he was young and charismatic. As the first Catholic president, he represented a new stage of American maturity. As an eloquent speaker, he embodied a sense of the new vigour of the 1960s: "Now the trumpet summons us again—not as a call to bear arms, though arms we need; not as a call to battle, though embattled we are—but a call to bear the burden of a long twilight struggle, year in and year out ... a struggle against the common enemies of man: tyranny, poverty, disease, and war itself."

Kennedy surrounded himself with advisers from universities and progressive thinkers who, along with visiting artists and writers, formed a "Washington court." Some writers referred to that period as Camelot (as you read about earlier in this chapter). In 1965 the eminent American historian Samuel Eliot Morison wrote: "With the death of John Fitzgerald Kennedy something died in each one of us. Yet the memory of that bright, vivid personality, that great gentleman whose every act and appearance appealed to our pride and gave us fresh confidence in ourselves and our country, will live in us for a long, long time."

Historians today still acknowledge Kennedy's charisma, but their assessment of his record shatters the myth. Some point to failures in his international policy, especially in Latin America and Vietnam. One summed up his career as follows: "Fairy stories are necessary for children. Historians ought to know better. In fact, John F. Kennedy was a mediocre president." Yet new perspectives can also add to Kennedy's image. The president, who had been wounded in World War II, suffered from Addison's disease, which left him in constant pain. His stoic determination to serve should be acknowledged in judging his career in Camelot.

### Try It!

1. Re-examine the Gulf of Tonkin resolution in the light of Johnson's declassified telephone transcripts, online at www.emp.ca/ah.
2. Assess the career of John F. Kennedy under the headings "Popular Image" and "Presidential Achievements." There are many relevant websites and print sources (try to find books from the 1960s to 1970s as well as recent works so that you can compare interpretations).
3. Debate: "Resolved that President Kennedy was a great president."

# STUDY HALL

## Thinking

1. State, in the form of a question, the problem Kennedy faced with Cuba when he became president.
2. The roots of the civil rights movement go back to the Civil War and the freeing of slaves. In what sense can this movement be called the fulfillment of the Civil War?
3. Some people thought of Vietnam as the world's first "television war." What are the positive and negative aspects of covering a war on television?
4. Debate the following issues:
   a. Resolved that separate cannot be equal.
   b. Resolved that non-violent tactics such as sit-ins and freedom rides are more effective than militancy and violence.
   c. Resolved that the Vietnam War was worth fighting.
   d. Resolved that the feminist movement is now outdated and old-fashioned.
   e. Resolved that the baby boomers were self-centred and selfish.

## Communication

5. Was President Kennedy a great president or was his greatness a myth? In a two-column chart, list the myths and realities about President Kennedy and draw your own conclusions.
6. In a web diagram with the term "segregation" at its centre, demonstrate how segregation affects the education of children. Then, identify which of these effects are illustrated in the painting in Figure 12.6.
7. How would anti-war leaders persuade students to stage a strike or sit-in to voice opposition to Vietnam? Using facts about the war and from American history, write a historically based speech for such a leader.
8. The Soviets set up two types of nuclear-armed missiles in Cuba. One had a range of 2,037 kilometres, and the other a range of 4,074 kilometres.
   a. On a map of North and South America, show the range of these missiles and the major cities within their range.
   b. What would be an appropriate title for this map from the point of view of each of the following: the US, the USSR, Cuba, Canada, other countries in Central and South America, and the Caribbean?
   c. What does the map reveal about how the Soviet missiles may have changed the Cold War?

## Application

9. Research the Kennedy assassination. Was Kennedy the victim of a conspiracy or was there just a lone gunman?
10. Research the race to the moon, its accomplishments, and its contributions to science and daily life. Was it was worth the cost? Explain.
11. How would you test the effectiveness today of the Voting Rights Act, the Civil Rights Act, and the Indian Civil Rights Act? Consider criteria such as the number of US cities with African-American mayors. Make a list of other criteria you would use to conduct research, and present your conclusions.
12. Assess the definition of "equal work" in the Equal Pay Act of 1963. What criteria will you use? Suggest a modern-day rewording of "equal work."

# 13 A Time of Crises (1972–1989)

## KEY CONCEPTS

In this chapter you will consider:

- The Watergate scandal leading to the resignation of President Nixon
- The energy crisis and its economic consequences
- The rise of environmentalism and the broadening of the civil rights movement
- The influence of religion on US social and political policy
- The effects of "Reaganomics" on the middle class, industry, technology, and science
- Social challenges, including the backlash against feminism, peace activism, gay activism, and the AIDS crisis

## The American Story

During the 1970s and 1980s, a series of national crises provoked great anxiety and doubt in many Americans. In the early 1970s, the federal government was shaken by the Watergate scandal and the resignation of President Nixon, and at the end of the decade the Iran Hostage Crisis suggested America had lost much of its prestige and influence on the international stage. In the 1980s, Americans were outraged to learn that President Reagan's administration had flagrantly broken federal laws to provide a rebel movement in Nicaragua with arms and money. Yet, the bicentennial celebrations in 1976 and the fall of the Berlin Wall in 1989 gave Americans cause for hope and pride in their accomplishments and history. But what would the future hold? How would the American people and their state react to their new-found status as the world's only superpower?

## TIMELINE

**1972**
- Nixon re-elected; visits China
- Watergate scandal

**1973**
- Vietnam War ends
- Oil crisis

**1974**
- Nixon resigns; Ford becomes president
- 1.8 million employees affected by strikes/lockouts

**1975**
- Indian Self-Determination and Cultural Assistance Act

**1976**
- US bicentennial

## IMAGE ANALYSIS

**Figure 13.1** East and West Germans celebrate the dismantling of the Berlin Wall, 1989. After World War II, Berlin, like the rest of Germany, was divided into four zones of occupation: British, French, American, and Russian. As the Cold War heated up, Soviet-allied East Germany built the Berlin Wall in 1961 to keep East Germans from escaping to the West. The Wall symbolized the political, economic, and cultural Iron Curtain between the communist East and the democratic West. In October 1989, following the escape of more than 13,000 East German tourists to Austria via Hungary, mass demonstrations broke out all over East Germany. When the East German Minister of Propaganda announced that "East Berliners will be allowed to cross the border with proper permission ... effective immediately," East Berliners flooded the checkpoints into West Berlin. November 9, 1989 is considered the date the Wall fell.

Millions around the world watched history unfold on television as ordinary German citizens spontaneously rose up, taking sledgehammers to the Wall. The media proclaimed a heroic victory for democratic ideals, the end of the Cold War, and the dawn of a new era. The dismantling of the Wall was the first step toward German reunification. Imagine how Germans felt watching the fall of the Berlin Wall, which had for so long divided their families, their country, and the world. What do you think this event meant for the United States?

- **1978**
  - ▸ Camp David Accords
- **1979**
  - ▸ Hostage taking at US embassy in Iran
  - ▸ Equal Rights Amendment dies
- **1981**
  - ▸ First cases of AIDS diagnosed
  - ▸ Ronald Reagan's presidency begins
- **1982**
  - ▸ Largest peace demonstration in US history
- **1989**
  - ▸ Free Trade Agreement becomes law
  - ▸ Fall of Berlin Wall; end of Cold War

# INTRODUCTION

If you were a young American in high school at the beginning of the 1970s, you would probably have grown up thinking the United States was the greatest country on earth. If you were a member of a middle-class family, you would have expected affordable post-secondary education and a well-paying job. However, in the early 1970s, circumstances might have forced you to question the beliefs you held as a child.

Your generation would come of age during America's humiliating military defeat in Vietnam. You would hear of serious wrongdoings in the White House, the CIA, and the FBI. You would see America's traditional economic assumptions shaken and its industrial predominance threatened. When the time came to celebrate your country's bicentennial in 1976, there would be political, economic, and social unrest. However, at the end of this period of questioning, you would witness the fall of the Berlin Wall. People around the world would celebrate the end of the Cold War and hold unprecedented hope for a new world order.

# POLITICAL AND ECONOMIC STRIFE

The 1970s began with Americans bitterly divided over US involvement in the Vietnam War. The economy was also under strain, largely as a result of funding that war. As well, there was a political scandal.

## Watergate and Its Aftermath

The events that led to the Watergate crisis began on June 13, 1971, when the *New York Times* published its first installment of the "Pentagon Papers," the classified summary of 30 years of US involvement in Vietnam that you read about in Chapter 12. President Richard Nixon, who was anxious to control the flow of information that reached the American public, asked the US Supreme Court to stop the publication; instead, the court cited the constitutional right to freedom of speech and allowed the newspaper to publish its summary. Nixon responded by setting up a White House Special Investigation Unit. This unit, which later became known as "the Plumbers," was assigned the job of finding and stopping information leaks to the press. Its mandate was also to create disinformation, and to unearth material that would discredit Nixon's opponents. In one of their first ventures, the Plumbers broke into the office of the psychiatrist of Daniel Ellsberg, the man who had originally leaked the Pentagon's classified information to the *Times*. The Plumbers were looking for information to discredit Ellsberg, but they found nothing of interest.

Such domestic espionage had not been common in US politics; under the Nixon administration, however, it became so. Determined to win a second term as president in 1972, Nixon and his aides established the Committee to Re-Elect the President (CREEP). In June 1972 a group of ex-CIA agents, anti-Castro Cubans, and others directed by members of CREEP broke into the office of the National Committee of the Democratic Party, which was located in the Watergate complex in Washington, DC, in order to install phone taps. They were caught, and in court the next day, most of them were identified as ex-CIA agents. Surprisingly, at first nothing much came of this affair, and it seemed to disappear from public notice. However, over the next few months, reporters Carl Bernstein and Robert Woodward of the *Washington Post* followed the case closely, establishing links between CREEP and White House aides. They relied in large part on tips from an informer with the code name "Deep Throat" (who in 2005 was revealed to be William Mark Felt Sr., the second in command of the FBI at the time).

Thanks to the persistence of Bernstein and Woodward, Watergate acquired new life. Twenty-five people, including Nixon's attorney-general and senior White House aides, were tried and convicted of a variety of criminal offences and sentenced to jail terms. The investigation also revealed that Nixon taped nearly all conversations and interviews in the Oval Office. At first, Nixon claimed executive privilege over the tapes and refused to release them to investigators. Eventually, however, heavily edited versions were released. The edited tapes revealed that Nixon had discussed possible payments for "dirty tricks" against political opponents during the 1972 presidential election. In July 1974 the US Supreme Court unanimously ordered Nixon to surrender the original tapes, and the president complied. The tapes, though containing an unexplained 18.5-minute gap, demonstrated that six days after the Watergate break-in Nixon ordered the CIA to stop the FBI from investigating it. It was Nixon's attempt to cover up the illegal activities that proved more damaging to his presidency than the break-in itself. And it was the tapes that provided the "smoking gun" that revealed the president had been deeply involved in the cover-up.

Following these revelations, the House Judiciary Committee approved three articles of impeachment, charging Nixon with obstruction of justice, abuse of power, and contempt of Congress. By this time, Nixon knew that his support in Congress, even among Republicans, had evaporated, and he would certainly be convicted and quite possibly sentenced to prison. Before the charges could be formally filed, he became the first US president to resign from office.

"I had always assumed, working for the CIA for so many years, that anything the White House wanted done was the law of the land. I viewed [the Watergate burglary] like any other mission. It just happened to take place inside this country."

—E. Howard Hunt, mastermind of the Watergate burglary

To learn more about impeachment, go to www.emp.ca/ah.

**Figure 13.2** "I have never profited … from public service. I have never obstructed justice … I am not a crook." (Richard Nixon, November 17, 1973.) Had Nixon not resigned in August 1974, he may have been the first US president found guilty of charges warranting impeachment in a trial before the Senate.

| The Presidents: 1972–1989 | | |
|---|---|---|
| **Richard Nixon*** | Republican | January 20, 1969 – August 9, 1974 |
| **Gerald Ford** | Republican | August 9, 1974 – January 20, 1977 |
| **Jimmy Carter** | Democrat | January 20, 1977 – January 20, 1981 |
| **Ronald Reagan** | Republican | January 20, 1981 – January 20, 1989 |
| **George H.W. Bush** | Republican | January 20, 1989 – January 20, 1993 |

* resigned

Following Nixon's resignation on August 9, 1974, Vice-President Gerald Ford was sworn in as president. Ford retained Henry Kissinger, Nixon's Secretary of State, as the architect of US foreign policy. In a controversial decision, Ford also pardoned Nixon in September 1974, as he believed it was essential to preserve the dignity of the office of president from further controversy. Those staff members who were prosecuted and jailed for involvement in Watergate served relatively short sentences in minimum-security prisons.

In 1975, congressional investigations of the FBI and CIA uncovered numerous instances of abuse of power and rights violations by these two organizations against foreign governments and American citizens. The CIA, for example, had been involved in a series of assassination plots against Cuba's Fidel Castro, and had introduced the African swine fever virus into Cuba in 1971. The CIA had also been involved in numerous efforts at "regime change" around the globe, such as the 1963 overthrow of the South Vietnamese government of President Ngo Dinh Diem, who was assassinated by the South Vietnamese military (see Chapter 12). Domestically, the FBI acknowledged that it had committed 92 burglaries between 1960 and 1966. Both the FBI and the CIA admitted that they had illegally opened mail and engaged in wiretapping without applying for the necessary warrants.

In 1978, Congress passed a law that made it illegal to monitor phone calls of Americans inside the United States without first obtaining a warrant from the Foreign Intelligence Surveillance Court. (This is the law that George W. Bush's administration was accused in 2006 of violating by circumventing the Surveillance Court to monitor phone conversations of suspected terrorists.) The CIA also had its powers curtailed so that it could not carry out surveillance or espionage operations within the United States.

## Economic Woes

Since the end of World War II, Americans had viewed themselves as citizens of the most prosperous and powerful nation on earth. Their country also politically dominated what they called "the free world" against the Soviet Bloc during the Cold War. This situation changed, however, in the 1970s and 1980s. America's defeat in Vietnam showed that its armed forces were not omnipotent, and the country's dependence on foreign oil would weaken it economically. The attempt by President Lyndon Johnson's administration to maintain the normal level of domestic spending while financing the Vietnam War had led to large federal deficits and damaging levels of inflation. Things were about to get worse.

## The Energy Crisis

In October 1973, the Organization of Petroleum Exporting Countries (OPEC), an oil-exporting **cartel** dominated by Arab oil-producing states, raised its prices, partly in response to US support for Israel during the **Yom Kippur War** of 1973. This action caused worldwide inflation, which added to the inflationary trend already present in the US economy. In addition to raising its prices, OPEC then sharply reduced oil production and placed an embargo on supplies to the United States. American reserves quickly dropped. This resulted in long line-ups at gas stations and a staggering increase in prices for gas and other hydrocarbon-based fuels. Gasoline prices shot up to four times what they had been before the Yom Kippur War.

The age of cheap oil, the foundation for US prosperity and growth in the postwar era, seemed to be over. Readily available oil at affordable prices had not only benefited America's auto industry and utility companies; it had also accelerated the spread of suburbanization and stimulated consumerism. By 1973, the United States, which was home to 6 percent of the world's population, consumed over a quarter of its oil. In the face of OPEC's embargo, the government called for lowering thermostats, cutting air travel, and reducing speed limits; it also encouraged car pools and the use of mass transit. Factories reduced work hours to conserve fuel; universities cancelled sessions during the winter months. The government also increased the licensing of nuclear power stations. A new focus on increasing domestic oil production had the effect of shifting wealth and power from northern and eastern regions of the United States to the South and the West.

Usually, inflation occurs either because of scarcities in goods or because of an increase in the amount of money in circulation. During this period,

**Figure 13.3** Gas stations were the scene of long line-ups during the 1973 oil crisis.

inflation occurred because of both scarcities (caused by the OPEC embargo) and increased money flow (caused by government spending on domestic programs and Vietnam).

Rising prices usually lead to an expansion in the economy, but the combination of the oil crisis, vigorous foreign competition, and large federal government deficits led to economic decline, especially in manufacturing. Unemployment rose to 7.4 percent in 1974, over double the rate of the 1950s and 1960s. "Stagflation" (an economic condition characterized by simultaneous inflation, slow growth, and high unemployment) also led to a fall in real income for workers and their families for the first time since the Depression of the 1930s.

## Industrial Decline

The early 1970s marked the beginning of the decline of American industrial strength. The oil embargo was partly responsible for this decline, but other forces were at work as well. Industries in Europe, devastated by World War II, had not only recovered; they had also modernized. Now they were able to produce technologically advanced and sophisticated industrial goods and consumer products in efficient factories that could easily compete with American factories for markets both at home and abroad. Similarly, many Asian nations, such as Japan, Taiwan, and Korea, were now capable of producing goods of high quality at a cost below that charged by US manufacturers.

For example, before 1973, US auto producers dominated the US market, with over 90 percent of total sales. Japanese and European cars were thought to be too small and of poor quality. American cars, by comparison, were perceived as luxurious, sophisticated, and solid. By the end of 1973, perceptions were shifting. Many people were beginning to view American cars as gas-guzzlers and imported ones as sophisticated and efficient. This change in perception marked the beginning of the erosion of American auto producers' dominance of the US market. In 1973, US auto sales dropped by 11 million, and the US auto manufacturers that were once major industrial players found themselves in trouble. In 1980 Chrysler, saved from collapse by a controversial $1.5 billion loan guarantee by the federal government, was forced to dismiss nearly half its workforce.

It was not long before the whole American industrial sector began to shrink. Prosperous industrial and

**Figure 13.4** A family in Detroit, Michigan stands in front of their house, from which they were evicted in the wake of the oil and energy crisis. During the 1970s, General Motors laid off thousands of employees and closed numerous plants in the northern and midwestern United States.

manufacturing cities across the United States began to lose workers and become "rust belts" of abandoned mills and factories. High-paying industrial jobs, even for the unskilled, were replaced by jobs in the services sector, including transport and warehousing, finance and insurance, and retail and wholesale trade. The AFL–CIO, a national American trade union federation, complained that the United States was becoming "a nation of hamburger stands" and "a country stripped of industrial capacity and meaningful work." According to the US Census Bureau, in 1974–75, the number of people classified as poor had risen 12 percent to include approximately 34 million people. The economic shocks of the early 1970s, reflected in the industrial decline, resulted in 1.8 million employees being affected by strikes and lockouts in 1974. Labour unions, long established in the industrial and manufacturing sectors, began to decline in size and influence.

## Tax Revolt

The American government's spending on the Vietnam War and the Cold War, along with other government spending, had created huge deficits. As a result, taxes remained high and were perceived by many ordinary Americans to be increasingly burdensome—especially in a period of stagflation. Americans on the right of the political spectrum adhered to a notion of individualism that resented government spending, perceived

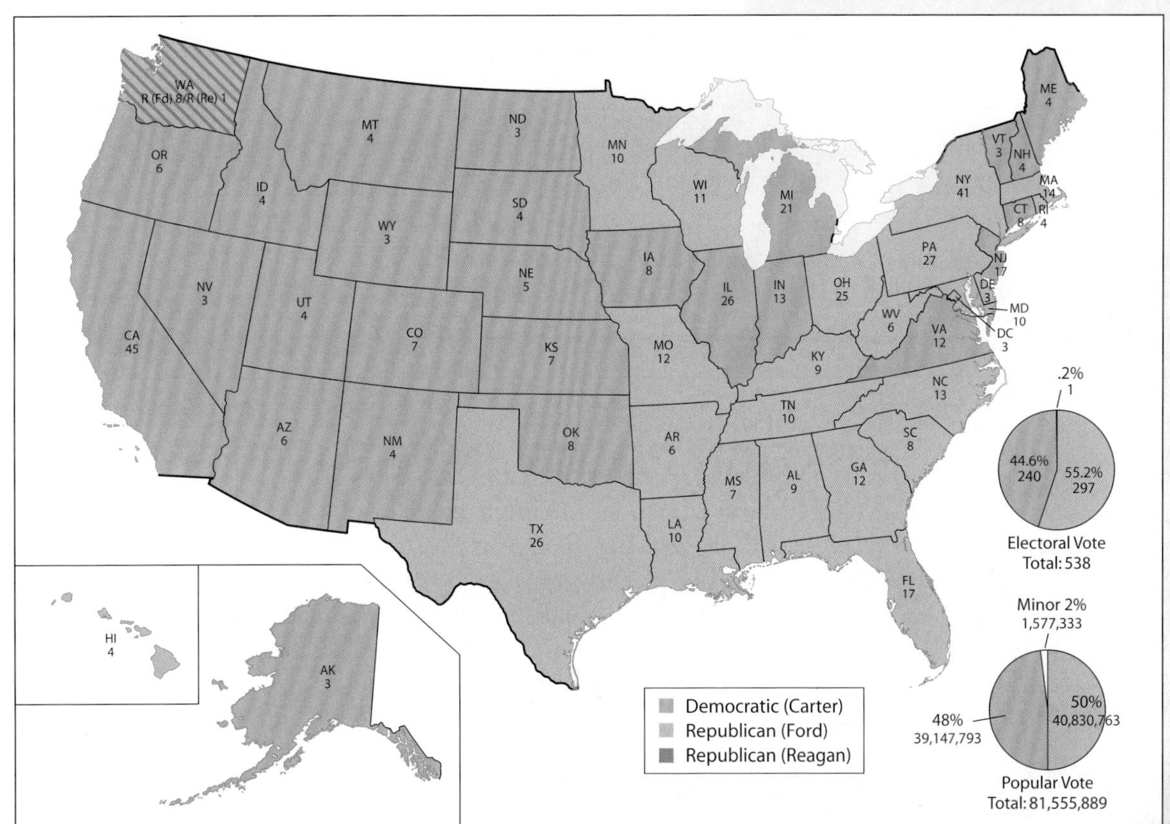


**Figure 13.5** Results of the 1976 presidential election. Republican Gerald Ford was saddled with a slow economy and paid a political price for his pardon of Nixon. Democrat Jimmy Carter ran as an honest Washington "outsider" and reformer, winning a narrow victory. Ronald Reagan received one write-in electoral vote.

social programs as creating dependency, and disliked what they saw as a bloated bureaucracy. In 1978, they began a campaign to lower taxes, reasoning that if less revenue was coming in, government would have to shrink. What followed was a tax revolt that began in California.

In many states, the public were able to bypass legislative bodies by putting legislative initiatives directly to voters in referendums. Proposition 13, a tax reduction initiative, found its way onto the ballot in California and was supported by voters. The immediate result was a 57 percent decrease in state taxes. Revolts against property taxes followed in 37 states, and against state income taxes in 28 states. By the 1980s, millions of taxpayers were calling for rollbacks of taxes and the shrinkage of "big government." At the same time, those who wanted to pay lower taxes were confronted with the results: diminished public services, with police officers, firefighters, teachers, and other civil servants being laid off; repairs of roads and other infrastructure postponed; and many other public works delayed or cancelled. Across the country, governments cut back long-standing social programs and refused to undertake new ones.

What started in the states was echoed at the federal level. Jimmy Carter, who succeeded Gerald Ford as president in 1977, introduced $18 billion worth of federal tax cuts in 1979. However, the cuts for the most part affected those who were paying high tax rates, and therefore mainly benefited wealthy individuals and corporations. Exxon's profit, for example, rose 56 percent in 1979, a year in which 3,000 independent gas stations went out of business.

### CHECK YOUR UNDERSTANDING

1. What was the purpose of the White House Special Investigation Unit (the Plumbers) set up by President Nixon?
2. Why was the role of Bernstein and Woodward crucial in the Watergate scandal?
3. What did the White House tape recordings reveal?
4. How did OPEC nearly destroy the US economy?
5. How were US voters able to stage a tax revolt?

## FOREIGN POLICY IN THE 1970s

Under Richard Nixon, the US implemented a policy of **détente** in its foreign relations. Détente, an attempt to relax the strained impasse between the United States and its Cold War adversaries—both the Soviet Union and China—was seen in Washington as a means for the United States to stabilize diplomatic relations with its opponents and reduce the likelihood of armed conflict, especially nuclear conflict. But there were other concerns as well: Nixon also wanted to advance US interests in other parts of the world, such as South America and the Middle East.

## WE THE PEOPLE
### *Henry Kissinger*

**Figure 13.6** Henry Kissinger gives a press conference in 1973.

> "Henry Kissinger is, plain and simply, the best secretary of state we have had in 20, maybe 30 years—certainly one of the two or three great secretaries of state of our century."
>
> —Ted Koppel, former ABC News anchor

Who was this larger-than-life figure in American foreign policy?

Born in 1923 to Jewish parents, Henry Kissinger's family fled Germany in 1938. In World War II he served in the US army as an interpreter and intelligence officer. After the war he had a brilliant career at Harvard University, becoming a professor of government and international affairs in 1957.

Kissinger served as foreign policy adviser to presidents Kennedy and Johnson, and promoted a "flexible response" strategy. When Nixon became president, he appointed Kissinger his national security adviser. Working together, they set out to reshape US foreign policy. Kissinger saw Russia as a rival superpower, and sought to achieve a global power balance through a policy of cooperation known as détente.

Kissinger concentrated foreign policy making within the White House under the National Security Council, giving him more influence than the Secretary of State. From 1973 on, he held both jobs. Kissinger and Nixon favoured secret negotiations to lay the groundwork for foreign policy decisions during the 1970s. These included establishing détente with the Soviet Union, and solving the oil crisis and other conflicts in the Middle East, for which they used a technique of frequent visits to competing sides called "shuttle diplomacy."

One of the long-running secret negotiations was with North Vietnam to settle the war. Although the negotiations for peace failed, both Kissinger and North Vietnam's Le Duc Tho shared the Nobel Peace Prize in 1973.

Kissenger had more success in engineering a new relationship with communist China. His secret negotiations with Chinese foreign minister Chou En-lai—which bore fruit in Nixon's historic visit to China in 1972 and meeting with party leader Mao Zedong—made Kissinger a media celebrity.

When Nixon resigned in August 1974 and Ford took office, Kissinger retained his position and his influence in foreign affairs. He was never connected to Watergate. Over the years, his reputation and his policy directions came under attack from many sides. Conservatives claimed that détente allowed the Soviet Union to build up its military arsenal. Liberals accused Kissinger of ignoring human rights with his policies on communist countries and Latin America. He also failed to end the Vietnam War peacefully.

Kissinger left office with President Ford in 1977. He has since taught at Georgetown University and been a media commentator and consultant to many groups, including the White House on policy in Iraq.

### Think It Through

1. Under what circumstances should foreign policy be conducted in secret in a democracy? Were Nixon and Kissinger justified in their techniques?
2. Given their failure to end the Vietnam War, research why Kissinger and Le Duc Tho won the Nobel Peace Prize in 1973.

## China

Richard Nixon had built his political career, beginning with his election to Congress in 1948, by accusing others of being "soft" on communism. By the 1970s, his reputation as an anti-communist "Cold Warrior" was well established. At the same time, Nixon and Henry Kissinger, his national security adviser, saw themselves as political realists who were uninterested in ideology and concerned with promoting a stable and orderly balance of power in the world. They approached this task by attempting to stabilize US relations with China and the Soviet Union.

As the 1970s began, the United States was on hostile terms with communist China and had no diplomatic relations with the mainland government; since 1949, it had recognized the island republic of Taiwan as the sole legitimate government, and continued to do so when Nixon took office in 1969. In 1971 Kissinger paid a secret visit to China. This was followed by Nixon's historic 1972 visit, which formally normalized relations between the United States and China. Relations between the two countries were also slightly thawed by "ping-pong diplomacy." During an international table tennis tournament, a champion US ping-pong player became friends with members of the Chinese team, a friendship that received sanction by the Chinese government, which in turn invited the US team to visit China. Ultimately, the two countries relaxed their diplomatic approaches to each other. They began to enter into a more friendly relationship, which included an increased volume of trade.

The establishment of a positive relationship between the United States and China had great strategic importance because it defused the likelihood of armed confrontation. It also allowed Nixon to play China off against the Soviet Union, whose relationship with China was already tense, despite their shared communist ideology. This meant that China supported the United States' condemnation of the Soviet invasion of Afghanistan in 1979. It also allowed the US to gain the upper hand in the worldwide public relations battle against the Soviets. If the US could be friends with China, the Soviets were becoming increasingly isolated, even in the communist world.

Because of Nixon's reputation as a resolute anti-communist, he could establish a friendly relationship abroad with a communist regime without facing much criticism at home. Nixon won re-election in 1972, in part because of his pursuit of détente with China. However, it was not until 1978, during the

**Figure 13.7** Mao to Nixon: "I like rightists." Nixon to Mao: "Those on the right can do things which those on the left can only talk about."

administration of President Carter, that the United States established formal diplomatic relations with China.

## The Soviet Union

During the 1970s, the United States also pursued a policy of détente with the Soviet Union. As you know from Chapter 12, a long-standing irritant for the US had been Soviet support for the communist government of Fidel Castro. In 1970 the Soviets agreed to stop building a submarine base and arming Cuba with offensive missiles. In exchange, the Americans promised to stop trying to topple Castro's regime.

In 1969 the United States and the Soviet Union began talks in Helsinki, Finland aimed at limiting the arms race, in particular, by limiting the numbers of intercontinental ballistic missiles (ICBMs) used to launch nuclear warheads. The result, in 1972, was the Strategic Arms Limitation Treaty (SALT I). Signed by Nixon in Moscow, the treaty was largely symbolic. While it limited the stockpiling of missiles and nuclear weapons, it did not stop missile production in progress, nor bar the development of sophisticated anti-missile defence systems. The Ford and Carter administrations tried to negotiate a further slowing of the arms race. However, after the Soviet invasion of Afghanistan in 1979, the US Senate refused to ratify SALT II.

These 1970s arms reduction efforts gave way in the 1980s to President Ronald Reagan's military buildup. This buildup included not only the creation of the MX and cruise missiles, which were tested in Canada, but also the establishment of Reagan's "Star Wars" program. Reagan exploited a loophole in SALT I that permitted the development of anti-missile systems in his attempt to create missile shields in space.

## Chile

In 1970 the Chilean people elected a Popular Unity government headed by President Salvador Allende, a Marxist. Allende was seen by the United States as a major threat to its influence in South America. An ally of Castro, he was anti-American and challenged the capitalist democratic model of government. Nixon used the CIA in an attempt to prevent Allende from being elected. When this effort failed, the CIA supported a coup led by General Augusto Pinochet, during which the army seized power and Allende was killed. During the Pinochet regime, more than 3,000 Chileans who

**Figure 13.8** Thousands of demonstrators in Rome, Italy protest the military coup in Chile on September 12, 1973. Some carry a large portrait of the late Chilean president, Salvador Allende.

**WEB LINKS**

To learn more about declassified documents relating to US involvement in Chile, go to www.emp.ca/ah.

opposed the government disappeared or were killed, and the use of torture by police and other officials became widespread.

The mid-1970s discovery of US involvement in overthrowing Allende and helping establish Pinochet created a major scandal that led to a US Senate investigation but did little to change Chile's brutal regime.

Chile eventually returned to democratic rule in 1990. There were several attempts to try Pinochet for various offences, including murder and corruption. However, Pinochet died in 2006 without being brought to trial.

## The Middle East

In the Middle East, US foreign policy met with both success and failure. As a result of the devastating effects of OPEC's 1973 oil embargo, which occurred in part because of US support for Israel in the Yom Kippur War, the United States resolved to improve its relationship with Arab states.

### Israel and Egypt

Since Israel's declaration of independence in 1948, the United States had been its closest ally. This alliance, along with the US's position as leader of the Western bloc of nations, made involvement in Middle Eastern affairs a significant aspect of American foreign policy in the postwar period. It also put the US at odds with many Middle Eastern countries that did not recognize Israel. (Many Arab and Muslim countries, such as Egypt and Syria, felt that Israel's creation had denied Palestinians their own state.) As a result, Israel and the

**Figure 13.9** The Middle East in the 1970s.

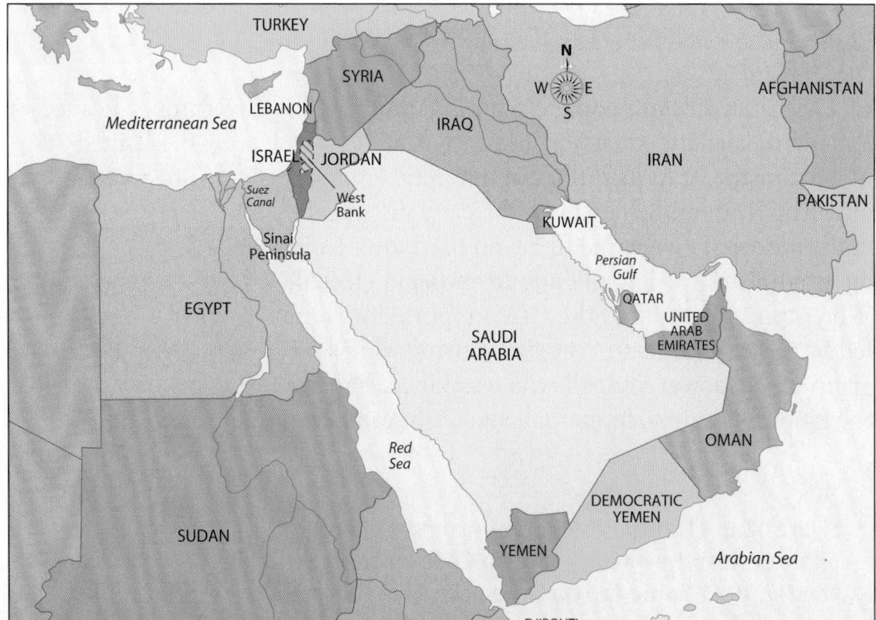

Arab world—including Egypt, Syria, Iraq, and others—faced off in a number of armed conflicts, including the 1948 Israeli war of independence, the 1956 Suez Crisis, the 1967 Six-Day War, and the 1973 Yom Kippur War. Many of these wars were fought primarily along the Sinai Peninsula, an area adjacent to the Israeli border controlled by Egypt but which Israel occupied following the 1967 war.

The United States wished to maintain good relations with both Israel and Egypt, the latter being a leader of the Arab world and of Africa. The US pressed Israel to accept a ceasefire with Egypt and to move toward a permanent peace treaty after the Yom Kippur War. Henry Kissinger then helped produce an accord in which Israel returned large parts of the Sinai to Egypt. In 1974 Israel and Egypt agreed to establish diplomatic relations. Eventually, in 1978, President Jimmy Carter managed to broker a peace treaty between Israel and Egypt with the Camp David Accords. This was a significant breakthrough for Middle Eastern peace, and a diplomatic triumph for Carter.

**Figure 13.10** US President Jimmy Carter witnesses the handshake between Egyptian President Anwar Sadat (left) and Israeli Prime Minister Menachim Begin at the 1978 signing of the Camp David Accords.

## Iran

If the achievement of peace between Israel and Egypt was a successful US foreign policy initiative, American support for the regime of the Shah of Iran was not. The United States had long supported the Shah's regime diplomatically, through foreign aid and arms sales, because the Shah was a strong US ally in the Middle East. However, the Shah was also a dictator who ruthlessly suppressed all internal opposition in Iran. When a combination of secular and religious elements, each with a different agenda, combined to overthrow the Shah in the Iranian Revolution of 1979, President Carter offered him asylum in the United States.

**SOUND BITE**

"[A] number of countries with deplorable records of human rights observance are also countries where we have important security and foreign policy interests."

—Report by Carter administration to Congress, 1977

In Iran, the Ayatollah Khomeini, an Islamic fundamentalist opposed to US policy, took power. On November 4, 1979 some of his followers stormed the US embassy in Tehran and took 53 people hostage. They held the hostages captive for 14 months, during which time the US could neither weaken the Ayatollah's regime (through economic sanctions) nor free the hostages. A rescue mission launched by the United States in 1980 ended disastrously. Highly trained US soldiers established a secret desert landing base inside Iran, but the mission failed when two of the eight helicopters that were supposed to swoop into Tehran crashed in a massive sandstorm. Eight US soldiers were killed, and the mission was aborted. Details of the failed mission led to further criticism of Carter.

Canada's heroic role in the hostage taking deserves mentioning. On November 4, 1979 when the crisis erupted and the US embassy personnel were seized, six Americans who were outside the compound avoided capture.

**Figure 13.11** American hostages are presented to the press at the occupied US embassy in Tehran.

They were, however, stranded in Tehran and were unable to leave the country. When they appealed for help, they were welcomed by Ken Taylor, Canada's ambassador to Iran. Until January 29, 1980 they were permanent "houseguests" at the Canadian embassy, where they were given refuge from the Iranian revolutionary regime. Canadian Prime Minister Joe Clark authorized Canadian passports to be issued to the US diplomats, and Taylor coordinated the "Canadian Caper" that allowed them to leave Tehran in the guise of a scouting crew for a fictitious film production company. They returned to a hero's welcome in the United States, and the American public was grateful toward Canada.

**Figure 13.12** Results of the 1980 election. Republican Ronald Reagan won a landslide victory over Jimmy Carter, due in part to the Iran hostage crisis and the wage and price controls that Carter imposed in 1978 as part of his anti-inflation program.

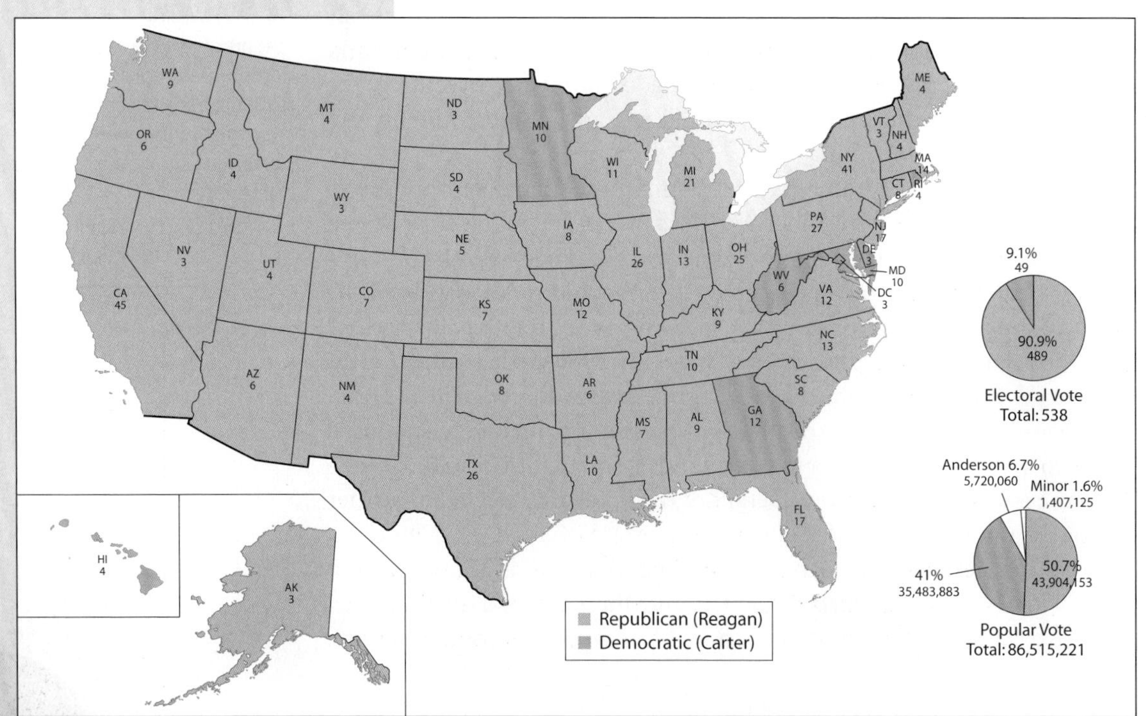

Nevertheless, America's apparent weakness on the international stage was a major embarrassment for Jimmy Carter, and Ronald Reagan won the 1980 presidential election partly because of his promise to free the hostages in Iran. In fact, Iran was unwilling to risk an all-out war with the US and released the hostages on the day of Reagan's inauguration, which did much to establish the new president's reputation for competence in foreign policy.

**CHECK YOUR UNDERSTANDING**

1. What was the importance of Nixon's China policy?
2. How was Nixon's China policy also a part of his policy toward the Soviet Union?
3. Why was the Strategic Arms Limitation Treaty (SALT I) of 1972 only symbolic?
4. Why did the United States involve itself in Middle Eastern affairs?
5. What was the link between US support for the Shah of Iran and the Iranian Revolution of 1979?

# PUBLIC PESSIMISM IN THE 1970s

How did Americans feel about these crises? The 1970s were a period of disillusionment with politics and politicians in America. The Watergate scandal, and Nixon's resignation under threat of impeachment, deeply affected the American people, who were forced to come to terms with widespread corruption at the highest levels of government. The defeat in Vietnam and the hostage crisis in Iran embarrassed the US internationally, undermined the myth of American omnipotence, and created an impression of a government that was inept and ineffective.

This was also a period of economic pessimism. The United States was no longer able to solve its economic problems arising from inflation, debt, de-industrialization, and the energy crisis. As the *New York Times* noted, "no longer will hard work and a conscientious effort to save money bring … a nice home in the suburbs." Americans were slow to accept this economic transition. They continued to make expensive consumer purchases, greatly increasing the use of credit, while expecting to receive high rates of return on investments. As a result, personal consumer debt rose dramatically while savings rates declined.

Socially, many Americans appeared to be less community-oriented than they had been in the 1960s. Writer Tom Wolfe characterized the 1970s as the "Me Generation," an expression that captured an increased focus on the individual's needs and desires as opposed to those of the community. This focus, combined with the prevailing spirit of pessimism, was reflected in two musical genres of the time. On the one hand, there was disco: an invitation to lose yourself in dance while forgetting all about unemployment, inflation, and dead-end

**Figure 13.13** The 1976 bicentennial celebrations in Washington, DC drummed up a degree of patriotism in anxious times.

jobs. On the other hand, there was punk: a counterculture that reflected disillusionment with social institutions and a widespread contempt for and disregard of authority.

A momentary bright spot was the 1976 bicentennial of the United States, the 200th anniversary of the signing of the Declaration of Independence. In the words of George Idelson, a resident of Washington, DC:

> In the winter of 1976 America was still hurting from the wounds of the Vietnam War. Officially it was over. The boys had come home. Not to ticker tape, but to tortured second-guessing. Those who had avoided the war fared little better. In truth, we were still at war—with ourselves.
>
> ... The year of the Bicentennial, the two-hundredth anniversary of the Declaration of Independence, had already begun ... As they have so many times before, they converged on the National Mall to celebrate ... There were no speeches. No music. Just people, thousands of people, enjoying themselves and each other, basking in the sun and a glow of unspoken pride and patriotism ... And when darkness arrived, and the fireworks began, it seemed as though this joyous burst of streamers, starts and explosions were the last gasps of the bitterness that divided us.
>
> In truth it didn't all end that day. But something remarkable happened. We were family again. We could find ways to forgive, if not to forget.

## Reaganomics

Tax cuts, which were the outcome of the tax revolts of the 1970s, accelerated when Ronald Reagan took office in 1981. Reagan's economic proposals, referred to as "Reaganomics," concentrated on further federal tax reductions, cost cutting, and shrinkage of government social programs. But it also featured enormous military expenditure, which resulted in increased government deficits. Reagan's answer to the shortfall in revenue was **supply-side economics**. Supply-siders claimed that economic problems stem from excessive taxation, which inhibits new investment that will stimulate economic growth. If taxes were reduced, they argued, investors would be able to invest more capital and generate more wealth, thus creating jobs and prosperity for all. Supply-side economics created more wealth for wealthy individuals and corporations. However, not much of this wealth trickled down to ordinary working people and their families.

Reagan proposed $40 billion in budget cuts to programs unrelated to military expenditure, and he obtained most of them, reducing federal income tax by 23 percent over three years. The economy in fact did grow, with minimal inflation thanks to a **tight money policy** at the Federal Reserve Board, lower oil prices that resulted from OPEC's inability to restrict oil supplies and maintain high prices, and the deregulation of natural gas prices. The tight money policy meant that interest rates were high; it benefited wealthy people because they were able to charge more for lending money and accumulate a large amount of interest. Deregulation of the pricing and distribution of natural gas led to lower costs, and the pent-up demand for goods following the 1979–82 recession boosted consumer spending.

While the economy improved, government finances did not. The deficit, fuelled by spiralling military expenditures, tax cuts, and increases in the cost of Medicare and Social Security (programs that benefited older Americans), rose dramatically. In response, Congress passed the Gramm–Rudman–Hollings Act in 1985, requiring major deficit reductions over five years. To achieve this goal, social programs continued to be cut back, with serious consequences for many citizens in need of assistance. Social Security disability benefits were terminated for 350,000 people in this period. For those at the bottom of the economic pile, life was becoming more difficult; as economic insecurity increased, many people had no access to good health insurance, and poverty rates grew seriously.

In the mid-1980s, for example, the US unemployment rate was usually 8–10 percent, far higher than the 4–6 percent that had been the norm for most of the post-1945 period. Since most health insurance in the United States was based upon employee plans, unemployment increased the number of uninsured persons as well: in 1987, 31 million Americans, or 12.9 percent of the population, had no medical coverage. Since that time, the figure has increased to over 45 million people.

## Effects of Reaganomics on the Middle Class

By the mid-to-late 1980s most middle-class Americans had begun to recover financially from the widespread economic insecurity that accompanied the shift from a manufacturing to a service economy. They moved into white-collar jobs, bought homes, and increased their spending on consumer goods. The economy had brightened by 1982, and modest economic growth followed through the rest of the decade. But many Americans continued to live beyond their means; their increased use of credit cards resulted in indebtedness and reduced rates of savings. Families tended to live in larger homes than in earlier decades, and to equip themselves with electronic goods and services such as VCRs, computers, answering machines, and cable television, most of which were produced outside the United States. Responding to the material culture of the period, historian James Patterson commented: "The more people consumed, the more they seemed to want … Sensing that something was missing, many Americans, while doing better, still seemed to feel worse."

## 49th PARALLEL

# The Free Trade Agreement

The friendship that developed between US President Ronald Reagan and Canadian Prime Minister Brian Mulroney resulted in one of the most controversial agreements in Canadian history. Wanting to make this agreement a reality, Mulroney went straight to the person who could make it happen: his friend and fellow conservative, Ronald Reagan. Both leaders agreed on the necessity of **free trade**, saying that lowering tariffs and other barriers was a way to increase prosperity for both countries. Economic slowdown and adjustment were issues on both sides of the 49th parallel: not surprising, since Canada and the US were each other's largest trading partner. In 1911 Liberal Prime Minister Wilfrid Laurier had negotiated a free trade agreement with the US. That was one of the issues that ended 15 years of Liberal government. Conservative Prime Minister Robert Borden killed the treaty, arguing that it would lead to the Americanization of Canada, and because of the Alaska Boundary Dispute (see Chapter 9).

To help Canada get the best deal possible, Mulroney appointed Simon Reisman, a veteran negotiator from the 1965 Auto Pact, while America appointed Peter Murphy, a diplomat with little experience. As might be expected, the negotiations were difficult. A treaty was signed in 1987 between the governments, although it had to be approved by Congress and Parliament. The Liberals and New Democrats accused the Conservatives of selling Canada to the US. Business was in favour of the agreement; some provinces (including Ontario), unions, cultural groups, and women's groups were not. The treaty was ratified in 1988 and became law January 1, 1989.

The Free Trade Agreement (FTA) meant the elimination of tariffs and reductions in non-tariff trade barriers on goods. By January 1, 1998, with a few exceptions, all tariffs on goods originally manufactured in Canada and the United States were eliminated. Canada retained the right to protect its cultural industries and such sectors as education and health care. Some resources, such as water, were left out of the agreement.

After the agreement came into effect, trade between Canada and the US began to increase rapidly. But the FTA has failed to liberalize trade in some areas, most notably softwood lumber. There have been Canadian complaints that Americans have repeatedly violated the agreement and refused to abide by the rulings of Canada–US trade dispute resolution panels.

**Figure 13.14** Ronald Reagan and Brian Mulroney at the "Shamrock Summit" in Quebec City, St. Patrick's Day 1985, singing "When Irish Eyes Are Smiling." How did Reagan's and Mulroney's friendship help cement the Free Trade Agreement?

Although the FTA is still controversial, it is no longer at the forefront of Canadian politics. It was incorporated into the North American Free Trade Agreement (NAFTA) between Canada, the US, and Mexico on January 1, 1994. This happened despite promises during the Canadian 1993 federal election to renegotiate key parts of the agreement. Besides expanding the FTA trade zone to include Mexico, NAFTA has added free trade in other sectors.

Despite general public support for the FTA/NAFTA, opinion polls tend to show that Canadians (and Mexicans) see their own country as a loser in NAFTA, while Americans are divided on the question.

## Think It Through

1. Research the FTA negotiations at www.emp.ca/ah. How big a deal was it for the United States?
2. How important is the FTA/NAFTA in today's global economy? Explain your views.

## Environmentalism

While many Americans were preoccupied with the economy, some worried about the environment. The modern environmental movement, which began in 1962 with the publication of Rachel Carson's *Silent Spring* (see Chapter 12), gained momentum during the 1970s and 1980s. In this period, environmentalists fought suburban overdevelopment, nuclear power, acid rain, depletion of the ozone layer, and the wasteful use of energy. Memberships in environmental organizations climbed steadily from 125,000 in 1960 to 6.3 million by 1990.

Concern about the environment by ever-increasing numbers of Americans began slowly to result in action by government and business: catalytic converters (devices to minimize pollutants) were introduced on automobiles; they, along with the unleaded gasoline introduced in the 1970s, reduced the toxicity of tailpipe emissions by 75 percent over the next two decades. Drinking water became purer, polluted lakes were cleaned up, and rivers were regenerated. In the late 1970s, President Carter signed federal clean air and clean water bills, along with legislation to control strip mining. The powers of the federal Environmental Protection Agency (EPA) (see Chapter 12) were strengthened.

In 1980 environmentalists won two significant victories:

- The Alaskan Lands Law doubled the acreage of Alaskan lands set aside as wilderness and national parks.
- A Superfund established by Congress provided $1 billion to clean up toxic waste sites; some of the funds came from federal revenue and some came from taxes imposed on those most likely to create toxic waste sites: chemical, oil, and mining companies. The need for such a fund had become apparent, as toxic waste sites began to be revealed. Perhaps the most notorious site was Love Canal, New York in 1978, where the inhabitants of an entire residential district had to abandon their homes and move when dangerously high levels of toxins from industrial waste were found in the soil.

**Figure 13.15** This 1986 poster was published by the Union of Concerned Scientists to encourage Americans to use less fossil fuel.

In the 1970s Americans were looking to nuclear power as a way of reducing reliance on foreign energy sources. But an accident that resulted in a near meltdown on March 28, 1979 at the Three Mile Island nuclear power plant in Pennsylvania shattered the popular faith in this alternative energy source. (In an eerie twist of fate, a Hollywood film about such a disaster, *The China Syndrome*, was released just 12 days before the real-life events at Three Mile Island.) Although no one was killed in the Three Mile

Island accident, the partial meltdown of the reactor was a public relations disaster for the nuclear energy industry. The much more serious Russian nuclear plant meltdown at Chernobyl on April 26, 1986 further soured many Americans on nuclear power. Although other nuclear plants continued to operate, no new plants were built in the United States.

Increased consumption of natural resources and increased spending on consumer goods blunted attempts to reduce energy consumption and clean up the environment. California, which experienced a population explosion in the 1970s and 1980s, became the largest consumer of water in the United States, drawing billions of litres of water from rivers and aquifers in the Southwest. Automobiles, though running cleaner, increased in number during the 1980s. From 1974 to 1980, energy consumption had fallen by 10 percent; this was partially the result of slow economic growth and oil shortages, but it also stemmed from many efforts at reducing both consumption and pollution. However, as energy prices fell in the mid-1980s, production of gas-guzzling vehicles began to increase as the first minivans and SUVs hit the market.

Environmentalism suffered a setback with the election of Ronald Reagan in 1980. Reagan proposed to replace tough mandatory enforcement laws with voluntary ones. The new administration ignored efforts to develop alternative energy sources using wind, water, and solar power, focusing instead on nuclear power. As the government retreated from environmental regulation, citizens' groups took action. For example, the Citizens' Clearinghouse for Hazardous Wastes, formed in the early years of the Reagan administration, acted as a resource for over 8,000 local environmental groups. One of these groups in Oregon brought a series of lawsuits, which succeeded in compelling the EPA to clean up unsafe sources of drinking water.

## Rights for African-Americans

As you saw in Chapter 12, the civil rights movement of the 1950s and 1960s combined court challenges, political organizing, marches, and demonstrations to bring an end to legal segregation in public services, education, voting, and other civil and political spheres. The movement was more successful in defeating aspects of segregation that resulted from legal inequities than those that resulted from economic realities and social customs. Approaches other than legislative reform were needed to combat the effects of racism that could not be overcome by ending legal segregation.

### Affirmative Action

One approach to advancing the rights of African-Americans and other minorities was **affirmative action**. Affirmative action programs took many forms, but what they had in common was that they gave preferential treatment to members of minority or disadvantaged groups. If, for example, an African-American sought entrance to a university, the fact of being African-American would operate to the advantage of the applicant. Another applicant, say from the white middle class, would not enjoy the same consideration. The rationale for affirmative action was that it would help to redress a long history of exclusion from access to education and employment.

Affirmative action programs soon became contentious. Critics charged that the programs primarily benefited women and upwardly mobile minorities without offering much assistance to lower-income minorities. However, because affirmative action was required in the public sector as a result of a 1961 presidential decree by John F. Kennedy, slowly but surely African-Americans began gaining employment as firefighters, police officers, and other high-profile public servants. By the mid-1980s many large corporations had voluntarily established affirmative action programs.

During the 1970s, affirmative action was challenged in the courts. Opponents claimed that it created "reverse discrimination" and argued that preferential treatment on the basis of race deprived other citizens of "equal protection of the laws," as guaranteed by the Constitution. In October 1977 *University of California Regents v. Bakke* was argued before the United States Supreme Court. Bakke, a white man, had been refused admission to medical school, although his admission scores were higher than those of many minority applicants who had been admitted under affirmative action quotas. He argued that these quotas deprived him of his constitutional equal protection rights.

In June 1978 the court ordered the university to admit Bakke. The majority ruled that his constitutional right to equal protection of the laws had been violated; it held that the 1964 Civil Rights Act, which prohibited federal funding for institutions that discriminated on the basis of race, had been violated as well. However, the court stated that the university was entitled to use race as one of its qualifications for admission. The judges' refusal either to outlaw or to fully endorse affirmative action programs reflected the deep divisions within US society as to the means by which African-Americans were to become full participants.

## Social and Political Recognition

During the 1980s, despite disappointing progress in employment and education, African-Americans began to acquire social and political recognition. The decade saw the declaration of Martin Luther King Day, as well as the election of African-American mayors in Chicago, Philadelphia, and Washington. In 1984 Jesse Jackson became the second African-American to compete for the Democratic Party's presidential nomination (Congresswoman Shirley Chisholm, in 1972, was the first). African-Americans also began to appear on television in non-stereotypic roles. For example, *The Cosby Show* began broadcasting in 1984, and *The Oprah Winfrey Show* followed in 1985.

**Figure 13.16** *The Cosby Show*, a popular situation-comedy, presented a non-stereotypic view of the modern African-American family. How would such shows have helped the cause of civil rights for African-Americans?

**Figure 13.17** Native Americans participate in the 1978 Longest Walk in Washington, DC to protest legislation that would have infringed their treaty rights. What were the key grievances put forth by the Native American civil rights movement of the 1970s and 1980s?

## Rights for Native Americans

The action of the American Indian Movement (AIM) at Wounded Knee in 1973 (see Chapter 12) marked a turning point in Native Americans' relationship with non-Natives. While AIM had support among some Native Americans, others found its approach too confrontational. However, AIM did articulate some clear new goals to improve the life of Native Americans that enjoyed broad support.

A key issue was that the federal government honour existing treaties and protect Native legal rights under the US Constitution. Treaties were important to Native peoples because they were agreements between equal and sovereign nations and were a means not only of exerting rights, but of ending dependency. Natives actively began to use US federal courts to enforce treaty rights.

Natives sought greater control over their own education in order to rebuild and strengthen their distinct cultures. In 1975 Congress passed the Indian Self-Determination and Cultural Assistance Act, which enabled Native communities to establish community-based and community-controlled schools. The reform of education was closely tied to the improvement of living standards and demands for job training programs. Natives also benefited from affirmative action programs in employment and education that were introduced in the 1980s.

In 1978 thousands of Native Americans took part in the Longest Walk, a five-month march from San Francisco to the Washington Monument. The purpose of the march was to protest proposed legislation that would alter treaty provisions on tribal government, hunting and fishing rights, and Native schools and hospitals.

In the 1980s Natives took control of re-establishing Native cultures and reforming education, increasing workforce participation, and raising health and living standards.

### CHECK YOUR UNDERSTANDING

1. What factors led to the growth of the US economy during the Reagan presidency?
2. Explain why a significant percentage of Americans have no health insurance coverage.
3. What specific steps were taken to protect the environment in the 1960s and 1970s?
4. How did Shirley Chisholm and Jesse Jackson achieve national recognition for African-Americans?
5. What is the purpose of affirmative action programs? Research how they benefited Native Americans.

# NEW DIRECTIONS IN AMERICAN THOUGHT

## Industry, Technology, and Science

The 1980s were a period of advancement in technology and science. Computers had been in use in the United States since the late 1940s, first by the government and the military, then in American universities, mostly for military, engineering, and weather simulations. The electronics industry, stimulated by the Cold War and funding for military research, began to develop and produce personal computers in the early 1980s. Seattle, Washington and Silicon Valley, California flourished as Microsoft and Apple pioneered the mass marketing of personal home computers. Cable television also made its debut, as did various cordless technologies, most notably cellphones.

The first "test tube" babies were conceived through in vitro fertilization outside of a woman's body, setting off a fierce debate about ethical and religious issues arising from the new reproductive technologies. Some social and religious conservatives attacked reproductive technologies as unnatural, dangerous, and contrary to ethical and religious doctrines. But for many women, in vitro fertilization presented options to a childless future.

## Religion in the 1970s and 1980s

With advancements in technology and science came ethical and religious debate. The United States has always been a religious society. Throughout American history there have been periods of religious growth. (You read about one such episode, the Great Awakening in the 1730s, in Chapter 2.) In the 1970s and 1980s, American religions appeared to be healthy, claiming

**Figure 13.19** An example of a "mega-church," a phenomenon that emerged in the 1970s and 1980s.

AMERICAN ARCHIVE

## The *Chakrabarty* Case and Its Implications

Ananda Mohan Chakrabarty was an engineer who developed a genetically modified microbe that consumes oil spills by breaking down crude oil. To protect his invention, he applied to the US Patent Office.

A patent is a form of intellectual property that gives the owner the right to prevent others from using an invention without permission. Permission to use a patented invention is typically granted in exchange for money. If an invention is successful, the inventor can sell the patent or charge others to use the invention. In a market-driven economy, the prospect of being paid for their inventions encourages inventors, and inventions generally lead to a better society. In fact, the United States is a world leader in both patent law and inventions.

The US Patent Office refused to issue a patent to Chakrabarty because it believed that the law did not cover living organisms. Several appeals followed, and ultimately the dispute was heard by the US Supreme Court. In its 1980 ruling in *Diamond v. Chakrabarty*, the court decided in favour of Chakrabarty by a margin of 5 to 4.

The case came down to an interpretation of the Patent Act. The law, the court noted, is written in broad terms: "Whoever invents or discovers any new and useful process, machine, manufacture, or composition of matter ... may obtain a patent." Chief Justice Warren E. Burger, writing for the majority, said that "in choosing such expansive terms ... Congress plainly contemplated that the patent laws would be given wide scope." On that basis, Chakrabarty's micro-organism "plainly qualifies as patentable subject matter."

Four other justices disagreed with this view. Justice William J. Brennan, writing for the dissenting minority, argued that while Congress had explicitly allowed patents for living organisms in other laws, such as the 1970 Plant Variety Protection Act, it had not done so in the Patent Act. Thus, he concluded, "Congress never meant to make items outside the scope of the legislation patentable."

The issue in *Chakrabarty* was narrow—an interpretation of patent law—but the case raises larger public policy questions. How far should property rights go? In 1988 the US Patent Office, following the court's decision in *Chakrabarty*, issued a patent for a genetically modified mouse used in cancer research, the so-called Harvard mouse. The property rights in a patent may be the economic engine that drives inventions, but what about the ethical issues around one's ability to "own" the genetic makeup of a living organism? Is there a limit to what people should be permitted to patent?

**Figure 13.18** Chakrabarty's patented microbes were used to clean up the *Exxon Valdez* disaster in 1989, one of the world's worst oil spills.

### Think It Through

1. How do patents create incentives for inventors? Using an example, show how incentives propel a capitalist economy. What are the drawbacks?
2. What are the ethical implications of allowing inventors and companies to patent living organisms? Come up with arguments for and against.
3. In interpreting legislation, should courts consider the social, economic, and ethical implications of their decisions? Or are these issues best left to the legislative branch of government? Explain your views.

more followers than ever before. Conservative Protestant churches gained the most followers. **Evangelical Christianity**, usually characterized by an intensely felt conversion experience and a literal interpretation of the Bible, led the way. It moved away from mainstream Protestantism into a more fundamentalist and politically motivated grassroots movement that involved millions of Americans, including President Jimmy Carter.

Many, but not all, evangelicals were **fundamentalists** who believed that everything in the Bible is literally true. Evangelicals were expected to live by a strict moral code. What prompted many evangelicals to become engaged in mainstream political and social issues was their concern that **secular humanism** was dominating schools and colleges and being advanced by mass media and political parties. By the early 1980s fundamentalists and evangelicals owned 40 television stations and 1,300 radio stations; in 1989 there were 336 television ministries. They collected about a billion dollars annually. In these decades as well, there emerged a broader-based alliance of fundamentalists, evangelicals, Mormons, and conservative Catholics and Jews. This new "religious right" was united in opposition to abortion, the ban on school prayer, court rulings facilitating the circulation of pornography, and other issues.

## Politics and Religion

The best-known organization of the new Christian right was the Moral Majority, founded by Jerry Falwell in 1979, which denounced divorce, abortion, feminism, and homosexuality, while supporting "free enterprise" and a strong American presence in the world. In 1978–79 the Moral Majority flexed its political muscles by forcing the city of Miami to repeal a pro-gay rights ordinance. Falwell's movement downplayed its religious focus, concentrating instead on organizing politically to build a strong, socially conservative movement open to many faiths. Its political action committee raised funds for conservatives, in 1979–80 raising $100 million for various campaigns. Its executive director, Robert Billings, left the Moral Majority in 1980 to work for Ronald Reagan's presidential campaign, creating an alignment between Christian fundamentalists and Republican policies.

One of the religious right's first targets was the US Supreme Court, which in 1962 and 1963 had strictly interpreted the constitutional requirement of separation of church and state by banning prayer in public schools. Another famous case was *Roe v. Wade* (1973), which you read about in Chapter 12. The judicial pronouncements in this case were directly opposed to the beliefs of many religious groups about abortion.

In response to the court's decisions, the religious right became highly politically motivated. It mobilized the growing evangelical movement to protest abortion, picketing clinics and exerting pressure on politicians to affirm their anti-abortion views publicly. Evangelical religious leaders and groups such as the Moral Majority became increasingly influential owing to their advocacy and organizational efforts.

## Backlash against Feminism

The religious right opposed feminist views. You saw in Chapter 12 how the 1970s women's movement successfully expanded education, employment, and reproductive rights that created choices for women. The 1980s was a period of reaction. The coalition of politically active right-wing Christians and other social conservatives attempted to undo feminists' hard-won victories. This coalition had support from the Reagan administration. Women's appointments as federal judges dropped from 15 percent under Carter to 8 percent under Reagan, who also eliminated women identified as feminists from the administration of federal programs. Popular magazines featured articles on high divorce rates, questioning whether career-focused women, who put their children in daycare, made adequate mothers.

The Equal Rights Amendment (ERA), approved by Congress in 1972, died for lack of state support in 1979. Although the deadline for ratification was extended to 1982, Reagan did nothing to support this measure, which feminists had been working for since the 1920s. The defeat of the ERA symbolized this backlash, which was also reflected in employment and income statistics. Despite decades of struggle, women represented two-thirds of adults living in poverty. The vast majority of women—75 percent—earned less than half the wages paid to men. By the end of the 1980s, 80 percent of women were still employed in jobs traditionally considered "women's work," such as nursing, teaching, cleaning, or secretarial services.

Much of the backlash focused on abortion. Those in support of abortion rights for women (pro-choice) consider abortion an option that must be available to women. Those opposed (pro-life) represent the rights of the unborn, portraying abortion as murder. Debate centred on philosophical, moral, medical, ethical, and legal principles and on the sacredness of life. Clashes were rooted in the conflicting assessments of legislation and court decisions regarding the freedom of choice or the degree of social control in the regulation of abortion. A 1986 *Washington Post–ABC News* poll found that 54 percent of Americans believed that women should have the right to an abortion no matter what; 34 percent agreed only in certain circumstances; and 20 percent disagreed in all cases.

Within a year of the Supreme Court's decision in *Roe v. Wade*, 50 bills were proposed at

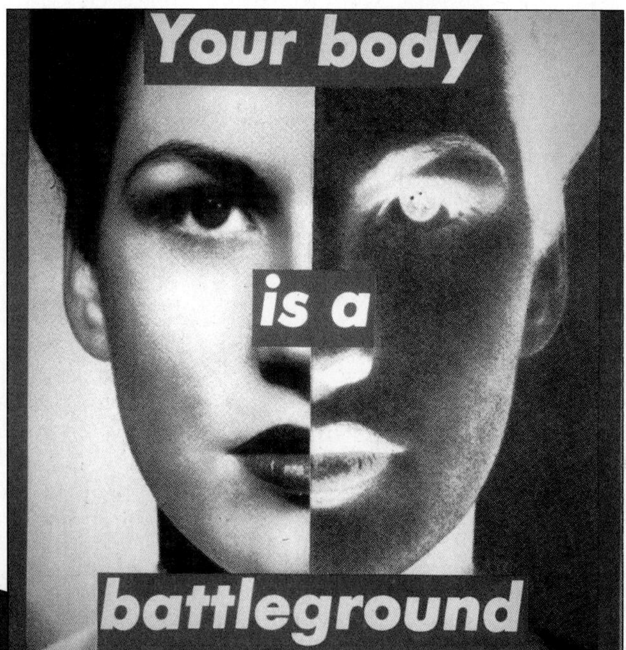


**Figure 13.20** This 1989 photographic silk-screen by American artist Barbara Kruger depicts the conflict surrounding women's reproductive health issues. Why did the issue of reproductive rights polarize US public opinion?

# Culture Notes

## Judy Chicago's The Dinner Party

*The Dinner Party* is a celebration of women: their history, their art forms, and their bodies. When the work was first exhibited at the San Francisco Museum of Modern Art in 1979, it attracted record-breaking crowds from all over the world. The installation had been five years in the making and involved the labour of hundreds of artists, craftspeople, and researchers under the direction of artist Judy Chicago. In explaining her work, Chicago said, "*The Dinner Party* was meant to end the ongoing cycle of omission in which women were written out of the historical record."

The installation consists of a triangular table with 13 place settings on each of its 15-metre sides. The guests of honour are 39 women drawn from mythology and history. For example, Ishtar, the Mesopotamian goddess who gives and takes life, dines in the company of the mediaeval abbess, musician, and scientist Hildegarde of Bingen. Mary Wollstonecraft, who wrote *A Vindication of the Rights of Woman* in 1792, sits next to American abolitionist Sojourner Truth. On the white floor underneath the table, the names of another 999 women are inscribed in gold.

Using a traditionally feminine institution—the dinner party—and traditionally feminine art forms—needlework, china painting, and ceramics—*The Dinner Party* is also a celebration of women's culture. Each guest is represented by embroidered table linens, a painted porcelain plate, a chalice, and eating implements. The sexual imagery on the plates ensured that the work would be highly controversial when it first appeared.

Chicago began work on *The Dinner Party* in 1974. A year and a half later, she realized that she needed help to complete it. Little by little, others joined her, and by the time the work was finished, hundreds of people had assisted. Her studio, she said, "operated according to feminist principles—which means flexible roles, an emphasis on honest interaction, the recognition that people's personal problems affect their work, and the integration of group-process techniques to facilitate personal expression." There were lectures, discussions, and potluck dinners for all who participated in the project.

After the San Francisco show closed, the installation went into storage, and many galleries refused to exhibit it. However, grassroots groups petitioned museums for exhibition space and acquired space on their own. Over the next 25 years *The Dinner Party* was shown in six countries to more than one million people. In 2007 *The Dinner Party* was permanently installed in the Brooklyn Museum as part of the Elizabeth A. Sackler Center for Feminist Art.

### Think It Through

1. In what sense is *The Dinner Party* a feminist statement?
2. Do you agree with Judy Chicago that women have been "written out of the historical record"? Explain your view.

**Figure 13.21** Judy Chicago's *The Dinner Party* installation, 1979, and a detail showing the place setting for Sojourner Truth.

the state and federal level to restrict the 1973 case's impact. The legislative backlash against the court's decision included efforts to limit abortion, such as the 1976 Hyde Amendment, which eliminated federal funding for abortions. More than 30 states passed legislation restricting the right to abortion by imposing consent and notification requirements on women. While support for abortion rights remained high, efforts of opponents made access to abortion difficult. By 1987 abortion services were unavailable in 85 percent of the nation's counties. The efforts of social conservatives also resulted in a drying up of support for family planning and birth control clinics.

By 1975 Catholic groups had begun sit-ins at family planning and abortion clinics. Evangelical Protestant groups joined the movement, and by the end of the 1980s they accounted for a majority of anti-abortion activists. Their activities prompted legal responses from women's and abortion rights organizations. Pro-choice groups confronted pro-life protesters at clinics and lobbied to stop anti-abortion bills going through state legislatures. They organized to elect pro-choice candidates to office. Pro-choice women's groups, such as the National Abortion Rights Action League (NARAL) and the National Organization for Women (NOW), petitioned, protested, and lobbied to protect women's right to choose.

## Peace Activism

There was also a backlash against the politics of war and nuclear weapons. A vigorous peace movement had developed by the late 1960s and early 1970s with the primary goal of ending the Vietnam War. On his first day in office in January 1977, President Carter formally pardoned Vietnam draft dodgers.

Peace activism in the United States went into a lull in the late 1970s but experienced a resurgence in the 1980s with the heightening of the Cold War during Ronald Reagan's two terms in office.

Reagan's massive military buildup of the 1980s—although supported by conservative and fundamental Christian groups—provoked opposition from a broad spectrum of peace activists, particularly those concerned about nuclear weapons. Women, such as Dr. Helen Caldicott, were at the forefront of the anti-nuclear movement; scientists and doctors organized to educate the public about the consequences of nuclear war. Some religious leaders, including the National Council of Catholic Bishops, declared their opposition to nuclear weapons. In July 1982 the largest demonstration in American history took place in Central Park in New York City, where one million people gathered to show their determination to end the arms race. This event was followed by smaller demonstrations around the country throughout the rest of the 1980s as the public continued to voice its desire for peace.

## Gay Activism and the AIDS Crisis

Another important issue was **acquired immune deficiency syndrome** (**AIDS**). With the widespread use of antibiotics after World War II, infectious diseases ceased to be much of a threat in the developed world. Health research during the 1950s, 1960s, and 1970s focused on other issues, especially heart disease and cancer. This began to change, however, in the 1980s. In 1981 the first cases of AIDS were observed. By 1985, 5,600 Americans had died of the disease. By 1989 the Centers for Disease Control (CDC) had confirmed 82,764 cases, with 46,344 deaths reported. The CDC estimated that there were actually ten cases for each one reported. Because the disease was first diagnosed among homosexual men, social and religious conservatives saw AIDS as a "gay plague" that was the consequence of a sinful lifestyle.

In 1987 gay activists formed ACT UP (AIDS Coalition to Unleash Power), an organization whose position was: "Turn anger, fear, and grief into action." The group's first effort was to stage a parade of half a million people in New York City in 1987 as a way to mobilize the public to fight the disease. At that time President Reagan, noting general public concern about the epidemic, declared AIDS to be "public enemy number one," but refused to endorse condom use or to acknowledge that the disease had spread to include many Americans outside the gay population. But by 1992, as a result of persistent lobbying from ACT UP and other groups, Congress approved a $2 billion program to fight AIDS.

**Figure 13.22** The conservative Reagan administration was slow to respond to the AIDS epidemic, and paid little attention to the problem until the famous actor and undeclared homosexual Rock Hudson died of the disease in 1985.

## CHECK YOUR UNDERSTANDING

1. How did the computer industry change in the 1980s?
2. What groups make up the US religious right?
3. How did social and religious conservatives take action to oppose the Supreme Court decision in *Roe v. Wade*?
4. Why were there large-scale peace protests in 1982?
5. From 1981 to 1992, what was the impact of persistent lobbying from activist groups such as NOW and ACT UP?

# FOREIGN POLICY IN THE 1980s

What was happening outside the United States during the 1980s? The US continued to see itself, and continued to be seen abroad, as the dominant political and military leader of the free world. However, US leadership in a bipolar world, which saw nations stalemated into "free" and "communist" camps, came to an end when the Soviet Union was dissolved at the end of the 1980s. Closer to home, the United States also continued to exercise close control in the parts of the world it dominated, particularly in Central and

South America. In the Middle East, the US attempted to exercise influence with mixed results.

## Central and South America

Following the Monroe Doctrine, the United States had always seen itself as the dominant power in Central and South America, with the right to intervene in the interest of maintaining political stability, exercising economic control, and preserving uncontested military predominance. American intervention usually took the form of military or economic support of conservative, pro-American, business-oriented regimes in the face of leftist opposition. When countries challenged American influence, the US often responded by intervening directly in the country's domestic affairs.

In the 1980s the United States intervened on numerous occasions to support right-wing dictatorships: El Salvador in 1981 and Honduras between 1983 and 1989. In 1983, the US, with the support of several Caribbean nations, launched an invasion of Grenada after a Marxist government seized power in a coup and established close relations with Cuba and the Soviet Union. Although many in Grenada welcomed the intervention, the United States' actions reflected its willingness to use military force to stop the spread of communism. The US also intervened in Panama in 1989 (see Chapter 14).

### Nicaragua

In 1979, Nicaragua's conservative Somoza regime was overthrown by a popular movement known as the **Sandinistas**. Influenced by Marxist revolutionary ideas, the Sandinistas were regarded with suspicion by the United States. The new regime threatened US economic interests in the country, particularly the banana industry. In response, the United States began offering secret funding and military training to the Contras, a right-wing coalition opposed to the Sandinistas. Eventually, however, opposition to secret CIA involvement with the Contras led Congress in 1982 to pass the Boland Amendment, limiting further US government assistance to the Contras.

Ignoring the amendment, Reagan's administration began to provide military and financial support illegally to the Contras. In 1986 the Nicaraguan government brought a case before the World Court accusing the United States of supporting armed aggression. The court condemned

**Figure 13.22** President Daniel Ortega of Nicaragua addresses the UN Security Council condemning the US's refusal to abide by the World Court's ruling against aid to Contra rebels.

the US for the unlawful use of force, and ordered it to desist and pay reparations to the Nicaraguan government. The US ignored the World Court's decision. Nicaragua took its case to the UN Security Council, where the United States vetoed a resolution condemning its aggression.

## The Middle East

Behind its foreign policy in the Middle East lay the United States' long-standing belief that the region was in need of stabilizing, as well as a commitment to find peace that supported US strategic interests. This included the need to ensure continuing supplies of crude oil.

US Middle East policy sought to maintain a strong alliance with Israel, providing it with financial and military support. At the same time, the United States also supported countries such as Saudi Arabia, which was a major oil supplier but had never officially recognized Israel's right to exist. The US also supported Saddam Hussein, the Iraqi leader who was fighting a war with Iran during the 1980s, by providing him with financial aid and selling him US arms. This was not an uncommon arrangement. The US government lent countries money they subsequently used to purchase US arms; in turn, the US purchased commodities from them, such as oil from Iraq.

In 1982 the United States sent troops to help stabilize Lebanon, which was in a civil war that lasted from 1975 to 1990. During that same interval, Israel invaded Lebanon to protect itself from the incursions of the Palestine Liberation Organization, which was operating out of Lebanon at the time. Although Israel rejected President Reagan's Lebanese peace plan of September 1982, this did not alter the US's favoured relationship with that country.

## The Soviet Union

During the 1980s tension between the United States and the Soviet Union continued. In 1979 the Soviets invaded Afghanistan. The United States countered the Soviet invasion by supporting groups that opposed the Soviet occupation. The Northern Alliance, a group of indigenous Islamic Afghanis, mounted a long-standing guerrilla war against Soviet occupation that ultimately defeated and forced the withdrawal of the Russians.

In 1982 Reagan made a speech in which he referred to the Soviet Union as "the Evil Empire" and accused it of sponsoring world terror. He refused to discuss arms limitation agreements unless the Soviets agreed to end their involvement in the affairs of other nations. Reagan's hard-line rhetoric was admired by many on the American right who advocated a more "muscular" approach to US–Soviet relations. Other Americans saw Reagan's comments as a needless provocation of the Soviets. The president, however, was committed to forcing the situation, moving from a long-established American strategy that "contained" the Soviets to one that confronted them directly.

In 1983 Reagan took a further step in the arms race by proposing "Star Wars," a program to develop a space-based weapons system designed to shoot down enemy missiles. The Soviets claimed that this program would escalate the arms race, and refused to discuss disarmament until the United States abandoned it. Reagan announced a trillion dollars' worth of increased military spending on weapons of all kinds.

## The End of the Cold War

The Soviet government, which could no longer afford the arms race that Reagan had ushered in, began to relax its control of its Eastern European satellite states, and withdraw its forces. Communist regimes fell throughout Eastern Europe, and the Soviet Union was peacefully dissolved. The collapse of the Soviet Union was one of the pivotal events of the post–World War II period.

The transformation of the Soviet Union was brought about in part by a determination to seek a more rational and less confrontational international arena. Soviet Premier Mikhail Gorbachev sought to lessen tensions, proposing mutual reduction of nuclear arsenals by 50 percent on both sides in 1986. But Reagan, committed to his "Star Wars" dreams, refused to make any commitment. In 1989, however, Gorbachev and Reagan agreed to eliminate all intermediate-range missiles from Europe. This was the most significant arms control agreement of the nuclear age. Gorbachev further reduced tensions by withdrawing the defeated Soviet forces from Afghanistan, leaving it to the Northern Alliance and the **Taliban**, a fundamentalist Islamic movement that would rule Afghanistan between 1996 and 2001.

In November 1989 the Berlin Wall fell, and East and West Germany were reunited shortly thereafter. It appeared that clashes between superpowers and the threat of nuclear war were over. The United States now found itself in a world in which it was the sole superpower, with apparent political, financial, and military influence over its allies and its enemies alike. The 1990s and the dawn of the 21st century would show that the international arena was more complicated than it appeared to be in 1989. But at that time, the United States was hopeful about its future. As incoming President George H.W. Bush noted, there was a "new world order." In his inauguration speech, Bush voiced the hope that the world would be a place of peace and prosperity.

**Figure 13.23** US president Ronald Reagan (centre) and president-elect George Bush with Soviet Premier Mikhail Gorbachev, December 7, 1988, in front of the Statue of Liberty. Consider how the fall of the Berlin Wall photo (Figure 13.1) and this photo depict a new world order.

# PAST VOICES

## Francis Fukuyama and "The End of History?"

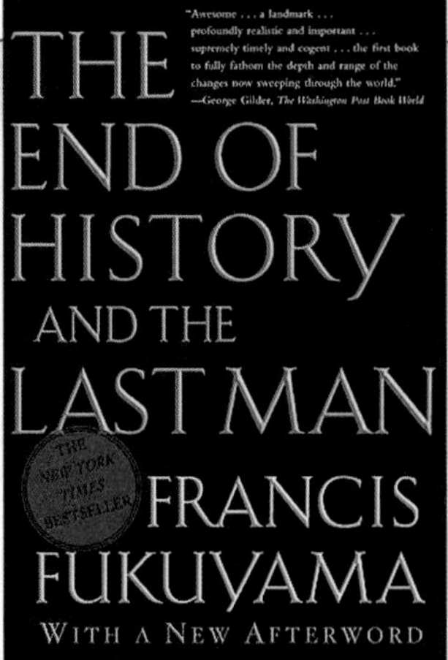


**Figure 13.24** Francis Fukuyama's *The End of History and the Last Man*, first published in 1992.

> What we may be witnessing is not just the end of the Cold War, or the passing of a particular period of post-war history, but the end of history as such: that is, the end point of mankind's ideological evolution and the universalization of Western liberal democracy as the final form of human government.
>
> —Francis Fukuyama, "The End of History?," 1989

With the end of the Cold War a number of major issues in the 20th century seemed to be settled. In economics, capitalism won and communism lost. In politics, democracy and freedom triumphed over dictatorship and tyranny. The "Evil Empire" was gone. What was next?

Perhaps nothing, suggested Professor Francis Fukuyama in a 1989 essay and a 1992 book, *The End of History and the Last Man.*

There have been many theories to explain the changes over time that make up history. One was based on the writings of Karl Marx. Followers of this theory, including the Soviet Union and communist China, believed that history would end with the triumph of the workers, and that class conflicts that came from this system would end with the fall of capitalism. Fukuyama argued that the conflict between these ideologies was over and that liberal democracy was the final winner.

He based his view on the following argument. Since the Industrial Revolution in Europe and America, democracy in one form or another has become the choice for a majority of the world's governments. Dictatorships from the end of the 20th century have largely been discredited. Communism as an economic system is not compatible with market economics, so that within democracies the market system has become the general system for economic growth.

The events of the previous 50 years seemed to prove Fukuyama right. Nazi Germany and Imperial Japan were crushed in World War II. The postwar period ending in the Reagan era saw Western democracies grow in prosperity while the Soviet Union imploded. The 1980s also saw the end of dictatorships and oppressive governments from Argentina, Brazil, and Chile to eastern Europe once the Soviet Union collapsed. Even communist China was beginning to embrace capitalist-style markets.

It is important to note that Fukuyama did not mean that history was "ending" in the sense that it was finished. Rather, he meant that history *as it had been defined* for over a century was finished. Not only would liberal democracy be the form of government within which history would unfold; it would not be replaced by some "better" form of government.

### Think It Through

1. What is Fukuyama's thesis, and how did he justify it?
2. If history was really to end, why is Chapter 13 not the final chapter of this book? Research what Fukuyama now says about the "end of history."

# CHECK YOUR UNDERSTANDING

1. Why did the Reagan administration oppose the Sandinista regime in Nicaragua?
2. What complex problem did the US face in the Middle East in the 1980s?
3. What role did oil play in US policy in the Middle East?
4. What did President Reagan's "Evil Empire" speech in 1982 signal about US policy toward the Soviet Union?
5. What were causes and effects of the fall of the Berlin Wall?

# THE HISTORIAN'S CRAFT

## Historical Mindedness

You have read in previous Historian's Craft features about how historians bring intellectual curiosity to their work. There is more to being historically minded, however, than just having an inquiring mind. Historians are alert to the history around them in historic buildings, monuments, street names, and older people who have lived through history. As well, historians are conscious of the academic, practical, and personal value of history.

### Academic Value

Historical knowledge about people, government, politics, the economy, international affairs, the arts, popular culture, and society provides you with an intellectual base for understanding the world. Knowledge of the nature of history and of concepts such as "cause and effect" and "conflict and change" helps you understand the human story as well as many scientific and technological developments.

You know that history is more than a matter of learning key facts and important concepts. Historians—and history students—also use skills of research, interpretation of evidence, and presentation of findings. These valuable history skills are important in many subjects and in the world outside school.

### Practical Value

You may be interested enough in history to make it the basis for a career—for example, as a teacher, professor, writer, archivist, or museum curator. Even if your interests lie elsewhere, history still has employment-related value. Besides the knowledge and skills described above, history prepares you to understand others—other political positions, other points of view, and other beliefs. Such understanding is essential for dealing with the complexities and pleasures of travel, multicultural societies, the global economy, and international communication.

### Personal Value

The wide scope and interdisciplinary nature of history allows you to capitalize on personal interests in the study of it. For example, in this chapter you might pursue your interest in the entertainment industry by researching the first minority-focused TV programs, or your interest in popular music through a project on punk rock's impact on American society.

In recent times, historians have become interested in historical consciousness: the way individuals make sense of history and find personal meaning in it based on their socio-economic, ethnic, and personal makeup. You might already be aware that family and personal background make the study of some topics more meaningful for some people than others. For example, an African-Canadian student might feel a strong personal connection to the civil rights movement covered in Chapter 12. A student with strong personal and religious or cultural views about reproductive issues might make sense of this chapter's sections on reproductive rights and feminism in a way that differs from other classmates. Recognizing your historical consciousness—and understanding that of others—enriches your understanding of the nature of history.

### Try It!

1. How could what you have learned in history help you pursue an occupation?
2. Make a list of three of your favourite leisure activities. Research one of these activities for the period of American history covered in this chapter.
3. Choose a topic from this chapter that you and two other students find particularly interesting. Write down why you find it interesting. Consider how this topic has special meaning for you personally, perhaps in terms of your family's background or your ethno-cultural heritage. After your classmates have completed the same exercise, compare notes. Examine the similarities and differences in meaning and emphasis that you have identified for the same topic.

# STUDY HALL

## Thinking

1. State, in the form of a question, the problem faced by President Nixon after the Supreme Court upheld the right of newspapers to print the leaked, secret "Pentagon Papers."
2. "Only a fervent anti-communist could normalize relations between China and the US." Do you agree? Why or why not?
3. Do the civil and religious protests described in this chapter indicate a decline in the United States, or are they the signs of an active, healthy democracy? Do they reflect something else? Explain your views.

## Communication

4. Debate the following issues:
   a. Affirmative action is just another form of racism and should be banned.
   b. All schools should receive equal per-pupil funding, regardless of the wealth of the community.
   c. Politics and religion should be kept separate.
   d. The struggle over reproductive rights and the rights of women is an issue for women alone.
   e. Ronald Reagan was responsible for the fall of communism in Europe.
5. In a diagram, show how OPEC's oil-pricing policy could affect the prices of US-made goods and US–world trade. Consider such products as tractors, medicines, and computer equipment.
6. Script a dialogue between President Reagan (defending the need for tax cuts and less government regulation) and an environmentalist (defending the need for government regulation to protect the environment).
7. In a two-column chart, show how each of the following had an impact on the Cold War: Nixon's China visit, SALT I, SALT II, Star Wars, Reagan's arms race, the Grenada invasion, Reagan's Nicaragua policy, the "Evil Empire" speech.

## Application

8. Find a transcript of the Nixon White House tapes. What is revealed about Nixon as a person and as a leader? What impact do you think the tapes had on public opinion?
9. Look at E. Howard Hunt's statement on page 441. What does it reveal about his attitude toward the rule of law?
10. Investigate Henry Kissinger's role in the Middle East, especially in the 1973 Yom Kippur War. Did he live up to his reputation as a "political realist" (see page 448)?
11. Research the Canadian role in the Iran hostage crisis. What is revealed about the nature of Canada–US relations?
12. If you had been living during the Reagan presidency, how might you have dealt with the 23 percent cut in income taxes? Calculate the change in income for a person who had been paying $10,000 per year in income tax. What would you have done with the money? How would similar decisions by millions of Americans have affected the economy?

# 14 Into a New Century (1989–Present)

## KEY CONCEPTS

In this chapter you will consider:

- The role of the United States in a new world order
- The impact of 9/11
- The "war on terror" and the war in Iraq
- Political, economic, and social challenges in recent times
- Historical perspectives on the present and the future

## The American Story

The end of the Cold War suggested an opportunity for American leaders to redirect the nation's wealth away from arms production toward social, health, and educational programs. The economy was strong and the future looked bright. It soon became clear, however, that the promise of peace and prosperity was an illusion. The United States continued to spend on the military, and became embroiled in interventions overseas. After the terrorist attacks of September 11, 2001 American leaders had to confront terrorism at home and abroad, and could devote little attention to domestic needs. The United States' anti-terrorist policies and its invasion of Iraq have divided American and world opinion.

## TIMELINE

| 1991 | 1992 | 1994 | 1995 | 1997 |
|---|---|---|---|---|
| ▸ Collapse of USSR<br>▸ Gulf War | ▸ Los Angeles Riot | ▸ NAFTA becomes law | ▸ US joins WTO | ▸ Kyoto Protocol |

## IMAGE ANALYSIS

**Figure 14.1** In 2003, the United States invaded Iraq as part of its "war on terror." Although it had allies—the "coalition of the willing"—it also had international critics. Here, protesters in Bangladesh march against the US, claiming that American policy was driven by its oil interests. The demonstrators' placards represent many of the anti-US sentiments felt by other international citizens—and some Americans.

Where do you stand on the US invasion of Iraq? What would you say in support of, or opposition to, the protesters in the photo?

- 1998: Attempt to impeach Clinton
- 1999: WTO protest in Seattle
- 2001: 9/11; USA PATRIOT Act
- 2003: War in Iraq
- 2005: Hurricane Katrina

# INTRODUCTION

In this chapter, for the first time in your study of American history, you will deal with events that you have lived through. This quality of "living history" presents challenges for historians and history students alike, since much of US history since 1989 has not been written. A good deal of the primary evidence is not yet available. The long-term effects of many events are still unknown. There is plenty of commentary, but most of it is partisan and emotional because the writers are living through the times.

You can gain perspective on recent developments, however, by seeing them in relation to historical patterns. Many of the events in this chapter relate to the key ideas in American history that are identified on page x. You can think about modern events in light of these ideas and other historical trends that you have identified. In the process, you will better understand both the past and the present—and you may anticipate some of America's future, too.

# A NEW WORLD ORDER

In the two years following the dismantling of the Berlin Wall, East and West Germany were reunited, the nations of the Eastern Bloc broke free from Soviet influence, and the USSR itself was dissolved. The US forged agreements with Russia to cut back nuclear arsenals and phase out multiple-warhead missiles. Hard-line communism was softening in China as its government allowed the development of peasants' markets and private businesses, and demonstrated more tolerance toward Western culture. These changes seemed to mark the "end of history" (see Chapter 13)—or at least the end of a dangerous stage in it. In the face of these dramatic changes, some Americans hoped for a "**peace dividend**." Funds redirected from the huge US military budget could now be applied toward Americans' social needs.

## Foreign Policy in a Changed World

President George H.W. Bush (father of President George W. Bush) capitalized on the new state of the world by negotiating with Russia's leader, Boris Yeltsin, to reach agreements on further armaments cuts and on the removal of Cold War economic barriers to stimulate the growth of Russian capitalism. The US was prepared to deal with this former totalitarian state in the post–Cold War era. It also remained ready to fight dictatorships in the Western Hemisphere and around the world.

### Panama

In 1988, General Manuel Noriega, a former ally of the US, seized power in Panama. Noriega ruled brutally, spouted anti-American pronouncements, and threatened the security of the Panama Canal. As part of their campaign to stem the flow of drugs into the United States, American authorities indicted him for drug trafficking. In December 1989, the US launched Operation Just Cause, sending 26,000 troops—the biggest US troop deployment since Vietnam—into Panama to depose Noriega. He was captured, taken to the United States, and convicted on the drug charges. Both Congress and the public supported this intervention. Not only had the US removed a brutal dictator and drug lord, but it also had reasserted American influence over both Panama and the Canal itself.

## The Gulf War

You know from earlier chapters that a unilateral US intervention in the Americas was nothing new. What was new was the United States' ability as the sole superpower to take the initiative in persuading other nations to intervene in a world trouble spot. In 1990, Iraq's President Saddam Hussein invaded Kuwait, secured valuable oil fields, and threatened Saudi Arabia. In response, the United Nations called for an immediate withdrawal. When Saddam refused, the UN applied economic sanctions to obtain his compliance. In the face of this crisis, President Bush addressed a joint session of Congress outlining US objectives: Saddam's unconditional withdrawal; restoration of Kuwait's government; security and protection of US citizens—and the creation of a "new world order" in which the strong protected the rights of the weak.

The UN directed Saddam to withdraw from Kuwait by January 15, 1991 or face action by a UN force. When the Iraqi leader refused to pull back, President Bush gained authorization from Congress to act against Saddam. On January 16, the UN-sanctioned coalition launched its first air strikes against Iraq. The coalition consisted of more than two dozen nations, including Britain, France, Italy, Kuwait, Saudi Arabia, and Canada. The US contingent was by far the largest, but the allies provided a wide range of support. For example, the Canadian contribution amounted to over 4,000 military personnel including medics, naval forces, and air crew.

**SOUND BITE**

"If Canada had stood aside we would have betrayed our own national interests, repudiated our own responsibilities and dishonoured our own traditions. Canada did not stand aside in two world wars and Korea. Canada did not stand aside to the hard work of seeking a peaceful end to the Iraqi occupation of Kuwait and … Canada is not standing aside tonight from giving effect to the United Nations resolutions in the Persian Gulf."

—Prime Minister Brian Mulroney, 1991

Once the air war was launched, events moved quickly in what the Americans dubbed Operation Desert Storm. On February 24, coalition ground forces, again mostly American, began their attack. By February 27, Kuwait City was liberated as Iraqi forces retreated. On February 28, the coalition declared a ceasefire. The objective of the UN resolution—the Iraqi withdrawal from Kuwait—had been achieved. The Gulf War was over. In the aftermath, the UN subjected Iraq to supervision of its weapons and restrictions on its military activities.

**WEB LINKS** 

To learn more about the chronology of the Gulf War, visit www.emp.ca/ah.

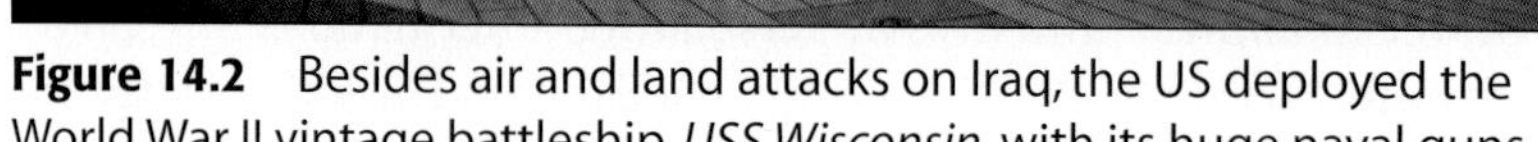

**Figure 14.2** Besides air and land attacks on Iraq, the US deployed the World War II vintage battleship, *USS Wisconsin*, with its huge naval guns.

**SOUND BITE**

"The Gulf War was a real watershed because it brought back the myth of war ... War became noble again. War became respectable ... The old lie resurrected itself in full glory, and the ghosts of Vietnam were vanquished."

—Chris Hedges, *Reporting America at War*, 2003

The Gulf War was a victory both for the UN and the United States. Saddam had been humiliated and US objectives had been met. The devastating land attack had lasted only 100 hours, and the Americans sustained only 750 casualties. American news reporters and on-air military analysts enthusiastically chronicled US successes. The impression given was that the number of Iraqi civilian casualties was low. Television coverage highlighted images of "smart bombs" in a high-tech, bloodless war—images far removed from the body bags of the Vietnam era. The president had declared that this conflict would not be another Vietnam, and had delivered on that promise. Most of the American public supported the war.

**Figure 14.3** Even after the Gulf War ended, US planes enforced a "no-fly zone" over Iraq to keep Saddam Hussein in check.

### A Second Look

A second look at the Gulf War raises critical questions. Was it as popular as the press coverage suggested? Was it a military triumph? Even during the war, there were protests by Vietnam veterans, pacifists, and others. Some critics noted that the United States had been trading for oil with Iraq almost up to the invasion and that the main goal of US intervention was to protect oil supplies. Others pointed out that the US had long supported Saddam with arms shipments—including chemical weapons. At the war's end, some condemned President Bush for not finishing the job he had started. By declaring an end to the war before allied troops occupied Iraq, Bush allowed Saddam to remain in power and to nurture a growing anger toward the United States and its allies. Many Americans who lived through the Gulf War still see US actions as justified and appropriate—perhaps not as many now as in 1991, however. What all may agree on was that the Gulf War heralded the "new world order"—one in which the United States would take decisive action in leading other nations to intervene for what is "right," or at least what the US decided was right.

### CHECK YOUR UNDERSTANDING

1. How did international affairs change dramatically in the early 1990s?
2. Compare the US invasion of Panama with its other interventions in Latin America (see Chapters 8, 9, and 13).
3. On what grounds could the Gulf War be considered a success for the United States?

# DOMESTIC AFFAIRS TO 1992

The United States may have enjoyed a military triumph in the Gulf War, but all was not well at home. Defence spending still consumed much of the federal budget, and there were other issues: a financial crisis, a growing gap between rich and poor, and racial violence.

## Defence Spending: A Permanent Pattern

The United States' interventions in Panama and the Gulf War underscored that there would be no post–Cold War peace dividend to spend on domestic matters such as poverty or health care. By the 1990s it was evident that military spending had become a core component of the modern US economy. President Eisenhower's warning about the emerging military–industrial complex (see Chapter 11) now seemed like an accurate prediction.

Since the 1950s there had been peaks in defence spending: the Korean War, the Vietnam War, and Ronald Reagan's military projects. Yet at no time

**Figure 14.4** US defence spending, 1950–2008.

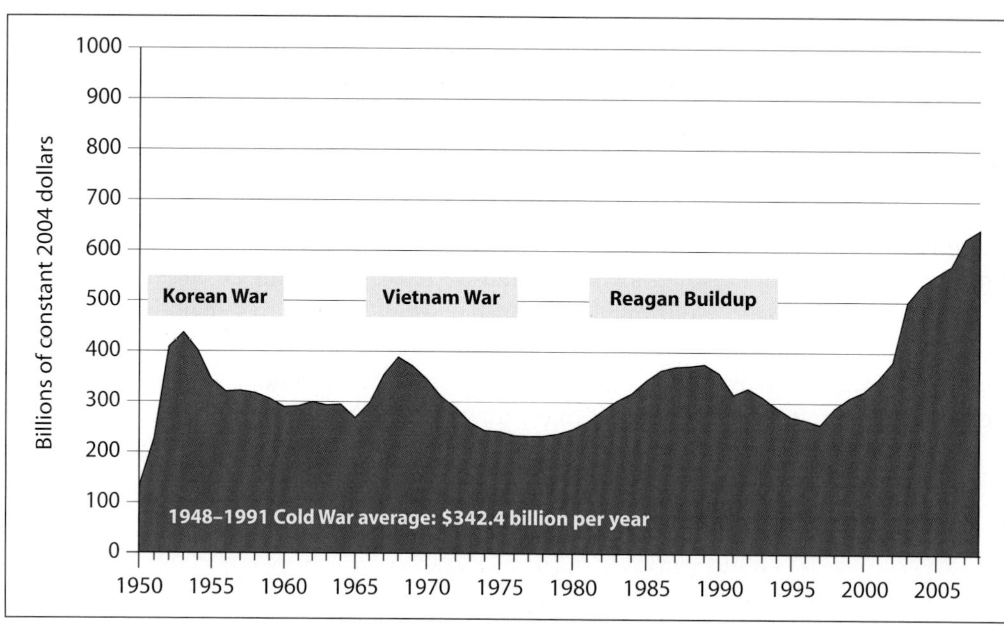


in the whole period since 1953 did defence spending return to pre–Cold War levels. This sustained level of military spending fundamentally changed the American economy and much of its politics in the second half of the 20th century. Military contracts drove the economy of many states, and members of Congress, regardless of their party, found themselves in the position of having to support huge military expenditures to preserve local defence industry jobs.

## Economic Problems

Some Americans were unaware of the extent of military spending, but many were all too aware of a financial crisis within the country. Savings and loans institutions had multiplied as a result of loosened financial regulations during the period of Reaganomics. In the late 1980s, however, hundreds of these lenders went bankrupt or were closed by federal regulators because of unsound practices. Investors' losses were close to $125 billion, and the federal government had to create a new agency to provide restitution and regulation. The federal payout to investors drove up the budget deficit. Democratic members of Congress, fearing a serious recession, pushed President Bush to support a tax increase. The president had little choice but to agree, even though he had promised not to raise taxes. In the mid-term congressional election of 1990, the Republicans lost seats largely because of that broken promise.

Thousands of Americans were affected by the savings and loans fiasco and the tax increases. Confidence in the economy was shaky; many people worried about health care, job security, and pensions. The decline in traditional industries that had begun in the 1970s and 1980s (see Chapter 13) continued.

Even some of the oldest and most stable industries were affected: the telecommunications giant AT&T cut one million jobs, and General Motors revealed plans to close 21 plants. By the 1990s, there was also growing awareness that the gap between the rich and the poor was expanding. In that decade, the pay of chief executive officers (CEOs) of US companies increased by 571 percent, while the pay of average workers grew by only 37 percent. Nowhere was the effect of pay disparity more evident than in the ghettos of American cities.

## Los Angeles Riot

In 1991, Los Angeles police officers were videotaped beating an African-American, Rodney King, as they arrested him. The video images were shown repeatedly on national television. In 1992, a predominantly white jury found one of the officers guilty of the minor charge of using excessive force in the arrest, but cleared the other police officers. When the verdicts were announced, a riot erupted in Los Angeles. The National Guard was sent in to quell the violence and looting. When order was restored five days later, more than 50 people had been killed and 4,000 injured, and more than a billion dollars in property had been destroyed or damaged.

Clearly, the old problems of poverty, violence, and racial tensions were still evident within the US. But in 1992, advances in technology made the violence even more immediate. Now ordinary people had video cameras and could record footage that would later be broadcast on national networks. Moreover, almost all Americans now owned televisions, and both the networks and the all-news channels flooded the airwaves with coverage of the riot.

President Bush recognized the impact of the media coverage: "Television has become a medium that often brings us together. But … the America it has shown us on our screens these last 48 hours has appalled us … It's as if we were looking in a mirror that distorted our better selves and turned us ugly." On the other hand, historian Mike Davis saw the riot as an accurate mirror of America: "It was a revolutionary democratic protest characteristic of African-American history when the major institutions have thwarted demands for equal rights. It was also a major post-modern bread riot—an uprising of not just poor people but particularly of those strata of poor in southern California who've been most savagely affected by the recession."

**Figure 14.5** Damage from the Los Angeles Riot. Compare the causes of this riot with those of the 1960s (see Chapter 12).

# PAST VOICES

## Anita Hill

In 1991, President Bush nominated Clarence Thomas to fill a vacancy on the US Supreme Court caused by the retirement of Thurgood Marshall, the first African-American justice and a liberal voice on the court. Thomas, another African-American, was a contentious nominee because he held conservative views on such matters as affirmative action and legalized abortions. As well, he had limited experience as a federal judge—only two years.

Thomas's confirmation hearings were moving through the US Senate when a bombshell hit the proceedings. Law professor Anita Hill, who had once worked for Thomas, accused him of sexual harassment. Thomas vigorously denied the charge. In the absence of conclusive proof, the Senate narrowly approved the nomination.

The Hill–Thomas episode reflected several key elements in US history: the system of checks and balances reflected in the Senate's review of presidential appointments and the practice of providing a balanced outlook on the Supreme Court. It also brought to the surface the issue of workplace harassment by those in positions of power—and the difficulties faced by those who choose to speak out. In the Senate, Hill said: "Telling the world is the most difficult experience of my life … I was aware, however, that telling at any point in my career could adversely affect my future career."

Hill's testimony—and the heavy media coverage of it—contributed to a dramatic increase in the number of reported sexual harassment cases. As well, many American women took note of the overwhelmingly male makeup of the Senate that had overlooked Hill's charges. An increase in female election victories in both houses of Congress (five female senators and 24 congresswomen) marked the 1992 election.

In 2005, Hill reiterated the reason that her testimony had been important: "I thought it showed how he dealt with issues of power generally and … how he viewed women generally, which would impact his role as a Supreme Court justice." She also reflected on the legacy of the episode in terms of gender politics:

**Figure 14.6** Anita Hill testifying before the Senate. Issues of race complicated the Hill–Thomas affair. He claimed that the televised hearings constituted a "high-tech lynching." Some black Americans did not relish seeing one African-American publicly criticizing another who was about to be appointed to a powerful position.

> I think there's better understanding today. And there's a better appreciation for the fact that if any community is going to prosper, if any community is going to be seen at its best, … the women in that community have to be viewed as equally as important as the men. And [women] have to be able to live outside of boundaries that are placed on them because of their gender.

### Think It Through

1. Use the Internet to research Thurgood Marshall and Clarence Thomas and compare their careers.
2. Why might Anita Hill be considered an important voice in American history?

| The Presidents: 1989–2008 | | |
|---|---|---|
| **George H.W. Bush** | Republican | January 20, 1989 – January 20, 1993 |
| **Bill Clinton** | Democrat | January 20, 1993 – January 20, 2001 |
| **George W. Bush** | Republican | January 20, 2001 – incumbent |

## Changing of the Guard

Economic uncertainty, tax increases, the Hill–Thomas affair, and urban unrest all contributed to the declining popularity of President Bush. As well, his initial success against Iraq was tarnished by subsequent events in that country. Saddam Hussein continued to brutalize his opponents within Iraq and refused to allow UN inspectors to look for prohibited weapons. In the 1992 election, Bush, the last of the presidents to have served in World War II, campaigned on his experience and dependability. Arkansas Governor Bill Clinton, 20 years younger and a former Vietnam War protester, campaigned on the need for change. The incumbent pointed to his success in the Gulf War, but Clinton—sensing the public mood—focused on domestic matters. Bush touted Reaganomics-era policies on tax cuts and minimum government interference in the economy. Clinton proposed a vigorous role for the federal government in the economy and in issues such as health care. Clinton appeared more relaxed and confident on television, both in debates and on late-night talk shows. A third candidate, Ross Perot, gained almost 20 percent of the popular vote and drained support from Bush, helping Clinton win.

### CHECK YOUR UNDERSTANDING

1. How had Eisenhower's warning about the military–industrial complex come to seem like an accurate prediction?
2. List the economic problems that the US faced in the early 1990s.
3. What were the long-term and immediate causes of the Los Angeles Riot?
4. Why did Bill Clinton win the 1992 presidential election?

# US FOREIGN POLICY IN THE NEW WORLD ORDER

Based on his campaign, Clinton was expected to move in new directions. He did reduce the defence budget—but only by 5 percent. By 1994, bowing to defence critics and Republican complaints, he agreed to a 10 percent increase—thereby following the post-1950 pattern of military spending described in earlier chapters. Moreover, like his predecessor, the new president soon committed American forces to interventions around the world.

**Figure 14.7** Mogadishu, Somalia, 1992. American troops had to deal with famine, civilian casualties, and violent warlords.

## Somalia

In 1992, the United States committed troops to a UN peacekeeping mission in Somalia, where civil war was raging. Operation Restore Hope had big goals—to deliver humanitarian aid and to establish representative government. The operation, however, turned into a hopeless task for peacekeepers trying to deal simultaneously with rival warlords and starving Somalis. A US helicopter was shot down, and the corpses of American soldiers were dragged through the streets of Mogadishu, the Somali capital. When Americans saw these actions on television, some questioned the whole operation; others criticized the newly elected Clinton for not providing enough backup for the peacekeepers. When a shaky peace agreement was reached among the warlords, Clinton seized the opportunity to withdraw American soldiers from Somalia in 1994.

## More Problems with Iraq

After the Gulf War, Saddam Hussein resisted UN weapons inspections. The UN imposed economic sanctions, but these excluded oil production to allow Saddam to rebuild essential services destroyed in the Gulf War. The Iraqi leader, however, used the oil profits to add to his personal wealth and that of his family. The US worked with the British government to enforce the existing "no-fly zones" over Iraq to monitor and contain Saddam. The US also called for Iraqi compliance with the weapons inspection process. When Saddam halted the inspections completely in 1998, Clinton ordered air strikes as a warning. These attacks were renewed in 1999, and continued sporadically until the US-led invasion of Iraq in 2003.

## The Balkans

While old problems with Iraq remained troublesome, a crisis developed in another part of the world. During the Cold War, Yugoslavia had consisted of six republics—Bosnia, Croatia, Macedonia, Montenegro, Serbia, and Slovenia—as well as the semi-independent provinces of Kosovo and Vojvodina. After the Cold War ended, strong nationalist sentiments tore the country apart. Slovenia, Croatia, Macedonia, and Bosnia declared independence in 1991–92. With the support of Yugoslavian president Slobodan Milosevic (a Serb), Serbs in Kosovo rebelled against the predominantly Albanian Muslim majority and seized power. Milosevic also sent troops into Croatia and Bosnia to support ethnic Serbs' claims.

The fighting was fuelled by bitterness from all sides, but it became clear to the world that Muslim populations were the victims of "ethnic cleansing" (genocide on the basis of ethnic origin). UN peacekeepers sent to the former Yugoslavia could not contain the crisis. In 1993–94, the international community tried a new tactic. Aircraft from several NATO countries, predominantly the United States, enforced a no-fly zone over the troubled nations to limit the violence. NATO planes took part in several aerial engagements against Serbian jets—the first shots ever fired by NATO forces since its formation in 1949.

In 1995, the US helped forge a peace accord for Bosnia. A NATO peacekeeping force—including American troops—moved into the troubled areas but became engaged in fighting with Serbian forces. Adding to the turmoil, the Islamic majority in Kosovo revolted against Serbian rule in 1998. When diplomatic attempts for peace failed, the US led a NATO bombing campaign against Yugoslavia, which resulted in an uneasy ceasefire. Working with NATO was a new twist on the role of the US in the new world order. NATO had been created during the Cold War to counter the threat of the Soviet Bloc (see Chapter 11). Now, US and NATO forces were engaged in combat, not to defend the West against the USSR, but to impose peace in a former communist nation.

To learn more about Yugoslavia in the 1990s, visit www.emp.ca/ah.

## The Middle East

In the 1990s, American policy toward the Middle East followed a familiar pattern: strong support for Israel and concern for stability in the region, both for peace's sake and to guarantee oil supplies (see Chapter 13). Following the Gulf War, the US lobbied hard to get the Israelis and the Palestinians to the bargaining table. The result was a summit in Madrid in 1991. In 1992, the Clinton administration capitalized on this event, and on a change of government in Israel, to encourage direct negotiations between the leaders of Israel and the Palestinian people. Meetings in Norway led to a breakthrough, known as the Oslo Accords. The Palestinians agreed to recognize Israel in exchange for Israel's promise to begin withdrawing some of its occupation forces from Palestinian territory. This breakthrough was formalized at the White House in 1993 when Israeli Prime Minister Yitzhak Rabin and Palestine Liberation Organization (PLO) leader Yasser Arafat shook hands over their agreement in principle.

**Figure 14.8** The handshake! Reflect on how this photograph represents the concept of expectation versus reality.

In the following year, Israel and the PLO reached a working agreement on implementing their 1993 handshake. An agreement for dividing the West Bank into zones of control was reached in Washington, but then in late 1994, Rabin was assassinated by an Israeli who opposed the accommodations with the Palestinians. Neither changes in the Israeli prime minister's office nor the election of Arafat as president of the Palestinian Authority could resolve matters. Washington continued to push Israel to withdraw its settlers from land ceded to Palestinian control, but the 1990s closed with tensions unresolved.

## A New Threat: International Terrorism

During the 1990s the United States had to deal with a new threat—international terrorism undertaken by Muslim extremists who opposed both US support for Israel and American values. The first evidence of this new development was a car-bomb attack on the World Trade Center in New York City in 1993. Seven people were killed and hundreds were injured. American authorities arrested and prosecuted the bombers, in the process discovering plans for attacks on other targets in New York, including tunnels, federal buildings, and the UN.

The terrorist threat took on new dimensions in the later 1990s with the emergence of **al-Qaida**, a terrorist network founded in the mid-1990s by Osama bin Laden. A wealthy and well-educated Saudi Arabian, bin Laden embraced the teachings of Muslim extremists who denounced the excesses of wealthy, secular, and materialistic Western civilization. Since the United States was the most powerful nation in the West, it became the obvious symbolic target.

In 1998, al-Qaida staged almost simultaneous bomb attacks on American embassies in Kenya and Tanzania, killing more than 200 people and injuring thousands. In response, President Clinton ordered bombing raids on al-Qaida training bases in Afghanistan and on a plant in Sudan that was suspected of manufacturing chemical weapons. These retaliations may have been counterproductive, however, as they provided the little-known bin Laden and his network with widespread notoriety.

**Figure 14.9** The results of the devastating attack on the US embassy in Nairobi, Kenya in 1998.

**Figure 14.10** Another attack attributed to al-Qaida took place in 2000. Suicide bombers rammed an explosive-packed speedboat into the destroyer *USS Cole*, which was on a courtesy visit to Yemen. The ship was badly damaged and 17 American sailors were killed. How might terrorists capitalize on this photograph? How might Americans?

The president's advisers proposed aggressive measures for dealing with bin Laden, including landing troops in Afghanistan to capture him and dispatching assassins to murder him. Clinton chose not to follow up on such suggestions. The extent of the threat posed by al-Qaida was unclear in the 1990s; perhaps Clinton saw the terrorist acts as unpleasant but occasional costs that the US had to pay for being the most powerful nation in the world.

## CHECK YOUR UNDERSTANDING

1. Summarize the main elements of Clinton's foreign policy.
2. Why was the US the target of terrorist attacks?
3. What was the symbolic importance of the handshake between Rabin and Arafat in 1993?

# A BOOMING AMERICA

The middle and later 1990s were good years for the US economy. The economic growth rate was high and the inflation rate was low. In 1998, the US poverty rate was at its lowest level in 20 years. In 1992 the unemployment rate was 7.4 percent, but by 1996 it was 5.4 percent. By 2000 it had fallen to 3.9 percent, the lowest in 30 years.

Clinton aimed at lowering the deficit by reduced spending and tax increases, especially on the wealthy. Despite Republican predictions of chaos, the policy worked. In 1992 the deficit was $290 billion, but Clinton managed a staggering reversal: there was a surplus of $124 billion by 1999. As the rate of economic growth soared, inflation and interest rates stayed low. Working Americans had plenty of disposable income, and the US economy was the world's strongest.

## Military Spending and Arms Sales

This prosperity occurred at a time when traditional manufacturing industries—for example, iron and steel, coal, and textiles—were continuing to decline. Part of the explanation was military spending that fed prosperity not only in states like California, centre of the aerospace industry, but also in states across the country where military bases fuelled the local economy. As well, US arms producers were making huge profits in overseas sales. By 1997, the United States was selling more arms abroad than all other nations combined. In just a four-year span from 1997, the US sold $44.82 billion in arms. The next closest armaments supplier was Russia at $17.35 billion.

## Information and Communication Technology

Another contributor to strong economic activity was the revolution in information and communication technology (ICT). Consumers marvelled at a whole new range of products—including mobile phones and the first practical, powerful, and inexpensive personal computers. Business demand for ICT hardware and software kept suppliers busy and created new kinds of jobs: software designers, technical support workers, and ICT managers. Even a potential ICT disaster, Y2K (computer disruptions as the year turned from 1999 to 2000), proved to be a bonus. There was no ICT meltdown at the turn of the new millennium, but sizable profits were made by companies that had developed Y2K-friendly equipment and security software.

The ICT impact was strong in many traditional industries, too. With rapid communication and data manipulation, industrial productivity increased and goods moved more quickly to retailers. Completely new approaches were introduced in manufacturing. "Just-in-time" inventories eliminated the need for huge warehouses, and the use of high-tech robots became widespread, especially in the car industry.

**Figure 14.11** Innovations in mobile phone technology in the 1990s paved the way for modern cellphones in the 2000s.

## Free Trade and a Stock Market Boom

Another economic impetus in the US economy was free trade. Building on the earlier FTA (see Chapter 13), Canada, the United States, and Mexico signed the North American Free Trade Agreement (NAFTA). Despite opposition from trade unionists, environmentalists and some Democrats, Clinton managed to get Congress to approve the agreement, and NAFTA came into effect on January 1, 1994. Clinton's support for free trade extended to the global context, and in 1995 the US joined the newly created World Trade Organization.

Finally, the economy was boosted by a healthy US stock market, buoyed by the high rate of economic growth, the ICT boom, and strong global markets. There were declines, of course—one followed an Asian currency crisis and the subsequent losses on the Hong Kong stock market in the fall of 1997. But by the end of that year, American stocks had not only recovered but had reached record levels of value. Another "blip" occurred the next year, when a Russian stock market collapse sent worldwide stock prices plummeting. Again, the US market recovered within six months. Enthusiasm for stock market speculation at times echoed that of the 1920s, leading Federal Reserve Chairman Alan Greenspan to caution against "irrational exuberance." There were signs that the economy was slowing by 2000–2001: oil prices were rising and economic growth slowed. Yet, like their predecessors in 1929, few investors could foresee how events on a single day could trigger a stock market collapse. That day was September 11, 2001.

### CHECK YOUR UNDERSTANDING

1. List the causes of the economic boom of the late 1990s.
2. How much credit should be given to President Clinton for this economic boom? Explain.
3. Research Y2K on the Internet. What fears did Americans have about this event? How did it turn out to be an economic benefit?
4. What parallels are there between the stock market boom of the 1990s and that of the 1920s (see Chapter 10)?

# TROUBLES AT HOME

Although this period was marked by economic confidence, it was also a troubling time for Americans. They had to grapple with political dissent and violence, failures in social reform, a presidential scandal, and a controversial election.

## Domestic Terrorism

In April 1995, two right-wing extremists, both US army veterans, bombed the Oklahoma City Federal Building, killing 168 people including 19 children in a

**Figure 14.12** Domestic terrorism in Oklahoma: the effects of a home-made truck bomb. Search the Internet to see how the victims have been commemorated.

daycare centre. The Oklahoma City bombers had planned the attack to mark the second anniversary of an incident at Waco, Texas in which members of the Branch Davidians, an anti-government religious cult, were killed by federal agents who had tried to search the group's compound for weapons and explosives.

Right-wing anti-government movements, citizens' militia organizations, and conspiracy theory groups (all fearful that the government was conspiring to take away constitutional rights) attracted some disaffected Americans in various parts of the nation. Members of such groups proclaimed they stood for true American values, opposed government interference with individual liberties (especially the right to own and use guns), and harboured a wide range of suspicions about Washington—for example, that the UN controlled the US government. Many of these groups also held racist, homophobic, anti-abortion, anti-Islamic, and anti-Jewish views. Although extremists were few in number, their willingness to use violence meant their impact was disproportionate, in terms of both damage and the news media.

**WEB LINKS**

To learn more about domestic terrorism in the 1990s, visit www.emp.ca/ah.

## Protests against the Globalized Economy

There was also dissent on the left. Protesters demanded that both American and foreign global corporations take greater responsibility for their employees' well-being and for the environment. Besides corporations, they targeted organizations such as the World Trade Organization (WTO) and the G7 (known as the G8 after Russia joined in 1997), where the richest countries meet to decide on trade issues and financial policies. One of the most dramatic protests took place at the WTO meeting in Seattle in late 1999. So extensive were the demonstrations that the police ran out of tear gas, the central business district closed, and the WTO sessions were disrupted.

**Figure 14.13** Police move in on anti-WTO protesters in Seattle in 1999. Examine the WTO website and that of an anti-WTO group to appreciate the differences in their points of view.

## Poverty, Welfare, and Health Care

By the 1990s, an economic trend that had developed over at least two decades became even more obvious—the plight of the poor. America's top 1 percent of wage earners owned 35 percent of the country's wealth. Meanwhile, millions of Americans were living at or below the poverty level, a quarter of US children lived in poverty, and millions of Americans had no health care. President Clinton introduced a variety of measures to address this dismal picture, including welfare reform. His most ambitious plan, however, was to provide health care coverage for every American.

The president set up a national health care committee and appointed his wife, Hillary Clinton, to head it. No previous presidential spouse had ever been handed such a major role in developing policy. Republican opponents attacked both the idea and the process; so did the private health care and health insurance industries. The committee undertook its work in secret on this vital issue and left out Congress from its consultations. The committee did produce a comprehensive report in 1993, but it was so massive—at 1,350 pages—that few Americans could come to terms with it. Republican opposition continued, and the private health industry produced television advertisements to convince middle-class Americans that their own health coverage was threatened. President Clinton had to abandon the health care initiative. Not only was this a humiliating defeat, but it helped contribute to Republican gains in the 1994 congressional elections.

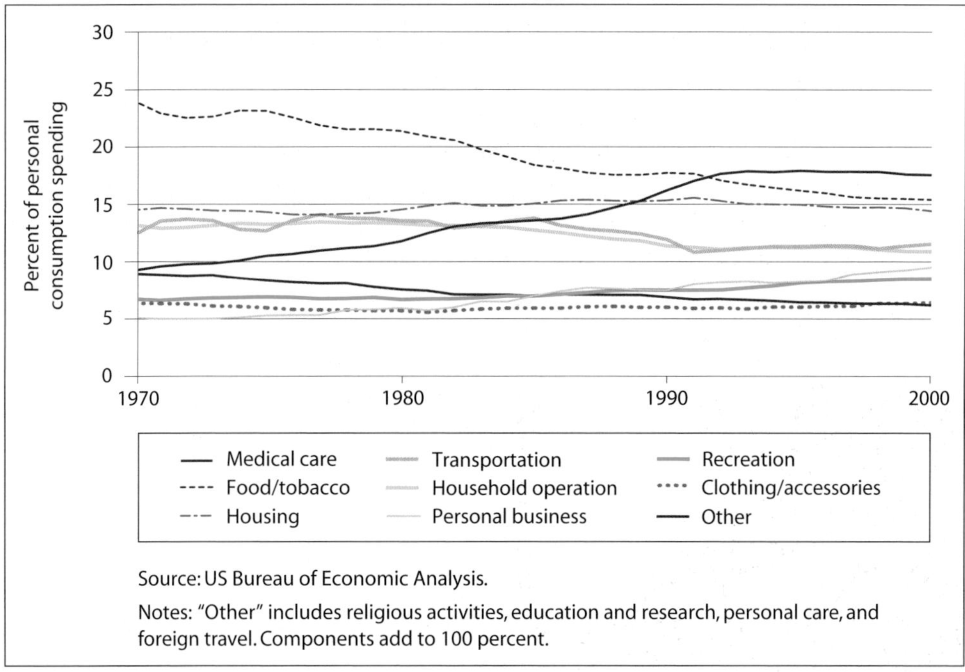


**Figure 14.14** Personal US consumption spending, 1970–2001. How much did per capita medical care spending increase between 1970 and 2000?

# WE THE PEOPLE

## Two Voices

In the 1990s, a voice emerged to speak for children and women. That voice was Hillary Clinton's. Before moving to the White House and afterward, she championed children's legal and medical rights. She headed the American Bar Association's Commission on Women in the Profession, highlighting such issues as sexual harassment and unequal pay. In a 1995 speech at the UN World Conference on Women, Clinton described women's rights in the United States and worldwide:

> Women comprise more than half the world's population ... Women are the primary caretakers for most of the world's children and elderly. Yet much of the work we do is not valued—not by economists, not by historians, not by popular culture, not by government leaders.
>
> Women around the world are giving birth, raising children, cooking meals, washing clothes, cleaning houses, planting crops, working on assembly lines, running companies, and running countries.
>
> Women also are dying from diseases that should have been prevented or treated; they are watching their children succumb to malnutrition caused by poverty and economic deprivation ... and they are being barred from the bank lending office and banned from the ballot box.

A second voice, that of black US Senator Barack Obama, also emerged to speak for another largely under-represented group, African-Americans. Obama is of Nigerian ancestry (through his father), Hawaiian by birth, and rooted in the state of Kansas (through his white mother). As a former community worker in inner-city Chicago, he has seen urban poverty and black alienation. As a graduate of Columbia University and Harvard Law school, he understands the value of higher education.

Obama also speaks to the nearly lost tradition of stirring oratory in US politics, as his words at the Martin Luther King Memorial in 2006 illustrate:

**Figure 14.15** (*Left*) Hillary Clinton became a US senator in 2001 and in 2007 mounted a campaign for the Democratic presidential nomination. (*Right*) Barack Obama speaks for African-Americans and for the diversity of the United States.

> [A]t some point, I know that one of my daughters will ask ... "Daddy, why is this monument here? What did this man do?"
>
> How might I answer them? ... at no time in his life did he hold public office. He was not a hero of foreign wars ... By his own accounts, he was a man frequently racked with doubt, a man [who] more than once questioned why he had been chosen for so arduous a task—the task of leading a people to freedom, the task of healing the festering wounds of a nation's original sin.
>
> And yet lead a nation he did. Through words he gave voice to the voiceless ... He endured the humiliation of arrest, the loneliness of a prison cell, the constant threats to his life, until he finally inspired a nation to transform itself, and begin to live up to the meaning of its **creed**.

### Think It Through

1. Read Hillary Clinton's speeches on her home page. How does she address children's and women's issues in her most recent speeches? What other issues are central topics in her recent speeches?
2. Research Barack Obama. What is your position on the statement: "Obama represents the American story: the child of modest means who overcomes adversity and makes good."

## Scandal and Impeachment

**Figure 14.16** The Clinton scandal provided fodder for the news media for months. How might the extensive coverage help explain Clinton's continued popularity?

Despite the failure of his health care initiative, Clinton's charisma—and the country's strong economy—carried him to victory again in the 1996 election. Clinton's second term, however, was marked by scandals. First, the president and his wife were accused of improper financial dealings in Arkansas before he became president. Then in early 1998, news broke that the president had entered into a sexual affair with a young White House intern. Questioned under oath, Clinton denied the story. As more evidence surfaced, Clinton stuck to his story, and the media fanned public speculation. Finally, Clinton admitted that he had engaged in "inappropriate" conduct; he continued to deny, however, that he had lied or ordered any cover-up.

Despite his denials, the House of Representatives Judiciary Committee charged the president with perjury and obstruction. For the second time in US history, a president would be tried for impeachment (see Chapter 7). The impeachment trial began in early 1999 in the Senate, as the US Constitution required, but it was evident that the two-thirds majority required for a guilty verdict would not be achieved. The president's behaviour might have been unsavoury but it did not include the impeachable acts of "treason, bribery, or other high crimes and misdemeanors" specified in the Constitution. Clinton was acquitted and remained in office to serve out his term.

Surprisingly, after his acquittal Clinton's approval rating went up. Apparently many Americans felt that the private behaviour of the president was his and his family's business, not the business of the nation. Reinforcing this position was Hillary Clinton's dignified response to the embarrassing scandal. As well, some Americans saw Republican pursuit of the impeachment proceedings as going beyond partisanship to malice. Americans were satisfied with their president being censured rather than removed.

## A Contentious Presidential Election

The election of 2000 pitted Al Gore, Clinton's vice-president, against Republican George W. Bush, governor of Texas. Gore, with his concern for the environment and for the have-nots in America, was politically to the left of Clinton, while Bush, with his Reaganomic views and his robust Christianity, was to the right of his father, the former president. Corporate gadfly Ralph Nader ran well to Gore's left as the candidate of the Green Party. Former White House adviser and television news host, conservative Pat Buchanan, ran on the Reform Party ticket.

The vote was so close that it created a crisis in the electoral process. The results in Florida could have determined the outcome, but balloting there was marked by voting irregularities. Months of recounts and legal wrangling followed. Eventually, the Supreme Court ruled against a further recount and declared Bush the winner. An investigation by the US Commission on Civil Rights later reported that the Florida election was marked by an abnormal level of disenfranchisement, especially of African-American and Hispanic voters, inferior voting equipment and ballot design, and polling stations inaccessible to disabled people. The report cited a general failure of leadership on the part of those running the election (including Governor Jeb Bush, George W. Bush's brother).

To learn more about the US Commission on Civil Rights' report on Florida voting, visit www.emp.ca/ah.

In office, Bush turned to his conservative domestic agenda. Convinced that the education system needed shaking up, he launched his "No Child Left Behind" program, which linked funding to improved test scores. He introduced a tax cut and suggested a drastic overhaul of the social security system that would allow for private pensions within the government scheme. The president's attention to his conservative domestic agenda was entirely diverted, however, on September 11, 2001.

**Figure 14.17** Results of the 2000 presidential election. The final vote was closer than the map suggests: Gore won the popular vote (48.38 percent compared to 47.87 percent for Bush), but Bush won more Electoral College votes (271 to 266).

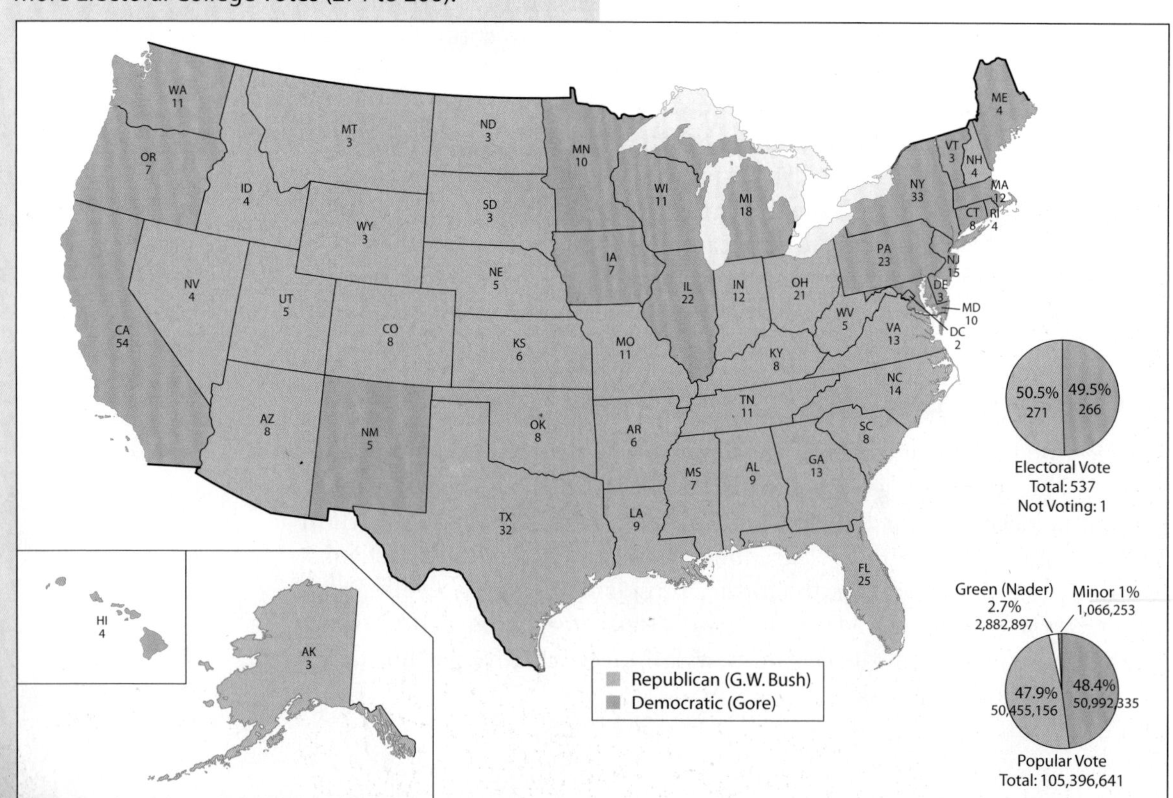

## CHECK YOUR UNDERSTANDING

1. What beliefs did some right-wing American fanatics hold?
2. Why were protesters targeting the WTO?
3. Review the graph in Figure 14.14 (page 491). Which spending levels remained constant? Which fell? Which rose? Speculate on the reasons for these trends.
4. Why did President Clinton remain popular despite scandal and attempted impeachment?
5. Why was the 2000 presidential election "contentious"?

# 9/11 AND ITS IMPACT

Some dates are landmarks in American history—for example, the "where were you?" events referred to in Chapter 12. In this chapter, one date stands out—September 11, 2001. The events of "9/11" remain raw in the minds of Americans, who still feel sorrow, anger, and patriotism. The attack on that day has shaped US history and both international and domestic policy.

## An Unprecedented Attack

On September 11, 2001 terrorists crashed two planes into the Twin Towers of New York's World Trade Center; the second attack occurred on live television. Another hijack crew crashed into the Pentagon, near Washington, DC. As passengers desperately fought the terrorists in a fourth plane, the hijackers were forced to crash it into the Pennsylvania countryside. Their target had been the US Capitol.

**WEB LINKS** 

To learn about the reconstruction of the World Trade Center and the on-site memorial, visit www.emp.ca/ah.

**Figure 14.18** New York, September 11, 2001.

This was the most devastating foreign attack on the US in history, exceeding the death toll from the Japanese attack on Pearl Harbor (see Chapter 11). Moreover, whereas casualties were mostly military in 1941, most of the 9/11 casualties were civilian. The 2001 attack was especially devastating because of the immediacy of the experience. In 1941, Americans heard radio reports of Pearl Harbor soon afterward, but they had to wait days for newspaper pictures and even longer for news films to reach local cinemas. In 2001, television broadcast every grim detail in real time and in replays. The attack on 9/11 seemed like an attack on every American.

The effects of 9/11 went beyond the immediate shock. The financial district of New York was so badly damaged that the New York Stock Exchange shut down. When it reopened, the Dow Jones Industrial Average recorded its biggest drop in history. A mild recession became a more serious one as concerns for security and economic stability drove the markets down. The biggest effect was fear—of further attacks and of the unknown. President Bush, whose immediate response to the attacks was shaky, soon took decisive action. He strongly backed the USA PATRIOT (Uniting and Strengthening America by Providing Appropriate Tools to Intercept and Obstruct Terrorism) Act, and identified the source of the attack: Osama bin Laden and al-Qaida.

## Homeland Security and Afghanistan

On October 26, 2001 Congress passed the USA PATRIOT Act, which gave law enforcement bodies extraordinary powers of search, wiretapping, seizure of records, and detention without charge. Civil liberties advocates pointed out that its provisions violated the constitutional rights of individuals, but Bush declared the Act was a necessity in the new "war on terror." Bush also created the Department of Homeland Security (DHS) to coordinate security matters at home. Still reeling from 9/11, most Americans supported these measures.

Bush also took the fight abroad. The Americans suspected the fundamentalist Muslim Taliban in Afghanistan of harbouring bin Laden and his training camps. The US air force struck at these camps, and Special Forces and CIA operatives worked on the ground with Afghan rebels to overthrow the Taliban

**SOUND BITE**

"Many of the tools the Act provides to law enforcement to fight terrorism have been used for decades to fight organized crime and drug dealers. One senator exclaimed during debate about the Act, 'the FBI could get a wiretap to investigate the mafia, but they could not get one to investigate terrorists. To put it bluntly, that was crazy!'"

—*Congressional Record*, October 25, 2001

"There are significant flaws in the PATRIOT Act, flaws that threaten your fundamental freedoms by giving the government the power to access your medical records, tax records, information about the books you buy or borrow, without probable cause, and the power to break into your home and conduct secret searches."

—American Civil Liberties Union website, November 14, 2003

regime. However, the Americans failed to capture bin Laden, who escaped either into Afghanistan's mountains or into a near-**feudal** district of northern Pakistan. The US failed to bring stability to Afghanistan but, unlike its disastrous mission in Somalia, committed itself to a long-term military and reconstruction strategy. American forces are still in Afghanistan in the NATO International Security Assistance Force, a coalition that includes Canadian soldiers and advisers.

**WEB LINKS**

To learn more about Canadians in Afghanistan, visit www.emp.ca/ah.

## The War in Iraq

By 2002, the United States had decided that there were more enemies than bin Laden—Iraq, Iran, and North Korea. President Bush characterized these nations as an "axis of evil." The basis for grouping these three—other than their anti-American stances—was murky, but any uncertainty was forgotten in Bush's decision to focus on one of them, Iraq. There was no proven link between Iraq and 9/11; indeed, it had become clear that the 9/11 terrorists were mostly Saudi Arabians. Still, Bush and his cabinet characterized Saddam Hussein as a dangerous enemy in the "war on terror." The Americans, along with some other nations, believed that Saddam had stockpiled weapons of mass destruction (WMD) and was attempting to develop nuclear weapons.

The US supported calls for renewed UN weapon inspections, but in the meantime Bush got congressional support to use force against Iraq. In late 2002, the UN Security Council directed Iraq to provide full access to arms inspectors. Saddam agreed but continued to frustrate their work. In January 2003, the head of the UN inspection team reported that not all WMD could be accounted for, and recommended more time to complete the process.

Some nations, including a number of European allies, wanted to give the UN inspectors more time. Bush's advisers, especially Vice-President Dick Cheney and Secretary of Defense Donald Rumsfeld, pushed for military action. Realizing that it would not get UN Security Council support for such action, the United States put together a "coalition of the willing" consisting of Britain, Australia, Italy, Spain, and some former Eastern Bloc nations.

In March 2003, a force of mostly American and British troops invaded Iraq. There were pockets of bitter fighting, but Baghdad was taken in early April. In mid-April American military officials declared the military campaign was over. That message was repeated by President Bush on May 1 on board the aircraft carrier *USS Abraham Lincoln*: "Major combat operations in Iraq have ended. In the Battle of Iraq, the United States and our allies have prevailed. And now our coalition is engaged in securing and reconstructing that country."

Securing and reconstructing Iraq proved to be no easy matter. The US took steps to secure oil industry installations, but gave limited attention to protecting ordinary citizens or cultural institutions. Looting broke out in many cities; museums and archaeological sites were ransacked, and hit-and-run attacks were launched against coalition forces. Protected by coalition

**Figure 14.19** President Bush addresses the troops on board the *USS Abraham Lincoln*. The "mission accomplished" sign was put up by the crew to mark the end of their tour—but it provided a great photo opportunity for Bush. What impression would this photograph give the American public?

troops, the UN inspectors returned but found no stockpiles of WMD. This news discredited Bush's original justification for the invasion and raised doubts about the whole venture.

American forces searched for Saddam and his top advisers while the US administration worked with the UN to set up a **provisional government**. When Saddam was captured in December 2003, hopes rose for a return to normality. Yet violence continued as his former supporters and other anti-coalition groups continued to attack the occupying troops. Meanwhile, Iraqi citizens tried to rebuild their lives in ruined neighbourhoods and in a shattered economy.

## The US and Iraq Today

The 2004 presidential election campaign was waged as violence in Iraq continued. The Democrats raised questions about the accuracy of pre-war intelligence, preparations for the occupation of Iraq, and a vision for building peace—questions about the honesty and leadership of President Bush. Yet Bush's opponent, John Kerry, failed to capitalize on such issues because his own policy for Iraq was unclear. Bush presented himself as a decisive war-time president, playing up his record of tax cuts and traditional Republican family, moral, and religious values (see Chapter 13). The incumbent had enjoyed strong support among fundamentalist Christians in 2000 and targeted this group in his 2004 campaign. Voter turnout was about 20 percent higher than in 2000, and the result was clear-cut: Bush won 51 percent of the popular vote to Kerry's 48 percent.

Meanwhile, the "coalition of the willing" was collapsing. Coalition partners withdrew from Iraq, not just because of the difficulties there, but also because of dangers at home. For example, Spain recalled its troops after terrorist attacks in Madrid and subsequent anti-war demonstrations. British Prime Minister Tony Blair remained a staunch ally, but bitter anti-war criticism in the UK over his support for Bush hastened his retirement. Still, the president and his supporters pointed to signs of progress, such as the free elections held in Iraq in January 2005.

The new Iraqi government, however, failed to deal with the crisis. Essential services still had not been restored. The economy was in ruins. The new government brought Saddam Hussein to trial and executed him in late 2006, but that further inflamed tensions. Sunnis who had benefited from Saddam's regime carried out violent suicide missions and other attacks, and extremist Shiite militia retaliated. Car bombings, detonation of improvised explosive

## AMERICAN ARCHIVE

# War by PowerPoint Presentation

Although the United States achieved a quick military victory in the Iraq War, Americans later found that securing and reconstructing Iraq would be difficult. On what evidence did Bush and his advisers base their assumptions about rebuilding Iraq? Their thinking must have been partly based on reports prepared by US Central Command military analysts. These analysts briefed Bush, Rumsfeld, Vice-President Cheney, the National Security Council, the Joint Chiefs of Staff, and generals in August 2002. Recently declassified, the briefing notes include PowerPoint slides. They indicate that military strategists made hugely optimistic assumptions about how many US troops would be necessary to stabilize Iraq, and how long they would have to stay.

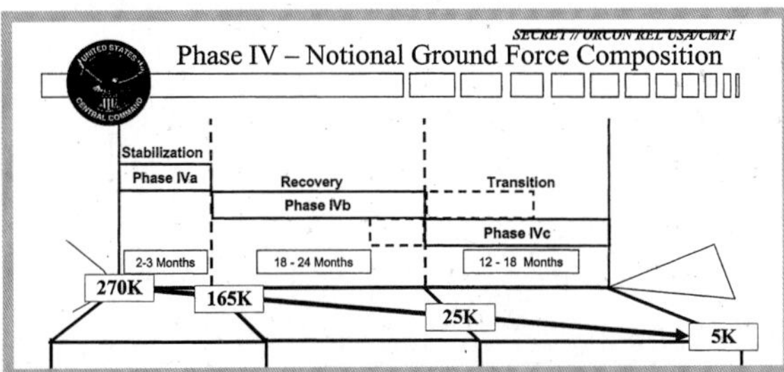


**Figure 14.20** This PowerPoint slide projects the number of US troops needed from the time of the invasion (270,000 troops) to 18 months afterward (5,000).

The planners assumed there would be a stable Iraqi government in place almost immediately after the invasion, and that there would be no resistance to US occupation. These assumptions appear in excerpts from another PowerPoint slide (Figure 14.21).

By the time the US invaded Iraq in March 2003, another plan had been developed based on a greater number of troops. The president and his advisers, however, remained optimistic about reconstruction plans. These documents not only reveal planning assumptions about Iraq; they suggest the impact of ICT on executive decision making. Military analyst Lt. Gen. David McKiernan declared:

> It's quite frustrating the way this works, but the way we do things nowadays is combatant commanders brief their products in PowerPoint up in Washington ... In lieu of an order, or a frag [fragmentary] order, or plan, you get a set of PowerPoint slides ... [T]hat is frustrating, because nobody wants to plan against PowerPoint slides.

- Opposition groups will work with us
- Co-opted Iraqi units will occupy garrisons and not fight either US forces or other Iraqi units
- Regional states will not challenge US military operations with conventional forces
- DoS [Department of State] will promote creation of a broad-based, credible provisional government—prior to D-day

**Figure 14.21** Key planning assumptions of the US invasion.

These war plan slides are not the only examples of "War by PowerPoint." In January 2003, the Defense Department proposed a "Rapid Reaction Media Team." It would begin to broadcast to a free Iraq immediately after victory, and then train Iraqis to contribute to American-style programming. Figure 14.22 shows key points from that PowerPoint proposal.

VISION: In 12 months, reconstitute indigenous Iraqi media as a model for free media in the Arab world.

FIRST MONTH IMPACT: Inform the Iraqi public about USG/coalition intent and operations, stabilize Iraq and provide Iraqis hope for the future.

REQUIREMENTS NECESSARY FOR FIRST MONTH:
Select, train, and deploy Iraqi rapid reaction media teams for:
- 24 x 7 national radio network (with pre-selected programming)
- 12 x 7 national television network (with pre-selected programming)

**Figure 14.22** Excerpts from the US Defense Department's slide presentation, "Indigenous Iraqi Media."

## Think It Through

To you, what is the most surprising piece of evidence in these briefing notes? Explain your views.

**Figure 14.23** American soldiers in the Green Zone, Baghdad. Why might this secure area be named "green"?

devices (IEDs) in roadways, attacks on mosques, kidnappings, and murders became the norm in Baghdad and other Iraqi cities. The Iraqi government remained unable to rule, and was able to meet only in Baghdad's Green Zone, a fortified district protected by American troops.

In the face of all this turmoil, Bush and his advisers stuck to their script—progress was being made to end the violence, the elected government was moving forward, US troops had to "see the mission through." Yet, Iraqis complained that conditions were no better than under Saddam. Within the United States, Bush's handling of the war—his faulty justification for the invasion based on WMD and his patent failure to plan for the reconstruction of Iraq—caused an outpouring of condemnation. A group of American historians declared him among the worst presidents ever. **Civil libertarians** had opposed extreme measures like the USA PATRIOT Act from the start, but now many other Americans began to raise concerns about detentions without trials, abuses of Iraqi prisoners in American custody, and the practice of **rendition** (transporting suspected terrorists to countries where the Americans knew they would be tortured). Even military lawyers and judges refused to take part in the legal proceedings against detainees at Guantanamo Bay. Protests against the war became commonplace, and the president's approval rating plummeted.

The 2006 mid-term congressional elections reflected the deep divisions over the war. The Democrats won majorities—easily in the House of Representatives and just barely in the Senate. The Democrats made clear that they

**Figure 14.24** The US declared terrorist captives **"illegal combatants"** rather than prisoners of war so that the administration did not have to abide by recognized standards for treatment of prisoners. Many of those detained have been held at the US base at Guantanamo Bay, Cuba since 2001.

**Figure 14.25** Among those protesting against US policy in Iraq have been the mothers of American troops.

would deal with the issue that had won them their seats: bringing home American troops. Recognizing the electoral message, Bush dismissed his much-criticized secretary of defence and talked about cooperation with the newly Democratic Congress. Yet soon after, the president ordered an increase in troop numbers in Baghdad on the grounds that a "surge" would be the final step needed to restore order.

In the spring of 2007, the Democratic-controlled Congress passed legislation linking American troop withdrawals with further military funding for Iraq. Bush vetoed this legislation in May 2007, four years after his speech on the *USS Abraham Lincoln*. The American public remains divided on critical issues regarding Iraq. Could Democrats, Republicans, and citizens of all stripes discuss an end to US occupation without being accused of betraying the troops or without putting those forces in greater danger?

**Figure 14.26** The possibility of history repeating itself. Are the two wars comparable? Is this cartoon a fair comment on the situation in Iraq? Explain.

## 49th PARALLEL

# Canada and the US in the Post-9/11 World

On 9/11, Canadian authorities immediately closed airports and air space to accept diverted American flights, carrying 33,000 passengers. Meanwhile, ordinary Canadians who had watched the terrorist attacks on television grieved the death of 25 Canadians in the Twin Towers, and realized that Canada's world had also changed.

Heightened security measures for air travel within and from Canada were soon introduced. In October 2001, Parliament passed legislation to guard against domestic terrorism, to work with other countries against terrorist threats, and to "prevent the Canada–US border from being held hostage by terrorists" to the detriment of the Canadian economy. Prime Minister Jean Chrétien expressed support for American attacks on Afghanistan and pledged Canadian troops toward that campaign. As of 2007, about 18,000 Canadian soldiers had served there.

Canada and the US have become close allies in combatting terrorism. Yet there have been tense moments in this relationship. A minor irritant was President Bush's failure to mention Canada when thanking other nations for their help after 9/11. More serious was a policy difference: Canada's decision not to become part of the "coalition of the willing" in Iraq. Continuing anti-terrorism issues have caused further friction.

Canadian Omar Kadr, captured in Afghanistan at age 15 and declared an "illegal combatant," was still being detained at Guantanamo Bay in 2007. Rights advocates in both Canada and the US have campaigned for his just treatment and possible return to Canada. The Canadian government appears to have been reluctant to intervene in the case, probably to avoid complicating already tricky relations with the US over anti-terrorist policy.

Canadian citizen Maher Arar was arrested by American authorities during a stop-over in New York and—under the US policy of rendition—subsequently flown to his native Syria, where he was interrogated and tortured. The Americans had acted on information provided by Canadian authorities as part of the intelligence sharing authorized by anti-terrorist legislation. Arar eventually was freed and returned to Canada, where an inquiry proved that he had no terrorist links. The Canadian government apologized to Arar and compensated him, but the Americans have refused to remove his name from their terrorist watch list.

**Figure 14.27** Maher Arar.

Easy passage between the countries has been replaced by tighter requirements for documentation and aggressive US customs and immigration policies for tourists and business travellers. American demands for passport identification for air travellers between the countries led to delays at passport offices, as well as a campaign by provincial and state politicians to modify the land-crossing requirements. A 2007 Canadian government report indicated that the costs to airlines, railroads, and shipping and truck lines to respond to US and Canadian border security measures amounted to $2.5 billion Canadian. As American patrols along the border increase, and as Canadian officials receive firearms, the historical image of the **"undefended border"** comes into question.

## Think It Through

1. Where do you stand on this statement: "Supporting American anti-terrorist measures is good Canadian policy"?
2. Review the 49th Parallel features in Chapters 4, 5, and 12. In the light of Canada–US history in these features—and with what you have learned elsewhere in this text—what do you predict will be the nature of future Canadian–American relations?

## CHECK YOUR UNDERSTANDING

1. What memories do you or your family have of 9/11? What insights do these give you into Americans' reaction to the attack?
2. List the reasons for the US invasion of Iraq. Which do you think best explains the decision to invade?
3. How might the briefing notes (see American Archives in this chapter) have influenced President Bush and his advisers in their policy on Iraq?
4. In two sentences, state the dilemma facing President Bush regarding the continuing occupation of Iraq.

# DOMESTIC AFFAIRS SINCE 9/11

Most of US history since 9/11 has been dominated by its "war on terror," and many domestic issues have been set aside. Still, there have been a number of key developments at home since 2001, as indicated in the following sections.

## Hurricane Katrina

Hurricane Katrina struck the Gulf Coast in August 2005. One of the worst natural disasters in American history—and the costliest in terms of damage—the storm killed at least 1,300 people, injured thousands, and forced tens of thousands from their homes. New Orleans was particularly hard hit as the storm breached levies in low-lying districts until 80 percent of the city was under water. Not only were people forced from their homes, but local emergency services were incapacitated either by the storm and floods, or by power and communication failures.

After the storm passed, the disaster worsened because of chaotic rescue and relief responses. Even days after the storm, rescue efforts still appeared to be inadequate and disorganized, especially in New Orleans. Graphic news coverage showed residents trapped on roofs, the homeless begging for food and water at the Superdome and Convention Centre, and disaster victims walking out of the city with a few salvaged belongings.

**Figure 14.28** Demonstrators carry anti-Bush signs calling for aid for victims of Hurricane Katrina in front of an armed forces recruiting centre in New York City, September 2005. About 100 people gathered to call for money to be redirected from the war in Iraq to Katrina victims.

In the aftermath, many questions were asked about the ineffective response in New Orleans. Some pointed fingers at the mayor and the Louisiana governor, others at the federal government. The director of the Federal Emergency Measures Agency (FEMA) resigned. Congress set up a committee to investigate the affair, and there were other investigations. These reports attributed most of the blame to the Department of Homeland Security set up after 9/11 to deal with all threats to the United States. Besides detailing the lack of training, communication, and coordination within the DHS and across federal agencies, these reports also concluded that the DHS had spent most of its energy and resources preparing for terrorist attacks instead of natural disasters. Nor did President Bush escape criticism, as the Republican-controlled Congress concluded that his earlier involvement could have speeded the response.

The failed relief response might be explained by incompetence, but Hurricane Katrina brought issues of race into frank public debate. Black residents made up 67 percent of the population of New Orleans, and many of them lived in the poorest districts in the low-lying parts of the city. Inevitably, many who lost their homes or were trapped by the flooding were black. Blanket television coverage of the disaster highlighted the effects of systemic black poverty.

Some commentators pointed out that evacuation plans called for people to leave in their cars, even though it was well known that poor blacks owned far fewer cars than white citizens. Others seized on the terrible conditions faced in the Superdome or on highway overpasses, where those who had been unable to evacuate took refuge. Hungry and homeless black people interviewed on television charged that their plight had been ignored because of their race. Despite the heroic efforts of those rescuers—local, state, and federal—who did reach New Orleans, the legacy of incompetence and neglect that followed Hurricane Katrina still feeds political debate in the US.

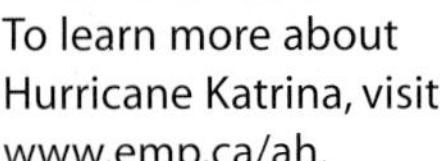


To learn more about Hurricane Katrina, visit www.emp.ca/ah.

## The Environmental Crisis

The environment has been an important concern for Americans since the 1960s, but problems such as air and water pollution and waste disposal have gained attention in recent years. Yet, scientific studies have identified an even greater threat: the depletion of the atmospheric ozone layer responsible for protecting the earth from the sun's ultraviolet rays. Throughout the world, people began to realize that climate warming required a global effort to reduce greenhouse gases, especially carbon dioxide ($CO_2$), which cause the problem.

In response, the UN developed a Framework Convention on Climate Change in 1992, and identified $CO_2$ emission limits (for example, from cars, industries, and coal-fired electricity plants) in meetings at Kyoto, Japan in 1997. Since then, 169 countries have ratified this Kyoto Protocol. The United States has not. The US is not alone in resisting the Kyoto Protocol. Australia did not sign, and some nations that did (including Canada) have failed to initiate steps to meet the emission caps by 2012.

As the biggest emitter of $CO_2$, and as the home base of many global corporations, the United States' absence from the protocol seriously weakens it. The US did institute other environmental pollution controls, but these were far less rigorous than those called for by Kyoto. Moreover, the US government's failure to

**SOUND BITE**

"Kyoto is, in many ways, unrealistic. Many countries cannot meet their Kyoto targets. The targets themselves were arbitrary and not based upon science. For America, complying with those mandates would have a negative economic impact, with layoffs of workers and price increases for consumers."

—George W. Bush, 2001

"The Bush plan is a recipe for more of the same—more pollution and more climate change ... Once again, the US is turning its back on the global fight against climate change. Instead, we have a unilateral American approach that undermines climate stability as well as global cooperation."

—Gerry Scott, director, David Suzuki Foundation, 2002

accept the Kyoto Protocol lent support to those Americans who were suspicious of the science behind global warming reports. Generally, environmental issues received less attention than the "war on terror"—except by environmentalists.

As evidence of global warming has mounted (changing storm patterns, extremes in floods and droughts, rising temperatures in northern zones), US attitudes and policy have shifted. Several state governments have taken the lead in the battle against carbon dioxide emissions by either suing the worst polluters (the strategy of eight eastern states plus New York City) or introducing tough emission caps for vehicles and industries (the strategy of California and several other Western states). These initiatives—some by Republican governments—along with increased corporate awareness of the reality of global warming may explain a new policy direction by President Bush in 2007. At the G8 meeting in Germany, he proposed talks among the world's biggest polluting nations to develop targets for reducing emissions of greenhouse gases. Yet the president proposed neither hard limits nor any monitoring mechanism.

For its part, the Senate is debating a bill to promote both clean energy from sources such as windmills and solar power, and alternative fuels for cars. The House of Representatives, with its Democratic majority, is considering direct limits on greenhouse gas emissions. Meanwhile, celebrities—including former Vice-President Al Gore—are speaking out about saving the environment, and many ordinary Americans are trying to limit their own **ecological footprint**, for example, by reducing air travel, driving fuel-efficient cars, and minimizing household energy consumption. Concerns about the impact of such measures on jobs and lifestyle, however, may mean that not enough will be done to come close to meeting the Kyoto standards.

**Greenhouse Gas Emissions**

- US emissions rose by 0.7 percent in 2005 to a record 7.24 billion tonnes and were 16.3 percent above 1990 levels.
- Emissions by 27 European Union members dipped by 0.8 percent to 5.18 billion tonnes and were 8.0 percent below 1990 levels.

—Reuters News Service, May 2007

**Figure 14.29**

## Rights: Progress and Challenges

As you have seen in earlier chapters, issues of rights have been prominent in American history from colonial times, through the Emancipation Proclamation and up to the modern period (see Chapters 12 and 13). Today, activist groups and principled individuals continue to meet the challenge of protecting rights that have been won and fighting to gain new ones. The US system of government also plays a role in meeting these challenges. The three examples below show how three parts of that system—the federal government, state governments, and the judiciary—promote rights in the United States today.

In 2004, Congress passed a Civil Rights Act that included provisions to protect the rights of a wide range of Americans:

- banning discrimination on the basis of race, national origin, or colour in accessing federally funded services
- forbidding the harassment of students based on race, gender, national origin, colour, or disability

- outlawing discrimination against older workers on the basis of age
- providing victims of discrimination based on sex, disability, or religion with remedies equal to those available for other forms of discrimination
- enhancing enforcement of the Equal Pay Act

At the state level, children's rights to medical care have been advanced through the State Children's Health Insurance Program (SCHIP) (federally and state funded, and run by individual states). All the states subscribe to the plan either by running SCHIP programs separately or by combining them with existing Medicaid for low-income people. Since the first year of the plan (1998), visible minorities have especially benefited. By 2004 the number of uninsured Latino, African-American, Asian-American, and Pacific Islander children had dropped by 30 to 50 percent since 1998, depending on the group.

To learn more about the Civil Rights Act of 2004 and SCHIP, visit www.emp.ca/ah.

The judiciary has made recent rulings protecting the legal and human rights of those detained by the United States in combatting terrorism. In 2004, a District of Columbia court ruled that Guantanamo detainees have the right to an attorney. In 2006, the Supreme Court ruled that the president lacked the authority to set up military commissions to try suspected terrorists (forcing Bush to get Congress to pass an act setting them up). In 2007, a federal appeals court in Virginia ruled that federal authorities could not declare civilians in the US to be illegal combatants and have the military hold them indefinitely. In the fall of 2007, the Supreme Court will consider the appeal of Guantanamo detainees on whether they have the right to challenge their detention in court. While such rulings centre on terrorist detainees, they will also affect Americans who advocate justice for all, and who defend the United States' reputation as a champion of legal rights.

## The Economy

Many of the economic trends that you read about in Chapters 12 and 13 and earlier in this chapter are evident in the United States today. Some of those trends are reflected in these **economic indicators**:

- The United States rebounded from the recession of 2001, and gross national product (GNP) rose in 2002–2003 to levels unseen since 1984. The US retains its position as the world's biggest economy in terms of GNP.
- Despite the impact of 9/11 and a further fall in 2002 (a four-year low), the US stock market—the world's largest—showed its resiliency in recovering by 2003.
- Unemployment rates have remained low—at about 5 percent (4.5 percent in 2007)—since Clinton's presidency.
- Over 8 million jobs were created between 2003 and 2007, more than all other large industrialized countries combined. Many of those jobs were in high-tech and service industries as traditional manufacturing industries continue to decline.

At the same time, some of the troublesome aspects of the economy that you read about in earlier chapters are still apparent.

Military expenditures continue to play a significant role in the economy. The defence budget in 1967 was $70 billion; defence budget estimates for 2008 amount to over $620 billion. Defence spending pushed up federal expenditures so that by 2004 the deficit was $413 billion.

President Bush introduced three major tax cuts, even though federal expenditures had risen. These tax cuts are scheduled to expire in 2010, but the political will to restore higher taxes may be lacking. If so, paying down the deficit will be difficult.

**Figure 14.30** Despite the introduction of high-tech processes in manufacturing, that economic sector has declined as the service sector has become more important.

Despite high employment rates, the gap between rich and poor is growing. The average income of the top 300,000 American wage earners was 440 times that of a worker in the bottom half of the income scale, double the 1980 gap.

There have also been some new directions in recent years. For example, the US is still a strong player in the global economy, but there are signs that its status may be diminishing. The euro has replaced the US dollar as the key currency of the international bond market. China's economy is expanding at a rate to replace the US as "number 1" in terms of GNP—it already produces more cars than the US.

Overall, these trends compose part of the United States' history of remarkable economic change. A subsistence economy was replaced by an agricultural one, then by manufacturing industries. In turn, manufacturing has been replaced by ICT and service industries as the main drivers of the economy. The direction of future developments may not be predictable, but economic change will continue as a strong theme in the American story.

To learn more about current economic indicators, visit www.emp.ca/ah.

## The American People and the American Dream

What does it mean to be American today? In the colonial period, being American meant independence and self-reliance. In revolutionary times, it meant a society where "all men are created equal." In the 1830s, de Tocqueville saw "equality of condition among the people" as America's defining quality (see Chapter 5). By the 20th century, Americans saw themselves as a free, enterprising, and strong people with a way of life that was the envy of many. Being American also meant offering to others a new life on an equal footing: "Give me your tired, your poor, / Your huddled masses yearning to breathe free" (see Chapter 8).

For those who immigrated, being American meant becoming Americanized. In a 1908 play that toured the United States, America was described as "the Great Melting-Pot where all the races of Europe are melting and reforming." The image of the melting-pot has been used frequently in describing US

**SOUND BITE**

"Our task is to combine due appreciation of the splendid diversity of the nation with due emphasis on the great unifying ideas of individual freedom, political democracy, and human rights. These are the ideas that define the American nationality."

—Historian Arthur Schlesinger Jr., *The Disuniting of America*, 1991

# Culture Notes

## Art in a Networked Society

**Figure 14.31** Hand-held histories as "hyper-monuments."

Today's United States is a networked society to a degree unimaginable in previous generations. Since 1990, cellphones with text messaging and camera facilities have become common, Web television was invented, the Internet grew and became more accessible, and powerful computers became relatively inexpensive. Besides having a huge impact on communication and accessing information, these ICT changes have also had an impact on culture. Internet radio and television, online movies, and downloadable music changed the way Americans experience popular culture. Suddenly, they gained more personal power to preview, select, and manage the forms of entertainment they want to enjoy.

These changes also allow Americans to become part of popular culture themselves by posting commentary on events, publishing essays, books, and poetry online, sharing personal videos and photographs, and even presenting their own cartoons and movies to the wired world.

ICT has affected more formal culture, too. Take the example of art. First, art has become much more accessible in a wired world. Americans can visit one website at The Virtual Library to access more than 1,500 museums in the United States, or they can view a virtual exhibit of paintings at New York's Metropolitan Museum of Art—all without leaving their own homes. The Internet also provides access to great paintings, prints, textiles, multimedia works, and photographs in art galleries around the world. An American in pre-Internet times would have had to spend thousands of dollars on travel or art books to enjoy these same works of art so fully.

Second, the Internet has provided a new vehicle for American artists to produce innovative works. It allows some artists to showcase their computer-generated works online—see, for example, the website of the Museum of Computer Art. Cyberartists present virtual interactive works that allow an exchange of ideas and emotion between artist and viewers in cyberspace. Artists and viewers find cyberart exciting because it

- exists virtually, outside of the limits of time and space that characterize traditional art
- is an authentic expression of the artist (i.e., not judged or filtered by art gallery staff or the market)
- is immediately accessible and reaches a global audience in potentially millions of places simultaneously
- may invite interaction with the piece of art or contact with the artist.

Naturally, cyberartists are found at their websites, but a more traditional exhibition was held in 2007 at The Boston Cyberarts Festival involving more than 50 museums, galleries, theatres, and public spaces in Boston.

### Think It Through

1. Visit the online sources described above through the links at www.emp.ca/ah.
2. Through the link above, visit Virtualmuseum.us to view visual art, and then Histories of Hyper-Monuments to view "hand-held histories." Compare art in this form to traditional art in a gallery.
3. Find another online American art gallery and view works of art from your favourite period in American history.

society—after all, the Great Seal of the United States has carried the Latin motto *E Pluribus Unum* (out of many, one) since its adoption in 1782.

In the 21st century, that image is being challenged as a myth that overlooks the diversity of US society throughout history. This image also ignores the reality that some Americans have been marginalized (for example, Native Americans, African-Americans, and the poor) and that others have held on to old views and prejudices, either as immigrants or against immigrants. At the same time, there are questions as to whether the modern influx of people from outside Europe and the Judeo-Christian tradition forces a reconsideration of the melting-pot image. People from around the world still flock to the United States (in 2005, the country had over 20 percent of the world's migrants living in it), but many of them retain their culture and religion while becoming Americans. Today, Americans debate how much *Pluribus* and how much *Unum* should prevail in US society.

**Figure 14.32** What comment is the cartoonist making about the American dream today?

There are many questions about the American dream. Will today's immigrants find as much opportunity and success as their predecessors? Can people still rise from humble beginnings to become financially secure? Could a modern-day Lincoln become president of the United States? The huge gap between rich and poor, as well as the vast expense involved in mounting an election campaign, raises doubts about these matters. Still, as you have seen in this text, Americans have always been vigorous, enterprising, and adaptable to change. Moreover—despite negative images associated with recent American foreign policy, and despite the extremes in wealth and position in today's US—most Americans still believe in the founding ideas of liberty, democracy, equality, and opportunity. How these ideas are pursued in the future will determine the character of the American people, and the shape of the American dream.

## CHECK YOUR UNDERSTANDING

1. Why were relief efforts so chaotic in New Orleans following Hurricane Katrina?
2. What are President Bush's stated reasons for not supporting the Kyoto Protocol? Speculate as to other reasons.
3. How do the Civil Rights Act of 2004 and SCHIP address some of the rights issues identified in earlier chapters of this unit?
4. What patterns are clear in the American economy over the period covered by Chapters 12 through 14?
5. What evidence have you seen of the American dream at work in earlier chapters? How is the dream different today?

# THE HISTORIAN'S CRAFT

## Historical Perspectives: Past, Present, and Future

Refer to the ideas in Features of This Text (page x): *liberty*, *democracy*, *equality*, and *opportunity*. Consider how these ideas are evident in history right up to recent times:

- How does the idea of liberty weave through topics from colonial times and the Constitutional Convention to the recent USA PATRIOT Act?
- What links those persons denied the right to vote in the past—Native Americans, women, and slaves—with those disenfranchised in the 2000 Florida election?
- Consider issues of equality in relation to 19th-century immigration, the formation of unions, and women's rights.
- Think about opportunity in the United States in terms of the Homestead Act, early industrialization, and today's income gap between rich and poor.

Consider the future. How will the long struggle for civil rights unfold in the years ahead? What economic and technological opportunities will enterprising Americans next seize? Has the US become an empire? If so, will the historic tensions between involvement and isolation lead it elsewhere? Your study of the United States' past allows you to raise questions like these, and provides you with an informed perspective for observing the US in the future.

Think about the role historians play in bringing the perspective of time to recent events that first appear as news stories. For example, news coverage of the Gulf War suggested that it was a "clean" war marked by precision bombing, limited impact on Iraqi civilians, and few American casualties. Historians have since provided a broader understanding by revealing that bombing was less than precise, that civilians suffered because of damage to essential services such as water and power, and that American casualties should include veterans suffering from Gulf War Syndrome (physical and mental illnesses related to stress, injury, and exposure to hazardous materials).

Remind yourself of the importance of primary evidence. In this chapter you have seen how recently declassified US Central Command briefing notes provide deeper understanding about the US strategy toward Iraq. Every year, historians uncover new evidence to provide fresh insights into history, from the times of the earliest Native American settlements up to events of the last decade.

As you think about the historian's work, remember that all the history you have read in this text has been crafted by people. Historians selected the evidence and produced the historical narratives that the authors used to write this text. These historians and writers made choices about what to emphasize and how to present the history. Sometimes the choices were dictated by the historical period. For example, in this last chapter, 9/11 and the "war on terror" demanded most of the attention, so there is less coverage of social history than in some other chapters. At other times, the choices were subjective—for example, choosing a painting or photograph that best reflects the times. You make choices, too. You might consciously choose to explore one part of history in depth—perhaps because of a personal interest in American music. You will also "choose" subconsciously to see events differently from others simply because of who you are based on your own personal, family, and cultural history.

Keeping in mind the ideas and themes in American history that you have read about in this text, and reminding yourself of the nature of the historian's craft, allow you to make sense of the United States today and tomorrow.

### Try It!

1. Visit the US National Security Archive online through the link at www.emp.ca/ah and choose one topic that interests you. How does the primary evidence there add to your understanding of the historic event?
2. Choose one chapter in this text. Explain how the ideas of liberty, democracy, equality, and opportunity are evident in the history described in that chapter.

# STUDY HALL

## Thinking

1. "The United States is a nation shaped by ideas" (see Features of This Text, page x). In the period 1989 to the present, what ideas helped shape (a) American politics and (b) American diplomacy?
2. What criteria make someone a hero in history?
   a. Would Anita Hill meet your criteria? Explain.
   b. Choose two historical figures from earlier chapters who do meet your criteria and support your choices.
3. Review the sections of Chapters 7, 11, and 14 that deal with the three presidents who faced the possibility of impeachment (Johnson, Nixon, and Clinton). What was similar in each of these three cases? What was different?
4. What dilemma faces President George W. Bush with regard to Iraq? How does the theme of intervention versus isolation that runs through American history relate to this dilemma?

## Communication

5. a. Update President Eisenhower's speech warning about the military-industrial complex (see Chapter 11) with data on military spending from this chapter and additional research on the US defence industry.
   b. Debate this question: Is American militarism the greatest danger facing the United States today?
6. Prepare a series of cartoons (storyboard style) that illustrate the voting abuses identified in Florida during the 2000 election. In an accompanying one-page statement, explain how these abuses violate the ideas that have guided American development: liberty, democracy, equality, and opportunity.
7. Review the American Archive feature, "War by PowerPoint Presentation" (page 499). Prepare your own PowerPoint slides to present "assumptions" that could have led Bush and his advisers to a different decision about the invasion of Iraq.
8. Visit American cyberartists' websites (see www.emp.ca/ah). Choose three examples of art that make a political statement about US history or society. Present them to your classmates and explain why you chose these examples.

## Application

9. In this chapter, one date stands out—September 11, 2001 (page 495). Review material in this chapter about the aftermath of 9/11, and write a paragraph explaining why this date stands out. Select another single date from an earlier period in American history and explain why it was equally important.
10. Choose your favourite cartoon in this book. Applying what you have learned about the history related to this cartoon, write your own caption for it. (If the cartoon already has a caption, write a new one.)
11. Review the topic of civil rights in Chapters 12 to 14. On the basis of the recent history of civil rights in the United States, speculate as to the next steps in the campaign for equality.
12. "As the 1930s came to a close, most Americans still held to the promise of the American dream: people could achieve great success if they only had faith in themselves and worked hard" (Chapter 10, page 359). Write an equivalent statement that applies to the US today.

# Appendix

## The Declaration of Independence

### In CONGRESS, July 4, 1776.

**The unanimous Declaration of the thirteen united States of America,**

When in the Course of human events, it becomes necessary for one people to dissolve the political bands which have connected them with another, and to assume among the powers of the earth, the separate and equal station to which the Laws of Nature and of Nature's God entitle them, a decent respect to the opinions of mankind requires that they should declare the causes which impel them to the separation.

We hold these truths to be self-evident, that all men are created equal, that they are endowed by their Creator with certain unalienable Rights, that among these are Life, Liberty and the pursuit of Happiness. —That to secure these rights, Governments are instituted among Men, deriving their just powers from the consent of the governed, —That whenever any Form of Government becomes destructive of these ends, it is the Right of the People to alter or to abolish it, and to institute new Government, laying its foundation on such principles and organizing its powers in such form, as to them shall seem most likely to effect their Safety and Happiness. Prudence, indeed, will dictate that Governments long established should not be changed for light and transient causes; and accordingly all experience hath shewn, that mankind are more disposed to suffer, while evils are sufferable, than to right themselves by abolishing the forms to which they are accustomed. But when a long train of abuses and usurpations, pursuing invariably the same Object evinces a design to reduce them under absolute Despotism, it is their right, it is their duty, to throw off such Government, and to provide new Guards for their future security. —Such has been the patient sufferance of these Colonies; and such is now the necessity which constrains them to alter their former Systems of Government. The history of the present King of Great Britain [George III] is a history of repeated injuries and usurpations, all having in direct object the establishment of an absolute Tyranny over these States. To prove this, let Facts be submitted to a candid world.

He has refused his Assent to Laws, the most wholesome and necessary for the public good.

He has forbidden his Governors to pass Laws of immediate and pressing importance, unless suspended in their operation till his Assent should be obtained; and when so suspended, he has utterly neglected to attend to them.

He has refused to pass other Laws for the accommodation of large districts of people, unless those people would relinquish the right of Representation in the Legislature, a right inestimable to them and formidable to tyrants only.

He has called together legislative bodies at places unusual, uncomfortable, and distant from the depository of their public Records, for the sole purpose of fatiguing them into compliance with his measures.

He has dissolved Representative Houses repeatedly, for opposing with manly firmness his invasions on the rights of the people.

He has refused for a long time, after such dissolutions, to cause others to be elected; whereby the Legislative powers, incapable of Annihilation, have returned to the People at large for their exercise; the State remaining in the mean time exposed to all the dangers of invasion from without, and convulsions within.

He has endeavoured to prevent the population of these States; for that purpose obstructing the Laws for Naturalization of Foreigners; refusing to pass others to encourage their migrations hither, and raising the conditions of new Appropriations of Lands.

He has obstructed the Administration of Justice, by refusing his Assent to Laws for establishing Judiciary powers.

He has made Judges dependent on his Will alone, for the tenure of their offices, and the amount and payment of their salaries.

He has erected a multitude of New Offices, and sent hither swarms of Officers to harass our people, and eat out their substance.

He has kept among us, in times of peace, Standing Armies without the consent of our legislatures.

He has affected to render the Military independent of and superior to the Civil power.

He has combined with others to subject us to a jurisdiction foreign to our constitution and unacknowledged by our laws; giving his Assent to their Acts of pretended Legislation:

For Quartering large bodies of armed troops among us:

For protecting them, by a mock Trial, from punishment for any Murders which they should commit on the Inhabitants of these States:

For cutting off our Trade with all parts of the world:

For imposing Taxes on us without our Consent:

For depriving us, in many cases, of the benefits of Trial by Jury:

For transporting us beyond Seas to be tried for pretended offences:

For abolishing the free System of English Laws in a neighbouring Province, establishing therein an Arbitrary government, and enlarging its Boundaries so as to render it at once an example and fit instrument for introducing the same absolute rule into these Colonies:

For taking away our Charters, abolishing our most valuable Laws, and altering fundamentally the Forms of our Governments:

For suspending our own Legislatures, and declaring themselves invested with power to legislate for us in all cases whatsoever.

He has abdicated Government here, by declaring us out of his Protection and waging War against us.

He has plundered our seas, ravaged our Coasts, burnt our towns, and destroyed the lives of our people.

He is at this time transporting large Armies of foreign Mercenaries to compleat the works of death, desolation and tyranny, already begun with circumstances of Cruelty and perfidy scarcely paralleled in the most barbarous ages, and totally unworthy the Head of a civilized nation.

He has constrained our fellow Citizens taken Captive on the high Seas to bear Arms against their Country, to become the executioners of their friends and Brethren, or to fall themselves by their Hands.

He has excited domestic insurrections amongst us, and has endeavoured to bring on the inhabitants of our frontiers, the merciless Indian Savages, whose known rule of warfare, is an undistinguished destruction of all ages, sexes and conditions.

In every stage of these Oppressions We have Petitioned for Redress in the most humble terms: Our repeated Petitions have been answered only by repeated injury. A Prince whose character is thus marked by every act which may define a Tyrant, is unfit to be the ruler of a free people.

Nor have We been wanting in attentions to our British brethren. We have warned them from time to time of attempts by their legislature to extend an unwarrantable jurisdiction over us. We have reminded them of the circumstances of our emigration and settlement here. We have appealed to their native justice and magnanimity, and we have conjured them by the ties of our common kindred to disavow these usurpations, which, would inevitably interrupt our connections and correspondence. They too have been deaf to the voice of justice and of consanguinity. We must, therefore, acquiesce in the necessity, which denounces our Separation, and hold them, as we hold the rest of mankind, Enemies in War, in Peace Friends.

We, therefore, the Representatives of the united States of America, in General Congress assembled, appealing to the Supreme Judge of the world for the rectitude of our intentions, do, in the Name, and by the Authority of the good People of these Colonies, solemnly publish and declare, That these United Colonies are, and of Right ought to be Free and Independent States; that they are Absolved from all Allegiance to the British Crown, and that all political connection between them and the State of Great Britain, is and ought to be totally dissolved; and that as Free and Independent States, they have full Power to levy War, conclude Peace, contract Alliances, establish Commerce, and to do all other Acts and Things which Independent States may of right do. And for the support of this Declaration, with a firm reliance on the protection of divine Providence, we mutually pledge to each other our Lives, our Fortunes and our sacred Honor.

—John Hancock

[The signers of the Declaration represented the new states as follows:]

**New Hampshire**
Josiah Bartlett, William Whipple, Matthew Thornton

**Massachusetts**
John Hancock, Samuel Adams, John Adams, Robert Treat Paine, Elbridge Gerry

**Rhode Island**
Stephen Hopkins, William Ellery

**Connecticut**
Roger Sherman, Samuel Huntington, William Williams, Oliver Wolcott

**New York**
William Floyd, Philip Livingston, Francis Lewis, Lewis Morris

**New Jersey**
Richard Stockton, John Witherspoon, Francis Hopkinson, John Hart, Abraham Clark

**Pennsylvania**
Robert Morris, Benjamin Rush, Benjamin Franklin, John Morton, George Clymer, James Smith, George Taylor, James Wilson, George Ross

**Delaware**
Caesar Rodney, George Read, Thomas McKean

**Maryland**
Samuel Chase, William Paca, Thomas Stone, Charles Carroll of Carrollton

**Virginia**
George Wythe, Richard Henry Lee, Thomas Jefferson, Benjamin Harrison, Thomas Nelson, Jr., Francis Lightfoot Lee, Carter Braxton

**North Carolina**
William Hooper, Joseph Hewes, John Penn

**South Carolina**
Edward Rutledge, Thomas Heyward, Jr., Thomas Lynch, Jr., Arthur Middleton

**Georgia**
Button Gwinnett, Lyman Hall, George Walton

# The Constitution of the United States

*We the People*

*of the United States, in Order to form a more perfect Union, establish Justice, insure domestic Tranquility, provide for the common defense, promote the general Welfare, and secure the Blessings of Liberty to ourselves and our Posterity, do ordain and establish this Constitution for the United States of America.*

## Article I.

**Section 1.** All legislative Powers herein granted shall be vested in a Congress of the United States, which shall consist of a Senate and House of Representatives.

**Section 2.** The House of Representatives shall be composed of Members chosen every second Year by the People of the several States, and the Electors in each State shall have the Qualifications requisite for Electors of the most numerous Branch of the State Legislature.

No Person shall be a Representative who shall not have attained to the Age of twenty five Years, and been seven Years a Citizen of the United States, and who shall not, when elected, be an Inhabitant of that State in which he shall be chosen.

Representatives and direct Taxes shall be apportioned among the several States which may be included within this Union, according to their respective Numbers, which shall be determined by adding to the whole Number of free Persons, including those bound to Service for a Term of Years, and excluding Indians not taxed, three fifths of all other Persons.

The actual Enumeration shall be made within three Years after the first Meeting of the Congress of the United States, and within every subsequent Term of ten Years, in such Manner as they shall by Law direct. The Number of Representatives shall not exceed one for every thirty Thousand, but each State shall have at Least one Representative; and until such enumeration shall be made, the State of New Hampshire shall be entitled to choose three, Massachusetts eight, Rhode Island and Providence Plantations one, Connecticut five, New York six, New Jersey four, Pennsylvania eight, Delaware one, Maryland six, Virginia ten, North Carolina five, South Carolina five and Georgia three.

When vacancies happen in the Representation from any State, the Executive Authority thereof shall issue Writs of Election to fill such Vacancies.

The House of Representatives shall choose their Speaker and other Officers; and shall have the sole Power of Impeachment.

**Section 3.** The Senate of the United States shall be composed of two Senators from each State, chosen by the Legislature thereof, for six Years; and each Senator shall have one Vote.

Immediately after they shall be assembled in Consequence of the first Election, they shall be divided as equally as may be into three Classes. The Seats of the Senators of the first Class shall be vacated at the Expiration of the second Year, of the second Class at the Expiration of the fourth Year, and of the third Class at the Expiration of the sixth Year, so that one third may be chosen every second Year; and if Vacancies happen by Resignation, or otherwise, during the Recess of the Legislature of any State, the Executive thereof may make temporary Appointments until the next Meeting of the Legislature, which shall then fill such Vacancies.

No person shall be a Senator who shall not have attained to the Age of thirty Years, and been nine Years a Citizen of the United States, and who shall not, when elected, be an Inhabitant of that State for which he shall be chosen.

The Vice President of the United States shall be President of the Senate, but shall have no Vote, unless they be equally divided.

The Senate shall choose their other Officers, and also a President pro tempore, in the absence of the Vice President, or when he shall exercise the Office of President of the United States.

The Senate shall have the sole Power to try all Impeachments. When sitting for that Purpose, they shall be on Oath or Affirmation. When the President of the United States is tried, the Chief Justice shall preside: And no Person shall be convicted without the Concurrence of two thirds of the Members present.

Judgment in Cases of Impeachment shall not extend further than to removal from Office, and disqualification to hold and enjoy any Office of honor, Trust or Profit under the United States: but the Party convicted shall nevertheless be liable and subject to Indictment, Trial, Judgment and Punishment, according to Law.

**Section 4.** The Times, Places and Manner of holding Elections for Senators and Representatives, shall be prescribed in each State by the Legislature thereof; but the Congress may at any time by Law make or alter such Regulations, except as to the Place of Choosing Senators.

The Congress shall assemble at least once in every Year, and such Meeting shall be on the first Monday in December, unless they shall by Law appoint a different Day.

**Section 5.** Each House shall be the Judge of the Elections, Returns and Qualifications of its own Members, and a Majority of each shall constitute a Quorum to do Business; but a smaller number may adjourn from day to day, and may be authorized to compel the Attendance of absent Members, in such Manner, and under such Penalties as each House may provide.

Each House may determine the Rules of its Proceedings, punish its Members for disorderly Behavior, and, with the Concurrence of two-thirds, expel a Member.

Each House shall keep a Journal of its Proceedings, and from time to time publish the same, excepting such Parts as may in their Judgment require Secrecy; and the Yeas and Nays of the Members of either House on any question shall, at the Desire of one fifth of those Present, be entered on the Journal.

Neither House, during the Session of Congress, shall, without the Consent of the other, adjourn for more than three days, nor to any other Place than that in which the two Houses shall be sitting.

**Section 6.** The Senators and Representatives shall receive a Compensation for their Services, to be ascertained by Law, and paid out of the Treasury of the United States. They shall in all Cases, except Treason, Felony and Breach of the Peace, be privileged from Arrest during their Attendance at the Session of their respective Houses, and in going to and returning from the same; and for any Speech or Debate in either House, they shall not be questioned in any other Place.

No Senator or Representative shall, during the Time for which he was elected, be appointed to any civil Office under the Authority of the United States which shall have been created, or the Emoluments whereof shall have been increased during such time; and no Person holding any Office under the United States, shall be a Member of either House during his Continuance in Office.

**Section 7.** All bills for raising Revenue shall originate in the House of Representatives; but the Senate may propose or concur with Amendments as on other Bills.

Every Bill which shall have passed the House of Representatives and the Senate, shall, before it become a Law, be presented to the President of the United States; If he approve he shall sign it, but if not he shall return it, with his Objections to that House in which it shall have originated, who shall enter the Objections at large on their Journal, and proceed to reconsider it. If after such Reconsideration two thirds of that House shall agree to pass the Bill, it shall be sent, together with the Objections, to the other House, by which it shall likewise be reconsidered, and if approved by two thirds of that House, it shall become a Law. But in all such Cases the Votes of both Houses shall be determined by Yeas and Nays, and the Names of the Persons voting for and against the Bill shall be entered on the Journal of each House respectively. If any Bill shall not be returned by the President within ten Days (Sundays excepted) after it shall have been presented to him, the Same shall be a Law, in like Manner as if he had signed it, unless the Congress by their Adjournment prevent its Return, in which Case it shall not be a Law.

Every Order, Resolution, or Vote to which the Concurrence of the Senate and House of Representatives may be necessary (except on a question of Adjournment) shall be presented to the President of the United States; and before the Same shall take Effect, shall be approved by him, or being disapproved by him, shall be repassed by two thirds of the Senate and House of Representatives, according to the Rules and Limitations prescribed in the Case of a Bill.

**Section 8.** The Congress shall have Power To lay and collect Taxes, Duties, Imposts and Excises, to pay the Debts and provide for the common Defence and general Welfare of the United States; but all Duties, Imposts and Excises shall be uniform throughout the United States;

To borrow money on the credit of the United States;

To regulate Commerce with foreign Nations, and among the several States, and with the Indian Tribes;

To establish an uniform Rule of Naturalization, and uniform Laws on the subject of Bankruptcies throughout the United States;

To coin Money, regulate the Value thereof, and of foreign Coin, and fix the Standard of Weights and Measures;

To provide for the Punishment of counterfeiting the Securities and current Coin of the United States;

To establish Post Offices and Post Roads;

To promote the Progress of Science and useful Arts, by securing for limited Times to Authors and Inventors the exclusive Right to their respective Writings and Discoveries;

To constitute Tribunals inferior to the supreme Court;

To define and punish Piracies and Felonies committed on the high Seas, and Offenses against the Law of Nations;

To declare War, grant Letters of Marque and Reprisal, and make Rules concerning Captures on Land and Water;

To raise and support Armies, but no Appropriation of Money to that Use shall be for a longer Term than two Years;

To provide and maintain a Navy;

To make Rules for the Government and Regulation of the land and naval Forces;

To provide for calling forth the Militia to execute the Laws of the Union, suppress Insurrections and repel Invasions;

To provide for organizing, arming, and disciplining the Militia, and for governing such Part of them as may be employed in the Service of the United States, reserving to the States respectively, the Appointment of the Officers, and the Authority of training the Militia according to the discipline prescribed by Congress;

To exercise exclusive Legislation in all Cases whatsoever, over such District (not exceeding ten Miles square) as may, by Cession of particular States, and the acceptance of Congress, become the Seat of the Government of the United States, and to exercise like Authority over all Places purchased by the Consent of the Legislature of the State in which the Same shall be, for the Erection of Forts, Magazines, Arsenals, dock-Yards, and other needful Buildings; And

To make all Laws which shall be necessary and proper for carrying into Execution the foregoing Powers, and all other Powers vested by this Constitution in the Government of the United States, or in any Department or Officer thereof.

**Section 9.** The Migration or Importation of such Persons as any of the States now existing shall think proper to admit, shall not be prohibited by the Congress prior to the Year one thousand eight hundred and eight, but a tax or duty may be imposed on such Importation, not exceeding ten dollars for each Person.

The privilege of the Writ of Habeas Corpus shall not be suspended, unless when in Cases of Rebellion or Invasion the public Safety may require it.

No Bill of Attainder or ex post facto Law shall be passed.

No capitation, or other direct, Tax shall be laid, unless in Proportion to the Census or Enumeration herein before directed to be taken.

No Tax or Duty shall be laid on Articles exported from any State.

No Preference shall be given by any Regulation of Commerce or Revenue to the Ports of one State over those of another: nor shall Vessels bound to, or from, one State, be obliged to enter, clear, or pay Duties in another.

No Money shall be drawn from the Treasury, but in Consequence of Appropriations made by Law; and a regular Statement and Account of the Receipts and Expenditures of all public Money shall be published from time to time.

No Title of Nobility shall be granted by the United States: And no Person holding any Office of Profit or Trust under them, shall, without the Consent of the Congress, accept of any present, Emolument, Office, or Title, of any kind whatever, from any King, Prince or foreign State.

**Section 10.** No State shall enter into any Treaty, Alliance, or Confederation; grant Letters of Marque and Reprisal; coin Money; emit Bills of Credit; make any Thing but gold and silver Coin a Tender in Payment of Debts; pass any Bill of Attainder, ex post facto Law, or Law impairing the Obligation of Contracts, or grant any Title of Nobility.

No State shall, without the Consent of the Congress, lay any Imposts or Duties on Imports or Exports, except what may be absolutely necessary for executing its inspection Laws: and the net Produce of all Duties and Imposts, laid by any State on Imports or Exports, shall be for the Use of the Treasury of the United States; and all such Laws shall be subject to the Revision and Control of the Congress.

No State shall, without the Consent of Congress, lay any duty of Tonnage, keep Troops, or Ships of War in time of Peace, enter into any Agreement or Compact with another State, or with a foreign Power, or engage in War, unless actually invaded, or in such imminent Danger as will not admit of delay.

## Article II.

**Section 1.** The executive Power shall be vested in a President of the United States of America. He shall hold his Office during the Term of four Years, and, together with the Vice-President chosen for the same Term, be elected, as follows:

Each State shall appoint, in such Manner as the Legislature thereof may direct, a Number of Electors, equal to the whole Number of Senators and Representatives to which the State may be entitled in the Congress: but no Senator or Representative, or Person holding an Office of Trust or Profit under the United States, shall be appointed an Elector.

The Electors shall meet in their respective States, and vote by Ballot for two persons, of whom one at least shall not lie an Inhabitant of the same State with themselves. And they shall make a List of all the Persons voted for, and of the Number of Votes for each; which List they shall sign and certify, and transmit sealed to the Seat of the Government of the United States, directed to the President of the Senate. The President of the Senate shall, in the Presence of the Senate and House of Representatives, open all the Certificates, and the Votes shall then be counted. The Person having the greatest Number of Votes shall be the President, if such Number be a Majority of the whole Number of Electors appointed; and if there be more than one who have such Majority, and have an equal Number of Votes, then the House of Representatives shall immediately choose by Ballot one of them for President; and if no Person have a Majority, then from the five highest on the List the said House shall in like Manner choose the President. But in choosing the President, the Votes shall be taken by States, the Representation from each State having one Vote; a quorum for this Purpose shall consist of a Member or Members from two-thirds of the States, and a Majority of all the States shall be necessary to a Choice. In every Case, after the Choice of the President, the Person having the greatest Number of Votes of the Electors shall be the Vice President. But if there should remain two or more who have equal Votes, the Senate shall choose from them by Ballot the Vice-President.

The Congress may determine the Time of choosing the Electors, and the Day on which they shall give their Votes; which Day shall be the same throughout the United States.

No person except a natural born Citizen, or a Citizen of the United States, at the time of the Adoption of this Constitution, shall be eligible to the Office of President; neither shall any Person be eligible to that Office who shall not have attained to the Age of thirty-five Years, and been fourteen Years a Resident within the United States.

In Case of the Removal of the President from Office, or of his Death, Resignation, or Inability to discharge the Powers and Duties of the said Office, the same shall devolve on the Vice President, and the Congress may by Law provide for the Case of Removal, Death, Resignation or Inability, both of the President and Vice President, declaring what Officer shall then act as President, and such Officer shall act accordingly, until the Disability be removed, or a President shall be elected.

The President shall, at stated Times, receive for his Services, a Compensation, which shall neither be increased nor diminished during the Period for which he shall have been elected, and he shall not receive within that Period any other Emolument from the United States, or any of them.

Before he enter on the Execution of his Office, he shall take the following Oath or Affirmation:

"I do solemnly swear (or affirm) that I will faithfully execute the Office of President of the United States, and will to the best of my Ability, preserve, protect and defend the Constitution of the United States."

**Section 2.** The President shall be Commander in Chief of the Army and Navy of the United States, and of the Militia of the several States, when called into the actual Service of the United States; he may require the Opinion, in writing, of the principal Officer in each of the executive Departments, upon any subject relating to the Duties of their respective Offices, and he shall have Power to Grant Reprieves and Pardons for Offenses against the United States, except in Cases of Impeachment.

He shall have Power, by and with the Advice and Consent of the Senate, to make Treaties, provided two thirds of the Senators present concur; and he shall nominate, and by and with the Advice and Consent of the Senate, shall appoint Ambassadors, other public Ministers and Consuls, Judges of the supreme Court, and all other Officers of the United States, whose Appointments are not herein otherwise provided for, and which shall be established by Law: but the Congress may by Law vest the Appointment of such inferior Officers, as they think proper, in the President alone, in the Courts of Law, or in the Heads of Departments.

The President shall have Power to fill up all Vacancies that may happen during the Recess of the Senate, by granting Commissions which shall expire at the End of their next Session.

**Section 3.** He shall from time to time give to the Congress Information of the State of the Union, and recommend to their Consideration such Measures as he shall judge necessary and expedient; he may, on extraordinary Occasions, convene both Houses, or either of them, and in Case of Disagreement between them, with Respect to the Time of Adjournment, he may adjourn them to such Time as he shall think proper; he shall receive Ambassadors and other public Ministers; he shall take Care that the Laws be faithfully executed, and shall Commission all the Officers of the United States.

**Section 4.** The President, Vice President and all civil Officers of the United States, shall be removed from Office on Impeachment for, and Conviction of, Treason, Bribery, or other high Crimes and Misdemeanors.

## Article III.

**Section 1.** The judicial Power of the United States, shall be vested in one supreme Court, and in such inferior Courts as the Congress may from time to time ordain and establish. The Judges, both of the supreme and inferior Courts, shall hold their Offices during good Behavior, and shall, at stated Times, receive for their Services a Compensation which shall not be diminished during their Continuance in Office.

**Section 2.** The judicial Power shall extend to all Cases, in Law and Equity, arising under this Constitution, the Laws of the United States, and Treaties made, or which shall be made, under their Authority; to all Cases affecting Ambassadors, other public Ministers and Consuls; to all Cases of admiralty and maritime Jurisdiction; to Controversies to which the United States shall be a Party; to Controversies between two or more States; between a State and Citizens of another State; between Citizens of different States; between Citizens of the same State claiming Lands under Grants of different States, and between a State, or the Citizens thereof, and foreign States, Citizens or Subjects.

In all Cases affecting Ambassadors, other public Ministers and Consuls, and those in which a State shall be Party, the supreme Court shall have original Jurisdiction. In all the other Cases before mentioned, the supreme Court shall have appellate Jurisdiction, both as to Law and Fact, with such Exceptions, and under such Regulations as the Congress shall make.

The Trial of all Crimes, except in Cases of Impeachment, shall be by Jury; and such Trial shall be held in the State where the said Crimes shall have been committed; but when not committed within any State, the Trial shall be at such Place or Places as the Congress may by Law have directed.

**Section 3.** Treason against the United States, shall consist only in levying War against them, or in adhering to their Enemies, giving them Aid and Comfort. No Person shall be convicted of Treason unless on the Testimony of two Witnesses to the same overt Act, or on Confession in open Court.

The Congress shall have power to declare the Punishment of Treason, but no Attainder of Treason shall work Corruption of Blood, or Forfeiture except during the Life of the Person attainted.

## Article IV.

**Section 1.** Full Faith and Credit shall be given in each State to the public Acts, Records, and judicial Proceedings of every other State. And the Congress may by general Laws prescribe the Manner in which such Acts, Records and Proceedings shall be proved, and the Effect thereof.

**Section 2.** The Citizens of each State shall be entitled to all Privileges and Immunities of Citizens in the several States.

A Person charged in any State with Treason, Felony, or other Crime, who shall flee from Justice, and be found in another State, shall on demand of the executive Authority of the State from which he fled, be delivered up, to be removed to the State having Jurisdiction of the Crime.

No Person held to Service or Labour in one State, under the Laws thereof, escaping into another, shall, in Consequence of any Law or Regulation therein, be discharged from such Service or Labour, But shall be delivered up on Claim of the Party to whom such Service or Labour may be due.

**Section 3.** New States may be admitted by the Congress into this Union; but no new States shall be formed or erected within the Jurisdiction of any other State; nor any State be formed by the Junction of two or more States, or parts of States, without the Consent of the Legislatures of the States concerned as well as of the Congress.

The Congress shall have Power to dispose of and make all needful Rules and Regulations respecting the Territory or other Property belonging to the United States; and nothing in this Constitution shall be so construed as to Prejudice any Claims of the United States, or of any particular State.

**Section 4.** The United States shall guarantee to every State in this Union a Republican Form of Government, and shall protect each of them against Invasion; and on Application of the Legislature, or of the Executive (when the Legislature cannot be convened) against domestic Violence.

## Article V.

The Congress, whenever two thirds of both Houses shall deem it necessary, shall propose Amendments to this Constitution, or, on the Application of the Legislatures of two thirds of the several States, shall call a Convention for proposing Amendments, which, in either Case, shall be valid to all Intents and Purposes, as part of this Constitution, when ratified by the Legislatures of three fourths of the several States, or by Conventions in three fourths thereof, as the one or the other Mode of Ratification may be proposed by the Congress; Provided that no Amendment which may be made prior to the Year One thousand eight hundred and eight shall in any Manner affect the first and fourth Clauses in the Ninth Section of the first Article; and that no State, without its Consent, shall be deprived of its equal Suffrage in the Senate.

## Article VI.

All Debts contracted and Engagements entered into, before the Adoption of this Constitution, shall be as valid against the United States under this Constitution, as under the Confederation.

This Constitution, and the Laws of the United States which shall be made in Pursuance thereof; and all Treaties made, or which shall be made, under the Authority of the United States, shall be the supreme Law of the Land; and the Judges in every State shall be bound thereby, any Thing in the Constitution or Laws of any State to the Contrary notwithstanding.

The Senators and Representatives before mentioned, and the Members of the several State Legislatures, and all executive and judicial Officers, both of the United States and of the several States, shall be bound by Oath or Affirmation, to support this Constitution; but no religious Test shall ever be required as a Qualification to any Office or public Trust under the United States.

## Article VII.

The Ratification of the Conventions of nine States, shall be sufficient for the Establishment of this Constitution between the States so ratifying the Same.

Done in Convention by the Unanimous Consent of the States present the Seventeenth Day of September in the Year of our Lord one thousand seven hundred and Eighty seven and of the Independence of the United States of America the Twelfth. In Witness whereof We have hereunto subscribed our Names.

George Washington—President and deputy from Virginia

New Hampshire—John Langdon, Nicholas Gilman

Massachusetts—Nathaniel Gorham, Rufus King

Connecticut—William Samuel Johnson, Roger Sherman

New York—Alexander Hamilton

New Jersey—William Livingston, David Brearley, William Paterson, Jonathan Dayton

Pennsylvania—Benjamin Franklin, Thomas Mifflin, Robert Morris, George Clymer, Thomas Fitzsimons, Jared Ingersoll, James Wilson, Gouvernour Morris

Delaware—George Read, Gunning Bedford Jr., John Dickinson, Richard Bassett, Jacob Broom

Maryland—James McHenry, Daniel of St Thomas Jenifer, Daniel Carroll

Virginia—John Blair, James Madison Jr.

North Carolina—William Blount, Richard Dobbs Spaight, Hugh Williamson

South Carolina—John Rutledge, Charles Cotesworth Pinckney, Charles Pinckney, Pierce Butler

Georgia—William Few, Abraham Baldwin

Attest: William Jackson, Secretary

## Bill of Rights

*Amendments 1–10*
*Ratified December 15, 1791*

**Amendment 1**

Congress shall make no law respecting an establishment of religion, or prohibiting the free exercise thereof; or abridging the freedom of speech, or of the press; or the right of the people peaceably to assemble, and to petition the Government for a redress of grievances.

**Amendment 2**

A well regulated Militia, being necessary to the security of a free State, the right of the people to keep and bear Arms, shall not be infringed.

**Amendment 3**

No Soldier shall, in time of peace be quartered in any house, without the consent of the Owner, nor in time of war, but in a manner to be prescribed by law.

**Amendment 4**

The right of the people to be secure in their persons, houses, papers, and effects, against unreasonable searches and seizures, shall not be violated, and no Warrants shall issue, but upon probable cause, supported by Oath or affirmation, and particularly describing the place to be searched, and the persons or things to be seized.

**Amendment 5**

No person shall be held to answer for a capital, or otherwise infamous crime, unless on a presentment or indictment of a Grand Jury, except in cases arising in the land or naval forces, or in the Militia, when in actual service in time of War or public danger; nor shall any person be subject for the same offense to be twice put in jeopardy of life or limb; nor shall be compelled in any criminal case to be a witness against himself, nor be deprived of life, liberty, or property, without due process of law; nor shall private property be taken for public use, without just compensation.

**Amendment 6**

In all criminal prosecutions, the accused shall enjoy the right to a speedy and public trial, by an impartial jury of the State and district wherein the crime shall have been committed, which district shall have been previously ascertained by law, and to be informed of the nature and cause of the accusation; to be confronted with the witnesses against him; to have compulsory process for obtaining witnesses in his favor, and to have the Assistance of Counsel for his defence.

**Amendment 7**

In Suits at common law, where the value in controversy shall exceed twenty dollars, the right of trial by jury shall be preserved, and no fact tried by a jury, shall be otherwise re-examined in any Court of the United States, than according to the rules of the common law.

**Amendment 8**

Excessive bail shall not be required, nor excessive fines imposed, nor cruel and unusual punishments inflicted.

**Amendment 9**

The enumeration in the Constitution, of certain rights, shall not be construed to deny or disparage others retained by the people.

**Amendment 10**

The powers not delegated to the United States by the Constitution, nor prohibited by it to the States, are reserved to the States respectively, or to the people.

**Amendment 11**

*Ratified February 7, 1795*

The Judicial power of the United States shall not be construed to extend to any suit in law or equity, commenced or prosecuted against one of the United States by Citizens of another State, or by Citizens or Subjects of any Foreign State.

**Amendment 12**

*Ratified June 15, 1804*

The Electors shall meet in their respective states, and vote by ballot for President and Vice-President, one of whom, at least, shall not be an inhabitant of the same state with themselves; they shall name in their ballots the person voted for as President, and in distinct ballots the person voted for as Vice-President, and they shall make distinct lists of all persons voted for as President, and of all persons voted for as Vice-President and of the number of votes for each, which lists they shall sign and certify, and transmit sealed to the seat of the government of the United States, directed to the President of the Senate;

The President of the Senate shall, in the presence of the Senate and House of Representatives, open all the certificates and the votes shall then be counted;

The person having the greatest Number of votes for President, shall be the President, if such number be a majority of the whole number of Electors appointed; and if no person have such majority, then from the persons having the highest numbers not exceeding three on the list of those voted for as President, the House of Representatives shall choose immediately, by ballot, the President. But in choosing the President, the votes shall be taken by states, the representation from each state having one vote; a quorum for this purpose shall consist of a member or members from two-thirds of the states, and a majority of all the states shall be necessary to a choice. And if the House of Representatives shall not choose a President whenever the right of choice shall devolve upon them, before the fourth day of March next following, then the Vice-President shall act as President, as in the case of the death or other constitutional disability of the President.

The person having the greatest number of votes as Vice-President, shall be the Vice-President, if such number be a majority of the whole number of Electors appointed, and if no person have a majority, then from the two highest numbers on the list, the Senate shall choose the Vice-President; a quorum for the purpose shall consist of two-thirds of the whole number of Senators, and a majority of the whole number shall be necessary to a choice. But no person constitutionally ineligible to the office of President shall be eligible to that of Vice-President of the United States.

**Amendment 13**

*Ratified December 6, 1865*

1. Neither slavery nor involuntary servitude, except as a punishment for crime whereof the party shall have been duly convicted, shall exist within the United States, or any place subject to their jurisdiction.
2. Congress shall have power to enforce this article by appropriate legislation.

**Amendment 14**

*Ratified July 9, 1868*

1. All persons born or naturalized in the United States, and subject to the jurisdiction thereof, are citizens of the United States and of the State wherein they reside. No State shall make or enforce any law which shall abridge the privileges or immunities of citizens of the United States; nor shall any State deprive any person of life, liberty, or property, without due process of law; nor deny to any person within its jurisdiction the equal protection of the laws.
2. Representatives shall be apportioned among the several States according to their respective numbers, counting the whole number of persons in each State,

excluding Indians not taxed. But when the right to vote at any election for the choice of electors for President and Vice-President of the United States, Representatives in Congress, the Executive and Judicial officers of a State, or the members of the Legislature thereof, is denied to any of the male inhabitants of such State, being twenty-one years of age, and citizens of the United States, or in any way abridged, except for participation in rebellion, or other crime, the basis of representation therein shall be reduced in the proportion which the number of such male citizens shall bear to the whole number of male citizens twenty-one years of age in such State.

3. No person shall be a Senator or Representative in Congress, or elector of President and Vice-President, or hold any office, civil or military, under the United States, or under any State, who, having previously taken an oath, as a member of Congress, or as an officer of the United States, or as a member of any State legislature, or as an executive or judicial officer of any State, to support the Constitution of the United States, shall have engaged in insurrection or rebellion against the same, or given aid or comfort to the enemies thereof. But Congress may by a vote of two-thirds of each House, remove such disability.

4. The validity of the public debt of the United States, authorized by law, including debts incurred for payment of pensions and bounties for services in suppressing insurrection or rebellion, shall not be questioned. But neither the United States nor any State shall assume or pay any debt or obligation incurred in aid of insurrection or rebellion against the United States, or any claim for the loss or emancipation of any slave; but all such debts, obligations and claims shall be held illegal and void.

5. The Congress shall have power to enforce, by appropriate legislation, the provisions of this article.

**Amendment 15**

*Ratified February 3, 1870*

1. The right of citizens of the United States to vote shall not be denied or abridged by the United States or by any State on account of race, color, or previous condition of servitude.

2. The Congress shall have power to enforce this article by appropriate legislation.

**Amendment 16**

*Ratified February 3, 1913*

The Congress shall have power to lay and collect taxes on incomes, from whatever source derived, without apportionment among the several States, and without regard to any census or enumeration.

**Amendment 17**

*Ratified April 8, 1913*

The Senate of the United States shall be composed of two Senators from each State, elected by the people thereof, for six years; and each Senator shall have one vote. The electors in each State shall have the qualifications requisite for electors of the most numerous branch of the State legislatures.

When vacancies happen in the representation of any State in the Senate, the executive authority of such State shall issue writs of election to fill such vacancies: Provided, That the legislature of any State may empower the executive thereof to make temporary appointments until the people fill the vacancies by election as the legislature may direct.

This amendment shall not be so construed as to affect the election or term of any Senator chosen before it becomes valid as part of the Constitution.

**Amendment 18**

*Ratified January 16, 1919,*
*later repealed by Amendment 21*

1. After one year from the ratification of this article the manufacture, sale, or transportation of intoxicating liquors within, the importation thereof into, or the exportation thereof from the United States and all territory subject to the jurisdiction thereof for beverage purposes is hereby prohibited.

2. The Congress and the several States shall have concurrent power to enforce this article by appropriate legislation.

3. This article shall be inoperative unless it shall have been ratified as an amendment to the Constitution by the legislatures of the several States, as provided in the Constitution, within seven years from the date of the submission hereof to the States by the Congress.

**Amendment 19**

*Ratified August 18, 1920*

The right of citizens of the United States to vote shall not be denied or abridged by the United States or by any State on account of sex.

Congress shall have power to enforce this article by appropriate legislation.

**Amendment 20**

*Ratified January 23, 1933*

1. The terms of the President and Vice President shall end at noon on the 20th day of January, and the terms of Senators and Representatives at noon on the 3d day of January, of the years in which such terms would have ended if this article had not been ratified; and the terms of their successors shall then begin.

2. The Congress shall assemble at least once in every year, and such meeting shall begin at noon on the 3d day of January, unless they shall by law appoint a different day.

3. If, at the time fixed for the beginning of the term of the President, the President elect shall have died, the Vice President elect shall become President. If a President shall not have been chosen before the time fixed for the beginning of his term, or if the President elect shall have failed to qualify, then the Vice President elect shall act as President until a President shall have qualified; and the Congress may by law provide for the case wherein neither a President elect nor a Vice President elect shall have qualified, declaring who shall then act as President, or the manner in which one who is to act shall be selected, and such person shall act accordingly until a President or Vice President shall have qualified.

4. The Congress may by law provide for the case of the death of any of the persons from whom the House of Representatives may choose a President whenever the right of choice shall have devolved upon them, and for the case of the death of any of the persons from whom the Senate may choose a Vice President whenever the right of choice shall have devolved upon them.

5. Sections 1 and 2 shall take effect on the 15th day of October following the ratification of this article.

6. This article shall be inoperative unless it shall have been ratified as an amendment to the Constitution by the legislatures of three-fourths of the several States within seven years from the date of its submission.

**Amendment 21**

*Ratified December 5, 1933*

1. The eighteenth article of amendment to the Constitution of the United States is hereby repealed.

2. The transportation or importation into any State, Territory, or possession of the United States for delivery or use therein of intoxicating liquors, in violation of the laws thereof, is hereby prohibited.

3. The article shall be inoperative unless it shall have been ratified as an amendment to the Constitution by conventions in the several States, as provided in the Constitution, within seven years from the date of the submission hereof to the States by the Congress.

**Amendment 22**

*Ratified February 27, 1951*

1. No person shall be elected to the office of the President more than twice, and no person who has held the office of President, or acted as President, for more than two years of a term to which some other person was elected President shall be elected to the office of the President more than once. But this Article shall not apply to any person holding the office of President, when this Article was proposed by the Congress, and shall not prevent any person who may be holding the office of President, or acting as President, during the term within which this Article becomes operative from holding the office of President or acting as President during the remainder of such term.

2. This article shall be inoperative unless it shall have been ratified as an amendment to the Constitution by the legislatures of three-fourths of the several States within seven years from the date of its submission to the States by the Congress.

**Amendment 23**

*Ratified March 29, 1961*

1. The District constituting the seat of Government of the United States shall appoint in such manner as the

Congress may direct: A number of electors of President and Vice President equal to the whole number of Senators and Representatives in Congress to which the District would be entitled if it were a State, but in no event more than the least populous State; they shall be in addition to those appointed by the States, but they shall be considered, for the purposes of the election of President and Vice President, to be electors appointed by a State; and they shall meet in the District and perform such duties as provided by the twelfth article of amendment.

2. The Congress shall have power to enforce this article by appropriate legislation.

**Amendment 24**

*Ratified January 23, 1964*

1. The right of citizens of the United States to vote in any primary or other election for President or Vice President, for electors for President or Vice President, or for Senator or Representative in Congress, shall not be denied or abridged by the United States or any State by reason of failure to pay any poll tax or other tax.
2. The Congress shall have power to enforce this article by appropriate legislation.

**Amendment 25**

*Ratified February 10, 1967*

1. In case of the removal of the President from office or of his death or resignation, the Vice President shall become President.
2. Whenever there is a vacancy in the office of the Vice President, the President shall nominate a Vice President who shall take office upon confirmation by a majority vote of both Houses of Congress.
3. Whenever the President transmits to the President pro tempore of the Senate and the Speaker of the House of Representatives his written declaration that he is unable to discharge the powers and duties of his office, and until he transmits to them a written declaration to the contrary, such powers and duties shall be discharged by the Vice President as Acting President.
4. Whenever the Vice President and a majority of either the principal officers of the executive departments or of such other body as Congress may by law provide, transmit to the President pro tempore of the Senate and the Speaker of the House of Representatives their written declaration that the President is unable to discharge the powers and duties of his office, the Vice President shall immediately assume the powers and duties of the office as Acting President.

Thereafter, when the President transmits to the President pro tempore of the Senate and the Speaker of the House of Representatives his written declaration that no inability exists, he shall resume the powers and duties of his office unless the Vice President and a majority of either the principal officers of the executive department or of such other body as Congress may by law provide, transmit within four days to the President pro tempore of the Senate and the Speaker of the House of Representatives their written declaration that the President is unable to discharge the powers and duties of his office. Thereupon Congress shall decide the issue, assembling within forty eight hours for that purpose if not in session. If the Congress, within twenty one days after receipt of the latter written declaration, or, if Congress is not in session, within twenty one days after Congress is required to assemble, determines by two thirds vote of both Houses that the President is unable to discharge the powers and duties of his office, the Vice President shall continue to discharge the same as Acting President; otherwise, the President shall resume the powers and duties of his office.

**Amendment 26**

*Ratified July 1, 1971*

1. The right of citizens of the United States, who are eighteen years of age or older, to vote shall not be denied or abridged by the United States or by any State on account of age.
2. The Congress shall have power to enforce this article by appropriate legislation.

**Amendment 27**

*Ratified May 7, 1992*

No law, varying the compensation for the services of the Senators and Representatives, shall take effect, until an election of Representatives shall have intervened.

# Presidents of the United States

| | President | Took office | Left office | Party | Vice-president | Term |
|---|---|---|---|---|---|---|
| 1 | George Washington | April 30, 1789 | March 4, 1797 | No party | John Adams | 1/2 |
| 2 | John Adams | March 4, 1797 | March 4, 1801 | Federalist | Thomas Jefferson | 3 |
| 3 | Thomas Jefferson | March 4, 1801 | March 4, 1809 | Democratic-Republican | Aaron Burr / George Clinton | 4/5 |
| 4 | James Madison | March 4, 1809 | March 4, 1817 | Democratic-Republican | George Clinton[1], vacant / Elbridge Gerry[1], vacant | 6/7 |
| 5 | James Monroe | March 4, 1817 | March 4, 1825 | Democratic-Republican | Daniel Tompkins | 8/9 |
| 6 | John Quincy Adams | March 4, 1825 | March 4, 1829 | Democratic-Republican | John Calhoun | 10 |
| 7 | Andrew Jackson | March 4, 1829 | March 4, 1837 | Democratic | John Calhoun[2], vacant / Martin Van Buren | 11/12 |
| 8 | Martin Van Buren | March 4, 1837 | March 4, 1841 | Democratic | Richard Johnson | 13 |
| 9 | William H. Harrison | March 4, 1841 | April 4, 1841[1] | Whig | John Tyler | 14 |
| 10 | John Tyler | April 4, 1841 | March 4, 1845 | Whig, no party[3] | vacant | |
| 11 | James K. Polk | March 4, 1845 | March 4, 1849 | Democratic | George Dallas | 15 |
| 12 | Zachary Taylor | March 4, 1849 | July 9, 1850[1] | Whig | Millard Fillmore | 16 |
| 13 | Millard Fillmore | July 9, 1850 | March 4, 1853 | Whig | vacant | |
| 14 | Franklin Pierce | March 4, 1853 | March 4, 1857 | Democratic | William King[1], vacant | 17 |
| 15 | James Buchanan | March 4, 1857 | March 4, 1861 | Democratic | John Breckinridge | 18 |
| 16 | Abraham Lincoln | March 4, 1861 | April 15, 1865[4] | Republican National Union[5] | Hannibal Hamlin / Andrew Johnson | 19/20 |
| 17 | Andrew Johnson | April 15, 1865 | March 4, 1869 | Democratic National Union[5] | vacant | |

| | President | Took office | Left office | Party | Vice-president | Term |
|---|---|---|---|---|---|---|
| 18 | Ulysses S. Grant | March 4, 1869 | March 4, 1877 | Republican | Schuyler Colfax, Henry Wilson[1], vacant | 21/22 |
| 19 | Rutherford B. Hayes | March 4, 1877 | March 4, 1881 | Republican | William Wheeler | 23 |
| 20 | James Garfield | March 4, 1881 | September 19, 1881[4] | Republican | Chester A. Arthur | 24 |
| 21 | Chester A. Arthur | September 19, 1881 | March 4, 1885 | Republican | vacant | |
| 22 | Grover Cleveland | March 4, 1885 | March 4, 1889 | Democratic | Thomas Hendricks[1], vacant | 25 |
| 23 | Benjamin Harrison | March 4, 1889 | March 4, 1893 | Republican | Levi Morton | 26 |
| 24 | Grover Cleveland (2nd term) | March 4, 1893 | March 4, 1897 | Democratic | Adlai E. Stevenson | 27 |
| 25 | William McKinley | March 4, 1897 | September 14, 1901[4] | Republican | Garret Hobart[1], vacant / Theodore Roosevelt | 28/29 |
| 26 | Theodore Roosevelt | September 14, 1901 | March 4, 1909 | Republican | vacant, Charles Fairbanks | 30 |
| 27 | William H. Taft | March 4, 1909 | March 4, 1913 | Republican | James Sherman[1], vacant | 31 |
| 28 | Woodrow Wilson | March 4, 1913 | March 4, 1921 | Democratic | Thomas Marshall | 32/33 |
| 29 | Warren G. Harding | March 4, 1921 | August 2, 1923[1] | Republican | Calvin Coolidge | 34 |
| 30 | Calvin Coolidge | August 2, 1923 | March 4, 1929 | Republican | vacant, Charles Dawes | 35 |
| 31 | Herbert Hoover | March 4, 1929 | March 4, 1933 | Republican | Charles Curtis | 36 |
| 32 | Franklin D. Roosevelt | March 4, 1933 | April 12, 1945[1] | Democratic | John Garner, Henry Wallace, Harry S. Truman | 37/38, 39, 40 |
| 33 | Harry S. Truman | April 12, 1945 | January 20, 1953 | Democratic | vacant, Alben Barkley | 41 |
| 34 | Dwight D. Eisenhower | January 20, 1953 | January 20, 1961 | Republican | Richard Nixon | 42/43 |
| 35 | John F. Kennedy | January 20, 1961 | November 22, 1963[4] | Democratic | Lyndon B. Johnson | 44 |
| 36 | Lyndon B. Johnson | November 22, 1963 | January 20, 1969 | Democratic | vacant, Hubert Humphrey | 45 |
| 37 | Richard Nixon | January 20, 1969 | August 9, 1974[2] | Republican | Spiro Agnew / Spiro Agnew[2], vacant, Gerald Ford | 46/47 |

| | President | Took office | Left office | Party | Vice-president | Term |
|---|---|---|---|---|---|---|
| 38 | Gerald Ford | August 9, 1974 | January 20, 1977 | Republican | vacant, Nelson Rockefeller | |
| 39 | Jimmy Carter | January 20, 1977 | January 20, 1981 | Democratic | Walter Mondale | 48 |
| 40 | Ronald Reagan | January 20, 1981 | January 20, 1989 | Republican | George H.W. Bush | 49/50 |
| 41 | George H.W. Bush | January 20, 1989 | January 20, 1993 | Republican | Dan Quayle | 51 |
| 42 | Bill Clinton | January 20, 1993 | January 20, 2001 | Democratic | Al Gore | 52/53 |
| 43 | George W. Bush | January 20, 2001 | Incumbent (term expires January 20, 2009) | Republican | Dick Cheney | 54/55 |

**Notes**

1. Died in office of natural causes.
2. Resigned.
3. Former Democrat who ran for vice-president on Whig ticket. Clashed with Whig congressional leaders and was expelled from the Whig Party in 1841.
4. Assassinated.
5. Abraham Lincoln and Andrew Johnson were, respectively, a Republican and a Democrat who ran on the National Union ticket in 1864.

# Map of the United States

# Glossary

**ace:** a fighter pilot who shoots down a specific number of enemy aircraft in combat

**acquired immune deficiency syndrome (AIDS):** a disease of the immune system, caused by exchange of bodily fluids with an infected person, that results in increased susceptibility to infection and certain cancers

**affirmative action:** a program that seeks to redress historical injustices by giving preferential treatment to members of minority or disadvantaged groups, especially in employment and education

**Agent Orange:** a herbicide, now known to be extremely toxic, used by US forces during the Vietnam War to clear jungle vegetation and expose enemy forces to attack

**agrarian:** of or relating to the land, especially its ownership or cultivation

**aide-de-camp:** a military officer who acts as a confidential assistant to a senior officer or general

**al-Qaida:** a terrorist network founded in the mid-1990s by Saudi Arabian Muslim radical Osama bin Laden

**Allies:** the nations united against the Axis powers in World War II, which included Britain and the Commonwealth (including Canada), France, and later the Soviet Union, the US, and China

**American dream:** the American belief that everyone in the United States has the chance to achieve success and material prosperity

**amphibious:** a military invasion involving forces landing by sea

**anarchist:** an advocate of anarchism (the belief that all government should be abolished) or of political disorder

**annexation:** the incorporation of another's territory into one's own

**anti-Federalists:** opponents of the new constitution after the American Revolution

**anti-Semitism:** views, actions, or policies that are hostile to or prejudiced against Jewish people

**armistice:** an agreement to cease armed conflict

**arms race:** a competition between nations for superiority in the development and accumulation of weapons

**arsenal:** a government building where weapons and ammunitions are stored and manufactured

**artisan:** a person who is skilled in a particular craft, such as pottery or weaving

**atomic bomb:** an explosive device involving the massive release of energy from the fission of heavy nuclei by neutrons sustaining a rapid chain reaction

**autonomy:** the right of political independence and self-government

**baby boom:** a temporary large increase in the birth rate, especially in the 15 years following World War II

**ballot:** a single round of voting

**beatnik:** a member of the beat generation, a movement of young people in the 1950s who rejected the conventions of society in their beliefs, habits, and dress

**Black Codes:** laws passed by most Southern states after the Civil War that restricted the labour rights of blacks, prevented land ownership by former slaves, and prohibited interracial marriages

**Black Tuesday:** the day the New York stock market crashed, Tuesday, October 29, 1929

**bootlegger:** a person who unlawfully produced, transported, or sold alcohol during Prohibition (1920–1933)

**boycott:** a refusal to purchase or handle goods from a particular person, company, nation, etc., in order to coerce them into behaving differently or to punish them

**brinkmanship:** the policy, especially in international relations, of taking a dispute to the brink of conflict in the hope of pressuring one's opponent into making concessions

**capital:** money that can be used to produce further wealth—for example, by starting a business

**capitalism:** an economic system characterized by a free competitive market and motivation by profit, and based on the private ownership of the means of production and distribution of goods

**carpetbaggers:** post–Civil War agents, responsible for putting the policies of Radical Reconstruction into practice, who used Reconstruction as an opportunity to seek and profit from political office

**cartel:** a group of producers or suppliers who collaborate to set prices, control production, and limit supply and competition

**censure:** to express official disapproval or condemnation of a person or thing—for example, by a vote of a legislature

**charter:** a written grant, issued by the sovereign power of a country, bestowing certain rights and privileges on a person, a corporation, or the people

**cholera:** an infectious and often fatal disease of the small intestine resulting in severe vomiting and diarrhea, usually caused by ingesting food or water contaminated with the bacterium *Vibrio cholerae*

**civil libertarians:** civil rights activists

**civil war:** a war fought between citizens or opposing groups within a country

**codify:** to arrange laws, rules, principles, etc., into an organized system or code

**colonialism:** a policy in which a country acquires or maintains colonies and develops trade for its own benefit

**commission system:** a system of municipal government in which executive, legislative, and administrative powers are in the hands of an elected commission

**Commonwealth:** an intergovernmental organization composed of Britain and many nations that were formerly members of the British empire

**communism:** a political ideology that seeks to bring about economic equality in society by seizing power from those who own property and distributing it to those who do not; in practice, it is characterized by government ownership of the means of production and centralized planning of the economy

**concentration camps:** military prison compounds for holding large numbers of captured enemy soldiers and/or their families, first used by Spain in Cuba in the late 19th century; unsanitary conditions in the camps often resulted in many deaths caused by disease

**conductor:** a person who acted as a guide or leader along the Underground Railroad

**confederacy:** an alliance of Native American people formed to allow them to pursue common goals

**Confederacy:** see *Confederate States of America (CSA)*

**Confederate States of America (CSA):** the confederation of the 11 Southern states (Alabama, Arkansas, Florida, Georgia, Louisiana, Mississippi, North Carolina, South Carolina, Tennessee, Texas, and Virginia) that seceded from the United States in 1861, an act that triggered the beginning of the American Civil War (also called the *Confederacy*)

**conquistador:** a conqueror, especially one of the Spanish soldiers who conquered Mexico, Peru, and Central America in the 16th century

**conscientious objector:** a person who objects to conforming to military service for religious or other reasons

**conspicuous consumption:** the acquisition and display of expensive goods in order to impress others

**constitutional monarchy:** a political system in which a king or queen rules as head of state to the extent permitted by a constitution

**consumerism:** the preoccupation with consumer goods and their acquisition

**Continental:** a banknote issued by the Continental Congress during the American Revolution

**contraband:** anything that has been smuggled, imported, or exported illegally

**copperhead:** a member of the Northern Democratic Party who opposed the war against the Confederacy, calling for an end to the draft and negotiated settlement; some were accused of conspiring with the Confederacy and imprisoned

**corporation:** a legal entity that allows many owners to act together as a single company, distinct from the individuals who own it, particularly in business

**council–manager system:** a system of municipal government in which an elected city council makes policy and passes bylaws, and hires a city manager to supervise government operations and implement its policies

**coup:** the violent or illegal overthrow of a government and seizure of political power, especially by the military

**creed:** a set of fundamental beliefs, such as a philosophy of life

**Croix de Guerre:** a French military award for heroism in battle

**Crusades:** the military expeditions made by European Christians in the 11th, 12th, and 13th centuries in response to centuries of Muslim wars of expansion

**cultural imperialism:** the powerful influence of one nation's culture in other nations

**deflation:** a policy or process of reducing general economic activity, including lower prices and a reduced money supply

**democracy:** a system of government by the entire population or all the eligible members of a state, either directly or through elected representatives; any organization governed by democratic principles

**desertion:** the act of running away from military service without permission and intending not to return

**despotism:** a government or political system under the control of a ruler who exercises absolute power

**destroyer:** a small, fast warship with light armour that is used to protect other ships, attack submarines, etc.

**détente:** the attempt to ease tense relations between countries

**domino theory:** the Cold War theory that the spread of communism to one nation would lead inevitably to communist control over neighbouring nations (the domino effect), particularly in Southeast Asia

**Dow Jones Industrial Average:** an index measuring the average level of share prices on the New York Stock Exchange

**draft:** the compulsory order to join the armed services in time of war

**draft dodger:** a person who illegally tries to avoid performing compulsory military service

**ecological footprint:** a measure of sustainability in which a unit of land area is used to demonstrate the ecological pressure caused by residents of a country

**economic disparity:** the gap between people who have low incomes and those who are rich

**economic indicators:** numerical measures—such as gross national product (GNP); national debt; and rates of unemployment, job creation, and inflation—that are used to assess the overall performance of a country's economy

**effigy:** a crude representation in the form of a sculptured figure or dummy of somebody or something who is disliked, and intended especially for ridicule, scorn, etc.

**elector:** a person who votes or is entitled to vote in an election

**emancipation:** the act of being freed from some restriction, especially from slavery

**Emancipation Proclamation:** a proclamation issued by President Abraham Lincoln that declared freedom for all slaves in states still in rebellion against the federal government, effective January 1, 1863

**embargo:** an official restriction on commerce, usually temporary, prohibiting trade in a given commodity or with a particular nation

**Enlightenment:** an 18th-century philosophical movement in western Europe in which reason and individualism were emphasized at the expense of religious and political traditions

**Espionage Act:** legislation passed in 1917 that made it a crime to convey information that would interfere with the "operation or success" of US armed forces in World War I or "promote the success of the enemy"

**evangelical Christianity:** a Christian belief system characterized by an intense and personal Biblical faith

**exceptionalism:** the idea that the creation of America was a unique historical experiment and that America holds a special position in the world

**excise tax:** a duty or tax on goods and commodities produced or sold within the country of origin

**excommunicate:** to officially exclude a baptized Christian from taking part in Communion or from other formal activities of the Church

**existential:** believing that each person is free to act but is isolated in a world that is beyond one's ability to control

**expatriate:** a person who, by choice or otherwise, lives in a country other than the one in which he or she was born

**fascist:** of or related to fascism, a system of government characterized by dictatorship, repression of opposition, and extreme nationalism

**Federal Reserve Board:** the central bank system of the United States (also called "the Fed")

**Federalists:** supporters of the new constitution after the American Revolution

**feminism:** the belief in the need to secure, or a commitment to securing, equality of the sexes in terms of rights and opportunities

**feudal:** a traditional system of political organization, dominated by nobles or warlords who each control their own territory largely independent of any central government authority

**fiscal:** relating to financial matters in general or to public revenues, especially the revenue from taxation

**forty-niner:** a person who participated in the California gold rush of 1849

**Fourteen Points:** President Woodrow Wilson's declaration of goals in World War I, including open international agreements and free trade, minimal use of armaments, and the formation of an international agency to promote world peace and security

**franchise:** the right to vote in elections

**free state:** any of the states that prohibited slavery before the American Civil War

**free trade:** international trade free from protective duties and quotas

**French Revolution:** the revolutionary movement that shook France between 1787 and 1799, reaching its first climax in 1789 and ending the *ancien régime*

**frontier:** the border area between white settlements and Native American territory; a region at the edge of a settled area

**fundamentalist:** any religious movement that seeks to return to the founding principles of a faith in the belief that holy texts are the literal and authentic word of God

**generation gap:** the difference in attitudes, behaviour, and interests between people of different generations, especially between parents and their children

**gold standard:** a system of defining the value of a currency in terms of gold, for which the currency may be exchanged

**Great Depression:** the economic crisis in the United States and other countries that began with the crash of the New York stock market in October 1929 and continued through most of the 1930s; it was characterized by mass unemployment and widespread poverty

**gross national product (GNP):** the total value of goods produced and services provided within a country in a year

**hippie:** a young person, especially in the 1960s, who rejected accepted societal values, advocated peace and free love, and adopted an unconventional physical appearance, usually with long hair, jeans, beards, etc.

**holding company:** a company that operates by buying enough stocks or bonds in one or more other companies to give it a controlling interest in each

**Hoovervilles:** shantytowns established in US cities during the Great Depression, named contemptuously after President Herbert Hoover

**Hundred Days:** the first three months of President Franklin Roosevelt's administration, during which more than a dozen new laws were passed and numerous federal agencies were created to address economic and social problems

**ideology:** a set of values, beliefs, and opinions that inform the thoughts and actions of an individual or a group

**illegal combatants:** the term used by the George W. Bush administration to describe prisoners taken in Afghanistan and Iraq so that the administration would not have to abide by recognized standards for treatment of prisoners of war in dealing with them

**impeachment:** the removal of a president from office by Congress for having taken part in criminal activity

**imperial:** involving or relating to the authority of a country over other countries or colonies

**indentured servant:** an immigrant to North America between the 17th and 19th centuries who agreed to work for an employer for a number of years in exchange for the cost of his or her voyage to North America, food, and shelter

**Indian agent:** an official who acts as a government representative to communities of Native Americans

**Indian Removal Act of 1830:** a law that in effect evicted all Native Americans from their hereditary lands in the East and sent them to lands west of the Mississippi in what are now the states of Oklahoma and Arkansas

**individualism:** the idea that people should live in a way that makes them independent and self-reliant, rather than subordinate to collective interests

**Industrial Revolution:** the social and economic transformation of society as a result of the majority of the working population shifting from agriculture to industry, especially that which occurred in Britain in the second half of the 18th century and the first half of the 19th century

**inflation:** an increase in the supply of currency relative to the availability of goods and services, resulting in a general increase in the price of goods and services and a fall in the purchasing value of money

**insurgent:** a person who rebels against authority, especially one who belongs to a group involved in an uprising against the government or a ruler of a country

**integrate:** to allow all to share the same facilities and opportunities regardless of race, ethnicity, religion, gender, or social class

**International Monetary Fund (IMF):** an agency of the United Nations established in 1945 to promote international monetary cooperation and the stabilization of exchange rates

**internment:** the confinement of a person or people considered a security threat, especially during war

**Iron Curtain:** the Cold War boundary between the Soviet Bloc countries of eastern Europe and the western European countries; the term was coined by British Prime Minister Winston Churchill in March 1946

**isolationism:** a government policy of non-involvement with the affairs of other countries, based on the belief that national interests are best served by avoiding economic and political alliances with other countries

**Jim Crow laws:** laws passed by Southern state governments following the US Supreme Court decision in *Plessy v. Ferguson* in 1896 to segregate black and white citizens; "Jim Crow" was a euphemism for "black"

**kamikaze:** during World War II, a Japanese aircraft loaded with explosives and deliberately crashed onto a target by its pilot

**Kremlin:** the government of Russia or the former Soviet Union

**Ku Klux Klan:** a secretive organization, founded in the South after the Civil War, that opposed Reconstruction and that assaulted and murdered former slaves and the Northerners who had come to assist them; it was revived in the early 20th century, harassing and intimidating blacks and other minorities

**laissez-faire:** an economic policy of government non-interference in the economy (from French, "let act")

**League of Nations:** an intergovernmental organization dedicated to preventing armed conflict, promoted by US President Woodrow Wilson in 1919 following World War I; it grew to 63 member states and was dissolved in 1946 after the founding of the United Nations

**Lost Generation:** the generation that came of age during or just after World War I, viewed as cynical and disillusioned

**Loyalists:** American colonists who supported Britain during the American Revolution, many of whom later migrated to Canada

**lynch:** to seize a person and put him or her to death, especially by hanging, for an alleged offence immediately and without a legal trial

**magazine:** a structure on land or on a ship where military equipment or supplies—including weapons, ammunition, and explosives—are stored

**malaria:** an infectious disease common in hot countries, characterized by recurring chills and fever, and caused by a parasite that is transmitted by the bite of infected mosquitoes

**manifest destiny:** the powerful 19th-century idea that the US should expand to occupy the entire continent, from the Atlantic to the Pacific

**Mason-Dixon Line:** the boundary that separated Pennsylvania from Maryland, and that represented the dividing line between free and slave states in the years before the American Civil War

**Mayflower Compact:** the document signed by 41 of the male passengers onboard the *Mayflower* prior to the ship's landing in Plymouth, Massachusetts, which became the foundation of that colony's government

**mayor–council system:** a system of municipal government in which an elected mayor and city council share legislative and administrative authority

**mercantilism:** an early modern European economic theory and system that advocated the establishment of colonies to provide raw materials and markets

**mercenary:** a professional soldier serving in a foreign army in exchange for payment

**Middle Ages:** the period of European history generally considered as beginning with the fall of the Roman empire in the 5th century and ending with the beginning of the Italian Renaissance in the 14th century

**military-industrial complex:** a nation's military and the industries supplying it considered as a combined influence on public policy

**militia:** a military force raised from the civilian population that can serve full time in an emergency; a reserve army that is not part of the regular armed forces but that can be called up during emergencies

**misogyny:** hatred of women

**missionary:** a person sent to another country by a church to spread its faith or to perform social or medical work

**Mormon:** a member of the Church of Jesus Christ of Latter-day Saints, founded in 1830 by Joseph Smith and now centred in Salt Lake City, Utah

**muckraker:** a critic who spreads information about real or alleged scandals, usually for political purposes

**napalm:** a highly flammable jelly, produced by mixing a thickening agent with gasoline and used in flamethrowers and firebombs

**Napoleonic Wars:** a series of campaigns fought under Napoleon I against Austria, Russia, Great Britain, Portugal, Prussia, and other European powers, lasting from 1800 to 1815 and ending with Napoleon's defeat at the Battle of Waterloo

**Nation of Islam:** a black Islamic organization founded circa 1930, which became prominent under the influence of Malcolm X and whose members are known as Black Muslims

**nationalize:** to take over (a business, property, industry, etc.) from private ownership on behalf of the state

**nepotism:** favouritism shown by a person in power to relatives, especially in offering employment or other privileges

**neutrality:** the state of being neutral, characterized by non-involvement in wars and disputes, not taking sides, and not joining alliances

**New Deal:** the economic and social policies introduced by Franklin D. Roosevelt in the 1930s to counteract the effects of the Great Depression

**nuclear weapon:** a missile, bomb, etc., involving the release of energy by nuclear fission, fusion, or both

**nullification:** the doctrine or theory that state governments have the right to declare void (nullify) laws within their borders that they believe violate the Constitution

**pacifism:** the belief that war and violence are morally unjustified and that all disputes should be resolved peacefully

**pacify:** to bring peace to an area, people, situation, etc., often ending conflict or unrest through the use of military force

**Palmer Raids:** raids against communists, radicals, and immigrants ordered by Attorney General Mitchell Palmer in 1920 after a bomb blast outside his house; the raids resulted in some 6,000 arrests and 600 deportations

**Panama Canal:** a canal completed in 1914 across the Isthmus of Panama, connecting the Caribbean Sea (Atlantic Ocean) and the Pacific Ocean and controlled by the United States until 2000

**partisan:** showing strong loyalty to a political cause or group

**Patriot:** a colonist who favoured radical action against the British authorities in colonial America

**patronage:** the practice of appointing friends and political supporters to public office

**peace dividend:** an anticipated redirection of funds from military spending to social programs after the end of the Cold War

**Pilgrim:** one of the English Puritans who sailed to North America on the *Mayflower* and founded a settlement at Plymouth, Massachusetts in 1620

**planter:** a person who owns or manages a plantation

**platform:** the publicly announced policies of a political party seeking election, understood as forming the basis of its actions in the event that it should come to power

**plutocracy:** the rule of a society by the wealthy

**polygamy:** the custom of having more than one wife or husband at the same time

**Progressivism:** an early 20th-century political movement that promoted policies such as slum improvement, public health, and women's suffrage, intended to reform the US government, economy, and society

**proletariat:** working-class people

**protectionist:** a supporter of protectionism, the economic theory or practice of protecting domestic industries

**provisional government:** a temporary system of government, usually established in a time of crisis

**proxy war:** a war instigated by a nation that does not itself become involved in the conflict

**pull factors:** influences that compel people to immigrate to (be pulled to) one place from another

**Puritan:** a member of a group of Protestants in England in the 16th and 17th centuries and America in the 17th century who called for strict religious discipline as well as the simplification of the ceremonies of the Church of England

**push factors:** influences that compel people to emigrate from (be pushed from) one place to another

**radical:** a person who holds extreme views or ideas or belongs to a political party holding extreme views

**ratification:** the process of making something valid by formal confirmation or approval

**recall:** a voting mechanism that allows citizens to remove from office a politician who has been unresponsive to the needs of constituents

**Reconstruction:** the period following the Civil War during which the Confederate states were reorganized under federal control and blacks were granted civil and economic rights

**redcoat:** A British soldier serving overseas, especially during the American Revolution

**referendum:** a direct yes–no vote by the electorate on a policy proposal

**Renaissance:** the period in western European history from the 14th to the 16th century, characterized by intensified classical scholarship and major cultural and artistic change, and generally held to be the transition between the Middle Ages and the modern world

**rendition:** the secret practice of transporting suspected terrorists to countries where they will almost certainly be tortured

**republic:** a state in which supreme power is held by the people, their elected representatives, or an elected or nominated president, instead of by a monarch, etc.

**Roosevelt Corollary:** an amendment to the Monroe Doctrine claiming the right of the United States to intervene in stabilizing the economic affairs of small nations in the Caribbean and Central America if those nations were unable to pay their international debts

**sachem:** the supreme chief of some Native North American people

**salutary neglect:** Britain's policy of interfering very little in colonial affairs from about 1690 to 1760

**Sandinista:** a member of a revolutionary organization that controlled Nicaragua from 1979 to 1990

**secede:** to formally withdraw from an alliance, a federal union, or other organization

**sectional:** of, relating to, or characteristic of a section or sections of a country, society, community, etc.

**secular humanism:** a philosophy that affirms the ability of people to lead ethical lives without reference to the supernatural and that seeks to separate religion from politics

**sedition:** acts or words intended to provoke or incite rebellion against government authority

**Sedition Act:** legislation passed in 1918 that extended the powers of the Espionage Act and criminalized speaking against the draft and military recruiting, encouraging soldiers to disobey orders or defect, discouraging the public from buying Liberty Bonds, or encouraging resistance to the United States or promoting the success of its enemies

**segregate:** to enforce racial separation of people, in a community, etc.

**settlement house:** as centre providing community services in an underprivileged area

**sharecropping:** a system in which families received a plot of land, which they were free to cultivate, in exchange for paying one-third to one-half of their crop to the landowner at harvest time

**slave state:** any of the 15 states in which slavery was legal until the American Civil War

**slave trade:** the business of capturing human beings and buying and selling them as slaves, especially the transporting of African blacks to the United States to be sold into slavery

**smallpox:** a highly contagious viral disease marked by high fever and pustules, usually leaving permanent scars

**social Darwinism:** a discredited social theory, advanced in the late 19th century, that applied Charles Darwin's theory of natural selection to the study of human society to argue that individuals, groups, and peoples gain advantage over others due to genetic or biological superiority

**socialist:** one who espouses socialism, a political and economic system in which the means of production and distribution of goods are owned collectively and political power is exercised by the whole community

**sovereignty:** the right to autonomy or self-government of a community, nation, etc.

**Soviet Union:** the communist state established following the Russian Revolution (1917), which included Russia and neighbouring territories (Ukraine, Georgia, Kazakhstan, etc.)

**space race:** the competition between the US and the Soviet Union in developments and achievements in the field of space exploration

**speculator:** someone who invests in something in the hope of making a profit but with the possibility of loss

**spirituals:** religious songs derived from the musical traditions of African-Americans in the Southern US

**suffrage:** the right to vote in political elections

**superpower:** a nation with supreme power and influence, especially the United States, and formerly the USSR

**supply-side economics:** an economic philosophy that favours reducing taxes in order to spur investment and create jobs

**Taliban:** a fundamentalist Islamic movement that ruled Afghanistan between 1996 and 2001

**tariff:** a duty or duties levied by a government on a particular class of imports or exports

**temperance movement:** the 19th-century reform movement that stressed the damaging effects of alcohol on the economy and family life, and sought to reinforce middle-class virtues of sobriety and thrift

**tenant farmer:** a farmer who farms rented land and pays the owner in cash or with produce

**tenement:** a large residential building with self-contained apartments or rooms rented cheaply and with only basic amenities, especially in a poor area of a city

**Terror:** the period of the French Revolution between September 1793 and July 1794 during which the ruling faction attempted to eliminate domestic and foreign opposition to the Revolution and over the course of which 40,000 French citizens were executed (also called "the Reign of Terror")

**three-fifths rule:** the rule agreed on by the delegates at the Constitutional Convention whereby, for purposes of calculating the states' populations for representation in Congress, five slaves were counted as three freemen

**Three R's:** principles on which President Franklin Roosevelt based his first New Deal: relief, recovery, and reform

**tight money policy:** an economic policy of restricting credit by maintaining high interest rates

**Transcendentalism:** a philosophical system that emphasizes intuition or the divine, especially associated with Ralph Waldo Emerson and other New England writers

**trust:** a group of corporations in a single industry (such as steel, oil, sugar, or railroads) that organize themselves into a single entity

**U-boat:** a German submarine used in World War I; short for "undersea boat"

**undefended border:** the border between Canada and the United States, which historically has had only civilian customs stations along its nearly 9,000-kilometre length

**Underground Railroad:** a secret network established to help fugitive slaves escape from the Southern US to the North or to Canada in the years before the American Civil War, consisting of safe houses and transportation

**unilaterally:** carried out in a unilateral way, that is, decided or acted on by only one involved party or nation irrespective of what the others do

**Union:** **1.** the United States of America; **2.** the side of the Northern states during the American Civil War, or its armed forces

**United Nations (UN):** an international organization of nations formed in 1945 to succeed the League of Nations and promote international peace, security, and cooperation

**utopia:** a place or state of things considered ideal or perfect; a condition of social or political perfection

**war bond:** a bond issued by a government to help finance war expenditures

**xenophobic:** of or characterized by a deep dislike or fear of foreigners, or foreign customs, cultures, or things

**Yom Kippur War:** the 1973 Arab–Israeli War, fought from October 6 (the day of Yom Kippur) to October 24, 1973, between Israel and a coalition of Egypt and Syria

# Index

# Credits

## IMAGES

### Chapter 1

Page 3: The Granger Collection. Page 5: Department of Anthropology, University of Missouri. Page 8: The Granger Collection. Page 9: Iroquois Setting Out on an Expedition, engraved by J. Laroque (coloured engraving), Grasset de Saint-Sauveur, Jacques (1757–1810) (after) / © Collection of the New-York Historical Society, USA / The Bridgeman Art Library International. Page 11 (top to bottom): The Granger Collection; The Granger Collection. Page 12 (left to right): Library of Congress; © Stapleton Collection/CORBIS. Page 15 (top to bottom): © Bettmann/CORBIS; Library of Congress. Page 18: The Granger Collection. Page19 (left to right): © Bettmann/CORBIS; The Granger Collection. Page 21: The Granger Collection. Page 22: The Granger Collection. Page 23: © Burstein Collection/CORBIS. Page 25 (top to bottom): The Granger Collection; © The Print Collector/Alamy. Page 26: The History Project. Page 27: © Museum of the City of New York/CORBIS. Page 28: © Bettmann/CORBIS. Page 30: Examination of a Witch, 1853 (oil on canvas), Matteson, Tompkins Harrison (1813–84) / © Peabody Essex Museum, Salem, Massachusetts, USA / The Bridgeman Art Library International.

### Chapter 2

Page 35: The Death of General Wolfe (1727–59), c. 1771 (oil on panel) (see also 105409, 119752 & 124902), West, Benjamin (1738–1820) / Private Collection, Phillips, Fine Art Auctioneers, New York, USA / The Bridgeman Art Library International. Page 39: Olaudah Equiano alias Gustavus Vassa, a slave, 1789 (mezzotint) / British Library, London, UK, © British Library Board. All Rights Reserved / The Bridgeman Art Library International. Page 40: © SuperStock, Inc./SuperStock. Page 41: Library of Congress. Page 42: The Granger Collection. Page 44: Edward E. Ayer Collection/Newberry Library. Page 46: Massachusetts Historical Society. Page 47 (top to bottom): Connecticut Historical Society Museum. Gift of Rufus Matthewson; © CORBIS. Page 49 (top to bottom): © steve bly/Alamy; The Granger Collection. Page 51 (top to bottom): George III (1738–1820) (oil on canvas), Ramsay, Allan (1713–84) (studio of) / Scottish National Portrait Gallery, Edinburgh, Scotland / The Bridgeman Art Library International; The Colonial Williamsburg Foundation. Page 52: © North Wind Picture Archives/Alamy. Page 55: The Granger Collection. Page 57: © CORBIS. Page 58: The Granger Collection. Page 59: The Granger Collection. Page 60: The Granger Collection. Page 61: The Granger Collection.

### Chapter 3

Page 65: William Walcutt, Pulling Down the Statue of George III, o/c, 1857. Lafayette College Art Collection, Easton, Pennsylvania. Page 67 (top to bottom): The Granger Collection; The Granger Collection. Page 69: The Granger Collection. Page 70: The Granger Collection. Page 71: The Granger Collection. Page 72 (top to bottom): The Granger Collection; The Granger Collection. Page 75: The Granger Collection. Page 76: The Granger Collection. Page 77: The Granger Collection. Page 80: The Granger Collection. Page 81: The Granger Collection. Page 85: © CORBIS. Page 87: Library and Archives Canada, c-002001. Page 88: The Granger Collection. Page 91: The Granger Collection. Page 92: The Granger Collection. Page 93 (top to bottom): The Granger Collection; The Granger Collection.

## Chapter 4

Page 101: The Granger Collection. Page 102: Eno Collection, Miriam and Ira D. Wallach Division of Art, Prints and Photographs, The New York Public Library, Astor, Lenox and Tilden Foundations. Page 103: The Granger Collection. Page 104 (top to bottom): The Granger Collection; © Bettmann/CORBIS. Page 105: The Granger Collection. Page 106: © Visions of America, LLC/Alamy. Page 107: The Granger Collection. Page 108: The Granger Collection. Page 109: The Granger Collection. Page 112: Library of Congress. Page 113 (top to bottom): The Granger Collection; Thomas Jefferson Foundation, Inc. Page 114: Thomas Jefferson Foundation Inc. Page 116: The Granger Collection. Page 120: The Granger Collection. Page 121: The Granger Collection. Page 123: The Granger Collection. Page 124: Archives of Ontario, 971.034.LOS, The Pictorial Field-Book of the War of 1812 by Benson J. Lossing. Page 125: Library and Archives Canada, c-040894. Page 127: © Visual Arts Library (London)/Alamy. Page 131: © Bettmann/CORBIS. Page 132: The Granger Collection.

## Chapter 5

Page 137: Library of Congress. Page 139: The Granger Collection. Page 140: © Visual Arts Library (London)/Alamy. Page 141: © CORBIS. Page 143: The Granger Collection. Page 144: The Granger Collection. Page 145: Chief Justice Marshall (1755–1835) (oil on canvas), Harding, Chester (1792–1866) / Private Collection, Photo © Boltin Picture Library / The Bridgeman Art Library International. Page 146: The Granger Collection. Page 147: Library and Archives Canada, c-0052571. Page 148 (left to right): The Granger Collection; The Granger Collection. Page 149: © Sandy Felsenthal/CORBIS. Page 150: The Granger Collection. Page 151: © Bettmann/CORBIS. Page 152: © Bettmann/CORBIS. Page 155: Clipper Ship Poster, 1849 (print), American School (19th century) / Private Collection, Peter Newark American Pictures / The Bridgeman Art Library International. Page 157: The Granger Collection. Page 158 (top to bottom): LDS Church Archives; The Granger Collection. Page 159: © Bettmann/CORBIS. Page 160: Thomas Cole, American, 1801–1848, Distant View of Niagara Falls, 1830, Oil on panel, unframed: 47.9 × 60.6 cm (18⅞ × 23⅞ in.); framed: 27¾ × 31½ in. (70.5 × 80 cm), Friends of American Art Collection, 1946.396, The Art Institute of Chicago. Photography © The Art Institute of Chicago. Page 161: The Granger Collection. Page 162: I.N. Phelps Stokes Collection, Miriam and Ira D. Wallach Division of Art, Prints and Photographs, The New York Public Library, Astor, Lenox and Tilden Foundations. Page 163 (top to bottom): The Granger Collection; The Granger Collection. Page 164: The Granger Collection. Page 165: The Granger Collection. Page 166: The Granger Collection.

## Chapter 6

Page 171: Duke University Library. Page 172: The Granger Collection. Page 173 (top to bottom): The Granger Collection; Library of Congress. Page 175 (top to bottom): American Slave Market, 1852 (oil on canvas), Taylor (fl.1852) / © Chicago History Museum, USA / The Bridgeman Art Library International; The Granger Collection. Page 179: The Granger Collection. Page 180: The Granger Collection. Page 183: © Bettmann/CORBIS. Page 184: © CORBIS. Page 185: © CORBIS. Page 187 (top to bottom): © CORBIS; The Granger Collection. Page 191: © CORBIS. Page 193: The Granger Collection. Page 194 (clockwise): The Granger Collection; The Granger Collection; The Granger Collection. Page 195: The Granger Collection. Page 198: Library of Congress. Page 200: © Bettmann/CORBIS. Page 201: © Bettmann/CORBIS. Page 202: Library of Congress. Page 203: The Granger Collection. Page 204: Library of Congress. Page 205: © CORBIS. Page 206: © CORBIS.

## Chapter 7

Page 211: "Across the Continent, Westward the Course of Empire takes its way," 1868 (colour litho), Palmer, Frances Flora Bond (Fanny) (c. 1812–76) / Private Collection, Peter Newark American Pictures / The Bridgeman Art Library International. Page 214 (clockwise): © Bettmann/CORBIS; © CORBIS; The Granger Collection. Page 215: The Granger Collection. Page 217: The Granger Collection. Page 219: The Granger Collection. Page 221 (left to right): © CORBIS; The Granger Collection. Page 222: © Bettmann/CORBIS. Page 223: The Skating Pond, pub. by Currier and Ives, New York, 1862 (litho), Parsons, Charles (1821–1910) (after) / © Museum of the City of New York, USA / The Bridgeman Art Library International. Page 224: © Bettmann/CORBIS. Page 226: American Premier Underwriters, Inc. Page 230 (top to bottom): The Granger Collection; © CORBIS. Page 232: Library of Congress. Page 234: Kansas State Historical Society. Page 235: © Hulton-Deutsch Collection/CORBIS. Page 237: Library and Archives Canada, c-018737. Page 238:

Library of Congress. Page 239 (top to bottom): © CORBIS; The Granger Collection. Page 240 (top to bottom): Smithsonian; The Granger Collection. Page 241: The Granger Collection. Page 242: Smithsonian.

## Chapter 8

Page 247 (top to bottom): © Kevin Fleming/CORBIS; The Granger Collection. Page 248: The Granger Collection. Page 249: The Granger Collection. Page 251 (top to bottom): The Granger Collection; © CORBIS; © Bettmann/CORBIS. Page 252: Mary Evans Picture Library. Page 253: The Granger Collection. Page 254 (top to bottom): The Granger Collection; Ewing Galloway/Hulton Archive/Getty Images. Page 255 (left to right): The Granger Collection; The Granger Collection. Page 256: © Bettmann/CORBIS. Page 258 (top to bottom): The Granger Collection; The Granger Collection. Page 259: © CORBIS. Page 263: © CORBIS. Page 266 (left to right): © CORBIS; The Granger Collection. Page 267: Wikipedia. Page 267: The Granger Collection. Page 270: Portrait of Emma Goldman (1869–1940), 1926 (b/w photo), American Photographer (20th century) / Schlesinger Library, Radcliffe Institute, Harvard University / The Bridgeman Art Library International. Page 271: The Granger Collection. Page 272: © Culver Pictures, Inc./SuperStock. Page 274: © Bettmann/CORBIS. Page 275: The Granger Collection. Page 276: The Granger Collection. Page 277: The Granger Collection. Page 278: The Granger Collection. Page 279: The Granger Collection. Page 281: The Granger Collection.

## Chapter 9

Page 285: The Art Archive/Imperial War Museum. Page 286: © Bettmann/CORBIS. Page 287 (top to bottom): © CORBIS; © CORBIS/Bettmann. Page 288 (top to bottom): The Granger Collection; © CORBIS. Page 289: The Granger Collection. Page 290: © Bettmann/CORBIS. Page 291: © Bettmann/CORBIS. Page 292 (top to bottom): © David J. & Janice L. Frent Collection/CORBIS. Page 293: © CORBIS. Page 294 (top to bottom): © Bettmann/CORBIS; © Bettmann/CORBIS. Page 296: © CORBIS. Page 298: © Underwood & Underwood/CORBIS. Page 299: © Bettmann/CORBIS. Page 300: The Granger Collection. Page 303 (top to bottom): The Granger Collection; © CORBIS. Page 305: © Bettmann/CORBIS. Page 306: Mary Evans Picture Library. Page 308: The Granger Collection. Page 309: The Granger Collection. Page 310: © Bettmann/CORBIS. Page 311 (top to bottom): © Bettmann/CORBIS; From the book *Nurse Helen Fairchild WWI*, by Nelle F.H. Rote, niece of Nurse Fairchild. Page 312: The Granger Collection. Page 313: The Granger Collection. Page 315: © Bettmann/CORBIS. Page 317: © Bettmann/CORBIS. Page 318: Newman Library / Baruch College (CUNY). Page 319: Derek Grant. Page 320: The Granger Collection.

## Chapter 10

Page 325: © Geoffrey Clements/CORBIS. Page 326: © CORBIS. Page 330: © Bettmann/CORBIS. Page 332 (left to right): © Bettmann/CORBIS; The Granger Collection. Page 333 (top to bottom): © Underwood & Underwood/CORBIS; © Bettmann/CORBIS; © Bettmann/CORBIS. Page 334: © Bettmann/CORBIS. Page 335 (clockwise): © Bettmann/CORBIS; © Michael Ochs Archives/CORBIS; The Granger Collection; The Granger Collection. Page 336: Smithsonian. Page 337 (top to bottom): The Granger Collection; © Underwood & Underwood/CORBIS. Page 340: © CORBIS. Page 341: The Granger Collection. Page 343 (top to bottom): © Bettmann/CORBIS; © Bettmann/CORBIS. Page 346: © Museum of History and Industry/CORBIS. Page 347: © CORBIS. Page 348: © Michael Ochs Archives/CORBIS. Page 350: © Bettmann/CORBIS. Page 351 (left to right): © Underwood & Underwood/CORBIS; The Granger Collection. Page 353: © Bettmann/CORBIS. Page 354 (top to bottom): Wikipedia; The Granger Collection. Page 357: © Bettmann/CORBIS. Page 358: The Granger Collection.

## Chapter 11

Page 364: © CORBIS. Page 365: The Kobal Collection. Page 370: © Bettmann/CORBIS. Page 371: © Bettmann/CORBIS. Page 372: Margaret Bourke-White/Time & Life Pictures/Getty Images. Page 374: AP Photo/Joe Rosenthal. Page 375: Hulton Archive/Getty Images. Page 376 (top to bottom): © Oscar White/CORBIS; Hulton Archive/Getty Images. Page 377: © CORBIS. Page 378 (top to bottom): Time & Life Pictures/Getty Images; © Bettmann/CORBIS. Page 380: © CORBIS. Page 382: The Granger Collection. Page 383: © Bettmann/CORBIS. Page 387: Margaret Bourke-White/Time & Life Pictures/Getty Images. Page 388: © Bettmann/CORBIS. Page 390: © Bettmann/CORBIS. Page 391: © Bettmann/CORBIS. Page 392: The Granger Collection. Page 393: © Bettmann/CORBIS. Page 395 (top to bottom): © Bettmann/CORBIS; © Burstein Collection/CORBIS. Page 396: © Allen Ginsberg/CORBIS. Page 397: The Granger Collection.

## Chapter 12

Page 401: © Bettmann/CORBIS. Page 404: © Bettmann/CORBIS. Page 405: © Bettmann/CORBIS. Page 406: © Bettmann/CORBIS. Page 408: © Bettmann/CORBIS. Page 409 (top to bottom): © Geoffrey Clements/CORBIS; Don Cravens/Time & Life Pictures/Getty Images. Page 410: Don Cravens/Time & Life Pictures/Getty Images. Page 411: © Bettmann/CORBIS. Page 412: © Bettmann/CORBIS. Page 414: © Bettmann/CORBIS. Page 415 (top to bottom): © Bettmann/CORBIS; Lee Lockwood/Time & Life Pictures/Getty Images; © Bettmann/CORBIS. Page 417: © Bettmann/CORBIS. Page 419: Bettmann/CORBIS. Page 420: Hulton Archive/Getty Images. Page 421: © Bettmann/CORBIS. Page 422: John Filo/Hulton Archive/Getty Images. Page 423: © Bettmann/CORBIS. Page 425: © JP Laffont/Sygma/CORBIS. Page 426: © Ted Streshinsky/CORBIS. Page 428: © Bettmann/CORBIS. Page 429 (top to bottom): © Hulton-Deutsch Collection/CORBIS; Judith F. Baca, "Division of the Barrios and Chavez Ravine." Detail from: The Great Wall of Los Angeles, began 1976. © SPARC www.sparcmurals.org. Page 431: Bettmann/CORBIS. Page 432: Time & Life Pictures/Getty Images. Page 433: NASA. Page 434: Time & Life Pictures/Getty Images. Page 435: © George Steinmetz/CORBIS.

## Chapter 13

Page 439: © Wolfgang Kumm/dpa/CORBIS. Page 441 (top to bottom): © Bettmann/CORBIS; © Wally McNamee/CORBIS. Page 443: Time & Life Pictures/Getty Images. Page 444: © JP Laffont/Sygma/CORBIS. Page 447: © Wally McNamee/CORBIS. Page 448: AFP/Getty Images. Page 449: © Bettmann/CORBIS. Page 451 (top to bottom): © CORBIS; © Bettmann/CORBIS. Page 452: © Bettmann/CORBIS. Page 454: © Wally McNamee/CORBIS. Page 456: CP/Bill Grimshaw. Page 457: Union of Concerned Scientists. Page 459: © Content Mine International/Alamy. Page 460: © Wally McNamee/CORBIS. Page 461: © Vince Streano/CORBIS. Page 462: © Natalie Forbes/CORBIS. Page 464: Kruger, Barbara: Untitled (your body is a battleground), 1989; photographic silkscreen on vinyl, 112 × 112 inches; courtesy The Broad Art Foundation, Santa Monica and The Mary Boone Gallery, New York. Page 465 (left to right): © Judy Chicago/SODRAC (2007). Page 467: © Photo B. D.V./CORBIS. Page 468: © Bettmann/CORBIS. Page 470: © Bettmann/CORBIS.

## Chapter 14

Page 475: © Reuters/CORBIS. Page 477: CP/Robert Galbraith. Page 478 (top to bottom): © CORBIS; CP/RNS; US Department of Defense. Page 481: AFP/Getty Images. Page 483: © Bettmann/CORBIS. Page 484: Getty Images. Page 485: © Reuters/CORBIS. Page 486: © Gilbert Liz/Sygma/CORBIS. Page 487: © Reuters/CORBIS. Page 488: © FogStock/Alamy. Page 490 (top to bottom): © Greg Smith/CORBIS; © Callahan Loren/Sygma/CORBIS. Page 492 (left to right): © Shawn Thew/epa/CORBIS; © Stefan Zaklin/epa/CORBIS. Page 493: © Najlah Feanny/CORBIS. Page 496: © Reuters/CORBIS. Page 496: Istockphoto. Page 498: AFP/Getty Images. Page 500 (top to bottom): © Faleh Kheiber/Reuters/CORBIS; © Ron Sachs/CNP/CORBIS. Page 501 (top to bottom): Getty Images News; The Economist, January 6, 2007, p. 7. Page 502: Reuters/Landov. Page 503: Getty Images. Page 507 (top to bottom): Istockphoto; AP/Joseph Major. Page 509: Mick Stevens © cartoonbank.com.

# Text

## Chapter 11

Page 377: Copyright 1953 from *Nisei Daughter* by Monica Sone. Reprinted with permission of author. Page 382: Franklin and Eleanor Roosevelt Institute. Page 388: Collections and Archives, Tufts University. Page 396 (top to bottom): From *On the Road* by Penguin Group, Viking Press; From *Howl* by Allan Ginsberg published by Harper Collins.

## Chapter 12

Page 409: Rose and Raymond Parks Institute for Self Development. Page 412: Martin Luther King Jr. Estate. Page 421: Hyperion Books an imprint of Buena Vista Books. Page 423: Martin Luther King Jr. Estate. Page 425 (top to bottom): Betty Friedman Estate; Reprinted by permission of the National Organization for Women. The 1966 NOW Statement of Purpose is a historical document and may not reflect the current language or priorities of the organization. Page 432: Alfred Publishing Co. Inc. www.alfred.com. Page 434: Houghton Mifflin Company.